D1565243

# FEMINIST PERSPECTIVES IN THERAPY

# FEMINIST PERSPECTIVES IN THERAPY

## Empowering Diverse Women

### SECOND EDITION

*Judith Worell and Pam Remer*

**John Wiley & Sons, Inc.**

*Library of Congress Cataloging-in-Publication Data:*

Worell, Judith, 1928–
    Feminist perspectives in therapy : empowering diverse women / Judith Worell, Pamela Remer.—2nd ed.
        p. cm.
    Includes bibliographical references and index.
    ISBN 0-471-37436-9 (cloth : alk. paper)
    1. Feminist therapy. I. Remer, Pam. II. Title.
RC489.F45 W69 2002
616.89′14′082—dc21

                                                                2002069120

Printed in the United States of America.

10  9  8  7  6  5  4  3  2  1

To our four feminist daughters,
Amy, Beth, Randa, and Wendy

# *Preface* ————————————————————————

The field of counseling and psychotherapy with women is relatively new. The first book on counseling women was published in the 1970s. On a parallel track, the development of a feminist approach to counseling and psychotherapy is also relatively recent. Several new journals have appeared and are now thriving that address the psychology of gender and women, as well as therapeutic issues in treating women clients. The research is expanding, new applications of feminist principles are appearing in the literature, and more theorists are paying attention to both the goals and the process of feminist therapy with women. As a result, many of the theories and research data that now appear in mainstream literature, such as those related to sexual assault and violence against women, were introduced and promoted by the insightful work of feminist researchers. As new applications and insights develop, there is a need to organize and expand on current views, to integrate them with contemporary theoretical positions, and to suggest applications of these ideas to practical case materials with a diverse range of clients.

The changing demographics of the United States and the globalization of concern for issues of importance to women have added new dimensions to our understanding of women and the multiple problems that confront them. No longer do we speak of the universal woman. Rather, we recognize that the diversity of cultures, religions, ethnicities, and individual characteristics of our clients requires us to attend to the meanings that each client assigns to her life experiences. Thus, we explore each client's concerns within the framework of her personal and social identities. The convergence and integration of feminist and multicultural perspectives in psychotherapy is critical and timely. In the second edition to this book, we have created a new model that moves toward achieving this goal.

A number of core issues related to the psychological health of women suggest the need for a specialty in feminist psychological practice with women. Among these issues are (a) the special problems that women bring into the therapeutic setting; (b) the continuing gendered socialization and institutionalized oppression of women; (c) the inadequacies of contemporary theory, research, and practice in addressing the lives of diverse women; and (d) the development of innovative approaches to conceptualization and intervention with women. The application of feminist and multicultural principles to psychological intervention with women calls for additional integration of theory with practice. Finally, topics requiring additional consideration include diagnosis and assessment, ethical practices in counseling with women, research applications, and the training of psychological practitioners.

In this book, we have synthesized the diverse strands of feminist theory to create *Empowerment Feminist Therapy*. This model integrates both feminist and multicultural perspectives. Individual chapters address core issues in counseling women in the context of these two major perspectives and apply them to a sample of clients with diverse identities. The book is useful both to beginning graduate students as an introduction to counseling women and to more advanced and professional clinicians. Advanced professionals may want to discover and integrate these emerging approaches into their therapeutic repertoire, or they may selectively adapt text materials for workshops and continuing education training. Each chapter contains a self-assessment pretest on knowledge or attitudes, an introductory overview, a chapter summary, and activities to enhance self-awareness and application. The self-assessment and applied exercises are excellent learning strategies and contribute to the usefulness of this book as a classroom or continuing education text. The underlying theme of the text emphasizes that effective psychological practice with women clients requires an awareness of personal stereotypes about these client populations, an understanding of self in relation to the diversity of women, and a sensitivity to the special psychological and social environments within which women's development takes place.

The authors are both feminist clinicians with wide experience in teaching, research, and therapeutic practice with women. As educators, we have an understanding of the principles of effective instruction, and we include components in the text that contribute to the learning process. As feminist educators, we believe learning is a collaborative process, and our students have contributed in important ways to our perspectives. As clinicians, we have both been active in the establishment and administration of a community mental health clinic. In this capacity, we infused our ideas about feminist principles into the values and operation of the agency. As psychologists, we have both been active in a range of feminist organizations and have participated in numerous conferences that address feminist and multicultural issues. Many of the ideas in this book have grown out of our experiences with putting feminist ideas into action.

Coming from clearly different theoretical viewpoints and employing a contrasting range of therapeutic goals and strategies, we each contribute to this project in unique ways. Through exposition in theory and case materials, we demonstrate how therapists with differing views can apply the principles of Empowerment Feminist Therapy with a diversity of women and can integrate these principles into their practice. Thus, the approach may be useful for individuals who prefer particular theoretical positions and who may differentially emphasize experiential, affective, cognitive, or behavioral strategies in their practice. Because more than two-thirds of the clients in nonresidential settings are women and increasing numbers of diverse women are in need of psychological services, it is incumbent on the therapist in training to become knowledgeable and competent in the important issues surrounding the well-being of all women.

Since the first edition of this book, we have developed many new understandings. Among these is an increased appreciation for the ways in which each individual constructs her personal and social identities. We have become more aware of the importance of addressing the complex intersects of these identities as they function in the context of women's lives. This insight required that we revise and expand the principles of feminist therapy to incorporate the impact of diverse social locations on problems in living. The process of revising our model involved reflecting anew on who we are and what social locations we occupy. We acknowledge a limitation in our expertise. As White, married, able-bodied, middle-class, and relatively privileged women, we struggle to understand and appreciate the lives of our diverse sisters. Throughout the book, we include applications to women from heterogeneous groups, but we necessarily view them through our own lens. The reader who wishes to apply the principles in this book to groups other than those we cover may wish to supplement the suggested references with further reading. We also made hard decisions about what topics to cover. We mention briefly many issues for women that require a much lengthier volume: body image, eating disorders, multiple concerns with health, sexuality, growing older and aging, distressed relationships, and so on. We hope that the selected sample of women's concerns will provide a model for feminist practice and research with other issues as they arise in your professional experiences.

We believe it is important to communicate to the reader about the way in which the book was written. As committed feminists, we dedicated ourselves to a collaborative and cooperative project. We view collaboration as a process in which each contributor has an equal part, but in which each may contribute in differing ways. For us, the collaborative venture involved an interrelated set of processes that included trust, protection, egalitarianism, respect, flexibility, self-disclosure, and affirmation.

In trusting ourselves and each other, we felt free to take risks with ideas and suggestions without fear of ridicule or criticism. In respecting each other's identity, we each valued and validated the other's theoretical and epistemological views. Neither of us attempted to mold the other to her own image. In maintaining an egalitarian working relationship, we each reserved the right to contribute our own knowledge, skills, and expertise to the format and content, and to contribute more substantially to those chapters in which we felt most competent. In doing so, we each maintained respect for the other's expertise and the legitimacy of her views, even when disagreements occurred, as indeed they did. In negotiating conflict, we each valued the other's perspective as real and legitimate, and we tried to apply our counseling skills to the process of active listening and offering constructive feedback. Throughout the process of writing this book, we attempted to maintain flexibility and openness, looking at each issue from alternative perspectives.

In applying feminist principles to the lives of other women, we tried as well to apply them to ourselves. In this context, we valued personal self-disclosure and shared the events in our lives that helped to frame current perspectives. We discovered that we are both survivors; between our two lives we have experienced incest, rape, wife abuse, sexual harassment, career and employment discrimination, dual-career marriages, motherhood, divorce, single parenting, grandparenting, and the professional superwoman syndrome. We have coped with our "Woman's Body" through menstruation, pregnancy, childbirth, hysterectomy, menopause, growing older, and an endless obsession with thinness. For us, then, the personal became political as we considered the external forces that shaped our lives and the personal triumphs that enabled us to emerge empowered with strength and self-affirmation.

We have come to realize that all women are survivors, having faced and met special challenges as a result of being women in a society that devalues women. We celebrate our success in meeting stress and challenge with creative solutions. In writing this book, we shift the focus from "Woman as Problem" to "Woman as Survivor and Thriver." In doing so, we acknowledge our own strengths as we affirm each other. And we celebrate and appreciate the many wonderful and courageous women whose lives have contributed to the collective tapestry of this book.

## ACKNOWLEDGMENTS

First, we want to extend a very special appreciation to the men who share our lives, Rory Remer and Bud Smith, for their continuing support and encouragement.

We also want to recognize the many people who were important to us in the process of completing this task: friends, students, mentors, clients, family, reviewers, and the many women whose lives construct the fabric of this book. Naming some of these people probably leaves out some others—in particular, the following played important roles:

| | |
|---|---|
| Diane Banic | Sherman Lee |
| Adena Bargad | Jeanne Marecek |
| Adam Blatner | Lori Montross |
| Andrea Blount | Melissa Moose |
| Redonna Chandler | Roberta Nutt |
| Carolyn Enns | Danielle Oakley |
| Linda Forrest | Rory Remer |
| Rachel Hare-Mustin | Damon Robinson |
| Carl Hollander | Sherry Rostosky |
| Janet Hyde | Janice Steil |
| Dawn Johnson | Rhoda Unger |
| Norine Johnson | Karen Wyche |
| Shirley Lange | Alice Zollicoffer |

# Contents

# *Prologue*

*We are born into, grow up, and grow old in a society that teaches us that the democratic phrase "all men are created equal" does not include women.*

Benokaritis & Feagin, 1986

This is a book about women, but it is also a book about yourself. In reading this book and its perspectives on the lives of women, you may arrive at a place that is different from where you started. You may revise your views and thinking about some theories, clinical interpretations, and information about women's experiences in contemporary society. In your journey through the book, you may begin to revise some of your attitudes toward women's roles and your ideas about the value of feminism in professional practice. We hope you begin to view the world through a different lens.

The self-assessment "Self and World Views" that follows will be a useful way for you to evaluate some of the ways in which your ideas and attitudes change. Before you start to read the book, take a few minutes to complete the inventory and to score yourself on the four factors on the profile. At the end of the book, we ask you to complete the inventory once more, thereby evaluating the extent of change, if any, on each of the four factors. We hope this exercise will lead to some insights for you. The best way for you to determine its utility is to commit yourself to a pre- and postassessment. Your scores should be your own personal property, but sharing the outcomes with a partner or friend may be an enlightening experience. Please try it.

## SELF-ASSESSMENT: SELF AND WORLD VIEWS

Look at the series of statements that follow. Some of these statements represent ideas about how the world works. Other statements are about how people might describe themselves. Read each statement carefully and decide to what degree it currently describes you or your ideas about the world. Then select one of the five answers that best describes your present agreement or disagreement with the statement.

For example, if you strongly agree with the statement, "I like to return to the same vacation spot year after year," you would rate the statement by writing the number 5 in the space provided. Remember to read each statement carefully and decide to what degree you think it describes your views at the present time.

| 1 | 2 | 3 | 4 | 5 |
|---|---|---|---|---|
| Strongly disagree | Disagree | Neither agree nor disagree | Agree | Strongly agree |

_____ 1. I don't think there is any need for an Equal Rights Amendment; women are doing well.

_____ 2. I used to think that there isn't a lot of sex discrimination, but now I know how much there really is.

_____ 3. I just feel like I need to be around people who share my feminist point of view right now.

_____ 4. I want to work to improve women's status.

_____ 5. I think that most women will feel most fulfilled by being a wife and a mother.

6. It only recently occurred to me that I think it's unfair that men have the privileges they have in this society simply because they are men.

_____ 7. Being a part of a feminist community is important to me.

_____ 8. On some level, my motivation for almost every activity I engage in is my desire for an egalitarian world.

_____ 9. I've never really worried or thought about what it means to be a woman in this society.

_____ 10. When you think about most of the problems in the world—the threat of nuclear war, pollution, discrimination—it seems to me that most of them are caused by men.

_____ 11. My social life is mainly with women these days, but there are a few men whose friendship I enjoy.

_____ 12. I have a lifelong commitment to working for social, economic, and political equality for women.

_____ 13. If I were a woman married to a man and my husband was offered a job in another state, it would be my obligation to move in support of his career.

_____ 14. It makes me really upset to think about how women have been treated so unfairly in this society for so long.

_____ 15. I share most of my social time with a few close friends who share my feminist values.

_____ 16. It is very satisfying to me to be able to use my talents and skills in my work in the women's movement.

_____ 17. I do not want women to have equal status with men.

_____ 18. Recently, I read something or had an experience that sparked a greater understanding of sexism.

_____ 19. Especially now, I feel that the women around me give me strength.

_____ 20. I care very deeply about men and women having equal opportunities in all respects.

_____ 21. I think that men and women had it better in the 1950s when married women were housewives and their husbands supported them.

_____ 22. When I see the way most men treat women, it makes me angry.

_____ 23. If I were to paint a picture or write a poem, it would probably be about women or women's issues.

| 1 | 2 | 3 | 4 | 5 |
|---|---|---|---|---|
| Strongly disagree | Disagree | Neither agree nor disagree | Agree | Strongly agree |

_____ 24. I feel that I am a very powerful and effective spokesperson.

_____ 25. I don't see much point in questioning the general expectation that men should be masculine and women should be feminine.

_____ 26. I am angry that I've let men take advantage of women.

_____ 27. Particularly now, I feel most comfortable with others who share my feminist point of view.

_____ 28. I am very committed to a cause that I believe contributes to a more fair and just world for all people.

_____ 29. I am not sure what is meant by the phrase "women are oppressed under partriarchy."

_____ 30. I am willing to make certain sacrifices to effect change in this society to create a nonsexist, peaceful place where all people have equal opportunities.

_____ 31. Generally, I think that men are more interesting than women.

_____ 32. I think that rape is sometimes the woman's fault.

## Scoring

The scale that you have just completed is a revised version of the Feminist Identity Development Scale (FIDS) discussed in Chapter 12. Both women and men can use this scale for self-assessment. To score your responses, please follow the following format. For each factor, add the numbers you assigned to each item in the scale to determine the total. Then, divide by the number of items in the factor: Insert this score in the grid provided, under the column for Pretest.

| | | |
|---|---|---|
| Factor I: | Items 1, 5, 9, 13, 17, 21, 25, 29, 31, 32 | Total/10 |
| Factor II: | Items 2, 6, 10, 14, 18, 22, 26 | Total/7 |
| Factor III: | Items 3, 7, 11, 15, 19, 23, 27 | Total/7 |
| Factor IV: | Items 4, 8, 12, 16, 20, 24, 28, 30 | Total/8 |

| | | Score | |
|---|---|---|---|
| **Factor** | | **Pretest** | **Posttest** |
| I: | Acceptance | ☐ | ☐ |
| II: | Revelation | ☐ | ☐ |
| III: | Embeddedness | ☐ | ☐ |
| IV: | Commitment | ☐ | ☐ |

At the completion of the book, we ask you to take the scale once more. After scoring your responses again, insert the factor scores in the column under Posttest. Assess any change and discuss with a friend or colleague. What have you discovered? See p. 318 for a display of scores.

# PART 1

# FOUNDATIONS OF FEMINIST THERAPY

The groundwork for becoming a feminist therapist extends far beyond a discussion of theory and technique. Working with women who seek help requires that you are aware of and understand the full context of their experiences and development across the lifespan. Readers may wonder why we have limited our focus to counseling and therapy with women, since many of the techniques and strategies of feminist therapy are applicable to both women and men. Excellent materials on the psychology of men and masculinity (e.g., Good & Sherrod, 2001; Levant, 2001), and on feminist family therapy for heterosexual couples (Silverstein & Goodrich, 2001) provide valuable sources for redefining the male self and patterns of relationship between women and the men that impact their lives. However, the extensive volume of recent theory and research as well as the scope of our own expertise led us to concentrate this book on issues that are relevant to the lives of girls and women.

New research on the importance of cultural diversity and pluralism on women's experiences made it critical that we integrate multicultural and feminist perspectives into a cohesive model for feminist practice. The task of integrating the experiences of inequality and oppression across the diversity of women with the goals and practices of feminist counseling and therapy is a challenging one. In this book, we attempt to meet this challenge with the full recognition that it offers not a recipe for practice, but a guidepost to helping you on your journey to becoming a competent multicultural feminist practitioner.

Part 1 provides the foundation for feminist therapy by offering a perspective in which to view the experiences of girls and women from the diverse context of their lives. The two introductory chapters set the stage for viewing the development of women's personal and social identities in contemporary society. First, we provide a rationale for recognizing the field of counseling and therapy with women as a separate specialty. In this framework, we explore concepts related to sex, gender, feminism and feminist psychology, multicultural diversity, and empowerment. We outline a feminist empowerment model of women's mental health that we apply to the process and outcomes of Empowerment Feminist Therapy (EFT) with women. This model offers a positive and enabling approach to intervention for the concerns that motivate women to seek help. Next, we

1

review the changing roles for women and men in contemporary Western societies, and relate these changes to the issues that women bring to counseling. We consider the psychological worlds of developing women from a range of social identity locations, pointing to the complex interplay of variables such as gender, ethnicity, sexual and affectional orientation, age, socioeconomic class, culture, physical characteristics and abilities, national and regional origin, and religious commitment. We consider how these factors intersect to influence gendered socialization practices and other external forces that shape who we are as women and men. Finally, we explore the psychological advantages of egalitarian relationships.

The remaining two chapters of Part 1 expand the discussion of feminist therapy and explore its application to diagnosis, assessment, and theory transformation. First, we describe the worldview assumptions that underlie EFT. The four principles of EFT are presented and we provide specific goals and strategies for each principle. We then assist you in integrating your current theorizing about how to do counseling and therapy in an empowerment feminist format. Finally, we present a critique of mainstream assessment and diagnosis and offer alternative strategies that are more compatible with a feminist perspective.

Each chapter begins with a self-assessment and ends with experiential exercises and further readings. The self-assessments are designed to encourage you to be reflective about your attitudes, values, and beliefs about women and men from differing cultural and social standpoints. Many of the self-assessments involve stereotypes that are commonly held by members of Western cultures. Although you may believe that you are unbiased, we challenge you to complete these self-assessments conscientiously. Do any of your current attitudes reflect biased attitudes or stereotyped thinking? Are these stereotypes primarily negative or positive? It might be interesting to retake each self-assessment after you have read the chapter and compare your two sets of responses. The exercises, on the other hand, bring you into more personal contact with the material covered in the chapter by asking you to apply some of the concepts to your own experiences. The exercises may be completed alone, but you will find it more enjoyable and enlightening to share your responses with a colleague or friend. At the end of the book, a final assignment is to retake the "Self and World Views" assessment on page 331 and consider how your progress through this book has altered your overall views and attitudes about women and men in all their diversities, and about yourself.

**Chapter 1** ———————————————————————————————

# *FOUNDATIONS OF FEMINIST COUNSELING AND THERAPY*

## SELF-ASSESSMENT: RELATIONSHIPS BETWEEN WOMEN AND MEN

A series of statements concerning women and men and their relationships in contemporary society follow. Please indicate in the space to the left the degree to which you agree or disagree with each statement using the following scale:

---

0 = Disagree strongly; 1 = Disagree somewhat; 2 = Disagree slightly;

3 = Agree slightly; 4 = Agree somewhat; 5 = Agree strongly

_____ 1. No matter how accomplished he is, a man is not truly complete as a person unless he has the love of a woman.

_____ 2. Many women are actually seeking special favors, such as hiring policies that favor them over men, under the guise of asking for "equality."

_____ 3. In a disaster, women ought not necessarily be rescued before men.

_____ 4. Most women interpret innocent remarks or acts as being sexist.

_____ 5. Women are too easily offended.

_____ 6. People are often truly happy in life without being romantically involved with a member of the other sex.

_____ 7. Feminists are not seeking for women to have more power than men.

_____ 8. Many women have a quality of purity that few men possess.

_____ 9. Women should be cherished and protected by men.

_____ 10. Most women fail to appreciate fully all that men do for them.

_____ 11. Women seek to gain power by getting control over men.

_____ 12. Every man ought to have a women whom he adores.

_____ 13. Men are complete without women.

*(continued)*

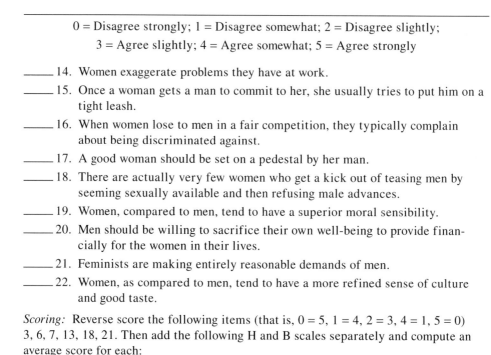

0 = Disagree strongly; 1 = Disagree somewhat; 2 = Disagree slightly;
3 = Agree slightly; 4 = Agree somewhat; 5 = Agree strongly

_____ 14. Women exaggerate problems they have at work.

_____ 15. Once a woman gets a man to commit to her, she usually tries to put him on a tight leash.

_____ 16. When women lose to men in a fair competition, they typically complain about being discriminated against.

_____ 17. A good woman should be set on a pedestal by her man.

_____ 18. There are actually very few women who get a kick out of teasing men by seeming sexually available and then refusing male advances.

_____ 19. Women, compared to men, tend to have a superior moral sensibility.

_____ 20. Men should be willing to sacrifice their own well-being to provide financially for the women in their lives.

_____ 21. Feminists are making entirely reasonable demands of men.

_____ 22. Women, as compared to men, tend to have a more refined sense of culture and good taste.

*Scoring:* Reverse score the following items (that is, 0 = 5, 1 = 4, 2 = 3, 4 = 1, 5 = 0) 3, 6, 7, 13, 18, 21. Then add the following H and B scales separately and compute an average score for each:

H = 2, 4, 5, 7, 10, 11, 14, 15, 16, 18, 21

B = 1, 3, 6, 8, 9, 12, 13, 17, 19, 20, 22

*Source:* Peter Glick and Susan T. Fiske, 1996, "The Ambivalent Sexism Inventory: Differentiating hostile and benevolent sexism." *Journal of Personality and Social Psychology, 70,* 491–512. Reprinted with permission.

In reading these questions, you probably noticed that some of the items appear to reflect stereotyped attitudes about women. Some statements also appear more hostile (H) and some more benevolent (B) than others. These two attitudes are exactly what Glick and Fiske (1996) intended to measure. They constructed the Ambivalent Sexism Inventory to reflect two conflicting attitudes toward women: the negative response of prejudice, defined as "antipathy based upon a faulty and inflexible generalization" and benevolence, or "viewing women stereotypically and in restricted roles but that are subjectively positive . . . and typically categorized as prosocial" (p. 491). Now, review your responses to the statements on this scale and (a) determine if you can detect those that are hostile versus those that are benevolent and (b) reflect on your responses to these two sets of items in terms of how you believe you rate yourself on sexist attitudes toward women.

## OVERVIEW

New approaches to women's psychological health have emerged in the wake of the revitalized Women's Movement. Since 1970, we have achieved public recognition of the separate forces that impact on women and men in Western societies. National and global organizations were formed to address the inequalities in the treatment of women's physical and psychological problems and to lobby for change. New scholarship and research on the psychology of women introduced the "second sex" into the medical and psychological literature and brought the life span issues of women into sharper focus. The social construction of gender relocates women's problems from individual and internal to societal and external. The feminist construction of gender redefines the nature of women's and men's relationships in terms of the expression and maintenance of power. The multicultural construction of gender identifies the intersects of gender, ethnicity, socioeconomic class (SES), and sexual orientation that shape our personal and social identities. The changes that have transpired in the past 30 years hold enormous implications for the ways in which psychological practice with women takes place.

Emergent client populations were "discovered" where problems were invisible and never believed to exist. The challenges of these new client populations stimulated the development of theories, research, and procedures to address their concerns. The combined efforts of women's groups in both the lay and professional communities have resulted in new agendas for women's mental health. The foundation for these agendas is rooted in the history and expression of feminism, which nurtures and promotes the goal of equality in all aspects of women's and men's lives, and among diverse groups of people.

This chapter presents an overview of these historic trends and provides an introduction to the remainder of the book. After reading Chapter 1, you will be able to:

- Discuss the rationale for a specialty in counseling and therapy with women.
- Explain the concepts of sex, gender, gender roles, and diversity.
- List the advantages and drawbacks of both alpha and beta bias in considering gender and diversity.
- Present at least three differing views of feminism.
- Apply these views of feminism to the principles of empowerment feminist therapy.
- Compare a symptom-reduction approach with the therapeutic goal of empowerment.

## RATIONALE FOR A SPECIALTY IN COUNSELING AND THERAPY WITH WOMEN

As emergent ideologies challenged traditional views, the field of psychology began to expand in new directions. The result of this expansion has been a wealth of new research and knowledge about women and men, revised theories to explain and account for psychological development, and a demand for creative applications to prevent and remediate human problems. The fledgling discipline of the Psychology of Women was established, providing the foundation for an applied science dedicated to counseling and therapy with women.

In the field of mental health, the consideration of sex, gender, and cultural diversity in the prevalence, etiology, diagnosis, and treatment of a range of human problems was conspicuously absent until recently. Two epidemiological surveys of community samples sponsored by the National Institute of Mental Health (NIMH) revealed that a high proportion of individuals with signs of depression, anxiety, panic, simple phobia, and agoraphobia are women, whereas men are overrepresented in the categories of substance abuse and antisocial behaviors. According to these surveys, in the United States, overall health and community mental health utilization rates are higher for women than for men. Women are prescribed a disproportionate share of psychoactive drugs, many of which have deleterious or unknown side effects (McBride, 1987; McGrath, Keita, Strickland, & Russo, 1990). Dissatisfaction with existing theories, knowledge base, and treatment approaches motivated a call for change.

In response to their growing awareness of personal dissatisfaction and unexplained malaise, groups of women began to congregate to discuss their life situations. In sharing experiences of restricted and stereotyped expectations for how they should conduct their lives, they discovered that their problems were voiced and mirrored by others. These discussions led to the awareness that the personal problems of individual women were rooted in their subordinate status in their families and society. The growing awareness of asymmetrical gender expectations and widespread discrimination and injustice for women resulted in the conclusion that "the personal is political." Consciousness-raising groups were therapeutic for many (Brodsky, 1973; Kravetz, Marecek, & Finn, 1983) and were instrumental in the early call for change in the sexist and oppressive social structures that characterized a patriarchal, or male dominated, society.

## Dissatisfaction with Traditional Treatment

Consciousness-raising groups were directed toward accomplishing social change rather than healing personal wounds. The impetus for seeking alternative approaches to women's well-being came from many directions, as researchers and clinicians voiced their concerns. Expression of these concerns covered a broad range of issues that addressed both the deficits in our psychological knowledge about women and the problems that existed with current intervention models and practices in the mental health field. As we shall discover, many of the issues that stimulated the formation of feminist perspectives remain problematic today. A sample of these early concerns follows:

1. Dissatisfaction with traditional theories of female and male development and behavior that depicted stereotyped male traits as the norm and females as deficient by comparison (Broverman, Broverman, Clarkson, Rosenkrantz, & Vogel, 1970; Gilbert, 1980).

2. Frustration with the continuing omission of women from the knowledge base of psychology (M. Crawford & Marecek, 1989; Grady, 1981; McHugh, Koeske, & Frieze, 1986).

3. Challenging gender stereotypes that defined traditional views of "femininity" for women and "masculinity" for men as the most desirable and psychologically healthy adjustments (Bem, 1974; Broverman et al., 1970; Constantinople, 1973).

4. Recognition that many of the reported sex differences in behavior, personality, and psychiatric diagnosis reflect inequalities in social status and interpersonal power between women and men, and between diverse groups of women (Henley, 1977; Unger, 1979).

5. Exposing evidence of gender bias and gender-role stereotyping in counseling and psychotherapy (American Psychological Association, 1975; Hare-Mustin, 1978; Schlossberg & Pietrofesa, 1978; J. A. Sherman, 1980).

6. Consideration of gender stereotyping and gender bias in psychiatric diagnoses (Franks, 1986; M. Kaplan, 1983; Lerman, 1996).

7. Determination that women's "intrapsychic" problems frequently originate from sources external to themselves (G. W. Brown & Harris, 1978; Miles, 1988; Rawlings & Carter, 1977).

8. Concern about disregard by many mental health professionals for the validity of women's self-reported experiences (Hare-Mustin, 1983; Holroyd, 1978).

9. Challenging the practice of attributing blame and responsibility to women for their experiences of sexual and physical violence (Koss et al., 1994; Resick, 1983; Walker, 1979).

10. Rejection of "mother-blaming" in family functioning that pathologized women's interdependence and involvement (by labeling these as enmeshment and overinvolvement), and removed responsibility from men for their lack of involvement or abuse of power (Bograd, 1986; Caplan & Hall-McCorquodale, 1985).

11. Negating the assumption in family therapy of a normative family hierarchy that rank-ordered gender roles, based on father as economic provider and head of household and mother as responsible for the emotional functioning of family members (Hare-Mustin, 1978; Margolin, 1982).

12. Concern for the increasing medicalization of women's psychological problems, including issues of diagnosis and prescriptive drugs (McBride, 1987; Worell, 1986).

13. Unwillingness to tolerate the continuing neglect of women's mental health concerns in both research and practice (Brodsky & Hare-Mustin, 1980; Sobel & Russo, 1981).

At a later stage in the development of therapeutic interventions for women, previously silenced voices addressed additional concerns that reflected the following:

14. Disagreement with diagnostic categories that diagnosed alternative sexualities as pathological, and growing awareness of the diverse range of women's sexuality (Espin, 1984; B. Greene, 1994b; Wilkinson & Kitzinger, 1993).

15. Neglect in the professional literature of the multiple sources of discrimination and exclusion in women's lives based on ethnicity and national origin, physical ability, sexual orientation, and other devalued minority group statuses (Comas-Diaz, 1991; B. Greene, 1986).

## CATALYSTS FOR CHANGE

In response to these concerns, new approaches to intervention with women were envisioned. The emergence of a specialty area in counseling and psychotherapy with women was predicated on four factors that supported its development (Comas-Diaz & Greene, 1994; Worell, 1980):

1. The Psychology of Women became a reality, providing a substantial body of theory and knowledge about the diverse biological, cultural, and psychological characteristics of women.

2. New client populations emerged whose needs for intervention and treatment were not addressed by current traditional approaches to therapy.

3. Revised models of women's mental health and well-being integrated new information about women and proposed innovative goals for women's empowerment.

4. Alternative counseling models were developed that addressed the unique characteristics and goals of underserved populations.

In the wake of these developments, training programs in the specialty of counseling and psychotherapy with women were initiated and implemented. We discuss each of these factors further in terms of their contributions to the specialty of counseling and psychotherapy with women.

Throughout this book, we use the terms *counseling* and *psychotherapy* interchangeably. Counseling has been applied historically to interventions that assist clients in understanding and resolving ongoing problems in living. As such, counseling tends to focus on positive aspects of psychological health and well-being. Psychotherapy, in contrast, has been applied traditionally to medical or illness models that locate problems in persons and that aim to reduce or "cure" pathology in patients. Because we adhere to an empowerment model that addresses women's pain and despair, but focuses its strategies and goals on supporting their strength and well-being, we use these terms interchangeably.

## THE PSYCHOLOGY OF WOMEN AND GENDER

The first requirement for the development of a specialty area is the accumulation of a body of knowledge that serves as a database for theory, research, and applications to practice. Four major outcomes of innovative research on women and gender include:

1. New information about women and the diversity of their lives in contemporary society.
2. Revised views of sex, gender, gender roles, and gender-related behavior.
3. Diversity and multicultural perspectives.
4. Feminist psychology, feminist theory, and implications for training and practice.

### New Information about Women

Early research related to the psychology of women focused on a search for sex-related differences, or those that might be found between girls and boys, women and men. In exhaustive searches of the literature published between 1967 and 1982, Mary Roth Walsh (1985) found over 13,000 citations related to the psychology of women. Kay Deaux (1985) reported 18,000 citations that covered sex-related differences and sex roles. Since then, the psychological literature on women and gender has increased geometrically as the burgeoning research fills both old and new journals. In the early publications, attention centered on characteristics assumed to differentiate the sexes, such as self-esteem, intellectual abilities, achievement variables, career development, interpersonal relationships, aggression, dominance, and verbal and nonverbal behavior.

Initial reviews of this research by Eleanor Maccoby and Carol Jacklin (1974), and later meta-analyses reported by Janet Hyde and Marcia Linn (1986) concluded that sex-related differences in personality and cognitive abilities have been overemphasized, accounting for no more than 1% to 5% of the variance in female and male responses. Other authors pointed out that it may be more important to look at within-group than between-group variance on any characteristic, since the differences among women or among men exceed the discrepancies between them (Feingold, 1994; Hyde, 1994; Lorber, 1994). From this perspective, perhaps one day "sex differences" will reflect only basic reproductive variables such as female pregnancy and male ejaculation.

## Situational Contexts

Later research broadened the areas of interest and focused on situational, personality, and contextual correlates of sex-related behaviors on a variety of tasks. These studies looked at areas such as expectancies and attributions for success and failure; interpersonal interactions and group processes; leadership and power tactics; personality traits associated with masculinity, femininity, and androgyny; sex-related attitudes and stereotypes; and an increasing number of variables related to the intersects of gender with a diversity of group characteristics. In these areas, differences between female and male groups were found to vary with the ethnic and sexual identities of the samples, the nature and domain of the task (e.g., mathematics vs. English, sports vs. sociability), the sex and ethnicity of the experimenter or target persons, and relevant attitudes and stereotypes. Identification as female or male was seldom the sole determinant of behavior. Nevertheless, the search for differences between girls and boys, and women and men remains salient in the psychological literature and is increasingly visible in the popular press (e.g., *Men Are from Mars, Women Are from Venus*).

## Women's Lives

Feminist psychology encouraged moving research on women out of the laboratory to look at the meaningful contexts of their lives. This research brought us new information about women in relation to the roles they occupy in Western societies (e.g., daughter, wife, lover, partner, mother, worker), the discriminatory practices that restrict their opportunities in almost all societies (e.g., in education, employment, politics, public life), the victimization and violence they experience in most societies (e.g., incest, rape, sexual harassment, physical battering), the diverse groups with which they affiliate (e.g., women of color and differing subcultures, lesbians, older women, disabled), and their psychological processes (e.g., well-being, self-esteem, stress, anger, depression, anxiety). As women's experiences are explored in the context of their diverse lives, innovative research strategies and approaches have been developed to address the complex questions that were not previously considered. The illumination of women's lives in context also leads us to ask creatively about how the sum and interaction among these experiences frame our sense of personal and social identity (Deaux, 1996; Deaux & Stewart, 2001; T. L. Robinson, 1999).

## Revised Views of Sex, Gender, Gender Roles, and Gender-Related Behavior

Although the call for change rallied around the issues that faced contemporary women, it soon became clear that women's concerns could be reinterpreted in the broader context of gender. That is, researchers in the field hypothesized that behaviors and attitudes previously believed to be determined by sex (female or male) were socially and situationally created rather than intrinsic to the individual. Some research provided evidence that women's and men's behaviors could be understood in the context of the status inequalities between the two sexes (Eagly, 1987; Henley, 1977) as well as between members of dominant and subordinate subcultures in the United States (Healy, 1997). Thus, many of the obtained gender-related behaviors could be interpreted as evidence of unequal power relations between socially defined groups (M. Crawford & Marecek, 1989; Sherif, 1982). These insights with respect to gender lead us to redefine our constructs and revise our research strategies.

## Sex or Gender?

*Sex* refers here to a descriptive and biologically based variable that is used to distinguish two categories of individuals: females or males. You may have been asked to respond to a questionnaire or form that said: "What is your sex?" and you checked one of the two choices, either female or male. In reality, there may be more than two sexes, based on the complex interplay of genetics, hormones, and reproductive structures (Unger & Crawford, 1993); however, most societies find it convenient to divide people into two groups. In the research literature, sex is frequently used as an independent variable to compare females and males on some characteristic. Aside from certain physical and reproductive capabilities, however, few, if any, characteristics can be explained by sex alone (Burn, 1996; C. F. Epstein, 1997). Sex has also been used in research as a stimulus variable (Unger, 1979) to structure and define what is observed by others. Such comparisons between females and males become reflections in the eye of the observer, usually in the form of stereotypes. "Stereotypes are sets of beliefs about a group of people . . . a mental list or picture of the traits, characteristics, and behaviors a particular social group is likely to possess [in this case, female or male]. While such beliefs exist in people's minds, they originate in the culture of those individuals" (Gollwitzer & Moskowitz, 1996, p. 387).

You may wish to review the responses you made to the self-assessment exercise at the start of this chapter. Do any of your ratings reflect your own biases or stereotypes about women? If so, your evaluations are not based on sex but on your gender stereotypes about what you believe to be true of most women, leading us into a discussion about gender.

## Gender

We define *gender* as culturally constructed beliefs and attitudes about the traits and behaviors of females and males (Deaux, 1984; Lott, 1997). Since many of these beliefs conform to dominant culture norms about others, we may be unaware that they are not necessarily "true." Gendered beliefs and practices vary across cultures, may change through historical time, and differ in terms of who makes the observations and judgments. According to many scholars, the language that we use to describe our experience of the world and that of others profoundly influences our "meaning-making" and understandings (M. Gergen, 2001). From this point of view, we construct our own meanings about reality and about gender that represent culturally shared agreements about what is "really" there. We take the position in this book that the personal characteristics typically attributed to gender are not "true" attributes of females and males, but are socially constructed categories that function to maintain female-male dichotomies and dominant group power structures (Hare-Mustin & Marecek, 1988; Lott, 1997; Unger, 1983, 1989).

Gender constructions also vary within and across socially identified groups in a society. For example, concepts of womanhood and femininity may be quite different for a Latina or an Asian woman in the United States, yet in each of these broad ethnic groups, separate subcultures may retain their own distinctive gender expectations (Peplau, Veniegas, Taylor, & DeBro, 1999). As we add more variables that intersect with gender, understanding the functions of gender becomes "both more and less important" (Unger, 1995, p. 416).

The social construction of gender, as it intersects with other social status identities, creates in each of us a self-image of who we are as females and males and how we should behave. Thus, our gender stereotypes are both descriptive and prescriptive (Fiske & Stevens, 1998; Lorber, 1994). The cognition that "I am a woman" functions to activate my entire experience of femaleness in society, and serves as a general schema or cognitive framework that shapes my current and future activities (Frieze, Bailey, Mamula, & Noss, 1989). The cognition that "I am an African American (Asian, Latina, Native American, bicultural, immigrant) woman" creates alternative images as each individual constructs her personal and social identities from the complex matrix of her culture and personal experience.

Gender also structures the expectations and behaviors of those with whom we interact, resulting in self-fulfilling prophecies, or behavioral confirmation, that in turn shape our behavior to meet the expectations of important others (Rosenthal, 1994; Snyder & Dyamot, 2001; Towsen, Zanna, & MacDonald, 1989). In Chapter 2, we review research that demonstrates how the social construction of gender influences socialization practices with girls and boys, and frames the separate roles of women and men in differing cultures.

*Gender Roles*

For many professionals in the field, gender becomes the major issue in working with women. "The social construction of gender plays a major role in the definition and diagnosis of illness, timing and expression of symptoms, treatment strategies, and theoretical explanations. Thus, mental illness is as much a social as a personal event" (Travis, 1988, p. 2).

For others, "gender and gender oppression are not the primary locus of identity or oppression for all women" (Greene & Sanchez-Hucles, 1997, p. 183). From this perspective, diversity takes primacy, with gender being only one site of women's disadvantage and oppression, joined by those of race and ethnicity, poverty, social class status, sexual orientation, disability, and aging. Figure 1.1 is a model of gender role functioning that includes many of the factors that interact on individuals to produce the gendered female or male self. We say more about gender issues in later chapters.

## Diversity and Multicultural Perspectives

Discussions in the psychological literature about diversity and multiculturalism in counseling and psychotherapy have paralleled those about women and gender. Only recently have there been attempts to integrate these perspectives in counseling and therapy with women (e.g., L. Brown & Root, 1990; Comas-Diaz & Greene, 1994).

*Diversity*

Although we tend to think of race or ethnicity when we speak of *diversity,* the concept embraces many other aspects of our personal or group identities. Diversity encompasses all aspects of a person's social realities: gender, culture, ethnicity and national origin, immigration and acculturation status, sexual and affectional orientation, age, education, socioeconomic status (SES), physical characteristics and abilities, intellectual abilities, and religious affiliation. These variables are some of the major characteristics that connect us to others as well as distinguish us from one another. They form the basis of our personal identity (T. L. Robinson & Howard-Hamilton, 2000). The complex intersect of diverse social locations and identities for each of us creates both a personal self-concept and a group consciousness that frame our values and world views.

The consideration of diversity in counseling and therapy is important for two major reasons: First, it is critical for the therapist to understand and be responsive to the

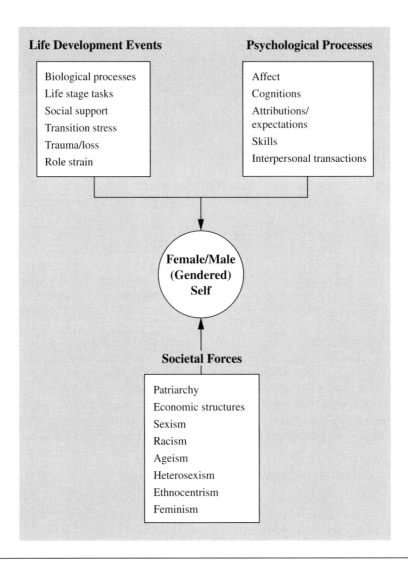

**Figure 1.1  Model of gender-role functioning.**

cultural context and personal meanings of the client's behavior and her current concerns. Second, the social locations by which she identifies herself and is identified by others provide opportunities for her to experience both pride and oppression. Clients may gain self-esteem and personal empowerment by identifying with groups they view as socially valued. But many of these socially identified groups are culturally stigmatized by negative attitudes, stereotyped beliefs, and active discrimination; these are the conditions that lead to oppression. We define *oppression* as a systematic denial of access to valued community resources to members of groups defined as inferior, undeserving, or different. Because oppression may be internalized as a reflected self-image, it creates a toxic environment that often produces illness and decreased well-being. We say more about how oppression affects client well-being in subsequent chapters.

In considering the diversity of social locations by which we identify ourselves and are identified by others, we refer to ethnicity and nationality rather than to race. Although racism is a toxic element in most societies that creates stigma and oppression for individuals in socially identified groups, biologists and anthropologists tell us that "race" is also a socially constructed category (Pederson, 1997; Phinney, 1996). As such, it does not represent the reality of genetic difference but rather, reflects the power of dominant social groups to define who is "in" and who is "out." Because the concept of race highlights presumed differences that are immutable, we prefer to speak of ethnicity, as inclusive of both "race" and the cultural and language frameworks that influence how people construct meanings and lifestyles. But because physical features and skin color also provide stimuli for inferring "race," it is also important to speak of racism in terms of the ways in which dominant cultures stigmatize and discriminate against those whom it defines as racially different or "inferior." Just as we define sexism in terms of negative attitudes, stereotypes, and discrimination against girls and women, we consider racism as a similar set of negative beliefs, attitudes, and behaviors toward certain ethnic groups.

## Multiculturalism

As women from non-White groups voiced their concern about their marginal status and invisibility in feminist psychology, increased attention was focused on the multiple identities that characterize us as women. A broad definition of multiculturalism presents it as "a philosophy that affords the development of flexibility and diversity of orientations to life and for the development of pluralistic identities" (Sparks & Park, 2000, p. 205). Hope Landrine (1995) proposed a multicultural feminist psychology that incorporates the contextual meanings of behavior for all cultures. By *culture,* we mean shared learned behaviors and values of a particular group that are transmitted across generations (Ridley, Li, & Hill, 1998). Culture includes external components such as institutions, language, and visible artifacts, social norms and social roles (rules and expectations for behavior), and internal components such as attitudes, values, world views, and ways of thinking about the self in relation to the collective. According to Helen Markus and her associates (1996), "Communities, societies, and cultural contexts provide the interpretive frameworks—including images, concepts, and narratives, as well as the means, practices, and patterns of behavior—by which people make sense (lend meaning, coherence, and structure to their ongoing experience) and organize their actions" (p. 858). We say more about these distinctions in Chapter 2 in discussing dimensions of identity.

Derald Sue and David Sue (1999) called for a multicultural counseling model that places cultural identity at the center. Their multicultural approach counteracts the racial and ethnic biases encountered by people of color. These biases tend to define people of color as the "problem," identifying their differences as due to genetic deficiency (they are intellectually inferior), cultural deficiency (they are culturally deprived), and pathology (they are abnormal or deviant). Instead of problematizing minority groups, the multicultural model is based on the assumption of difference rather than deviance, viewing cultural and ethnic experiences as strengths that are valuable to both the person and society.

In a broader view of multicultural counseling, Leroy Baruth and Lee Manning (1999) include differences in culture, world views, and the nature of reality as well as the variables of gender, sexual orientation, and life stage. Concepts of diversity and multiculturalism vary, depending on the perspectives of the authors. We use the term *diversity* rather than *multicultural* in this book to emphasize both the similarities and the differences among us. Throughout, we take an integrative and inclusive approach that recognizes, respects, and values the diverse factors that impact the lives of women while also identifying our commonalities. For any individual, these factors may include, among others, ethnocultural identity, gender, culture, nationality, language, religion, sexual orientation, physical characteristics and abilities, and socioeconomic class. We say more about diversity and identity in Chapter 2.

## The Meaning of Difference

In addition to the consideration of diversity, it is important to consider two major approaches to gender-related characteristics, those that exaggerate the differences between females and males within and across diverse groups, and those that ignore them. Rachel Hare-Mustin and Jeanne Marecek (1990) refer to these two stances as *alpha bias* and *beta bias.* They maintain that bias toward either approach to gender is problematic for women. We apply this concept as well to other aspects of diversity.

Alpha bias assumes an "essentialist" position, that there are real and enduring differences between the orientations, abilities, and values of women and men, as well as between women and men from diverse groups. This position tends to dichotomize women and men, to support different roles based on their presumed natural dispositions, and to encourage separatism. Examples of alpha bias that heighten the valuing of women include beliefs about women's special "ways of knowing" (Belenky, Clinchey, Goldberger, & Tarule, 1986); and views of woman as more intrinsically relational, caring, and connected than men (Chodorow, 1978; Gilligan, 1982; Jordan, Kaplan, Miller, Stiver, & Surrey, 1991).

Examples of alpha bias that are used to devalue women are found in sociobiology and endocrinology. Here, obtained gender differences are attributed to evolutionary processes such as reproductive strategies (Buss, 1996; Kendrick & Trost, 1993) or to the presumed effects of androgens (male hormones) on brain functioning. In the former case, men's "promiscuity" and social dominance are regarded as natural and rooted in the outcomes of successful mate selection over the centuries. The stronger and more dominant males were able to win many desirable females through successful combat and thus reproduced themselves in greater numbers. In the latter case, sex differences in performance, such as in spatial relations, are attributed to the selective effects of male androgens on the right cerebral hemisphere (brain lateralization). In both examples, gendered patterns of behavior are assumed to result from endogenous or biological variables that reflect "true" sex differences. Based on her examination of extensive data, Ruth Bleier, a biologist, concluded that there is no firm evidence for a biological basis of behavioral differences between females and males (Bleier, 1984, 1988).

Alpha bias has also been used to the disadvantage of the African American woman. By picturing her as "matriarchal" and dominant in her family, she is seen as contributing to the problems encountered by African American men in Western society. In this case, the assumption of difference blames these women for the external barriers of discrimination and exclusion that impede their men (Lott, 1997).

Alpha bias becomes useful, however, in asking new questions about women's experience and in looking at the particular circumstances of their lives apart from those of men. We see in Chapter 10 that a feminist approach to research suggests that specific questions about the lives of women may be generated as a result of considering their unique psychological environments. Alpha bias also allows us to assert that gender as female-male distinction is not the only locus of difference that affects women's lives. The multicultural view of gender affirms the distinctive perspectives of women from diverse social identities. However, to the extent that these perspectives, such as the assumption of female nurturance, are seen as exclusive or "essential" to the identity of all women in diverse social groups, alpha bias may fall into the same problematic space as other essentialist views.

Beta bias ignores or minimizes differences between women and men. Traditional psychological research has erred in the direction of beta bias by (a) ignoring questions related to the diverse lives of women, and (b) assuming that findings based on male samples could be generalized to explain all women's experience and behavior. Minimizing gender and diversity differences frequently leads to disadvantaging many women, for example, assuming that they have equal access to resources and equal opportunities in relationships, employment, and leadership positions. Ignoring questions about women's lives has created a void in the psychological literature about half of the human population. Hare-Mustin and Marecek (1990) caution the helping profession in particular that alpha or beta bias in the context of counseling can be either facilitative or disadvantageous to the client.

Because sex-related attributions and expectations are so heavily dominated by gender conceptions, we may never be able to extricate the "true" effects of sex from those of gender; that is, the direct influence of gender begins well before birth, as expectant parents impose their own gender stereotypes on the unborn child, thus confounding the two variables (Karraker, Vogel, & Lake, 1995). In Chapter 2, we discuss the influence of culturally framed gender expectations on the development of girls and boys.

*Gender Roles*

The concept of gender roles refers to patterns of culturally approved behaviors that are regarded as more desirable for either females or males in a particular culture. The social construction of gender in any culture will function to determine broad expectations for female and male social roles that are consistent with attitudes and world views in that culture. Thus, gender conceptions define what we believe is appropriate behavior in various situations for ourselves as well as for other women or men.

Gender roles in any society are influenced by a large number of variables and will vary within different subcultures and across historical time. We conceptualize the individual's gender-role functioning as multidetermined by both positive and negative societal forces, by life development events, and by the person's own psychological processes (see Figure 1.1). Consistent with our discussion of gender, we assume that being female or male influences the expression and experience of each variable in the model, with the complex intersect of these variables producing the gendered self. For many feminist psychologists, one goal of psychological development is to challenge the primacy of a gendered self, so that culturally prescribed gender roles become more flexible and optional, if not obsolete. With a transcendence beyond assigned gender roles, both women and men would perceive themselves and others as humans with equal options for alternative behaviors (Bem, 1985, 1993; Lott, 1985a, 1997; Worell, 1981).

In Chapter 2, we discuss traditional and emerging flexible gender roles, and possibilities of a gender-flexible individual. One of the aims of a feminist approach to counseling is to assist individuals in freeing themselves from the constrictions of rigid role prescriptions. There is some evidence that traditional gender roles have become more relaxed both in the United States and in other countries over the past 30 years (Sidhu,

2000). The ideal of a gender-flexible self for women, however, is far from realized in any society in which gender and other social status variables determine many of their life-course events.

## Feminist Psychology

Research and scholarship in the psychology of women is not necessarily feminist (Worell, 2000). There is a great deal of overlap and the major scholarly journal, the *Psychology of Women Quarterly,* is feminist in its goals, procedures, and content (Worell, 1990, 1994). In this section, we define feminism and provide examples of feminist orientations to personal and social issues and applications to clinical practice. Feminist research is covered in Chapter 10. Feminist assessment, counseling, and psychotherapy are explored in greater detail in Chapters 3, 4, and 5.

### Defining Feminism

The range of belief systems attached to the term *feminist* is broad. Over 20 years ago, *Webster's New World Dictionary* (1978) defined feminism as (a) "The principle that women should have political, economic, and social rights equal to those of men," and (b) "the movement to win such rights for women" (p. 514). Thus, the dictionary definition included an appeal to social justice and advocacy for social change. We expand this definition to include "equality among women" as well as between women and men, to acknowledge the status and power inequities that may exist across women of differing social locations. With these seemingly benign definitions, it is curious why the statement "I am a feminist" so often elicits a negative reaction. Is it because some people believe that women should not have rights equal to those of men? Or to each other?

Those who identify themselves as feminists express both common and diverse themes. For example, in an interview study with 77 feminist professors of psychology, Faye Crosby and I (JW) asked this question: When you say, "I am a feminist," what do you mean? For our sample of academic women, four common themes expressed their feminist identity: (1) a social construction view of gender, (2) concern with societal power structures that disadvantage women and other subordinate groups, (3) valuing the experience of all women, and (4) willingness to advocate for social change. The most strongly committed in this group ("I always call myself a feminist"), were the most active in the service of social change (Worell, 1996).

From a broader theoretical perspective, feminist theories have addressed the question of how to explain the inequality between women and men in almost all cultures and across all historical times, and how this injustice should be remedied (Enns, 1997). We briefly summarize five major positions in feminist theory: liberal, cultural, radical, women of color, and lesbian (Table 1.1).

The *Liberal* feminist viewpoint targets inequalities in legal, political, and educational arrangements and promotes laws to redress inequities in opportunity for education and employment. In contrast, the *Cultural* feminist addresses the male-dominated culture that devalues women's relational qualities and seeks to empower women by celebrating the unique qualities of women, viewing them as caring, intimate, cooperative, and connected to others. These qualities are valued and become the major source of power and liberation. From a *Radical* feminist approach, however, women's oppression is rooted in patriarchy, or the unequal allocation of power in society to men. The source of women's oppression lies

**Table 1.1    Who is the "real" feminist?**

| Feminist Theory | Sample Attitudes |
| --- | --- |
| Liberal | "I want social, economic, and political rights equal to those of men." |
| Cultural | "If women ran things, the ethic of caring and cooperation would rule." |
| Radical | "The real issues for women are the systems of patriarchy and unequal power." |
| Women of color | "We are oppressed by poverty, racism, and the ethnocentrism of White privilege." |
| Lesbian | "We are oppressed by sexism, heterosexism, and homophobia." |

in institutional male dominance and control of all aspects of women's lives. The identification of patriarchy as a system of male privilege leads to solutions that go beyond "equal pay for equal work," and leads logically to requirements for activism to achieve social and institutional change.

*Women of Color* feminism identifies institutional racism as the major source of women's oppression. Thus, patriarchy, a system of male domination, is not the only source of oppression; both White women and men of color can be oppressors as well as being the oppressed (Comas-Diaz & Greene, 1994). Social change must come through acknowledging and reducing White privilege, honoring the values and culture of oppressed minority groups, and eliminating both institutional racism and sexism. Finally, *Lesbian* feminism identifies both patriarchy and heterosexism as bases for the oppression of women. The assumption that heterosexuality is "normal" frames alternate sexualities and lifestyles as deviant and undesirable, leading to discrimination, exclusion from public life, and restricted civil rights of women who love and live with other women. One proposed solution to challenging heterosexism, albeit not the only one, has been to advocate legislative action toward equality for sexual minorities under the law. As another solution, the promotion of "gay pride" has empowered many in this community to reject social bias and discrimination and to affirm their self-esteem.

The range of definitions and theories about feminism leads us to conclude that feminism, as a social and political movement, is broad and multifaceted. It is clear that many differing attitudes and values are associated with being a feminist, but all roads lead to a simple conclusion: Equality of opportunity, respect, and fair treatment for all persons is essential.

## Defining Feminist Psychology

The applications of the diverse views of feminism have resulted in conflicting definitions in the professional field. Since we take a constructionist view of gender, we shall also do so for feminism: That is, by agreement, we select feminist principles that are most reflective of the values and beliefs to which we subscribe. We are indebted to Barbara Wallston (1986) for her cogent articulation of a similar set of feminist values, and we expand on these to embrace more diverse populations. At the base of these views is the conviction that women's problems cannot be solved in isolation from the institutionalized politics of the larger social structure.

For our purposes, feminist psychology embraces eight tenets:

1. *We advocate inclusiveness.* We acknowledge that the social impact of gender is experienced unequally and unfairly for women with diverse personal and social
   identities, including ethnicity and culture, sexual and affectional orientation, socioeconomic status, nationality, age, and physical characteristics.
2. *We advocate equality.* We recognize that the politics of gender are reflected in
   lower social status and unequal access to valued resources for a majority of
   women in most societies.
3. *We seek new knowledge.* We value and advocate increased understanding about
   the diversity of women's experience as it is framed by multiple personal and social identities.
4. *We attend to context.* Women's lives are embedded in the social, economic, and
   political contexts of their lives and should not be studied in isolation.
5. *We acknowledge values.* Personal and social values enter into all human enterprises; education, science, practice, and social advocacy are never value-free.
6. *We advocate change.* We are committed to action to accomplish social, economic,
   and political change toward establishing equal justice for all persons.
7. *We attend to process.* Decision-making processes that affect personal and group
   outcomes should be consensual and consistent with feminist principles of mutual
   respect and honoring all voices.
8. *We expand psychological practice.* We recognize that feminist principles can be
   applied to all professional activities in which we engage: theory building, prevention, counseling and therapy, assessment, pedagogy, curriculum development, research, supervision, leadership, and professional training.

You may see more than the bare outlines of Webster's Dictionary definition of feminism in these eight principles. We emphasize inclusiveness first and the diversity of oppressed groups, because the politics of racism, ageism, ablism, homophobia, and poverty
deprive individuals of their human dignity and liberties. A feminist lens encourages us
to look at the uses of power and how status hierarchies deprive women from all social locations of their respect, freedom, and equality. In valuing women's experiences, we legitimize the study of women in all their diversities as an important scientific enterprise,
and we encourage innovative methods of research to explore these experiences. We reject
the notion of totally objective science or practice related to behavior and call on educators, researchers, and practitioners to acknowledge their values and biases.

We believe that few individual women can achieve equity alone and that the commitment to feminism requires both individual and collective action for social, institutional,
and political change. We recognize that we may have to accomplish change through the
mechanisms of current power structures, but we endeavor to promote decision-making
processes that are consistent with feminist principles. Finally, we extend our concepts
of feminist practice to all the professional activities in which we engage (see Worell &
Johnson, 1997). Overall, our feminist psychological practice approach seeks a dual outcome: assisting women toward empowerment in their own lives and seeking change in
whatever social power structures form the basis of many of their problems. Although
you may subscribe to many or all of the eight principles, you may not have thought of

yourself as a feminist. In Chapter 11, we discuss further your personal decision to identify as a feminist or a feminist therapist.

## Implications for Training and Practice

The advances of the Psychology of Women in terms of theory and knowledge provide exciting implications for training programs in counseling and psychotherapy. In Chapter 12, we offer a model of training that incorporates this knowledge and uses it in the service of educating and sensitizing prospective practitioners. As a student, we want you to be aware of the diverse gender and cultural stereotypes you may hold, your attitudes toward nontraditional or gender-flexible roles for women and men, and your understanding of the politics of gender as it intersects with other social identities. In particular, you will want to understand the social impact of violating traditional gender roles in the context of multicultural constraints and the price that women (and men) from differing social locations may pay for doing so.

An effective program for training counselors for women incorporates a research component that avoids gender and multicultural bias in method and content, and that explores the diverse lives of both women and men. The program also includes a feminist analysis of client issues and careful supervision to provide constructive feedback to the therapist. We believe that without such awareness, you are likely to impose your stereotypes on your clients. In doing so, you may unwittingly support them in "adjusting" to the status quo and in remaining in subordinate life positions. As you read this book, please complete all the self-assessment and awareness activities. These activities are designed to assist you in evaluating and changing, if necessary, your social constructions of sex, gender, and diversity. The goal of these activities is to promote the effective and ethical treatment of women.

## EMERGENT CLIENT POPULATIONS

The second requirement for a specialty in counseling and therapy with women is a client population whose needs and goals are not being met by traditional practices and procedures. How does the population of women clients differ from those of the past? What are their special needs that require advanced knowledge, skills, and specialized training?

### Family Role Shifts

Dramatic changes in the formation and maintenance of family roles in the past 20 years have lead to a shift in many women's lifestyles, in the situations they face, and in the problems with which they cope. In particular, women are remaining single more frequently and for longer periods of time, finding partners or marrying later, having fewer children, entering the paid labor force at an unprecedented rate, developing new career paths, separating and divorcing more often, coping with single parenting and stepparenting, reentering higher education at later ages, experiencing interrupted careers and employment paths, and repartnering or remarrying. They are growing older and living longer, and may find themselves "sandwiched" between growing children and elderly parents, or living alone. New definitions of "family" have encouraged marginalized groups such as lesbian and bisexual women to confront their relationship needs more openly. Each of these life events may present situational coping problems and issues for which women seek help.

The increase of women in the paid labor force confronts them with a host of new issues: managing multiple roles, negotiating dual-career and egalitarian relationships, coping with role conflict (work-family balance) and role strain (work-family stress), nontraditional career development and change, employment discrimination, pay equity, professional isolation, sexual harassment, management and leadership training, assertiveness concerns, workforce reentry, and retirement. Figure 1.2 displays the dramatic increase in women's labor force participation from 1975 through 1995.

The prevalence of singleness and high divorce rates opens up issues of finding new relationships, establishing sexual satisfaction, developing social support networks, divorce counseling, child custody and maintenance decisions, managing stepchildren and reconstituted families, and coping with financial stress and loneliness. Chapters 6 and 7 consider clients who seek counseling because of family and work-related conflicts.

## Women and Violence

The exposure of violence and sexual assault to public scrutiny in the past 20 years has had two positive effects on client populations. First, more women are seeking assistance following violent experiences such as rape or physical and emotional abuse. Second,

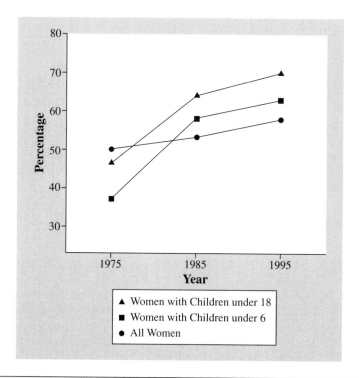

**Figure 1.2    Percentage of women in the labor force in the United States.** *Source: U.S. Office of Labor Statistics.*

women who have been abused through incest or sexual assault as children are coming to terms with the long-term impact of their early victimization. The establishment of crisis centers for sexual assault and woman-battering has encouraged many women who formerly would have suffered in silence to seek assistance. The "normalization" of this violence may appear frightening when we look at prevalence rates: Depending on the particular survey, one in four adult women have been sexually assaulted at some time in their lives (Koss et al., 1994), and 20% to 35% of women report being or having been in an abusive or battering relationship (McHugh, Frieze, & Browne, 1993). Public attention to violence has had the salutary effect of encouraging women to confront their abuse by saying, "No more secrets." Chapters 8 and 9 deal with clients who were physically and sexually abused.

## Women and Body

Certain syndromes have increased in reported frequency as society places continuing demands on women to conform to gender-role standards, and as women are becoming concerned with the care and maintenance of their bodies. There is a rising prevalence of girls and women concerned with body image and weight control, as evidenced by eating disturbances such as anorexia, bulimia, and obesity (Striegel-Moore & Cachelin, 1997). Women also seek psychological help in dealing with medical and physical concerns: AIDS, mastectomy, menstrual-related distress, reproductive issues including pregnancy, unplanned pregnancy and infertility, and problems concerning the abuse of addictive substances such as alcohol and prescription drugs.

## Women with Diverse Identities

Finally, we are increasingly aware of higher risk for women with diverse group identities. Women in high-risk groups are those with issues that are compounded by exclusion and discrimination as a result of experiences of racism, ageism, homophobia, immigration, and poverty (see Figure 1.1). Women from high-risk groups have been reluctant to seek help from the mental health community, partly because they anticipate and frequently experience a reenactment of societal discrimination in psychotherapy. As new multicultural approaches to counseling and therapy are developed and practiced, more of these women are encouraged to seek help in dealing with their particular concerns.

The emergence of multiple and complex lifespan issues for women in contemporary Western societies provides a sufficient rationale for the development of new approaches for addressing these issues. The implications of diverse client populations for both research and practice are evident.

## A FEMINIST RESEARCH AGENDA

The third requirement for a specialty in counseling and psychotherapy with women is a firm foundation of research related to their mental health concerns. There is a pressing need for increased research to broaden the knowledge base about women's mental health concerns. More information is required to gain a firm understanding of the multiple factors that contribute to stress and distress in all groups of women, as well as to their strengths and resilience.

Alternative and creative methods of research become important to gain new knowledge, enabling a fuller exploration of women's lives in context (M. C. Crawford & Kimmel, 1999; S. Reinhardz, 1992; Riger, 1992). The application of feminist principles to the conduct and content of research has brought about a transformation in how we go about our research activities (Grossman et al., 1997; Worell & Etaugh, 1994). During the past 30 years, a plethora of scholarly journals that focus on women's lives have been established. The most visible include *Psychology of Women Quarterly, Sex Roles, Violence and Victims, Women and Therapy, Journal of Interpersonal Violence, Feminism and Psychology, Women and Health,* and the *Journal of Feminist Family Therapy.* Many other research journals in counseling psychology and related areas have begun to include articles related to women's health and well-being. The research base on women's lives is dynamic, alive, and expanding. We discuss issues in feminist research in Chapter 10.

## NEW MODELS AND EMERGENT PROCEDURES

It has been evident to many of us in the professional arena that traditional approaches to prevention and intervention for women were inadequate. Methods of treatment entrenched in the medical model tend to label the woman as disordered and to locate the problem in her biology, personality, or deficient skills; we regard these as insufficient to address the multiple forces that impact on women's well-being. New information on cultural norms suggests that the expression of distress and pain may be evaluated differently across cultural groups; what is normal for one culture may appear very deviant to another (S. R. Lopez & Guarnaccia, 2000). We take the position here that "fixing" the woman to return to her former status and adjustment is unsatisfactory and unacceptable. The psychiatric concept of *remission* as a definition of a positive outcome for psychotherapy exemplifies this traditional approach. Models of counseling and psychotherapy that aim to remove pathology are frequently inappropriate for women (and especially for some in minority groups), by targeting inappropriate or limited aspects of their lives. Innovative approaches and strategies are clearly required. Chapters 3, 4, and 5 present a framework for reconstructing an alternative view of the counseling and therapy process for women that focuses on building strengths, empowerment, and resilience.

The final step in developing a specialty in feminist psychological practice leads us to introduce innovative models and procedures. Dissatisfactions with and perceived limitations of traditional therapies paved the way for major changes in the treatment of women. The development of feminist approaches to intervention with women signaled a dramatic break from previous therapies in many aspects of values and procedures. In addition to the general principles of feminist therapies, specialized interventions that target the unique issues and concerns of underserved or inappropriately served client groups have been formulated. In recognition of an essential component of any practice, ethical principles in counseling and therapy with women have been developed by feminist groups.

### Feminist Psychological Practice

The development of feminist principles and procedures in counseling stretches from the early beginnings of consciousness-raising groups (Brodsky, 1973; Kravetz, 1980) to the 1982 establishment of the Feminist Therapy Institute for advanced psychotherapists (Rosewater & Walker, 1985). Following these two developments, many talented practitioners and scholars have contributed creatively to the growing literature in this field. The 1993 First National Conference on Feminist Practice brought together more than 90 scholars and practitioners to develop an agenda for the future of feminist practice. This group expanded the concept of practice by including 10 separate but interconnected areas: Theory, Assessment, Therapy, Research, Curriculum, Teaching, Diversity, Supervision, Postdoctoral Training, and Student Voices (Worell & Johnson, 1997). We add two important areas of feminist practice to this model: Prevention and Leadership. The principles developed through consensus at this important conference are discussed throughout this book.

New horizons in feminist practice have gradually evolved. The Feminist Academy (L. Brown, 1996) was established to provide continuing education for new and seasoned practitioners. A specialty in Feminist Psychological Practice was developed for submission to the American Psychology Association for inclusion in the accreditation procedures (Remer, Enns, Fisher, Nutt, & Worell, 2001). Revised Guidelines for Counseling Women were drafted to replace the earlier ones (Enns, Nutt, & Rice, 2002). We credit our thinking about feminist practice to the accumulated writings, dialogue, and practical experiences of innumerable colleagues.

## Principles of Feminist Practice

From the diverse theories and aggregate wisdom discussed, we adopt an integrative perspective based on four essential principles of feminist practice:

1. *Attention to the diversity of women's personal and social identities.* The intersects of women's multiple identities, whether consciously experienced or unaware, are explored and examined for their influences on client expectations and behaviors, and on their experiences of privilege or oppression.
2. *A consciousness-raising approach.* Clients are helped to differentiate between the politics of the sexist, racist, or homophobic societal structures that influence their lives and those problems over which they have realistic control. Intrapsychic causation for problems in living is supplanted by exploration of gender-role messages mediated by their culture, societal expectations, and institutionalized sexism, racism, or homophobia.
3. *An egalitarian relationship between client and therapist.* The client is encouraged to set personal goals and trust her own experience and judgment. Power differentials between client and therapist are minimized.
4. *A woman-valuing and self-validating process.* Communal qualities of interdependence, concern for others, emotional expression, and cooperation are valued and honored. Women are encouraged to identify their strengths, to value and nurture themselves, and to bond with other women. Language forms that devalue women are reframed from weakness to strengths (e.g., terms such as *enmeshed* and *fused* may be reframed as *caring, concerned,* and *nurturing*).

## An Empowerment Model

We present an empowerment model of counseling that incorporates and expands on the theoretical perspectives and principles described earlier. Empowerment is a broad goal of feminist intervention that enables individuals, families, and communities to exert influence over the personal, interpersonal, and institutional factors that impact their health and well-being (Worell, 2001; Wyche & Rice, 1997). The overall goals of personal and social empowerment emphasize client strengths and resilience in coping with past, current, and future trauma and stress.

## Why Empowerment?

Does it appear that we suggest a focus on clients' empowerment rather than on symptom reduction or a return to their baseline functioning prior to entering therapy? Of course we want clients to feel better after they terminate therapy than before they sought services. We believe that empowerment encompasses both goals. To understand the importance of an empowerment frame, we need to consider briefly four critical concepts: power, oppression, empowerment, and resilience.

*Power* has been defined in many ways and is a term that communicates both positive and negative meanings. Power hierarchies can exist at many levels: individual, interpersonal, organizational, and societal (Ragins & Sundstrom, 1989). In practice, these categories probably overlap. In the typical therapy dyad, power is reflected in "the amount of unshared control possessed by one member of a dyad over the other member . . ." (Georgeson & Harris, 2000, p. 1239). At a more societal level, Carolyn Sherif (1982) described power as control over social institutions and their various resources, enabling the power holder to establish rules, initiate action, make decisions, and impose rewards and punishments on others. Although power is typically associated with gender, males holding more than females in most societies, power also interacts with other socially defined groups. Thus, there are dominant (more powerful) groups in all societies that have control over many of the resources available to subordinate (less powerful) groups. The use of their legitimized power by dominant social groups leads to oppression, or the exclusion of less powerful groups from valued resources.

*Oppression* is also defined in many ways. We define oppression as ownership or access to valued resources by members of dominant social groups while denying or limiting access to these resources for members of subordinate groups. For the dominant group, oppression can be justified by defining subordinate groups as different or inferior, and thus they can be seen as less in need or less deserving of these resources. Oppression creates a toxic environment for subordinate groups that may result in illness and alienation. We do not imply that the process of oppression is necessarily conscious or intentional; it may vary from benign to hostile, and from covert to overt. For example, by constructing the "true" nature of women as passive, nurturant, indecisive, and emotional, they become clearly more suited than men for household duties, child care, and other care, and less suited for business or organizational leadership. Since both women and ethnocultural minority groups are subordinate in Western societies, empowerment may enable them to reclaim the asymmetry in access to valued resources.

Empowerment is conceptualized in two ways in the context of therapy. First, clients are empowered in dealing with their life situations through achieving skills and flexibility in problem solution, and developing a full range of interpersonal and life skills. They learn to identify and cherish their personal strengths and assets as well as recognize their responsibility for change. Cultural and personal identities are explored for their contributions to client concerns and for their relevance in strengthening personal and cultural pride. Second, empowerment encourages women to identify and challenge the external conditions of their lives that devalue and subordinate them as women or as members of minority groups, and that deny them equality of opportunity and access to valued social, economic, and institutional resources—those sources of reward, suste-nance, support, or opportunity that are identified as important and meaningful by each group or individual.

Feminist approaches to empowerment thus incorporate both internal and external contributions to personal distress and well-being, and assist women to discriminate be-tween them. This discrimination functions to free them from feelings of being different, deficient, "crazy," or out of control; it replaces their sense of powerlessness with strength and pride in their ability to cope with current and future challenges. These new feelings and skills lead to increasing resilience in coping with stress and adversity.

Resilience and thriving are new ways to look at the mental health outcomes of fem-inist therapy (Worell, 2001; Worell & Johnson, 2001). Empowerment is assumed to lead to resilience through supporting the knowledge and skills that facilitate effective coping with future situational inequities, discrimination, exclusion, and interpersonal stress. The resilient person is able to respond to increased stress and negative life events with effective coping skills that enable her to maintain her sense of well-being and effective functioning. These may be skills and attitudes that are learned early in life, capabilities acquired through survival following aversive events, or skills devel-oped through an affirmative and empowering therapy experience. We think of empow-erment and resilience as more than the absence of pathology. There is also evidence that some individuals move beyond resilience to thriving, or positive growth, following the resolution of trauma and stress (Tedeschi & Calhoun, 1995). That is, they may find new meanings and a new sense of purpose in life. More research is needed to under-stand how clients move from empowerment to resilience to thriving. Chapter 3 de-scribes the empowerment model in the context of the four principles of Empowerment Feminist Therapy and provides multiple goals and specific strategies that represent each principle.

### Measuring Empowerment

To conceptualize empowerment as a testable model, it is first necessary to identify its components and then to develop measures to assess them. The Empowerment Model of Women's Well-Being (Worell, 1993b, 2001) provides 10 variables that contribute to em-powerment and resilience (see Table 1.2). The model offers a theoretical conceptualiza-tion that can guide therapy goals, interventions, and the evaluation of therapy outcomes. The utility of this model in assessing therapeutic effectiveness is discussed further in Chapter 10.

The ten hypothesized outcomes of the Empowerment Model are supported by the lit-erature on women's health and well-being. The healthy woman in a healthy environment is envisioned as having positive self-evaluation and self-esteem, a favorable comfort-distress balance (more positive than negative affect), gender-role and cultural identity awareness, a sense of personal control and self-efficacy, self-nurturance and self-care, effective problem-solving skills, competent use of assertiveness skills, effective access to facilitative social, economic, and community resources, gender and cultural flexibil-ity in behavior, and socially constructive activism. In brief, she is confident, strong, connected to a supportive community, and resilient.

To measure empowerment as an outcome in feminist practice, the Personal Progress Scale (PPS) was developed to measure each of the ten hypothesized outcomes of femi-nist empowerment therapy (Worell, Chandler, Johnson, & Blount, in press). In Chapters 2 and 3, we introduce the PPS; and in Chapter 10, we present the outcomes of feminist

**Table 1.2    Empowerment model of women's well-being**

| Outcome | Description |
| --- | --- |
| Self-evaluation | Improved self-esteem, self-affirmation. |
| Comfort-distress ratio | Less distress and more comfort. |
| Gender- and culture-role awareness | Behaviors informed by gender- and culture-role and power analysis of continuing life situations. |
| Personal control/self-efficacy | Improved perception of personal control and self-efficacy. |
| Self-nurturance | Increase in self-nurturing behaviors and avoidance of self-abusing behaviors. |
| Problem-solving skills | Improved problem-solving skills. |
| Assertiveness | Increased use of respectful assertiveness skills. |
| Resource access | Increased access to social, economic, and community support. |
| Gender and cultural flexibility | Flexibility and choice in beliefs and behaviors informed by gender and cultural identity. |
| Social activism | Involvement in social activism, institutional change. |

*Source:* J. Worell, (1993, November). *What Do We Really Know about Feminist Therapiest. Approaches to Research on Process and Outcome.* Invited presentation to the Texas Psychological Association, Austin, Texas.

therapy using the PPS as well as several other measures of feminist therapy process and outcome.

*Feminist Strategies*

As we have seen, the tenets of feminist counseling and therapy cut across diverse theories and specific techniques. Feminist therapists endorse a range of theoretical views and employ many different kinds of strategies and specific interventions. We are personally committed to two different, but not incompatible, theoretical views: cognitive-behavioral, and psychodrama. Each of us has adapted a basic theoretical orientation and techniques to render it compatible with EFT principles and procedures. In Chapter 4 we provide a method for transforming a theory of counseling to render it more consistent with feminist views. Some theories may be more conducive to this transformation process than others, depending on the extent to which they endorse gender-biased or ethnocentric concepts or procedures. Ethnocentric concepts assume that the language and constructs that apply to one group are universal across all groups.

Across various theories, however, some techniques are used commonly by most feminist therapists. Strategies that may be common to most feminist approaches include gender-role analysis, power analysis, and demystifying methods. In gender-role analysis, clients are helped to identify how societal structures and expectations related to traditional gender arrangements have influenced their lives. Power analysis explores the power differential between women and men (and/or between oppressed and dominant groups) in Western societies and assists clients in understanding both the destructive and effective uses of personal and institutional power. In demystification, clients are provided with information about therapeutic procedures and the process of change, and with the tools for evaluating and monitoring their own progress. While demystification is not unique to feminist approaches, it is used strategically as a means of reducing the power differential between client and therapist and thus empowering the client.

More recently, multicultural perspectives have emphasized the importance of a cultural analysis, recognizing that psychological intervention always occurs in a cultural context. Clients are encouraged to explore their personal and social identities, and how their assimilation of the dominant or external culture matches or conflicts with their internally generated cultural messages and values. In the context of therapy, cultural differences across the three-way interaction among client, therapist, and the intervention setting may produce tensions and misunderstandings (Ridley et al., 1998). The use of each of these strategies requires the development of specialized competencies that include relevant sensitivity, knowledge, attitudes, and skills. We describe these strategies and competencies more fully in Chapter 3.

## Ethical Principles

The development of ethical principles specifically designed for intervention with women represents another area in which approaches to interventions with women have been advanced (Rave & Larson, 1995). Following a major survey in which gender-biased practices of psychotherapists were uncovered (American Psychological Association, 1975), several groups in the American Psychological Association formulated ethical principles in practice with women. These principles are further described and explained in Chapter 11. One indicator of the legitimacy of a discipline or field is the presence of an ethical code. We believe that the adoption of ethical procedures should become routine for all the helping professions, working not only with women but also with minority or oppressed groups.

## DIRECTIONS FOR CHANGE

Feminist views of intervention with women incorporate a mandate for public action and social change. It is insufficient to "fix" the woman for functioning in a dysfunctional society. Our model of intervention for empowerment includes an outreach component with action on three levels: community involvement, consumer enlightenment, and social policy.

At the community level, we involve ourselves with agencies and local groups that work on behalf of women's issues. The consumer enlightenment level encourages us to disseminate information about women to relevant groups, so that this information can be integrated toward modifying prevailing attitudes, beliefs, and practices. Relevant groups might include professional organizations, law enforcement, parents, teachers, schools, and the public media.

Action on social policy goes further to influence legislation, funding, and public policies that will eliminate gender-based and racial/ethnic stereotypes, prevailing power differentials, and support of discriminatory practices. As professional practice, consumer enlightenment, and social policy work together to effect social change, we will see new visions of what we are and what we can become.

## SUMMARY

In this chapter, we presented the outlines for developing and implementing a specialty in feminist practice with women. The requirements for this specialty include a field of knowledge about the psychology of women, a population of clients whose needs are not being met by current approaches, a research agenda that provides a blueprint for future research needs, and a therapeutic approach that is tailored to the population of clients being served. The outlines for this specialty require new training programs to implement the guidelines for change and an outreach plan that effects changes in policies across educational, government, and political structures.

## ACTIVITIES

**A.** As a woman—look back at your life as a woman. Consider the challenges you faced, and assess your strengths as you met and survived these challenges. Appreciate and take pride in your strengths. Share your thoughts with a partner or friend.

**B.** As a man—think about the important women in your life. Select one or several and consider the challenges they faced as women. Assess their strengths as they met these challenges. Appreciate and take pride in their strengths. Share your ideas with a partner or friend.

## FURTHER READINGS

Hare-Mustin, R. T., & Marecek, J. (1990). *Making a difference: Psychology and the construction of gender.* New Haven, CT: Yale University Press.

Landrine, H. (1995). *Bringing cultural diversity to feminist psychology: Theory, research, and practice.* Washington, DC: American Psychological Association.

Silverstein, L. B., & Goodrich, T. J. (2001). Feminist family therapy. In J. Worell (Ed.), *Encyclopedia of women and gender: Sex similarities and differences and the impact of society on gender* (Vol. 1, pp. 447–456). San Diego, CA: Academic Press.

Worell, J., & Johnson, N. G. (Eds.). (1997). *Shaping the future of feminist psychology: Education, research, and practice.* Washington, DC: American Psychological Association.

# Chapter 2

# *SOCIALIZATION FOR WOMANHOOD: DEVELOPING PERSONAL AND SOCIAL IDENTITIES*

*Others are central to the existence and possibility of being an individual. Because of the formative quality of the person-other relationship, there can be no individuality without collectivity, no independence without interdependence. . . .*

Edward Sampson, 2000

*How do we understand and incorporate the "other"? How do we reconcile being the other?*

Bonnie R. Strickland, 2000

## SELF-ASSESSMENT: EXPLORING PERSONAL IDENTITY

Each person has some answers to the question "Who am I?" Most of us respond to this question in ways that are both similar and different from how others respond. Some of the group identities that individuals use to define themselves are listed next. In the spaces to the right, briefly in your own words state "who you are" or how you define yourself. For example, for the space marked *nationality,* you might write "American" or "Chinese." For the space marked *ethnicity,* you might write "African American," "Caribbean," "Chinese American," or "Mandarin," to define your ethnic identity. There are no right or wrong answers.

Sex                              _____

Age                              _____

Educational level                _____

Nationality                      _____

Sexual orientation               _____

Ethnicity                        _____

Race/skin color                  _____

Religious orientation            _____

Social class status               _____

Immigration/citizenship status     _____

Primary/secondary language(s)      _____

Physical characteristics/body image   _____

Physical ability/disability         _____

Other                             _____

Each of the these categories provides an opportunity to locate yourself in a position of relative social advantage (privilege) or disadvantage (oppression). If you identified yourself as male, American, Caucasian (or White), middle class, heterosexual, English-speaking, Protestant or Christian, a citizen born in the United States, tall, muscular, and athletic, you have described what is referred to as "seats of privilege." That is, these are characteristics that enable individuals to access and benefit from a variety of community resources with relative ease. You have described characteristics that are valued and "privileged" in the broad U.S. culture. On the other hand, if you described yourself as female, dark-skinned, Arabic, recent immigrant, Muslim, short, heavy, and elderly, you have described some of the general characteristics that may present barriers in U.S. society and may lead to experiences of discrimination or disadvantage (oppression) for you. That is, these are characteristics that signal that you are less valued and less respected in some venues, such as education or employment, and may provide barriers to you in accessing valued community resources. Few of us occupy social locations that are all either privileged or undervalued.

Now compare your responses to the categories appearing in the model in Figure 2.1. Can you identify each of these responses as representing privilege or oppression (barriers to access or opportunity) for you in your experience? Does an identity that represents privilege in contemporary society make you feel proud and empowered, or defensive and uncomfortable? Do you dislike the idea that you may be disadvantaged or excluded because of who you are? Keep these ideas about privilege and oppression in mind as we discuss the development of our personal and social identities.

## OVERVIEW

We know that in all cultures, females and males grow up in environments that are physically and psychologically different in important ways. All levels of sociocultural environments have been found to exert significant pressures on developing individuals to adapt and conform to prevailing expectations for gender-typed behavior. These external influences on gender socialization include a person's cultural background and community; the family; the educational system; the media; public, political, and religious institutions; and the workplace. An important outcome of these socializing agents for individual development is the gradual formation of a sense of self or personal and social identity, represented by the simple, yet complex, question "Who am I?" We consider this question first in the context of the link between personal and social identities that constructs for each of us a multifactored and intersecting matrix of self-definition. We

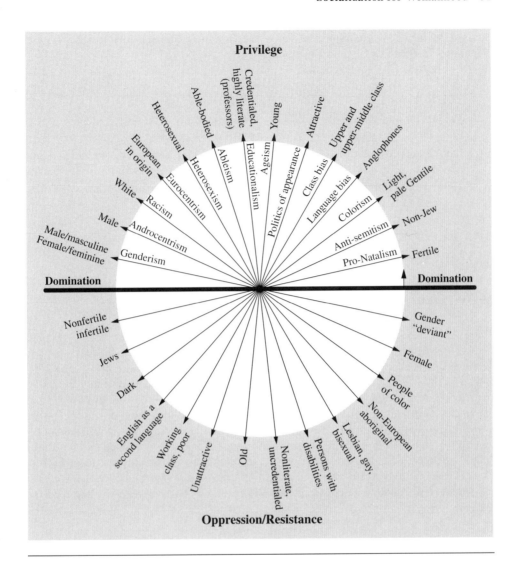

Figure 2.1   Intersecting axes of privilege, domination, and oppression. *Source: From The Gender Question in Education: Theory, Pedagogy, and Politics, by A. Diller, B. Houston, K. P. Morgan, and M. Ayim, 1996, Boulder, CO: Westview Press. Reprinted with permission.*

present a model of personal and social identity, and we link these identities to the process of counseling and therapy.

Socialization influences on individual development are then viewed from four major perspectives: the family, the educational system, the media, and the workplace. We discuss the implications of these socialization agents and social role expectations for personal and interpersonal functioning. Even as new social roles and revised standards for social behavior emerge, however, both the dominant and minority or ethnic cultures continue to transmit messages that support moving women into traditional institutionalized social structures. We examine these processes for their contributions to the problems and issues that women bring to counseling.

After reading Chapter 2, you will be able to:

- Discuss how personal and social identities are interdependent.
- Explain how each level of identity development for any aspect of a person's identity (e.g., ethnicity, gender) may influence personal functioning and well-being.
- Define and describe the impact of SEARCH (sexism, ethnocentrism, ableism and ageism, racism, classism, and heterosexism) variables on personal well-being.
- Describe the dimensions of family socialization that differentiate the experiences of girls and boys.
- List the contributions of schools, the media, and the workplace to the barriers that face today's women.
- Discuss the advantages of egalitarian relationships.

## EXPLORING PERSONAL AND SOCIAL IDENTITIES

Each client who seeks help in redesigning her life situation is a unique person. Her individual life pattern and experiences, just like her DNA, are matched by no other person. However, each client is also a member of multiple groups that can be defined by categories such as age, life stage, sexual orientation, nationality, physical characteristics such as skin color, ethnic origin, cultural identity, religious or spiritual orientation, employment status, educational attainment, physical or mental disability, or socioeconomic level. Identification with any of these groups (as well as other groups not listed) is accompanied by implicit or explicit norms and standards that may define and structure the client's beliefs, attitudes, values, expectations, and interpersonal transactions. Each of us is connected to a network of social categories or groups that influence the ways we experience the world, how we construct meanings, and how we are perceived and received by others.

### Identity Characteristics

Social identities can be characterized by the way others react, as well as the way in which we react to ourselves. The impact of social identities is influenced by *visibility, situational salience,* and *social privilege.* Some categories, such as skin color and other visible characteristics, are relatively public and easily discernable by others. In contrast, some categories are relatively invisible until disclosed, such as sexual orientation or religious affiliation. The dimension of *visibility* may impact individuals differentially at various levels of their awareness or identity development for that category. Although the multiplicity of social locations and their associated meanings are interconnected and exist simultaneously for any individual, they may not be *salient* or operational until primed by situational or life stage contexts. Your identity as an African American woman, for example, will probably be more salient for you in a business meeting with a group of all-White men than when you are at home with family or close friends. Additionally, each point of identity, such as ethnicity, may reflect unique experiences, norms, and cultural ethics. And each aspect of identity may reflect socially conferred *privilege* and entitlement or oppression, discrimination, and powerlessness. Figure 2.1 displays a useful model for visualizing the intersects of social identities that clients may experience, representing institutionalized advantage (privilege) or disadvantage and bias (oppression) for them. How do these identities match your own life experience?

The impact for any individual of the socialization variables we discuss next are mediated by the complex matrix of the person's social locations and their experiences in them. We agree with Kay Deaux (1993) that "personal identity is defined, at least in part, by group memberships, and social categories are infused with personal meanings" (p. 5). Thus, social and personal identities are interdependent and intersecting. The intersect of identities implies that in any situation, one or more may be relevant for the individual and more salient in personal awareness. Thus, Janet, a woman of color who uses a wheelchair for locomotion, is more aware of her disability than her ethnicity when confronted with a flight of stairs. However, if Janet is the only woman of color in a large male-oriented business office, her ethnic and gender identities are more likely to be present in her concerns. Finally, if Janet is then fired from her job, she may wonder which of the three identities (gender, ethnicity, disability) influenced the decision or perhaps none of them if her work was unsatisfactory. It is important in the counseling relationship to assist clients in the process of understanding and appreciating the significance of her multiple locations.

### Searching for Bias

This model of diversity shows that there are many opportunities for individuals to experience either positive or negative outcomes because of their personal and social identities. Clients such as Janet who are seeking psychological help may be dealing with one or more aspects of institutional bias and discrimination. Throughout this book in our discussions of bias and oppression, we use the term *SEARCH* as an inclusive description. *SEARCH* represents sexism, ethnocentrism, ableism and ageism, racism, classism, and heterosexism, but your search for external sources of oppression should extend beyond these seven variables. In the process of assessment, diagnosis, and interventions with clients, it is important for you to "search" for the influence of external pressures, as well as attend to the client's internal processes.

## Personal/Social Identities in the Counseling Relationship

For each client, both acknowledged and unacknowledged identification with social locations that are important to her functions to shape many of the expectations, attitudes, and behaviors that she brings to the counseling relationship. Similarly, your own group identities and experiences will have shaped your personal biases, attitudes, values, and expectations about others. Both client's and therapist's personal and social identities, then, influence the course of therapist-client interactions. We believe that an awareness and understanding of the client's important group identities is essential to the practice of ethical and effective counseling.

Therapists and counselors who work with clients who are different from themselves in functionally important ways (age, ethnicity, sexual/affectional orientation, etc.) need to develop multiple skills to enable them to approach each client with empathy and sensitivity to her particular group identities, as well as to her individual issues (B. Greene & Croom, 2000; Sue & Sue, 1999). The skills for working with clients who differ from the therapist in important ways been described as *multicultural competencies,* which consist of three broad components: attitudes/beliefs, knowledge, and skills (T. L.

Robinson & Howard-Hamilton, 2000; Sue & Sue, 1999). For the feminist therapist, it is particularly critical to recognize the implicit power imbalance that occurs when the client's important identities lie with culturally oppressed groups. The multicultural counseling skills presented in Table 2.1 assist the therapist in identifying and modifying those attitudes and behaviors that communicate inequality and distance to the client. We return to further discussion of these competencies in later chapters.

What is the importance to counselors and therapists of understanding both your own and your clients' personal/social identities and the level of awareness or development for each of these identities? First, your awareness and exploration of your own identities may provide pathways or barriers to understanding and facilitating awareness for your clients. The greater the similarity of your cultural background, for example, to that of your client, the easier it may be for you to understand, accept, and respond appropriately to her values and world views. In contrast, as you and your client diverge in cultural background and levels of awareness, the greater the possibility that you will misunderstand, misinterpret, or mishandle her communications and her concerns. For example, in a cross-cultural study examining the question "Who am I?" college students in the United States described themselves in relatively unique and positive terms that reflected personally valued and stable internal traits. In contrast, students in Japan were more modest or self-critical, and their self-descriptors were more situational and connected to particular social contexts (Kanagawa, Cross, & Markus, 2001). In the absence of understanding

**Table 2.1   Characteristics of the multiculturally skilled feminist therapist**

| | |
|---|---|
| Knowledge | Has a good understanding of the sociopolitical system's operation in the dominant culture with respect to its treatment of minorities. |
| | Possesses specific knowledge and information about the particular group with whom she/he is working. |
| | Is aware of institutional barriers that prevent minorities from using mental health services. |
| Attitudes | Is aware and sensitive to her or his cultural heritage and to valuing and respecting differences. |
| | Is aware of her or his own values and biases and how they may affect minority clients. |
| | Is comfortable with differences that exist between self and client in terms of ethnicity, age, culture, sexual orientation, socioeconomic status (SES), and beliefs. |
| | Is sensitive to circumstances (personal biases, sociopolitical influences, etc.) that may suggest referral of the minority client to a member of her own reference group. |
| Skills | Can generate a wide variety of verbal and nonverbal responses. |
| | Can send and receive both verbal and nonverbal responses accurately and appropriately. |
| | Is able to exercise institutional intervention skills on behalf of her or his client. |

Adapted from *Counseling American Minorities* (5th ed.), by D. R. Atkinson, G. Morton, and D. W. Sue, 1998, Boston: McGraw-Hill.

these diverse cultural contexts, a therapist might misconstrue a Japanese client in this case as indecisive and as having low self-esteem.

Second, both you and the client will want to explore her level of awareness for each of her social identities as they become salient to her concerns. This awareness has two functions. For the client, awareness of her social locations can facilitate her self-understanding and self-acceptance. For you as therapist, your knowledge of her identity development on any dimension may suggest an appropriate entry point and possible strategies for intervention.

## Dimensions of Identity Development

Models of identity development were developed to account for individual differences in self-knowledge, attitudes, and behaviors of individuals from ethnic and cultural minority groups (Sue & Sue, 1999). Examples of these include models for nigrescence or Black awareness (Cross, 1980), lesbian identity (Cass, 1979), feminist identity (Downing & Rousch, 1985), racial/cultural identity (Atkinson, Morton, & Sue, 1998), and White racial identity (Helms, 1990). The utility of these models is at least threefold: to (1) deconstruct stereotypes, (2) guide intervention, and (3) evaluate outcomes (see Table 2.2). Thus, if Charmaine is in denial about her bicultural heritage (Level 1, Table 2.3), your suggestion that she reach out to her extended family for support may fall on deaf ears for Charmaine, who perceives herself as autonomous, independent, and perfectly able to take care of herself.

The major models of identity development just listed consist of a series of relatively discrete stages, with persons moving from the lowest stage of unawareness (naïveté, denial, or conformity) through to the highest stage of awareness (integration, appreciation, internalization). In contrast, we prefer to conceptualize the process of personal/social identity development as a graded set of dimensions, each of which varies from low to high in terms of how an individual might be categorized or conceptualized. Thus, a person may identify with components of each dimension, rather than being located at only one stage. Further, we believe it is important to understand how these dimensions of personal/social identity are impacted by whether they reflect social advantage (privilege), create risk for discrimination and exclusion (oppression), or by a mixture of both. In the personal/social identity model presented next, we illuminate how aspects of both oppression and privilege can operate simultaneously at each level.

**Table 2.2    The utility of identity development models**

| Application | Rationale |
| --- | --- |
| Deconstruct stereotypes | Monolithic conceptions by both therapists and clients of diverse cultural groups are dismantled to illuminate the range of beliefs and attitudes for individuals in these groups. |
| Guide interventions | Possible points of entry for therapeutic interventions are considered in light of clients' primary level of identity for relevant social locations. |
| Evaluate outcomes | Effectiveness of interventions for therapeutic, educational, or community change will be reflected in client movement along the identity development continuum. |

**Table 2.3   Personal/social identity development**

**Level 1: Preawareness**

*Privilege/Advantage*

    Conforms to majority norms and values; believes these are universal.

    Accepts cultural stereotypes of the oppressed group.

    Believes own group is better than others.

    Is unaware of or denies own privileged status; accepts it as normal and deserved.

    Has access to valued societal resources.

    Believes in a just world in which meritocracy determines personal outcomes (I deserve the good things I have in life).

*Oppression/Disadvantage*

    Conforms to majority norms and values.

    Deprecates own group and appreciates majority group.

    Accepts negative stereotypes about own group.

    Is self-deprecating and self-blaming.

    Has low access to societal resources.

    Believes in a just world (I don't deserve more than I have).

**Level 2: Encounter**

*Privilege/Advantage*

    Becomes aware of privileged status.

    Acknowledges that privilege is connected to groups status.

    Becomes aware of discrimination and stereotyping.

    Is uncomfortable with possibility of self as oppressor.

    Experiences cognitive dissonance, conflict, or guilt.

    Experiences conflict with prior views of self and others.

*Oppression/Disadvantage*

    Becomes aware of oppression as member of own group.

    Has conflicting views of self and others.

    Is conflicted over valuing self and valuing dominant group.

    Is aware of oppressed status of one's own entire group.

    Experiences relief: It's not my fault.

    Becomes angry about the injustice and harm to self and group.

**Level 3: Immersion**

*Privilege/Advantage*

    Becomes informed about oppressed group and their concerns.

    Understands impact of discriminatory practices on oppressed group.

    Appreciates positive qualities and values of oppressed group.

    Instigates increasing contact with members of oppressed group.

    Increases awareness of self as oppressor.

    Establishes collaborative rather than competitive relations with oppressed group.

**Table 2.3**   *(Continued)*

*Oppression/Disadvantage*

   Becomes self-appreciating.

   Becomes group appreciating.

   Increases knowledge about oppressed group.

   Increases anger at the oppression and at the oppressors.

   Immerses self in activities that center on own group; excludes oppressors.

**Level 4: Integration and Activism**

*Privilege and Oppression Combined*

   Is willing to share personal and public resources.

   Is able to move comfortably between the worlds of both groups.

   Appreciates values and qualities of both groups.

   Understands social, political, and economic status of both groups.

   Rejects and confronts negative stereotypes and discriminatory practices.

   Works actively to instigate change toward social justice.

## A MODEL OF PERSONAL/SOCIAL IDENTITY DEVELOPMENT

In developing the Personal/Social Identity Model, we acknowledge our debt to the contributions of previous models of identity development that provided the groundwork for our conceptualization. The strength of the model presented in Figure 2.1 lies in the inclusion of both privilege and oppression characteristics at each level, in recognition of the social reality that these locations intersect for any individual. Table 2.3 lists some of the characteristics that might be descriptive of individuals on each dimension; the model is divided by whether it appears to be representative of advantage/privilege or disadvantage/oppression. You may notice that these descriptors refer variously to attitudes and beliefs as well as to behaviors. The motivational or emotional components represented by attitudes extend for each client across a continuum of negative reactions such as shame and self-hatred, to positive reactions such as self/group affirmation and pride. Not all of the descriptors are characteristic of any one client, and clients may be located at relative points along more than one dimension at any particular time or situation. As you read the characteristics included in each dimension, you may want to select one of your personal identities (gender, ethnicity, etc.) and place yourself on one or more of these locations in terms of the way that you now see yourself. With any of these personal identity locations, do you experience discomfort and shame or do you feel satisfaction and pride?

   To summarize this model of personal/social identity development, we see that the process of becoming aware, understanding, and appreciating the positive qualities of both one's own and other groups on a range of social locations is complex. In contrast to other models, we emphasize the interdependency of identities. For any client, some identities are more salient than others to the process of therapy. To place this process in the framework of the larger social structure, we now turn to some of the sociocultural practices and institutions that shape our gender development and inform us about who we are.

## LEARNING GENDERED IDENTITIES

Interdependency of identities implies that each person's gender identity is multideter-mined. Thus, gender variables intersect with ethnicity, culture, sexual orientation, so-cial class, and other social status markers that influence the personal and social self. The literature on diversity in ethnicity and culture in these intersects is sparse and pro-vides only limited information about identity development across cultural divides (Ohye & Daniel, 1999; Reid, Haritos, Kelly, & Holland, 1995; Vasquez & de las Fuentes, 1999). All life maps cannot be covered here; therefore, we offer samples of gender learn-ing patterns, acknowledging that multiple cultural patterns remain to be explored. Socialization and identity development in each culture can be interpreted as a rule-governed and observational process of learning that teaches us what to believe and what to value, how to behave, how to present ourselves to others, and how to feel about our-selves and others. Every culture appears normal to those who grow up in it. Gendered patterns of beliefs and behaviors that occur frequently and repetitively in the culture in which we develop, that appear in many diverse situations, and that are evident across a range of institutional contexts, seem "normal" and "appropriate" to us. Thus, the culture constructs our realities and identities in many contexts, providing invisible barriers to considering other possibilities.

### Learning the Rules

The process of gender-role and identity development is a lifelong journey. Although ear-lier theories of gender-typing assumed that gender identity and preferences are devel-oped by middle childhood, later formulations support a lifespan approach (Bussey & Bandura, 1999; P. A. Katz, 1979; Worell, 1981). That is, gender-role orientation can be considered as a composite of attitudes, beliefs, interests, skills, and activities that be-come integrated with gender in ways that are qualitatively and quantitatively different across major life periods and social locations.

Early learning can predispose individuals to accept and enact the gendered behaviors and attitudes that are widely practiced in their social and cultural environments. During adolescence, major changes take place as girls enter a period of critical identity develop-ment (N. G. Johnson, Roberts, & Worell, 1999; D. L. Tolman & Brown, 2001). Girls are increasingly confronted with conflicting messages about attractiveness and body image, sexuality, career goals, relationships, and what it means to be a "woman" in their culture as well as in the broader contemporary society (Basow & Rubin, 1999; de las Fuentes & Vasquez, 1999; D. L. Tolman, 1999; Worell, 1989b). Later experiences, however, may dramatically alter their perceptions and values. New demands on women's time and skills may precipitate a reorganization of values and priorities. Exposure to new settings and opportunities can expand one's behavioral range and encourage greater flexibility in gen-der-related activities. Across the life span, gendered behaviors and beliefs tend to be-come less restrictive.

For members of ethnic communities and those who have recently immigrated to a new country, exposure to the expectations of the majority dominant culture presents new challenges (de las Fuentes & Vasquez, 1999). Experiences of immigration, accultura-tion, assimilation, and bicultural disparities open new opportunities or may present ad-ditional barriers to gender flexibility (Hurtado, 1997). Thus, we assume that gender-role adoption is an organic and fluid process, influenced by many variables, and not a com-pleted product at any particular life period (C. F. Epstein, 1997).

## Rule-Governed Learning

Nevertheless, most of us develop and mature in families that transmit many traditional messages, or rules, about appropriate behavior for girls and women. In rule-governed learning, differential treatment and responses to females and males are abstracted by each individual into generalized rules for living (Constantinople, 1973; Pleck, 1985). These gender-related rules are applied to self and others in two general forms: (1) gender stereotypes that serve as personal guidelines or ideals for behavior in many situations (e.g., rules that may vary across cultures for being the good girl, good daughter, good woman, or good mother), and (2) self-imposed expectations and standards that function as personal mandates (I can, I should, I must), or restrictions (I can't, I shouldn't, I won't). Thus, each individual learns many of the prevailing gender stereotypes promoted by the dominant culture as well as gender messages that characterize her social and cultural heritage. Layered on the base of these mandates, she also incorporates specific gender learning as a function of her own experiences within family, school, peers, and community.

### Gender Awareness

Gender awareness appears in children as early as two years of age. By middle childhood, the consistency of children's knowledge about gender rules is well established (Huston, 1983; Powlishta, Sen, Serbin, Poulin-Dubois, & Eichstedt, 2001; Serbin, Powlishta, & Gulko, 1993; Worell, 1982). Elementary schoolchildren typically can verbalize many established gender rules, such as what behaviors are expected of girls and boys in the areas of toy and activity choices, clothing and hairstyles, and adult gender roles and occupations. These rules may differ across groups and cultures, as seen, for example, in the head or whole body covering practiced by many Muslim girls and women. Knowledge of prevailing rules, of course, does not dictate compliance, and variability occurs across gender, individuals, and historical time. Length of hair, for example, is less of a gender-marker today, as many girls adopt shorter hairstyles and boys frequently grow their hair below their shoulders.

### Gendered Bodies

Visible use of cosmetics, skirts or dresses, and shoes designed to draw attention to narrow feet and exposed legs, however, remains clearly gendered in North American society. Despite some cultural variations in standards of beauty, rules about the importance and forms of personal attractiveness for girls and women exist across most Western nations. Girls become aware of these expectations as early as the elementary school years, with resulting concerns about weight and appearance that heighten as they enter adolescence (Striegel-Moore & Cachelin, 1999). More than males, females are socialized to "emphasize external evaluations and view their bodies as ornamental rather than instrumental" (Srebnik & Saltzberg, 1994). In this manner, girls are socialized to monitor themselves as objects of observation and evaluation by others. In turn, more positive evaluations of women accrue to those who are relatively youthful and thin. According to Cheryl Travis (2001), it is impossible to escape cultural messages such as ". . . beauty is a central feature of women's identity and worth" (p. 190). Attractiveness may be defined differently across groups, however, related to cultural norms and values related to body size and appearance. Variations have been noted especially for African American women, who generally experience less body dissatisfaction than do women from other groups (Harris, 1995).

One outcome of this "culture of beauty" is a heightened sense of body dissatisfaction and excessive concern with weight management and dieting among most girls and women. Indeed, up to 70% of North American females consider themselves to be overweight, with consequent unhealthy eating and dieting behaviors (Jackson, 1992). The culture of "thinness" adds to these concerns, driving some girls to restrictive eating patterns that may result in anorexia—excessive loss of weight and body mass due to restrictive eating, or bulimia—dieting and binge eating with resultant unhealthy behaviors such as smoking, purging, or drug ingestion (Smolak & Striegel-Moore, 2001; Striegel-Moore & Cachelin, 1999). However, extensive research on unhealthy eating patterns suggests that there are multiple and complex paths to the development of eating disorders. Figure 2.2 displays a model that summarizes the research on both risk and protective factors in the development of bulimia (Striegel-Moore & Cachelin, 1999). We say more about women's body dissatisfaction in later chapters, especially as it relates to depression (Chapter 6).

## Gendered Careers

Changes have occurred over the years in children's occupational aspirations. Recent research suggests that children are aware of gender segregation in occupations (what jobs are mostly for boys or mostly for girls). However, many girls now reject the teacher-nurse-secretary stereotype traditionally reserved for women in favor of high status and high-paying male-dominated careers, such as veterinarian, doctor, and lawyer. Elementary and adolescent age boys, in contrast, are maintaining their occupational preferences for traditional masculine-typed (and high-paying) careers, such as engineering, medicine, and the law (Helwig, 1998). Although traditional gender rules are becoming more flexible across cultures and subcultures in the United States, current research suggests that many of these expectations for "appropriate" girls' behavior have not disappeared (Basow & Rubin, 1999; N. G. Johnson et al., 1999). Chapter 7 discusses factors that influence women's career decision making.

## Gender-Related Belief Systems

As adult women and men, we continue to incorporate many gender rules into our personal guidelines for living. As a result, we may tend to feel virtuous and appropriately "female" or "male" when we conform to personal gender beliefs, and we may feel uncomfortable, threatened, or "unfeminine" or "unmasculine" when we violate them. It is also important to recognize that violations of gender norms for behavior frequently have social consequences in both interpersonal and work-related situations. In some situations, for example, openly assertive women may be seen as "bitchy" if they insist that others do not interrupt them when speaking; and women's refusal to conform to prevailing norms related to cosmetic makeup and clothing may lead to their termination from employment (Fiske & Stevens, 1998). Fear of such negative consequences can train us to be more gender-conforming than we might like in situations that are important to us.

## Gender Rules

Two types of gender rules are relevant here. The first way to approach gender-based social rules considers prevailing stereotypes and beliefs about the traits and behaviors of women and men in contemporary society, and views them as organizing rules for those who endorse them. A second way is to identify cultural attitudes or ideologies about how women and men should relate to each other and what should be their appropriate social

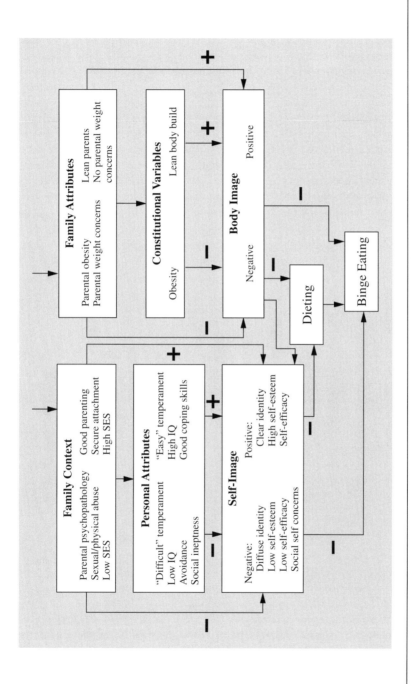

**Figure 2.2   A model of risk and protective factors for eating disorders.** *Source:* From "Body Image and Disordered Eating in Adolescent Girls: Risk and Protective Factors," by R. H. Striegel-Moore and F. M. Cachelin, 1999, in *Beyond Appearance: A New Look at Adolescent Girls* (pp. 85–108), Washington, DC: American Psychological Association. **Reprinted with permission**

roles. Traditional gender ideologies are those that position men as more important than women and thus entitle them to legitimate privileges, control, and dominance. Most studies find that women are more likely than men to accept egalitarian gender-role beliefs. However, in a cross-cultural study comparing gender ideologies between women and men in 14 countries, John Williams and Debra Best (1990) reported that "the effect of culture was greater than the effect of gender" (p. 223). Figure 2.3 displays this relationship, with more egalitarian ideologies appearing to the left and more traditional ones to the right.

*Trait Stereotypes*

Early studies on adult gender stereotypes in the United States identified clusters of traits that differed for women and men; being rated high on one cluster implied being low on the other. A communal, expressive, or "feminine" orientation, such as being warm, emotional, nurturant, kind, and concerned with the welfare of others, was believed to be proper and healthy for women. Agentic, instrumental, or masculine traits such as competence, leadership, aggressiveness, competitiveness, and independence were considered more appropriate and healthy for men (Broverman et al., 1970). Similar stereotyped

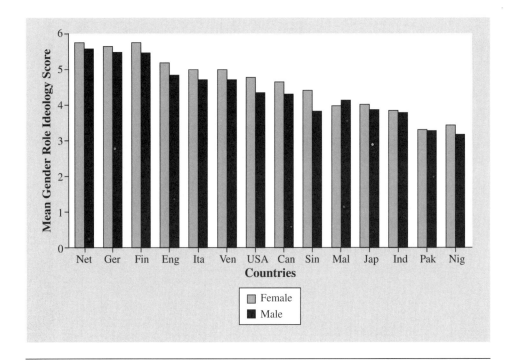

Figure 2.3    Gender ideologies in 14 countries. *Note:* Mean Sex-Role Ideology scores for female and male subjects in 14 countries (Netherlands, Germany, Finland, England, Italy, Venezuela, United States, Canada, Singapore, Malaysia, Japan, India, Pakistan, Nigeria). From *Measuring Sex Stereotypes: A Mmultinational Study* (p. 91), by J. E. Williams and D. L. Best, 1990, Beverly Hills, CA: Sage. Copyright 1990 by Sage Publications. Reprinted by permission.

clusters have been replicated many times in the United States and internationally (T. Ruble, 1983; Spence & Helmreich, 1978; Williams & Best, 1990). Expectations in most cultures that women and men differ on these characteristics extend to gendered stereotypes for a wide range of human behaviors, including personality traits, interpersonal behavior, choice of clothing, language forms, nonverbal mannerisms, occupational and career decisions, and leisure activities. Thus, women in most cultures tend to be associated more with home activities and child care, and men more with activities that involve power, work, and achievement. However, in subsequent research, these gender attributes have been shown to be loosely connected, such that attitudes toward one area do not necessarily predict beliefs about others (Twenge, 1999).

In an attempt to dislodge these bipolar gender stereotypes, Sandra Bem (1974) proposed that an equal balance of feminine and masculine traits that she termed *androgyny* would promote the best psychological health outcomes by enabling individuals of both sexes to be flexible across situations. Although the concept of androgyny as a mental health outcome was popular for a while and is certainly intriguing, it has since fallen into disuse as more extensive and inclusive formulations of gender were developed. Bem (1993) has since pointed out that *androgyny* implies gender difference and polarity in that there are gendered trait clusters that are more typical of women or men. Bem added that the concept of equal balance of traits for women and men suggests a heterosexual bias and fails to "acknowledge the existence of gender inequality" (p. 123). Since those early studies were conducted, some changes have transpired both in the United States and globally toward more egalitarian expectations for women and men (Spence & Hahn, 1997).

Research with cultures other than White middle class suggests that gender stereotypes are modified by variations in cultural norms (Lips, 1999; McNeill et al., 2001), as well as by contextual variables such as individual family environments, ethnicity or cultural identification, rural or urban residence, sexual orientation, and so on. For example, in two large samples of Japanese college students, men were found to attribute more feminine than masculine traits to themselves, despite the cultural norm of male dominance (Sugihara & Katsurada, 2000). The authors speculate that the hierarchal nature of the Japanese workplace encourages men to incorporate many of the traits that are typically endorsed by subordinate groups such as women (e.g., being polite, considerate, cooperative, and friendly). Such traits are less likely to be endorsed by U.S. males. Hope Landrine (1999) reported that perceived stereotypes differed for stimulus persons who were presented as either Black or White and either poor or middle class (respondents were mainly White U.S. college students).

*Gender Ideologies*

Although modern gender ideologies tend to move in the direction of more equality between the sexes (Twenge, 1997; Williams & Best, 1990), research using measures of *Modern Sexism* (Swim & Cohen, 1997), *Neosexism* (Tougas, Brown, Beaton, & Joly, 1995), and *Ambivalent Sexism* (Glick & Fiske, 1996, 1997) tells another story. That is, just as with racism, overt sexist attitudes have gone underground by becoming more subtle and covert. The *modern or neosexist* is one who opposes affirmative action, believes that women already have enough, has negative attitudes toward both the women's movement and homosexual persons, and attributes the asymmetry in social roles for women and men to biology (B. Campbell, Schellenberg, & Senn, 1997). In turn, the *benevolent sexist* maintains power through being protective of (or seeking protection for) the "weaker sex," while the *hostile sexist* feels superior to women and desires to dominate them (Glick & Fiske, 1997). For counselors and clients, it is important to note that many women are socialized to accept these gender belief systems, thereby supporting the system that subordinates and belittles them. With clients in counseling, it is useful to discover some of their personal rules and messages about growing up as a girl and woman, and the possible sources of these messages; this process is called *gender-role analysis.* We discuss gender-role analysis next and more fully in Chapter 3.

## GENDER-ROLE ANALYSIS

One of our goals in counseling women is to help clients become aware of the unwritten rules or messages they use to guide their lives. Although we use the language of communication in referring to "messages," it is likely that most of these rules are not typically within active awareness for most people. Gender-related messages may need to become explicit if clients are to assume meaningful control over their daily lives. The technique of gender-role analysis encourages women and men to examine the gender rules that guide their thoughts, feelings, and behavior. In the process of gaining gender-role awareness, clients can explore how the rules were learned, consider how well these rules function for them now, and make decisions about which of their gender-driven messages they would like to revise.

For example, in most families there are implicit and explicit rules about family and work both in and outside the home. In both the two-parent, single-earner and dual-earner, heterosexual family, the rule for most women that home and children come before job or career is embedded in a network of daily and intermittent tasks. These tasks are usually controlled by rules about who in the family plans and cooks meals, shops for food, plans and manages social contacts, picks up a sick child from school, calls and arranges child care, sews clothes or mends a torn shirt, does the laundry, shops with children for clothes, arranges (or does) the housecleaning chores, visits the school on PTA night and consults with teachers, bakes cookies for the homeroom party, plans and officiates at the children's birthday parties (or weddings), and takes grandma to her medical appointments, and other chores. These are only a sample of the multiple tasks involved in home and family management. Although the specifics of these tasks vary by culture, the fact that women who are wives or mothers (as well as providers) still do the majority of these tasks is clearly related to the traditional socialization of women for the wife/mother role in most cultures (Lips, 1999; Silverstein, 1996; Steil, 1997).

Many women in dual-earner heterosexual families are attempting to equalize the home/child responsibilities. However, both their own and their partners' gender-socialized messages, as well as certain cultural norms, frequently interfere with their egalitarian intentions. When home and child care tasks are delayed or left undone, women, more than men, are likely to feel uncomfortable and guilty. The process of gender-role analysis may be useful and therapeutic to a woman struggling with the self- and externally imposed demands of home care and child care. In the process of gender-role analysis, she may be helped to understand how the external messages become internalized. She can then ask herself why she feels she must assume the major portion of these tasks in addition to her employment outside the home, and how she can plan to disengage her self-messages from those imposed by others. In the application of gender-role analysis to women's socialization messages, it is helpful to understand the social processes through which gender-related rules have been adopted and internalized by each of us. We can then interpret these processes to clients and assist them in meaningful plans for change.

## THE ROLE OF SOCIAL INSTITUTIONS

Social institutions teach gender rules according to similar principles. Because gender stereotypes are common throughout most cultures, individuals learn these rules as an integral part of their environments. In addition to explicit gender teachings, the total effect of institutional gender rules provides a "hidden curriculum" (Worell & Stilwell, 1981), in which the messages are frequently implicit rather than explicit. The subtle and pervasive existence of both explicit and implicit gender messages at all levels of each culture informs women and men about who they are, what they may become, and how they should view themselves.

An important agenda of the women's movement, both in the United States and globally, has been to articulate and make public the sexist and discriminatory practices that exist at all levels of social communities. The contributions of multiculturalism have also expanded the range of public awareness to other kinds of exclusion and discrimination. As a result, revised social practices in many communities, as well as numerous legal remedies in the United States, have challenged and/or moderated the extreme effects of societal sexism as well as other "isms." Nevertheless, voluminous research on the influences of families, the public media, schools, peers, and working environments attests to the persistence of gendered and culturally stereotyped messages in both the private and public domains.

## SOCIALIZATION IN FAMILIES

In all cultures, families form the earliest classroom in which gender rules are learned. We speak of families in the broadest sense, including those that are two-parent, single-parent, multigenerational, or extended (that include a network of other relatives, godparents, and friends), and those that are either heterosexual or lesbian/gay. Although most parents and caretakers deny that they treat their girls and boys differently, observational studies in homes, schools, and clinical settings support the contributions of parents to the gender-defined training of their children (Bussey & Bandura, 1999; D. Ruble & Martin, 1998). The gender attitudes of parents provide a foundation for this training. In replicating the results of an earlier study, it was found again that mothers of newborn daughters described them as more feminine, more delicate, and less strong than did mothers of newborns who rated their sons (Karraker et al., 1995). Of course, gender socialization practices may vary across ethnic and cultural groups. Research in these areas, however, is limited to a select group of cultures, and most samples have been drawn primarily from the dominant U.S. culture. We know relatively little about the range of diversity in family life both within and across cultures (Segall, Lonner, & Berry, 1998). Finally, some studies find little or no relationship between parental beliefs and their actual behaviors with their young children (Bornstein, Cote, & Venuti, 2001), which speaks to the importance of observing what people do as well as what they say.

## Teaching the Rules

The degree to which parents and caretakers actively participate in gender typing varies by individual family, as well as by sex of the parent, socioeconomic class, cultural or ethnic group, degree of acculturation, and the parents' own gender-role beliefs. One of the more salient variables here is the sex of the parent, with fathers more than mothers in most cultures being relatively more traditional in expectations for both their daughters and sons.

The more traditional orientation of fathers appears in both direct behavior toward their children and in their role behaviors in the home (Barry, 1980; Block, 1979; Fagot, 1978; Langlois & Downs, 1980; Lytton & Romney, 1991). Fathers in most cultures spend more time and are more involved with their sons, and promote their intellectual and cognitive development more than for their daughters (Bronstein, 2001; Starrels, 1994). In families with strong cultural norms for father dominance, the father effect becomes more pronounced. For example, in Mexican American families, the norm for *respecto* "governs all family relationships . . . and dictates appropriate deferential behavior . . . on the basis of age, gender, and authority status. The traditional role of the father includes discipline of the children and expectations of obedience." In contrast, women in these families are expected to be submissive and self-sacrificing as wives, and nurturing and protective as mothers (McNeill et al., 2001, pp. 12–13). Angela Ginorio and her associates (Ginorio, Gutierrez, Cauce, & Acosta, 1995) point out, however, that in second- and third-generation families in the United States, these gender rules are changing as Latinas enter the labor force and begin to assert their desire for more egalitarian family roles. This gendered father effect is also consistent with the findings that African American fathers were found to gender type both their daughters and sons more than a comparison sample of White fathers (Price-Bonham & Skeen, 1982). Mothers, of course, are not immune to prevailing gender expectations and are found in many studies to allow more freedom for their boy children and to assign more household responsibilities to their girls (Wolleatt & Marshall, 2001).

Personal gender-role beliefs can also mediate one's parenting behaviors. Parents who are flexible and less traditional in their gender-role beliefs have been found to stereotype less in their parenting behaviors and to produce more gender-flexible children (Brooks-Gunn, 1986; Jackson, Ialongo, & Stollak, 1986; P. A. Katz & Ksansnak, 1994; Kelly & Worell, 1976; Spence & Helmreich, 1978; Weisner, Garnier, & Loucky, 1994). Personal beliefs may also interact with cultural patterns that encourage distinct forms of gender training. For many African American girls, for example, this training may take the form of "resistance for liberation" that aims to "empower African American females through confirmation of positive self-conceptions" (V. Ward, 1996, p. 95). Although many African American mothers tend to be controlling with their daughters, they also promote assertiveness and independence as a means of encouraging self-protection skills to combat racism (Cauce et al., 1996). According to Pam Reid and her associates (1995), African American women are themselves less willing than most North American White women to conform to established societal gender typing and tend to expect more egalitarian family relationships. In contrast, Mexican American families tend to be fairly indulgent and child-centered with young children, but then exert more control as girls approach adolescence (Ginorio et al., 1995). And in Caribbean American families, girls are put under greater control and restrictions than boys, especially in adolescence (Waters, 1996).

In the following section, we explore some general findings on parental socialization practices suggested by current research, and we consider the differential messages that girls and boys may receive in family settings. In individual or group work with women, however, it is important for each client to explore her personal gender training as she experienced it, and as it impacted her behavior and the messages she continues to give herself.

## How Families Teach

Families socialize for gender-related behavior in two major ways: (1) by modeling patterns of behavior that are observed and imitated by children, providing expectations about future gender-related behavior; and (2) by providing direction and encouragement of gender-typed behavior. Encouragement may take the form of attention, approval or disapproval, by teaching gender-related content and skills, and by providing environmental structure and opportunities for exploration and new learning. We consider each of these socialization functions next.

### Modeling

Families provide models of gender-traditional or gender-flexible behavior. The activities and roles that parents perform in the household provide patterns for current behavior and expectations about future goals and relationships. Mothers who work outside the home, especially those in high status careers, for example, are more likely to have daughters who assume responsibility for themselves, work during adolescence, work outside the home when they become mothers themselves, and have higher levels of career aspirations and success than daughters of homebound women (Hoffman, 1979; Serbin et al., 1993). Fathers in dual-earner homes are also likely to play a less traditional role, providing daughters with a more cooperative and flexible model of family relationships. In one study of two-paycheck homes with alternating workshifts, fathers and mothers frequently assumed equal shares of both homemaker and provider roles (Deutsch & Saxon, 1998); both girls and boys in such families might be expected to learn that fathers (and men) can be caretakers and nurturers and that mothers can be equal in the provider role. However, it is still the case in the United States that although over 70% of married women with children under 18 years old are employed, they do nearly twice the amount of housework and up to two-thirds of child care (Steil, 2001). This pattern is also evident across various groups of ethnic families (John, Sheldon, & Luschen, 1995) as well as globally (United Nations, 1995). Thus, for developing girls and boys, asymmetrical patterns of family work are likely to be viewed as normal and thus to be replicated in their own adult relationships. As Janice Steil points out:

> Children are introduced to gender-based patterns of labor at an early age. Studies of children as young as age six, studies of children through the school years, and studies of adolescents all show that boys are allowed to spend more time in leisure activities than girls; and girls are asked to spend more time in household tasks and childcare and to contribute a greater share of family work than boys. (2001, p. 350)

However, in single-parent or lesbian families, different patterns of family and work roles are modeled. Most single mothers are employed; and in lesbian homes, the sharing of employment and family roles tends to be egalitarian (Peplau & Beals, 2001; Steil, 2001).

Parents also model patterns of interpersonal relationships. Children can observe and learn about how people in families express emotionality, love, detachment, control, and dominance. Regardless of maternal employment, many two-parent families continue to present patterns of father dominance, control over important decisions, and access to favored resources such as leisure time. Some families provide patterns of paternal violence, wife battering and rape, child incest and abuse, and desertion. Children in these families are learning about the place of girls and women in relationships and about how women (their mothers and themselves) cope with violence and abuse. Both girls and boys in violent and abusive families develop dysfunctional beliefs and behaviors related to interpersonal affection and control. These children may carry over such patterns into their future relationships. Persistence of issues related to family violence and abuse are detailed further in Chapter 9.

*Direct Encouragement*

Parents actively instruct and teach their children with gender-related messages and skill development that prepare them for distinctive future roles. Girls are more often instructed in domestic skills, for example, while boys are usually taught to throw balls and encouraged to be athletic. Boys are taught not to cry, while girls may be encouraged to be more attentive to the feelings of others and to "behave like a lady." Especially salient here are the distinctive clothes and toys that parents provide, the freedom they allow both in and away from the home, and the expectations they communicate about future educational and occupational commitment. Typical girls' clothes, such as dresses, are less conducive than are boys' clothes for active play. Girls' toys encourage quiet play in proximity to parents and are frequently imitative and uncreative (tea sets, makeup kits, housekeeping toys). Parents also encourage girls to remain closer to home than boys and are more concerned with their supervision and monitoring (Block, 1983; Bronstein, 2001; Huston, 1988).

Observational studies confirm that parents tend to give preschool children more positive attention when they are engaged with gender-typed toys and play, and they tend to reprimand cross-gender play (Fagot & Hagen, 1991; Langlois & Downs, 1980). Fathers engaged in a learning task with their preschool children were more likely to steer their boys back to task completion and their girls toward interpersonal socializing and play (Block, Block, & Harrington, 1975). And preschool boys who believed their fathers disapproved of cross-gender play were the most highly stereotyped in their toy choices (Raag & Rackliff, 1998).

## Cognitive Outcomes

These differential parent patterns may not be verbalized by the child, but they carry clear messages about what activities the parents believe are desirable and appropriate, and what opportunities they make available for learning and play. Jeanne Block (1983) proposed that gendered parental practices establish "metamessages" that communicate important developmental information about the self in relation to the environment. As parents interact with children in a multitude of ways, they are telling girls and boys about their self-worth, their personal goals, and their world views. These metamessages help to channel children into directions for development that may be functionally different for girls and boys. On the basis of an extensive review of research, Block suggested that, in contrast to boys, many girls tend to develop low self-efficacy or belief in one's ability to master important tasks, less curiosity and independent exploration of the environment, and low risk-taking behavior in the face of requirements for problem solution. These aspects of cognitive orientation, according to Block, leave such girls with impaired strategies and skills for independent action in the face of conflict, and inadequate skills for mastery and overcoming obstacles.

Aletha Huston (1988) proposed that the close supervision of girls and their continual proximity to adults, especially the mother, leads girls to become compliant, attentive to the wants of others, obedient, quiet, and unassertive. Close bonding with adult socialization agents, however, also fosters "communal behaviors promoting group cohesion and caring about others" (p. 16). Accordingly, the close contact with adult agents results in women's capacity for maintaining close emotional ties with others.

Finally, the emphasis in many families on affectional behavior expressed by girls and independent mastery behavior by boys may communicate to girls that relationships are both their major source of self-definition and their primary responsibility (Cancian, 1987; Miller, 1976). In future encounters, women are likely to believe that they must be attached to a man if they are to find meaning in their lives. Further, that if a relationship fails, it is their "job" to mend it and their fault when one partner exits. As a result of these metamessages, a common issue presented by women in psychotherapy centers on intimate relationships, as women struggle with "finding them, understanding them, untangling them, changing them, repairing them, or escaping them" (Worell, 1988a). The focus on the woman as caretaker of the relationship further reduces a woman's power and control over important resources in her life, and renders her dependent on the intimate partner to fulfill her self-image.

Reinforcement of passive and compliant behavior may be highlighted for girls who experience paternal or sibling incest. In these families, the girl is given attention and praise for "colluding" with the sexual perpetrator, "cooperating" with the abuse, and "keeping the secret" from others. Experiences in which compliant behavior to male sexual abuse is repeatedly reinforced in childhood may predispose the girl to further compliance with later abuse. This is part of the process of "revictimization" (Wyatt, Guthrie, & Notgrass, 1992), which we discuss further in Chapter 8.

## Teaching New Rules

Changes brought about in the latter half of the twentieth century—movement of women into the workforce, altered expectations for marital and motherhood status, and revised conceptions of appropriate gender-role behaviors—leave both women and men with changing norms for personal well-being and life adjustment. Current definitions of *family* are clearly in flux; only 3% of U.S. families are classified as traditional father provider and homebound mother; indeed, over 71% of married women with children under 18 are currently in the labor force (U.S. Bureau of Labor Statistics, 1997). Employed women who are single, cohabiting, or in committed lesbian relationships may also be mothers, and they expand the corpus of employed parents in the United States. These changes also lead to new sources of personal and culturally based satisfaction and stress. Although women who are not employed outside the home may take sole responsibility for home and child care, as well as volunteer for community projects, their work differs from paid employment. Full-time homemakers receive no direct wages, they are seldom rewarded with recognition for their efforts and skills, and they have difficulty in restricting their hours of working to a predictable eight-hour schedule. They also have no opportunity for advancement or for bettering their position and remuneration. And most full-time homemakers may never have the opportunity to retire from their home duties or to receive retirement compensation.

With a change in personal and cultural attitudes toward traditional gender roles, many families are attempting to break new ground. Many families now strive to provide egalitarian role models, to monitor carefully their sex-differentiated practices, to teach their girls and boys about equal opportunity, and to increase the nonsexist environment of their children. Girls are more often encouraged in individual and competitive sports, and many boys (and men) are learning the pleasures and challenges of preparing meals. Indeed, in comparison to less active girls, higher self-esteem has been reported for high school girls who were encouraged toward athletic participation (Delaney & Lee, 1995). While doubtless these efforts have had some success in promoting gender-flexible behavior (P. A. Katz & Boswell, 1986), parents also find that patterns for gender-distinct expectancies are rampant in the culture, as mediated by television, magazines and books, and the realities of social institutions (Weinraub & Brown, 1983). Even the most "liberated" parent may feel frustrated by the transmission of societal messages that conflict with values and ideals practiced at home. Both authors have been told at some time by their young daughters that they could not possibly be doctors because doctors are men!

## Implications for Counseling

In summarizing the diversity of family patterns and the changing roles for women as wives, mothers, and workers, it is important to separate our personal ideals and preferences from the realities of women's lives. As women face new choices, the decision-making tasks become more difficult. In counseling with both employed and nonemployed clients, it is important to emphasize that a large body of research supports the conclusion that multiple roles improve the quality of women's lives and lead to more satisfaction than to stress (Barnett & Rivers, 1998; Crosby, 1991; Steil, 1997). We also know that relationships that are perceived as egalitarian in terms of balance of power, decision making, household and child care, respect, and support bring more satisfaction and a sense of intimacy and well-being to both partners than asymmetrical relationships (Dion & Dion, 2001; Steil, 1997, 2001; Worell, 1988a). Both counselors and clients will want to adjust their conceptions and solutions to the actualities of today's families and the new expectations that confront both women and men. As these role expectations change, moreover, we experience revised conceptions of how women and men ought to behave as females and males. The changing conceptions of appropriate gender and family roles in today's increasingly diverse society are certainly very important advances in the lives of contemporary women and men.

The family is only one of the cultural agents that constructs a framework of gender-role messages for women's development. We now consider some of the other social institutions that form a background for family transmission of gender information. In particular, the general media, schools, and work environments all contribute their share of gender, ethnic, and sexuality stereotypes and discriminatory practices.

## MEDIA MESSAGES

The public media projects gender stereotypes from many sources, including language, television, videotapes, the Internet, music, art, dance, books, magazines, and newspapers. Assume that these media sources probably add to (or perhaps multiply) the effects of the major sources of public media gender learning.

# Language

Gender rules embedded in written and spoken language inform children (and adults) about the place and value of women and the relationship between women and men. Mary Crawford (2001) asserted that "language shapes social reality . . . and help[s] perpetuate gender inequality" (p. 229). All forms of the media refer to the "opposite sex," establishing difference and implying inequality. This terminology also implies a generic or universal woman and ignores the diversity among groups of women (Crawford, 2001). Susan Basow (1992) proposed that "language plays a major role in defining and maintaining male power over women" (p. 141). She suggested that this outcome is accomplished through three major formats: ignoring, labeling, and deprecating.

*Ignoring* women occurs most blatantly in the public media through the widespread use of the generic masculine. That is, masculine pronouns (he, him, his) and word forms (mankind, manpower) are used to denote all persons, both male and female. It has been estimated that the average individual will encounter the generic *he* more than 10 million times in a life span (MacKay, 1980). The generic masculine eliminates women from the public domain, rendering them invisible. It has also been demonstrated to influence the evaluations and perceptions of both children and adults. When individuals of both sexes are presented with a sentence such as "All men are created equal," both their verbal and visual images are primarily those of a man (E. Wilson & Ng, 1988). We challenge you to notice in your academic and public reading materials whether the generic masculine still appears or is replaced with gender-free pronouns and terminology.

As a function of many feminist groups taking an activist stance, new guidelines for language have entered the public domain. For example, we now speak of *police officers* and *mail carriers,* framing the concept that both women and men can enter these job categories. The American Psychological Association adopted nonsexist language guidelines for all its publications in 1981 (American Psychological Association, 1983). Since then, feminist scholars and researchers have introduced into public awareness the realities of the invisible woman through naming their experiences of sexual harassment, date rape, sexism, and battered woman. These terms are now common in the cultural lexicon, but that did not exist 20 years ago.

*Labeling and deprecating* are two other sources of gender and ethnically based social messages. Labels for women are frequently differentiated in such a way that the woman is thrown into a subordinate role. Examples include the "I pronounce you man and wife" wedding ceremony and "Mrs. John Smith" following marriage. The traditional order of gender referencing (boys and girls, men and women) also implies male primacy. Which of the two sexes is presumed to be more important? We hope you have recognized by now that in this book, we reversed the custom by frequently referencing women before men. *Deprecation* of women occurs when language referring to them is derogatory (*bitch*), belittling (*girls*), or depersonalizing (*chick*). Many researchers have demonstrated that deprecating words are applied more frequently to women than to men (D. Holland & Davidson, 1984; Pearson, 1985). Activists in both the feminist and ethnic communities have worked to establish terminology that provides more positive perspectives. To circumvent the gendered stigma of being identified as single or spinster, many women now use the term *Ms.* in place of *Miss* or *Mrs.* To reduce stigma from one's sexual orientation, homosexuality has been replaced by *lesbian* and *gay.* To remove racist stigma and establish community pride, African Americans have modified their identity from *colored, Negro,* and *Black.* Labels can belittle and deprecate, or inform and affirm.

## Television, Video, and the Internet

Television consumes the attention of the average North American child between four and five hours every day, with about 20,000 commercials each year. The average North American watches more than 700 advertisements weekly. All aspects of televised programming—children's programming, prime time, daytime soaps, and especially the commercials—present stereotypes that are disadvantageous to ethnic minorities and to women. We see three issues of concern regarding portrayals of women and men in the visual media.

### Stereotyping

First, research on portrayals of girls and women in the media over the past 40 years has consistently shown that they appear less frequently than men and are typically cast in traditional and stereotyped roles (L. M. Ward & Caruthers, 2001). In particular, ethnic or minority women are almost invisible, or are portrayed in exaggerated stereotypic ways, and seldom appear in major roles. Girls in comparison to boys are depicted as less active, less assertive, and less knowledgeable. More than men, women tend to be portrayed as home-oriented and to be concerned with their appearance and that of their floors, laundry, and furniture. The persistence of stereotypes includes women as submissive and indecisive, frequently helpless, and usually as sex objects (Pacheco & Hurtado, 2001). Portrayal of women on afternoon "soaps" shows women who are frequently divorced, raped, abandoned, misunderstood, or otherwise in some kind of personal difficulties (Pearson, 1985).

Children and adults from all ethnic and cultural groups are receiving some clear messages from commercial television: White men are the most important, the most competent, and they make the major decisions. Further, the more that people watch television, and the stronger their initial stereotypes, the more entrenched they become in traditional views of women and men (McGhee & Freuh, 1980; M. Morgan, 1982; L. M. Ward & Caruthers, 2001). Although efforts have been made to include women as competent role models in some programming, the proportion of competent to incompetent and ethnic to White women remains unfavorable for purposes of effective modeling outcomes.

### Violence

Second, the depictions of violence against women, and especially those that portray coerced or violent sex, increase the probability that male viewers will entertain violent thoughts about women and will increase their acceptance of prevalent rape myths (Briere & Malamuth, 1983; Malamuth, 1998; Scott, 2000; Chapter 8 discusses rape myths in detail). Videotapes that are commercially available for rental or purchase in thousands of retail outlets are a major source of portrayals of both sexual and nonsexual violence against women. Gloria Cowan and her associates (Cowan, Lee, Levy, & Snyder, 1988) surveyed a sample of widely available X-rated videos in California, reporting that physical violence against women appeared in 73% of the films, and 51% of the films showed a man raping a woman.

Detailed reviews of the effects of violence in the media (Donnerstein, 2001; Linz, Donnerstein, Bross, & Chapin, 1986) concluded that (a) depictions of violence against women influence the viewer's attitudes toward violence and aggression, and (b) the pairing of sex and aggression may encourage the association of violence with sexual arousal for men and lowers the threshold for subsequent aggressive acts. Repeated exposure to violent sexual acts toward women reduces male empathy for the victim and increases his belief that she enjoys being violated.

*Body Images*

Finally, the physical images of women in both visual and printed media as slim, White, blonde, and stereotypically attractive by Western standards provide an impossible model for all girls and women to achieve. They learn to set unrealistic standards of female beauty and thinness, leading to distorted body image and chronic body dissatisfaction. For many North American girls and women, these images provide a background for the emergence of self-destructive eating patterns and eating disorders (Lavine, Sweeney, & Wagner, 1999). Despite these media influences, body image concerns are less prevalent in women from cultures that place less emphasis on being thin as a criterion of female beauty (Striegel-Moore & Cachelin, 1999). African American adolescent girls, for example, have been found to experience less social pressure to be thin and report a higher level of self-esteem and more confidence in their attractiveness than a comparable sample of White girls (Eccles, Barber, Jozefowicz, Malenchuck, & Vida, 1999). However, with greater exposure to mainstream cultural pressures, African American girls are as likely as their White peers to feel dissatisfied with their weight and to diet excessively (Schreiber et al., as cited in Striegel-Moore & Cachelin, 1999).

## THE EDUCATIONAL SYSTEM

Children spend about one-third of their waking lives in school. Although children arrive at school with well-established gender stereotypes, all aspects of the school setting have been shown to contain gender messages. These gender messages are transmitted through personnel and administrative arrangements, textbooks, curriculum, teacher and counselor behavior, and through differential allocation of resources, such as in athletics.

Although Title IX of the Elementary and Secondary Education Act prohibits sex discrimination across certain practices of educational institutions, limited progress has taken place with regard to gender equity. Curriculum arrangements frequently encourage girls to enter language and home economics courses and boys to focus on advanced math and technical training. Counselors are not always helpful in encouraging the educational aspirations of girls toward economic self-sufficiency and nontraditional career choices. Athletic programs have been heavily weighted in favor of boys' participation and competition, and programs for girls and women are still insufficiently financed and supported. Schools may not be the primary vehicle for gender-related learning, but research has consistently supported the view that most schools are doing little to counteract or modify traditional gender stereotypes and beliefs (Eccles & Hoffman, 1984; Stockard et al., 1980; Worell, 1982, 1989a). In the following sections, we summarize some of the findings of comprehensive reviews of school culture and practices in the United States related to gender, ethnicity, and sexual orientation (see American Association of University Women [AAUW], 1992, 1993, 1995; DeZolt & Henning-Stout, 1999; Sadker & Sadker, 1994).

### What Children Learn

Children are learning about who has the power. The large majority of elementary and high school teachers are women, and most principals and school superintendents are men. Children are also learning to consolidate their previous stereotypes about how to be a girl or boy and what they may expect to become as they mature into women and men. In many textbooks, girls "are often rendered as stereotypic, invisible, misrepresented, and marginalized" (DeZolt & Henning-Stout, 1999, p. 256). Girls have been more frequently depicted in school texts as passive, fearful, unwilling to take risks, and asking for help when in trouble. Girls have been less frequently shown in heroic, brave, adventurous, and achieving roles. Through higher frequencies of White men and boys in both text and pictures, and role-restricted portrayals of both Anglo and ethnic girls and women in their assigned school readings, children are learning about who the culture believes to be important and worthy of admiration and respect.

Children are also learning that schools may not be safe. Although there is a current flurry in the United States about children who shoot children, we know that children experience other forms of virulent violence in their schools on a daily basis. Two major types of violence are prevalent: sexual harassment, and both physical and verbal harassment of students that are identified as "different" on many dimensions. These dimensions may include physical size (too small, too thin, too fat), sexual orientation, skin color, religious practices, or other ethnocultural variables. For example, surveys of lesbian and gay youth reveal increasing levels of verbal and physical violence directed toward them. In the AAUW 1993 survey of eighth- through eleventh-graders, 81% of girls and boys reported some kind of sexual harassment in school, including "mooning and flashing," unwanted touching and grabbing at their genitals or breasts, and being called *queer* or *faggot*. Further, 44% reported sexual harassment by a school staff member. We know that the sequelae of sexual harassment may be as great as that of sexual assault or rape (Gutek & Done, 2001; see also Chapters 6 and 8). Racism also abounds in schools, targeting students who are visibly identified with various ethnocultural groups. For example, following the September 11, 2001, tragedy in the United States when the World Trade Center in New York City was destroyed by Islamic extremists, many communities reported a backlash against people who appeared to be Islamic or Arabic in origin. Across the country, Islamic students in some school systems reported verbal and physical harassment, especially against girls who adhered to the cultural custom of covering their heads in public.

Among other reactions, harassed girls reported increased anger, fear, shame, humiliation, helplessness, confusion, dislike and avoidance of school, less participation in class, and lower grades. Victims frequently blame themselves, preferring not to report the experience to anyone, and then take responsibility for the harassment. The high prevalence of harassment suggests that many schools do not take these events seriously, further reinforcing the culture of violence and disrespect. What kinds of messages are girls receiving about their bodies, their developing intimate relationships, and whom they can trust to protect them when they are violated?

## What Teachers Teach

Most teachers are unwilling to declare that they view girls and boys differently, or that they interact with girls in any way other than they deal with boys. Some research supports these egalitarian views; however, many studies suggest otherwise. First, it is important to note that many teachers subscribe to the same stereotypes as the general population, that is, tending to see girls as emotional, neat, quiet, concerned about appearance, easily hurt, and harboring a dislike for math and science. It seems unlikely that teachers who believe in stereotyped gender differences can avoid transmitting those attitudes to their students in various ways.

Repeated observational studies disclose that boys receive more teacher attention both when they succeed and when they fail, and are given more talk time in class. Teachers tend to provide higher-level questions to boys and respond more quickly to their requests for help. Boys with high math achievement are praised more often and receive more teacher interaction than girls with similar math abilities. Although girls receive grades in school that are at least as good as those received by boys, girls' interest and engagement with math and science begin to dwindle at about the seventh grade. Lack of interest in advanced math by adolescent girls has been associated with its identification as a field "for boys," as well as with active teacher discouragement of mathematically talented girls. As a result, girls become less assertive in class over time and are less likely to select higher level math and science courses.

Finally, as more women enter advanced educational institutions, both overt and covert discriminatory practices follow them through college. In the Project on the Status and Education of Women, Bernice Sandler (1982) identified more than 35 kinds of situations that functioned to create "a chilly climate in the classroom" for women students in institutions of advanced education. This large-scale study concluded that both female and male faculty undermine women's self-confidence and career aspirations. Examples of these discriminatory situations include: (a) overt discrimination (disparaging comments in class, questioning women's career commitment, sexual harassment), (b) subtle discrimination (being more attentive to men students), and (c) rendering women invisible (interrupting them more, ignoring women who volunteer, calling on women less frequently). Thus, at all levels of education, women can expect to find a differential atmosphere of academic encouragement and equity.

## Implications for Counseling

Current and past experiences with school-based sexism can provide rich materials for exploration with women who have career or achievement conflicts. In considering some of the messages they may have learned at school, these women can begin to reconsider the sources of their work and relationship-related distress. When women experience institutional gender-based discrimination, they tend to attribute their difficulties to their personal characteristics or lack of competency. In Chapters 6 and 7, we discuss how to help clients untangle their gendered messages from the realities of their current life situations, thereby releasing them from the torments of self-deprecation and depression.

## THE WORKPLACE

Women are socialized to the expectations of the workplace long before they seek employment outside the home. From early childhood through adolescence, we have seen that young girls maintain traditional stereotypes about what jobs are "appropriate" for women. For some girls, employment aspirations have been restricted by the cultural stereotypes that surround them at home, in school, and in the media. Women have expected to work at a restricted range of jobs, to earn less than their male counterparts in the same or similar jobs, and to accept discriminatory limits placed on their promotion and advancement (Fassinger, 2001). For women who continue to follow traditional lines of employment, the messages they may carry with them convey low status, a lack of control over their work-place conditions, and little hope for a better tomorrow.

Contemporary changes in attitudes toward women's work and career aspirations have motivated many women to challenge the boundaries of sexism and to seek educa-tion and job placement in fields that have been traditionally reserved for men. As women begin to infiltrate the male world of work, new demands and sources of stress enter their lives. Women in nontraditional jobs face many of the barriers and stresses of women in all employment settings: discrimination in the form of lower wages than men, gender stereotypes, sexual harassment, and restricted opportunity for advance-ment. They are meeting new obstacles as well, through biased expectations of compe-tent women, isolation as token female, denial of access to higher-level positions, and a lack of powerful role models (Kanter, 1977; Lott, 1985b). It is important for women to understand that barriers to equality in the paid labor market may provide continuing sources of stress and negative messages that contribute to the development of destruc-tive symptomology: anxiety, self-deprecation, exhaustion, and depression. We consider career and working environments and their implications for counseling more fully in Chapter 7.

## APPLICATIONS TO CLIENTS

The cultural messages provided to women, as well as the barriers they meet along the path of self-development, impact women differentially. When we see a woman in clini-cal consultation who presents syndromes of adjustment to her life situation that appear dysfunctional for her, we explore collaboratively with her the range of her personal and social identities. We then look to the societal influences on these identities and on her presenting issues. Next we explore how the client has interpreted and internalized the messages she receives from the many streams of her social environment, and we consider how these messages have contributed to the distress and pain in her current life. Con-sider a sample of the clients who arrive at our office with syndromes that appear to be intimately connected with widespread cultural messages.

> Sylvia, a 40-year-old highly educated African American woman, was distraught over her latest romantic breakup. She showed signs of depression (sleeplessness, loss of appetite, self-deprecation) and anxiety (gastric upset, fear of being alone). She was certain that life would never be better for her and that she could never find another man from her own eth-nic community to love her.

> Irene, a 37-year-old legal secretary of English descent, confessed that she had been taking diet pills for years and feared that she was addicted to them. Nevertheless, she was proud of her slim figure and terrified to relinquish the assurance offered by the medication that she would remain attractive to her spouse. Despite a medical assessment that she was well within her weight range for her age and height, she insisted she was "too fat" and wanted referral to a diet center.

> Joyce, a 55-year-old homemaker, was brought in infancy from Poland to the United States by her parents. Joyce was brought to the office by her husband because she refused to drive alone. She seldom left her house and was convinced she would have a panic attack and be-come "stranded" if she were to leave home alone. She remained essentially homebound ex-cept when her husband accompanied her.

Gwat-Yong was a 43-year-old Cambodian woman who had recently immigrated to the United States. She had lost her husband during the Cambodian war and subsequently fled her village, accompanied by her four children. They spent time in a refugee camp, and she married another refugee. Together they managed to obtain legal immigrant status in the United States. She was referred by her supervisor at the hotel where she worked as a maid after the supervisor observed severe bruises on Gwat-Yong's face and neck. Although reluctant to self-disclose, Gwat-Yong agreed to counseling to keep her job. Despite her limited English, we learned that her husband, whom she had married out of convenience in the refugee camp, had been unable to find employment and was resentful of his economic dependence on her. He also expected total obedience from her and became violent when she did not perform all the household duties he expected. Aside from her bruises, she presented symptoms of exhaustion, apparent depression, guilt about leaving her children in day care after school, and concern that her eldest boy was becoming a delinquent. She was caught between fear of losing her job, pressure for economic survival, and attempts to placate and serve an abusive husband whom she did not love or respect.

Alice and Jean were both in their early twenties and of Scandinavian background. They were in disagreement about whether Alice should "come out" to Jean's family during their holiday visit. Alice was not ready to declare her lesbian identity publicly for fear of repercussions with her own family as well as at work. Jean wanted to maintain an honest and open communication with her parents and wanted them to know and accept her committed relationship with Alice.

We could enumerate many more concerns that women bring to counseling that have interconnections to the cultural messages that women receive and take in. It becomes important for these clients to understand that they are similar to many other women in their stressful situations, and that the troubles facing them may have important antecedents in their cultural conditioning. This is not to avoid the contributions of each woman's ongoing behavior to the outcomes of her personal life. Through a gender-role analysis, however, she is helped to distinguish between the messages she receives from others and those she continues to provide for herself.

## SUMMARY

This chapter proposed that the process of becoming a woman in contemporary Western societies is embedded in the intersects of our personal and social identities. These identities in turn are influenced by the cultural contexts in which we develop and the extent to which we regard ourselves as advantaged (privileged) or disadvantaged (oppressed). We offered a personal-social identity model that outlines levels of development in moving from unawareness to awareness and integration of each aspect of personal identity. We discussed the development of gender belief systems and the manner in which they may influence how others regard us and how we regard and value ourselves. We then reviewed the contributions of the family, the media, and the educational system to the socialization experiences of women and men. We viewed gender-role socialization as a rule-governed process through which the differential treatment of women and men is abstracted by each individual into gender-specific rules for living. These rules are then translated into stereotypes about others as well as into internalized standards for personal behavior. We explored how major social institutions provide a variety of gender messages that limit and restrict opportunities for women and that erect barriers to women's full development and well-being. We considered the implications of women's socialized gender-role messages for the problems that women present in psychotherapy in the areas of depression, body image, excessive dependency, marital abuse, home-career conflicts, sexual harassment, and lesbian relationships.

## ACTIVITIES

### Assessing Your Social Locations

In Chapter 3, you learn that the first principle of empowerment feminist therapy (EFT) is that *Personal and Social Locations are Interdependent*. Thus, assessing for clients' social locations is a fundamental part of EFT. While a client's social locations may be assessed in several different ways, the following exercise gives you a basic way to assess. In this exercise, we ask you to apply the assessment to yourself.

### *1. Label Your Social Locations*

At the beginning of this chapter, you labeled your personal/social locations. Refer to this labeled list for the next steps.

### *2. Determine Saliency/Primacy of Your Locations*

Because the saliency of your social locations may vary from situation to situation, choose a personal issue or situation that you want to explore. (This is similar to having chosen a content or goal focus for client sessions.) For example, you might choose to explore a sexual harassment situation at work, a conflicted interpersonal relationship, a past traumatic experience, a personal strength you possess, or a decision you need to make.

With your chosen focus in mind, look over your personally labeled list of social locations and rank order (1–5) the five social locations you occupy that are most important to your chosen issue.

### *3. Identify the Identity Development Level of Your Social Locations*

For this step, focus on the social location you ranked number 1 (most important) in Step 2. Begin by thinking about whether you consider this location to be a seat of advantage/privilege or a seat of disadvantage/oppression. The following continuum represents where you perceive this location to lie in contemporary Western society.

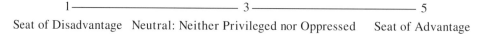

1————————————— 3 ————————————— 5

Seat of Disadvantage   Neutral: Neither Privileged nor Oppressed     Seat of Advantage

List several reasons for your placement on this continuum.

Consult Table 2.2, which describes levels of identity development. At what level of identity development on this social location are you?

### *4. Repeat for Another Social Location*

Repeat Step 3 for the social location you ranked number 2 in Step 1.

## 5. Assess the Impact of Your Social Locations on Your Chosen Issue

Focusing on your two most salient social locations and on your primary level of identity development on each, think about the impact of each of these locations on the personal issue you chose to explore in Step 1. The following questions help you assess this impact. What sociocultural messages have you received related to each location, especially messages related to the personal issue you chose? What role models relevant to each location have been salient for you? What opportunities and reinforcements or barriers and punishments for each of these locations have you experienced? How do these two social locations intersect in their impact on your issue?

## Uncovering Cultural Messages

Select one of the cases discussed in the final section of this chapter and complete the following:

1. List the possible socialization factors that might have contributed to the presenting problem.
2. Generate at least two messages that the client may have internalized (i.e., accepted as her own) that may be serving to maintain her present patterns.
3. For each self-generated message you listed in number 2, restate the message in terms that might enable the client to view the issue differently and more productively for herself.

## FURTHER READINGS

Bem, S. L. (1993). *The lenses of gender: Transforming the debate on sexual inequality.* New Haven, CT: Yale University Press.

Deaux, K. (2002). Social identity. In J. Worell (Ed.), *Encyclopedia of women and gender: Sex similarities and differences and the impact of society on gender* (Vol. 2, pp. 1059–1068). San Diego, CA: Academic Press.

Peplau, L. A., & Garnets, L. (Eds.). (2000). Women's sexualities: New perspectives on sexual orientation and gender. *Journal of Social Issues, 56*(2). Whole issue.

# Chapter 3 ─────────────────────────────────

# *EMPOWERMENT FEMINIST THERAPY*

> *. . . all feminisms share an explicit political urge—to reform or remake the world in line with a deeply held conviction that women have been the victims of faulty and exploitive social institutions.*

J. B. Elshtain, 1991, p. 128

## SELF-ASSESSMENT: THERAPY WITH WOMEN

For each of the following statements, decide to what degree it describes your approach to counseling and psychotherapy with women. Write the number in the space to the left of each statement that best describes your approach to working with women clients. If you are a trainee who has not yet counseled clients, respond with the way you plan to work with clients.

| Almost Never True | | | Sometimes True | | Almost Always True | |
|---|---|---|---|---|---|---|
| 1 | 2 | 3 | 4 | 5 | 6 | 7 |

In my counseling and psychotherapy with clients, I:

_____ 1. Establish an egalitarian relationship with my client.

_____ 2. Disclose my values, when appropriate, to my client.

_____ 3. Disclose personal experiences relevant to my client's issues.

_____ 4. Help my clients trust their feelings and experiences.

_____ 5. Consider my clients as experts on their experiences, thoughts, and feelings.

_____ 6. Indicate to my clients that their problems should be considered through a gender-role perspective.

_____ 7. Encourage my clients to work actively for social change as it impacts women's improved status.

| Almost Never True | | | Sometimes True | | Almost Always True | |
|---|---|---|---|---|---|---|
| 1 | 2 | 3 | 4 | 5 | 6 | 7 |

_____ 8. Suggest to my clients that differences between women and men are predominantly the result of socially constructed gender roles.

_____ 9. Routinely ask my clients about physical or sexual abuse occurring in the present or in the past.

_____ 10. Share with my clients the environmental input to their expressed problems.

_____ 11. Directly identify myself as a feminist in my interactions with clients and other professionals.

_____ 12. Am sensitive to, and address with my clients, the special issues of gender, minority or ethnic status, race, disability, and sexual orientation.

_____ 13. Work actively for social change as it impacts women's improved status.

_____ 14. Believe psychiatric diagnostic labels are frequently gender-biased against women.

_____ 15. Am committed to working with clients who experience discrimination and subordination in our culture.

## Scoring

Sum the total for your responses. Scores range from 15 to 105. Scores near the 105 end of the range indicate that you use (or intend to use) therapeutic strategies that are consistent with Empowerment Feminist Therapy (EFT) as well as other feminist therapy approaches.

This instrument is an abbreviated version of the Therapy with Women Scale (TWS; D. Robinson & Worell, 1991) and has been used to differentiate therapists who are "woman-centered" in their practices from those who are not. In a study of therapists embracing a range of theoretical orientations and their clients, therapists who had higher endorsements of feminist therapy strategies (i.e., higher scores on the TWS) had clients with scores significantly higher on a measure of empowerment (Worell et al., in press). See Chapter 10 for a detailed description of this instrument and related research.

## OVERVIEW

In this chapter, we acquaint readers with Empowerment Feminist Therapy (EFT) and its philosophical underpinnings, goals, and techniques. After reading Chapter 3, you will be able to:

• Discuss the assumptions and values that form the foundation of feminist practice.
• Present the four basic principles of EFT.
• Describe the goals and interventions of EFT.
• Identify how your own beliefs and value systems fit with those of EFT.
• Explain the EFT techniques of demystification, cultural analysis, gender-role analysis, power analysis, reframing, and relabeling.

## FEMINIST THERAPIES: FOUNDATIONS AND EXPANSIONS

Feminist therapy approaches developed as a result of the feminist movement of the 1960s. As discussed in Chapter 1, leaders of the feminist movement criticized traditional therapists for being agents of society, for encouraging women to adapt to traditional gender roles while also labeling women "sick" when their adaptation was too complete (e.g., labeled "masochistic" for being submissive to their abusive husbands; Caplan, 1985), and for ignoring the mental health concerns of women. Consciousness-raising and self-help groups developed as an alternative to traditional therapy. Some of the people who participated in those consciousness-raising groups were traditionally trained mental health professionals. They took the newly acquired awareness about themselves as women and men and about institutionalized sexism and created a new therapeutic approach to working with female and male clients. This new approach, called *feminist therapy,* was based on feminist beliefs.

### Range of Feminist Therapies

A range of feminist therapy theories have emerged from a variety of feminist philosophies (Enns, 1997). Carolyn Enns identified four major types of feminist therapies: (a) Liberal, (b) Radical, (c) Cultural, and (d) Women of Color. Her descriptions of each are summarized next (see also Chapter 1):

- *Liberal* feminist therapists believe that traditional stereotyped socializations restrict the development and options of women and men and that ending these restrictions can be achieved by providing equal opportunities and "gender-neutral policies" (Enns, 1997, p. 119) via rational arguments. The identification of gender bias is a key component of Liberal feminist therapy. While Liberal feminist therapists substantiate the existence of gender bias in social institutions, the main thrust of therapy is to facilitate clients' recognizing and challenging internalized gender bias to achieve personal aims.

- *Radical* feminist therapy is based on the belief that sexist, racist, classist, and heterosexist societal structures oppress and victimize women. Personal struggles are redefined as social/political problems shared by many women. Society, not the individual woman, is sick. Consciousness-raising about oppression and about how it has been internalized, establishing collaborative client-counselor relationships, and facilitating change of patriarchal and other oppressive societal structures are crucial components of Radical feminist therapies.

- In contrast to Liberal and Radical feminist therapists, *Cultural* feminist therapists view women and men as essentially (biologically) different. They observe that women's experiences, perspectives, values, and abilities are given less societal value; and this devaluation contributes to both societal and individual problems. Cultural feminist therapists place importance on acknowledging and revaluing women's perspectives (e.g., subjective, connected knowing, interdependence, and relational caring). Therapeutic strategies include establishing an empathic relationship through which the therapist facilitates clients' valuing of traditionally female traits and perspectives, acquiring increased ability to be self-empathic, and learning to connect to others in mutually empathic relationships.

- *Women of Color* feminist therapies focus on racism and the interactive effects of the diverse forms of other societal oppressions (e.g., sexism, ethnocentrism, classism). Earlier forms of feminist therapy are critiqued for their assumptions that White women's experiences of oppression are universal and normative for all women, thus minimizing or ignoring the effects of social class and racism. Women of Color feminist therapies emphasize the importance of researching and understanding the lives of diverse groups of women. Counseling interventions are aimed at identifying societal racism and other forms of oppression. Values embraced by diverse cultures of women (e.g., harmony, collectivism, interdependence) are acknowledged and respected. Clients are helped to challenge the internalized negative impact of these societal oppressions and to work for social change.

**Table 3.1    First National Conference on Education and Training in Feminist Practice: Final plenary session common themes**

*Feminist Practice*

1. Includes therapy/intervention, teaching, political action, consultation, writing, scholarship, research, supervision, assessment and diagnosis, administration, and public service.
2. Promotes transformation and social change.
3. Assumes that the personal is political.
4. Embraces diversity as a requirement and foundation for practice.
5. Includes an analysis of power and the multiple ways in which people can be oppressed and oppressing.
6. Promotes empowerment and the individual woman's voice.
7. Promotes collaboration.
8. Promotes the value of diverse methodologies.
9. Promotes feminist consciousness.
10. Promotes self-reflection on a personal, discipline, and other levels as a lifelong process.
11. Promotes continued evaluation and reflection of our values, ethics, and process, which is an active and reflective feminist process.
12. Asserts that misogyny and other inequalities are damaging.
13. Encourages demystification of theory and practice.
14. Views theory and practice as evolving and emerging.

The process of feminist practice is part of the content of feminist practice.

The contextual framework that looks at the psychological and political is important.

Learning integrates thoughts, knowledge, feelings, and experience.

*Source:* From *Shaping the Future of Feminist Psychology: Education, Research, and Practice* (p. 249), by J. Worell and N. G. Johnson (Eds.), 1997, Washington, DC: American Psychological Association. Copyright © 1997 by the American Psychological Association. Adapted with permission of the American Psychological Association.

## First National Conference on Education and Training in Feminist Practice

While feminist therapists embrace a wide range of perspectives, they share a common core of beliefs. In 1993, at the First National Conference on Education and Training in Feminist Practice in Boston, feminist psychologists (practitioners, theorists, and researchers) met to discuss the current state of and future directions for feminist psychological practice. This conference, often referred to as the *Boston Conference,* was created and sponsored by the Society of the Psychology of Women (Division 35) of the American Psychological Association. Conference participants unanimously agreed on a set of "Common Themes" of Feminist Psychological Practice (see Table 3.1 on page 63). The unanimous consensus by this group of 77 feminist psychologists from diverse backgrounds and theoretical perspectives attests to the existence of a core set of values that underlies feminist psychological approaches.

## Integrating Feminist Approaches

Given the range of views of feminist therapies, in this book we present an approach to feminist therapy that represents our integration of these perspectives. The Empowerment Model of Feminist Therapy introduced in Chapter 1 incorporates many of the ideas from the four major types of feminist therapy identified by Enns (1997) and of the common themes identified at the *Boston Conference.* However, our EFT model most closely resembles the one labeled *Radical* since we focus on women's low social power as the basis of many of their problems, and we believe that both social and individual changes are needed. Our current conceptualization of EFT also integrates many aspects of the Women of Color feminist therapy approaches, but we have done so using a broad and inclusive definition of diversity.

In this chapter, the assumptions, principles, goals, and techniques of EFT are explored in detail. Because feminists' assumptions about the world form the foundation of feminist therapy, and because these beliefs influence the choice of therapeutic goals and techniques, the worldview assumptions of EFT are presented first.

## EMPOWERMENT FEMINIST THERAPY

### World View Assumptions

Some feminist therapists consider their only theoretical orientation to be that of the "feminist therapist." However, many feminist therapists embrace a wide range of theoretical orientations related to practice (e.g., Psychoanalytic, Cognitive Behavioral, family systems, Gestalt). Although their therapeutic goals and techniques may vary in accordance with their various theoretical orientations, the goals, techniques, and concepts that emerge are evaluated against a broad system of interrelated beliefs that most feminist therapists embrace. Concepts and techniques in each therapist's repertoire that violate that feminist belief system are modified or replaced. (See Chapter 4 for a more detailed explanation of this theoretical transformation process.) Thus, a core set of beliefs forms the foundation on which our EFT is built and can be stated as a set of basic assumptions. The assumptions presented next are a selective synthesis of the existing literature (Enns, 1997; Gilbert, 1980; Greenspan, 1983; Rawlings & Carter, 1977; Sturdivant, 1980; Worell & Johnson, 1997; Wyche & Rice, 1997):

1. Women have individual problems because of living in societies that devalue them; limit their access to resources; and discriminate against them economically, legally, and socially. Thus, sexism is institutionalized in all areas of society—families, religion, education, recreation, the workplace, and laws—and is a major source of problems.

2. Racist, classist, heterosexist, ageist, ethnocentric, and handicapped oppressions are also important sources of societal pathology.

3. An end to all forms of oppression in societies requires both changes in how people are socialized and structural changes in major social institutions. Political, institutional change is necessary to eradicate sexism, racism, heterosexism, ageism, and ableism.

4. All societal opportunities should be open to both women and men regardless of culture, ethnicity, physical characteristics, age, sexual orientation, handicaps, or social class. Gender or identified groupings should not be used to determine or judge individual behavior or to restrict opportunities for personal competence and flexibility in all areas of living.

5. Psychopathology, which is defined by the dominant culture, is primarily environmentally induced. Likewise, what is considered "normal" is defined and maintained by the dominant culture.

6. Women and men do not have equal status and power. In most cultures, women are oppressed and in a subordinate power position.

7. Contrary to theories of biological determinism, women differ from men primarily because social forces encourage differential constructions of gender. These gender-role-stereotyped constructions limit the potential of all human beings. All people have the capacity for all characteristics and behaviors. Both women and men are victims of gender-role socialization. Gender-role socialization is one major source of individual pathology for both women and men.

8. Relationships between people should be egalitarian. Committed relationships (e.g., marriage, cohabiting partners) should be a partnership between equals. Traditional, hierarchical power differentials are detrimental to women and to members of all oppressed, subordinate groups.

9. Women's perspectives, female value systems, and female experiences should be given weight and focus equal to male perspectives. Likewise, diverse ethnic and subcultural perspectives should be understood and respected.

10. Nonfeminist, nonmulticultural therapeutic approaches have been developed primarily from Western, White, male, heterosexual perspectives and value systems. Without transformation, these therapeutic approaches can be detrimental to oppressed and culturally diverse populations.

11. Therapy is a value-laden process. All therapists communicate their own values in the therapy session, with or without their awareness. Therapists who are aware of their own values and explicitly state their relevant values to clients minimize the imposition of their values on clients.

## Overview of Empowerment Feminist Therapy

Four basic principles of EFT emerge from the previously described worldview assumptions and guide the work of empowerment feminist (EF) therapists:

I.   Personal and Social Identities Are Interdependent.
II.  The Personal Is Political.
III. Relationships Are Egalitarian.
IV.  Women's Perspectives Are Valued.

These principles represent how feminist beliefs and assumptions are applied to the content and process of therapy. These four principles form the core beliefs about the nature and conduct of EFT. The goals of EFT encompass a wide range of possibilities that reflect both the therapist's theoretical orientation and the specific issues of individual clients. The following section presents the four principles of EFT and related counseling goals.

## I: Personal and Social Identities Are Interdependent

EF therapists begin by understanding their clients in the context of their sociocultural environments. As discussed in Chapter 2, every individual occupies several social locations (e.g., gender, ethnicity, social class, sexual orientation, age, physical abilities, and characteristics) within a complex sociocultural matrix. Each of these locations is socially constructed through a network of dominant and subordinate cultural expectations that contribute to the individual's personal identity. In a given society, some of these locations are seats of privilege (e.g., White, male, heterosexual, physically able), and others are seats of oppression (e.g., female, Person of Color, lesbian, physically disabled).

In Chapter 2, we also presented a model of Social Identity Development, which integrates an individual's awareness of her seats of privilege and oppression (see Table 2.3). We use this Social Identity Development Model as the foundation for understanding our clients' sociocultural contexts (Principle I), for raising their awareness of the impact of these social locations on their personal identities (Principles I and II), and for facilitating their movement through the relevant identity development levels (Principle I).

### Identifying Social Locations

In Principle I, the EF therapist begins by collaboratively identifying with the client all of her relevant social locations. The client is encouraged to discuss the meaning to her of each of these locations. The counselor assesses the client's level of identity development for each of these locations. (Individuals may be at different levels of identity development for each of their relevant social locations.) Therapists also facilitate clients' awareness of the intersecting nature of these locations.

### Assessing Saliency of Social Identities

During the initial exploration of social locations, the EF therapist assesses which of the client's identities are salient and which ones have primacy for her. Client perceptions of saliency; recognition that a particular social location has personal relevancy; and primacy, recognition that a particular social location is central or crucial to her personal identity, are influenced by both her level of identity development and the situational context. For example, an African American woman who is primarily at the Immersion level as related to her ethnicity, but mainly at the Preawareness level of her gender identity, will probably perceive her ethnocultural location to be central to her identity and life situation and her gender location to have little relevance or saliency.

Treating clients as experts on themselves, EF therapists first focus the counseling on the social locations most primary to clients. Since EF therapists believe social locations are intersecting and interdependent, they later expand explorations to include any of the individual's social identities that are relevant to the client's issues. These explorations facilitate the client's psychological process of perceiving her own experiences of both injustice and privilege. "The oppression of women is seen as filtered through the multiple lenses of historical, social, political, economic, ecological, and psychological realities" (Wyche & Rice, 1997, p. 65).

Exploring social locations and their accompanying cultural value systems often results in clients becoming aware of cultural conflicts occurring both internally and externally. Throughout the EFT process, these conflicts are explored, navigated, and challenged. Ideally, clients eventually mediate these conflicting loyalties so that they are living comfortably within the interdependence of their social locations (Worell, 2001).

## Summary

We envision Principle I as the major vehicle for integrating diversity into a feminist therapy framework. Diverse sources of oppression (and privilege), not just gender, are identified and interactively explored for their contribution to clients' issues. EF therapists heighten their clients' awareness of all their social identities, which facilitates their forward movement in identity development for these locations. Framing clients' issues in their cultural contexts is a key factor in empowering clients. To explore the interdependent strands of clients' cultural contexts, we identify their relevant, intersecting social locations and their level of identity development in each of these locations.

In our revised model of EFT, gender is not assumed to have primacy over other social identities; rather, primacy is determined within clients' phenomenological perspectives. However, we do believe gender will be relevant and salient for most client issues. That is, although racism, heterosexism, ethnocentrism, and other "isms" may be primary for a particular client, sexism and gender issues are often an accompanying subtext. Within multiple social locations, we believe that the meaning of gender (i.e., what it means for a client to be a woman or man) varies in its social construction across cultural contexts. But we also assert that gender is a source of oppression for most women. ". . . the commitment to address women's subordination and disadvantaged status in society serves as a unifying thread linking all feminist psychologists" (Wyche & Rice, 1997, p. 63).

## Counseling Goals for Principle I

The following statements are possible feminist therapy goals related to Principle I, *Personal and Social Identities Are Interdependent*. The therapist helps the client:

1. Increase awareness of her social locations and identity development within these locations.
2. Separate "internal from external representations" of her social locations (Worell & Johnson, 2001).
3. Accept and appreciate herself within her social locations.
4. Cope comfortably within the interdependence of her social locations.
5. Prize herself and the groups to which she belongs.

## II: The Personal Is Political

The Personal Is Political principle encompasses feminist beliefs about gender-role stereotyping, institutionalized sexism, and all forms of oppression. Since traditional gender-role socialization and the institutionalized separation and discrimination of people based on gender, ethnicity, sexual orientation, physical characteristics, age, and socioeconomic status (SES) are judged to limit the potential of all individuals, the external environment is considered a main source of clients' problems. Thus, a primary source of a client's "pathology" is not intrapsychic or personal, but rather, social and political (Gilbert, 1980). Acknowledgment of the societal sources of women's individual issues is the core of feminist therapy (Wyche & Rice, 1997). This "consciousness-raising" about the "isms" involves making visible the often-invisible forms of oppression and inequality.

Despite the centrality of Principle II in EFT, we believe that Principle II extends Principle I and cannot stand apart from it. That is, the oppressions associated with all the client's social locations interact and influence the development of problems in living.

### Separating the External from the Internal

Feminist therapy focuses on helping clients identify the influence of social rules, gender-role socialization, institutionalized sexism, and other kinds of oppression on personal experience, so that they can separate the external and internal sources of their problems. This process involves several steps, including: First, individuals must recognize the existence and the negative influence of oppressive societal practices (e.g., racism, sexism). Second, they must begin to see a relationship between these external experiences and the issues they have brought to counseling. Third, they must decide whether they want to change themselves (e.g., their internalized messages) and/or their environments (social change). Finally, they must implement the desired changes. The priority in EFT is to identify dysfunctional environmental factors rather than to concentrate only on intrapsychic factors. Further, the focus is on changing the unhealthy external situation and the internalized effects of that external situation, rather than on helping the client adapt to a dysfunctional environment.

### Reframing Pathology

Subordinated individuals are not blamed or pathologized for thinking, feeling, and behaving in ways that are congruent with living in an oppressive society. Their "symptoms" are seen as strategies for coping with an unhealthy environment (Wyche & Rice, 1997). For example, women's depression may be seen as a natural, logical response to being oppressed (Greenspan, 1983). The recognition that there is not something inherently wrong with them ("I'm not crazy"), that their reactions are "normal" given the patriarchal, racist, classist heterosexist society in which they live, empowers clients to make changes in themselves and in their environments. A natural outcome of consciousness-raising about the external sources of women's issues is for women to become angry at their oppressors and at their unfair treatment. EF therapists believe that it is important not only for women to learn to express their anger, but that it is also crucial for women to use their anger as a source of energy for changing their environments and themselves. Individuals are not to blame for personal issues that have their etiology in toxic social environments, but are responsible for working toward change.

One focus of this change is on helping clients modify the beliefs they have internalized from their toxic environments. For example, in relation to sexism, clients identify the culturally constructed gender-role messages they learned about what is appropriate for females and males, evaluate the costs and benefits of that socialization, and then challenge and reconstruct those messages that have a high cost. Feminist therapists encourage clients to develop all aspects of themselves. Individuals are encouraged to develop a full repertoire of behaviors.

## Initiating Social Change

It is not sufficient to change clients' internalized societal messages. For example, even children who are raised in stereotype-free families still have to live in a world of discrimination and gendered expectations. The ultimate goal of feminist therapy is to create a society in which sexism and oppression of minority groups does not exist. Thus, change of our institutions (e.g., the family, schools, religion, the workplace, economics, laws, political structure) is crucial, since these are the means by which society perpetuates sexism and other forms of oppression. Mental health cannot be achieved solely by women acquiring healthier behaviors. Society must be changed and women from all groups must have increased social power as well as increased personal power (Wyche & Rice, 1997).

These social-change goals of feminist therapy are difficult to integrate into the individual focus of counseling. One way to accomplish this integration is to view social change as having a continuum of levels—from large, macrolevels to smaller, microlevels. For example, a macrolevel social change would be a change in policies by a political party (e.g., including more female and minority convention delegates). Other macrolevel change examples are the changes in rape laws that have occurred in the past two decades. An example of change at a microlevel is a woman confronting her supervisor about racist or sexist practices in the workplace and the resulting changes in office procedures and/or her supervisor's attitude. Client action for environmental changes, especially at the micro level, is often a spontaneous outcome of identifying the external sources of one's problems, of not blaming the victim. Social change that is facilitated by feminist therapy is more likely to occur at the micro level. However, microlevel changes made by individuals often result in macrolevel societal changes (e.g., the changing roles of women discussed in Chapter 2). Macrolevel changes are also accomplished by a group of individuals working for social and political change. EF therapists encourage clients to join groups where they can work with others for these changes. This group alliance increases the individual's social power and contributes to the empowerment of her group and community.

Feminist therapists also involve themselves in their communities in working for social change. They model skills directed at institutional change. This institutional change involvement is also important as a preventive strategy—changing the environmental conditions so that they will not continue to cause problems for women (i.e., to make environments healthier). For instance, recently the American Psychological Association (APA) Society for Women in Psychology (SWP) formed a Task Force on Women and Poverty that was charged with the responsibility to review and summarize research related to this area. The summary was used as the basis for a paper submitted to all members of the U.S. Congress to challenge existing legislation that appeared to be holding low-income women responsible for problems created by social structures.

Because feminist therapy targets social (political) change, it has been criticized for being political. These criticisms are usually based on the assumption that other psychological theoretical orientations are objective, value-free, and nonpolitical. We assert that all theoretical orientations have values and are political. With respect to traditional

theories, we wonder why helping women adjust to existing political and social structures and realities is not viewed as political. We believe that both challenging social
structures (feminist therapy) and supporting social structures (traditional theories) are
"political acts."

An obvious and major implication of the *Personal Is Political* principle is that societal
and cultural practices are critiqued through feminist and diversity lenses. Limiting and
oppressive practices and values are challenged. Feminist therapy approaches have always
involved consciousness-raising about inequities and working to change both the internalized messages and the external structures that maintain the inequities. On an individual
level, clients have sectors of tolerating inequality, which occur when the cultural benefits
of that inequality to the individual outweigh individual costs. While this toleration can be
affected by heightening clients' awareness of individual and societal costs, ultimately it is
the client's decision whether to change internal and external vestiges of oppression.

## Summary

Embracing the *Personal Is Political* principle results in major transformations in client
case conceptualization. Attention to the social origins of psychological distress challenges traditional theories' attributions to individual pathology. The focus of therapeutic interventions is on empowerment of women and the transformation of oppressive
societal structures. This empowerment of women and of all oppressed groups includes
fostering their resiliency and well-being and viewing their responses to toxic social contexts as coping skills (Worell, 2001).

## Counseling Goals for Principle II

The following statements are possible feminist therapy goals related to the *Personal Is
Political* principle. Therapists help clients:

1. Become aware of their own gender-role socialization process.
2. Identify their internalized oppression messages and beliefs.
3. Replace internalized stereotyped beliefs with more self-enhancing self-talk.
4. Develop a full range of behaviors that are freely chosen, not dictated, by the
   dominant White, heterosexual culture (e.g., to become more flexible and competent and less gender typed).
5. Evaluate the influence of social factors on personal experiences.
6. Understand how society oppresses women and other minority groups.
7. Identify sexist and oppressive societal practices that negatively affect them.
8. Acquire skills for enacting environmental change.
9. Restructure institutions to rid them of discriminatory practices.
10. Develop a sense of personal and social power.

## III: Relationships Are Egalitarian

Feminist therapists believe that interpersonal relationships should be as egalitarian as
possible. This principle is related to the observation that women in most societies do not
have equal status and power with men and that minority groups are subordinate in status
to majority groups (United Nations, 1995).

One of the major complaints by the Women's Movement was that traditional therapists used their power to encourage and/or coerce women to adapt to an unhealthy environment, and thus, were agents of patriarchal social control. The gender-role-stereotyped values of therapists negatively influenced clients (Rawlings & Carter, 1977). Feminist therapists believe that it is crucial to build an egalitarian relationship between the client and counselor for two reasons. First, egalitarian client-counselor relationships minimize the "social control" aspects of therapy (Sturdivant, 1980). In an egalitarian therapeutic model, counselors have less of a power base from which to impose their values on clients. Second, the client-counselor relationship should not reproduce the power imbalances women and other subordinate groups experience in society. The therapeutic relationship should be a model for egalitarian relationships in general.

## Empowering the Client

In EFT, clients and counselors are considered to be of equal worth. One is not the "expert" and the other "sick." Therapy is to be a collaborative process in which clients are considered to be experts on themselves. Treating clients as experts on themselves honors their lived experiences. Counselors' expertise is based on their specialized training (knowledge of human behavior, of therapy, and of institutionalized oppression) and on their own life experiences. Feminist therapists use several strategies to minimize the power differential between them and their clients. First, because therapy is a value-laden process, feminist therapists make their relevant values known to their clients in the beginning of counseling. This declaration of values by counselors minimizes imposition of their values on clients (i.e., clients are free to accept or reject counselors' values if they are made explicit).

## Demystifying the Therapy Process

Feminist therapists share their beliefs about society and educate their clients about the theory and process of feminist therapy. This allows clients to make an informed choice, to be an educated consumer about therapy (Gilbert, 1980; Greenspan, 1983; Sturdivant, 1980; Wyche & Rice, 1997). Clients are encouraged to shop around for a therapist. Feminist therapists teach their clients relevant therapeutic skills, such as using a gender-analysis lens through which to view their life experiences. Counseling goals are collaboratively determined by the client and counselor, and written contracts are often used to spell out the conditions of therapy.

## Balancing Power

Contrary to many traditional approaches to therapy, feminist therapists use selective self-disclosure (share information about their current and past life experiences) when relevant to client issues and self-involvement (share their here-and-now reactions) with clients. A female counselor's self-disclosure to a female client may facilitate identifying the common social conditions that they share as women. This is an important way to move from an intrapsychic focus to a relevant social, external focus (Greenspan, 1986). Counselor self-disclosure may also illuminate differences between the client and therapist. For example, if an African American therapist who has a history of domestic violence victimization by an ex-husband is counseling a White client who is also a victim of domestic violence, they would share some dimensions of sexism related to their abuse histories. Yet, their cultural gender-role socialization messages would differ. The counselor might self-disclose that, in contrast to the client's gender-role socialization, the

African American gender-role messages allow women to be strong and economically independent. This examination of two differing sets of cultural messages about how to be a woman would be a powerful illustration to the client that gender-role messages are socially constructed values and not biological truths. Self-disclosure may also reduce the role distance and power differential between client and therapist.

Self-involving responses conveying how the therapist is emotionally reacting to the client, or to what the client is saying, are important for several reasons. First, the client receives feedback about how she is impacting another person. Second, therapists allow their own vulnerabilities to be present by sharing their feelings. Third, the therapist models effective communication skills, including modeling direct expression of anger—an emotion that is discouraged for women by traditional gender-role socialization in many cultural groups. Self-disclosure and self-involvement must be used with care. They are used when they are relevant to the client's issues, when they can be appropriately handled by the client, and when their use will be in service of the client's psychological growth.

In advocating egalitarian client-counselor relationships and counselor self-disclosure, EFT embraces a female perspective on the therapeutic process that conflicts with many beliefs of traditional therapies that are based on stereotyped Western male values. The objective, emotionally distant, expert-therapist model of many traditional therapies is replaced by a model that emphasizes empathy, nurturance, and mutual respect. Collaboration and mutual respect between client and therapist contribute to the creation of a supportive and safe (believing, not blaming) therapeutic environment in which clients learn to trust themselves, challenge self-blame, and become empowered to accomplish individual and social change.

Client "transference" issues are also treated differently. Client reactions to the therapist are not treated solely or primarily as transference of previous relationships to the therapeutic relationship. Rather, much consideration is given to the reality of the client-counselor relationship—that the client is having legitimate here-and-now reactions to the real attributes and behaviors of the therapist. Thus, in feminist therapy, these client reactions are not usually interpreted as transference, but are accepted as valid (Greenspan, 1983). The counselor-client relationship is explored and counselors are open to client feedback. This feedback is especially important when clients express anger at the therapist. Since many females are systematically taught not to express their anger, a major goal of feminist therapy is to facilitate clients' expression of anger. For therapists to interpret clients' anger toward them as really being transferred anger invalidates clients' angry feelings, punishes their initial attempts at expressing their anger, and violates the feminist concept of clients being experts on themselves.

### Affirming the Woman

In further promotion of egalitarian therapeutic relationships, feminist therapists emphasize identification of client strengths in addition to exploration of problems. Often identification of these strengths involves reframing of previously negatively valued traits, ones that are negatively valued using an androcentric or ethnocentric perspective, but are reappreciated from a gynocentric or culturally flexible perspective. This revaluing of self is a part of the fourth principle of EFT, which is discussed later in this chapter.

### Summary

Egalitarian therapeutic relationships are difficult to achieve. The establishment of an egalitarian relationship with clients is more of an ideal that is continually strived for, rather than an accomplished reality for all or even most therapeutic relationships. Striving for egalitarian relationships may conflict with the values of some ethnic groups. Given that oppression of groups of people usually involves power imbalances, we believe that confronting the negative impact of hierarchial relationships in a society is a crucial element of EFT.

## Counseling Goals for Principle III

The following statements are possible feminist therapy goals that are related to the *Relationships Are Egalitarian* principle. Counselors help clients:

1. Develop egalitarian relationships—both in therapeutic relationships and in the client's life generally.
2. Develop competencies to be economically autonomous. Most feminist therapists believe that women should maintain the ability to be financially independent so that they will not be in a "one-down," subordinate position.
3. Develop a balance of independence and interdependence in relationships.
4. Develop a full range of interpersonal and life skills.
5. Be appropriately assertive.
6. Develop skills for dealing with interpersonal conflicts that come from living in oppressive environments.
7. Express and use anger appropriately in service of implementing constructive change.
8. Identify and value personal strengths and assets.

## IV: Women's Perspectives Are Valued

A common misconception about feminist therapy is that its goal is to make women more like men. On the contrary, a major premise of EFT is that women and men need to be able to increase their appreciation of women's perspectives of life and of culturally embedded female value systems.

In Chapter 1, we pointed out that socially constructed conceptions of gender have segregated and devalued many sets of behaviors that are traditionally socialized in women. Reconstruction of our gender conceptions requires that we reevaluate these female-stereotyped traits and affirm them as important and valuable human characteristics for both women and men. Feminist therapy assists women in identifying the devalued aspects of their socialized selves and in reconceptualizing weakness into strength and negative deficit into positive advantage.

The devaluation of female-related characteristics results in a double bind for women. They are reinforced for being "appropriately" female and at the same time are devalued for being that way. For example, many women are taught to be nurturing of their families, to put their family members' needs before their own, and to devote their life energies to "making the home." Yet women are criticized for being enmeshed with their families and for being dependent on men economically. The concept of *codependency,* typically applied to women, is a prime example of how women are pathologized for providing the nurturance and attachment behaviors they were taught to give to men (van Wormer, 1990). Many cultures expect women to nurture others. Yet, nurturance is devalued in White patriarchal cultures, as is evidenced by the low pay associated with "nurturant" professions like nursing and teaching, and by the low status that nurturing by the therapist has in most traditional therapy approaches. Women often internalize this androcentric double bind by following the gender-role norm, while devaluing themselves and their femaleness (Greenspan, 1983). Societal, White male-stereotyped norms invalidate women's experiences.

## Revaluing Women

Feminist therapists believe that women need to reject androcentric definitions of womanhood, to learn to value their personal characteristics, and to validate their own, woman-centered views of the world. Women are encouraged to self-define, based on trusting their own experiences. Sturdivant (1980) called this phenomenon the "woman-defined-woman" (p. 92). Female-typed characteristics and personal characteristics valued by subordinated ethnic cultures that have been defined as deficits when compared to White, Western male characteristics are "revalued" as strengths in feminist therapy. Thus, empathy, nurturance, cooperation, intuition, interdependence, and relationship focus are valued and given priority. Needs for nurturance and interdependency are viewed as legitimate and not as pathological. Peaceful negotiation is valued against competitive and aggressive solutions to conflict. Heterosexuality is not seen as healthier than other sexual orientations, such as being lesbian, gay, or bisexual.

## Outcomes of Revaluing Women

This revaluing and redefining process has many implications for both women and the feminist therapy process. First, learning to value previously devalued characteristics facilitates women's use of a large role repertoire (i.e., they not only acquire desirable additional traits they have been taught to suppress—becoming more androgynous—but also prize and use desirable traditionally female-typed traits). Second, they learn to value other women and their relationships with women. Increased bonding with other women is seen as an important way for women to understand the common social conditions that underlie their life problems. Thus, consciousness-raising groups and all-female therapy groups are viewed as very desirable alternatives to replace or augment individual therapy. These groups provide ways for women to heal women and for women to see that their individual power is bound to the power of women as a group. However, we also acknowledge that women, because of their diverse life circumstances (e.g., ethnic origins, sexual orientations, age, physical abilities, social class), may have differing or even conflicting needs and perspectives. These differences should be understood, valued, and incorporated into the endeavors of the group. Women cannot be empowered solely through intrapsychic change. Real empowerment of women can be realized only through social change (Greenspan, 1983). A third implication of the revaluing process is that women learn to nurture themselves (Gilbert, 1980).

Fourth, EFT incorporates these female-based value systems. Clients are treated as experts on themselves, thereby facilitating clients' trusting themselves, their inner wisdom, and intuition. In EFT, the subjective experiences of both therapists and clients are valued. Meeting client needs (rather than frustrating them), nurturing clients, being empathic, and establishing collaborative, egalitarian relationships are important aspects of feminist therapy. (For a more detailed account of how androcentric and ethnocentric values influence traditional therapeutic approaches, see Greenspan, 1983, and Comas-Diaz & Greene, 1994.) Feminist therapists believe that when clients experience therapists' empathic understanding and support, they are more likely to love and nurture themselves (Greenspan, 1983). EFT embraces a holistic approach to therapy whereby cognitive, emotional, physical, spiritual, and environmental dimensions of the client are valued.

## Counseling Goals for Principle IV

The following statements are possible feminist therapy goals related to the *Women's Perspectives Are Valued* principle. Therapists help clients:

1. Trust their own experiences as women.
2. Redefine womanhood from female perspectives.
3. Appreciate female-related values.
4. Trust their intuition as a legitimate source of knowledge.
5. Identify personal strengths.
6. Identify and take care of their own needs and nurture themselves.
7. Value themselves as women.
8. Value other women and their relationships with them.
9. Deemphasize androcentrically and ethnocentrically defined physical attractiveness.
10. Accept and like their own bodies.
11. Define and act in accordance with their own sexual needs rather than someone else's sexual needs.

## THE CHALLENGE AND PROCESS OF INTEGRATING DIVERSITY INTO EMPOWERMENT FEMINIST THERAPY

Integrating diversity perspectives into the EFT framework is a challenging process that requires us and you, the practitioner, to be ever vigilant about cultural and group differences and about the effects of power differentials. As we struggled with the structural changes needed, we became even more aware of both the similarities and tensions between feminist and multicultural approaches. Integrating these two perspectives requires making structural value decisions, decisions that might be made differently by others attempting the same task. Thus, in the spirit of Principle III of disclosing relevant values, we have listed the major integration decision rules we developed and followed.

1. EFT values are the foundation into which we integrated diversity perspectives.
2. For each woman, gender may not be a primary social location, but gender will almost always be salient.
3. We employed a broad definition of diversity rather than a more narrow version of multiculture so that all forms of oppression could be addressed.
4. We believe that to be an effective EF therapist, each of us must examine all our seats of privilege (advantage) and oppression (disadvantage). EF therapists work against all forms of oppression.
5. Culture is not sacrosanct. Although diverse cultures must be understood and respected, most cultural contexts have both positive and toxic elements. Feminist

therapy has always challenged cultural beliefs and practices that subordinate, discriminate against, and limit the potential of groups of people.

6. The practice of EFT requires cultural knowledge and flexibility in the choice of therapeutic interventions so that the specific needs of diverse clients may be met. However, the four principles of EFT remain the foundation for the counseling of these diverse clients.

## TECHNIQUES OF EMPOWERMENT FEMINIST THERAPY

EF therapists use a wide variety of techniques to accomplish the goals of feminist therapy. Some techniques, such as gender-role analysis and power analysis, are unique to feminist therapy, while others are drawn from other theoretical orientations. All techniques that EF therapists use must first be evaluated for their compatibility with EFT principles. Those techniques that violate these principles are modified or discarded. For example, most feminist therapists do not use paradoxical interventions, such as prescribing the symptom (Levant, 1984), if the therapist uses the technique without the client being aware of its purpose. This "manipulation" of the client violates the egalitarian relationship principle. In the next section, we define and discuss several techniques central to EFT. These techniques of feminist therapy are displayed in Table 3.2.

**Table 3.2    Techniques of Empowerment Feminist Therapy**

| Principle | Techniques |
|---|---|
| Principle I<br>Personal and social identities are interdependent. | Social identities analysis<br>Identity development level analysis |
| Principle II<br>The personal is political. | Cultural analysis<br>Gender-role analysis<br>Power analysis<br>Bibliotherapy<br>Reframing<br>Assertiveness training<br>Consciousness raising |
| Principle III<br>Relationships are egalitarian. | Demystifying strategies<br>Collaborative goal setting<br>Therapist self-disclosure<br>Therapist self-involving responses<br>CR groups |
| Principle IV<br>Women's perspectives are valued. | Relabeling<br>CR groups |

## Cultural Analysis

As discussed in Chapter 2, the issues women bring to counseling cannot be adequately understood apart from their cultural context. Thus, issues raised by clients are examined for their general cultural contexts and for multiple sources of oppression. The following questions can be used to structure that examination. Therapists can ask themselves these questions when conceptualizing about client issues and/or the questions can be explored with clients:

1. What definition does the White, Western, male, heterosexual dominant culture give to the client issue (e.g., rape, wife battering, career choice)? How are the dominant culture's values reflected in the definition? That is, how has the dominant culture socially constructed the issue? What aspects of societal context are ignored by this definition? When societal contributions to the problem are ignored, victims are blamed for what has been done to them. What definition would be less intra-psychic and more consistent with women-diversity-centered perspectives?
2. What is the incidence rate for this issue among various groups of people (e.g., men, women, Whites, People of Color, heterosexuals, gays, lesbians, people at higher and lower SES levels)? Disparate rates among groups may signal the effects of oppression.
3. Which of the client's social locations are related to the issue? If the client blames self for the problem, how is her social identity development level related to the self-blame?
4. What myths exist in the society about the issue? What is the source of these myths and how are they being maintained? What stereotyped gender-role beliefs are connected to the myths? What societal power differentials are connected to the myths?
5. What labels, language, or diagnoses are connected to the issue? How do these locate the problem in the individual and ignore social context?

In a cultural analysis of the client issues, the answers to these questions are collaboratively explored using a variety of therapeutic strategies including, but not limited to, information giving, bibliotherapy, client self-reflection, theme identification, and counselor self-disclosure. A complete cultural analysis also includes two more specific kinds of analyses: gender-role analysis and power analysis.

## Gender-Role Analysis

Gender-role analysis is designed to increase clients' awareness of how societal gender-role-related expectations adversely affect them and how women and men are socialized differentially (Sturdivant, 1980). The content of gender-role messages varies from culture to culture. For members of subordinated groups, gender-role analysis is applied both to expectations internalized from the dominant culture and to gendered expectations of the minority cultures. The first step of gender-role analysis is for clients to identify the direct and indirect gender-role messages (verbal, nonverbal, modeled) they have experienced across their life spans. Second, they identify both the positive and negative consequences to them and to society of those gender-role messages. Third, they identify how they have internalized these external messages in the form of conscious and unconscious self-talk. Fourth, they decide which of these internalized messages they want to change. Fifth, they develop a plan for implementing the change (e.g., cognitive restructuring). Sixth, they implement the change. They also learn skills for counteracting negative environmental reactions to their implemented changes. Gender-role analysis can be used in many variations (see Remer & Remer, 2000). One structured exercise on gen-der-role analysis is presented in the Activities section at the end of this chapter. Many feminist therapists believe that gender-role and power analyses are more effectively done in groups of women (Kravetz, 1980).

## Power Analysis

Power analysis has two purposes:

1. To increase clients' awareness of the power differential existing between domi-nant and subordinate groups in a society (e.g., between women and men, between heterosexuals and those with other sexual orientations).
2. To empower clients to have influence on the interpersonal and institutional exter-nals affecting their lives.

We define *power* as the ability to access personal and environmental resources to effect personal and/or external change. Actual use of power depends on access to and/or pos-session of different kinds of power, the decision to use that access, and the ways in which the power is exerted.

Power analysis can involve several steps. First, both the therapist and client can re-view the variety of existing definitions of power and then choose the one that best fits for them. Second, clients are taught about the different kinds of power (e.g., role, re-source, legal, institutional, normative, reward, physical, referent). Third, information can be given about the differential access-dominant and subordinate groups have to these kinds of power (P. B. Johnson, 1976; Lips, 1999). Clients are encouraged to iden-tify which kinds of power they possess or to which they generally have access. Fourth, clients can be introduced to P. B. Johnson's (1976) structure for understanding the vari-ous ways power can be exerted (e.g., direct vs. indirect, personal resources vs. concrete resources, and competence vs. helplessness). Since Johnson concludes that women gen-erally exert power through indirect, personal resources, and helplessness means, women clients especially need to identify the modes they typically use in exerting power and to learn about alternative strategies. Fifth, clients are asked to explore how societal mes-sages (e.g., internalized stereotyping) and environmental barriers (institutionalized sex-ism, racism, ethnocentrism, classism, heterosexism, etc.) are affecting their use of power. Challenging and changing their internalized messages is an important prerequi-site to clients' using a wider range of kinds of power and of power strategies. Clients also assess the risks, costs, and benefits to them of using alternate types of power. The final step in power analysis encourages clients to try out additional or alternative kinds of power and power strategies, thereby increasing their power-role repertoire.

Individuals from both dominant (privileged) and subordinate groups can benefit from analyzing the destructive and effective uses of power. Both sides of the power structure are analyzed, especially the "effects of too little power and authority on women and the effect of too much power and authority on men" (J. Brickman, 1984, p. 61).

## Assertiveness Training

Traditional gender-role socialization of many, but not all, cultural groups of women prohibits women from acting assertively and directly (Jakubowski, 1977). Thus, training to be assertive, to stand up for one's own rights while not trampling the rights of others, is crucial for women if they are not to be powerless victims. Assertive skills are important for women to possess to impact the environment effectively and to bring about social change. Since assertiveness skills are so important to both effecting institutional change and to having egalitarian relationships, feminist therapists must possess assertion-training skills (Gilbert, 1980). Jakubowski has developed a four-component assertiveness training program for women, which includes teaching clients to differentiate between assertive, passive, and aggressive behaviors, to develop a belief system that supports their rights to assert their needs and have them met, to reduce psychological blocks (e.g., traditional gender-role messages) to their being assertive, and to develop assertiveness skills through behavioral rehearsal.

## Consciousness-Raising Groups

Consciousness-raising (C-R) groups, a creation of the Women's Movement, are groups of women meeting regularly to discuss their lives as women. As the women in a C-R group share information about their individual lives, they begin to identify the commonalities in their experiences and then to see the social/external roots of those experiences that are related to living in oppressive environments. The women explore their gender-role socialization process and its negative and positive effects on their lives (gender-role analysis), and they examine the one-down power position of women in society (power analysis). A feminist-diversity C-R group would also include a cultural analysis where all forms of oppression and privilege are examined. Generally, C-R groups are leaderless and egalitarian, are growth-oriented, and focus on working toward social change. The content may range from cognitively oriented discussions to more personal, emotional sharing. They share similarities with self-help groups (Kravetz, 1980). The C-R group goals and format are often adapted by feminist therapists to counseling women in all-women groups with the therapist as leader. These all-women therapy groups follow the feminist therapy principles and are seen as having several advantages over individual counseling. First, the interpersonal sharing is spread over many individuals, rather than just the client and counselor, thus providing a wider base for identifying the commonalities and differences in the women's experience. Second, the women are sources of healing for each other, often taking turns at being the healed and the healer—a process that helps turn "victims" into "survivors" (Figley, 1985) and empowers the individual woman. Third, the women can work toward social change more effectively together than alone. Thus, although C-R groups were more prevalent earlier in the Women's Movement, we believe they are still a very important way that EFT can be implemented.

## Bibliotherapy

Feminist therapists often encourage clients to read books and articles relevant to their therapeutic issues. The client's learning about herself and her environment through reading is called bibliotherapy. Resocialization (away from traditional gender-role stereotypes) and education of clients about sexism and all forms of oppression are facilitated by clients' reading. Bibliotherapy is also a good way for clients to learn life coping skills. Bibliotherapy can also increase the expertise of the client vis-à-vis the therapist, thereby reducing the power differential between them.

## Reframing and Relabeling

In the family therapy literature, *reframing* is a technique in which the counselor changes the frame of reference for looking at an individual's behavior. It usually refers to a shift from an intrapersonal to an interpersonal definition of the client's problem (Grunebaum & Chasin, 1978). In feminist therapy, the reframing shift is usually from intrapersonal and individual to societal and political and is accomplished by identifying the contribution of the external environment to the individual's problem. For example, depression, which is usually viewed as being a result of dysfunctional thought, feeling, and behavior patterns of the individual, may be reframed by EF therapists as a natural response to women being in a subordinate power position. Thus, reframing is a very useful technique for the *Personal Is Political* principle of feminist therapy.

*Relabeling* usually refers to counseling interventions that change the label or evaluation applied to the client's behavior or characteristics, usually shifting the focus from a negative to a positive evaluation. Related to the *Women's Perspectives Are Valued* principle of EFT, clients learn to relabel previously evaluated weaknesses (based on androcentric norms) as strengths (based on gynocentric norms). For example, a woman who has been told she is "too emotional" relabels herself as having the ability to express feelings and to be empathic to others' feelings.

## Therapy-Demystifying Strategies

Feminist therapists use a variety of techniques to demystify the therapy process for clients. The more clients know about therapy in general and specifically about therapy with this particular therapist and share in decisions related to their therapy, the greater is the chance for developing an egalitarian relationship between the therapist and client.

Having access to information is one way to increase women's personal power. EF therapists teach clients about therapy so that they can be informed consumers. In initial sessions with clients (some feminist therapists provide this session free of charge), EF therapists describe their theoretical orientation and therapeutic strategies, their relevant personal and professional values, their general expectations for both themselves as therapists and for clients, and clients' rights as consumers of therapy. Fees for therapy are also negotiated. They often encourage clients to shop around for a therapist by interviewing other therapists and finding the best match. For example, the New York Chapter of the National Organization for Women (1978) has published the booklet *A Consumer's Guide to Nonsexist Therapy* to educate potential clients about their rights and to help them in their search for a therapist.

Once the client has decided on a therapist, the client and feminist therapist develop a therapeutic contract (either verbal or written) that articulates the conditions of therapy (fee, session time, length of therapy, etc.) and the therapeutic goals toward which they will work. The goal setting is done collaboratively, with input from both the client and counselor and with the client having the final say.

EF therapists also teach relevant counseling skills to clients. For example, many counseling skills are basically good interpersonal communication skills (e.g., confrontation skills, active listening) that can be important for clients to add to their behavioral repertoire. Self-awareness and self-monitoring skills give clients control over their behaviors and thus increase their choices. Feminist therapists also teach and encourage clients to evaluate the counseling relationship and to evaluate progress toward therapeutic outcomes. Identifying and expressing needs and wants is an important change for many women because of gender-role rules that dictate that women should subordinate their needs to the needs of others. By giving feedback to the therapist about how the therapist is impacting the client, and by evaluating whether her needs are being met in therapy, the client learns how to assert herself. EF therapists see client disagreement with the counselor as a positive reflection of her experience rather than as client resistance.

Demystifying strategies are not the exclusive domain of feminist therapists. Indeed, they are strategies for applying ethical practices in counseling sessions for all kinds of therapies (Hare-Mustin, Marecek, Kaplan, & Liso-Levinson, 1979). However, in feminist therapy, demystifying strategies serve the additional purpose of reducing the power differential between client and therapist, thus increasing the possibility of an egalitarian therapeutic relationship.

## CHARACTERISTICS OF EMPOWERMENT FEMINIST THERAPISTS

First and foremost, EF therapists must have a commitment to the beliefs of feminism and a set of values that are consistent with the EFT principles. We believe EF therapists must apply feminist principles to their own lives and should model the incorporation of these principles. Thus, feminist therapists must explore their own social locations and assess their levels of identity development related to these locations. Being an effective EF therapist requires constant vigilance about one's seats of oppression and of privilege. EF therapists engage in continuing education and self-examination, which enhances their development through the identity levels of their various social locations. EF therapists identify and challenge any values and beliefs they hold that oppress or devalue any subordinate group. They are also involved in their communities in bringing about social change to lessen all forms of oppression. Thus, EF therapists must make a commitment to challenge all forms of oppression in their lives including confronting and working for change in the privileged groups to which they belong. For example, a Christian, heterosexual, African American male who wants to be an EF therapist must examine and challenge his own male and heterosexual privileges and work to change the beliefs in his church congregation that homosexuality is sinful.

EF therapists are knowledgeable about the psychology of women, about women's issues (especially about the external sources of women's concerns), and about multicultural psychology. They use this professional and personal awareness in the counseling process to listen to what clients say and to conceptualize and reframe client experiences from a feminist perspective. They are active in the therapeutic process. They initiate explorations of how gender-role socialization and environmental sexism and other relevant "isms" impact client issues. They challenge clients to consider a full range of choices. For example, if a female client expresses interest in nursing and medical technology, the feminist therapist would encourage her to add physician to her list of career alternatives. Feminist therapists are often advocates on behalf of clients.

Sturdivant (1980) suggested that feminist therapists also need to be warm, empathic, and spontaneous—to be capable of expressing their feelings and willing to self-disclose and self-involve. Feminist therapy deemphasizes therapist "objectivity," since the need to be objective distances both the client and counselor from their own feelings. EF therapists value emotional involvement with clients as well as having cognitive understanding. Since expression of anger is often important for women, counselors must be comfortable with their own expression of anger and with clients' expressions of anger in sessions.

## EMPOWERMENT FEMINIST THERAPY: A CASE ANALYSIS

In this section, EFT is applied to a client case. Our intention is to show you a comprehensive case analysis of how an EF therapist would counsel "Nina," an incest survivor. (Other case applications are described in subsequent chapters.)

### Nina: A Childhood Sexual Abuse Survivor

Nina is a 31-year-old White, heterosexual, middle-class female who comes to therapy because of periodic bouts of unexplained depression, a low level of sexual desire, and low self-esteem. She is the only female stockbroker in a medium-sized company. She and her husband have two children and have recently been in marriage counseling for their sexual difficulties (unmatched levels of sexual desire). She entered individual therapy because she felt that the sexual difficulties were "her fault." She reports being repeatedly sexually abused by her older brother from the time she was 5 years old until she was 11 years old. She never told anyone about the abuse and mentions it in therapy only after careful open-ended questioning by her therapist. Nina reports terrifying, frightening nightmares in which she sees her brother in her bedroom and she awakens feeling frightened.

## Empowerment Feminist Strategies with Nina

EF therapists would approach Nina's issues quite differently than a traditional therapist might. They would reject incest myths (e.g., that incest only occurs in low SES families), assess for sexual trauma, educate about incest and sexual violence, reinterpret family power dynamics, remove blame from the victim, and empower the client to become a survivor.

### Assessing for Sexual Trauma

Because EF therapists are well educated about the reality of women's lives (e.g., high occurrence rate of rape, sexual abuse, wife or partner abuse), they routinely assess for these experiences in all their clients. For example, at the beginning of therapy, the therapist would ask Nina if she had had "any uncomfortable, unwanted, or unpleasant sexual experiences." Also, because of their knowledge about specific women's issues, EF therapists would know about the range of symptoms often found in incest survivors and would recognize that Nina's four presenting issues (depression, sexual difficulties, nightmares, and low self-esteem) are symptomatic of sexual abuse trauma (B. M. Hughes, 1999).

### Identifying Social Identities

Nina's therapist would educate her about personal and social identities, seats of oppression, and seats of privilege. Nina would then diagram her social identities as illustrated by the exercise in Chapter 2. The diagram of her social identities is depicted in Figure 3.1. Based on clinical interview questions, Nina's therapist would assess her level of identity

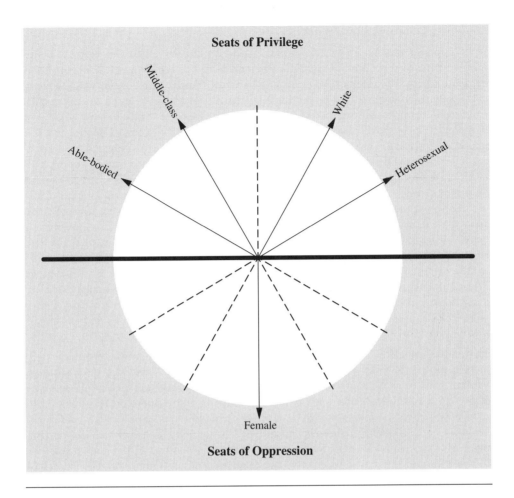

**Figure 3.1   Diagram of Nina's social identities.**

development along these locations, revealing that she is primarily in Pre-awareness on all her identities.

### Removing Victim Blame

As the memories and the feelings of the incest surface, the therapist would share her knowledge about incest with Nina, helping her to connect her present behavior and feelings to her trauma. This reduces Nina's feelings that she is going crazy. Brother-sister incest would not be viewed as less traumatic than parent-child incest. Nina's brother would be held responsible for his abusive behavior, and his behavior would be defined as rape, an act of sexual violence. EF therapists believe that the victim is never to blame. Intrusive, abusive offenders use their power to achieve self-gratification in a way that traumatizes less powerful victims (J. Brickman, 1984). Nina would learn that orgasm can be a purely physiological response to genital touch and that her orgasmic response to her brother did not signify that she wanted to be abused, nor that she really wanted to have sex with her brother.

*Analyzing Family Power Dynamics*

In EFT, power and authority are seen as important underlying issues. The power that Nina's brother had because he was older and male would be explored, as would Nina's and her mother's possible lack of power as females in the family. Nina's mother would not be held solely responsible for not protecting Nina. Nina's father's role (as an equally responsible coparent) in not having protected Nina would be explored. Since the dynamics of an individual family are strongly influenced by the societal norms of male dominance, it is important for the power differential between males and females in Nina's family and in society in general to be addressed (Herman, 1981). Society's view of incest, as depicted in incest myths and the media, would also be discussed. For example, many people believe that incest is perpetrated only by "crazy" family members and that children's failure to disclose the abuse means they wanted to be abused or that they were not really hurt by it. More than likely, Nina's experience of the sexual abuse would be different from society's depiction of incest. By helping Nina challenge the myths she has learned, the therapist facilitates Nina's beginning to trust her own feelings and perspective. For example, the role of sexual violence in helping to keep women subjugated through fear would be addressed. Incest is directly connected to men having sexual power over women (J. Brickman, 1984).

*Equalizing Power*

The feminist goal of building egalitarian therapeutic relationships would be especially important with Nina so as not to recreate, in the therapy relationship, the controlling victimizer-helpless victim dynamics of her abuse. The feminist therapist would appropriately self-disclose. If the therapist is herself a rape or incest survivor, she would share some of her own experiences as a victimized female and as a survivor. Goals would be collaboratively decided and might include claiming her sexuality for her own pleasure (rather than restoring her sexual functioning for her husband), learning to like and nurture her own body, trusting her own perspective and experience of her trauma, valuing her femaleness, nurturing herself, identifying her strengths as a survivor, increasing her assertion skills, learning not to blame herself, expressing all of her feelings related to the incest (especially anger), and learning to channel her anger for effecting external change.

*Reinterpreting "Symptoms"*

Nina's "symptoms" would be viewed as normal reactions to traumatic experience, not as indicators of pathology. The counselor and Nina would explore how her symptoms are connected to her specific trauma and how they helped her to cope with the trauma. Nina would probably be encouraged to join a therapy group for incest survivors. Through group sharing, Nina would learn to feel less different and isolated. She would also have the opportunity to help other victims to heal, an experience that Figley (1985) says is important in becoming a "survivor." Finally, the feminist therapist and/or Nina might work at changing society, especially its contribution to the existence of incest and society's myths about incest. Social change is seen as crucial. For example, near the end of therapy, Nina urged her stockbroker firm to contribute to a nonprofit clinic that provides medical and counseling services to children who have been abused.

However, Nina's incest trauma is only one source of her symptoms. Nina's depression and low self-esteem also would be partially viewed as normal reactions to Nina's status as a woman in a patriarchal society (i.e., they are a reflection of her societal subordination as a woman). The feminist counselor would inquire about Nina's experiences as the only professional woman in her office and of her experiences pursuing a nontraditional career. In what ways is she being discriminated against in the workplace? Nina's possible role strain and role overload would also be discussed. Strategies for changing her environment and others' expectations of her (rather than giving up her work) would be explored.

## SUMMARY

The four principles of EFT—*Personal and Social Identities Are Interdependent, the Personal Is Political, Relationships Are Egalitarian,* and *Women's Perspectives Are Valued*—constitute a therapeutic approach very different from most traditional therapies. The EFT approach requires that all of a person's gendered, racist, ethnocentric, heterosexist, classist, ableist, and ageist perspectives and assumptions about both the world and therapy be considered anew. Becoming a feminist therapist means putting your androcentrically and ethnocentrically defined view of the world and your androcentrically and ethnocentrically based professional training into a basket, mixing up the contents, and then putting them into a feminist-designed sieve that requires major reconstruction and/or disposal of existing psychological concepts. Correspondingly, clients of EF therapists acquire a new way of looking at and responding to their world. For both the counselor and the client, this shared journey of empowerment can be frightening, angering, and exhilarating.

## ACTIVITIES

After reading this chapter, retake the Therapy with Women Scale at the beginning of the chapter to see if you have changed any of your responses.

### Gender-Role Analysis Exercise

This exercise is designed to help you identify the advantages and disadvantages of gender-role messages you learned while growing up and by which you may continue to be influenced. Complete the following steps:

#### 1. Gender-Role Message Identification

Beginning with your early childhood experiences and continuing developmentally up to the present day, list all the messages you received about how you should and should not behave because you were female or male. Make two lists: one of "Shoulds" and one of "Shouldn'ts." You may want to include rules about how you should dress, what role you should play in your family, how you should interact with the other sex, and so on. These lists represent the composite of the gender-role rules that you have learned.

Remember that these messages may have been verbal or nonverbal; they may have been reflected in ways you were rewarded, punished, or ignored; and they may have been modeled by others. These messages may have come from a variety of sources: significant others, acquaintances, the media, printed materials, or from institutional structures and policies. In recalling these messages, it is useful to work with developmental periods of your life (e.g., junior high) and to focus on those factors and people who were influential in your life during that period. If you live within two or more cultural groups, you may have two or more conflicting sets of gender-role messages. Be sure to include all of these messages and their sources on your list.

## Gender-Role Restructuring

a. Look over the lists you have just made. Put a mark by each message that still influences your present behavior. Select one of these marked messages to explore further here.

b. Identify sources of the message. Think about how and where you originally learned this message (e.g., in your family, in school, in church, from peers, on television). List all the sources from which you learned this gender-role rule.

c. Name current reinforcers and punishments. In what ways and by whom are you currently reinforced for behaving in accordance with, or punished for not behaving in accordance with, your gender-role rule?

d. Perform a cost-benefit analysis. What benefits do you gain by following your gender-role rule? What does this gender-role rule cost you; how does it limit you? What benefits do you see that society gains by women (or men) living in accordance with your gender-role rule? What are the costs to society of this gender-role rule?

e. Make the decision to change. Based on your personal and societal cost-benefit analysis, decide whether you want to change this internalized gender-role message. If you decide not to change it, stop here. If you decide to change it, proceed to the next step.

f. Reconstruct the message. Rewrite your gender-role rule into a self-message that is more self-enhancing and less restricting. What behaviors do you need to change to live in accordance with your newly constructed message?

g. Implement the new message. Brainstorm strategies that help you implement your new message and its corresponding behavior changes. Make a commitment to yourself about which of these strategies you will use.

## FURTHER READINGS

To expand your understanding of feminist therapy and related diversity issues, see the following resources:

Enns, C. Z. (1997). *Feminist theories and feminist psychotherapies: Origins, themes, and variations.* New York: Harrington Park Press.

Remer, P., & Remer, R. (2000). The alien invasion exercise: Creating an experience of diversity. *International Journal of Action Methods: Psychodrama, Skill Training, and Role-Playing,* 147–154.

Worell, J., & Johnson, D. (2001). Feminist approaches to psychotherapy. In R. K. Unger (Ed.), *Handbook of the psychology of women and gender* (pp. 317–329). New York: Wiley.

Worell, J., & Johnson, N. G. (Eds.). (1997). *Shaping the future of feminist psychology: Education, research, and practice.* Washington, DC: American Psychological Association.

Wyche, K. F., & Rice, J. K. (1997). Feminist therapy: From dialogue to tenets. In J. Worell & N. G. Johnson (Eds.), *Shaping the future of feminist psychology: Education, research, and practice.* Washington, DC: American Psychological Association.

# Chapter 4

## FEMINIST TRANSFORMATION OF COUNSELING THEORIES

*Psychological theories provide abstractions about human phenomena. . . . If integration means drawing methods from different sources, the mechanisms should be grounded in a unified theoretical framework.*

Albert Bandura, 1997

## SELF-ASSESSMENT: CLARIFYING YOUR THEORETICAL POSITION

Before you begin to use feminist theory in your practice with clients, you need a clear conception of your theoretical position in psychotherapy and counseling. That is, how do you currently use theoretical conceptions in your approach to human functioning and behavior change? Before reading Chapter 4, complete the following format for clarifying your current theoretical approach to therapy. At the end of this chapter, we ask you to apply your understanding of Empowerment Feminist Therapy (EFT) principles to revising and adapting the theory of your choice to a feminist format.

1. Briefly trace the historical basis of the theory. Who were the theoretical grandparents, and how did they gather data to develop and support their theorizing?
2. List the key constructs or concepts of the theory.
3. How does the theory explain personality development and change?
4. How does the theory explain psychopathology, mental illness, maladjustment, or problems in living that bring clients into contact with the helping professional?
5. How does the theory integrate diversity in personal and social identities?
6. What is the role of assessment and diagnosis?
7. What is the role of the therapist and of the client?
8. List the major therapeutic techniques or strategies.
9. Develop a brief statement about how this theoretical approach fits your personal views of human functioning and behavior change.

## OVERVIEW

This chapter develops an understanding of how to integrate traditional theoretical views with EFT principles. We start with a comparison of traditional and EFT models to theory building, and we provide a format for assessing the compatibility of any theory with EFT principles. Two theoretical approaches to psychotherapy and counseling are offered as examples of the adaptation process: Cognitive-Behavioral theory and Psychodrama. We challenge you to perform a similar transformation exercise on a theory of your choice. After reading Chapter 4, you will be able to:

- Compare traditional with feminist-compatible models of theory construction.
- Determine the compatibility of your preferred or chosen theory with EFT principles.
- Revise the chosen theory to fit compatibly with EFT principles.

## A GUIDE TO THEORY TRANSFORMATION

### Advantages of Theoretical Integration

As noted in Chapter 3, some feminist therapists embrace feminist therapy as their sole theoretical orientation. More commonly, however, they combine feminist therapy with one or more traditional therapy approaches. This combining of two or more theories is often executed at the technique level, with therapists pragmatically choosing interventions. In contrast, when more traditional theories are combined with EFT, we advocate integrating the multiple approaches at both theoretical and applied levels. We believe that therapeutic change is most effectively accomplished when therapists are well grounded in a cohesive theory that enables them to conceptualize the client's issues, to select appropriate interventions, and to anticipate their effects. Throughout the book, we define a *traditional theory* as one that: (a) neglects to integrate all aspects of diversity into its constructs and assumptions, (b) omits the impact of external oppression of subordinate groups on individual development and functioning, and (c) overtly or covertly embraces values of the dominant culture to the exclusion of alternative value systems.

We have several reasons for advocating theoretical integration. First, a theory provides a consistent resource for conceptualizing functional and dysfunctional behavior patterns and for selecting interventions that are tailored to the needs of the client. Thus, theory-based interventions are more likely to follow a rational process of hypothesis testing and revision of strategy than a trial-and-error approach that attempts "whatever will work" (Bandura, 1997). Second, theory-based interventions are also more likely than randomly chosen techniques to be subjected to systematic research evaluation. A research base can provide valuable information to the clinician about how the intervention functions with differing types of problems and with various client populations. Third, we believe that for the purposes of working effectively with women clients, theoretical assumptions and working hypotheses should be explicit, rather than implicit, in the awareness and functioning of the clinician. Finally, theoretical integration is difficult or impractical when certain constructs and interventions of traditional therapies are incompatible with EFT. In our view, most contemporary theories of psychotherapy and counseling contain elements that render some of their applications undesirable for use with women and minority clients. Some theories of behavior development and change are more conducive than others to integration with feminist views.

The following sections offer a format for analyzing a current theory of behavior change for its compatibility with EFT principles. First, we summarize the characteristics of theories that are inconsistent with effective treatment strategies for women. Then, we suggest four criteria for developing a feminist-diversity format for theories of counseling and psychotherapy. We complete the analysis with a set of guidelines for transforming a given theory into a format that meets the criteria for EFT.

## Characteristics of Traditional Theories

The purpose of a psychological theory is not to mirror nature or to establish truth, but to present an image of nature that appears useful for understanding individuals (Levy, 1970). Similar to the concept of gender, a theory is a construction of reality that reflects the understandings that exist at the time of social history in which the theory is developed (K. J. Gergen, 1985; Morowski, 1987; Morowski & Bayer, 1995). Many psychological theories were born during a period in history in which gender was viewed as a dichotomous property of being female or male. Observed social arrangements were assumed to be rooted in the nature of gender, so that women and men were assumed to possess different characteristics and were therefore suited for divergent life pathways. Consequently, some theories currently in use bear the reflections of our historical heritage regarding the "true" nature of women and men. Furthermore, these traditional theories do not acknowledge the influence of cultures on both women and men, and the multiple social locations of each individual.

The following analysis presents six characteristics of traditional theories that reflect biased or outdated assumptions about the place of gender and diversity in human functioning. These characteristics are displayed at the left of Table 4.1. A theory can be gender biased or culturally biased if its content and constructs can be characterized in any of the following ways: (a) androcentric, (b) gendercentric, (c) ethnocentric, (d) heterosexist, (e) intrapsychic, or (f) deterministic.

**Table 4.1    Characteristics of theories**

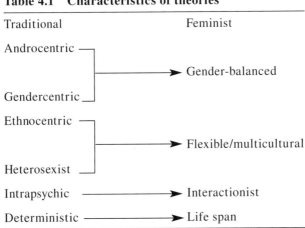

## Androcentric

An *androcentric* theory constructs the lives of persons according to an understanding of the lives of men (Doherty, 1978; P. A. Katz, 1979; Rosser, 1990; Worell, 1981, 1989b). The theory may use male-oriented constructs such as "penis-envy," or may draw assumptions about "normal" human development from an observation of men's developmental sequences of behavior. Examples of androcentrism are found in Freud's (1948, 1965) description of male identity development, in which the boy's defensive identification with a father figure leads to the formation of a healthy superego and internalization of high moral standards. Since girls do not progress through the same Oedipal sequence as boys, their superego development is never quite as consolidated, resulting in the assumption of a lower level of moral development in women. Women, in Freud's view, are by nature passive, emotional, masochistic, narcissistic, and have a lesser sense of justice.

Other examples of androcentric theories are found in Erikson's (1963, 1968) description of identity development in women and men. For the adolescent male, a sense of secure identity comes from adopting a philosophy of life and choice of a career. For women, however, identity is normally deferred until "they know whom they will marry and for whom they will make a home" (1968, p. 123). A woman's identity is therefore defined not by ideology or career commitment, but by her fusion with the roles of wife and mother.

Some theories contain Eurocentric, White, male-defined conceptions of the healthy personality. Some family systems theories, for example, emphasize hierarchy, differentiation, and firm interpersonal boundaries (Bograd, 1986). In Murray Bowen's theory, the differentiated self (ideal adjustment) is characterized by a rational and objective stance, and the capacity to free the self from relationship contexts (Hare-Mustin, 1978). Michele Bograd (1988) pointed out that by these male-defined standards, women are viewed as "enmeshed, undifferentiated, or over-involved, where the prototypically male pole is valued and the prototypically female pole is defined as unhealthy" (p. 97).

Clinicians who base their understandings of women and men on either of these theories may arrive at conclusions about women clients that are biased and inaccurate for any particular woman. Although thoughtful therapists might argue that these parts of Freud's, Erikson's, or Bowen's theories do not play a role in their current therapy, it seems possible that unverbalized influences of the theory may exist.

## Gendercentric

*Gendercentric* theories propose two separate paths of development for women and men. The theories of Freud and Erikson previously discussed are both gendercentric and androcentric. Other theories that posit separate paths of development, however, do not necessarily devalue women but view them as separate and different from men in their personality structure, needs, or values. An example is Object Relations Theory (Chodorow, 1978; Miller, 1976). Recent formulations of psychoanalytic approaches to personality structure and development are also reflected in the Self-in-Relation theory promoted by the Stone Center (Jordan et al., 1991). These theorists propose that women and men differ fundamentally in their needs for attachment and separation, and in their valuing of intimacy and connection in relationships. The differences in personality structure are assumed to evolve from early experiences with the mother, who functions as a prime force in determining the female and male orientation to self and others. As a result, "for girls, 'being present with' [others] psychologically is experienced as self-enhancing, whereas for boys it may come to be experienced as invasive, engulfing, or threatening" (Surrey, 1991, p. 55).

Therapists who adopt a gendercentric theory reveal alpha bias (see Chapter 1). They tend to view women and men as dichotomous in their relationship needs and skills, emphasizing how women and men differ rather than how they intersect (Worell & Johnson, 2001). Although there are some demonstrable differences between women and men in relationship styles, these differences are small, overlapping, and frequently a function of situational constraints or self-presentation strategies rather than personality structure (Deaux, 1984; Deaux & Major, 1987). We believe that it is counterproductive to attribute patterns of behavior to sex or gender, rather than to sets of attitudes and beliefs that are modifiable. Although we may focus on socially based gender messages that women and men internalize and transfer into behavior as they mature, these messages and behaviors are viewed as changeable, rather than deeply rooted in personality structure or biological sex.

Therapists who are gendercentric and/or androcentric may embrace the belief that women and men should behave in traditionally gender-role stereotyped appropriate ways. Thus, therapists using these approaches may believe that for women to be psychologically healthy, they should reflect some or all of these characteristics: emotionally expressive, compliant, nurturant, and fulfilled through their roles as wives, mothers, and helpmates. They may assume that for a man to be psychologically healthy, he ought to be aggressive, independent, unemotional, competitive, and economically successful. Whether consciously or not, traditional therapists may thus promote gendered, rather than flexible, behaviors and may encourage client conformity to established gender-role patterns (Sturdivant, 1980).

### Ethnocentric

*Ethnocentrism* is built into the structure of many theories that base their observations on Anglo European populations. Ethnocentric theories assume that the facts of development and human interaction are similar across cultures, ethnic groups, and nations. In addition to rendering other cultures invisible, ethnocentric theorists define the norm using dominant cultural beliefs and values. Consequently, patterns of beliefs and behavior of other cultural groups may be viewed as deviant and changeworthy.

From a Western dominant-culture perspective, individual needs and self-determination are highly valued. In contrast, many collectivist cultures value the welfare of the group and social harmony over individual needs (Lykes & Qin, 2001; Triandis, 1995). The "invisible" individualistic values of most traditional therapeutic modalities render them inappropriate for clients from most non-Western cultures (Sue & Sue, 1999). These values also conflict with the interdependent and communal values of EFT's principles I and IV.

Additional examples of ethnocentrism in theorizing are seen in assumptions about "normal" family functioning, including the hierarchy and privileging of the two-parent heterosexual family, the relative power position of women and men in families, and the place of children in the family structure. Assumptions about "working mothers," children's day care, extended family arrangements, and who should have jurisdiction over children in contested custody suits can all be influenced by the clinician's theoretical view of appropriate family functioning.

Therapists who adhere to traditional systems theory may also impose their values on Black, Hispanic, Asian, or other ethnic group families whose concepts and values of appropriate family functioning may vary considerably from White, middle-class American culture. Conceptions about appropriate amounts of "enmeshment" and "individuation" (or attachment and separation), for example, may vary across ethnic groups, allowing the potential for misuse of these constructs with families that adhere to culturally different lifestyles. Clinicians from diverse theoretical persuasions may need to examine their assumptions and beliefs about both individual and family healthy functioning to avoid an ethnocentric position with clients.

## Heterosexist and Monosexist

Psychology has been generally *heterosexist* in its theory, research, and practice (Kitzinger & Wilkinson, 1993). Most traditional theories of psychological development and therapeutic change view heterosexual orientation as normative and desirable, and they devalue lifestyles that are oriented toward same-sex partners. In classical psychoanalytic theory, for example, an orientation other than heterosexual was viewed as a failure to achieve normal gender identity; therefore, the preference for same-sex intimate partners was treated as a personality disorder. Heterosexism was built into earlier diagnostic systems, and only in 1973 did the American Psychiatric Association remove homosexuality as a category of mental illness from the *Diagnostic and Statistical Manual of Mental Disorders (DSM-II)*.

*Monosexism* is also evident in most theoretical perspectives. Monosexism assumes a static model of sexual orientation, preference, and behavior. Most cultures adhere to a monosexist ideology, whereby we are attracted romantically and sexually to same- or other-sex individuals throughout our lives. In contrast, current research and theory suggest that a proportion of those who are attracted to heterosexual attachments are also drawn to same-sex relationships; the current term for this orientation is *bisexual* (Rust, 2000). And recent theorizing by Anne Peplau and Linda Garnetts (2000) suggests that women's sexuality is neither bipolar or even tripolar, but is multidetermined, flexible, and fluid over time, as depicted in Table 4.2. The importance of understanding heterosexism

**Table 4.2    Conceptualizing women's sexuality**

| Old Perspectives | New Perspectives |
| --- | --- |
| Heterosexuals are normal and mentally healthy; sexual minorities are abnormal and psychologically impaired (illness model). | Sexual orientation is not associated with psychological adjustment or mental health. |
| Gender conformity is central to sexual orientation; heterosexual women are feminine and lesbians are masculine (inversion model). | There is no inherent link between gender conformity and sexual orientation; this link varies across different social contexts. |
| Biological determinants of sexual orientation are emphasized. | Biological influences are limited, indirect, and differ across specific contexts. |
| Sexual orientation is an enduring, unchanging disposition. | Women's sexual orientation is potentially fluid and changeable over the life span. |
| Sociocultural influences are not considered; observed patterns are often assumed to be universal. | Sociocultural influences are emphasized, including cultural views of gender and sexuality. |

*Source:* Adapted from "New Paradigm for Understanding Women's Sexuality and Sexual Orientation," by L. A. Peplau and L. D. Garnetts, 2000, *Journal of Social Issues, 56,* pp. 329–350. Reprinted with permission.

and monosexism for both theory and practice cannot be underestimated. We discuss client issues of women's sexuality in future chapters.

New avenues of research suggest the need for at least four revisions of classical heterosexist theory:

1. Preference for same-sex partner (gay or lesbian) or for partners of either sex (bisexual) is a stable historical fact. In a survey of 3,000 English-speaking people in the United States, 4.3% of the women and 9.1% of the men had some same-sex experience since age 18; of these, 25% also had a heterosexual partner in the past 12 months (Laumann, Gagnon, Michael, & Michaels, 1994).

2. Personality functioning in lesbian women and gay men differs mainly from heterosexual samples in that these individuals tend to be more egalitarian and less gender-typed in their interpersonal behavior (Blumstein & Schwartz, 1983; Kurdek & Schmitt, 1986).

3. Standardized indices of pathology and mental health do not reveal differences between heterosexuals and lesbian, bisexual or gay individuals, couples, or parents (Peplau & Garnetts, 2000).

4. Sexual attractions may change or modify at differing points in the life span.

Clinicians who remain loyal to unsupported theories about sexual and affectional development and behavior may reveal homophobic and biased attitudes in their counseling practices that are unhelpful and possibly harmful to clients. For example, professional psychologists who believed that the "origin" of sexuality of lesbians and gay men is a personal choice (and thus could be voluntarily changed) were less likely than others to recommend child custody for those couples (I. Crawford, McLeod, Zamboni, & Jordan, 1999).

## Intrapsychic

Psychotherapeutic theories may be placed on a continuum from *intrapsychic* to *environmentally determined*. In contrast to intrapsychic theories that assume the source of personal problems are internal to clients (i.e., clients' personality structures, ineffectual thoughts, behaviors, and/or feelings), environmentally determined theories view the source of clients' problems as sociocultural. Theories that attribute all behavior to intrapsychic causes may fall in the position of "blaming the victim." Theories of development and therapeutic change that minimize or ignore the influence of the external environment on past and current behavior patterns may cast total responsibility on the woman for her actions and for the situations in which she finds herself.

Although we do not propose that clients be exempted totally from their individual contributions to the problems they encounter in life, or from their responsibility for change, an intrapsychic causation model suggests that changes should occur only with the client and not with her social, economic, or institutional environment. Clinicians who adopt an intrapsychic model tend to emphasize how the clients' personalities, internal conflicts, thoughts, or behaviors have contributed to their predicaments, and tend to ignore or minimize situational constraints and environmental stressors. Clients may be assured that they can "fix" themselves, regardless of a toxic or noxious life situation, by adjusting their behavior and thinking patterns. In intrapsychic approaches to therapy, aversive and unhealthy environments are accommodated rather than challenged.

Examples of intrapsychic theories include both Object Relations theory and some theories of cognitive change. In Object Relations theory (Chodorow, 1978; Marcus, 1987), women's failure to differentiate and separate from the mother figure may be seen as a factor in their unwillingness to leave an abusive marital relationship. In some rational cognitive-behavioral theories (e.g., Ellis, 1962), the client may be held responsible for her current situation because of her "irrational and faulty" thinking.

## Deterministic

*Deterministic* theories of development and behavior assume that current patterns of behavior were developed and fixed at an early stage in life. Concepts of causality tend to be linear, with past events predicting current behavior. As a result, gender-role conceptions and orientations are viewed as an inflexible part of personality and as relatively intractable at later stages. Clinicians who adhere to a deterministic view tend to expect an orderly sequence of change with clients and may assume that behavior is less affected by current situations than by past history and/or stable personality traits. A deterministic view of personality development may encourage clinicians to apply diagnostic labels that describe a stable property of the person (dependent personality, for example) rather than to describe situational behavior patterns (e.g., allows partner to make decisions for her).

In summarizing the characteristics of many traditional psychological theories, we find that they may contain attributes of androcentrism, gendercentrism, ethnocentrism, heterosexism, and monosexism, as well as intrapsychic and deterministic assumptions that are detrimental to effective counseling with women. Therapists using theories that are restrictive on any of these dimensions may overtly or covertly blame members of subordinate groups for the effects of societal oppression. Further, when more than one of these undesirable attributes is present, they dynamically interact to create even more toxic social and therapeutic environments for clients of subordinate groups. In the following section, we offer an alternative format in which any theory can be evaluated for compatibility with a feminist view.

## A Format for Empowerment Feminist Theory

Whether you decide to adhere strictly to one theoretical approach or you wish to develop a combination of theoretical strategies, you can examine your assumptions, concepts, and techniques for their compatibility with a feminist model. In contrast to the characteristics of traditional theories described, the EF format provides four criteria for evaluating a theory: (a) gender-balanced, (b) flexible/multicultural, (c) interactionist, and (d) life span (see Table 4.3).

## Gender-Balanced

Gender-balanced theories view women and men as similar in psychological makeup. These theories avoid stereotypes, or language that labels one sex as more socially desirable, mature, or valued than the other. Gender-balanced theories explain differences that might be found between women and men in terms of socialization processes, self-presentation strategies, and developmental aspects of cognitive and affective processing. That is, the theory avoids incorporating into its structure and concepts the sexist or stereotyped concepts of both dominant and subordinate cultures. Gender-balanced theories promote change toward reduced gender-role stereotyping in social roles and interpersonal behavior.

**Table 4.3   Theory transformation steps**

Step 1. Identify sources of bias in the theory. (Compare each of the following areas to the criteria listed under Comparison Criteria.)

    A.  Historical development of theory.

    B.  Key theoretical concepts.

    C.  Theory of personality development.

    D.  Sources of clients' problems.

    E.  Language and label usage.

    F.  Role of diagnosis and assessment.

    G.  Role of therapist and client.

    H.  Counseling techniques.

Step 2. Restructure theory's biased components.

Step 3. Determine viablity of theory.

Step 4. Identify compatiblility with feminist criteria.

Step 5. Highlight feminists components from chosen theory and add components from other theories that facilitate accomplishment of counseling goals related to Principles I, II, III, IV.

**Comparison Criteria**

Feminist Theory Format

    *Gender-free.* Women and men are similar in makeup; differences are due to socialization.

    *Flexible-multicultural.* A wide range of healthy lifestyles is acceptable. Theory applies to diverse client groups.

    *Interactionist.* Individual functioning is the result of interactions between individual and environmental variables.

    *Life span.* Development is a lifelong process.

**Empowerment Feminist Therapy Principles**

    I.  Personal and Social Identities Are Interdependent.

   II.  The Personal Is Political.

  III.  Relationships Are Egalitarian.

  IV.  Women's Perspectives Are Valued.

*Source:* Adapted from *Feminist Perspectives on Therapy: An Empowerment Model for Women,* by J. Worell and R. Remer, 1992. Chichester, England: Wiley.

## Flexible/Multicultural

A flexible theory uses concepts and strategies that may be adapted to apply to individuals or groups of any age, culture, ethnicity, gender, class, or sexual/affectional preference. A flexibility model can account for within-group as well as between-group differences in behavior, and allows for a range of healthy and satisfying gender roles and lifestyles for both women and men from diverse groups. A flexibility model suggests the possibility of multiple interpersonal arrangements and options for change, rather than prescribing the desirability of one behavioral outcome over the other. A flexible/multicultural theory requires that constructs and interventions be chosen with awareness of and sensitivity to the cultural and ethnic values of clients.

## Interactionist

A theory that hypothesizes a reciprocal interaction between the complex intersects of individuals' identities and a range of internal and external variables is essential to Empowerment Feminist and diversity approaches. Interactionist theories contain concepts that are specific to the individual (affective, behavioral, and cognitive) and to those that can encompass the situation or the broader environment (institutions, cultures, power, barriers). Interactionist theories tend to fall midpoint on the continuum between intrapsychic and environmentally determined. Interactionist theories consider multiple causes and influences on behavior, such that the individual cannot be understood outside the context of all relevant variables. Interactionist theories may respect important social or personal identities yet also invite the possibility of change in both individuals and situations. Because feminists tend to believe that culture structures how people think, feel, and behave, many feminist therapists take a position closer to the environmentally determined end of the continuum.

## Life Span

A life span view assumes that development is a lifelong process, in which behavior changes can occur at any time. Therefore, *maturity* is not an end-state nor can an ideal state of functioning be determined. Life span theories describe behavior according to multiple determinants that may induce continual change rather than emphasizing traits or orderly sequences of behavior (Baltes, Staudinger, & Lindenberger, 1999; Baruth & Manning, 1999). As applied to gender-related behavior, a life span theory suggests that these behaviors are not fixed in people, time, or situations, but are potentially in flux. From a life span perspective, individuals are embedded in their social-historical environment but remain capable of choice and self-determined change (Bussey & Bandura, 1999; Worell, 1981). Life span theories invite an open approach to behavioral change that encourages alternative options at all ages and at any point in the life story.

In summarizing the requirements for theories that are compatible with a feminist/ diversity perspective, we see that they encompass four characteristics: gender-balanced, flexible/multicultural, interactionist, and life span. In the next section, we offer a procedure for examining your preferred theory. With this procedure, you examine a selected theory for evidences of traditional concepts that are detrimental to counseling women and transform the theory to a format that is more compatible with EFT principles.

## Transforming a Theory to an Empowerment Feminist Format

Since many feminist therapists use one or more theories in addition to feminist therapy, a process for integrating the values, constructs, and interventions of multiple theories is necessary for achieving a congruent approach. Our proposed transformation process envisions EFT as the foundation of a person's theoretical integration. All aspects of other embraced theories must be compatible or must be transformed to be compatible with this Empowerment Feminist foundation. For a theory to become compatible with EFT, the theory should be thoroughly analyzed and compared to at least eight criteria. First, the theory should meet the four requirements (gender-balanced, flexible/multicultural, interactionist, life span) described in the previous section. Second, the theory should not violate and must be able to embrace the four principles of EFT. In this section, we present guidelines for adapting your theoretical orientation to EFT. Table 4.3 depicts five steps involved in transforming a theory to an Empowerment Feminist format.

## Step 1: Identify Sources of Bias

The first step in the transformation process is to analyze all major aspects of a particular theoretical orientation to identify the sources of bias in the theory. That is, what aspects of the theory are androcentric, gendercentric, ethnocentric, heterosexist, classist, intrapsychic, or deterministic? Different aspects of the theory are delineated and compared with the eight criteria listed in Table 4.3. There are eight substeps to this analysis.

**Historical Development of Theory**   Because many sources of theoretical bias are covert or subtle, it is important to know how the theory was developed and how the social-cultural era in which the theoretician lived influenced the development of the theory. More specifically, what were the cultural beliefs about appropriate roles for women and men during the time the theory was conceived? What were the social arrangements between groups of people in that society (i.e., structured hierarchies between dominant and subordinate groups)? How are these beliefs and arrangements reflected, ignored, or rejected in the theory? Whom did the theoretician observe or study in deriving the theory's constructs? If the criterion sample is restricted to one gender, social class, ethnicity, age, and so on, then application to other samples is likely to have androcentric, ethnocentric, heterosexist, classist, and/or gendercentric biases. For example, Super's (1957) original theory of career development was based on studying the career development of middle-class, English-speaking White males (androcentric, classist, ethnocentric).

**Key Theoretical Concepts**   What are the key constructs in the theory? How are the concepts applied to women and men? That is, are different constructs used for females and males (gendercentric)? Are the constructs applied similarly or differentially to females and males? What value judgments about femaleness and maleness are conveyed by the constructs? Do the constructs reflect individualistic or male-valued traits (androcentric; e.g., independence, differentiation, hierarchical power)? Do the constructs reflect dominant culture values (ethnocentric)? For example, are independence and individualism valued over interdependence and community when mental health is defined?

**Theory of Personality Development**   Cultural bias in a theory is often most clearly evident in how personality development is explained by the theoretician. How are any differences between females and males explained? Does female or male development serve as the norm against which the other sex is evaluated? Are different roles prescribed for females and males? How are mental illness and mental health defined? Are they defined differently for females and males (gendercentric)? Is the description of mental health based on Western values (ethnocentric)? What is the relative emphasis on a client's deficits versus strengths? What is the role of the environment and culture in personality development (intrapsychic)? Does the theorist acknowledge power differentials in the sociopolitical context? Is behavior seen as the result of single or multiple determinants? Are personality traits fixed at an early stage of life, and thus seen as difficult or impossible to change (deterministic)?

**Sources of Clients' Problems**   Most current psychotherapies focus primarily on the source of problems as located in the client (intrapsychic) or at least as being in the client's control. Even theories that acknowledge the impact of environmental events and situational context on individual behavior often frame the goals of counseling to focus solely on intrapsychic change. In accordance with *The Personal Is Political* principle, a feminist approach requires incorporation of environmental change goals. What are the internal and/or external sources of problems and pathologies in personality development? What are the impacts of external stressors on individual coping? How does culture influence individual development and behavior? Is the theory primarily intrapsychic or interactionist? What are the goals of counseling and do they include goals focused on social change? Does the theory "blame the victim" (and/or the victim's mother)?

**Language and Labels**   Traditionally, theories have used the generic masculine to refer to all persons. Only recently have writers and publishers suggested or required substituting plural nouns and pronouns for the generic *he*. Most theoretical orientations are written with the generic *he* because they were developed before these publishing changes occurred. The problem is that research has consistently shown that when individuals read *he* references, they are more likely to perceive that the subject matter applies to males than to females (Basow, 2001). Thus, most of our older theories have to be read compensating for the use of the generic *he*.

The labels applied to the theory's constructs are also crucial. Are the same behaviors in females and males labeled differently (gendercentric)? What value judgments are conveyed by the labels used (gendercentric, androcentric, heterosexist, ethnocentric)? Do the constructs reflect bias about SEARCH variables?

Even if the constructs and labels of a theory are neutral (e.g., family systems theory), the writings that explain the theory can apply it in a sexist, heterosexist, or ethnocentric manner. Thus, it is extremely important to examine the case examples given in the writings for evidence of bias. Do the case examples of functional or "appropriate" behavior reflect the client's traditional gender-role stereotypes? Do the case examples of dysfunctional or "inappropriate" behavior reflect departure from traditional gender-typed behavior, or is dysfunctional behavior represented only by members of subordinate groups?

**Role of Diagnosis and Assessment**   As we elaborate in Chapter 5, diagnosis and assessment can be biased in many ways. Most theories specify roles for the use of assessment strategies and diagnostic labels. Theories that use sexist diagnostic labels or diagnostic systems closely connected to Freudian theory are the least compatible with a feminist therapy approach. Diagnostic categories and labels that closely parallel traditional gender-role or cultural stereotypes usually pathologize or blame individuals for their own socialization or life circumstances (accuse women of masochism or African Americans of paranoia, for example). Theories that advocate a client-therapist collaborative approach to assessment and diagnosis are more compatible with EFT. A feminist-diversity theory also needs constructs and techniques for measuring external environmental variables and their impact on people's lives.

**Role of Therapist and Client**   According to Principle III of EFT, egalitarian relationships between client and therapist are valued because they do not recreate the power imbalances that subordinate groups experience in society. Thus, theoretical orientations that advocate a distant, expert role for the therapist vis-à-vis the client are incompatible with EFT. How are the desired roles of client and therapist described by the theory? Are differences between counselor and client acknowledged? How are differences between counselor and client expectations negotiated? How are counseling goals decided? How much validity is given to the client's perspective? How is client "transference" viewed? What is the role of "resistance" and how is it handled? Is therapist self-disclosure permitted or encouraged by the theory?

**Counseling Techniques**    Techniques that emphasize a significant power differential between the therapist and client are incongruent with EFT. Are the therapeutic techniques manipulative or hidden, as in paradoxical directives? How are the techniques and client-counselor therapeutic interactions related to collaborative or noncollaborative setting of counseling goals? How are empathy, self-disclosure, and other relationship-building techniques integrated into the theory? Are culturally relevant rituals acceptable?

### Step 2: Restructure Theory's Biased Components

In Step 1, the oppressive components of the theory were identified. In Step 2, these identified components are modified so that they are nonbiased. If modification is not possible, those aspects of the theory must be eliminated.

### Step 3: Determine Viability of Theory

Once biased components have been restructured or eliminated, the theory is reevaluated for its continued viability. If too many components have been eliminated or modified, the theory may have lost its basic structure and/or congruence. If the theory is judged to be no longer viable, another theory that is more compatible with the principles of EFT should be sought. If the theory is judged to be viable, then move to Step 4.

### Step 4: Identify Compatibility with Feminist Criteria

The theoretical and applied aspects that have survived Steps 1, 2, 3, and 4 are appreciated for their compatibility with EFT. They are also recognized for their potential contribution to the practice of feminist therapy (i.e., aspects of this theoretical orientation that can be borrowed by feminist therapists using differing primary theories). These contributions to other feminist orientations are the focus of Step 5.

### Step 5: Highlight Feminist Components

Many theories make unique contributions to feminist therapy. Many constructs and techniques from diverse theories facilitate the accomplishments of EFT Principles I, II, III, and IV goals. At this step, contributions from other theories are evaluated for possible inclusion in your own theory. It is helpful at this point to articulate, either verbally or in writing, how you have integrated your preferred theory within a feminist format that is compatible with EFT.

## APPLICATIONS OF THEORY TRANSFORMATION

In the following two subsections, we demonstrate the process of theory transformation with two selected theories: Cognitive-Behavioral, and Psychodrama. Each of the two authors of this volume employs a preferred theory in conjunction with EFT and discusses her view of how the theory can be integrated with feminist principles. The steps in theory transformation may vary according to both the theory and the individual who applies it. Thus, each application of theory transformation may be unique, despite some basic similarities. Here, we demonstrate a process of theory application and revision. As a prospective or practicing clinician, you should select and apply the theory of your choice in a similar manner.

## Cognitive-Behavioral Interventions

Cognitive-Behavioral (CB) theory and strategies embrace a broad range of learning-based and cognitive approaches. Most psychological theories are based on the dynamic interactions among three basic response dimensions: thinking (cognitions), feeling (emotions), and doing (behavior). Differences among theories tend to lie in how much emphasis is given to each of these three variables, such as those who maintain either a strictly behavioral or cognitive approach. More commonly, theorists from these two camps have arrived at creative ways of integrating these variables to establish a variety of useful and effective CB interventions. Many of these interventions have been developed and validated for specific client populations, such as for depression, anxiety, or Posttraumatic Stress Disorder. The two basic assumptions of all CB theories are: (a) The beliefs, emotions, and behaviors that bring clients to seek help are learned and maintained in the same manner as are all learned behaviors; and (b) those human responses that are learned can be unlearned or changed according to established psychological principles. Thus, this broad CB approach is very optimistic and positive about the prospects for developing effective interventions to address human distress. Extensions of CB to interventions with women emphasize multiple assessment strategies that are relevant to the individual lives of women (Allen, 1995; MacDonald, 1984; D. Robinson & Worell, 2002; Toner, Segal, Emmot, & Myron, 2000).

The scientific and philosophical foundations of learning theory and experimental psychology are reflected in the efforts of CB therapists to establish research-based support for their interventions. The emphasis on empirical validation of CB interventions encourages the use of theoretical constructs that can be clearly defined and measured, and the development of therapeutic procedures that can be taught to others and replicated across clinical settings. In the past decade, extensive efforts have been directed at establishing empirical validation, or treatment efficacy for a number of cognitive and learning-based interventions for selected diagnostic categories. Treatment *efficacy* of a therapeutic approach "refers to the ascertainment of the effects of a given intervention when compared to an alternative intervention or to no treatment in a controlled clinical context" (American Psychological Association, 1995, p. 7). Efficacy studies incorporate carefully controlled clinical trials that attempt to maximize internal validity (appropriate design, population, reliable and valid measures, etc.) and thus rule out competing hypotheses about what might be responsible for the outcomes (Jacobson & Christensen, 1996). Treatments that meet these stringent criteria are considered *empirically validated* (Chambless & Hollon, 1998; Kendall, 1998). There are both advantages and concerns about this approach to outcome assessment; however, it has been clear that learning-based and cognitive interventions have comprised the bulk of those therapies that are considered to be empirically validated by these criteria (Worell, 2001). We discuss issues related to outcome assessment further in Chapter 10.

In this section, we examine representative aspects of CB theory using an abbreviated version of the format for transforming a theory (Table 4.3). We next briefly overview the historical background and common components of CB interventions, provide a rationale for CB theory in terms of its compatibility with the principles of EFT, and suggest revisions in CB concepts and procedures that increase its compatibility with EFT principles.

## Historical Background

CB theory has a complex history, integrating concepts and strategies from at least five differing sources. Table 4.4 displays five of the most significant models, along with representative (not inclusive) treatment goals and techniques. These models reflect the historical roots of CB approaches: Behavioral (classical conditioning), Operant, Social Learning, Cognitive, and CB theories.

Behavioral theories use *classical conditioning* therapeutically to account for how our emotional reactions, such as preferences and fears, may be conditioned automatically through simultaneous pairing to specific objects, persons, or situations. These emotional reactions may then *generalize* to similar situations, making it more difficult for the individual to isolate and change the effects of the original stimulus. *Operant conditioning* is used therapeutically to alter behavior (or thoughts and feelings) by managing

**Table 4.4  Historical roots of cognitive-behavioral theory**

| Model | Treatment Goals | Representative Strategies |
|---|---|---|
| Behavioral learning | Reduce conditioned emotional reactions; decrease avoidant behavior. | Stimulus control. Relaxation techniques. Desensitization, exposure. In vivo practice. |
| Operant | Rearrange external contingencies; facilitate a reinforcing environment. | Contingency management. Differential reinforcement. Contracting. |
| Social learning | Facilitate self-regulation of thoughts and behavior; client as change agent. | Modeling, role play. Skill training, self-efficacy. Self-management. Information giving. Bibliotherapy, home assignment. |
| Cognitive | Modify dysfunctional beliefs, attributions, standards, and expectancies. | Cognitive restructuring. Relabeling. Reattribution training. Problem solving. |
| Cognitive-behavioral | Assist client to learn new cognitive, emotional, interpersonal, and behavioral skills. | All the above plus: Collaboration. Coping skills. Self-instruction. Stress inoculation. |

their consequences through self- or other-applied reinforcement, punishment, or extinction. The procedure for applying these consequences is called *contingency management.* The major contributions of *Social Learning Theory* (Bandura, 1977b) include an emphasis on cognitive variables and the development and validation of a sophisticated theory of observational learning, called *modeling,* to account for how verbal, pictorial, and behavioral images provided by others can function to change the attitudes, beliefs, and behaviors of the observer. One important principle is that of *vicarious experience,* whereby we learn from the outcomes that accrue to others. More recently, Bandura (1986, 1997) has proposed a *Social Cognitive Theory* with an emphasis on *self-efficacy* as an organizing principle in how people manage their lives. You may recall that our model of women's psychological well-being included the encouragement of self-efficacy.

Cognitive theories propose that the ways individuals structure their thought processes lead to both adaptive and problematic behavior. Some cognitive therapists (e.g., Beck, 1976; Ellis, 1962) proposed that the way we think influences the way we feel, so that interventions are aimed at clients' beliefs and "self-talk." Several other cognitive theories are drawn into the formulations, most notably *Information Processing* and *Attribution Theory.* For purposes of simplicity, we have incorporated these into the social learning and cognitive theories that have integrated their rationale and techniques in therapy. In your further readings, you may encounter concepts that relate to either of these two theories.

For example, information processing theory is incorporated into Bandura's (1986) theory of modeling to account for how people encode, retain, and retrieve information. Information processing may also be useful in identifying the ways in which clients "selectively attend to those cognitions and perceptions that confirm their explanatory hypotheses while selectively ignoring information . . . that is inconsistent with their beliefs" (Toner et al., 2000, p. 22). Attribution theory is closely related to the concept of learned helplessness, which is used by some cognitive therapists to understand and treat both depression and distressed or abusive relationships (Abramson, Seligman, & Teasdale, 1978; Baucom et al., 1996; Douglas & Strom, 1988; Metalsky, Laird, Heck, & Joiner, 1995).

Table 4.4 shows that clinicians who self-describe as cognitive-behavioral in their orientation tend to employ a variety of interrelated techniques and procedures selectively drawn from all five modalities. Some therapists have also proposed integrative approaches that expand the boundaries of a strict learning or cognitive point of view (see Craighead, Craighead, Kazdin, & Mahoney, 1994; N. Epstein, Schlesinger, & Dryden, 1988; Jacobson, 1987).

## Common Features of Cognitive-Behavioral Interventions

Donald Meichenbaum (1986) identified some of the commonalities among the diverse range of CB interventions. He pointed out that CB interventions tend to be relatively short, moderately structured, and encourage an active role by both counselor and client. CB therapists typically engage the client in a collaborative alliance, whereby the two parties embark on a "shared adventure" to understand and reconceptualize the client's problems. Although therapists frequently take the role of a teacher, they do not presume to be the expert. Rather, they engage clients in an "egalitarian relationship" in which they serve "as a consultant who is prepared to provide special skills, rather than as authority who can provide certain answers" (Piasecki & Hollon, 1987, p. 143). You may see how CB theory is compatible with Principle III of EFT.

Across CB approaches, Meichenbaum (1986) suggested that the therapist work with clients to:

1. Help them better understand the nature of their presenting problems.
2. View their cognitions (automatic thoughts, images) and accompanying feelings as hypotheses worthy of testing rather than as facts or truths.
3. Encourage them to perform personal experiments and review the consequences of their actions as evidence that may be contrary to their prior expectations and beliefs.
4. Learn new behavioral, interpersonal, cognitive, and emotional regulation skills (p. 347).

More recently, Frank Dattilio (2000) emphasized that the collaborative approach of CB therapies assists in establishing a warm, supportive relationship with the client and maintaining counselor-client rapport. As with other approaches, the therapeutic alliance has been shown to be a critical variable in encouraging and supporting the process of change. This collaborative stance includes jointly established therapeutic goals, use of assessment measures, and the productive application of homework tasks. The right-hand column of Table 4.4 displays a sample of the wide range of interventions that may be applied.

## Rationale for Cognitive-Behavioral Theory

We believe that CB theory is a comfortable choice for feminist therapists because so many of its tenets are compatible with our view of effective treatment for women. CB constructs and interventions meet the criteria for a feminist format discussed earlier, in that they are gender-balanced (do not differentiate constructs by gender), flexible (can be applied to all clients regardless of their social or personal identities), interactionist (attend to the reciprocal interaction between individuals and their environments), and can be applied across the life span.

### Feminist Format

Both behavioral and cognitive theories use language and concepts that are gender-neutral and can be flexibly applied to any group of individuals. Concepts such as *reinforcement, generalization, expectancy,* and *self-efficacy* are not embedded in a developmental structure that defines females and males or dominant and subordinate groups in differing terms. Social Learning Theory in general has emphasized that a positively reinforcing environment encourages flexibility of behavioral repertoires and has discouraged the use of negative procedures because they inhibit prosocial behavior. The concepts of cognitive and behavioral theories are free of age-related restrictions, and can be applied to thoughts, feelings, and behaviors at any age or stage of life. CB interventions may thus be tailored for use with individuals from differing age, ability, or gender groups, and from diverse ethnic and cultural populations.

### Feminist Therapy Principles

How can we match the broad range of CB interventions and concepts with the principles of EFT? A sample of this matching procedure is presented in Table 4.5. The articulation of CB and EFT is further elaborated for Principles I, II, III, and IV.

**I. Personal and Social Identities Are Interdependent**   The constructs of cognitive therapy are particularly relevant to helping clients and therapists work with issues

**Table 4.5    Cognitive-behavioral strategies: Congruence with Empowerment Feminist Therapy principles**

| Strategy | Principle | Application to EFT |
|---|---|---|
| Modeling | I, II, III, IV | Allows therapist to demonstrate competent behavior, wide-role repertoire, flexibility, self-disclosure. |
| Contracting | I, II, III | Provides equal participation in goal setting and choice of strategy; encourages client to initiate change in self and situation. Collaboration. |
| Functional analysis | I, II, III | Enables therapist and client to collaborate in determining situational and personal antecedents and consequences of problems. |
| Self-monitoring | I, II, III, IV | Assists client in identifying her thoughts and feelings in relation to situational events. |
| Self-reinforcement | I, II, III, IV | Enables client to nurture and empower self. |
| Stress inoculation | I, II, III, IV | Strengthens client coping skills; enables her to identify and appreciate her strengths. |
| Assertiveness training | I, II, III, IV | Assists client in meeting her needs, raising self-esteem and self-efficacy, and achieving personal goals. Leads to empowerment and personal pride. |
| Cognitive restructuring | I, II, III, IV | Provides for gender and cultural analysis, power analysis; reframes deficits as strengths. |

related to identity development and integration. Some of the cognitive concepts that function to mediate client emotions and behavior include *beliefs* about self and others, *attributions* (beliefs about the causes of particular events), and *self-efficacy* (perceived ability to perform a response or meet a challenge). Each of these concepts is activated through self- statements and *cognitive schemas* (broad underlying core beliefs) that are important to the understanding of how clients connect themselves in the context of their lives. All of these constructs may be implemented therapeutically in the process of identity exploration and gender-role analysis.

**II. The Personal Is Political**    First, the learning theory concepts of respondent and operant conditioning emphasize that all behavior is embedded in context and can be changed only in relation to the social and cultural situations in which it occurs (S. Hayes, 1987). Learning theory concepts can be used to encompass the external variables that influence women's well-being. These external factors include sources of stress in women's lives such as trauma and isolation (aversive stimulus, punishment, and reinforcement deficit) as well as sources of nurturance and satisfaction (reinforcing environments and events). For example, in behavioral marital therapy (Jacobson & Margolin,

1979; Walz & Jacobson, 1994), attention is given to the frequency and ratio of critical versus positive spouse comments (punishment and reinforcement), and to pleasing activities that the couple shares (reinforcing events). These variables, among others, are targeted for intervention, with the general goal of increasing shared pleasurable activities and positive partner comments and decreasing negative communications and withdrawal.

Second, the Social Learning Theory concepts of *observational learning* and *modeling* (Bandura, 1977b) are useful in gender-role analysis for conceptualizing social and historical influences on women's stereotyped images and messages. Bandura's (1978) concept of *reciprocal determinism* suggests that psychological functioning is a continuous reciprocal interaction between cognition, affect, behavior, and environmental consequences. Bandura pointed out that in this process, "the environment is influenceable, as is the behavior it regulates" (p. 195). The idea of an "influenceable environment" clearly sets the stage for implementing social change and coincides with our emphasis on assisting clients to effect change, whether small or substantial, in their life space.

Finally, the cognitive and CB components (Bandura, 1977a, 1977b, 1986, 1997; Beck, 1976; Ellis, 1962; Kanfer & Schefft, 1988; Meichenbaum, 1977; Rotter, 1954; Thoreson & Mahoney, 1974) are useful in a variety of procedures that integrate ongoing thought processes with procedures for overt behavioral and situational change. These procedures may include *cognitive restructuring* (reframing, relabeling), *reattribution* (revising the causality of events), anxiety management, problem solving, stress inoculation, and self-management. These strategies provide the client with self-managing coping skills that reassign blame, strengthen self-efficacy, and assist her efforts to effect change in both self and situation.

**III. Relationships Are Egalitarian**    Cognitive behavioral strategies can be implemented to promote client empowerment. In the three procedures of assessment, goal setting, and contracting, the client's role in CB therapy is one of negotiated partnership. Therapist and client collaborate to discover what the problems are, and to negotiate a contracted set of goals and possible alternatives. Meichenbaum's (1986) description of the process of CB therapy clearly highlights the collaborative nature of CB interventions. Instructions, suggestions, and homework activities are carefully explained and are consensual rather than prescribed. Failure to complete the self-managed activities between therapy sessions is seen as a problem to be explored and resolved, rather than to be interpreted as client resistance.

Three additional characteristics of CB interventions contribute to client empowerment. First, the central role of assessment and evaluation in CB interventions encourages the use of periodic assessment of client progress. Providing direct feedback for client progress (or lack of it) invites clients to share the therapeutic process and the strategies that may be negotiated when progress is impeded. Second, attention to skills training in domains that have been underdeveloped has been useful in such areas as career skills and situational assertiveness. Third, self-management procedures (*self-monitoring, self-instruction, self-evaluation*) are typically initiated and encouraged to fully empower the client as an active agent in her own therapy and behavior change.

## Revising Cognitive-Behavioral Theory to a Feminist Format

The forgoing discussion suggests that many aspects of CB theory are well-suited to EFT. This section reviews three modifications of CB theory that we believe increase its compatibility with EFT principles: (1) relabeling of pathologizing concepts, (2) focus on feelings, and (3) integration of social role theory.

## Relabeling Pathologizing Concepts

Although most concepts in CB theory and its historical relatives are generally bias-free with respect to gender and ethnicity, we encounter some examples of CB concepts that may be detrimental to women. In particular, certain cognitive concepts implicate individual pathology as the cause of individual problems, while placing minimal emphasis on the context or environment in which the behavior occurs. Are clients being told their thinking is *distorted, irrational,* or *faulty?* Some cognitive therapists in particular tend to use cognitively pathologizing concepts that locate the problem solely in the client's "illness," in effect blaming the client for her symptoms.

Since the feminist therapist accepts the client's experiences as *real data,* terms that label her thinking as *irrational* or *faulty* deny the client's perceptions and drive her further from trust in herself. Alternative ways to conceptualize client behavior when it does not appear to match reality should be considered. In particular, clients from cultural contexts other than that of the therapist may take a different approach to the relationship between thoughts and feelings. Labeling particular beliefs as *faulty* may represent an ethnocentric approach, imposing our Western emphasis on the ideal of rational and objective thought. Careful and sensitive questioning about the meaning of such beliefs to the client may reveal alternative construals that need to be respected and taken into consideration.

First, it may be that the client's perceptions do match the realities of her life situation. Extensive research on the accuracy of perception in depressed persons, for example, indicates that depressed persons probably see reality more accurately than those who optimistically believe that the environment is beneficial and that they can control their outcomes (Hammen, 1988). Lynn Rehm (1988) further amplified the depressed process, noting that "perception of the objective world is not distorted in depression. Depressed individuals accurately report specific events in their lives . . . (but) . . . depressed persons are more negative about themselves" (p. 167). Indeed, it appears that nondepressed persons show the most cognitive distortion; they tend to be higher in "illusions of personal control," show inflated (unrealistic) expectations of future success on experimental tasks, maintain a self-serving bias in attributions for positive outcomes, and they overestimate the amount of positive feedback they receive (Alloy & Abramson, 1988). Now, who are the real "distorters of reality"? Of course, positive distortion may be beneficial in maintaining an optimistic view of self and others and thus a means of warding off depression, but we tend to label this cognitive bias favorably as *optimism* and not *faulty thinking.*

In contrast to the expansive cognitive bias of nondepressed individuals, the negative self- and worldviews of many depressed clients lead us to explore the realities of their lives as well as the distortions in their thinking processes. The pessimistic attributions and expectations should cue the therapist to obtain a fuller understanding of the situational contributions to current dysphoric moods. In Chapter 6, we see that Sylvia's depressive symptoms, although accompanied by negative cognitions, were intimately related to her oppressive situations at home and at work.

Second, the client may be acting in accordance with her understanding of family and societal expectations for her behavior. A case example here is 32-year-old Margaret, who talked seriously of suicide following the break-up of her marriage. She was convinced she was a failure as a woman, she would never find another man (who else would want her?), and if she did, she would be too old to have children, and, therefore, life was no longer worth living. Rather than convince her of the irrationality of these thoughts, she was encouraged to explore socialized messages about women's proper role (a good woman marries and has children), mandates for the successful marriage (a good wife keeps the marriage together), stereotypes about single women (an unmarried woman is an old maid), and fears about living without a partner (women are helpless and need to be taken care of). Although these gender-based messages were not the only ones driving Margaret to desperate measures, she was able to explore how her acceptance of them was contributing to her sense of panic and helplessness.

In the process of a systematic situation/mood/thought pattern probe, we encourage clients to monitor their dysphoric or negative feelings in relation to specific situations, and then to self-monitor their gendered and cultural messages, pessimistic expectancies, negative self-talk, and detrimental attributions of self-blame and guilt. In Chapter 6, we provide a mood-situation rating form for client self-monitoring of feelings and related thoughts. Further, we may help clients to determine if they have been misinformed, uninformed, may not have taken all possibilities into consideration, may want to look further, reconsider the context in which the event occurred, and so on. It may also be useful to explore with clients the cultural sources of their feelings, such as guilt. In cultures that emphasize the collective over the individual, the client may feel responsible if she believes she has denied, shamed, or otherwise harmed her ethnic group. Thus, she may have culture-bound beliefs about atonement and relieving guilt that need to be explored. In this process, we assist clients in understanding that regardless of external realities, the repeated expression of negative self-evaluation and expectancies contributes to the dysphoric moods they experience. The cognitive restructuring techniques of CB therapy can then be effectively implemented, without the use of pathologizing labels and client-blaming attributions. Finally, we encourage clients to consider options for implementing changes in self-situation interactions that may ameliorate the internal and external conditions that contributed to the depressive symptoms.

## Focus on Feeling

As we have seen, CB interventions tend to view dysfunctional moods (negative emotions) in relation to the cognitive mediators that elicit and maintain them. Thus, sadness, anxiety, and rage are viewed primarily as the result of the person's cognitive appraisal of external stressors and a negative evaluation of the ability to cope (Lazarus & Folkman, 1984; Meichenbaum, 1977). In feminist counseling, we continue to employ CB strategies for dealing with disabling reactions of hopelessness, fearfulness, and associated avoidance behaviors, but we also explore women's responses to their angry feelings.

Traditional socialization in many cultures has encouraged women to avoid direct confrontation or negative assertion with others. When individuals feel underbenefited, ignored, overworked, humiliated, or powerless, angry feelings are likely to be evoked. In the absence of "permission" to express these feelings directly, women are likely to be more self-critical, self-blaming, and hopeless about changing the conditions that produce their unhappiness (Major, 1987). Feelings of helplessness, self-abasement, and hopelessness are frequently those that may lead to a diagnosis of depression. In the process of gender-role analysis, we are likely to uncover situations that might elicit legitimate anger from clients, and we help them to explore their anger in a safe environment. We also encourage them to identify and express their angry feelings in ways that benefit them without provoking alienation and violence from others. Such strategies are particularly critical in certain cultures where it may be dangerous for women to express themselves openly in opposition to the authority of husbands, fathers, and even brothers. In such circumstances, we explore with the client what she believes may be the limits and possibilities of her range of alternatives. However, we view the appropriate expression of anger and negative assertion as important for women as they strive to gain a sense of positive self-regard and empowerment in their lives.

## Social Role Theory

We select the broad concept of social role theory to encompass the socialized role expectations and power imbalances that influence people's lives. Adding some concepts from social role theory to CB interventions allows us to: (a) interpret current behavior in terms of gender socialization, and thus to complete a gender-role analysis (Principle II); (b) conceptualize situational behavior in a broader societal context, to perform a power analysis, and to examine the effects of patriarchy, sexism, and other types of bias and discrimination (Principles I, II); (c) add terminology that describes aspects of role behavior, such as role conflict, role strain, and role overload; and (d) relabel certain concepts, such as deficit behaviors, in terms of over- or under-socialization, thus reframing pathology into woman-valuing terms (Principle IV). In a social role framework, we can then talk about resocialization or reconstructing environments, rather than remediating deficit or dysfunctional behavior.

Consideration of women's position in the larger societal context also enables us to encourage clients to join women's support groups, to value the communal-typed traits they may possess (nurturance, caring for others, peacemaking), and to value their place in society as women. Relabeling of devalued traits (passivity, enabler, or codependency) in terms of women's socialization as peace-maker and keeper of relationships may enable clients to reframe their position more positively in their close relationships (Worell, 1988a). Because the structure of CB theory is based on an interactionist approach, the merger with social role theory produces a strong union.

## Reevaluation of Cognitive-Behavioral Theory

Our analysis of CB theory and its concepts and major strategies allows us to draw two conclusions. First, the theory is a viable one for feminist therapists, and its major concepts and interventions serve well in a feminist format. Second, we see that some adjustments in terminology and conceptualization must occur if feminist insights are to be integrated effectively. We provided several examples of pathologizing concepts that require revision and added concepts that facilitate a feminist analysis and intervention. For any theory of your choice, the transformation process can be successful and heuristic, provided that it does not violate the basic structure of the theory. In the case of CB theory, the major foundations and interventions remain intact.

# Psychodrama

*Psychodrama* is an interpersonally focused theory of psychotherapy developed by Jacob Moreno. Individuals exist in and react to their relationships with other people (L. J. Fine, 1979). Psychodrama theory regards humans as primarily social beings. Before critiquing psychodrama from a feminist theory perspective, the major concepts that form the basis of psychodrama theory are reviewed. The theory presented here is synthesized from the works of Fine (1979), H. A. Blatner (1996), A. Blatner (2000), Moreno (1946/1985), and Moreno (1959/1975).

Moreno viewed mentally healthy people as spontaneous creators of their own lives (L. J. Fine, 1979). *Spontaneity* is the ability to respond to life situations in a novel and effective way. Spontaneity is present at birth. External environments, which include significant others (social atoms) and the cultural context in which the person lives, can either facilitate or inhibit further development of spontaneity for the individual. Responses that at one time were spontaneous can become ritualized, patterned, and conserved if they are used repeatedly. *Conserves* are finished products or acts. They are the result of spontaneous and creative processes. *Cultural conserves* are products sanctioned by a given society. Examples of cultural conserves are works of art, laws, books, social rules and norms, and parameters for acceptable performance of roles. While cultural conserves contribute continuity to a social group, they also can restrict individual spontaneity and the evolution of the culture.

Moreno believed that modern society had come to worship conserves to the detriment of its own development. Thus, Moreno sought to change the culture and society as a whole, not merely to help individuals adapt to the environment. He advocated the healing of social systems. Likewise, because he believed many individual problems arise from environmental barriers of a social, economic, political, and cultural nature, he proposed that healing of the individual needed to take place in a supportive social context. He called this social healing *sociatry* and viewed it as a powerful source of therapeutic change.

Because the social environment is seen to play a significant role in human development, Moreno studied individuals in the structures of their intergroup relationships. These investigations into the relationships within groups is called *sociometry*. Sociometric interventions are the major tools that can be used to change society and social institutions.

Sociometric evaluations can be used to measure the attractions and repulsions between members of a group. These attractions and repulsions are influenced by two forces—transference and tele. While Moreno acknowledged the existence of transference, he believed that other therapies overemphasized its importance. *Tele* is a "two-way reciprocal knowing of each other by two people" (L. J. Fine, 1979, p. 432). *Tele* is "one person's correct, intuitive estimate of the actualities of the other" (Moreno, 1975, p. 84). Thus, *tele* is different from *transference,* in that *tele* is based on the real attributes of the two people, whereas *transference* is one person's unreal perception of and projection of attributes onto the other.

Role playing, role taking and role creating are related key concepts in psychodrama theory. The ability to respond spontaneously requires the person to have a large role repertoire. One source of pathology (i.e., lack of spontaneity) is a person having a limited role repertoire. For individuals to make novel and effective responses (i.e., spontaneous responses in a variety of life situations), they need to be able to perform (i.e., have the necessary skills) and feel free to express a wide range of behaviors (role repertoire). Individuals' role repertoires may be limited because they have had ineffective role models or because certain roles that are in their repertoires are blocked at an expressive level. Each culture has conserves that govern the acquisition and expression of roles in that culture. Adam Blatner and Alee Blatner (1988) pointed out how important it is for people to learn how to create and negotiate roles. "Roles may be assumed, modified, refined, elaborated and relinquished. This is a most liberating lesson. It invites us to re-evaluate whatever roles we play . . ." (p. 32). A feminist application of conserves to gender roles allows the psychodramatist to see how gender-role conserves limit the spontaneous behavioral responses of women and men in a given culture.

Leo Fine (1979) described psychodrama therapy as an action method of psychotherapy that ". . . employs dramatic interactions, sociometric measurements, group dynamics, and depends on role theory to facilitate changes in individuals and groups through the development of new perceptions and behaviors and/or reorganization of old cognitive patterns" (p. 428). In therapy, clients act out their personal problems in the here-and-now moment by recreating and working through scenes from their lives. These enactments are optimally done in a group setting where group members can take the roles of significant others in each other's scenes. However, psychodramatic theory and techniques can be adapted for individual therapy.

Taking unfamiliar roles in others' enactments facilitates the role repertoire expansion for all group members. Each group member is seen as the ". . . therapeutic agent of the other; consequently, group members assist in treatment and are as important as the therapist" (L. J. Fine, 1979, p. 429). The tele between all members of the group, including the therapist, is a healing force in the group. Tele between therapist and client is a powerful source for therapeutic change. Thus, it is important for the therapist to be open with and known to the client.

The goals of Psychodrama therapy are to facilitate individuals to reclaim their spontaneity, break free of cultural conserves, and expand their role repertoires. Further, psychodramatic interventions seek to create social environments that are open to change and where novelty is valued. Individuals are encouraged to explore group problems to develop social solutions.

## Rationale for Psychodrama Theory

We view Psychodrama theory and techniques as compatible with EFT. This section describes how psychodrama is congruent with a feminist format and with EFT principles.

### Feminist Format

Jacob Moreno began writing about Psychodrama theory in the early 1920s and continuing into the late 1960s. Although Moreno developed his theory in the context of European and American cultures that sanctioned traditional gender-role stereotypes for women and men, he advocated individual spontaneity and freedom from cultural conserves, including role restrictions, that inhibit individual spontaneity. His major concepts and terminology do not define females and males in differing terms, or apply differential standards of mental health to women and men. He uses nonstigmatizing labels. For example, the client in a psychodrama is called a protagonist. Thus, psychodrama is gender-free and is flexible/multicultural. According to psychodrama theory, an individual's behavior is a result of multiple determinants—innate spontaneity, heredity, social forces, and environmental forces. Thus, psychodrama meets the test for an interactionist theory.

Moreno believed that a person's past experiences influence present behavior. Past experiences in which spontaneity was blocked give rise to "act hunger" (A. Blatner, 1996). These blocked responses are often repeated in present experiences. However, these previous experiences are not limited to early childhood. Adult experiences can also give rise to act hunger. Change in adulthood is seen as possible. Indeed, Psychodrama puts much emphasis on role training and spontaneity training, which are aimed at enhancing individuals' present and future effectiveness. Development is viewed as a lifelong process. In summary, psychodrama meets the four feminist format requirements: gender-balanced, flexible/multicultural, interactionist, and life span.

## Empowerment Feminist Therapy Principles

Psychodrama fits smoothly with the four principles of EFT. Further, we believe that much of its theory that focuses on the role of the environment in creating problems for individuals can be a useful addition to other theoretical approaches that do not have such a component. A sample of psychodramatic techniques compatible with EFT principles is presented in Table 4.6.

**I. Personal and Social Locations Are Interdependent** Principle I stresses that every person occupies multiple social locations that are constructed by a complex of

**Table 4.6   Psychodrama strategies: Congruence with Empowerment Feminist Therapy principles**

| Strategy | Principle | Application to EFT |
| --- | --- | --- |
| Sociodrama (group exploration of common social problems). | I, II, IV | Allows women to identify common social problems and to identify personal collective solutions to social problems. |
| Double (person plays the role of protagonist's inner self). | I, II, III, IV | Facilitates client's fuller expression of feelings, thoughts, and behaviors. Clarifies unspoken gender and cultural rules and messages. |
| Role-reversal (client role-plays another person in order to understand other's perspective). | I, II, III, IV | Allows client to gain appreciation of diverse women's perspectives and gives clients permission to practice actions and skills not usually in their repertoire. Increases empathic understanding of others. |
| Role training (client practices new behaviors or skills in role-played scenarios). | I, II, IV | Allows clients to try out new responses in a safe environment where norms are supportive of nontraditional behavior for either gender or cultural expectations. |
| Role-taking, role-creating (in role-taking, client enacts a given role; in role-creating, client creates or expands a role). | I, II, IV | Helps clients learn that roles can be modified, refined, elaborated, and relinquished. Helps free clients from traditional gender conserves and to be creative in their expression of roles. |

dominant and subordinate cultural expectations. EFT therapists assess and raise clients' awareness about their social locations and empower clients by framing their issues within their sociocultural contexts. Similarly, the impact of cultural conserves on individuals' behaviors is a core focus of Psychodrama theory and practice. Psychodrama role theory addresses the culture-bound nature of roles, stresses the importance of understanding clients' cultural roles, and focuses on helping them challenge toxic cultural role restrictions by using role-creating strategies.

**II. The Personal Is Political**    Moreno believed that pathology could develop solely from environmental sources and that an overly conserved environment was often the primary source of pathology. Moreno (1975) pointed out that there were people who ". . . suffer deeply from a major maladjustment, but of a collective and not a private nature" (p. 359). There are cultural conflicts in which individuals are persecuted or restricted, not because of themselves, but because of the group to which they belong.

"Pathology occurs (a) with too rigid a social structure, where the individual is unable to grow and change, or (b) when relationships are not balanced" (Fine, 1979, p. 430). The opposite of this pathology is spontaneity. Adam Blatner and Alee Blatner (1988) point out that creativity and spontaneity ". . . threaten the stability and authority of the hierarchical social and religious systems" (p. 21).

Moreno sought to bring about changes at many levels. He stated frequently that his ultimate goal was to change the universe. Thus, the core of his theory embodies the notion that the personal is social. He developed techniques, such as sociograms, to assess social environments. He created sociodrama as a technique that could be used to change social environments, and he used group restructuring techniques to maximize cohesion, tele, and spontaneity and to minimize restrictive conserves in intact social groups. *Sociodrama* is a "form of psychodramatic enactment which aims at clarifying group themes rather than focusing on the individual's problems" (H. A. Blatner, 1973. p. 9). In sociodrama, the group chooses a common social problem to explore and for which to develop possible solutions. The aim of sociodrama is "not his (sic) own salvation, but the salvation of all members of his (sic) clan" (Moreno, 1985, p. 365). Thus, sociodrama can be used to help women and other oppressed groups explore their common life situations and search for creative, collective solutions.

There are several Psychodramatic techniques that relate to role functioning. *Role taking* is the technique of playing the collective and private parts of a given role (e.g., mother). Role taking can help clients explore the culturally and individually conserved aspects of a role. From a feminist therapy perspective, role taking facilitates clients' identification of gender-role messages. Through *role creating,* the individual or group is encouraged to move beyond the conserved, stereotyped role to a spontaneous, creative expansion of the role. Through this process, gender roles can be redefined and new roles created, thus expanding one's role repertoire. Practice with both role taking and role creating are key components in spontaneity and role training. The Psychodrama belief that it is important for individuals to choose spontaneously from a large role repertoire closely parallels feminist valuing of androgyny.

**III. Relationships Are Egalitarian**    One of Moreno's most important contributions to the therapy process was the change in the nature of the therapist-client relationship. The following quotations capture the essence of the collaborative client-therapist relationship that Moreno proposed:

Therapy is a reciprocal process between the therapist and patient, and not a one-way relationship. (Moreno, 1975, p. 37)

The therapist, before he (sic) emerges as the therapeutic leader, is just another member of the group. (Moreno, 1975, p. 9)

. . . both (therapist and client) on the same level—they are equal. (Moreno, 1985, p. 254)

The initiative, the spontaneity, the decision must all arise within the subjects themselves. (Moreno, 1985, p. 337)

. . . each patient is the therapeutic agent of the other. (L. J. Fine, 1979, p. 442)

Thus, Moreno's approach calls for an egalitarian relationship between therapist and client. In fact, he believed that the tele factor between client and therapist and between all the members of the group is a major source of therapeutic change and healing. Members of the group are trusted to contribute to and heal each other. Further, the therapist must be open with and self-disclose to the client to maximize tele. Every psychodrama session ends with members of the group and the therapist disclosing to the protagonist experiences from their own lives that are similar to the issues on which the protagonist has just worked. This process is called *sharing*. Sharing allows "for group members to discover their commonality" (L. J. Fine, 1979, p. 428). Feminist therapists can borrow this technique by ending sessions with personal sharing.

Moreno also believed that individuals were self-directed and self-correcting if they received accurate feedback. Moreno (1975) said that the individual was capable of ". . . meeting his (sic) own problems and patients as capable of helping one another" (p. 87). These beliefs closely parallel the feminist therapy concept regarding the client as an expert on self.

**IV. Women's Perspectives Are Valued**    Psychodrama theory values many aspects of women's experiences. Psychodrama theory emphasizes the importance of relationships to human beings. Tele between individuals is given a central role in therapeutic healing. The ability to role reverse—to put one's self in another's role and to take the other's perspective—is considered by psychodramatists to be the most important Psychodramatic technique. Both role reversal and doubling are techniques that rely heavily on empathy. Through the technique of doubling, the therapist or group members become the inner voice of the protagonist, helping her to express heretofore unexpressed feelings, thoughts, and behaviors. Doubles must have tele with the protagonist, use intuition, and draw on the life experiences they have in common with the protagonist. Doubling can be used by feminist therapists to help clients specify and concretize the gender-role messages that influence and limit their behavior, and to give a voice to the desire to take action that violates traditional female gender-role expectations. Tele, doubling, role reversal, and viewing individuals in relational contexts all demonstrate the important roles that female/communal values and strengths play in psychodrama. All female groups can facilitate women in exploring not only their common problems, but also their common strengths.

## Additional Potential Contributions of Psychodrama to Feminist Therapy

Psychodrama is an action form of therapy in which the past, present, and future can be explored on the stage. In enactments, concretization in space and action is highlighted. For example, from a feminist therapy perspective, inner struggle in a woman who wants to pursue a career but feels that she can be a good mother only by staying home full time, could be concretized by group members playing each side of her dilemma and actually pulling on her in different directions. Power dimensions in relationships are physically concretized in dramas by having the more powerful person stand on a chair while interacting with the less powerful person. Thus, feminist therapy power analysis can be enhanced by symbolizing and exaggerating, through high and low physical positions, the unequal power in relationships. Concepts or inanimate objects can be given form in a psychodrama or sociodrama. Thus, a feminist therapist can help a group embody a sexist, racist, or homophobic society, giving it a form and a voice. Group members can then be encouraged to engage in dialogue with that society (see Pam Remer & Rory Remer, 2000).

## Revising Psychodrama Theory to a Feminist Format

Our analysis shows that Psychodrama theory, techniques, and therapeutic goals are congruent with EFT principles. However, there are several modifications that would enhance further its compatibility with feminist-diversity therapy.

First, although the concept of cultural conserves obviously applies to traditional gender roles, the Psychodrama literature does not contain specific and in-depth analyses of gender-role rules as conserves. Similarly, although clients are seen to be damaged by socialization and the acculturation process, more needs to be written about how gender-role messages and institutionalized oppression can be explored on the Psychodrama stage.

Second, while the technique of role reversal reflects female values of empathy and understanding another's perspective, we believe that emphasizing role reversal or using it prematurely can be harmful to female clients. Premature role reversal interferes with women's identifying their own needs and wants. It replicates the female socialization process of being alert to what other people want and subordinating our own needs to them. Further, role reversal into another's role makes expression of anger to that person more difficult for female clients. Thus, role reversal with female clients should be used judiciously and be carefully timed (e.g., not done prior to the expression of anger).

Third, since Psychodrama as a mode of therapy was developed primarily for use with groups, and since many feminist therapists work primarily in individual sessions, adaptations need to be made in some of the techniques for their use in individual counseling. Fortunately, many psychodramatists have already made and written about these adaptations (A. Blatner & Blatner, 1988; Goldman & Morrison, 1984). The use of psychodrama in individual counseling is called *psychodrama-a-deux*. Thus, Psychodrama theory and most of the Psychodramatic techniques are used successfully in individual counseling.

## Reevaluation of Psychodrama Theory

Our evaluation of Psychodrama theory and techniques suggests that Psychodrama is compatible with an EFT approach. A Psychodramatic approach does not violate any of the eight comparison criteria listed in Table 4.3. The major constructs of Psychodrama remain viable throughout the transformation process. However, we point out two revisions that would enhance Psychodrama's congruence with a feminist therapy approach. Further, we suggest that several aspects of Psychodrama—its theory about the role of the external environment in individual problem development, its technique of physicalizing power differentials, and its technique of embodying or giving tangible form to abstract feminist concepts such as a *sexist, racist,* or *homophobic* society—can make valuable feminist contributions to other therapeutic orientations.

## SUMMARY

This chapter presents a model for merging traditional theories of psychotherapy with a feminist therapy format. We explored how the characteristics of many traditional theories may be incompatible with EFT principles. We regard a theory as biased if its content and constructs are androcentric, gendercentric, ethnocentric, heterosexist, intrapsychic, or deterministic. In contrast, a feminist theory format suggests that theories of behavior change should be gender-balanced, flexible/multicultural, interactionist, and life span in their structure and content. The model for transforming a theory to feminist format was further explored through the presentation of two theoretical approaches: Cognitive-Behavioral Therapy and Psychodrama. Each theoretical view was shown to be essentially compatible with feminist principles, yet lacking in certain concepts or dimensions that required revision. In the following activity, we challenge the reader to perform a similar analysis and transformation on a selected theoretical approach.

## ACTIVITY: TRANSFORMING YOUR THEORETICAL ORIENTATION

This activity builds on your responses to the self-assessment at the beginning of this chapter. In the self-assessment, you answered nine questions about your chosen theoretical orientation. These questions help you describe the basic concepts and techniques of your theory. Now use these answers as a basis for completing the transformation steps found in Table 4.3. Follow the transformation steps to help you determine how compatible your theory is with an EFT perspective.

## FURTHER READINGS

Blatner, A. (1996). *Acting-in: Practical applications of Psychodramatic methods.* New York: Springer.

Blatner, A. (2000). *Foundations of Psychodrama: History, theory, and practice.* New York: Springer.

Craighead, L., Craighead, W. E., Kazdin, A., & Mahoney, M. J. (1994). *Cognitive-behavioral interventions: An empirical approach to mental health.* Boston: Allyn & Bacon.

Epstein, N., Schlesinger, S. E., & Dryden (Eds.). (1988). *Cognitive–behavioral therapy with families.* New York: Brunner/Mazel.

Fine, L. J. (1979). Psychodrama. In R. Corsini (Ed.), *Current psychotherapies.* Itasca, IL: Peacock.

Follette, V. M., Ruzek, J. L., & Abueg, F. R. (Eds.). (1998). *Cognitive-behavioral therapies for trauma.* New York: Guilford Press.

# Chapter 5

# *A FEMINIST APPROACH TO ASSESSMENT*

*Culture "affects the way people label illness, identify symptoms, seek help, decide whether someone is normal or abnormal, set expectations for therapists and clients, give themselves personal meaning, and understand morality and altered states of consciousness."*

Charles Ridley, Lisa Li, and Carrie Hill, 1998, p. 828

*A crucial challenge for feminist assessment is to incorporate contextual variables beyond that of gender that define women's lives (e.g., race, culture, sexual orientation, age, immigration status) in a manner that reflects the meaning of that context for the particular woman for whom an assessment is being conducted.*

Santos de Barona and Dutton, 1997, p. 53

## SELF-ASSESSMENT: ASSESSMENT OF CLIENT DESCRIPTIONS[*]

Read each of the following client descriptions. Then, answer the questions that ask you to hypothesize about the client's gender, economic status, age, ethnicity, and marital status. If you cannot make a particular judgment, leave the space blank. You can compare your answers with those of other respondents on page 129.

### Client 1

This person passively allows others to assume responsibility for major areas of his or her life because of a lack of self-confidence and an inability to function independently. This person subordinates his or her own needs to those of others on whom he or she is dependent to avoid any possibility of having to be self-reliant. This person leaves major decisions to others. For example, this person will typically assume a passive role and allow

---

[*]*Source:* From "The Politics of Personality Disorder," by H. Landrine, 1989, *Psychology of Women Quarterly, 13,* pp. 325–329. Used with permission.

the spouse to decide where they should live, what kind of job he or she should have, and with which neighbors they should be friendly. This person is unwilling to make demands on the people on whom he or she depends for fear of jeopardizing the relationships and being forced to rely on himself or herself. This person lacks self-confidence. This person tends to belittle his or her abilities and assets by constantly referring to him/herself as "stupid."

This person is most likely to be:

1. Female _____     Male _____
2. Wealthy _____     Middle class _____     Poor _____
3. _____ Years old
4. Black _____     White _____
5. Married _____     Single _____
6. *DSM* diagnosis _____

## Client 2

This person habitually violates the rights of others. In childhood, this person engaged in frequent lying, stealing, fighting, truancy, and resisting authority. In adolescence, this person showed unusually early or aggressive sexual behavior, excessive drinking, and use of illicit drugs. Now in adulthood, this behavior continues, with the addition of inability to maintain consistent work performance or to function as a responsible parent, and failure to obey the law. This person shows signs of personal distress, including complaints of tension, inability to tolerate boredom, and the conviction (often correct) that others are hostile toward him or her. This person is unable to sustain lasting, close, warm, and responsible relationships with family, friends, or sexual partners.

This person is most likely to be:

1. Female _____     Male _____
2. Wealthy _____     Middle class _____     Poor _____
3. _____ Years old
4. Black _____     White _____
5. Married _____     Single _____
6. *DSM* diagnosis _____

## OVERVIEW

Assessment and diagnostic procedures are viewed by many mental health practitioners as crucial to understanding and defining client issues. Attention to the impact of cultural learnings and contexts on client reactions and clinician decision making have often been peripheral or entirely absent in these assessment and diagnostic procedures. Thus, a feminist-diversity approach to assessment and diagnosis diverges considerably from more traditional ones. We begin this chapter with a feminist critique of traditional mainstream approaches and conclude with feminist perspectives and strategies for assessment and diagnosis. After reading Chapter 5, you will be able to:

- Identify androcentric, ethnocentric, heterosexist, classist, ageist, racist, and other oppressive perspectives that underlie most traditional approaches to assessment and diagnosis.
- List the sources of gender and cultural bias in testing instruments.
- Discuss the major differences between traditional and Empowerment Feminist Therapy (EFT) approaches to testing and diagnosis.
- Understand the relationship between oppressions that women experience (e.g., sexism, racism, heterosexism, classism, ageism, ethnocentrism, ableism) and the "symptoms" they develop.

## TRADITIONAL APPROACHES TO ASSESSMENT AND DIAGNOSIS

As with other therapeutic interventions, assessment and diagnoses are governed by therapists' theoretical orientations and belief/value systems. In this section, traditional approaches to assessment and diagnosis are defined and then critiqued for their possible sources of bias.

### Assessment

Assessment in psychotherapy and counseling has many possible functions (Hansen, Stevic, & Warner, 1986; G. Meyer et al., 2001). Some of these functions are to:

- Identify the focus and goals of therapy.
- Identify and categorize the client's problems.
- Increase the client's understanding of self.
- Increase the counselor's understanding of the client.
- Identify appropriate therapeutic intervention strategies.
- Assess whether the therapist is competent to treat the client.
- Evaluate the client's progress and/or the effectiveness of therapy.
- Minimize legal risk and liability.

Assessment includes a wide variety of information-collection strategies such as interviewing, systematic observation, self-monitoring, life history taking, standardized objective tests, projective tests, analysis of person-environment interactions, and biopsychological assessment. Choice of assessment procedures and instruments varies depending on whether clinicians view the behavior as interactive with the environment/situation or caused by enduring personality characteristics.

In general, assessment procedures, including testing and diagnosis, are culturally biased to the degree that they stereotype females and males and discount or ignore the environmental context of clients' lives. Throughout this chapter, we are using the term *bias* to refer to all forms of cultural bias including sexism, ageism, ableism, ethnocentrism, classism, racism, heterosexism (SEARCH Variables). The ways in which bias may affect the assessment process are detailed in the following sections on testing and diagnosis.

*Sources of Bias in Testing*

Tests are one kind of strategy often used by therapists to collect assessment data about clients. Tests "provide greater standardization of stimulus conditions" and, thus, are "an objective aid to observation in the diagnostic process" (Hansen et al., 1986, p. 394). As with diagnostic classification systems, tests may be biased in many different ways.

In general, a test is biased if it:

1. Results in individuals being limited in their performance on the test on the basis of their group membership.
2. Limits individuals from considering (career) options or being eligible for opportunities on the basis of gender or other social locations.
3. Causes others to limit individuals from considering options or being eligible for opportunities on the basis of gender or other social locations.

Biased assumptions and values can be incorporated in tests in at least four different ways:

1. Tests may have biased items.
2. They use inappropriate norm groups for comparison of an individual's score.
3. They provide biased interpreting information.
4. The test construction concepts reflect sexist, racist, ethnocentric, heterosexist, and/or classist structures of society.

**Biased Items**    First, bias in test items exists if the terminology or language used is culture bound, and/or reflects SEARCH variables. For example, gender bias in test items can occur if sexist terminology is used or if the items give a gender-based experience advantage to either females or males. An example of sexist terminology is using *policeman* instead of *police officer* on a career interest inventory. Second, if test items are based on experiences that are more likely for some groups (e.g., males) in a culture than for other groups (e.g., females), the test has a group-based experience advantage. These group-based advantages usually favor the dominant cultural group (Ridley et al., 1998). For example, a test item on a math achievement test that asks, "How many total points are scored by a football team that makes two touchdowns plus a field goal?" has a male experience advantage (i.e., playing football), while one that asks, "How many ounces are in a cup of milk?" has a female experience advantage (i.e., cooking). Similarly, a general ability test item that asks, "Does the knife go to the right or left of the plate in a proper table setting?" has both a middle-class and female experience advantage (R. K. Payne, 1998). Third, biased items may exclude the perspective of a group. For example, life history questionnaires often assume a heterosexual perspective by asking numerous questions about heterosexually based experiences, such as marriage or divorce, and by not asking questions about homosexual ones or by phrasing questions about homosexual experiences that marginalize them. In general, testing instruments are almost always culture bound (Ridley et al., 1998).

The Scholastic Assessment Test (SAT), a test widely used in the United States for determining entrance into undergraduate institutions and awarding of some scholarships, is a good illustration of the use of biased items that have negative results for women. Noting that women scored higher than men on the verbal portion of the SAT, its developers replaced items that focused on the humanities and the arts with ones from science and business, thus removing the male disadvantage. However, despite women's poorer performance on the math section of the test, no similar revisions to balance the content of items has been made on the SAT-M (Betz, 1993). As a result, women's SAT scores underpredict their actual college grades, and use of these SAT scores result in lowered rates of admission for women (Fassinger, 2001; Hyde & Kling, 2001).

**Inappropriate Norm Groups**   Second, tests may be biased by using inappropriate norm groups against which to compare an individual's score. For example, before its revision into the Strong-Campbell Interest Inventory (SCII), the Strong-Vocational Interest Blank (SVIB) had separate tests for men and women. Many nontraditional (male-dominated) career options for women were not on the female form. If a woman wanted to know how her interests compared to those employed in male-typed fields, she had to take the man's form. Thus, her interests were compared to men working in those fields that gave her less likelihood of having "similar interests" and receiving encouragement to pursue those occupations further. While the issue of whether to use same-gender or mixed-gender norms is a complex and debated one, there is general agreement that using cross-sexed norms on interest inventories restricts women's exploration of nontraditional careers.

Many tests are normed on Caucasians, and the scores of diverse ethnic group members are interpreted based on these norms. The less biased approach is to norm tests on diverse groups and provide separate norms when appropriate (e.g., Trauma Symptom Inventory; Ridley et al., 1998; Santos de Barona & Dutton, 1997).

**Biased Constructs**   The third way that an instrument can be biased is if the theoretical basis for its construction reflects the oppressive structures of society. An excellent example of this problem occurs in the measurement of career interests, which can be based on one of two competing theories. One theory, the *Hypothesis of Social Dominance,* reflects the status quo of the current social and occupational structure. The other theory, the *Hypothesis of Opportunity Dominance,* is based on changing the status quo by broadening the individual's consideration and pursuit of nontraditional options (Cole & Hanson, 1978). Before further explaining these two theories, it is necessary to understand the nature of career interests. A person's interests (career-relevant likes and dislikes) are influenced by genetic factors, socialization experiences, observation of role models, and experience with an activity. Thus, career interest inventories measure gender-role and cultural learning processes.

Cole and Hanson (1978) posited two differing hypotheses about interests and subsequent satisfaction in careers. Their *Hypothesis of Social Dominance* stated that:

> Until the areas of socially accepted interest options become broadened during a person's development, the careers in which people will be satisfied will not broaden. (p. 499)

Under this theory, society and the socialization process must change before individuals' satisfactions in careers will change. The alternate *Hypothesis of Opportunity Dominance* states that:

> When career opportunities widen, people will find satisfaction in a wider range of careers in spite of limiting aspects of their earlier socialization. (p. 499)

Under this theory, making a wider range of career opportunities available to women should come first, which will, in turn, bring about changes in society and gender-role socialization.

Cole and Hanson (1978) contended that the measurement of a person's likes and dislikes and the comparison of those preferences with people currently employed in careers support the Social Dominance theory. The social dominance approach to assessment accentuates the existing racial and gendered arrangements in careers (e.g., fewer role models in high status, high-paying careers for women and members of oppressed groups). Instruments that use cross-sex norms, mixed-sex norms, or raw scores for women, and which lack appropriate norm groups for a variety of ethnic groups, are compatible with the Social Dominance theory. Although raw scores may represent existing realities in careers, they contribute to the continuation of occupational gender segregation. For instance, women and men have different gender-role socialization experiences that result in differential response patterns on interest inventories. Thus, using same-sex norms controls for these differing socializations by comparing individuals' scores with those who have had similar gender-role experiences (Zunker, 1998). Using instruments that predominantly measure individuals' stereotyped socialization experiences to career counsel women restricts their career options and perpetuates the status quo. Using instruments that de-emphasize socialization experiences and use same-sex norm groups for comparisons is compatible with the Opportunity Dominance theory.

The Self-Directed Search (SDS; J. L. Holland, 1994) is an example of an interest inventory that fits the Social Dominance Hypothesis. Of the five sections of the SDS, three directly assess past experiences. Thus, if a woman has in the past imagined herself being a nurse, teacher, or secretary; or has been a secretary and thus possesses office skills and clerical ability (i.e., can type and take shorthand), she will score high on the conventional scale of the SDS based primarily on what she has done, rather than scoring high on scales in which she might be satisfied and successful. Further, the SDS uses raw scores for determining compatible career areas. Because the SDS can be completed, scored, and interpreted with little or no counselor involvement, it is a low-cost, popular instrument. Thus, it is used with many women and minority group members, resulting in their being directed into occupations representing the status quo. For example, African American and Latina women are overrepresented in low-level occupations in Holland's Realistic typology (Stitt-Gohdes, 1997).

Contrastingly, the Nonsexist Vocational Card Sort (NSVCS), developed by Cindy Dewey (1974) as an alternative to standardized interest inventories, is an Opportunity Dominance assessment strategy. The nonsexist names of a wide range of career options are written on individual cards, the same set being used for both female and male clients. Individuals sort the cards into piles ranging from "would not choose" to "might choose." Then, in an interactive exchange with the counselor, clients clarify reasons for their sorting of the choices. Using an updated diversity perspective, the counselor and client collaboratively look for connecting themes, and the counselor challenges the client's stereotyped beliefs about careers and about the client's view of self.

Both the NSVCS and the Opportunity Dominance Hypothesis were created about 30 years ago, and we believe that neither have received the attention they are due. First, while both the theory and card sort were developed around a gender focus, we have described both here as they can be applied for expanding options for diverse groups. Second, we believe that the therapeutic outcomes associated with applying the Opportunity Dominance theory and using the NSVCS need to be researched. In addition, many more assessment strategies need to be developed that fit with the Opportunity Dominance perspective.

In summary, tests can be biased if the types of items they contain, the terms used in items, the norm groups used, the interpretation instructions provided in the manual, and the theory underlying their construction reflect SEARCH variables. Biases incorporated into the test then interact with any biased beliefs held by the clinician. Biased tests support the Social Dominance Hypothesis and help perpetuate a stereotyped society.

*Environmental Factors Impacting Test-Taking Performance*

Research has documented that test-taking conditions (e.g., gender and ethnicity of administrator, language used) can affect the testee's performance (Ridley et al., 1998). Claude Steele's (1997) concept of stereotype threat is an excellent example of how testing conditions, both immediate and long-term, may impact the testing performance of women and people of color. Stereotype threat is a situational, "social-psychological threat that arises when one is in a situation or doing something for which a negative stereotype about one's group applies" (p. 614). Steele hypothesized that stereotype threat would be cued by the awareness that "a negative group stereotype could apply to oneself in a given situation" (p. 617) and that one could experience stereotype threat whether or not one believes the stereotype; that is, the stereotype does not have to be internalized to affect how the individual responds. The experience of the stereotype threat produces anxiety that diminishes performance in the domain.

Steele (1997) investigated the impact of stereotype threat on two groups: college women taking a difficult math test and African Americans taking an intellectual ability test. When test-taking directions that cued stereotype threat were used (e.g., telling the women that gender-differences were expected), the participants had depressed test scores. When the directions did not cue stereotype threat (e.g., African Americans being told the test was not diagnostic of ability), the stereotyped groups' performance equaled the comparison groups (i.e., men or Whites). Thus, test-taking performance was influenced by test-taking instructions and group stereotypes. Steele summarized this impact by saying, "Thus, stereotype threat may be a possible source of bias in standardized tests, a bias that arises not from item content, but from group differences in the threat that societal stereotypes attach to test performance" (p. 622). Pamela Reid and Sue Zalk (2001) pointed out that situational testing factors are usually ignored or remain invisible, and then the individuals alone are blamed for the poor performance. Psychologists and educators need to be aware of the impact of stereotype threat when administering tests, interpreting test results, and creating educational interventions.

## Diagnosis

Diagnosis relates specifically to three assessment functions—identification of the problem, categorization of the problem, and determination of appropriate therapeutic interventions. Psychological diagnosis has its roots in the medical illness model. To determine a diagnosis, a therapist must have a diagnostic classification system and strategies for identifying, measuring, and labeling symptoms corresponding to the diagnostic classifications. Further, the therapist's theoretical approach, the diagnostic classification used, and the therapist's beliefs and prejudices interact to determine what criteria are used, what symptoms are looked for, in whom the symptoms are found, and, to some extent, how the symptoms are measured.

## Feminist Critique of Assessment and Diagnostic Approaches

Assessment and diagnostic approaches are susceptible to bias in five major ways:

1. Disregarding or minimizing the effect of the environmental context on individuals' behaviors.
2. Disregarding cultural norms and values.
3. Giving different diagnoses to different groups of people displaying similar symptoms.
4. Making misjudgments in selection of diagnostic labels because of stereotyped beliefs.
5. Using a biased theoretical orientation.

### Disregarding Environmental Context

First, assessment and diagnosis are biased to the extent that they focus solely or primarily on the behaviors and traits of the individual without regard to the environmental context (e.g., poverty, patriarchy, and powerlessness) and without regard to the effect of the environment on the individual's response (person-environment interaction). Feminist-diversity therapists believe that when the social conditions of women's lives are minimized or ignored, misdiagnosis and blaming the victim result (Santos de Barona & Dutton, 1997). For example, if therapists do not perceive that women live in a society that stereotypes and discriminates against them, therapists are more likely to judge the woman's response to her situation as an overreaction, or abnormal. Further, they will look for ways to explain her reactions that ignore the effects of her environment. Locating the pathology in female clients further stigmatizes and blames them for the results of their own socialization and society's oppression of them. This process reduces their self-esteem, increases depression, and increases feelings of powerlessness. For example, consider Nina, the woman in Chapter 3, who was sexually abused by her brother. She is more likely to be diagnosed as having a personality disorder if the therapist does not see her symptoms as related to possible sexual abuse and so does not assess for it, or if the therapist does uncover the sexual abuse but does not judge it to be traumatic. For diagnostic strategies to be free of SEARCH factors, they must incorporate an assessment of environmental factors and use diagnostic classification systems that allow for environmental stressors to be possible sources of pathology.

### Lack of Awareness of the Impact of Culture

Most traditional diagnostic classification not only de-emphasizes environmental, cultural contexts, and power differentials, but also disregards the impact of cultural norms on human behavior and on definitions of mental health and pathology (Enns, 2000; S. R. Lopez & Guarnaccia, 2000; Ridley et al., 1998; Santos de Barona & Dutton, 1997). Ridley et al. (1998) pointed out that cultural differences among people often result in members of the subordinate culture being defined as *abnormal*. "The misapplication of mental health criteria from one culture to another usually leads to the misdiagnosis of clients" (p. 861). Furthermore, Steven Lopez and Peter Guarnaccia (2000) asserted that "culture shapes the manner in which children and adolescents express psychological distress" (p. 584). The reaction to this distress does not usually violate cultural norms.

## Differential Diagnosis Based on Group Membership

Third, diagnostic approaches are biased if the structure and definitions of their categories lead to the application of different diagnoses based on the clients' social locations or group memberships to clients displaying similar symptoms. Misdiagnosis based on stereotype is more likely to happen if the symptom descriptors for categories mirror societal stereotypes. (See the self-assessment examples at the beginning of the chapter.) Further, the biases of therapists may interact with the biases of the diagnostic classifications used. Diagnostic category descriptors that use traits or adjectives are more susceptible to bias than are behavioral descriptors, because they require more inference by the clinician. For example, a category that uses *dependent* and *submissive* as descriptors is more likely to be applied to women, because the descriptors fit the traditional female gender-role stereotype and because as adjectives they are more open to the interpretive biases of the diagnostician. Thus, clinicians are more likely to "see" the symptoms in female clients than they are in male clients. A research study by Becker and Lamb (1994) illustrates this point. Clinicians were asked to diagnose hypothetical female and male clients based on written client descriptions with only the sex of the client varied. The client vignettes used symptom descriptors consistent with criteria for both Borderline Personality Disorder (BPD) and Posttraumatic Stress Disorder (PTSD). Clinician participants rated the female case clients higher for applicability of the BPD diagnosis than they did the male clients. Female clinicians gave higher ratings of the PTSD diagnosis than did male participants. The researchers concluded that gender of both client and of clinician influences diagnostic judgment.

## Therapist Misjudgment

A fourth source of bias in diagnosis and assessment is the belief system of the diagnostician/therapist. Therapists who have stereotyped beliefs may harbor preconceived ideas about the presence of symptoms in groups of people (i.e., ethnic groups, gender groups). They may also have preconceived ideas about the evaluative labels applied to these symptoms. For example, dependency is more likely to be "seen" in females (i.e., believing that females are economically dependent on males) and ignored in males (i.e., failing to see that men are dependent on women for maintaining their households) (Becker, 2001; Greenspan, 1983). Further, the clinician may apply androcentric and ethnocentric positive values to independence while viewing dependence as pathological. (In Chapter 3, we discussed the alternate feminist value of interdependence.) Because stereotyped beliefs are usually accepted as norms in a society, they are often applied without awareness by therapists. These preconceived beliefs, which are largely out of awareness, often lead clinicians to discount data that do not support their assumptions. The less that their bias is in their awareness, the more pervasive its influence is likely to be in their diagnostic evaluations, and the more confident of "misdiagnosis" they become.

## Theoretical Orientation Bias

Fifth, the degree of bias present in therapists' theoretical orientations also influences therapists' diagnostic evaluations. The theoretical orientation provides a framework for what is considered healthy and unhealthy and for explaining how individuals develop. If the theoretical orientation is biased, clinicians' conceptualizations of what symptoms are pathological, in whom they are pathological, and assessment strategies used for measurement of symptoms are all likely to be biased. In Chapter 4, we considered how biases can influence theoretical concepts and explanations of behavior.

## Interaction of Biased Components

A description of the interaction between components (cultural context, clinician, client) and the stages of bias in diagnosis is presented in Figure 5.1. Bias (e.g., institutionalized sexism and racism, gender-role socialization) in the culture impacts the clinician's responses, the client's responses, and each stage of the diagnostic process. The different ways that bias can enter into the diagnostic process are depicted. Each source of potential bias in the assessment and diagnostic process can occur in isolation or in combination with other sources. When more than one source is present, there is greater likelihood that a harmful diagnostic evaluation of the client will be made.

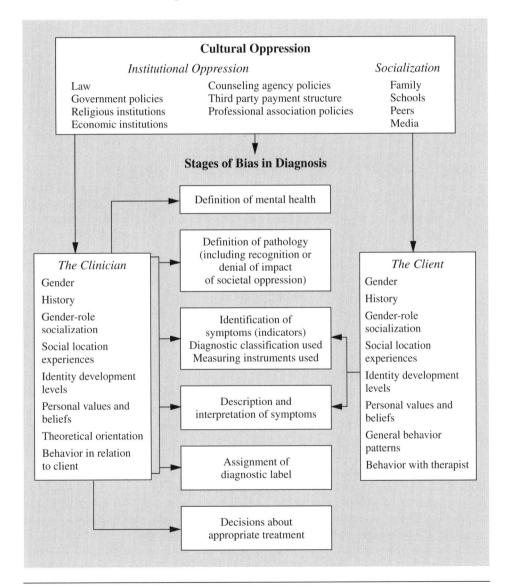

**Figure 5.1   Interactional components and stages of bias in diagnosis.**

## *DSM-IV*

The *Diagnostic and Statistical Manual of Mental Disorders, 4th Edition* (*DSM-IV*; American Psychiatric Association, 1994) is the most widely used mental disorder diagnostic classification system in the United States. Feminist psychological practitioners have criticized the *DSM-IV* and its predecessors for being sexist, ethnocentric, and culture-bound (Becker, 2001; Caplan, 1995; S. R. Lopez & Guarnaccia, 2000). We begin with a general feminist critique of the *DSM* and then, with a focused critique of several specific diagnostic categories.

### *A General Culture-Based Critique of the* DSM

The *DSM* incorporates cultural bias in several different ways: (a) focus on internal pathology; (b) clinician bias; and (c) use of trait descriptors.

**Focus on Internal Pathology**   The *DSM* was developed on the medical model. The disease model that underlies the *DSM* views distress as a disease, a disorder, and decontextualizes any external causes of the disorder (Becker, 2001). Using the *DSM* focuses clinicians primarily on diagnosing an individual's internal pathology. In fact, very few of its diagnostic categories locate the source of the problem in an environmental stressor. The *DSM* categories assign the locus of the problem to individual pathology with little or no regard for the impact of a sexist or oppressive environment (Becker, 2001). For example, a woman who has a history of unstable relationships, who abuses alcohol, has short bouts of depression, has been suicidal, and who has chronic feelings of emptiness will often be diagnosed to have a Borderline Personality Disorder if her environmental context of sexual abuse is not assessed and uncovered (Caplan, 1995).

Further, the organization and sequencing of the *DSM* results in diagnostic decisions about Axes I and II before contextual factors are considered on Axis IV (Becker, 2001; S. R. Lopez & Guarnaccia, 2000). Dana Becker concluded, "The priorities of the *DSM-IV* are clear: the attitudes of psychotherapy clients, the meaning these clients give to their symptoms, and the social and historical context of their distress are marginalized in the process of diagnosis" (p. 336). In addition, the culture-bound syndromes identified in the *DSM* come only from nondominant groups suggesting the dominant group's disorders are free of cultural influences (Lopez & Guarnaccia, 2000).

**Clinician Bias**   Diagnosis of a mental disorder requires the observation of a symptom in a person's behavior. The observer must make a judgment about the presence of a symptom and whether it constitutes impairment in functioning. The clinician must determine whether the symptoms are a maladaptive response to stress (i.e., what is a normal or abnormal reaction; Russell, 1986). Thus, both the response and the stressor are open to interpretation. Becker (2001) asserted that viewing problems in living as illnesses obscures the cultural values and politically influenced stereotyped beliefs of the diagnoser. (See Becker [2001] for an analysis of how the development of *DSM* categories has been influenced historically by social and cultural forces.) The clinician's values, biases, and theoretical orientation influence all diagnostic judgments.

Bias in therapists' diagnostic evaluations of mental health has been found in many studies (e.g., Becker & Lamb, 1994; Broverman et al., 1970; Ford & Widiger, 1989; S. Hamilton, Rothbart, & Dawes, 1986; Landrine, 1989). Further, if clinicians misjudge the extent of the stressor or ignore its existence altogether, the individual's symptoms are more likely to be evaluated as pathological.

**Use of Trait Descriptors**    A third related criticism of the *DSM* involves the types of descriptors used. In the *DSM-III* (American Psychiatric Association, 1980), several of the personality disorder categories (e.g., Histrionic Personality Disorder, Dependent Personality Disorder) with higher prevalence rates for women had trait or adjective descriptors that also described traditionally gender-role-socialized women (S. Hamilton et al., 1986). For example, a person with a histrionic personality disorder was described as "overly dramatic"; "reactive"; "often acts a role, such as 'victim' or 'princess' "; "there may be a constant demand for reassurance because of feelings of helplessness and dependency" (American Psychiatric Association, 1980, p. 313). Although changes have been made in the *DSM-IV,* its descriptors for Histrionic Personality Disorder still currently include "pervasive and excessive emotionality" and "overly concerned with impressing others by their appearance" (p. 655), descriptors that parallel traditional female stereotypes. While many of the revisions of the *DSM-IV* are in a positive direction, therapist judgment still plays a large role for certain categories.

**Prevalence Rates**    The *DSM-IV* reports differential prevalence rates for females and males for numerous disorders (e.g., Major Depressive Disorder, Borderline Personality Disorder). There are divided opinions about why these differential rates exist (Franks, 1986; Hartung & Widiger, 1998; M. Kaplan, 1983; Widiger & Spitzer, 1991). For example, Hartung and Widiger reviewed the research related to gender and diagnostic categories of the *DSM.* They identify sources of error in this research including sampling biases and biases in diagnostic criteria. They hypothesized that differential gender rates in *DSM* categories are influenced by women seeking treatment more often than men, biased clinical research trials, and diagnostic criteria that reflect stereotypic gender-role behavior favoring one sex. They made suggestions for future improvements while acknowledging the difficulty in creating gender-neutral diagnostic criteria. From a different perspective, Marci Kaplan argued that "masculine-biased assumptions about which behaviors are healthy and what behaviors are crazy are codified in diagnostic criteria and thus influence diagnosis and treatment patterns" (p. 786).

Kaplan's analyses of the sexist components of the *DSM* serve as a useful summary for all types of bias. She pointed out that there are three major assumptions underlying diagnosis that are influenced by gender bias. First is the belief that the trait or symptom is unhealthy, which is a value judgment. Second is the assumption that the symptoms are dysfunctional, rather than creative survival strategies for coping with oppression. Third, the symptom is described in and tied to a female (subordinate group) context, and the male (dominant group) context for the same symptom is exempted or ignored (e.g., dependency). Thus, Kaplan's explanation for the differential diagnostic rates in females and males for many *DSM* diagnostic categories is that sexism is incorporated in the *DSM.*

## Feminist Critique of Several DSM-IV Diagnostic Categories

We next explore the application of biases in the *DSM-IV* by employing a feminist critique of three specific diagnostic categories: Borderline Personality Disorder, Dependent Personality Disorder, Posttraumatic Stress Disorder.

**Borderline Personality Disorder**    Borderline Personality Disorder (BPD) is a diagnosis applied to individuals who have "a pervasive pattern of instability of interpersonal relationships, self-image, and affects, and marked impulsivity. . ." (American Psychiatric Association, 1994, p. 650). Becker (2001) reported that: (a) BPD is the most frequently used personality disorder; (b) a diagnosis of BPD is between two and nine times more likely to be given to women than to men; and (c) current definitions of BPD emphasize affective features that result in higher diagnostic rates for women. Further, while many women who receive the BPD diagnosis were abused as children, the *DSM* descriptions of BPD do not include this information (Becker, 2001; Becker & Lamb, 1994). A diagnosis of BPD is often given to "difficult" therapy clients who clinicians believe cannot be successfully treated (Becker, 2001; D. Robinson & Worell, 2002).

**Dependent Personality Disorder**   Dependent Personality Disorder involves "a pervasive and excessive need to be taken care of that leads to submissive and clinging behavior and fears of separation (American Psychiatric Association, 1994, p. 666). Among the characteristics of the disorder are passivity, difficulty in making decisions, trouble disagreeing with others, fear of appearing to be competent, and self-sacrificial. The criteria for Dependent Personality Disorder have been criticized for their similarities to traditionally socialized female characteristics and for excluding characteristics of male dependency (Becker, 2001; D. Robinson & Worell, 2002).

**Posttraumatic Stress Disorder**   The *DSM-IV* criteria for Posttraumatic Stress Disorder (PTSD) include: (a) experiencing or witnessing a traumatic event involving serious injury, death, or threat thereof to self or others; (b) intense horror or helplessness; (c) intrusive memories; (d) avoidance of cues reminiscent of the trauma; and (e) anxiety and panic reactions.

In a previous edition of this book (Worell & Remer, 1992), we emphasized the advantages of the PTSD diagnosis because it is one of the few *DSM* categories that locates the problem in an external source and is, therefore, less stigmatizing to the individual.

However, PTSD has also been criticized by feminist practitioners. For example, the current PTSD criteria do not include reactions to repeated traumas (e.g., childhood sexual abuse) or to chronic trauma exposure (insidious trauma). Insidious trauma, a concept proposed by Maria Root (as cited in Sanchez-Hucles & Hudgins, 2001), involves repeated, cumulative traumatic experiences such as racism, sexism, or heterosexism. Others (e.g., Herman & van der Kolk as cited in Sanchez-Hucles & Hudgins, 2001) have proposed a complex form of PTSD where the trauma is sustained and repeated (e.g., wife battering, experiences with oppression). This conceptualization of complex trauma and trauma reactions is included as a supplement to the *DSM-IV* PTSD category as DESNOS (disorders of extreme stress not otherwise specified).

Three additional limitations of PTSD as currently conceptualized are important. First, PTSD symptom criteria do not include all reactions to trauma. For example, depression, difficulty in interpersonal relationships, substance abuse, physical symptoms, and self-blame are not included; yet, they are substantiated outcomes of trauma (Ingram, Corning, & Schmidt, 1996; McCann, Sakheim, & Abrahamson, 1988). Failure to connect these symptoms to trauma experiences can result in treatment that does not help the victim heal from the trauma. Second, exposure to trauma and trauma reactions are influenced by cultural context. For example, people from oppressed groups (e.g., lesbian women, Women of Color, women living in poverty) are at increased risk of exposure to trauma. Indeed, 69% of all women have experienced at least one trauma (Sanchez-Hucles & Hudgins, 2001). As we discuss in greater length in Chapter 8, racism and sexism interact in the way society treats trauma victims, often holding them responsible for their own victimization. As noted earlier in this chapter, because cultural factors are not integrated into the diagnostic process in the *DSM,* trauma survivors from diverse groups may be treated inappropriately without taking their cultural contexts into account (Koss, Heise, & Russo, 1994). Third, labeling reactions to external trauma stressors as a disorder located in an individual victim, appears internally inconsistent (Becker, 2001). A PTSD diagnosis does not acknowledge the sociocultural contexts that create and sustain violent acts against women and that blame women for their own victimization afterward (Koss, Heise, et al., 1994).

## DSM: *Summary*

The location of pathology in the individual, the minimization of effects of oppressive environmental stressors, the use of category descriptions that parallel societal stereotypes, the use of trait rather than behavioral descriptors, and the lack of empirical research evidence to substantiate many categories all contribute to the biased structure of the *DSM*.

## FEEDBACK ON CHAPTER SELF-ASSESSMENT: CLIENT DESCRIPTIONS

In the self-assessment at the beginning of the chapter, you were asked to predict the groups to which each client belonged. These client descriptions were part of two studies conducted by Hope Landrine (1989). Her premise, which was supported by the results of these studies, was that social stereotypes would match (Hypothesis of Equivalence) the client descriptions that were based on various *DSM* personality disorder diagnoses. Client 1 in the self-assessment fits the *DSM* criteria for Dependent Personality Disorder. Respondents in Landrine's study described this person as a slightly older, married, middle-class, White woman. Client 2 in the self-assessment fits the *DSM* criteria for Antisocial Personality Disorder. Landrine's respondents described this person as a young, lower-class male. She concluded that the respondents, who were college students, relied on ordinary social stereotypes to complete the identification task. We want to add that the social stereotypes her respondents applied were also ethnocentric, Western cultural perspectives. We believe that this supports feminist contentions that many *DSM* personality disorder categories have stereotypes embedded in their descriptions and that evaluators also hold those stereotypes. We hope that by examining your cognitions and answers in completing the exercise, you can begin to identify the stereotypes that guide your judgments as a first step in challenging those stereotypes.

## EMPOWERMENT FEMINIST THERAPY APPROACH TO ASSESSMENT AND DIAGNOSIS

### Empowerment Feminist Therapy Assumptions

The following eight EFT assumptions, based on the four EFT principles, form the foundation for a feminist approach to assessment and diagnosis. (These assumptions are summarized in Table 5.1.) The perspective reflected in these assumptions challenges most of the assumptions that underlie traditional approaches to diagnosis. Indeed, EFT therapists redefine what is considered psychologically healthy.

**Table 5.1    Empowerment Feminist Therapy assumptions about assessment and diagnosis**

1. Gather information about clients' personal and social identities.
2. Integrate cultural context data into interpretation of other assessment and diagnostic data.
3. Create assessment strategies to promote social change.
4. Assess the environmental contexts of women's lives.
5. Empower clients by using a collaborative approach to assessment, diagnosis, and interpretation.
6. Reframe symptoms as ways of coping with oppressive environments.
7. Assess for client strengths and resiliencies.
8. Value and use multiple ways of knowing.

1. Accurate assessment and diagnosis require gathering information about clients' social identities and cultural contexts and using that information to guide the entire therapeutic process. Principle I, *Personal and Social Identities Are Interdependent,* and Principle II, *The Personal Is Political,* both emphasize the importance of understanding the social locations and cultural contexts of women's lives.
2. In accordance with both Principles I and II, cultural contexts must be an integral part of interpreting and using assessment and diagnostic data.
3. In relation to Principle II, assessment strategies should be created for and used to promote social change (Santos de Barona & Dutton, 1997).
4. EFT therapists minimize pathologizing the individual by including appraisals of the environmental societal contexts of women's lives in their assessments (Principle II).
5. EFT practitioners acknowledge that unequal power relationships influence the entire assessment process. In accordance with Principle III, *Relationships Are Egalitarian,* an EFT approach seeks to empower clients by collaborating with them about assessment and diagnostic purposes, strategies, uses, and interpretations.
6. In accordance with Principle IV, *Women's Perspectives Are Valued,* and Principle II, client responses to oppressive situations are viewed as coping strategies, not primarily as symptoms and deficits.
7. In concert with Principle IV, client strengths and resiliencies are an important focus of clinical assessments.
8. In line with Principle IV, multiple ways of knowing (e.g., rational, intuitive, objective, subjective) are valued (Santos de Barona & Dutton, 1997) and are used in the assessment process.

## Assessment for Personal and Social Identities

We agree with Ridley et al. (1998) that multicultural assessment must begin with identifying, interpreting, and using cultural data. Our model begins with a principle that emphasizes the multiple and interdependent social identities of women and men and that assesses for clients' levels of identity development and acculturation for each of their relevant identities. We disagree with approaches like the *DSM* that relegate cultural context to a secondary, almost afterthought, role. For the impacts and meanings of social, political, and cultural contexts to be integrated into an effective therapeutic approach, we begin by assessing these cultural identities.

Although we could confine ourselves to a feminist view of how to approach assessment issues in therapy, support for feminist perspectives can also be found in the multicultural arena. For example, Charles Ridley and his colleagues (1998) developed a Multicultural Assessment Plan model for working with diverse clients. Their model consists of three phases: (1) Identify cultural data, (2) interpret cultural data, and (3) incorporate cultural data. Thus, they stressed the importance of beginning assessments with a thorough understanding of the cultural influences and experiences of each client. They asserted that clinicians should always be asking, "How is culture relevant to understanding this client?" (p. 857)

Using Principle I, *Personal and Social Identities Are Interdependent,* as a guide, EFT clinicians assess for: (a) acculturation; (b) identity development level for each relevant social location; (c) client cultural values; (d) client experiences with oppression, discrimination, and being stereotyped; (e) experiences with gender-role socialization; (f) access to societal resources (e.g., health care, good nutrition, educational opportunities, social support); and (g) power arrangements in the home (Phinney, 1996; Ridley et al., 1998; Santos de Barona & Dutton, 1997). These assessment strategies are crucial to a feminist-diversity therapeutic approach.

By adding Principle I to our EFT model, we believe we have addressed Maryann Santos de Barona and Mary Ann Dutton's (1997) challenge for feminist assessments that integrate multiple contextual variables (e.g., ethnicity, gender, class, sexual orientation) that "define women's lives" (p. 53). Beginning EFT with detailed attention to the intertwining and defining social locations of women's lives provides the foundation for a contextually based understanding of their "personal" issues.

## Feminist View of Women's "Symptoms"

The contrast in approaches to assessment and diagnosis between feminist and traditional therapist is rooted in their different views of the "symptoms" women exhibit. Feminist-diversity therapists believe that failure to acknowledge the oppressive societal context in which women live leads many mental health professionals to mislabel and misevaluate women's responses to their environment as pathological. In most instances, feminist therapists do not see these responses as pathological symptoms, but rather as creative strategies for coping with society's oppression of women, and especially with its oppression of women of color. Sturdivant (1980) stated that "Symptoms do not become 'symptoms', until they are labeled so by someone" (p. 117).

Feminist therapists (L. S. Brown, 1994; Franks, 1986; Greenspan 1983; Smith & Siegel, 1985; Sturdivant, 1980; Walker, 1994) reinterpreted women's "symptoms" or behaviors as:

1. *Behaving in accord with traditional female roles* (i.e., women exhibit feminine socialized traits and then are labeled pathological). Oversocialized, overdeveloped traditional female gender-role traits fit into this category (e.g., Dependent Personality Disorder).

2. *Representing role conflict for women.* Women are often forced to choose between their own growth as individuals and their being "appropriate females." Further, women who are members of subordinate groups in a society are often forced to choose between the values of the subordinate group and the often-conflicting values of the dominant group. Both situations generate internal conflict that often surfaces as anxiety. For example, a woman who feels torn between being physically attractive to men and feeling angry about being judged primarily on her physical attractiveness develops a facial tic (Greenspan, 1983). Miriam Greenspan described these responses to being oppressed as "hidden protests" (p. 185), and Sturdivant (1980) referred to them as "survival tactics" (p. 124). Many women do not have enough safety or power to protest directly, and so must often resort to indirect, more passive modes of expressing their anger. Society's pressure to fit women into a limited set of stereotyped roles frequently leads to "symptom" formation in the individual.

3. *Representing a coping strategy for surviving all types of oppression and discrimination.* Sturdivant (1980) viewed women's anger as a healthy response to being oppressed; ". . . pain in response to a bad situation is seen as adaptive, not pathological" (p. 165). Manipulative and passive-aggressive behaviors are two examples of symptoms as coping strategies in an environment that punishes subordinate groups' (e.g., women's) direct use of power.

4. *Reflecting the result/consequence of female socialization.* Greenspan (1983) summarized this socialization factor when she said:

The major ingredient of depression—the feelings of hopelessness, helplessness, worthlessness, futility, and suppressed rage—are the affective components of the objective social condition of female powerlessness in male society. (p. 193)

We believe that her comments apply to all forms of powerlessness in a society.

5. *Representing societal pathological labeling of deviancy from traditional females' gender-typed behaviors.* For instance, women's assertive behavior in many cultural groups is often labeled *aggressive* or they may be called a *bitch*.

These reinterpretations do not represent distinct categories, but rather are overlapping reframes of what have previously been labeled pathological symptoms in women and other subordinated groups. (See Table 5.2 for a summary of EFT reframes of symptoms.) They are also explanations for the differential prevalence rates for women and men in many diagnostic categories. Feminist-diversity therapists believe that women's "symptoms" arise for good reasons and have their etiology in the pathological environment in which women live. Therapists need to help women see the strength and/or health embodied in women's responses to their subordinate status in society. In accordance with EFT principles, these symptoms are relabeled and reframed by EFT therapists as *coping strategies.* Women are empowered by reframing previously labeled *manipulative* or *crazy* responses as ". . . attempts to achieve the goals of control and influence under given social constraints" (Smith & Siegel, 1985, p. 14). In therapy, the underlying goal of a given behavior (symptom) is identified, the strength represented by the behavior is acknowledged, and, if desirable, a behavior that exercises more direct power may be searched for and practiced. (See Chapter 3 for a more detailed description of power

**Table 5.2  Empowerment Feminist Therapy reinterpretations of women's "symptoms"**

Women's "symptoms" are reinterpreted as:

1. Behaving in accord with traditional female roles.
2. Representing role conflict for women.
3. Representing a coping strategy for surviving all types of oppression and discrimination.
4. Reflecting the result/consequence of female socialization.
5. Representing societal pathological labeling of deviancy from traditional female gender-typed behaviors.

analysis.) Further, many feminist therapists avoid using the word *symptom*, substituting words such as *reaction, coping strategy, behavior, sign, indicator.*

## Contextual Assessment of Women's Lives

Therapeutic assessment procedures and diagnostic classifications often ignore the reality of women's lives (Santos de Barona & Dutton, 1997). For example, women are often the victims of domestic violence, rape, and sexual abuse. Many behaviors seen in female clients are the result of the high rates of abuse and violence in women's lives. Other behaviors are the result of the everyday stressors of being gender-role-stereotyped, living in poverty, and living in a society that is racist, heterosexist, and ableist (insidious oppression). EFT therapists move the locus of pathology from the individual to the environment. What appear as individual or intrapersonal factors are viewed as consequences of socialization and institutionalized oppression processes (i.e., women introject external, oppressive messages (L. S. Brown, 1994; Santos de Barona & Dutton, 1994). In most cases, both individual and environmental factors are seen as contributing to clients' problems. However, in EF therapy, it is possible that no individual or internal factors contribute to the problem; there is conceptual room to attribute the entire problem to a pathological environment. This EFT concept is grounded in social psychology research that demonstrates that pathological environments can, in a very short time, produce pathology in normal, psychologically healthy people (P. Zimbardo, personal communication, 1988).

Shifting the label of pathology from the individual (i.e., personality disorder) to external factors empowers the client, as she understands that there is not something innately wrong with her. Her behaviors, viewed in the contextual reality of her life, begin to make sense as reasonable responses to her often-traumatic environment. She gains a new sense of hope. More appropriate treatment interventions can be used. Further, external location of the problem makes clear the need to change environments that have such negative consequences for women. Preventive interventions at the micro- and macrosocietal levels can be identified. Notice that if clients' problems are internally located, as is the case in most of our theoretical orientations, needed changes in the environment are not addressed.

EF therapists are knowledgeable about the events that occur more often to women: rape, sexual abuse, woman battering, job discrimination, and sexual harassment. For example, about one in four women will be raped during her adult life (Lonsway & Fitzgerald, 1994); about one in three female children has been sexually abused (Russell, 1984);

about one in three women will be battered by a male/significant other during her adult life (Koss, Goodman, et al., 1994). Feminist therapists routinely assess for the presence of these events in their clients' lives (Browne, 1993). For example, they ask clients about "unpleasant or unwanted sexual experiences." They are knowledgeable about the effects on individuals of these aversive events and identify relevant client reactions as possible indicators of these experiences because clients may minimize or hide these events from the therapist. In Chapter 9, Rachel was in counseling for three months before she revealed, very reluctantly, the existence of repeated and severe physical battering in her marriage.

## Environmental Assessment Strategies

Since the heart of an EF therapy approach to diagnosis is environmental assessment, new strategies for this assessment are needed. Laura Brown (1987) developed a four-step process for evaluation of the individual's environment. First, the nature of the stressor is determined; is it interpersonal and/or cultural/environmental? Second, the frequency of the experience in the woman's life is calculated. Third, the nature of the consequences (positive, mixed, negative) to the individual from the stressor is identified. Finally, the interaction of developmental stages and tasks with the stressor is conceptualized.

Feminist therapy approaches, generally, and EFT, specifically, have interventions designed to assess environmental contexts. Gender-role analysis is used to assess for gender socialization experiences (in both dominant and subordinate cultures) of the client and on the ways those prescriptions have been internalized. Power analysis with its focus on hierarchial power distributions and differential access to both societal resources and various sources and use of power provides a vehicle for understanding the environmental context and how it restricts the possible responses of women. Further, the social location and identity development level identification interventions described in Chapter 2 are useful environmental assessment strategies (a cultural analysis). In addition, EF therapists need to look for and/or develop contextual assessment strategies. For example, the "Power and Control Wheel," which is popularly used to help individuals identify abusive relationships, is an excellent tool (see Figure 5.2). This wheel was developed by battered women in Duluth, Minnesota, based on their personal experiences—an excellent example of treating women as experts on themselves. In Chapter 4, we identified several Cognitive-Behavioral and Psychodrama interventions that are useful methods for assessing environments.

The need for and use of environmental assessment perspectives and strategies for both feminist and multicultural therapies have implications for clinician training. Typically, assessment courses in most psychology training programs place little or no emphasis on assessments of contexts or cultures. To train culturally competent therapists, we must expand beyond traditional assessment and diagnostic perspectives. Only when we develop, train for the use of, and implement environmental and contextual assessment strategies do we truly move away from an intrapsychic approach to therapy. Further, adequate tools for assessing societal and cultural oppression and toxicity are a crucial element in changing societal institutions.

Once the environmental context of a clients' life has been assessed, the therapist helps the woman to view her behavior in this context. As we indicated earlier, what may have first appeared as dysfunctional responses or "symptoms" may now be seen to be survival strategies for coping with the negative environment.

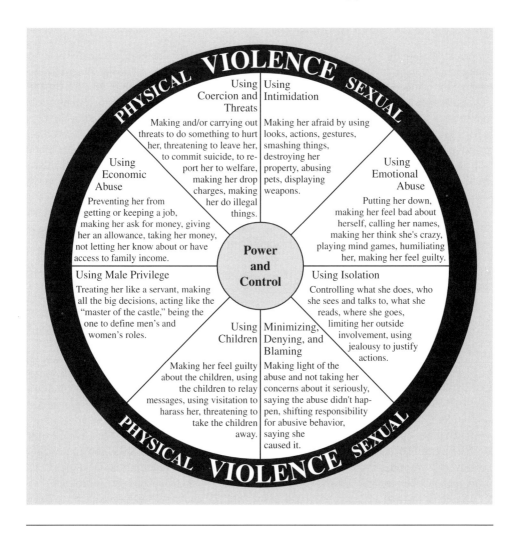

**Figure 5.2    Power and control wheel.** *Source:* **Domestic Abuse Intervention Project, 202 East Superior Street, Duluth, Minnesota 55802, 218-722-2781. Reprinted with permission.**

## A Collaborative Approach to Diagnosis

In most traditional diagnostic approaches, the expert therapist uses psychological tests, history taking, and the clinical interview to arrive at a diagnosis. The client answers the questions without much understanding of the diagnostic process. Feminist and multicultural therapists collaborate with their clients about the assessment process (Ridley et al., 1998; Santos de Barona & Dutton, 1997). If tests or other measures are used, their purpose and nature is explained to the client. If a diagnostic label is to be given, the label and its potential consequences are discussed with the client whenever possible. The therapist also discusses with the client the process used by the therapist to arrive at the diagnosis. Clients share in decisions about how the results will be used.

## To Diagnose or Not to Diagnose

Feminist therapists are divided about the use of diagnostic labels. The use of the *DSM* categories is seen as especially problematic. The realities of the economic marketplace in the United States render it difficult for a mental health provider to obtain third-party reimbursement from the government or private insurance company, or for clients to be reimbursed for their therapy costs if a *DSM* diagnosis is not used. As an alternative to personality disorders, a situational stressor diagnosis like PTSD can be used when appropriate. However, our experience with PTSD has not been free of problems. Clients who have been given a PTSD diagnosis have been later turned down for health insurance, despite our statements that the clients were now recovered. Feminist-diversity therapists find themselves caught between the evils of using a classification system that is sexist and that minimizes the impact of culture or of not having third-party reimbursement. Thus, for many middle- or low-income clients, failure to use a *DSM* diagnosis means that the therapist must either deny them services or provide free services.

## Feminist Approaches to Testing

Some feminist therapists eschew the use of tests in therapy, both because the tests reflect the sexist and racist cultural values and because the use of tests sets up the therapist in yet another expert role. However, some feminist therapists (Koss, Goodman, et al., 1994; Rosewater, 1985a; Walker, 1994) believe that testing can be useful if applied within feminist therapy principles. For example, testing results can be used to normalize and make sense of clients' social location experiences. Rosewater advocated collaboration between client and counselor in the use of test results as well as in the selection of tests. The results of tests are to be shared openly with clients and should be presented in a way that the client can understand. In accordance with treating the client as an expert on herself, she is encouraged to help make sense of the test results. Increasing clients' self-awareness and knowledge about their issues is an important empowerment strategy. Tests can be one valuable source for increasing their knowledge and self-awareness.

Lynne Rosewater (1985a) proposed using tests in nontraditional ways (i.e., to bring about social change). She said that feminist therapists armed with the knowledge of the oppression in women's lives should:

> . . . develop alternative interpretations for widely influential test instruments, interpretations that would be consistent with the philosophic base of feminism. (p. 267)

For example, Rosewater used a woman's Minnesota Multiphasic Personality Inventory (MMPI) profile to substantiate that she was a battered woman, as a defense in her trial for the murder of her abusive husband. In a related vein, standardized tests can be used to research women's issues. Rosewater (1985b) gave the MMPI to battered women, schizophrenic women, and women who had been given a Borderline Personality Disorder diagnosis. This procedure allowed her to develop a differentiated profile for battered women, which can then be used to identify other battered women or to refute misdiagnosis of battered women. Rosewater also identified similarities in the MMPI profiles between schizophrenic and battered women. Thus, she concluded that without additional information, clinicians were likely to misdiagnose the battered women. She emphasized the importance of therapists attaining thorough client histories that inquire about the violence in women's lives. Battering must be considered before diagnosing a woman as schizophrenic.

EF therapists emphasize the use of bias-free tests. They analyze tests for their biased components and, based on their findings, either modify the test by deleting or revising items or discontinue its use. EF therapists also use nonstandardized strategies for assessment, such as having clients self-monitor their own or others' behaviors. They use nonsexist assessment strategies like the Nonsexist Vocational Card Sort (Dewey, 1974).

## Collaborative Assessment Strategies

EF therapists emphasize assessment strategies that focus on collaboration between the therapist and client and that empower the client. As discussed in the Cognitive-behavioral section of Chapter 4, self-monitoring of behaviors, thoughts, and feelings and functional analysis can increase a client's self- and situational awareness, as well as expand the therapist's knowledge of the client and her life situation. Further, a client's continuous or periodic self-assessment and self-monitoring allows her to evaluate the effectiveness of her own therapy.

## Assessing for Women's Strengths and Positive Outcomes

Most therapeutic approaches, especially those driven by use of the *DSM* and medical models, focus primarily on symptom reduction (e.g., helping the client become less depressed or anxious). Feminist therapists have historically challenged this limited view of desired therapeutic outcomes and have pointed out the importance of assessing for both women's strengths and for the positive outcomes of therapy (e.g., empowerment). Recently, Martin Seligman (1998) focused the attention of the entire psychological community on a "positive psychology," which de-emphasizes pathology and emphasizes well-being, compassion, and thriving. Further, research has documented that individuals, especially trauma survivors, may evidence positive therapeutic outcomes and continuing symptomatology at the same time (Calhoun & Tedeschi, 1998; Zollicoffer, 1989). Thus, from several perspectives, assessment of positive therapeutic outcomes and client strengths is important and is highly compatible with EFT.

In this chapter and book, we have constantly emphasized the importance of assessing for clients' strengths, especially those skills they have used to cope with negative, oppressive, and/or traumatic environments. The concept of resiliency embodies this notion of strength and effective coping skills in the face of adversity (D. M. Johnson, 2001). We partially agree with Schissel's (1993) and Barnard's (1994) concepts of resiliency as the capacity to withstand the negative impacts of oppressive and traumatic life events. However, we also believe individuals can be strengthened by and find positive meaning from overcoming these negative events. Dawn Johnson asserted that "empowerment can be seen as giving women the skills to become more resilient . . ." (p. 58). Thus, she identified empowerment as a key factor in resiliency.

In our choice of the label *Empowerment Feminist Therapy* for our therapeutic approach, we strove to incorporate/embody the essence of what we want to achieve in counseling with women. Our goal is to help clients access internal and external resources to accomplish both internal/personal and external/societal change. Obviously, this goal aims far beyond symptom reduction. We believe that complete and thorough assessment at the beginning of counseling should include identifying client "survival" strengths.

Therapist awareness of clients' coping and thriving skills balances the usual symptom, deficit approach to assessment and gives the therapist a stronger foundation for trusting the client as an expert on self and for a collaborative therapeutic approach. Assessment of oppression, compassion, well-being, positive affect, resiliency, effective coping skills, and progression in identity development levels at the beginning and end of therapy results in documenting feminist therapy goals that are not adequately reflected with a focus on symptom reduction.

Instruments are needed to evaluate the positive outcomes of feminist therapy. Laying a foundation for measuring the positive impact of EFT, Judith Worell (1993b) developed ten outcome domains consistent with the four principles of EFT. (See Chapter 10 for a more detailed description of her outcomes.) Worell and Redonna Chandler (1996, 1999) created the Personal Progress Scale-Revised (PPS-R), which has items designed to measure these ten outcome domains and the four EFT principles, that is, the multiple dimensions of empowerment. The PPS-R is a promising instrument for measuring the positive outcomes of EFT and the multiple strengths that women possess. (You may take the PPS-R at the end of this chapter; we will further describe the PPS-R in Chapter 10).

## SUMMARY

We believe that feminist approaches to assessment and diagnosis are still in their infancy. Feminist therapists generally agree that bias enters into most traditional approaches to diagnosis and testing and that these factors must be eliminated from our assessment of clients. Beyond this basic agreement, feminist therapists have divergent approaches to assessment, falling along a continuum from avoidance of formal diagnostic and testing procedures at one end to the development of alternative methods for diagnosis and testing at the other. Our common goals are to develop and use assessment and diagnostic procedures that highlight the impact of sexism and oppression in women's lives, that reveal women's strengths and personal resources, that make our reality visible to ourselves and others, and that validate our experiences.

## ACTIVITY

### Personal-Social Identity Time Line

The purpose of this exercise is to increase participants' awareness of their experiences (both personal and social components) with oppression and privilege. These experiences are identified in a developmental lifeline format so that individuals can be more aware of the cumulative effects of these related experiences.

*Step 1*

Choose a personal location or identity to explore (e.g., gender, ethnicity, sexual orientation, class). (You may repeat this exercise multiple times with several of your identities.)

*Step 2*

Identify the events, experiences, and/or scenes in your life related to this location and label them on the developmental time line.

| Birth | 10 yrs. | 20 yrs. | 30 yrs. | 40 yrs. | 50 yrs. | 60 yrs. | 70 yrs. |
|-------|---------|---------|---------|---------|---------|---------|---------|

*Step 3*

Above the line and event label, list the feelings and thoughts elicited by each event.

*Step 4*

Below the line, briefly describe the societal context related to each event.

*Step 5*

What did you learn about your social location by completing your time line?

What events stood out most? What decisions or conclusions did you make as a result of these experiences?

As a result of completing this time line, do you believe that each of your social location is a seat of oppression or privilege? Why?

## Exercise Variations

1. Share one or more of your events with a partner or significant other.

2. A group can decide to simultaneously explore a particular location relevant to the whole group (e.g., gender, ethnicity). Compare events, feelings, thoughts, and societal contexts for everyone's time lines (in most groups, there will be members occupying seats of privilege and oppression related to the common location being explored).

## PERSONAL PROGRESS SCALE REVISED (WORELL & CHANDLER, 1999)

The following statements identify feelings or experiences that some people use to describe themselves. *Please answer each question in terms of any aspects of your personal identity that are important to you as a woman,* such as gender, race, ethnicity, culture, nationality, sexual orientation, family background. Write your answers in the space to the left of each question using the scale. For example, for the statement "I have equal relationships . . .", you would write 1 if this is almost never true of you now, 7 if this is true of you almost all the time, and 2 through 6 if the statement is usually not true, sometimes true, or frequently true for you in your life now. There are no right or wrong answers.

| Almost Never | | | Sometimes True | | | Almost Always |
|---|---|---|---|---|---|---|
| 1 | 2 | 3 | 4 | 5 | 6 | 7 |

_____ 1. I have equal relationships with important others in my life.

_____ 2. It is important to me to be financially independent.

_____ **3. It is difficult for me to be assertive with others when I need to be.**

_____ 4. I can speak up for my needs instead of always taking care of other people's needs.

_____ 5. I feel prepared to deal with the discrimination I experience in today's society.

_____ **6. It is difficult for me to recognize when I am angry.**

_____ **7. I believe that women like me have equal opportunities with other women and with men in today's world.**

*(continued)*

| Almost Never | | | Sometimes True | | | Almost Always | |
|---|---|---|---|---|---|---|---|
| 1 | 2 | 3 | 4 | 5 | | 6 | 7 |

_____ 8. I feel comfortable in confronting my instructor/counselor/supervisor when we see things differently.

_____ 9. I now understand how my cultural heritage has shaped who I am today.

_____ **10. I give into others so as not to displease or anger them.**

_____ **11. I don't feel good about myself as a woman.**

_____ 12. I have a great deal of respect for other women.

_____ **13. When others criticize me, I do not trust myself to decide if they are right or if I should ignore their comments.**

_____ 14. I realize that given my current situation, I am coping the best I can.

_____ 15. I am feeling in control of my life.

_____ **16. In defining for myself what it means for me to be attractive, I depend on the opinions of others.**

_____ 17. I believe that some of my problems are due to the sexism, racism, and/or homophobia in today's society.

_____ **18. I can't seem to make good decisions about my life.**

_____ **19. I have only myself to blame for my problems.**

_____ 20. I am aware of how I was socialized in my culture to do things just because I am a woman.

_____ 21. I believe that many of my problems are similar to those of other women like me.

_____ **22. I do not feel competent to handle the situations that arise in my everyday life.**

_____ 23. I am determined to become a fully functioning person.

_____ **24. I do not believe there is anything I can do to make things better for women like me in today's society.**

_____ 25. I recognize that some of my problems are a result of living in a society that does not value women like me.

_____ 26. I believe that a woman like me can succeed in any job or career that she chooses.

_____ **27. When making decisions about my life, I do not trust my own experience.**

_____ **28. It is difficult for me to tell others when I feel angry.**

_____ 29. I am able to satisfy my own sexual needs in a relationship.

_____ **30. It is difficult for me to be good to myself.**

_____ **31. It is hard for me to ask for help or support from others when I need it.**

_____ 32. I want to help other women like me improve the quality of their lives.

_____ **33. I feel uncomfortable in confronting important others in my life when we see things differently.**

_____ 34. I want to feel more appreciated for my cultural background.

_____ 35. I am aware of my own strengths as a woman.

_Note:_ Items in boldface type are reverse coded.

## FURTHER READINGS

Becker, D. (2001). Diagnosis of psychological disorders: *DSM* and gender. In J. Worell (Ed.), *Encyclopedia of women and gender: Sex similarities, differences, and the impact of society on gender.* San Diego: Academic Press.

Lopez, S. R., & Guarnaccia, P. J. J. (2000). Cultural psychopathology: Uncovering the social world of mental illness. *Annual review of psychology: Volume 51.* Palo Alto: Annual Reviews.

Ridley, C. R., Li, L. C., & Hill, C. L. (1998). Multicultural assessment: Reexamination, reconceptualization, and practical application. *Counseling Psychologist, 26,* 827–910.

Santos de Barona, M., & Dutton, M. A. (1997). Feminist perspectives on assessment. In J. Worell & N. G. Johnson (Eds.), *Shaping the future of feminist psychology: Education, research, and practice.* Washington, DC: American Psychological Association.

# PART 2

# LIFE SPAN ISSUES IN COUNSELING WOMEN

The issues that women bring to counseling are not easily classified into discrete categories. A presenting problem that appears to be the most salient at the time of initial contact with you may be revised, expanded, or ignored completely as therapy progresses. Some clients may be overwhelmed by emotional reactions that appear to be beyond their control, such as periods of intense anxiety, panic attacks, or unexplainable feelings of sadness and hopelessness. The internal and external sources of these reactions may become clear only after careful assessment and exploration of the client's personal and social identity, her life circumstances, and her perception of them.

Other clients may present a clear set of issues that they wish to address: I want to lose weight, change my job, find a satisfying career, reconsider my marriage, keep my husband from getting angry, find a life partner, deal with my mastectomy, decide whether to have a child, confront my rape, reduce my loneliness, get along better with my mother, or other issues. One client may focus on a single issue, while another may detail a list of problems that complicate her life. Whatever the presenting problems may be, clients experience a range of reactions that signal personal distress. In the process of assessment, you observe your clients' verbal and nonverbal communications of their affective states, their beliefs and attributions for their dilemmas, and the actions they have considered or attempted in their efforts to cope with their stress. You also view your clients from the perspective of their relevant history and social locations, their families, and their supportive communities. The sum of this information represents the client and her issues at any given time, and each may become a target for therapeutic inquiry and intervention within the context of each woman's unique life situation.

In Part 2, we consider a selected sample of the issues that bring a diverse population of women to counseling. Chapter 6 on depression explores one of the most frequent referrals for personal distress. The succeeding chapters explore more specific concerns that women bring to counseling, career decision making, sexual assault, and partner abuse. Each chapter defines the client population and the issues to be addressed, and summarizes the socialization, situational, cultural, and societal factors that may contribute to each client's personal distress. All four of the clients we consider are members of nondominant or minority social groups. These clients are not representative of their respective groups, but their clinical issues are relevant to the ethnic or cultural frames that structure their perceptions and worldviews, and that may influence the process and outcomes of our interventions.

The therapists for each client are trained and experienced with Empowerment Feminist Therapy (EFT), reflecting both EFT values and worldviews, as well as the use of representative strategies and techniques. Each therapist finds, as you will also, that her own life experiences, her personal values and biases, and her relevant social locations may influence the ways in which she responds and interacts with individual clients. The extent that therapists are aware and acknowledge these personal values to both self and client may structure the information that each chooses to self-disclose. Therapist self-awareness can also have a direct impact on client involvement and satisfaction with therapy, and on the progress and outcomes of intervention. Through the presentation of each client's personal story, the following chapters suggest how the feminist therapist works in the context of a target issue to apply the principles of EFT.

# Chapter 6 ─────────────────────────────────

# *DEALING WITH DEPRESSION*

*I feel dissatisfied with myself because I should be able to accomplish all the things people are supposed to be able to do these days. . . .*

Sylvia

## SELF-ASSESSMENT: BELIEFS AND FACTS ABOUT DEPRESSION

Fact and theory about the incidence, etiology, and treatment of depression suggest divergent and sometimes conflicting interventions. The following statements represent both fact and theory. For each statement, check the answer that best represents your belief, understanding, or knowledge about the broad range of reactions that indicate depression.

|  | Agree | Uncertain | Disagree |
|---|---|---|---|
| 1. Depression is caused by faulty thinking. | _____ | _____ | _____ |
| 2. Depressed persons overgeneralize about life's problems. | _____ | _____ | _____ |
| 3. Depression is really anger turned inward. | _____ | _____ | _____ |
| 4. Treatment of depression requires release of pent-up anger and rage. | _____ | _____ | _____ |
| 5. Depression is best treated by methods that alleviate the symptoms. | _____ | _____ | _____ |
| 6. Depressed people distort reality. | _____ | _____ | _____ |
| 7. The "empty nest" syndrome is a major cause of depression in older women. | _____ | _____ | _____ |
| 8. Depressive reactions are equally common in women and men. | _____ | _____ | _____ |

*(continued)*

|  | Agree | Uncertain | Disagree |
|---|---|---|---|
| 9. Postpartum depression seldom lasts beyond a few weeks. | ———— | ———— | ———— |
| 10. Depressed women tend to blame others rather than themselves for their problems. | ———— | ———— | ———— |
| 11. Depression is a biological and genetically based disease that is best treated with pharmacotherapy. | ———— | ———— | ———— |
| 12. Depression is frequently related to marital or relationship distress. | ———— | ———— | ———— |
| 13. Signs of depression may differ across diverse ethnocultural groups. | ———— | ———— | ———— |
| 14. Depressive moods in women are highly related to hormonal changes. | ———— | ———— | ———— |
| 15. A history of physical or sexual assault predicts subsequent depression. | ———— | ———— | ———— |

## Scoring

Statements 1 through 6 concern theory, and your answers may reflect your personal beliefs. The remaining items are statements of fact: 9, 12, 13, and 15 are true; 7, 8, 10, 11, and 14 are false. Use these statements to assess the accuracy of your store of knowledge about depression. Further discussion of these statements is found throughout the chapter.

## OVERVIEW

Regardless of the specific issues that women bring to counseling, many of your clients are likely to show evidence of depression and anxiety. The indices of emotional distress may differ across individual clients as well as between clients of diverse ethnic or cultural groups. We believe that interventions for presenting concerns should focus on helping clients to: (a) define and explore issues of concern to the client; (b) identify pertinent personal and social identities; (c) collaboratively set goals for therapeutic change; (d) examine relevant family, ethnocultural, gender role, societal, and personal factors; (e) formulate and initiate practical solutions to current life problems; and (f) plan for long-term maintenance of healthy behaviors. For many clients, you will also intervene to reduce intense emotional discomfort and debilitating patterns of cognition and behavior that interfere with effective functioning and personal well-being.

We consider the development of depressive reactions of women in the context of a case presentation of Sylvia. We first review some data on incidence of depression and definitions that clarify the range of feelings, beliefs, and behaviors that accompany a diagnosis of unipolar depression. We then discuss some of the factors that have been advanced to explain the disproportionate incidence of depressive reactions in women, including biological, societal, and gender-role socialization. The theories we use to conceptualize Sylvia's depressive episodes are related to the external factors of societal racism and sexism that produce ambiguous and aversive environments for women. We also consider gender-role socialization that encouraged Sylvia's self-silencing, self-blame, and feelings of psychological entrapment. Intervention strategies for Sylvia included ethnocultural analysis, gender-role and power analysis, assertiveness coaching, cognitive restructuring, reattribution training, relaxation skills, stress inoculation, problem solving, community connections, and behavioral activation through increasing pleasant activities.

After reading Chapter 6, you will be able to:

- Describe biological, societal, cultural, and gender-role explanations for women's depressive reactions.
- Provide support and critiques for each of the variables hypothesized to precede or accompany women's depressive reactions.
- Suggest ways in which each of the four principles of Empowerment Feminist Therapy (EFT) can be used to facilitate intervention with women's depressive reactions.

## SYLVIA'S STORY: HOPELESSNESS AND RESIGNATION

Sylvia, a 35-year-old African American woman, entered her first counseling session by stating that she probably did not belong here and was "pretty sure" we could not help her. She had been referred to therapy by her family physician, who believed that her reports of headaches, exhaustion, sleeplessness, and lack of appetite might be related to psychological rather than medical factors. Sylvia agreed to consult with a therapist, stating that she did not know what else to do. She spent most of the first session in counseling weeping uncontrollably. "I can't figure out what's the matter with me. I am tired all the time, and I cry a lot for no good reason; I can't seem to control it." In addition to periods of crying, Sylvia also reported difficulty in sleeping, patterns of wakefulness at 3:00 and 4:00 a.m., loss of appetite and consequent weight loss, and disinterest in sexual activity with her husband. She reported feeling exhausted after work, difficulty in concentrating on her work, fear of making errors (she was an accountant in a midsize firm), and periods of anxiety and crying at work. "Besides being tired all the time, it seems that my life just isn't going anywhere," she explained. "I'm not performing well at work and was passed up for promotion this year. They just don't seem to like me or my work. I supervise a younger guy and they promoted him over me. If that isn't the pits. And can you believe, he's the company Don Juan; he comes on to all the women at work. Maybe I am in the wrong profession. It feels like I can't do anything right."

In discussing her marriage with Clarence, Sylvia appeared resigned. "That's not working out either. I can't seem to please him or his family. He thinks I work too much and his mother and sister think so, too. And he's really not interested in my work or the problems that I have there. I can't find any way to keep this relationship alive; I feel like I'm alone all the time, even when we're together." In summing up her present life, Sylvia sighed despondently, "Nothing's coming together in my life; I just feel like a total failure. What's the use of going on? I can't find ways to make things better . . . Lord knows I've tried. He wants children, too, and his mom is always asking me about that . . . 'Sylvia, when are you going to start a family?' But I'm afraid I wouldn't even make a good mother. I guess I've waited too long, I'm almost 36, probably too old anyway. He's right, it wasn't good planning on my part to put all my energies into my career before starting a family. Now I've made a mess of my career and family life, too. I used to think I was smart, but I guess I've never been much of a success at anything . . . I don't know where to go from here."

## Assessment

Sylvia's initial presenting behaviors signaled to her therapist, Ellen, that she was considerably depressed and somewhat anxious. She also appeared suspicious of the counseling situation and reluctant to becoming engaged, possibly as a reaction to having a White therapist. However, Sylvia agreed to remain for an initial assessment and feedback. Ellen was a seasoned EFT and Cognitive-Behavioral practitioner with considerable experience with clients who were different from herself in age (48), ethnicity (Caucasian), religion (Catholic), and sexual orientation (heterosexual). Mindful of the cross-cultural context, Ellen attended to the goals for culturally informed behavioral assessment suggested by Tanaka-Matsumi, Seiden, and Lam (1996). These goals include (a) raising cultural issues at an early stage to indicate respect for the client's culture, (b) being sensitive to the particular norms for women's roles in the client's community, and (c) attending to client expectations regarding intervention. Ellen applied the Personal/Social Identity Scale (see Chapter 2) during the assessment phase to determine the level of Sylvia's gender and ethnocultural identity development. Her pattern of responses suggested that she was at Level 1 (Preawareness) on both dimensions. Ellen also used the Revised Personal Progress Scale (PPS-R; Worell & Chandler, 1999) to assess Sylvia's strengths and level of perceived personal empowerment. Again, Sylvia's responses reflected feelings of incompetence, self-blame, and an unwillingness to identify external sources as relevant to her personal experiences of stress.

The assessment interview also covered present concerns, history of previous episodes similar to this one, and family history of depression (there were none). Ellen asked about recent experiences of relationship termination or loss and continuing stressors such as financial problems, physical concerns, or care of elderly or disabled family members. She also screened for suicide risk and for evidence of present or previous physical and sexual abuse. Sylvia was invited to raise these issues at a later time if she felt uncomfortable addressing them at the outset of counseling. Ellen asked about substance use, both past and present, and obtained an inventory of medication. Sylvia had been taking an antidepressant and medication for hypertension, prescribed by her family physician, for about six months. She withdrew from both medications recently, saying that they gave her uncomfortable side effects, did not seem to help, and she feared becoming "drug-dependent."

Sylvia's responses to the Beck Depression Inventory (BDI-II; Beck, Steer, & Brown, 1996) revealed a pattern of negative self-worth, hopelessness, and somatic disturbances. Her elevated score was consistent with a diagnosis of moderately severe depression. Because she expressed feelings of isolation and loneliness, Ellen used the Young Loneliness Inventory (Young, 1982) to assess for more specific areas of distress. Her high score suggested that she felt isolated and without intimate supportive relationships in her current life. Ellen also administered the Silencing the Self Scale (Jack, 1991) to help uncover her apparent unwillingness (and possibly her unvoiced anger) to assert her needs in her important work and home relationships. The excerpt at the beginning of this chapter is Sylvia's endorsement of one of the items on this scale. Her pattern of responses was consistent with women diagnosed with varying signs of depression (Carr, Gilroy, &

Sherman, 1996). Finally, since anxiety and unipolar depression often coexist (Mineka, Watson, & Clark, 1998), Ellen assessed her level of anxiety on the State-Trait Anxiety Scale (Spielberger, Gorsuch, & Luchins, 1970). Her score was elevated but within the normal range.

Ellen then examined the range of Sylvia's attributions (perceived reasons and causes) for the present episode and fully explored her current life circumstances, especially those relating to family and work. She revealed that she and her husband Clarence lived in the town where his family lived and where he worked, which was 30 miles away from her job. This living arrangement required long hours of commuting for her and provided little time for friends or leisure activities. Her husband also expected her to be responsible for household management and meal preparation, providing additional stressors in her daily schedule. In response to questions about her husband's potential involvement in couples' counseling, she indicated that he had previously refused her efforts to engage him in relationship counseling, and that it was "useless" to attempt to gain his cooperation. Ellen sent her home after the initial session with a mood/situation rating sheet (see Table 6.1) and asked her to gather data at periodic intervals each day, relating her thoughts and feelings to current situational events, both positive and negative. The purpose of this assessment was to help both Sylvia and the therapist understand the situational (what was happening) and cognitive (automatic thoughts and self-talk) correlates of her dysphoric moods. Ellen also hoped that by asking her to record pleasant as well as unpleasant events, she might gain some understanding of the direction of her attention and thought patterns.

## Impression

Sylvia's story is not very different from that of many other women. Faced with stressful situations at both home and work, she attributed her "failures" to her own lack of competence in both domains. However, Ellen noted Sylvia's relatively fair, coffee-color skin, fashionable attire, and carefully straightened and styled hair. These observations suggested to Ellen that cultural and gender factors related to being an African American woman functioning in a corporate organizational structure might be important to address in counseling. An additional challenge for Ellen was her assessment of Sylvia's identity for both gender and ethnicity at the Preawareness levels. Although Sylvia acknowledged that discrimination is a fact of life for Black women in the United States, she denied that it applied to her. That is, by minimizing personal discrimination due to either of these identities, Sylvia was averting the stress produced by discrimination and protecting her self-esteem by maintaining her sense of control (K. R. King, 1998). Ellen surmised that Sylvia's attempts to follow traditional scripts for the "good wife" in her culture, and both the dominant and her own cultural scripts for the "successful career woman" had left her with demands from herself and others that she perceived to be beyond her ability to accomplish. Her depressive symptoms mirrored her experiences of helplessness in the face of seemingly unsolvable problems and hopelessness in believing that she could solve her present problems to her own satisfaction and meet the expectations of her husband and family at home and her supervisor at work. In both situations, she voiced responsibility and blame for her predicament and believed that others were justified in letting her know that she was not doing her job. And, like many other working women, Sylvia did not look beyond herself to consider the inequities in resources and power balance in both her home and employment settings that contributed to her feelings of incompetence

**Table 6.1  Sylvia's mood-situation rating form**

*Directions:* Describe your moods when you are feeling especially high or low, happy or sad, anxious, and so on, and rate them on a scale from 1 to 100 (least to most). Note what was happening, what you were thinking or telling yourself, then what you actually did.

| Day/Time | Situation | I Felt (Rate 1–100) | I Thought | I Did |
|---|---|---|---|---|
| Thursday 8:00 A.M. | Clarence complained about breakfast being cold. | Clutch in my gut, fear, anxiety? (60) | I can't do it all. | Told him I would cook him a hot one tomorrow. |
| 11:45 A.M. | Steve said he was going to a long lunch and if I would cover his Exigen account calls for him, he'd sure appreciate it. | Trapped into doing his work again, helpless, resentful. (80) | He's always doing this to me; he thinks I'm his secretary or something. | Covered his calls. |
| 2:45 P.M. | Steve came back, patted and hugged me, told me what a great trooper I was. | Confused (90), angry (75), maybe a little pleased. (20) (Rated later in session when she was better able to sort out her reactions.) | Well, at least he said something nice, but why should I want to please him? I'm all confused. | Smiled at him and said I was glad to help out. |
| 4:30 P.M. | Sitting at my desk, not doing anything useful. | Depressed, discouraged, feeling teary. (85) | I'm a mess, I can't think any more, I can't finish my own work, I always let him do a number on me—what a jerk I am. | Tried to work on my own accounts but couldn't keep my mind on work. Took it all home to do at night. |
| 8:00 P.M. | Finishing up dishes and Clarence says his mom and sister are coming over. | Clutch in my gut— resentment, fear. (90) | I don't want to talk to them, I can't do my work, I can't do it all, I guess I'll have to stay up late. What a mess. | Talked to his mom and sister, stayed up late to finish accounts, didn't even answer Clarence when he said goodnight. |

150

**Table 6.2   *DSM-IV* criteria for major depression**

1. Depressed mood: sad, tearful.
2. Loss of interest or pleasure in daily activities.
3. Loss or gain in appetite, significant weight loss or gain.
4. Difficulty in sleeping or night wakefulness.
5. Psychomotor agitation or retardation.
6. Fatigue or loss of energy.
7. Feelings of worthlessness or guilt, self-blame.
8. Difficulty in concentration, indecisiveness.
9. Recurrent thoughts of death or suicide.

*Source:* American Psychiatric Association, 1994, *Diagnostic and Statistical Manual of Mental Disorders* (4th ed.). Washington, DC.

and despair (Crosby, 1982). Throughout the assessment interview, Sylvia made no spontaneous mention of her strengths or of the pleasures in her life.

The combination of concerns voiced by Sylvia suggested a diagnosis of Major Depression, as defined by five or more criteria on the *Diagnostic and Statistical Manual of Mental Disorders, 4th Edition (DSM-IV)* and displayed in Table 6.2. This decision leads to considering intervention plans for Sylvia within the context of the extensive research literature on Cognitive-Behavioral approaches to treatment of depression. Ellen also considered Sylvia's situation from an EFT position, and she explored with her how the ethnic and cultural disparities between them might be important to consider as they worked together. In this context, Ellen then moved to discuss the dimensions of personal and social identity, which placed Sylvia at Level 1, Preawareness, on both ethnicity and gender (see Chapter 2). Sylvia believed that with hard work and "appropriate" behavior, she could achieve anything she set her mind to accomplish. But when her hard work did not result in reaching all of her goals, her response was self-blame and resignation.

During her counseling sessions, Ellen challenged this assumption of meritocracy in the light of further revelations about Sylvia's work situation. Ellen also explored with her how the context of her life situation; her cultural and gender-based socialization and self-expectations; the apparent bias and harassment in her work setting; the lack of parity in her marriage; her isolation from community, intimacy, and emotional support; and her habitual methods of responding and coping have contributed to her present state. In the context of these multiple issues, we consider how Sylvia helped herself to a new freedom through a reconstruction of her situation and a series of decisions that effected changes both in herself and in her interactions with others.

## DEPRESSION IN WOMEN

To view Sylvia's concerns in a broader context, we consider depression in terms of its incidence, the contributing factors, definitions, and some of the factors that research suggests contribute to its onset and persistence. We all experience transitory periods of sadness and feeling down, but normal depressive episodes tend to disappear and are seldom accompanied by prolonged disturbances in daily functioning.

## Incidence

Signs of depression are common in any clinical caseload. In contrast to occasional periods of feeling blue, more serious and persistent dysphoric reactions signal the need for effective clinical intervention. It is estimated that in the United States, more than 17 million persons suffer annually from serious depression. Prior to adolescence, girls and boys are equally vulnerable, but depression rates increase for girls in early adolescence. By the late teens, twice as many girls as boys are diagnosed with unipolar depression (Nolen-Hoeksema & Girgus, 1994). Across all studies of sex ratios in the epidemiology of depression, covering respondents from clinical settings as well as from nonclinical community surveys, women outnumber men by more than two to one. This female-male ratio varies by age, marital status, ethnicity, and nationality, but the gender difference remains significant across all groups. Divorced and widowed women have higher rates of depression than married women, who in turn have higher rates than never-married women. A history of depression is predictive of repeated depressed episodes. For women, repeated depression tends to be triggered by a variety of stressful and adverse life events such as relationship loss, sexual and physical violence, poverty, inequality, and overt discrimination (American Psychological Association, 2001; Whiffen, 2001).

## Definitions

Clinicians should be aware of *DSM-IV* criteria for the diagnosis of depression (see Table 6.2), as well as cutoff scores on major instruments for screening clients, such as the Beck Depression Inventory (BDI) and other similar measures. From an empirical approach, factor analytic studies of depressive signs reveal six major factors (Lewinsohn, Antonuccio, Steinmetz, & Teri, 1984). These factors, incorporating affective, cognitive, somatic, and behavioral manifestations of depression, include the following:

1. Dysphoric mood: Feeling sad, unhappy, helpless, hopeless, worthless, and incompetent. The future appears gloomy and unlikely to improve.
2. Reduced rates of behavior: Low activity level, inefficiency, inability to complete tasks, difficulties in concentration. Daily activities become effortful and are no longer pleasurable.
3. Conflicted interpersonal behavior: Marital and relationship distress and dissatisfaction, loneliness, social anxiety, and withdrawal.
4. Guilt: Being a burden to others, unable to perform responsibilities to family and work, self-deprecation, self-blame.
5. Material burden: Focus on external circumstances, financial problems, excessive demands by others.
6. Somatic complaints: Poor appetite, weight loss, sleep disturbances (too much or too little), headaches, fatigue, and loss of energy.

In addition to these indicators of depression, we screen for suicidal ideation. Depressed women are considerably more vulnerable than other client types to attempted or completed suicides, and this risk factor should be considered in treating a client with more than two of the six syndromes. It seems clear that *depression* is a broad label to cover a group of related signals of personal distress and dysfunctional response patterns.

Although no client is likely to manifest every response pattern, Sylvia displayed some indications of all the depression factors in her presenting problems.

## ISSUES IN WOMEN'S DEPRESSION

Aside from standard criteria for diagnosing depression in your clients, a major concern is to understand the disproportionate prevalence rates for women. The literature on depression is probably more extensive than on any other clinical syndrome at the present time, but questions concerning the disproportionate rate of women's depression were neglected until recently (American Psychological Association, 2002; Nolen-Hoeksema & Jackson, 2001). We consider three major factors related to women's depression: biological, societal, and gender-role socialization. Because depression is conceptualized here as a complex response pattern with cognitive, affective, behavioral, and somatic attributes, we anticipate that for any individual, several factors may be implicated in its development and maintenance. See Figure 6.1 for a range of potential factors.

### Biological Factors

Biological hypotheses about women's depressive episodes embrace both genetics and endocrinology. The genetic hypothesis proposes that depression is sex-linked and transmitted disproportionately to women. Although vulnerability to depression occurs in families, rates are equally distributed between women and men in first-generation relatives (Weissman, 1980). Thus, depression-proneness appears to be inherited equally by women and men.

Hormonal factors related to levels of estrogen and progesterone are implicated in studies on adolescent, premenstrual, and postpartum depression. Adolescent depression rates are inconsistently related to hormonal balance. However, girls who enter menarche at an early age are more vulnerable to depression as well as anxiety, eating disorders, and substance abuse (Graber, Lewinsohn, Seeley, & Brooks-Gunn, 1997). These changes in well-being appear related to dissatisfaction with body image rather than to raging hormones. For some adult women, both menstruation and childbirth are associated with an increase in vulnerability to depressive reactions. However, both situations are characterized by complex changes and are more likely to be associated with depression for women who have experienced previous depressive episodes.

### Premenstrual Depression

Periods of mild depression prior to menstruation may be influenced by increased body fatigue and bloating due to water retention, as well as to discomfort induced by intrauterine "cramps." In most cultures, women have been socialized to view the menstrual cycle with negative expectations, and women's attitudes toward menstruation have been shown to influence both its impact and its reported frequency (Reame, 2001). The slight increase in self-reported depression associated with the menstrual cycle is insufficient to account for women's twofold depression rates. For the small percentage of women who experience more functional premenstrual impairment, medication during the luteal phase may provide sufficient relief (American Psychological Association, 2001). In our view, the stigma associated with a psychiatric diagnosis of Premenstrual Menstrual Dysphoric Disorder (PMMD) should preclude the use of this diagnosis in EFT.

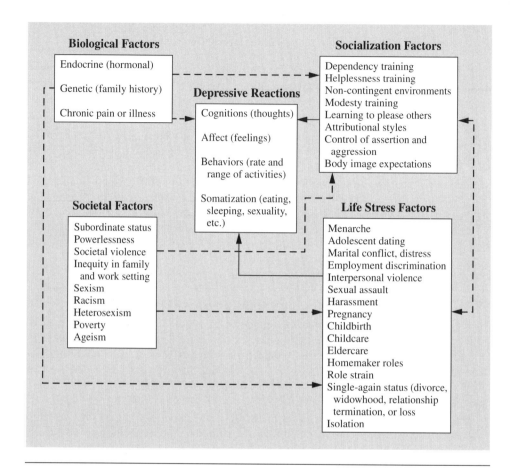

**Figure 6.1   Contributions to women's depression.** The multiple factors that may contribute to women's depression are divided here into categories that interact and overlap. Not all variables are discussed in text. The heavy lines indicate direct influences on depressive reactions. The dashed lines indicate influences that contribute to vulnerability and/or stress.

## Pre- and Postpartum Depression

During pregnancy and following childbirth, women commonly experience transitory depressive moods or "maternity blues" (O'Hara, 1989). Although hormonal factors may be implicated, we know that role transitions are also involved. Continued postpartum depression is inversely related to spousal support and is magnified by lack of sleep, stresses of new motherhood, household responsibilities, and marital strain. Women who remain depressed after several weeks postpartum, however, have been found to be depressed prior to childbirth (Whiffen, 2001). The risk of psychotic reactions also increases for women in the first three months following childbirth, but these severe reactions usually require hospitalization. The effects of continued depression on parenting may be profound, and treatment of both pre- and postpartum depression is important when it is prolonged and impairs effective personal and family functioning. The lack of evidence for hormones as a causal factor, however, suggests that EFT may be as effective as medical intervention for most women.

## Menopause

Finally, depression associated with menopause has not been supported by recent research. Individual reactions in midlife may be related to psychosocial changes such as divorce, widowhood, death of close friends and family members, and departure of children from the home. The term *menopause* was not in existence until the late nineteenth century. The meanings associated with the biological cessation of the childbearing years are likewise socially constructed, with diverse cultures assigning different meanings to its onset. In many cultures, freedom from menstruation, pregnancy, and child care signal a new liberty for women that is to be celebrated rather than mourned. Although hormone replacement therapy is commonly used to treat certain physical changes, it has not been effective in treating major depression (Sommer, 2001).

## Biological Factors: Conclusions

Although biological factors may well influence some mood fluctuations, these reactions tend to be mild and transitory. It is doubtful that these factors are responsible for the two-to-one discrepancy in rates of depression for women. The fact that more than 70% of the prescriptions for psychotropic drugs are written for women may reflect medical assumptions about the biological bases of women's depression and anxiety reactions (McBride, 1987). Indeed, we saw that Sylvia had been prescribed an antidepressant by her physician, with little ameliorative effect. We do not reject the short-term use of psychotropic intervention for depression, but suggest that it be administered and monitored carefully and in the context of psychological treatment that assists clients in confronting the life challenges associated with the depressive episodes. Both clinicians and clients should be aware that research comparing antidepressants to Cognitive-Behavioral psychotherapy for severe depression has failed to find a consistent advantage for either (DeRubeis, 1999; Jacobson & Hollon, 1996).

Although biological variables may interact with situational stressors in the etiology of depression, we found no evidence of a biological contribution to Sylvia's current state. Instead, we turn to psychosocial factors in attempting to understand her depression. We consider two broad categories: factors descriptive of the broader culture or society and factors that relate to women's gender-role socialization.

# Societal/Situational Factors

The social status hypothesis suggests that the structures of patriarchy and institutionalized sexism disadvantage women in many ways (see Chapter 2). Across the nations of the world, women, more than men, are subject to the stressors of poverty, violence, and inequality. Higher levels of anxiety, depression, and somatization have been found in women who have been subjected to sexual harassment and sexual assault (Koss, Heise, et al., 1994). Hope Landrine and her colleagues have shown that sexist discrimination contributes more to women's depression than do other major life stressors (Landrine, Klonoff, Gibbs, Manning, & Lund, 1995). For Women of Color, recurrent experiences of racism interact with sexism to multiply the stress and disadvantage (Wyche, 2001). For

Sylvia, it became clear that a number of sources of stress and bias were contributing to her depressive reactions.

With respect to the onset of depression, we consider those specific factors that suppress women's sense of mastery and control over their lives, and that relegate women to positions of diminished status, resources, and interpersonal power. For Sylvia, two major factors seemed salient: the quality of her marital and family relationships, and the circumstances in her workplace. Further, it appeared that her Preawareness level of ethnic identity and her belief in meritocracy (success comes to those who are competent and work hard) provided the cognitive structures that allowed her to blame herself for her "failures." It also served to isolate her from the possibilities of a supportive community, in that she wanted to "make it on my own terms."

For other clients, differing societal factors might be important to consider. In particular, the prevalence of violence toward women is a prime example. Note that we screen all clients for evidence of physical or sexual abuse, because these events have high probability levels in the lives of women and are correlated with evidence of depression. For example, in a sample of college students, Witt and Worell (1988) found that levels of depression on the BDI were significantly elevated for those who reported past or present physical abuse in a romantic relationship. Likewise, in a large probability sample of 3,132 community residents, sexual assault during some time in the respondents' lives (16.7% of the women) predicted later major depressive episodes, as well as substance abuse and a variety of anxiety disorders (Burnam et al., 1988).

## Marriage

Marriage appears to confer a protective advantage for men but provides a greater risk of depression for women. Marital distress has been consistently related to depressive disorders; in almost half of unhappy marriages, wives were found to be depressed (McGrath et al., 1990). In a survey of more than 700 corporate employees, married women holding positions that ranged from clerical to managerial to scientist reported more depressive symptoms than did married men (D. L. Hughes & Galinsky, 1994). In this study, negative well-being was correlated with women's lower employment satisfaction and more reported inequity in household and child care arrangements.

The research literature is unclear on whether women's satisfaction with work external to the home may serve as a barrier to the experience of depression in women. For the most part, multiple roles have contributed positively to women's self-esteem (Crosby, 1991), but this relationship is contingent on several factors, including satisfaction with work and support and equity in marriage. When marital arrangements are inequitable in terms of power and decision making, and household workloads are unevenly distributed, women continue to be disadvantaged and report more dysphoria and depressive symptoms (Steil, 1997). Adding "worker" to "homemaker" with little modification in the "wife" role leads to role overload and role strain. Although some studies characterize African American families as more egalitarian than those in the dominant White culture, significant levels of inequity still exist. Figure 6.2 displays the relative task loads reported by a sample of dual-earner middle-class African American families, showing that wives who worked either full- or part-time still assume the major burden of household tasks (Hossain & Roopnarine, 1993). Sylvia reported that despite her career and child-free status, her marital arrangement was relatively "traditional" in terms of expectations for her homemaker role and the understanding that she should place her husband's wishes, such as where they lived, ahead of her own. She felt that her efforts to communicate her needs

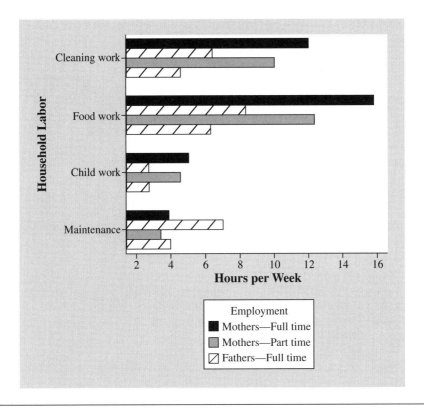

**Figure 6.2**    **Division of household labor in a sample of African American families in which mothers are employed either full time or part time. Adapted from "Division of Household Labor and Child Care in Dual-Earner African American Families with Infants," by Z. Hossain and J. L. Roopnarine, 1993, *Sex Roles, 29,* pp. 571–584.**

to him were fruitless and that he continued to "manage" the marriage to his own image. Both her husband and his family indicated their displeasure with her continued childlessness and thought she should settle down and be a good wife and mother.

In contrast to Sylvia's situation, a full-time homemaker client who presents similar depressive signs might suggest a different scenario. Since the homemaker role may be unrewarding to some women, we would explore the dimensions of her satisfaction and discontent with her household activities, as well as with her marital and community relationships. It is particularly important that psychotherapists who work with depressed women be cautious about viewing the resumption or "improvement" of their clients' traditional household role behaviors as a sign of recovery. For example, some structured programs for depression assigned tasks such as housecleaning, shopping, laundry, ironing, cooking, making beds, use of cosmetics, stylish clothing, and hair care as therapeutic strategies for women but not for men (cf. Liberman & Roberts, 1976). Evaluation of improvement, in this case, consists of reshaping the woman back into the role of the good wife. When working with prescribed social role behaviors, it is crucial that therapists explore carefully what activities are rewarding and satisfying to women apart from societal expectations for their roles.

*Employment*

For many women in the workforce, employment conditions are characterized by job segregation into low-paying and low-status positions that offer little opportunity for enrichment, advancement, or self-determination. For women in male-dominated professions, the picture is somewhat different. The societal expectations for women in nontraditional employment settings contain conflicting messages. Women are expected to be hard working and competent at their jobs (performance level), but are frequently not expected to achieve the same position as men (accomplishment level). They may be reminded of their status as women in both overt and covert ways, and they are frequently given little support for advancement despite their professional training and expertise.

In addition, sexual harassment is a common stressor for women in employment settings, especially in male-dominated contexts. *Sexual harassment* refers to sexual attention or coercion that is unwanted and offensive to the target person. In a series of surveys of federal employees from 1980 through 1994, the United States Merit Protection Board found that one-third of all women employees reported being the targets of sexually suggestive looks and comments; 25% reported unwelcome physical touching by coworkers and supervisors; one in six was asked for a date, and 10% were asked for sexual "favors" (Fitzgerald, Collinsworth, & Harned, 2001). All these acts create a hostile work environment and are prohibited in the workplace under federal civil rights laws. Like Sylvia, the majority of victims were avoidant rather than confrontive, ignoring or tolerating the behavior. Sexual harassment is not benign, however, and considerable research has documented that it places women at high risk for psychological harm. Typical responses to being harassed include embarrassment, humiliation, anxiety, depression, Posttraumatic Stress Disorder (PTSD), somatic complaints, interference with productive work, and lower job satisfaction. Sylvia experienced many of these reactions but did not connect her dysphoria with the aversive behaviors of her office mate. We return to sexual harassment issues in Chapter 7.

As an accountant in a midsized firm, Sylvia was the first and only woman, and the only African American, to be employed in her unit in other than a secretarial position. Her supervisor and coworkers expressed support and desire to increase their staff of women in the accounting division, but made no moves to hire others. Although she had more years of experience than Steve, her office mate, he made frequent suggestions about how she could improve her work and questioned her use of certain procedures. On Fridays, he occasionally left early and commented that she could finish up, since she had no children to look after at home. Further, he made sexually suggestive remarks and indicated in many ways that he was interested in her as an attractive woman rather than as a competent colleague.

In discussing these issues with her supervisor, she was told that Steve was "just trying to be friendly and helpful" and that she "shouldn't take things so seriously." In division staff meetings, she felt that her suggestions were not considered or implemented and that she seemed to have little impact on office procedures and decisions. The final blow was Steve's recent promotion in preference to her as first-line supervisor, a position she had expected to be offered. Sylvia knew that Steve had frequent lunches with their supervisor, but believed it was friendship rather than business. Looking back, she commented that her supervisor had never invited her to lunch.

In addition to sexism and racism in Sylvia's work situation, we see at least three elements of employment discrimination: isolation, sexual harassment, and devaluation of her competence. It appeared that her firm was satisfied to hire a token African American woman, but then expected her to remain "in her place." She was not accorded a pathway to administrative connections (socializing with the supervisor), and her reports of sexual harassment and coworker interference were minimized and disregarded. Her position in staff meetings was typical for that of a woman in a White male-majority group, in that her comments were ignored and her contributions were overlooked. In essence, she became invisible.

## Reinforcement Deficit Theory

The Social Status hypothesis of women's depression is compatible with formulations by Peter Lewinsohn that reinforcement deficits may function to precipitate and maintain depressive reactions (Lewinsohn, 1974). That is, depression is related to an unfavorable ratio between positive and negative person-environment outcomes. The low rate of positive outcomes is assumed to result in increasingly passive behavior and dysphoric mood, as the individual feels incapable of reaching personal goals and reacts with withdrawal and despair. These researchers do not specifically address the gender- and ethnicity-driven societal aspects of oppression as a reinforcement deficit in the lives of women. However, their theory is compatible with an EFT position since it emphasizes environmental contributions to the development of depression. A more recent contribution to this theory is offered by *Behavioral Activation* theory (Jacobson, Martell, & Dimidjian, 2001), which aims to increase behaviors that will elicit sources of environmental reinforcement. Although reinforcement deficit and behavioral activation theories recommend adding pleasurable activities to balance the reinforcement ratio, we believe that this approach is insufficient. In EFT, it is also necessary to effect a change in the individual's power position in interpersonal transactions. Establishing a favorable balance of say in decision making and access to valued resources empowers the client in the future as well as in the present situation.

In Sylvia's situation, the failure of both her family and her supervisor to respond favorably to her requests for support and parity in the marriage and recognition at work set the stage for her feelings of impotence and powerlessness. In addition, the theory suggests that individual skill deficits may contribute to depressive reactions by reducing the probability that the person is able to obtain reinforcing events or to reduce negative ones. We see that Sylvia's strategies for modifying conditions both at home and work were ineffective in producing desirable changes; thus, she attributed her failures to her own lack of ability.

## Societal/Situational Factors: Conclusions

In summarizing the societal contributions to Sylvia's current reactions, it seems clear that socialized expectations about her roles and behaviors were communicated clearly to her by both family and the workplace. Although the research literature provides inconsistent support for the hypothesis that women experience more general life stress than do men, we believe that this question has not been sufficiently addressed. The data show, however, that the occurrence of highly stressful events is closely connected to the incidence of depression. In summarizing the data from seven different interview studies of stress and depression in community samples of women, Carolyn Mazure (1998) found that more than 80% of the cases of depression were preceded by adverse life events (see Figure 6.3). Women's stressors may differ from men's in quality, content, and duration.

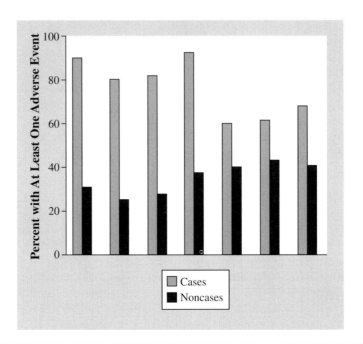

**Figure 6.3   Life stressors as risk factors in women's depression. Data from seven separate studies of clinical and community samples.** *Source: "Life Stress and Risk Factors for Depression,"* by C. M. Mazure, 1998, *Clinical Psychology: Research and Practice, 5,* pp. 291–313. Reprinted with permission.

Women's stressors may be more likely to leave women feeling helpless, incompetent, and out of control of their lives. The issue for understanding and treatment of women's depression is not whether women have more stressors than men, but to consider and explore the nature of societal events, images, and expectations for each client that produce continuing life stress.

## Gender-Role Socialization Factors

The societal expectations, rules, images, and messages that women receive throughout their lives become internalized and translated into individual modes of habitual reacting. Women are frequently unaware of how their automatic thoughts and behaviors are shaped and maintained by the gender-driven expectations of others. Some of the primary signs of depression, although demonstrated by men as well as by women, appear to be correlates of societal socialization for womanhood: withdrawal in the face of challenge, unassertiveness, feelings of incompetence, self-blame, crying, expectations below ability and achievement levels, and dysfunctional patterns of attributions for self-defined success or failure.

Although data suggest that African American girls and women are not typically deficient in self-esteem or assertiveness (Eccles et al., 1999; T. L. Robinson & Ward, 1995), Sylvia's pattern of responding was more consistent with her Preawareness identity position of denying the impact of racism and sexism on her life. That is, her desire to achieve in the financial world and her belief in meritocracy led her to follow dominant culture scripts for marriage and career achievement. When these patterns turned out to be ineffective, she felt that she had only herself to blame. We summarize briefly two major hypotheses related to female socialization that prepare the pathways for depressive reactions to stress and challenge: (a) learned helplessness/hopelessness, and (b) an interpersonal orientation toward pleasing others that motivates many women to be highly sensitive to the approval and support of others.

## Learned Helplessness/Hopelessness

One of the most frequently proposed hypotheses to account for these signs of depression is the learned helplessness/hopelessness model. The original model of learned helplessness (Seligman, 1975) proposed that as a result of repeated exposure to uncontrollable aversive outcomes, individuals may conclude that their behaviors have no effect on external events. Therefore, outcomes are believed to be uncontrollable. The cognitive, affective, and behavioral correlates of this belief are consistent with those of depression, including passivity in the face of challenge and lowered self-esteem. A reformulation of the learned helplessness model to account for individual differences proposed that the person's *attributions* for the uncontrollable events were the primary determinant of the helplessness/hopelessness response pattern (summarized by Seligman, 1981).

The pattern of attributions for greatest risk (we call this the *hopelessness triad*) is characterized by attributions of negative events to internal, stable, and global causes, and the attribution of positive outcomes to external, unstable, and specific causes. A meta-analysis of 104 studies on the relationship of attributional styles to depression found that the more people attributed negative events in their lives to internal, stable, and global causes, the more likely they were to evidence depressive symptoms (Sweeney, Anderson, & Bailey, 1986).

Thus, people like Sylvia who blame themselves for bad events ("Since I didn't get promoted, I must be a poor manager") experience a loss of self-esteem. Attributing bad events to internal stable causes that are unlikely to change ("I'm probably not fit to be in the business world") leads to feelings of incompetence over time in coping with future situations. And generalizing many situations ("I can't seem to make it anywhere in my life") results in chronic feelings of helplessness and hopelessness, and inability to cope effectively with stress. In contrast, when such individuals experience positive outcomes, they discount these by attributing their occurrence to an external unstable factor such as luck or chance ("I'm lucky even to have this job, because they needed a woman; I shouldn't complain"), once more diminishing their self-efficacy. Finally, the importance of the situation to the individual influences the severity and intensity of depressive symptoms. Thus, for Sylvia, the two areas of her life with most value, her marriage and her work, were the focus of her feelings of uncontrollability and failure. There is considerable evidence that women and girls, more than men and boys, use attributions that depress their performance and inhibit positive and assertive efforts to overcome adversity. These reactions may be related to gender-role socialization that encourages a "modesty" response in girls that prevents many girls from taking personal credit for their successful performances.

## Interpersonal Orientation toward Pleasing Others

Female socialization patterns in most cultures emphasize an orientation toward others rather than toward the self (see Chapter 2). When girls are encouraged to pay more attention to what others want of them to the detriment of their own wants and needs, the stage is set for excessive self-blame when important others are displeased. Fear of losing love and approval further motivates many girls and women to deny expression of their anger and to "self-silence," according to Dana Jack (1991). In Sylvia's case, a loving but de-manding family of origin had convinced her that she could achieve anything she wanted in today's society, and she worked hard to meet their expectations. Her perceived failure at both marriage and employment was combined with her reluctance to assertively con-front or antagonize her husband and his family or her boss. As a result, she felt unable to resolve her predicament, resulting in withdrawal and feelings of helplessness.

Susan Nolen-Hoeksema and Benito Jackson (2001) reported that depressed women, more than men, display a self-questioning mode of coping with stress, characterized by *rumination* rather than by active problem solution. Among other factors, they found that rumination was related to women's beliefs that they were responsible for maintaining positive relationships with others, and that they had relatively little control over impor-tant events in their lives. For Sylvia, we believe that this coping style was embedded in a larger frame that embraced both her desire to please (interpersonal orientation) and an attributional style that encouraged self-questioning and self-blame. In believing that she had no available solutions to her predicament, she resorted to ruminative "self-talk" that further convinced her of her past failures, her present incompetence, and her bleak out-look for the future. In this respect, Sylvia's rumination resembled the "negative triad" that Aaron Beck (1976) hypothesized as the cognitive basis of depression.

In addition to the foregoing contributions to depressive reactions, there are additional socialization factors (see Chapter 2) that for many women produce lower expectancies for success in male-typed tasks: low risk-taking tendencies and increased "compliance" and attempts to please authority. Together with the learned helplessness hypothesis, the accumulated effects of these gender-role socialization factors appear to contribute sub-stantially to the depressive syndromes more frequently observed in women.

## Gender-Role Socialization Factors: Conclusions

It is evident from Sylvia's dialogue that her reactions to her situation were character-ized by pervasive negative cognitions, but there were many factors in both home and work situations to induce such beliefs. There is considerable research to support the view that the negative cognitions of depressed individuals reflect their actual life cir-cumstances and the reactions of significant others (Krantz, 1985). Rather than presume that her dysphoric moods resulted from distorted thinking patterns or selective recall of negative events, the therapist explored further the details of her home and work situa-tions, and the specific interactions that left her feeling incompetent and out of control of her life.

## EMPOWERMENT FEMINIST THERAPY INTERVENTION STRATEGIES

Interventions for Sylvia were planned in the context of the real and oppressive situations that confronted her at home and in the workplace, the societal messages that she had in-ternalized and accepted as her own, the gender-socialized behaviors she tended to use in interpersonal situations, and the attributions she made for the outcomes of her interac-tions. Interwoven across these interventions were aspects of her personal/social identity that factored into the dyadic relationship and the choices that she made in her life.

## A Five-Phase Model

In counseling sessions with Sylvia, her therapist Ellen used a modified Cognitive-Behavioral approach. Plans for counseling followed a five-phase procedure:

1. Assessment and goal-setting.
2. Attention to Sylvia's personal/social identity levels and therapeutic implications of the cross-cultural dyad in counseling.
3. Exploration of thoughts, feelings, and behaviors in the context of both dominant and ethnic cultures and societal messages and Sylvia's situational patterns of reacting.
4. Initiation of problem-solving strategies, behavioral activation, experiments to test hypotheses, implementing new insights into Sylvia's work and home settings.
5. Planning of maintenance and generalization strategies to strengthen Sylvia's revised view of herself and her environment and to provide support for further change.

These phases may overlap or merge. In Cognitive-Behavioral interventions, assessment may continue periodically to provide feedback on progress to both therapist and client. Although a progression of strategies is planned, each of the four EFT principles may be implemented and revisited throughout the sessions in the context of the individual client's needs and progress.

### Phases 1 and 2

**Empowerment Feminist Therapy Principles I, III, and IV**    In Phase 1, EFT Principle III (Relationships Are Egalitarian) was addressed first. Ellen discussed the general procedures to be followed, shared her own views on how behavior change occurs, and provided feedback to Sylvia on the results of the assessment. At this point, Ellen also brought in EFT Principle I (Personal and Social Identities Are Interdependent) to explore Sylvia's perception and comfort with the cross-cultural therapy dyad. Although earlier Sylvia appeared reluctant to enter therapy, she denied that her reaction was based on discomfort with a White therapist and asserted that in most cases, race did not matter to her. It was apparent that Sylvia was not comfortable in discussing ethnocultural issues, and Ellen decided to defer further discussion of this factor for a more appropriate opportunity in the therapy process. Together they developed a set of goals and a written contract that would be reevaluated at the end of three months.

Ellen set the stage for implementing Principle III by pointing out that as a trained psychologist, she possessed knowledge of behavior change, but that Sylvia was the expert on herself. Counseling would be both a teaching and a learning process, in which each member of the dyad assumed the roles of teacher and learner. Together, they comprised a team with equal but differing contributions to the change process.

Sylvia initially rejected responsibility for her own progress, stating that she didn't know how she could be of any use because she was obviously a failure in solving her problems. Ellen countered these objections with questions about Sylvia's feelings and perceptions (Principle IV: Women's Perspectives Are Valued), validating them as "real" data that provided a unique perspective on Sylvia. Ellen was careful to avoid labeling any of Sylvia's reactions as *distorted, faulty,* or *irrational,* since these labels tend to lower self-esteem and further convince the client that she is out of control of her thoughts, as well as of her life.

**Empowerment Feminist Therapy Principles I and II**    Ellen then brought Principle II (The Personal Is Political) in by helping Sylvia to reframe some of her statements from self-blame ("I'm a failure at keeping my marriage together") to social messages ("I'm feeling responsible for keeping my marriage together because I was taught that relationships are supposed to be the woman's job"). Through careful questions about both her own and her parents' relationships, Sylvia was able to see that marriage is a shared partner responsibility and that the failure, if any, was not hers alone. Ellen shared some information on factors that contribute to women's relationship satisfaction, including intimacy, emotional support, and equity in the distribution of power (Lange & Worell, 1990; Steil, 1997; Worell, 1988a).

In a similar vein, her attributions for the problems at work were reframed in a manner that suggested the possible roles of sexism, isolation, ethnic discrimination, and sexual harassment in her employment setting. Ellen provided Sylvia with information about women in male-dominant work settings and the isolating effects of the solo woman on men's behavior in groups (Gutek, 2001b). Since Sylvia seemed somewhat skeptical, Ellen gave her a short form of a scale that measures the corporate working environment for women (Stokes, Riger, & Sullivan, 1995). Table 6.3 displays the six variables measured by this scale.

Sylvia was surprised and relieved to learn that most women, more than most men, viewed the corporate environment as hostile to women on all these variables. Ellen also challenged Sylvia to consider the intersect of sexism and racism (Principle I), questioning the possible sources of her isolation, harassment, and devaluation at work. Together they explored some of Sylvia's past experiences in which gender or ethnicity appeared to be a biasing factor. These insights into societal contributions to her dilemmas were both confusing ("Now I'm not sure what to believe") and exciting ("Maybe it's really not all my fault?"), and she felt challenged to explore them further. Since Sylvia appeared ready and interested, Ellen provided her with some readings on the lives of Women of Color and left Sylvia with open questions: "Who are you as an African American woman? What things are most important to you?" Ellen suggested that in answering these questions, it would be helpful for her to complete a genogram on her family of origin (see Box 6.1).

**Goal Selection**    In developing therapeutic goals, Ellen helped Sylvia to narrow her focus from general affect ("I want to feel better") to prioritizing more specific behavioral goals ("I want to feel better about my progress at work"). Sylvia decided that her marital concerns were complicated by her husband's nonparticipation and the demands of his family; therefore, these issues were set aside temporarily. She chose instead to work on her sleep and somatic problems and to explore her sense of failure and incompetence in relation to the work setting. She was also intrigued by Ellen's open approach to discussing racism and her personal identity and asked if they could talk more about these issues in relation to her work situation. In helping Sylvia set specific behavioral goals, Ellen was providing the foundation for a situational view of stress that removed the pathology from her ("I must be going crazy, I'm so mixed up") and focused instead on the specifics of her interpersonal transactions and her perceptions of them. Ellen was also concerned about Sylvia's decision to sidestep her marital difficulties, but

**Table 6.3   Measuring the corporate work environment**

1. *Opportunities and Mentoring* reflect differences in how women and men are treated on the job.

   "Compared to men, women in this office are appointed to less important committees and task forces."

2. *Inappropriate Salience of Gender* is reflected through behaviors based solely on gender.

   "In this office, people interrupt women more often than they interrupt men."

3. *Sexist Attitudes and Comments* are both present and tolerated in the workplace.

   "Jokes that are demeaning or degrading to women are told . . . in this office."

4. *Informal Socializing* tends to favor groups and activities for males over females.

   "Company social events generally appeal to both the female and male employees."

5. *Balancing Work and Personal Obligations* recognizes the difficulties in work-family balance.

   "Supervisors in this company are understanding when personal or family obligations . . . take an employee away from work."

6. *Remediation Policies and Practices* are open to addressing gender issues in the workplace.

   "People who raise issues about the treatment of women in this company are supported by other employees."

*Source:* From "Measuring Perceptions of the Working Environment for Women in Corporate Settings," by J. Stokes, J. S. Riger, and M. Sullivan, 1995, *Psychology of Women Quarterly, 19,* 533–550. Adapted with permission.

determined that Sylvia needed to set her own priorities and would consider the marriage when she was ready to do so.

## Phases 2 and 3

In practice, Phases 2 and 3 also tend to merge, and all four EFT principles are engaged. With Sylvia, a range of Cognitive-Behavioral and EFT strategies was used: progressive relaxation; increasing pleasant activities (self-nurturing); stress inoculation; gender-role, ethnocultural-role, and power analyses; cognitive restructuring; bibliotherapy; self-disclosure by Ellen related to some of her own work-related experiences; reattribution coaching; "homework" agreements; problem solving; role playing; and assertiveness practice. We summarize these procedures briefly.

**Relaxation, Stress Inoculation, Pleasant Activities**   Ellen suggested that Sylvia might be better able to cope with daily hassles at home and work if she were getting more sleep and could learn to relax. Ellen recommended a book that included relaxation instructions as well as other information about depression (*Control Your Depression;* Lewinsohn, Munoz, Youngren, & Zeiss, 1979). Progressive muscle relaxation was taught as a first strategy for helping Sylvia to "read" her body signals and to exert more control over her experiences of tension. Sylvia was given an audiotape with

---

### BOX 6.1

#### Constructing a Family Genogram

Draw a family tree representing at least three generations of your family. Gather information about your mother and as many female family members as you can for the following areas: occupations, childbearing pattern (mother's age at births, number and spacing of children, miscarriages), partner patterns (marriage, divorce, remarriage, death of partner, singlehood, same-sex partner, age at marriage or partnering, divorce or death of partner), nature and quality of female-male relationships in each family grouping (power differential, dysfunctional patterns), nature and quality of female-female relationships in each family grouping, significant characteristics of each female family member, female members who were outcasts/black sheep in the family. What traumas were experienced and how did the women cope with them? This information can be collected by reflecting on family stories you have heard, looking at family photo albums, and interviewing family members.

The major goal of the exercise is to get an intergenerational picture of what it means to be female in your culture and in your family and the nature of female-male relationships in your family. Listen for gender-role messages related to your cultural identity that have been passed on verbally or modeled from one generation to the next. Look for the commonalities and differences in the lives of females in your family's history. What positional status or power do women have in your family? What are their strengths? What have been the barriers to their full development as people? How are you currently living in accordance with or in reaction to the gender and cultural legacies of your family?

---

Ellen's spoken relaxation instructions, which Sylvia then used to help herself to sleep at night and to return to sleep during periods of insomnia. Ellen showed Sylvia how to use her self-monitoring data on sleep periods and ruminative thoughts to evaluate her progress.

Sylvia was also coached on how to use coping self-statements in real-life situations (stress inoculation) to strengthen her ability to cope with situational stress (Meichenbaum, 1986). Together they role-played some alternative ways that Sylvia could deal with work-related problems. Sylvia took to this approach quickly and found it effective in helping her to reduce body tension at work ("I can breathe deeply and relax my shoulders") as well as to confront and handle stressors ("I can deal with this situation") that interfered with daytime performance. Sylvia was pleased with her new competencies and encouraged by early progress in self-managing some of her debilitating patterns.

In addition to working with stress-produced tension and negative self-statements, Ellen recommended that Sylvia begin to self-nurture, with time set aside for things that she wanted to do just for herself. Sylvia objected at first, saying that she had no time for anything else in her life. Ellen directed her back to the *Control Your Depression* workbook and suggested that she begin to monitor her day for those activities that were very enjoyable to her. She was to monitor her mood at those times as well. Sylvia also completed a list of potentially pleasurable activities that were currently absent in her life.

The process of activating Sylvia to consider her personal needs and desires each day resulted in her realization of how little pleasure she allowed herself. As a first step, she decided on a project she had been wanting to do "forever": Join a health club and work out every day. Although Ellen suggested taking small steps at first, such as daily walks, Sylvia set larger goals for herself. She decided to investigate health clubs near both home and work, and she made a commitment to join one and work out three days a week. This commitment had to be renegotiated several times before Sylvia was able to convince herself that she had the time and the energy to carry it through.

**Gender, Culture, and Power Analysis**   Sylvia and Ellen further explored the work environment. They focused on the characteristics of employment for Women of Color managers in a White male-dominant corporate setting (power analysis), the interaction of gender and ethnic bias that may have compounded the attitudes and behaviors of her office mate and supervisor (ethnocultural analysis), and the messages that women in such situations give themselves (gender-role analysis). They also explored how all three dimensions were probably operating to encourage an atmosphere of sexual harassment in her office. Together they discussed ways in which Sylvia might pay attention to future transactions to test whether gender or ethnicity was the contributing factor to her supervisor's attitudes. Ellen also introduced Sylvia to the possibility of drawing a privilege/oppression diagram to help visualize her situation. Figure 6.4 displays the diagram that Sylvia constructed for herself. Ellen questioned the placement of childless status as a liability, and Sylvia pointed out that in her husband's family, it was expected that women bear children to maintain the strength and well-being of the entire community.

Ellen also recommended a book on organizational risks for women, *Games Your Mother Never Taught You* (Harrigan, 1977), to help Sylvia view her work-related problems in a different light. Sylvia was a cooperative client and completed the book in two days. She began to see how her isolation from supportive relationships at work; the overbearing, competitive, and seductive behavior of her office mate; and the discriminatory attitude of her supervisor were contributing to her feelings of incompetence and failure.

For each situational factor, Ellen and Sylvia explored together how Sylvia was feeling, what she was telling herself (attributions and automatic thoughts), and how her self-talk matched the realities of these situations. Ellen spoke briefly about how negative thoughts can influence feelings about self, and that feeling incompetent might reciprocally influence her subsequent performance and interactions. Ellen supported Sylvia's perceptions of the real power games that existed, but challenged her self-blame ("I just stood there and let them do that to me, what a dope I was") and her low sense of self-efficacy for change ("I'll never be able to make it in the business world"). Sylvia was encouraged to perform small experiments at work, testing out her hypotheses against the daily events and her responses to them.

At this point, Ellen shared some of her own experience in being the first and only woman in an all-male academic department (self-disclosure), and that she also reacted by withdrawing and feeling incompetent and said nothing to her supervisor when she did not receive a raise her first year when others, all men, were given salary raises. Ellen acknowledged that Sylvia's situation was more complex in that both ethnicity and gender may have been targets for corporate stereotyping and exclusion. Sylvia was able to reframe her attributions accordingly, and together they explored alternative ways to explain the events at work. Sylvia was encouraged to use her new perceptions to reevaluate

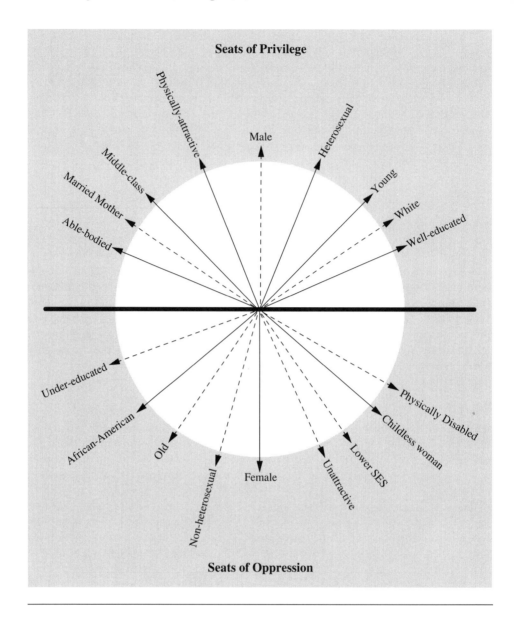

**Figure 6.4    Sylvia's social identities.**

the situation and to view her behavior and outcomes at work in a more positive and self-affirming manner (cognitive restructuring and reattribution).

**Problem Solving, Role Playing, Assertiveness**    Once Sylvia began to determine that her issues at work were related to real discriminatory practices involving both gender and ethnicity (Identity Development Level 2, Encounter), her anger at what had transpired became overwhelming to her. In her sessions, she alternately wept and raged at the "injustice of the system" and swore to even the score with her office mate and supervisor. Ellen supported her feelings of rage as legitimate and helped Sylvia consider how she could turn rage into energy for effective action: "How can you deal effectively with what has happened to you, and what do you want to do about it now?" Ellen's shared goal was to help empower Sylvia to initiate some changes in herself and in her work relationships to increase her positive experiences.

In considering alternatives and how to implement them, Ellen was careful to support Sylvia in her personal belief that work relationships should be friendly, cooperative, and supportive (Principle IV: Women's Perspectives Are Valued). Although one of Sylvia's solutions was to revise her values ("I'll just have to become like them—scheming, aggressive, and self-serving"), she realized that these traits were alien to her sense of fairness and equity. Ellen pointed out the differences between aggressive and assertive behavior, suggesting that Sylvia could choose assertive strategies that were both positive ("I want a separate office" to her supervisor) and negative ("No, I won't stay late so you can go home early" to her office mate) to improve her work environment.

Ellen and Sylvia role-played a range of strategies for altering the situation at work, including asking for a new office or another office mate, asking for a raise, reporting her office mate's harassment to a higher administrator, confronting her supervisor on her failure to be promoted, and so on. Each solution was role-played and evaluated for its possible outcomes. Sylvia also decided to consider employment in another firm, as she realized that each strategy in her present environment might be useless in changing things (see Stokes et al., 1995, for employee decisions to leave). Her decision to look at other job possibilities freed her to try new behaviors at work. When she confronted her supervisor, she was surprised and pleased to find that he agreed to give her a new office. However, the promotion issue was not resolved, and she became more depressed with the failure of her new assertiveness to get everything she wanted.

For a while she regressed, stopped her exercise program, and said she felt once more like a failure. Earlier cognitive and behavioral strategies were reinstated, and Sylvia was supported for the progress she had been accomplishing. Depressed women may need continuing support to acknowledge and take credit for their progress (Kaslow, 1989). Ellen continued to help Sylvia explore her ethnic and cultural identity (Principle I) and encouraged her to consider reaching out to others in her community. Sylvia decided to attend a local church with her mother-in-law and found a group of African American women there with whom she could "just be me." The experience of immersing herself in a supportive and culturally similar group was very empowering for Sylvia, and she began to voice more assertively her newfound indignation at her employment dilemma. Ellen provided her feedback about her movement from Preawareness (Level 1) to Encounter (Level 2) to Immersion (Level 3) in both her ethnic and gender identity development, and further explored with her the changes that had taken place in her beliefs and behavior. Toward the end of the counseling sessions, Sylvia reported that she had left her firm and accepted a position as first-line supervisor in another accounting firm. She felt proud of her newfound insights about corporate policies and related to Ellen that she was careful to question the new employer carefully about policies related to discriminatory practices. She was ecstatic as she reported on her new horizon and on her termination session with her own company, in which she confronted them with the sexism and racism in their corporate policies and the reasons she was leaving. She began to see that the changes in herself enabled her to make effective changes in others. Although she never knew the outcomes of her confrontation with her original firm, she felt very powerful at having been able to tell them what she had experienced. She hoped her information would help other women in that firm (Principle IV), but she was not willing to stay there under present conditions.

*Phase 5*

The outcome of Phases 1 through 4 was a new sense of self-efficacy and empowerment for Sylvia, as she began to view her problems in a different light and to take positive action toward change. She felt ready to terminate counseling for a while, even though she had barely touched her marital issues. Ellen supported Sylvia's decision to set the marital relationship aside temporarily, giving Sylvia time and space to try out a new set of perceptions and behaviors. She left the path open for Sylvia to return in the future, suggesting that over time, the marital difficulties might sabotage her new strategies for combating depression (Jacobson, Holtzworth-Munroe, & Schmaling, 1989). Further sessions might involve support and feedback on how Sylvia was functioning in the new job, her community, and family relationships, or they might begin to focus on the marriage situation as Sylvia became more prepared to deal with it.

The final issues for Ellen to raise with Sylvia concerned maintaining new skills and insights, coping with new situations, and continuing to engage with a support system. Recall that Sylvia scored high on the Young Loneliness Scale and indicated a lack of intimate support in her life. Her posttherapy score on Loneliness was reduced from baseline, but remained moderately high. Since the marital relationship was on hold, Ellen discussed the possibility of another support group with women who had similar professional issues (Principle IV). Ellen suggested several women's groups in Sylvia's work city and encouraged Sylvia to join one. A follow-up telephone call one month later revealed that Sylvia had joined a professional women's forum, finding three other woman accountants there; and she was enjoying the social and professional contacts. She decided to take an evening once a week for herself to meet and socialize with these new friends.

## Intervention Strategies: Conclusions

The counseling sessions with Sylvia covered a period of six months. Although she did not resolve all her presenting problems, particularly with respect to her marriage, her final evaluation on the BDI and the Silencing the Self Scale indicated success in decreasing the depressive symptoms. Her total score on the PPS, a measure of empowerment, increased significantly from baseline as well. She was sleeping fairly well, had gained some needed weight, no longer felt sad and hopeless, and was making many positive statements about her life. She felt apprehensive but optimistic about her new job situation, was taking time to renew and nurture herself, and felt a welcome sense of personal competence and ability to deal with problems as they arose. Her attributions of self-blame were being replaced by positive coping statements that acknowledged external barriers but focused on problem solution rather than withdrawal. She no longer believed that her life was a failure, and she even viewed her marriage differently ("There are some definite problems but perhaps we can work them out—we'll see"). She was spending quality time with two new women's support groups, one in the local church, of which she had become a member, and one in her professional community. With these added activities, her attendance at the health club was more sporadic but she maintained that exercise was important to her well-being and she would not let it disappear.

The combination of Cognitive-Behavioral and EFT strategies was particularly effective in working with this client. In addition to ameliorating her presenting symptoms of depression and hopelessness, the outcomes of her counseling sessions included an increased sense of personal and social empowerment, and resilience in confronting and coping with both present and future life situations.

## SUMMARY

An overview of the signs of depression in women included a summary of primary symptoms, the epidemiology of depression, and major hypotheses for the higher incidence of unipolar depression in women as compared to men. Three factors were discussed in relation to women's depression: biological, societal/situational, and gender-role socialization. The case of Sylvia was presented as an example of a woman whose depressive symptoms reflected a reaction to her feelings of powerlessness and failure both at home and at work.

Cognitive-Behavioral and EFT strategies were combined, using a five-phase model of intervention. The addition of culturally sensitive feminist principles and strategies to the more established Cognitive-Behavioral techniques enabled the client to consider her depressive reactions in the context of societal, situational, ethnocultural, and gender-role socialization factors. The outcomes of this time-limited therapy included reduction in symptoms of depression, an increase in self-reported efficacy, a new awareness of work-related variables that serve as barriers to women's achievement, a more positive and self-affirming style of attribution, and a growing awareness of self as a strong and resilient Woman of Color. Self-initiated changes in the client's work, home, and social situations provided new opportunities for personal development and a renewed sense of community and control in her life.

## ACTIVITIES

### Self-Assessment: Beliefs and Facts about Depression

After reading this chapter, retake the self-assessment at the beginning of the chapter to determine if you have revised any of your beliefs or have gained new information.

### Practicing a Feminist Case Analysis: Complete either 1 or 2 of the following cases:

1. Assume that you are Sylvia's therapist and that she has returned to you for a reexamination of her marriage. Once more, her husband will not join the counseling sessions. Review the five-phase model presented in this chapter and the strategies used to assist Sylvia with her work-related issues. List and discuss briefly:

   a. What issues should be addressed now with Sylvia.

   b. How EFT principles would enter the therapy process now.

   c. How can you be of help to Sylvia if her husband is a nonparticipant?

   d. How would your particular social locations impact the therapeutic process with Sylvia?

Pair yourself with a partner and role-play one session with Sylvia, addressing the issues outlined. Reverse roles and see if your partner would confront it differently.

2. Consider Sylvia's case from the perspective of a White middle-class woman with all the same information. What, if anything, might you do differently than with the case of Sylvia?

## FURTHER READINGS

To further your understanding of Cognitive and Behavioral approaches to the treatment of depression, see the following resources. Please note, however, that each approach contains strategies that may need to be modified to increase its compatibility with EFT principles.

Comas-Diaz, L., & Greene, B. (1994). *Women of Color: Integrating ethnic and gender identities in psychotherapy.* New York: Guilford Press.

Leahy, R. L., & Holland, S. J. (2000). *Treatment plans and interventions for depression and anxiety disorders.* New York: Guilford Press.

Lewinsohn, P. M., Antonuccio, D. O., Steinmetz, J. L., & Teri, L. (1984). *The coping with depression course: A psychoeducational treatment for unipolar depression.* Eugene, OR: Castalia.

Martell, C. R., Addis, M. E., & Jacobson, N. S. (2001). *Depression in context: Strategies for guided action.* New York: Norton.

Nolen-Hoeksema, S., & Jackson, B. (2001). Mediators of the gender differences in rumination. *Psychology of Women Quarterly, 25,* 37–48.

# Chapter 7 ————————————————

# *CHOOSING A CAREER PATH*

*In every country and every region of the world, there are jobs that are specifically defined as "women's work." They are usually considered beneath men's station.*

Seager and Olson, 1986, p. 45

*Men's jobs, on the other hand, are often well-paid and highly respected and women have a very hard time breaking into their ranks.*

Seager and Olson, 1986, p. 109

## SELF-ASSESSMENT: ANALYZING YOUR CAREER DEVELOPMENT

Using the age line on page 174, create a chart of the important events in, and influences on, your own career development. In following the step-by-step instructions, enter each indicated experience or influence on the line at the age or ages where it occurred. The left half of the page is for entering career-related events; the right half is for entering career choices you have fantasized, considered, or chosen at various ages.

1. To the left of the line, enter your major educational experiences (e.g., elementary school, graduate school).
2. To the left of the line, enter some of your major life events (e.g., marriage, partnering, divorce, birth of children, illnesses).
3. To the right of the line, enter all the careers you fantasized about, considered, and/or actually chose at various ages.
4. For the ages you have not yet reached, enter to the right of the line the career choices or positions you hope to have at future points.
5. As you look across your career dreams and choices, note how your choices have been affected by your being a woman or a man. Enter to the right of the line in red ink any critical turning points related to your gender and your career choices. Enter to the right of the line in a different color any critical turning points related to each of your social locations and your career choices.

---

*Personal Career Development Chart*

| Life Events | | Career Choices |
|---|---|---|
| | Birth | |
| | 5 Years | |
| | 10 Years | |
| | 15 Years | |
| | 20 Years | |
| | 25 Years | |
| | 30 Years | |
| | 35 Years | |
| | 40 Years | |
| | 45 Years | |
| | 50 Years | |
| | 55 Years | |
| | 60 Years | |
| | 65 Years | |
| | 70 Years | |
| | 75 Years | |
| | 80 Years | |
| | 85 Years | |
| | + | |

## OVERVIEW

The negative impact of stereotyping and institutionalized oppression on women's lives is visible in yet another area: women's career development and choice processes. Women earn about three-fourths of what men earn (U.S. Department of Labor, 1999) and continue to be employed in low-paying, lower-status occupations. The high percentage of women with household incomes below the poverty level is reflected in the phrase *feminization of poverty.*

While the career development process for women is complex and difficult to capture in a simple theoretical model, we present a sociocultural perspective for understanding women's career development and change agency—an EFT approach to meeting the career counseling needs of women. In this chapter, we meet Michelle, who sought career counseling because she was feeling dissatisfied as a high school math teacher. In counseling, Michelle explores how her career development has been affected by her social locations and begins to challenge these beliefs and to choose a career path more in line with her potential, abilities, and interests.

# MICHELLE'S STORY: NONTRADITIONAL CAREER INTERESTS

Michelle, a 32-year-old single, White, protestant woman from a middle-class family, was self-referred for career counseling to her therapist, Holly, who is a 40-year-old White, protestant, heterosexual Empowerment Feminist (EF) therapist. Michelle reported feeling slightly depressed and confused about her life direction and dissatisfied with her current career as a high school math teacher.

> I have had an uneasy feeling in the pit of my stomach for the past six months every time I think about my next (33rd) birthday. I feel restless and uncomfortable as a teacher. While I know well the content of the courses I'm teaching (advanced math classes), I'm having trouble getting the concepts across to some of the students, and disciplining them is a challenge. Yet, I'm afraid to let go of the teaching. I struggled to identify and enter this career three years ago. Before that, after graduating from college, I drifted from one temporary job to another. I was a store clerk, a secretary, a tax form preparer, and even a house cleaner. I just did not know what I wanted to do, and here I am again, doubting if I want to be a teacher.

When Michelle's therapist, Holly, inquired about Michelle's personal and educational history, she discovered that Michelle had been in honors classes through junior high and high school and had a 3.6 grade-point average as an undergraduate. Michelle remembered being tested by someone in junior high who, she thought, told her that her IQ was over 140. Michelle knew she had done well in school but was surprised when Holly used the word *gifted*.

Michelle and Holly contracted for 10 career counseling sessions over a four-month period. At that point, they agreed they would reevaluate and contract for additional sessions if needed. They decided to focus on two major areas: clarifying Michelle's long-term career goals and resolving her immediate conflict over whether to continue teaching. Holly informed Michelle she was an Empowerment Feminist therapist and explained to Michelle what that meant. Holly noted that Michelle was a gifted woman who seemed to have frequently chosen below her potential. Holly explained to Michelle that she felt it was important for them to explore the impact of her gender and other social locations on Michelle's past and current career choices to help her make future choices that were self-fulfilling. They also agreed to use an Empowerment Feminist decision-making model to guide their work together.

## DEFINITIONS

Michelle's situation can best be understood in the general context of women's career development. We examine this context by (a) defining career and career development, and (b) reviewing some of the factors that may influence women's career development.

The study of factors affecting women's career choices is directly linked to the ways in which career and career development are defined. Typical definitions of *career* found in the literature vary from broad and encompassing of all life activities to more narrow definitions that focus solely on paid work activities. An example of a broader conceptualization comes from Donald Super (1976), who defined career as "the sequence of occupations and other life roles which combine to express one's commitment to work in his or her total pattern of development" (p. 4). An example from the narrower end of the continuum is provided by Vernon Zunker (1998). He defined career as "the activities and positions involved in vocations, occupations, and jobs as well as related activities associated with an individual's lifetime of work" (p. 7).

Most theories of women's career development focus on the interaction between paid work and family responsibilities. From this perspective, broader definitions of career, like the one offered by Super, would seem to be the most compatible with an Empowerment Feminist Therapy (EFT) approach. However, Louise Fitzgerald and John Crites (1980) argued for a more narrow definition of career. They defined career as ". . . the developmental sequence of full-time, gainful employment engaged in by the individual during the course of his or her working life" (p. 45). Although they acknowledged that pursuing homemaking activities is an important factor affecting the career choice process, they do not consider homemaking to qualify as a career choice. Fitzgerald and Crites argued the importance of financial compensation for careers. They asserted that women will not achieve equity with men until they are no longer dependent economically on others. Thus, from this perspective, a more narrow definition of *career* is compatible with an EFT approach.

We agree that economic independence for women is crucial to achieving full equality. However, we also believe that to exclude homemaking, volunteer, and leisure activities from a definition of *career* denies not only the centrality of these activities in women's lives, but also the career-related skills that women develop as a result of participation in these activities. Thus, we define *career* as the "developmental sequence of all life experiences (including education, paid employment, leisure, homemaking, volunteer work) that affect one's commitment to and satisfaction with work."

Career development is affected strongly by environmental factors. These external factors include gender-role socialization, institutionalized oppression, cultural stereotypes, and economic, political, and educational structures. Thus, we use the American Counseling Association's (1994) definition of *career development:* "The total constellation of psychological, sociological, educational, physical, economic, and chance factors that combine to shape the career of any individual" (as cited in Zunker, 1998, p. 7). We give special attention to the environmental and cultural factors that create opportunities or barriers to women's career development.

## FACTORS AFFECTING WOMEN'S CAREER DEVELOPMENT

Our definition of career development reflects the variety of factors influencing women's career paths. In the following sections, we overview these factors. Further, we explore the interrelationships among these factors and the ways in which women's socialization and experiences with institutionalized oppressions and cultural stereotyping inhibit their career achievement. We begin by reviewing the problems with current theories of, and research on, women's career development.

Most of the widely used career development theories (e.g., Holland, Super) have been based primarily or entirely on the research studies of White, Western, middle-class males (see Zunker, 1998). Despite the fact that these theories have limited applicability for women, women's career development is often compared to these male-based norms. Moreover, Western career theories and career counseling models are based on values that do not fit with many cultures. For example, autonomy, independence, and future time perspective are value assumptions in most of these theories. Asian American individuals may choose in accordance with their parents' wishes not because they are career immature, but because of cultural values to be deferent to their parents (T. L. Robinson & Howard-Hamilton, 2000). Further, the career development process for women is complex, and, thus, is difficult to predict and capture in a theory. The complexity of women's career development processes is reflected in the plethora of research studies in the past 25 years related to women's career development, their career choice processes, and their achievement motivation.

Research on the variables affecting women's career development has produced some conflicting results. Frequently, the factors that are significant contributors to women's career achievement in some studies are not found in others. Research methodology, variance in how the factors are measured, population sample used, and which factors are included all contribute to the inconsistency of outcomes across studies. This research has a significantly limited perspective because it has focused primarily on the lives of White women.

Synthesizing this literature is beyond the scope of this chapter. Rather, we have chosen to focus on the internal and external factors most often theorized to enhance or inhibit women's career achievement. Further, we are emphasizing those factors that are impacted by or result from cultural oppressions.

Internal and external influences on women's career achievements are conceptualized here in the context of cultural bias. *Bias* includes any factor that limits career choices or career development based solely on a person's membership in a particular group. The Women's Career Wheel shown in Figure 7.1 illustrates the enormous impact of cultural bias and stereotyping on women's career choices and career development, and how bias, especially gender and ethnocultural bias, often results in women choosing careers below their potential.

The outer part of the wheel depicts external, environmental factors affecting women's career development. These social, economic, educational, and political forces can generally be viewed as embedded in cultural socialization and institutionalized oppression processes. We believe that all women's career development and career choices are embedded in these biased, external contexts. In turn, these environmental forces impact on, and interact with, factors internal to each of us. The wheel illustrates that what were originally environmental variables, external to women, become internalized. Thus, even factors appearing as internalized on the wheel largely began as externally induced factors.

As you read the following sections on external and internalized factors, consider which of these factors fit your own career development experiences. Return to the self-assessment exercise that you completed at the beginning of the chapter. Enter on your career line any additional social location-related experiences that have affected your career development.

## External Factors: Cultural Socialization and Institutionalized Oppression

Discrimination against women is evident in many sectors of society. Discrimination based on gender, ethnicity, age, religion, class, and sexual orientation is institutionalized in most political, economic, educational, occupational, and religious systems. Astin's (1984) theory of career development contains two elements dealing with these external influences: gender-role socialization and the structure of opportunity. Gender-role socialization is accomplished in families, at school, at work, and in play

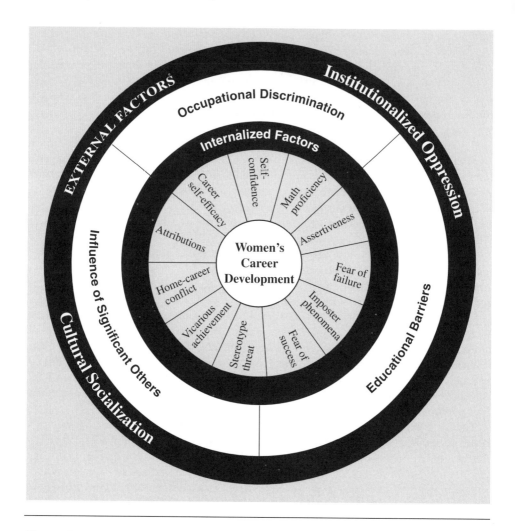

**Figure 7.1   Women's career wheel: Factors affecting women's career development.**

(see Chapter 2). Astin's *structure of opportunity* includes the distribution of jobs, gender typing of jobs, job requirements, discrimination, the economy, family structure, and reproductive technology. A diagram of Astin's model is presented in Figure 7.2. For our discussion here, we highlight three external influences: educational discrimination, influence of significant others, and occupational discrimination. In each of these areas, there is an interplay between cultural socialization and institutionalized oppression. While Astin's model focuses on gender-role issues, it can be modified to include multiple forms of discrimination and stereotyping to enhance its compatibility with EFT.

*Educational Barriers*

Most of us spend about half of our waking hours in school during the most formative years of our career development. Historically speaking, women's inclusion in educational institutions has been relatively recent. Until early in the twentieth century, education

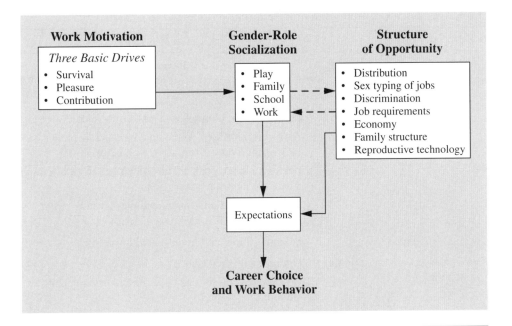

**Figure 7.2   Astin's career development model. A need-based sociopsycological model of career choice and work behavior.** *Source:* **"The Meaning of Work in Women's Lives: A Sociopsychological Model of Career Choice and Work Behaviors," by H. S. Astin, 1984,** *The Counseling Psychologist, 12,* **pp. 117–126. Reprinted with permission.**

was viewed as unhealthy for women. Further, women and People of Color were viewed as less intelligent than White males (Reid & Zalk, 2001). As discussed in detail in Chapter 2, discrimination in most educational systems has been well-documented and is manifested in several ways:

- Many studies have shown that teachers, counselors, and administrators respond differently to boys and girls in ways that reflect traditional gender-role stereotyping (Sadker & Sadker, 1994). In Table 7.1, we summarize some of these differential practices under "communication patterns" and "curriculum content." Some of these educational practices fit with hostile sexism and others fit with the concept of benevolent sexism (see Chapter 1).
- Textbooks, instructional materials, and tests have been demonstrated to be biased (Fassinger, 2001; Reid & Zalk, 2001; Sadker & Sadker, 1994; Stitt-Gohdes, 1997). These educational materials often show women and men in gender and ethnically stereotyped activities and occupations, use more male than female pronouns, underrepresent female contributions in all fields, and, in general, depict males more often than females. In addition, girls and women are often portrayed as incompetent, afraid, and unable to take effective action on their own behalf. Bias in textbooks exists at all grade levels from kindergarten through graduate school. Although there have been improvements in recent years, sexism, racism, and heterosexism are still present in educational materials.

**Table 7.1    Forms of educational discrimination relevant to women**

| Type | Description |
| --- | --- |
| Marginalizing communication patterns | Overt hostility toward women and minorities. |
| | Male and heterosexually based analogies and examples. |
| | Sexist, racist, homophobic jokes or remarks. |
| | Attribution of boys' poor academic performance to lack of motivation and girls' to lack of ability. |
| | Lack of encouragement for women and diverse groups to pursue nontraditional goals. |
| | Lower expectations for subordinate groups' achievement. |
| Intimidating behaviors | Sexual, ethnic, and homosexual harassment. |
| Curricular and extracurricular content and practices | Overuse of rote learning. |
| | Infrequent interactions between faculty and diverse students. |
| | Stereotypic presentation of women and diverse groups in textbooks. |
| | Lack of appropriate role models for diverse groups. |
| | Activities that exclude women or other diverse groups. |
| Institutionalized White, male power hierarchy | Women and minorities clustered in low-level positions. |
| | Lack of leadership role models and mentors for diverse groups. |
| | Sexist, racist, classist, heterosexist attitudes of educational leaders. |

- The administrative hierarchy of U.S. educational institutions also reflects bias. For example, colleges and universities are primarily constructed on patriarchal values and structures. Further, while the majority of elementary teachers in the United States are female, the percentage of female faculty and female administrators dramatically decreases as grade level increases. For example, less than 3% of public school superintendents are female (Fassinger, 2001). Only 19% of university full professors are female (Reid & Zalk, 2001). Further, in a 1999 study by the American Association of University Professors, male faculty in universities granting doctoral degrees earned 9.7% more than female faculty of equal rank (as cited in Reid & Zalk, 2001).
- School personnel often encourage females and males to enroll in gender-stereotyped courses and to pursue gender-stereotyped careers. As Table 7.2 shows, women have made significant strides, but more work to reduce barriers remains, especially for ethnic minority, lesbian, and lower socioeconomic (SES) women (Astin & Lindholm, 2001). Lack of encouragement (which creates a "null environment") or active

Table 7.2   **Percent of women enrolled in professional degrees by field and year**

| Field | 1960 | 1970 | 1980 | 1990 | 1997 |
|---|---|---|---|---|---|
| Dentistry | 0.0* | 1.1 | 13.3 | 30.9 | 36.9 |
| Medicine | 5.5 | 9.1 | 23.4 | 34.2 | 41.4 |
| Law | 2.5 | 7.1 | 30.2 | 42.3 | 43.7 |
| Business | 3.6 | 3.9 | 22.4 | 34.0 | 38.9 |

*Note:* Actual figure was 0.0008.
*Source:* Academic Aspirations and Degree Attainment of Women, by H. S. Astin and J. A. Linholm, 2001, J. Worell (Ed.), San Diego, CA: Academic Press. Reprinted with permission.

discouragement of nontraditional pursuits inhibits women from breaking from traditional gender-role socialization (Farmer, 1997; Fassinger, 2001).

Thus, through the biased attitudes and behaviors of school personnel, lack of nontraditional role models, bias in educational materials, sexism and racism in the administrative hierarchy, and differential patterns of encouragement for achievement, educational systems are a major source of oppressive experiences for many women. (See Table 7.1 for a summary of educational discrimination practices.) All these factors impact directly and indirectly on women's career aspirations and career development. Although the effects of a biased education on women are many, the primary outcome is that women tend to choose majors and careers consistent with gender-role, racial, and class stereotypes (Eccles, 2001; Farmer, 1997).

## Influence of Significant Others

The role of significant others, including parents, peers, partners, teachers, and mentors, demonstrates the influence of role models, of encouragers and rewards, and of discouragers (lack of reinforcement or punishment). In general, women who choose nontraditional careers are more likely to have had direct encouragement for, and role modeling of, nontraditional careers. For example, in Helen Farmer's (1997) longitudinal research comparing women who did and did not persist in scientific careers, nonpersisters changed their aspirations in part because their parents conveyed the importance of being a wife and mother. On the other side, she found that parents' support for their daughters' achievements had a positive effect on their career choices. Farmer's participants were also impacted negatively and positively by teachers' reactions, but generally indicated that school counselors had little or no impact. Richie and colleagues (1997) found that educator, parental, and spousal support were important for high-achieving African American and White women. In an achievement motivation literature review, Jacqueline Eccles (2001) cited research indicating that teachers were more likely to encourage high-achieving, White males to aim for college and high-level careers than they were other groups of students.

## Occupational Discrimination

Discrimination in the workplace involves stereotyping of groups (based on sexism, ethnocentrism, ableism and ageism, racism, classism, and heterosexism [SEARCH] variables) and institutionalized oppression. Both stereotyping and institutionalized oppression may be of the hostile or benevolent type (Glick & Fiske, 1996). Examples of hostile oppression are discrimination in hiring and promotion decisions and sexual or ethnocultural harassment. The benevolent type of oppression is usually more subtle and includes behaviors or policies differentially aimed at members of a group based on stereotypic beliefs about that group (Hyde & Kling, 2001). For example, a boss exempts a female manager (without her request) from attending an important regional staff meeting so that she will not have to be away from her husband and children overnight. Experiences with discrimination and stereotyping—whether hostile or benevolent, overt or subtle—can have dampening effects on women's career development, with high costs for both the individual and society (Auster, 2001; Clark, Caffarella, & Ingram, 1999; Farmer, 1997; Fassinger, 2001; Gutek, 2001a; Richie et al., 1997). Workplace discriminations are so pervasive that Farmer asserted that for high-achieving women to succeed in their careers, they must have coping skills to challenge and address the discrimination obstacles they face.

## Stereotyping in the Workplace

Women's roles in the workplace have undergone major transformations in the past 40 years. Women have entered nontraditional occupations at increased rates, a growing percentage of all women are working outside the home, and increased numbers of married women with families are in the labor market (Zunker, 1998). While women from all diverse groups have made significant strides, they still have not achieved full equity with White men (Gutek, 2001a).

Most women's career development is impacted by a culture's gender-role stereotypes, gender-role socialization, gender discrimination, and sexual harassment. Further, women who belong to additional disadvantaged groups are exposed to stereotyping, socialization processes, discrimination, and harassment based on stereotypes about those groups.

Gender stereotyped beliefs about appropriate cultural roles for women and men form the foundation for gender discriminatory practices in the workplace. The traits and behaviors stereotypically viewed as possessed by men in White, Western cultures (e.g., competitiveness and logical, initiating behaviors) lead people to see men as suited for certain occupations, especially ones involving leadership and professional or technical skills (Gutek, 2001a). On the other hand, White, Western stereotyped beliefs about women (e.g., nurturing ability, cooperation, gentleness) are associated with a more narrow range of occupations, clustered into caretaking, lower status, and lower paying careers. While gender-role stereotypes vary across diverse groups in the United States, the majority of these groups reflect patriarchal structures. Moreover, the U.S. workplace is still currently dominated by White, Western male cultural values; thus, these White gender stereotypes continue to impact how women of all diverse backgrounds are treated in the labor force. The impacts of these stereotyped beliefs are found in the workplace in several ways: (a) uneven distribution of groups across careers, (b) unequal earnings between women and men and between ethnic groups, (c) unequal power arrangements, and (d) harassment of women.

**Uneven Distribution**    The existence of gender typing of occupations is demonstrated by:

1. The gender-typed labels that have been applied (e.g., policeman, stewardess).
2. The uneven distribution of females and males in various careers.
3. Inequitable compensation given in female-dominated careers.

While gender-typed labels have gradually been replaced by nonsexist ones in textbooks and formal documents, they continue to exist in everyday conversation and in informal writings. Several generations are probably needed to eradicate the use of sexist language completely. Because Chapter 2 discussed the negative impact of sexist language, we merely summarize here: To the degree women have heard and used gender-typed labels for careers, they are at least somewhat less likely to view male-labeled careers as appropriate for them.

Segregation based on occupational stereotyping is reflected in the composition of various occupations. In Table 7.3, percentages of women, African Americans, and Hispanics in selected occupations for the years 1983 and 1999 are displayed. A comparison of the 1983 and 1999 figures for nontraditional occupations (for both women and other diverse groups) shows consistent improvement over time. However, the 1999 figures indicate that women, African Americans, and Hispanics are still underrepresented (proportional to their representation in the total workforce) in these occupations. Women continue to be clustered in the traditional careers of teaching, nursing, and clerical workers. This occupational gender segregation (A. J. Murrell, 2001) is especially evident in "the blue and pink collar labor markets where technical and unionized skill labor jobs are occupied primarily by men and pink-collar and other service-related skilled jobs are occupied primarily by women" (Eccles, 2001, p. 45). Even within science careers, women are found in less prestigious careers than men (Farmer, 1997). This gender segregation of occupations applies to females and males in most ethnocultural groups (Eccles, 2001).

**Unequal Earnings**    The effects of stereotyping are also reflected in the earnings of men, women, and ethnic minorities. As Table 7.4 shows, the highest median wages were earned by White males, followed by African American males, White females, and African American females (U.S. Bureau of Census, 2000). In 1999, a similar, but somewhat improved, pattern for minority groups is evident. White males are still the highest paid groups and Hispanic males and females are the lowest. The patterns suggest that:

1. Being female and being a person of color have depressing effects on a person's income.
2. Being female, regardless of ethnic status, lowers earnings when compared to men of the same group.
3. Being both a female and a Person of Color puts individuals at multiple risk.

Traditionally gender-typed occupations for women have lower pay than those occupations traditionally gender-typed as male even when education and skill level have been controlled (Fassinger, 2001). Despite Barbara Gutek's (2001a) conclusion that women generally do better in jobs that have specific educational requirements, the gender and ethnocultural pay gaps exist even in highly trained groups (Vasquez, 2001). Women in nontraditional careers typically earn less than men in those fields. For example, female faculty continue to earn less than male faculty even when seniority and academic discipline are held constant (American Association for University Professors, 1999 as cited in Vasquez, 2001). Women as managers earn less than their male counterparts (Wade, 2001). We began this chapter with a quotation by Seager and Olson (1986) based on their review of international data on women and the labor force. They concluded that internationally women are segregated into low-paying, low-status occupations.

**Table 7.3    Selected occupations: Percentage of workforce by gender and ethnicity**

| Occupation | 1983 | 1999 |
|---|---|---|
| *Total Workforce* | | |
| Women | 43.7 | 46.5 |
| Blacks | 9.3 | 11.3 |
| Hispanics | 5.3 | 10.3 |
| *Architects* | | |
| Women | 12.7 | 15.7 |
| Blacks | 1.6 | 2.3 |
| Hispanics | 1.5 | 4.4 |
| *Engineers* | | |
| Women | 5.8 | 10.6 |
| Blacks | 2.7 | 4.6 |
| Hispanics | 2.2 | 3.5 |
| *Mathematical and Computer Scientists* | | |
| Women | 29.6 | 31.1 |
| Blacks | 5.4 | 7.5 |
| Hispanics | 2.6 | 3.6 |
| *Physicians* | | |
| Women | 15.8 | 24.5 |
| Blacks | 3.2 | 5.7 |
| Hispanics | 4.5 | 4.8 |
| *Registered Nurses* | | |
| Women | 95.8 | 92.9 |
| Blacks | 6.7 | 9.6 |
| Hispanics | 1.8 | 3.1 |
| *Teachers* | | |
| Women | 70.9 | 74.8 |
| Blacks | 9.1 | 9.9 |
| Hispanics | 2.7 | 5.4 |
| *College and University Teachers* | | |
| Women | 36.3 | 42.4 |
| Blacks | 4.4 | 6.5 |
| Hispanics | 1.8 | 4.2 |
| *Administrative Support including Clerical* | | |
| Women | 79.9 | 78.7 |
| Blacks | 9.6 | 13.5 |
| Hispanics | 5.0 | 9.4 |

*Source:* United States Bureau of Census, 2000.

**Table 7.4   Comparison of U.S. full-time median weekly wages by gender and ethnicity: 1985 and 1999**

| Group | 1985 Weekly Wage[a] | 1985 Weekly Ratio[b] | 1999 Weekly Wage | 1999 Weekly Ratio |
|---|---|---|---|---|
| White males | $417 | 100% | $638 | 100% |
| African American males | $304 | 72.9% | $488 | 76.5% |
| White females | $281 | 67.4% | $483 | 75.7% |
| African American females | $252 | 60.4% | $409 | 64.1% |
| Hispanic males | Not available | | $406 | 63.6% |
| Hispanic females | Not available | | $348 | 54.5% |

[a] Weekly wage in dollars.
[b] Wage ratio compared to White males.
*Source:* United States Bureau of Census, 2000.

Seager and Olson (1986) asserted, "Women's relative underpayment in work is a major factor in the growing feminization of poverty" (p. 47). Similarly and more currently, Heidi Hartmann, Katherine Allen, and Christine Owens (1999) studied the U.S. wage gap between women and men and minorities and nonminorities. They analyzed the gendered wage gap, controlling for hours worked, educational level, age, and geographic location, and found that if women were paid earnings comparable to men, they would earn over $4,000 more a year and their poverty rates would be cut by half. These lower wages affect not only women, but also their children and families. Because of their lower earnings levels, at retirement, women have about half of the pension income of men, and female retirees are much more likely to be living in poverty than are male retirees (Vasquez, 2001). Given these consequences, Joy Rice (1997) advocated that poor women be counseled to pursue training that is "not traditionally gender-based" (p. 14) and is technologically based.

**Unequal Power**   The structure of occupational institutions is often based on White, male, Western values (e.g., competition, aggressiveness) and on norms of male experiences (e.g., men being primarily the "breadwinners"). These androcentric and ethnocentric biases pose additional problems for women in the workplace. For example, based on androcentric perspectives, most workplaces provide no child care facilities and few offer flexible working schedules to accommodate family needs. Since women still shoulder major child care and family responsibilities, lack of flexible policies and child care facilities negatively impacts women's careers (Clark et al., 1999; Farmer, 1997; Fassinger, 2001).

Women and minorities are also less likely to hold positions of power and leadership in most work environments (Gutek, 2001a). The stereotype of being a leader fits more closely the stereotype of being a White male (Gutek, 2001a; Heilmann, 2001; Wade, 2001). Further, this "envision a leader, envision a male" phenomenon appears to be global (Schein, 2001). Although these stereotypes and their associated myths about women as leaders have been challenged by actual research (primarily conducted by feminist scholars), Gutek concluded that the stereotypes and myths continue to influence interactions and decisions in the workplace because "sometimes the myths sell better than the realities" (p. 383).

Women and minority group members who hold leadership positions face several barriers. First, women leaders engaging in assertive, self-promoting behaviors are likely to be viewed more negatively than male leaders displaying those same behaviors (Fassinger, 2001). Second, lack of institutional resources (e.g., secretarial help, technical or lab resources, grants), lack of mentors, and exclusion from the "old-boy" network are especially problematic for women in nontraditional careers. Women are less likely to have mentors than men (Reid & Zalk, 2001). Role models and mentors serve several crucial functions:

- They provide examples of how to cope with life's challenges. Role modeling of strategies for confronting racism, sexism, ableism, ageism, classism, and heterosexism are important for helping women handle oppressive career experiences (Farmer, 1997).
- The role model may either support or challenge societal stereotypes.
- Mentors and role models with characteristics similar to the target women (e.g., gender, ethnicity, age, sexual orientation) are crucial for learning informal norms and rules and other information important to success (Farmer, 1997; Fassinger, 2001; Gutek, 2001a).
- Appropriate role models are important to the development of self-efficacy for nontraditional occupations for women (Betz, 1992).
- Women need mentors who can address and model strategies for combining home and family commitments (Farmer, 1997).

Based on a review of the literature, Ellen Auster (2001) concluded that for women, having a mentor is associated with having higher pay, more promotions, and greater career satisfaction.

**Sexual Harassment**    Title VII of the Civil Rights Act of 1964 and Title IX of the Educational Amendments of 1972 prohibit gender discrimination in employment and education in the United States (Zunker, 1998). Although overt sex and race discrimination in employment practices is generally prohibited by law, such practices still overtly and covertly exist. Employment discrimination varies from covert, subtle to overt, blatant, with even the most subtle oppressive experiences having accumulative effects over time (Fassinger, 2001; Stitt-Gohdes, 1997). For example, sex discrimination has been found to account for 55% to 62% of the variance in the career success of women (Fassinger, 2001).

Among the various forms of employment discrimination, sexual harassment has been one of the most studied and is one of the most pervasive. *Sexual harassment* (SH) is "any deliberate or repeated sexual behavior that is unwelcome to its recipient, as well as other sex-related behaviors that are hostile, offensive, or degrading" (Fitzgerald, 1993, p. 1070). In the quid pro quo type, the victim either benefits or suffers negative consequences for compliance or noncompliance with sexual requests. In the hostile environment type, an offensive (gender-based) work environment interferes with women's ability to work or learn.

In studies of sexual harassment in the workplace and in places of learning, about 50% of women have been found to be sexual harassment victims (Fitzgerald, 1993; Gutek, 2001a; Koss, Goodman, et al., 1994). Further, minority women (e.g., Women of Color, lesbian women) may be at increased risk for being sexually harassed and may be at risk for ethnic and lesbian-targeted harassment as well (A. J. Murrell, 2001; Reid & Zalk, 2001). For example, in a study of more than 1,000 university undergraduate and graduate women, the following percentages had experienced some type of sexual harassment: African American, 62%; Latina, 60%; European American, 56%; Asian, East Indian American, 46%. While 51% of heterosexual women had experienced SH, 81% of lesbian or bisexual women had been sexually harassed (Cortina, Swan, Fitzgerald, & Waldo, 1998). Sexual harassers may be peers or a person in a position of authority. In most cases, sexual harassment is an abuse of power, either of the harasser's position in the organization or of the harasser's societal privilege (e.g., male, White, upper class, heterosexual).

Sexual harassment has pervasive, negative career, psychological, and physical consequences for its victims (Fitzgerald, 1993; Hamilton et al., 1986; Koss, Goodman, et al., 1994; Reid & Zalk, 2001). Career-related consequences include disrupted work history, absenteeism, loss of seniority, decreased opportunity for advancement, and changing jobs or majors. Depression, anxiety, decreased self-esteem, self-doubt, fear, feelings of helplessness, and posttraumatic stress are some of the major psychological consequences. Health and physical consequences include headaches, nausea, gastrointestinal problems, sexual dysfunction, and sleep disturbance.

### Summary of External Barriers

Oppressive experiences, especially racism, sexism, ableism, and heterosexism, are plentiful in women's lives and create barriers to their educational and career achievements (Farmer, 1997). The oppressive societal messages sent to women have a threefold impact:

1. They convey that women are not as valuable or as competent as men, especially in traditional male gender-typed arenas (i.e., that "women can't").
2. They suggest that it is not appropriate for women to pursue traditional male careers (i.e., that "women shouldn't") (Heilmann, 2001; Terlau, 1991).
3. They suggest that, even when women are competent and do pursue a nontraditional career, they are not rewarded appropriately and may even be punished.

When women realistically perceive these barriers, they are less likely to choose nontraditional paths. These overt and covert structural barriers discourage women from considering, choosing, and persisting in nontraditional majors and careers.

## Multiple Jeopardy

Most of the achievement and career-related research on women has been conducted on White women (Gutek, 2001a; Hyde & Kling, 2001). Women who are also members of additional subordinate groups have increased vulnerability. For instance, based on her Women of Color data, Farmer (1997) asserted that experiences with racism impacted these women at every stage of development. She also pointed out that being from a low SES background sometimes motivated the career attainments of the women she studied and at other times restricted it. In general, the SEARCH forms of oppression interact to place women with multiple subordinate social locations in increased jeopardy in schools and the workplace (Byars & Hackett, 1998; Farmer, 1997). Further, stereotyping of each group varies and has additional and unique impact. Gender-role stereotyping also varies across each group and so impact varies correspondingly. For example, African American females receive more androgynous socialization than White or Latina females. Thus, both White and Latina women have lower self-efficacy for nontraditional careers (Byars & Hackett, 1998). Finally, Women of Color have to navigate between the White male culture of the workplace and the cultures of their communities (Auster, 2001).

The statistics in Tables 7.3 and 7.4 demonstrate how racism and sexism affect People of Color, and especially Women of Color. Pamela Reid and Sue Zalk (2001) commented: "The relationship between representation and level of prestige or importance is remarkably linear, such that the more important or prestigious a position or institution is, the less represented are women and people of color" (p. 30). Gutek (2001a) concluded that eliminating stereotyping (due to SEARCH factors) would significantly decrease women's employment difficulties: "In short, stereotypes are an important component in understanding both how women behave at work and how they are perceived by others, and those stereotypes often put women at a significant disadvantage" (p. 383). She also highlighted the importance of future research on the stereotypical experiences of marginalized women's subgroups.

It is beyond the scope of this chapter to detail the oppressive experiences and their internal impact for every diverse group of women. In lieu of detailing the specific experiences of each diverse group, we have chosen to describe some of the career issues for lesbian women. We chose this group because Michelle, our client for this chapter, is a lesbian woman.

## Career Issues for Lesbian Women

Lesbian women's identity development and career development processes are not linear; they intertwine and affect each other in unique ways for each woman. That is, a woman may become aware of her lesbian identity at any time across the life span (Morgan & Brown, 1991). The earlier she becomes aware of that identity, the more it affects her career choices. Women who identify as a lesbian later in the life span have to address how to integrate their current career choice with their lesbian identity.

Because sexual orientation identity is not visible the way skin color or gender is visible, lesbian women have a choice about whether to disclose this aspect of themselves. Disclosure to others, or "coming out," is affected by the social climate. That climate in the United States is generally hostile. First, heterosexuality is assumed, is highly valued, and serves as the foundational structure for most societal institutions (i.e., a heterosexist environment). Second, negative societal stereotypes are generally held about homosexual people (i.e., a homophobic environment). Growing up and living in this homophobic and heterosexist culture often results in lesbians having negative feelings about themselves. Earlier lesbian identity development models tied self-acceptance of identity to disclosure to others. More recently, these two processes have been conceptualized as separate, with lesbian individuals having to make repeated decisions about whether to disclose to others based on how "safe" each situation is (i.e., evaluating the benefits and costs of disclosing; Fassinger & Miller, 1996).

**Workplace Discrimination against Lesbian Women**   Lesbian women are likely to encounter workplace discrimination (Morgan & Brown, 1991). This discrimination can result in job loss and/or verbal and physical attacks (Rostosky & Riggle, in press). Legal protection varies across communities and organizations. However, in the last 10 to 15 years, some major businesses have instituted nondiscrimination policies and/or have extended health policy benefits to the partners of lesbian women and gay men. Given the severe outcomes of discrimination, lesbian women have difficult decisions to make about whether to disclose their sexual orientation in the workplace. They may disclose or not, choose a field or work setting that does not discriminate, or be self-employed (Morgan & Brown, 1991).

**Additional Career Factors for Lesbian Women**   Many lesbian couples value egalitarian relationships and eschew traditional gender-role behavior. Lesbian women have at least double minority status (gender and sexual orientation) and the gender pay gap affects lesbian couples doubly (Morgan & Brown, 1991).

**Being "Out" at Work**   Sharon Rostosky and Ellen Riggle (in press) surveyed lesbian, gay, and bisexual individuals (LGB) to explore the relationships among workplace policies, internalized homophobia, and job satisfaction for both individuals and their partners. Being "out" at work was associated with the individual's workplace having a nondiscrimination policy, the individual having lower levels of internalized homophobia, the partner's workplace having a nondiscrimination policy, and the partner having lower levels of internalized homophobia. They concluded: "disclosure in the workplace is associated with the degree to which gay and lesbian individuals perceive that they are safe in their organizations and self-accepting of themselves" (p. 20).

## Internalized Factors

In the following sections, we explore the more specific ways these external negative messages and structural barriers impact women's perceptions of themselves and their environments, and how these internalized perceptions influence their career-related choice behaviors. External oppressive messages and barriers impinge on women so pervasively that the messages are no longer perceived as external, but rather as something wrong or deficient in the women themselves (Fassinger, 2001). The impact of the external environment is reflected in career-related beliefs, interests, values, and goals (Astin & Lindholm, 2001). These relationships are depicted in the Women's Career Wheel in Figure 7.1. In the career wheel, we attempt to symbolize that women "are not born with these ideas" (Hyde & Kling, 2001, p. 374), but rather learn them through cultural socialization and by their experiences with institutionalized oppression.

The large number of internal factors on the career wheel demonstrates the many ways in which each woman may internalize her external experiences. Also, for any particular woman, any number of these factors may be working in combination. The whole impact is greater than the sum of the individual factors.

### Attributions

When men experience success, they are more likely to attribute their success to their ability, whereas women are more likely to attribute their successes to luck or effort (Eccles, 2001; Fassinger, 2001; Wade, 2001). Males are more likely to attribute their failures to chance or lack of effort, whereas females are more likely to attribute their failures to their lack of ability (Eccles, 2001). These attributions are theorized to be related to interpretations based on gender-role stereotyping. That is, women attribute their failure on a male-stereotyped task to lack of ability. Female attributions of success to external sources and of failure to internal sources contribute to women having less self-confidence and to their avoidance of some achievement situations. Attribution-making appears to be a socialized phenomenon. Yee and Eccles (1983) found that adults were more likely to tell task-succeeding girls that they were lucky and to tell task-succeeding boys that they did well because they were smart. The adults attributed the boys' task failures to lack of effort and the girls' task failures to lack of ability. Similarly, in a review of related research, Eccles (2001) pointed out that parents also make these gendered attributions about their children.

## Career Self-Efficacy

Career-relevant self-concept factors have long been a cornerstone of career development theories. One form of self-concept, self-efficacy, has been given a central role in career development (Eccles, 1994). *Career self-efficacy* is a specific form of self-efficacy; it refers to people's beliefs that they can successfully perform job activities that are part of specific occupations. In general, females report higher self-efficacy for traditionally female occupations than for nontraditional occupations (Eccles, 2001). Career self-efficacy is viewed as a mediating variable of career choice, in that, if individuals believe that they cannot perform the tasks required in a career, they will not aspire to that career (Betz, 1992, 1994; Betz & Hackett, 1981; Eccles, 2001).

Betz and Hackett (1981) theorized that women are lower in self-efficacy for nontraditional occupations because of traditional gender-role socialization. With respect to nontraditional careers, women have lower self-efficacy because they have less direct experience with nontraditional tasks, they lack same-sex role models, they receive less encouragement from others that they can perform the nontraditional tasks, and they experience higher anxiety in relation to the tasks. For the opposite reasons, women develop high self-efficacy for traditional occupations. Betz and Hackett concluded that traditional gender-role socialization directly affects development of specific career self-efficacies; career self-efficacy, in turn, directly affects women's traditionality of occupational choice. Indeed, researchers have found positive relationships between self-efficacy and career aspirations, social support, and career interests, and negative relationships between self-efficacy and barriers to careers (Betz, 1994; Fassinger, 2001; Hyde & Kling, 2001).

Michelle tended to attribute her successes to effort and, thus, did not think of herself as an intelligent woman. While she usually attributed her failures to not working hard enough, in the area of math she tended to attribute any poor performance to not having "enough" math ability. Thus, her self-efficacy for graduate work in math was lower than her actual performance achievements would suggest.

## Self-Confidence and Self-Esteem

In general, males tend to overestimate their abilities, while females underestimate theirs (Dweck, 1986; Fassinger, 2001). Both estimates are inaccurate, but the male perceptual error has a positive effect on performance and self-esteem, while the female error has detrimental effects. Gender differences in self-confidence and self-esteem vary across specific domains. Girls and women have higher self-confidence for female-stereotyped arenas, and self-confidence is not related to actual performance (Eccles, 2001; Hyde & Kling, 2001). For example, boys have higher self-confidence about math while girls are higher in self-confidence about English. Further, a woman's hierarchy of self-confidence across domains (i.e., compared to herself) also impacts her eventual career choices (Hyde & Kling, 2001). For example, if her self-confidence for writing is higher than for math (even if her self-confidence for math is high), she is more likely to choose a writing-related career. The underestimation by females contributes to fear of failure (i.e., "I don't have the ability, thus I am likely to fail") and to lower self-esteem. Higher self-confidence is also positively related to expectations for success. Girls' self-confidence erodes during adolescence, and this erosion impacts at especially critical career decision-making points (Eccles, 2001). For example, Michelle lacked confidence in herself in general and she consistently underestimated her intelligence.

## Math Proficiency

Males tend to excel at higher-level math courses, are more likely to enroll in higher-level math courses, and score higher on math on the Scholastic Aptitude Test (SAT). The issue of what accounts for the female-male differences has never been fully resolved. While some argue for biological differences, others argue that the differences in math performance are tied to gender-role socialization and institutionalized sexism. The latter is compatible with a feminist therapy approach. Ruth Fassinger (2001) reviewed the literature and concluded that gender-role socialization and the gender typing of math as a male domain were major factors in the math performance difference. She also pointed out that in addition to these factors, test bias, sexism in educational strategies, sexism in texts, and the "science nerd" image limit women's pursuit of higher math courses (p. 1173). Further, females have lower self-efficacy for math than males even when their actual performance is higher. Eccles (2001) concluded that lower self-confidence about a domain (e.g., math) may lead to a woman's not pursuing or dropping out of careers related to that domain. Moreover, math is a critical filter in the job market (Farmer, 1997) because math skills are crucial to so many fields and because math-related fields, such as engineering and accounting, are higher paying and are male dominated.

Janet Hyde and Kristen Kling (2001) reviewed research on gender and math performance. They concluded:

1. Math performance is composed of a complex of different skills, and gender differences are not consistent across skill types.
2. The age at which math performance is assessed affects gender differences found with girls in elementary school performing better than boys, suggesting that developmental life experiences impact gender differences.
3. Male superior performance on the math section of the SAT compared to female performance yields an effect size much larger than those found in other research data bases, suggesting some type of gender bias in the SAT math tests.
4. Women's enrollment in advanced math courses is affected by the value they give to math.
5. Within-sex differences are greater than between-sex differences.

Michelle had always been good at math and had received reinforcement for her math abilities from several of her teachers. In college, she took a nontraditional path by majoring in math. However, she also reported that she received little or no encouragement from her professors in her major, and none of her professors were female. Thus, although proficiency in math was a facilitating force in Michelle's career choice process, as she reached upper levels of math achievement, lack of role models and lack of encouragement from her professors impacted her decision not to pursue graduate training in math.

## Fear of Failure

*Fear of failure* is an expectancy that you will not be able to attain a particular goal. When individuals experience fear of failure, they are more likely to either not attempt to reach the goal or to become handicapped by anxiety while attempting to attain the goal. While both women and men may experience fear of failure, Sherman (1987) and Clance and O'Toole (1987) asserted that, because men are generally more confident and receive more encouragement than women, fear of failure has more negative impact for women. Fear of failure has been found to be related to lack of confidence, low self-esteem, low risk taking, and fear of success (Farmer, 1997; Sherman, 1987).

One of Michelle's early long-term goals had been to be a math professor. She had given up that goal in college because she feared she would not be successful in a doctoral program.

## Fear of Success

Horner (1972) characterized *fear of success* (FOS) as a motivation to avoid success, which she believed was a key factor accounting for differences in female and male motivation. Horner believed that FOS was a stable personality trait that developed early in childhood and was related to gender-role identity development. She believed that as long as achievement and being "feminine" were societally defined as conflicting, women would internalize these conflicts.

Horner's original findings have had mixed substantiation by subsequent researchers, and its theoretical underpinnings have also been critiqued. (See Hyde and Kling's 2001 review.) In particular, the context of the successful situation (e.g., success in a female- or a male-dominated occupation, success in a competitive or cooperative situation) changes individuals' FOS scores. Thus, what was originally conceptualized as a generalized trait is probably more a fear of transgressing gender-stereotyped expectations; therefore, researchers of FOS are probably actually measuring cultural attitudes and stereotypes. Hyde and Kling (2001) concluded that FOS research has been currently discarded.

We have retained a discussion of fear of success both because of its historical value in understanding research on women's career achievement and because it can be seen as a realistic appraisal by women of societal rewards and punishments for conformity to or deviation from gender-stereotyped norms in achievement situations. Thus, for the women who experience FOS, it is another example of the internalization of cultural restrictions on women.

In her longitudinal study of women who do and do not persist in science, Farmer (1997) found that science persisters had lower FOS than nonpersisters. Even women who choose nontraditional career paths may experience FOS conflict. Yuen and Depper (1987) concluded that FOS is really a fear of failure (i.e., being successful at a career, yet risking relationship loss). While most of the research on FOS has been conducted on White participants, some research suggests that African American women have less FOS than White women (as cited in Hyde & Kling, 2001).

## Impostor Phenomenon

The *impostor phenomenon* is a term used by Clance and Imes (1987) to describe a feeling of phoniness by high achievers. Individuals who have attained a level of success, but feel like impostors, assess that they do not deserve the achievement and expect to be "found out." *Impostors* do not enjoy their accomplishments and negate external evidence of their abilities (Clance & O'Toole, 1987). Many of the characteristics of *impostors* demonstrate the close ties between attributions, fear of success, fear of failure, self-confidence, and gender-role messages. *Impostors* tend to be anxious about failure when faced with evaluation or a new task, have difficulty internalizing positive feedback, underestimate their own abilities and chances of future success, attribute their successes to luck and hard work, avoid some accomplishments, and set goals below their potential (Clance & O'Toole, 1987; Thompson, Davis, & Davidson, 1997). Mixed results related to the prevalence of the impostor phenomenon in women and men have been found by researchers (Clance & O'Toole, 1987; K. Hayes & Davis, 1993; J. E. King & Cooley, 1995; Thompson et al., 1997). Ewing, Richardson, James-Meyers, and Russell (1996) investigated the impostor phenomenon in African American graduate students. They found that academic self-concept and being in the immersion-emersion stage of racial identity were significant negative predictors of feeling like an impostor. Beverly Greene (1994a) hypothesized that the internalized effects of both racism and sexism contribute to the impostor phenomenon in African American women.

Michelle consistently discounted positive feedback and tended to downplay all of her accomplishments. With the exception of her math ability, Michelle especially discounted skills and assets that stereotypically fall in the male domain. For example, although she possessed and used many leadership skills, she had been surprised when she was elected by her teaching peers to represent them on a districtwide committee. She was sure they had made a mistake.

## Stereotype Threat

In Chapter 5, we describe Claude Steele's (1997) concept of stereotype threat (ST). When a negative stereotype about a person's own group applies to a situation (e.g., taking a test), the threat of confirming the stereotype produces anxiety in the individual, which in return reduces effective performance. In Chapter 5, we also described the research documenting how ST affects the test performance of women and African Americans. Although the existing literature is small, preliminary results indicate that it also affects the performance of Latinas and Latinos and individuals from lower SES groups (Hyde & Kling, 2001). Further, we hypothesize that women who have social locations in multiple subordinate groups have intersecting impacts from stereotype threat. For instance, African American women may have additional anxiety and, thus, lowered performance on math ability tests.

Unlike the other factors on the inner part of the Women's Career Wheel, the societal stereotype about a person's own group does not have to be believed or internalized to affect women's behavior and career development. For example, ST has been used to explain women's lower performance on the SAT math test. Because the stereotypes operate outside the individual's belief system, society has to be changed to reduce ST's impact. These societal changes include eliminating society's stereotypes and revamping the learning environments of schools (Hyde & Kling, 2001).

Michelle earned a score of 650 on the SAT math test. Although this is a fairly high score and Michelle had excelled academically in math, she had not previously considered graduate work in math because she believed her score was not competitive enough. Stereotype threat may have lowered her score on this test.

## Lack of Assertiveness

Lack of assertiveness is an additional internal barrier to women's career achievements. Assertiveness skills are not typically taught or modeled for females and are not sanctioned for women from most cultural groups. Assertiveness skills are especially important for confronting and persisting in the face of discrimination barriers in educational and occupational systems.

Attributions made and the choice to be assertive may be influenced by whether the task is on behalf of others or on behalf of self. That is, women may be able to be more assertive when working on behalf of others (Wade, 2001). Although negotiating for pay and raises is an important aspect of career adjustment, making requests for themselves is not consistent with many cultures' view of feminine behavior. Based on gender-role socialization, women may accept lower pay especially when they have to declare their requests publicly. Further, assertive women may suffer negative consequences for being assertive that men do not. When they are not assertive, they are responding to accurate expectations of negative, external consequences and not out of low self-esteem or lack of skills (Heilmann, 2001; Wade, 2001).

Michelle had difficulty verbalizing her strengths and accomplishments to others. This particular lack of assertion was a career barrier for Michelle in interviewing situations.

## Vicarious Achievement

Vicarious achievers find personal fulfillment and satisfaction through a relationship with a directly achieving person with whom they identify (Lipman-Blumen & Leavitt, 1978), and they take pleasure both from the accomplishments of the other person and from their relationship with this person. Some degree of identification of the vicarious achiever with this other person is necessary; to some degree, vicarious achievers take as their own the goals, values, and interests of this person. In contrast, direct achievers derive pleasure by using self as a means to goals. Lipman-Blumen and Leavitt hypothesized that traditional gender-role socialization contributed to the development of vicarious achievement patterns in women and of direct achievement patterns in males. They found that vicariously achieving women were more likely to subscribe to traditional gender-role stereotypes and had lower expectations for continuing their education than direct achievers. They concluded that women with a vicarious achievement orientation often fulfill their achievement needs through their spouses' and/or children's accomplishments.

Over the past 20 years, discussion of and research on how vicarious achievement affects the career development of women had dwindled and almost disappeared, probably because so many women have entered the paid workforce. We debated dropping this section from this chapter; however, we both identified several women we know or have counseled who chose a more indirect approach to achievement through their husbands or children. Thus, although vicarious achievement may not be as prevalent or impactful as it once was, we believe that it still functions in some women's career development. We believe clinicians should be aware of the phenomenon because they may encounter it in a client; therefore, we have included it in the chapter.

As will be revealed later, Michelle eventually disclosed that she was lesbian to her therapist, Holly. Michelle told Holly that as a lesbian woman, she expected to support herself throughout her life. For her, being economically independent from her partner was an important factor in their maintaining an egalitarian relationship. Thus, vicarious achievement was not a significant influencing factor in Michelle's career development.

## Home-Career Conflict

Gender-role socialization in many cultures (e.g., Hispanic, Asian American) emphasizes the nurturing role for women. When women choose a career, they usually expect themselves, and are expected by others, to carry the majority of home maintenance, child care, and extended family (e.g., care of aging parents) responsibilities. They often believe their career achievement is acceptable only if they are first successful with their home responsibilities (Farmer, 1997). For example, White women usually value family over career while White men value family and career equally (Eccles, 2001). Further, both women and men believe that women should lessen involvement in one of these arenas to accommodate growing involvement in the other. On the other hand, men's commitments to career and family are viewed by both women and men as independent of each other (Benedetto & Tittle, 1990). Women often feel guilty about not giving 100% to each and push themselves to be perfect at both. Other women may resolve the home-career conflict by pursuing only one arena: to be wife and mother, or to have a career. High-achieving women feel particularly pulled between their achievement needs and expectations and gender-role expectations, often choosing less professional careers that can accommodate family roles (Farmer, 1997).

No matter which of these paths is taken, for many women, the home-career conflict has a significant impact on career development at decision points as well as on a daily basis. This impact is especially limiting for women in nontraditional careers (Fassinger, 2001; Gutek, 2001a). Because gender-role socialization varies across minority groups, minority women experience the home-career conflict with various degrees of intensity (Stitt-Gohdes, 1997). For example, Angela Byars and Gail Hackett (1998) reasoned that because of differences in cultural gender socialization, compared to White women, African American women have less home-career conflict and Latinas have higher home-career conflict. However, across diverse groups, women continue to bear the majority of child care and housework responsibilities, even in more egalitarian relationships (Fassinger, 2001; Stitt-Gohdes, 1997). In fact, Ruth Fassinger (2001) hypothesized that home-career conflicts may result if the woman has liberal career values and traditional family values.

Being married and having children has been found to be associated with lower salaries for women and higher salaries for men. Spousal support for the married woman's career is crucial to reducing stress and role conflict and for career success (Clark et al., 1999; Farmer, 1997). The home-career conflict has been cited as a major restricting factor on women's career achievement (Fassinger, 2001). Given that multiple roles have been found to have psychological, relationship, and career benefits for women (Barnett & Hyde, 2001), Ruth Fassinger (2001) asserted, "it is not simply the combining of multiple roles that creates stress and compromises women's well-being, but rather the lack of concrete support in the workplace and family, forcing women into personal responsibilities for impediments to role management that are beyond their control" (p. 1178).

Michelle and her partner, Anne, have committed to establishing and maintaining an egalitarian relationship; and because they are both women, they do not have to be constantly vigilant about traditional female-male patterns of interacting in their relationship. Thus, the home-career conflict is not currently a barrier for Michelle. Later, if she and Anne decide to have children, female gender-role messages may impact how they juggle their multiple roles.

## Internalized Factors: A Summary

Some women can identify one or more of these internalized factors as having inhibited their career development. Others, even those in leadership positions who have experienced large doses of sexism and/or racism, have little awareness of gender issues and fail to perceive gender discrimination as the culprit for their problems (Clark et al., 1999). Recall that Sylvia, the client in Chapter 6, whom we assessed to be primarily at Level one, Preencounter, in both gender and ethnocultural identity development, initially did not perceive that being a Woman of Color was impeding her career success. "Women need help to disentangle those values that are personally important to them from others they have been taught that may be less important" (Farmer, 1997, p. 17). Identifying these internal barriers, tracing them to their external sources, and challenging and changing both external and internal barriers form the foundation of a feminist therapy approach to facilitating women's career development. While almost all women bear the effects of stereotyping and institutionalized oppression, we and others (e.g., Eccles, 2001; Hyde & Kling, 2001) are distressed by the lack of research on how these internal factors apply to diverse groups. More specifically, Janet Hyde and Kristen Kling called for research to study the effects collectivist cultures have on achievement goals. They speculated that in these cultures, group goals are more important factors in predicting achievement than individual goals.

Although we have focused on the pervasive negative effects of oppression on women's career development, women do find ways to cope with and overcome these barriers. Indeed, despite the negative environment, many women triumph over these barriers. For example, almost all the participants in a study of high-achieving women were involved in some type of social action aimed at ending racism and sexism (Richie et al., 1997). In addition to their career achievements, they had each made strong commitments to equality and social justice.

## A CHANGE AGENT CAREER COUNSELING MODEL

In Chapter 4, we presented four conditions that must be met for a counseling theoretical approach to be compatible with EFT (see Table 4.1). In addition to meeting these four conditions, a feminist career counseling approach should address external factors affecting career development as well as internal ones, teach strategies for dealing with oppression, and include strategies for bringing about changes in economic and occupational structures (EFT Principles I and II). A feminist career counseling approach should account for the interaction between the individual's choices and environmental opportunities and barriers, as well as allowing for changes in both (Astin, 1984; Farmer, 1997; Fassinger, 2001; Stitt-Gohdes, 1997). The model should challenge the restrictions placed on women's potential by gender-role socialization and internalized SEARCH factors. In line with Principles I, II, III, and IV, an EFT approach to career counseling can enhance self-exploration of social location variables, facilitate the woman's trust in herself, and empower her.

*Agency,* the "tendency of the individual to respond proactively to situations representing educational and career opportunities" (Betz & Hackett, 1987, p. 299), is an important empowerment strategy. Agency includes creating opportunities and being assertive. Agency has been found to be a crucial behavioral competency for professional women (Betz & Hackett, 1987; Farmer, 1997; McLennan, 1999).

Holly, Michelle's counselor, used a career counseling approach with Michelle that directly incorporates teaching clients agency skills and encourages clients to use these agency competencies to challenge past, present, and anticipated career barriers. Holly's approach was based on a change agent career decision-making model called *Career Optimization through Change Agency* (COCA), developed by Pam Remer and Charles O'Neill (1978).

COCA is a 13-step decision-making model that focuses on teaching clients to be active agents in overcoming obstacles in the path of their most desired career choices. Approaching career choice in the context of total life planning and highlighting the developmental nature of career choices are also included in the COCA approach. Clients are taught to identify internal and external barriers to obtaining highly prized career goals and to perceive these barriers as problems that can be changed. Research on the use of the COCA model with undergraduate, undecided majors who took a semester-long course based on the model indicated that students became significantly more rational and less intuitive (i.e., impulsive) and dependent in their decision-making styles, more certain about their choices of an occupation, more crystallized in their vocational self-concept, and had fewer vocationally related identity problems. Further, they engaged in more career information seeking and were more likely to endorse change agent strategies for solving career problems that involved barriers (Remer, O'Neill, & Gohs, 1984).

The 13 steps of the COCA model are overviewed in Table 7.5. We highlight several of COCA's 13 steps as we summarize Holly's counseling of Michelle. However, it is beyond the scope of this chapter to present a complete description of the COCA model. (See Remer and O'Neill [1980] for a detailed explanation.)

## Michelle's Counseling: Discovering and Valuing Potential

During the initial phase of counseling at Steps 1 and 2 of the COCA model, Holly and Michelle clarified mutual expectations for counseling and began building a collaborative counseling relationship. In addition to suggesting that Michelle explore the impact of her social locations on her career choices, Holly recommended that Michelle learn a change agent approach to identifying and overcoming barriers that prevent her from reaching her full personal potential. Holly overviewed the COCA model for Michelle and taught her about the change agent approach. Their contracted goals were described earlier in the chapter.

**Table 7.5    Overview of "career optimization through change agency" decision-making steps**

| | |
|---|---|
| Step 1: | Admit I am confused or uncertain about my career decisions. |
| Step 2: | Commit myself to learning the decision-making process and to applying that process to my specific career-decision problem. |
| Step 3: | Collect information about myself. |
| Step 4: | Generate a list of careers. |
| Step 5: | Collect information about my career alternatives. |
| Step 6: | Eliminate any career alternatives that are obviously most incompatible with self. |
| Step 7: | Compare the self-evaluation with the career alternatives analysis. |
| Step 8: | Assess the advantages and disadvantages of each alternative. |
| Step 9: | Attempt to improve my chances in any alternative. |
| Step 10: | Weigh (assign priority to) ordering the alternatives of career alternatives. |
| Step 11: | Implement my decision. |
| Step 12: | Evaluate my decision. |
| Step 13: | Generalize what I have learned about how to make a decision. |

*Assessing for Career Potential*

At Step 3, Holly and Michelle engaged in a major career-related assessment, which began with an assessment of Michelle's relevant social locations. Further, in addition to the usual career assessment of a client's abilities, career interests, personality factors, and work values, Michelle and Holly explored Michelle's typical decision-making style, her gender-role orientation and beliefs, and her life goals. When useful and relevant, they chose standardized assessment measures but were careful to supplement with other less-traditional assessment strategies that were less prone to social location biases and social-dominance bias (see Chapter 5).

In the assessment of Michelle's social locations, she described herself as a White, middle-class, Baptist woman who was "behind" in her career development. Michelle initially indicated she had a female roommate (Anne), but disclosed during the social location assessment that she and Anne were really intimate partners. (Michelle had become aware of her lesbian identity in her mid-teens.) Anne is a clinical social worker who specializes in LGB issues and is involved in numerous LGB social action causes in the community. Thus, she is "out" in both her job and in the community. Michelle indicated that she is not "out" at work because she believes (probably accurately) that she would be viewed by parents as a threat to the children she teaches.

The fact that Anne is "out" in the workplace and community and Michelle is not is a source of tension between them. Michelle is in constant fear that Anne's visibility as a lesbian will inadvertently "out" Michelle at work and lead to reprisals there. Part of her current career dissatisfaction is not feeling safe in her workplace.

Michelle and Holly assessed that Michelle is primarily in Level 3, Immersion, of lesbian identity development. Especially as a result of her relationship with Anne, Michelle was aware of societal discrimination against LGB persons, had challenged most of her internalized homophobia, and was accepting of herself as a lesbian. When she began living with Anne three years ago, Michelle had disclosed to her parents. They initially struggled with her disclosure, but gradually accepted her relationship with Anne.

Holly assessed Michelle to be primarily in the second level (Encounter) of her identity development as a woman. As a result of her movement through the lesbian identity levels, she had begun to become aware of gender issues and sexism. However, this was a recent process for her, and she was largely unaware of how her experiences as a female had impacted her career choice process. Holly hypothesized to Michelle that Michelle's being both a woman and a lesbian had affected Michelle's career development. Holly asked her to complete the career lifeline exercise (found at the beginning of this chapter) focusing especially on these two social locations.

Michelle and Holly also discussed how Michelle felt about seeing a heterosexual therapist. Michelle said that she had been worried a therapist might be judgmental about her sexual orientation and had asked her lesbian friends to recommend a therapist who was "safe" and knowledgeable about lesbian issues. Her friends had recommended Holly, who had a good reputation for counseling LGB clients. Holly encouraged Michelle to confront her if she ever betrayed Michelle's trust or came across as judgmental.

*Abilities*

Because Michelle viewed herself as overachieving rather than as gifted, Holly suggested that she take an individual intelligence test. Michelle's score of 135 fell in the superior, gifted range. Michelle continued to express surprise, saying that she believed that she had obtained high grades in school only because she had worked so hard. She had previously given graduate school only passing consideration, since she believed that hard work would not be enough to succeed. Holly taught Michelle about women's typical attributions about their successes and failures, and about the impostor phenomenon. Michelle was able to see how her attributions of her successes to effort and her low academic self-confidence (despite the excellence of her academic performance) were linked to her socialization as a female. Holly suggested that Michelle complete a variety of abilities identification exercises. For example, Michelle identified her most significant life achievements and did an analysis of the specific abilities she used in each of these achievements. These abilities were stated as noncareer-content-bound functional skills (Figler, 1979), so that they could be applied easily across various career alternatives. For example, Michelle's skills doing calculus and other higher math functions were translated into the functional skills of abstracting, analyzing, calculating, organizing, predicting, and researching. As Michelle considered other careers besides math, she could apply these neutrally stated skills to those careers. Functional skills analysis is a particularly useful career counseling tool with women who have never been in, or have periods being out of, the paid workforce because these women can analyze their volunteer, home-related, and leisure activities/ achievements for the skills they possess; it is also useful for individuals who are considering career changes. These identified skills can then be translated into the abilities needed for various careers.

These exercises helped Michelle begin to "own" her abilities and challenge her self-defeating attributions of her successes to effort and luck. She also became aware of how her downplaying of her own accomplishments was in part linked to the lack of encouragement from her professors, which created a "null environment" for her. Michelle also read research articles about gifted women and learned that her conflicts between wanting to achieve and wanting to be seen as feminine are often heightened for gifted women. She discovered that, despite having majored in math, she had internalized "math nerd" images and so had internal conflicts about being a woman and being a mathematician. She was then able to challenge these images.

## Interests

Michelle's performance on the Strong Interest Inventory showed high basic interests in science and math, and high similarity scores to mathematicians, engineers, biologists, and lawyers. Holly gave Michelle the Nonsexist Vocational Card Sort (Dewey, 1974) that we reviewed in Chapter 5. Through the card sorting process, through a gender-role analysis, and with challenging from Holly, Michelle became aware that she held gender-role beliefs that were barriers to her considering careers that were in line with her potential. First, she identified that she had learned women were not supposed to be good at math and science. This belief contributed to her having some fear of success and feeling like an impostor in the nontraditional field of mathematics. She also connected this belief to her immediate postcollege years of underemployment. Second, she realized she had several nontraditional gender-role beliefs, ones that fit well with her lesbian identity. She believed in egalitarian relationships, and she wanted to work and be financially independent. However, given her spotty work history and her growing awareness of sexism and heterosexism in the workplace, the idea of being financially responsible for herself was frightening.

Holly suggested that Michelle identify potential role models and mentors for herself. Michelle asked several female acquaintances who were employed in different occupations related to mathematics to meet with her and describe their career experiences. Before meeting with these women, she and Holly developed a list of questions for them.

Several of these questions focused on their experiences with sexism because Michelle was beginning to realize how much of a role covert sexism and the lack of encouragement from her environment had played in her underemployment and in her reluctance to seriously consider graduate school in math. Two of the women she interviewed were lesbians. Michelle explored with them the climate for lesbian women in their workplaces and asked them to share how they coped with both sexism and heterosexism in their careers. Holly believed that these career interviews served three important purposes.

1. The interviews connected Michelle to relevant role models and potential mentors, both of which had been in short supply in Michelle's career development.
2. These nontraditional women helped challenge the "math nerd" stereotype Michelle held.
3. From these women, Michelle learned important strategies for dealing with discrimination barriers.

During the card sort, Michelle realized that she aspired to be a college math professor, a dream she had been reluctant to verbalize previously. Through her work with Holly, she was beginning to acknowledge that she was an intelligent woman who was quite capable of doctoral work. Whereas previously she had believed that the lack of encouragement from others meant she didn't have the needed ability, now she perceived it as covert forms of sexism.

This exploration by Michelle and Holly illustrates the application of change agency strategies to the career choice process. Michelle's gender-role beliefs were not treated as immutable facts to which Michelle needed to adjust. Rather, they were treated as mutable barriers to be challenged and possibly eliminated or reduced. Potential sexist and heterosexist-based discriminations were also treated as mutable barriers for which Michelle could develop coping strategies. Michelle was energized by these challenges and became motivated to become involved in lesbian social activism activities. She realized her choice of a career and educational and job sites had to have more safety for being "out" than did her current teaching job. Sharing these new realizations with her partner, Anne, helped relieve the tensions created by their current differences in being "out" at work.

### Values

Michelle and Holly explored Michelle's life and work values through a series of values clarification exercises. One advantage of this experiential approach, as compared to use of standardized tests, is that it gives clients practice with being experts on themselves. An especially helpful exercise for Michelle was writing a newspaper article about herself 20 years from now. Michelle wrote about being recognized for a significant professional contribution she had made and for which she was to receive an award. In the article, she also mentioned having the support of her partner and their child. Thus, she saw clearly that both achievement outside of the home and close family ties were very important to her. Michelle was surprised she had included a child in her story. As a result, she and Anne began to discuss the possibility of bringing a child into their relationship. This last point illustrates the close connection between career and personal counseling and the importance of focusing on the life goals of clients, not just their career goals.

## Generating Alternatives and Collecting Information

At Step 4 of the COCA model, Holly encouraged Michelle to brainstorm a quantity of possible career alternatives for herself. Brainstorming, with critical judgment suspended, is an especially useful technique for women whose range of alternatives has been limited by gender-role messages and institutionalized oppression. Michelle and Holly collaborated in the brainstorming process.

At Steps 5 and 6, Holly asked Michelle to collect some information about all of her brainstormed alternatives. The amount and variety of information varied according to how much information Michelle already possessed. Some alternatives that were grossly incompatible with Michelle were eliminated as she collected information. Holly challenged Michelle when she thought Michelle was eliminating alternatives prematurely, or on the sole basis of a barrier that could be changed. By the end of Step 6, Michelle had narrowed her alternative list to university math professor, community college math teacher, lawyer, or accountant.

### Analyzing the Alternatives

In Steps 7 and 8, Michelle applied a systematic process for identifying the short- and long-term advantages and disadvantages of each of her alternatives. During these steps, Holly also focused Michelle on her intuitive and emotional responses to each of her alternatives through imagery work. While in a relaxed state, Michelle imaged or fantasized herself in a typical day working at each of her alternatives. Michelle's feelings and the symbols that emerged in the imagery work were explored. In accordance with EFT Principles III and IV, Holly encouraged Michelle to trust her feeling reactions as an additional source to the rational approach they had been using.

### Identifying Change Agent Strategies

Holly and Michelle used a problem-solving approach to Michelle's internal and external career barriers that were encountered throughout the decision-making process. The disadvantages identified for each alternative at Step 8 can also be viewed as barriers that can be changed. Reducing or eliminating a disadvantage improves the desirability and probability of that alternative. Thus, at Step 9, Holly and Michelle reviewed the disadvantages of Michelle's alternatives. Michelle had listed "worry about her ability to be admitted to doctoral programs in math," which was the main barrier to her aspirations to being a college or university professor. Holly encouraged her to collect information about selection criteria used in several different programs. In addition, she and Michelle brainstormed ways Michelle could enhance her chances of acceptance. As a result of these discussions, Michelle decided to collect information from the current students in graduate programs she was considering about how LGB affirmative the programs were.

### Choosing and Implementing

At Step 10, Michelle rank-ordered her alternatives from most to least desirable as: university professor, community college teacher, accountant, lawyer. With Holly's help, Michelle developed a plan for implementing her first-ranked choice. The implementation plan included change agent strategies relevant to this choice. Michelle was pleased with her 1350 total Graduate Record Examination (GRE) scores and acknowledged without qualification that she was indeed an intelligent woman! Michelle applied to several doctoral programs in math and chose to attend a nearby university that was open to her lesbian identity and that had established a mentoring program for female graduate students.

## SUMMARY

Michelle's journey toward choosing a satisfying career path was facilitated by a combined EFT and change agent counseling approach. Michelle had confronted and worked to change several internal and external barriers that had limited her previous career development. She had learned how being a lesbian woman had affected her choices. She expanded the number and range of alternatives she was considering. She learned a decision-making process that she could apply to other life decisions and a problem-solving approach for challenging barriers to her desired goals. Further, she began to own and appreciate her intellectual and personal power.

Michelle's career journey represents only one type of career development problem encountered by women. Indeed, she had many financial, educational, and intellectual resources that many of our clients do not have. Her counseling needs would be different were she a single, divorced mother who had no labor force experience and little financial resources. Daily survival needs would then take precedence over career-self actualization needs.

In this chapter, we presented an overview of the many gender and other social location-based external and internal factors affecting women's career development. We asked you to identify how these factors have influenced your own career development, and we illustrated the interplay among some of those factors for Michelle. The challenge to feminist career counselors is at least twofold. In addition to using our knowledge and awareness at an individual level to "unyoke" ourselves and our clients from the restraints of our socialization and discrimination as women, we are challenged to change the social, economic, educational, and occupational structures that limit the career achievement of all women.

## ACTIVITIES

Make a list of the gender-role messages that have influenced your career-related decisions. Underline those messages that are currently restraining you from reaching your optimal career goals. Choose one of these messages and identify possible change agent strategies for changing and restructuring this message.

Complete the following imagery exercise in a quiet place. After relaxing yourself, imagine that you were born male (if you are a woman) or female (if you are a man). Slowly see yourself growing up as this gender. Imagine what activities you would choose and what messages you would hear. Now imagine yourself fantasizing about trying out, and choosing, career paths throughout your life. When you are finished with the imagery, note how your choices were different as the other gender.

## FURTHER READINGS

Byars, A. M., & Hackett, G. (1998). Applications of social cognitive theory to the career development of women of color. *Applied and Preventive Psychology, 7,* 255–267.

Gutek, B. A. (2001). Women and paid work. *Psychology of Women Quarterly, 25,* 379–393.

Hyde, J. S., & Kling, K. C. (2001). Women, motivation, and achievement. *Psychology of Women Quarterly, 25,* 364–378.

Remer, P., & O'Neill, C. D. (1980). Clients as change agents: What color could your parachute be? *Personnel and Guidance Journal, 58,* 425–429.

# Chapter 8 ———————————————————————

# *SURVIVING SEXUAL ASSAULT*

> *Fear. Paralysis. Powerlessness.*
> *Legs unwillingly pried apart,*
> *Stripped of clothes and personhood,*
> *Frozen in time.*
> *Soul-filled pain numbed with self-abandonment.*
> *An observer watching who once was me*
> *Unable to make him stop.*
> *Illusions of personal power and control stripped naked,*
> *Beliefs of a lifetime shattered.*

> Pam Remer, 1993

## SELF-ASSESSMENT: BELIEFS ABOUT RAPE

Your beliefs and knowledge about rape influence how you respond therapeutically to clients who are rape survivors. Use the numerical scale to rate your level of agreement with each statement.

| Very Much Disagree | | | Neutral | | | Very Much Agree |
|---|---|---|---|---|---|---|
| 1 | 2 | 3 | 4 | 5 | 6 | 7 |

_____ 1. Many women secretly desire to be raped.

_____ 2. In reality, women are almost never raped by their boyfriends.

_____ 3. When men rape, it is because of their strong desire for sex.

_____ 4. A woman who goes to the home or apartment of a man on the first date is implying that she wants to have sex.

_____ 5. If a woman doesn't physically fight back, you can't really say that it was rape.

_____ 6. Women tend to exaggerate how much rape affects them.

_____ 7. Rape accusations are often used as a way of getting back at men.

These seven items are taken from the Illinois Rape Myth Acceptance Scale (IRMA; D. L. Payne, Lonsway, & Fitzgerald, 1999). All of the questions represent common myths about rape. Higher scores represent greater acceptance of rape myths. Rape myths and facts are discussed in depth later in this chapter.

## OVERVIEW

The negative consequences of gender-role stereotyping of both women and men and of institutionalized sexism are most clearly reflected in the violence against women, which is so prevalent in contemporary society. Increasing numbers of our clients come to us directly or indirectly because they have been victims of adult rape, childhood sexual abuse, and/or wife battering. Feminist psychological practitioners must be knowledgeable about the occurrences of violence in women's lives, the impact of those traumas on women, and therapeutic strategies that facilitate healing from these traumas. In Chapter 3, we briefly discuss feminist therapy interventions with an adult survivor of incest, and in Chapter 9, we discuss feminist interventions with victims of wife battering. In this chapter, we describe an Empowerment Feminist Therapy (EFT) approach to working with Anna, a survivor of an adult, heterosexual, acquaintance rape. In addition, we discuss the prevalence of rape, rape myths, and assessment procedures appropriate for sexual assault survivors. Intervention strategies for Anna include cultural analysis, gender-role analysis, power analysis of rape, cognitive restructuring, desensitization, emotional catharsis and behavioral management of fears, and flashbacks.

After reading Chapter 8, you will be able to:

1. Describe the cultural context of rape.
2. Distinguish between rape myths and facts.
3. Develop a definition of rape compatible with EFT.
4. Recognize the symptoms associated with rape trauma.
5. Identify the stages of healing from rape trauma.
6. Describe an EFT model for counseling rape survivors.

## ANNA'S STORY: DELAYED POSTTRAUMATIC (RAPE) REACTION

Anna, a 30-year-old married Latina teacher who was the first person in her family to graduate from college, was referred by the local rape crisis center for therapy. She had called them because she began having nightmares about a forced sexual encounter she had while on a date in college. She reported waking up and feeling very anxious.

> I wake up three or four mornings a week in a state of terror. My heart races and it's hard for me to move. My last dream reminded me of a bad experience I had in college when my date drove to an isolated part of town, held me down, and threatened to beat me up unless I had sex with him. I tried to get away, but couldn't. I gave up fighting. But my reactions don't make sense. That experience was 10 years ago, and I didn't react much at the time. I felt lucky not to have been physically hurt, and I felt pretty stupid to have gotten myself in such a predicament. I didn't tell anyone until last week when I called the crisis line. I feel like I'm going crazy. I just don't usually get this overpowered by things.

During the first session, Anna revealed that although she and her husband, Tomas, have a happy marriage, recently she had started feeling irritated with him in the middle of making love—"for no reason."

In addition to the nightmares, Anna began having flashbacks about her rape, in which she saw the rape happening again and again and would feel like she was back in it. She also reported feeling "different" from others and isolated from them. At first, Anna had great difficulty in talking about her traumatic experience. Eventually she was able to relate the details of her experience to Diane, her therapist. She gave the following description:

> A male friend of mine suggested that I go on a blind date with a friend of his who was coming to visit for the weekend. This guy, Raul, was an important young man in the Latino community at a neighboring university, so I agreed to go. We went out for dinner and then went to a college-related party. Raul was a charming companion and I was flattered by his interest in me. Over the course of the evening, Raul and I had a couple of drinks, but toward the end of the evening Raul began drinking a lot. I wanted to walk back to my dormitory, but he insisted that he was sober enough to drive.
>
> Instead of going directly to my dorm, he turned toward the west side of town where there were a number of small farms. When I questioned him, he said he wanted to show me a beautiful view of the night sky. He pulled off onto a private road and stopped the car in an isolated meadow. He began to kiss me and put his hands on my breasts. I did not want to have sex with him. I was a virgin. I pushed him away and told him that I wanted to go back to my dorm. He responded very coldly that he was not going to take no for an answer. Suddenly he was very different from the charmer he had been all evening.
>
> He ripped open my blouse and I struggled to get free, but he was just too strong. He let me know that one way or another we were going to have sex and that we could do it with or without my being hurt. I felt paralyzed and numb. He took off my skirt and underwear easily because I stopped struggling. He dropped his trousers. While he held me down by my wrists, he ordered me to put his penis in my mouth. The whole idea nauseated me, but I complied. I remember thinking that if he would just ejaculate, everything would be over. Instead, after he came, he put his mouth on my genitals and tried to stimulate me. I felt so invaded and I was terrified that he would never let me go. I left my body at some point and became an observer. I don't remember many more details. Somehow I got my clothes on and he took me back to the dorm. He warned me not to tell anyone, saying no one would believe that I hadn't consented. Besides, he would tell everybody that I was a tramp. I went into the dorm, took a long shower, and said nothing to anyone.

## CULTURAL ANALYSIS OF RAPE

Rape occurs in a social context. Rape cannot be understood apart from that context, and the woman who has been raped cannot be treated effectively without understanding that context. An analysis of the cultural context of rape is best begun by viewing rape as one type of violent act perpetrated against women and by understanding rape in its global context. According to United Nations Resolution 48/104 (December, 1993), "Any act of gender-based violence that results in physical, sexual, or psychological harm or suffering to women, including threats of such acts, coercion, or arbitrary deprivations of liberty, whether occurring in public or private life" constitutes violence against women (as cited in Koss, Heise, & Russo, 1994, p. 510). Rape is one of the violent acts against women included in this declaration.

Male violence against women generally, and rape specifically, is a "manifestation of gender inequality" and "a mechanism for the subordination of women" (Koss, Goodman, Browne, Fitzgerald, Keita, & Russo, 1994, p. 4). Gendered social structures exist in most cultures and include: (a) unequal legal, economic, physical, and educational power distributions between women and men; (b) societal acceptance of violence against women; (c) cultural myths/beliefs that blame victims and that accuse them of lying; (d) heterosexual scripts that establish female-male relationships within a culture; and (e) gender-role expectations (Koss, Goodman, et al., 1994, p. 4; Koss, Heise, & Russo, 1994). These gendered social structures create and maintain rape globally.

## SOCIOCULTURAL PERSPECTIVES OF RAPE

Cultures differ in how they define rape and in how they treat rape victims and rapists. As definitions and consequences of rape vary culturally, so do rape prevalence rates. Patricia Rozee (1993) examined the cross-cultural context of rape by using a feminist conceptualization of rape. Focusing on female victims, she used the absence of the woman's choice to have sexual contact as the determining factor in whether a rape took place. Thus, she defined *rape* as "lack of female choice in genital contact. . . . The lack of choice is assumed where there is use of force, threat of force, or coercion; presence of multiple males; physical pain, loss of consciousness, or death; or when the woman is punished or suffers some other negative outcome if she refuses" (p. 502).

Rozee classified rapes as two types: normative and nonnormative. Unchosen genital contacts that do not result in real punishment of the perpetrator(s) are considered by Rozee to be "normative rapes" (i.e., ones that are condoned by society). Unchosen genital contacts that are not condoned (i.e., not approved of) by the society are classified as nonnormative rapes. Nonnormative rapes are usually narrowly defined in a culture, and the societal sanctions against perpetrators often vary depending on the social status of the victim. Thus, even in nonnormative rapes, perpetrators are not always punished and its victims may still be blamed.

According to Rozee (1993), normative, condoned rapes are not punished in a given society because they do not violate cultural norms. She posed six categories for condoned rape: marital, exchange, punitive, theft, ceremonial, and status. Exchange rape includes men offering other men sexual access to their women as a "bargaining tool, gesture of solidarity, or conciliation" (Rozee, 1993, p. 507). Punitive rape is often used on women who violate cultural gender-role expectations, who disrespect male authority, or whose husbands need to be punished. Theft rape includes rape used as a weapon of war, and ceremonial rapes include defloration rituals and virginity tests. Status rapes involve the use of status power (e.g., master to slave). Exchange rape was the most prevalent form of normative rape in the societies studied by Rozee. Koss, Goodman, et al. (1994) added date/acquaintance rape to Rozee's categories.

After analyzing rape cross-culturally using her definitions of normative and nonnormative rape, Rozee found that nonnormative rapes existed in 63% of the societies studied whereas 97% of the societies had normative rapes. Contrary to conclusions reached earlier by Peggy Sanday (1981) that societies are either "rape prone" or "rape free," Rozee asserted that all societies are rape prone.

## CULTURAL ANALYSIS OF WESTERN SOCIETIES

A cultural analysis of Western societies shows that we live in a society that often condones rape, misdefines it, blames victims for its occurrence, sets up women to be raped and men to be rapists, and offers inadequate services to aid survivors in their long-term recovery. The existence of rape and the trauma resulting from rape is strongly influenced by what a society teaches about rape, how it gender-role-socializes women and men, and by the power differentials that exist between women and men (Koss, Goodman, et al., 1994; Sanday, 1981). Thus, a cultural analysis of rape includes an analysis of rape myths, a gender-role analysis, and a power analysis. In the next sections, we present a brief overview of these three areas.

## Cultural Myths about Rape

Koss, Goodman, et al. (1994) assert that the "cultural beliefs that support rape also support sexual harassment, battering, sexual murder, and other forms of violence against women" (p. 7). They identify seven common themes in myths about male violence against women:

1. Victim masochism (e.g., "She wanted it").
2. Victim precipitation (e.g., "She asked for it").
3. Victim characteristics ("It wasn't really rape").
4. Victim fabrication (e.g., "She lied").
5. Male justification (e.g., "He didn't mean to").
6. Violent acts are not harmful (e.g., "Rape is a trivial event").
7. The acts are deviant (e.g., "Rape is a deviant act").

At the beginning of this chapter, you respond to seven statements that reflect rape myths taken from the Illinois Rape Myth Acceptance Scale (D. L. Payne et al., 1999). In developing and validating their instrument, the authors identified seven factors or categories of myths that closely parallel Koss, Goodman, et al.'s (1994) themes. Your agreement with any of the seven statements at the beginning of this chapter represents belief in rape myths. We hope that reading this chapter leads to your replacing rape myths with rape facts.

Rape myths are attitudes and beliefs that are generally false but are widely and persistently held, and that serve to deny and justify male sexual aggression against women (Lonsway & Fitzgerald, 1994, p. 134). Thus, rape myths operate as stereotypes shared by a particular culture. According to D. L. Payne et al. (1999), rape myths serve two functions. First, societal myths about rape obscure the high prevalence rates of rape and they justify and normalize the occurrence of rape. Second, rape myths divert attention for the causes of rape from societal structures (e.g., patriarchy) by blaming the individual victim. When the victim is blamed, harmful societal (patriarchal) structures are not challenged or changed.

Facts about rape often directly contradict the cultural myths about rape perpetuated by our society. For instance, most rapes occur not in "dark alleys" but in familiar locations, especially in victim's homes (Abbey, McAuslan, & Ross, 1998). In addition, at least 50% of rapes are committed by persons known to the victims (i.e., acquaintance rapes; D. M. Greene & Navarrim, 1998; Mills & Granoff, 1992; Mynatt & Algeier, 1990; Zollicoffer, 1989). Women of all ages, from all cultural groups, and of all types have been raped (Holzman, 1996). Women do not unconsciously desire to be raped, neither do they provoke rape by their appearance (e.g., manner of dress) or actions. Women cannot always stop a rape attempt by fighting back. In some cases, physical resistance may stop a rape; in others, it may lead to escalation of violence and greater physical injury in the victim.

Rapes are rarely reported to the police or disclosed to anyone (Mills & Granoff, 1992; Warshaw, 1988). In contrast to the myth that a woman "cries rape" to protect her reputation or to seek revenge, the truth is that most women who are raped do not report the incident (Lonsway & Fitzgerald, 1994). Victims of acquaintance rape are less likely to report the rape to authorities and are more likely to tell no one about their rape (Koss, 1985). Because acquaintance rapes differ markedly from society's definition of *real rape* and because they are condoned (i.e, are normative), many acquaintance rape survivors do not even label their forced sexual experience as *rape* (Koss, 1985). For example, Anna did not refer to her experience as *rape* until she had been in therapy for a while. By learning about rape myths and facts in counseling through a cultural analysis of rape, Anna was able to acknowledge that she had been raped.

Furthermore, rapists do not commit rape because of uncontrollable sexual urges. Research indicates that the primary motives for rape are aggression and need to control and subjugate (Groth, Burgess, & Holmstrom, 1977). That is, rape is a violent and aggressive act that is accomplished through sexual behavior. Rapists cannot be identified by their appearance, socioeconomic status, marital status, or educational level. In a study by Malamuth (1981), 35% of college men indicated a likelihood of committing rape if they would not be punished. In a more recent study by Rapaport and Posey (1991), 43% of college males anonymously admitted to coercing sex, and 15% said they had committed acquaintance rape.

Belief in rape myths are held by significant numbers of people in the United States; and these beliefs vary with regard to gender, race, and ethnicity (Lonsway & Fitzgerald, 1994). For example, African Americans and Hispanics demonstrate higher acceptance of rape myths (Dull & Giacopassi, 1987 and Williams & Holmes, 1981, as cited in Lonsway & Fitzgerald, 1994). Further, in general, men indicate higher endorsements of rape myths than do women (Lonsway & Fitzgerald, 1994).

Belief in rape myths also correlates with other negative factors. Kimberley Lonsway and Louise Fitzgerald (1994) cite research studies that indicate a positive relationship between greater acceptance of rape myths and (a) more traditional attitudes toward women, (b) "macho" gender-role identification, (c) more positive evaluations of rapists, (d) higher acceptance of aggression against women, (e) male sexual coercion, and (f) higher rates of victimization for females.

## Gender-Role Analysis

The incidence of rape in a society is related both to gender-role socialization of women and men and to a hierarchical power distribution in which women are dominated by men (Sanday, 1981). Through a cross-cultural analysis of 95 societies, Sanday found that societies that have higher rape prevalence (i.e., rape prone) were characterized by a tolerance for violence, encouragement of men to be aggressive, isolation of the sexes, devaluation of female traits and activities (especially nurturance and child care), noninvolvement of men in child care, and promotion of male dominance over females. She concluded that the way a society gender-role socializes its females and males determines its rape proneness.

## Gender-Role Prescriptions for Women

Weis and Borges (1977) asserted that gender-role socialization and dating rituals in the United States' dominant culture contribute to the prevalence of rape. Burkhart and Fromuth (1991) similarly concluded that gender-role socialization encourages acceptance of rape myths and of victim blame and creates dating scripts that normalize gender power differentials and sexual aggression against women. The following gender-role prescriptions for women set them up to be victims:

1. Women are property of men.
2. Women are responsible for controlling men's sexual behavior.
3. Women need to be protected by men.
4. Women should be kind, gentle, and physically nonaggressive.
5. Women should not be physically strong.
6. Women should always be polite.
7. Women should be dependent on men, passive, and childlike.
8. Good women are virgins.

Weis and Borges (1977) concluded that many women are socialized to ". . . internalize the psychological characteristics of defenseless victims who have not learned or cannot apply the techniques of self-defense and so must rely upon the protection of others" (p. 47). In an acquaintance rape, their protector is often the rapist. Thus, girls and women learn that their gender puts them at risk for victimization (Sanchez-Hucles & Hudgins, 2001). While these prescriptions for women's behavior vary some from subculture to subculture, these messages apply across many ethnic and class groups.

## Gender-Role Prescriptions for Men

Many men in the United States in both dominant and subordinate cultures are socialized to be sexually assertive and/or sexually aggressive by the following gender-role messages:

1. Men should be physically aggressive, powerful, and controlling.
2. Sex is to be viewed as a conquest. Women who say "no" really mean "maybe."
3. Men should pay for dates and women should "reimburse" them sexually.
4. Women are the possessions of the men who protect them.
5. Women are viewed as sexual objects.
6. Men should initiate sex and dominate women.
7. Men should be the bosses and women should obey them.

Thus, many males are socialized to be sexually aggressive, to view women as sexual objects, and to expect to be obeyed. These messages help set the stage for sexually aggressive behavior by some men. These lessons also help blur the distinction between seduction and rape for these men. For example, R. Remer and Witten (1988) found that men perceive more commonality between rape and seduction than do women, who see more commonality between rape and assault. Additionally, overidentification with the "macho" role may lead some men to adopt a rapist attitude. Such men may validate their masculinity by intimidating women and sexually aggressing against them. In a review of research on rape and college men, Berkowitz (1992) found that between 25% and 60% of men had engaged in some form of sexual aggression. The risk of sexual aggression is increased if the man is hostile toward women, blames rape victims, and initiated and paid for the date. Whaley (1998) described a socialization model for understanding sexual violence toward women. Whaley asserted that patriarchal societies encourage men to "do masculinity" including sexually objectifying women and reinforcing sexual conquest of women. Further, sexually aggressive behavior is not sufficiently nor consistently punished.

## Power Analysis

As a group, most men have more economic, physical, role, resource, and political power than most women. Although most ethnic minority men have less power than most White men, ethnic minority men still usually have access to more sources of power than do ethnic minority women. Given that most rape perpetrators and their victims are of the same ethnocultural group, a man can use his more powerful position to coerce a woman into sexual acts or can use his physical power (or threats) to overcome a woman's resistance. His role and economic power make it harder for her to report a rape. Her lower social value makes it less likely that she is believed and more likely that she is blamed for the rape (Koss, Goodman, et al., 1994). Further, due to racist attitudes and stereotypes, Women of Color, lesbian women, women with disabilities, and women living in poverty have even less role, resource, and political power than heterosexual, middle-class, White women.

## Interaction Effects

Gender-role messages interact with male power dominance and with rape myths to produce a rape victimization process. Weis and Borges (1977) defined victimization as ". . . the social process that before, during, and after the event simultaneously renders the victim defenseless and even partly responsible for it" (p. 35). Thus, society teaches women to accept responsibility for victimizing events that befall them, and teaches men to legitimize their sexual aggression against women. Further, this process makes it less likely that women will report or even talk about their sexual assault experiences because they are likely to be blamed for them: "Led to believe that she is responsible for any sexual outcome and faced with an unsupportive social environment . . . , the woman experiences herself as having only the choice of responsibility and self-blame, or denial" (Koss & Burkhart, 1989, p. 35). Thus, most women live in fear of being raped, and rape survivors become stigmatized and isolated.

## DEFINITION AND PREVALENCE OF RAPE

A feminist analysis of rape is enlightened by studying the historical definitions of rape. Early definitions were based on men's property rights, with women considered men's property. Thus, rape was considered to be theft of a daughter's virginity or of a wife's chastity (Brownmiller, 1975). From this perspective, a perspective that continued in law until recently, a wife could not be raped by her husband because he had a permanent right to sexual relations with her granted through the marriage contract. Historically, legal definitions of rape required a "fresh" complaint, evidence of physical resistance, and corroborating evidence because women were believed to falsely accuse men of rape (Friedland, 1991). Further, a "reasonable man standard" exists in the way rape laws are written and/or are interpreted by the police and courts. Under the reasonableness standard, a man is not guilty of rape if he reasonably believes that the woman gave her consent (Friedland, 1991; P. Lopez, 1992). Thus, this standard is based on his belief and not on the victim's experience, intention, or perception. Feminist legal scholars have called for legal reform that embraces a "reasonable woman standard" where the standard is whether the woman perceives she consented (Lopez, 1992).

## Definitions of Rape

A variety of definitions have been and are applied to the word *rape*. Although legal definitions vary from state to state in the United States, the most common legal definition of *rape* involves sexual intercourse by forcible compulsion with a woman. This definition is not compatible with feminist counseling because it is so narrow (e.g., sexual acts other than penile penetration of a vagina, rape of a male) are excluded. Legal definitions of *rape* exclude the experience of many rape survivors. A clinical definition of *rape* needs to be more encompassing of our clients' rape experiences.

The definition of *rape* that therapists use is influenced by their attitudes, experiences, and cultural values and, in turn, influences their reactions to clients who have been raped. As we discuss throughout this book, EF therapists examine carefully their attitudes and values in relation to their clients' issues and are open with their clients about these views. EF therapists who work with sexual assault survivors need to be aware of their own rape myths and gender-role stereotyping and work to change those attitudes and beliefs that revictimize their clients. EF therapists use definitions of *rape* that encompass a wide variety of rape experiences and that do not blame the victim.

A definition of *rape* is difficult to agree on, even for feminist therapists. As we wrote this chapter and its revision, we wrestled with finding a definition with which we both could live. One of us felt that defining *rape* very broadly (i.e., "any sexual activity imposed on one person by another") is crucial so as to be comprehensive and inclusive. The other felt that a definition of *rape* needs to be specific enough (i.e., "any coerced sexual activity in which a part of the body is penetrated") so that *rape* is distinct from other terms (e.g., sexual harassment). We both wanted a definition that included: (a) various kinds of sexual activity, not just penile penetration of a vagina; (b) various kinds of force or threat of force; (c) coerced sexual activity to a variety of victims, and (d) culturally normative and nonnormative forms of rape.

In a research study by Mary Koss (1985), sexual victimization was operationalized along four levels: highly sexually victimized, moderately sexually victimized, low sexually victimized, and not sexually victimized (see Table 8.1 for her definitions). We encourage you to review the variety of definitions of rape given here and then decide on your own definition of rape and/or sexual victimization.

## Prevalence of Rape

Estimates about the prevalence or incidence rates for rape vary according to the definition of rape used and the methods for gathering the data. Further, the number of unreported and unacknowledged rapes makes accurate tabulations of rape incidences difficult. For example, in a study of college women (Koss, 1985), 12.7% of the respondents fell into the

**Table 8.1   Koss' (1985) categories of sexual victimization**

| Category | Definition | Percent of Respondents in Group | Percent of Group Who Indicated They Had Been Raped |
|---|---|---|---|
| Highly sexually victimized | Experienced ". . . at anytime in the past oral, anal, or vaginal intercourse against their will through the use of force or threat of force." | 12.7% | 57% |
| Moderately sexually victimized | "Experienced sexual contact (fondling, kissing) or attempted sexual intercourse against their consent through the use of force or threat of force." | 24.0 | 0 |
| Low sexually victimized | Experienced "sexual intercourse when they did not desire it subsequent to the use of extreme verbal coercion, insistent arguments, false promises, or threats to end the relationship . . ." | 17.9 | 0 |
| Not sexually victimized | Did not experience any of the above. | 37.6 | 0 |

*Source:* "The Hidden Rape Victim: Personality, Attitudinal, and Situational Characteristics," by M. P. Koss, 1985, *Psychology of Women Quarterly, 9,* 193–212.

highly sexually victimized group, 24% into the moderately sexually victimized group, 17.9% into the low sexually victimized group, and 37.6% met the criteria for the not sexually victimized group. Thus, 62.4% of the women in her study had experienced some kind of sexual victimization.

Koss (1985) also asked all respondents if they had been raped. Of those who were highly sexually victimized, only 57% said they had been raped. Koss called this subgroup *acknowledged rape victims.* Of these acknowledged rape victims, 31% were romantically involved with the perpetrator, and 48% had not told anyone about the rape. Forty-three percent of those who were highly sexually victimized said that they had not been raped, even though they met the legal definition of rape. Koss called this subgroup *unacknowledged rape victims.* In the unacknowledged group, more than 50% had not told anyone; 100% had not reported to the police, a hospital or a rape crisis center; and 76% were romantically involved with the perpetrator. Thus, even when a woman experiences an event that meets the legal definition of rape, she may not self-define that event as rape, and this nonacknowledgment of the rape is more likely when the victim and perpetrator are romantically involved (e.g., date rape).

Far from being a rare occurrence, rape is a common happening in many women's lives. Prevalence figures from rape research vary from 12% to 46% of adult women having experienced a rape or attempted rape (D. M. Greene & Navarrim, 1998; Koss, 1985; Mills & Granoff, 1992; Mynatt & Algeier, 1990; Russell & Howell, 1983; Tjaden & Thoennes, 2000). The usual figure for completed rapes is that one in four women will be raped at least once during her adult life (Lonsway & Fitzgerald, 1994). Women account for 94% of all rape victims (Riggs, 2000).

## COPING WITH RAPE

Before describing the therapeutic interventions used to facilitate Anna's resolution of her trauma, it is important to understand the reactions of rape victims. Weis and Borges (1977) describe rape as "a total attack against the whole person, affecting the victim's physical, psychological, and social identity" (p. 72). Rape victims experience loss of control, fear for their lives, and physical violation of their bodies. "Directed, focused, intentional harm involving the most intimate interpersonal act—that is the nature of rape" (Koss & Burkhart, 1989, p. 31). The duration and intensity of rape-related reactions vary depending on situational circumstances, what recovery stage the survivor is in, how the symptoms are reacted to by others, and cultural myths and values. Both delayed reactions and long-term, ongoing symptoms have been found in rape survivors (Koss, 1993; Resick, 1993). Mary Koss, Lori Heise, and Nancy Russo (1994) describe three areas of rape impact: psychological, somatic/physical, and sociocultural. Short- and long-term psychological effects of rape include Posttraumatic Stress Disorder (PTSD), depression, rape-related fears, anxiety, substance abuse, interpersonal difficulties, sexual dysfunction, lowered self-esteem, and suicidal ideation and attempts (Koss, Heise, et al., 1994; Resick, 1993; Sanchez-Hucles & Hudgins, 2001). Physical and somatic effects of rape include pregnancy, sexually transmitted diseases, physical injury caused by the rapist, long-term increased use of medical care, and body violation (Koss, Heise, et al., 1994).

Koss, Heise, and colleagues also enumerate the sociocultural impacts of rape, including:

1. Living in fear and thus restricting daily activities to avoid rape.
2. Being shamed by family members after being raped, including spousal divorce and murder by a family member.
3. Victim suicide.

When the psychological, physical, and sociocultural costs of rape are viewed collectively, they argued that rape is best understood as a violation of women's human rights and as a major health issue.

## AN EMPOWERMENT FEMINIST THERAPY STAGE MODEL

Pam Remer (1986) developed a feminist-oriented stage model for understanding the short- and long-range reactions and methods of coping of rape survivors. This model delineates client needs and counseling strategies for each stage. Remer's model provided the underlying structure for Anna's EFT therapy.

## Stage One: Pre-Rape: Cultural Socialization about Rape

Bosnian women raped by war, degraded possessions then killed by their relatives.

A five-year-old child accused of sexual provocation.

"What did you do to entice him?"

"There is no such thing as rape. All you have to do is move."

One woman raped every six minutes.

Too many children raped by trusted caregivers.

"If you can't prevent it, you might as well lie back and enjoy it."

One in four women abused by men they love.

One in three female children sexually abused.

One in six male children sexually abused.

Nine in ten working women sexually harassed.

"You are responsible for a man's sexual behavior."

"Don't go out alone after dark."

"She asked for it."*

Because rape occurs in a social context of cultural norms and myths that misdefine rape and blame victims, Stage One of the Remer model, the Pre-rape stage, includes all of the life experiences, gender-role socialization and all the societal depictions of rape myths that a woman has had before being raped. The woman's learning at this stage influences how she feels and behaves during and after the rape, and even whether she defines her unchosen sexual activity as "rape."

Stage One also includes all women living with the constant fear of being raped. In this stage, many feminist therapists work politically and preventively to bring about changes in people's attitudes toward rape, in laws related to rape, and in the services and support available to rape survivors. Inclusion of this stage in the model underscores EFT Principle II, *The Personal Is Political.* Stage One emphasizes that sexism and racism are institutionalized in rape laws, court procedures, and blaming of rape victims, and that gender-role stereotyping and institutionalized sexism and racism contribute to the prevalence of rape. Reduction of the occurrence of rape in any society requires a restructuring of power relationships, challenging of institutionalized sexism and racism, and changing the way females and males are gender-role and culturally socialized.

During counseling for rape trauma, EF therapists do a cultural analysis of rape in general, and more specifically, an analysis of the client's pre-rape personal learning about rape, so that the client can understand more clearly her reactions during and after the rape. This client-counselor collaborative cultural analysis of rape is a foundational component of EFT rape counseling. This analysis is a crucial factor in the client's ability to stop blaming herself for her rape and in coming to define the event as rape.

## Stage Two: The Rape Event

Fear. Sadness.

Tears I can't quite touch.

Realizing how deep his violation and that moment reached into my soul and life.

Minutes that lasted hours,

A single experience relived a thousand times.*

Stage Two, the Rape Event, includes all the events immediately preceding, during, and following the rape. The rapist's behavior, the situation, and the victim's reactions are important details for the client to share with the therapist. Charles Figley (1985) suggested that therapists' knowledge of the trauma details enables them to refute clients' erroneous self-blaming. Further, describing the details of the rape facilitates the victim's cognitive processing of the rape (Chard, Weaver, & Resick, 1997; Resick & Schnicke, 1993).

The events immediately preceding the rape often influence whether the potential victim senses danger. For example, if the assailant is an acquaintance whom she trusts, she interprets his actions leading up to the rape in the context of that trust and is unlikely to realize she is in danger. Further, whatever the circumstances, the victim initially may deny the reality of what is happening to her. The more "time lag" there is in realizing the danger, the less likely it is that the victim can escape (Weis & Borges, 1977). The awareness of danger often begins vaguely and increases. The awareness depends on actual cues present (e.g., the man's behavior, her previous trust of him) and on the victim's prior learning. Victims often report feeling confused (Zollicoffer, 1989).

Once the reality of the rape is acknowledged, victims use a range of coping strategies. In a study of 88 rape survivors, Alice Zollicoffer (1989) found that survivors reasoned with the rapist (54.5%), struggled (44.3%), remained motionless and quiet (43.2%), pleaded (40.9%), numbed out (36.8%), cried (35.2%), and screamed (18.2%). Victims experience a wide range of emotions during the rape. The survivors in Zollicoffer's study reported feeling afraid (81.8%), helpless (80.7%), overwhelmed (65.9%), confused (60.2%), fear for their lives (59.1%), disgusted (46.6%), angry (38.6%), guilty (35.2%), and physical pain (33%). In Zollicoffer's study, rapists were reported to use various forms of coercion. Rapists physically entrapped victims (75%), made verbal threats (56.8%), physically restrained victims (56.8%), threatened physical harm (54.5%), shoved and hit victims (40.9%), and displayed a weapon (37.5%). In this study, 87.5% of the assaults involved vaginal sexual violations, 40.9% involved oral sexual violations, and 9.1% involved anal sexual violations.

Victims' needs during Stage Two are, first, to escape being raped. When they fail to escape, they focus on getting through the rape alive and on minimizing physical and psychological damage. Common responses include victims' dissociating from their physical bodies and perceiving time distortion.

EF therapists who work with sexual abuse survivors must be clear within themselves that the rape victim is never to blame for the rape. As we hear the details of a client's rape events, we need to listen for how the client's actions were influenced by her own myths about rape, by her experiences with oppression, and by her gender-role-socialization process. Two examples help illustrate this point. First, a rape victim who has been taught that rape is committed by strangers in dark alleys is less likely to perceive that she is in danger of being raped by someone she knows early enough in the encounter to enable her to prevent the assault or escape. Second, for most rape survivors, there is a point in the rape in which they realize that they are unable to escape being raped. Their behavior changes from trying to stop the rape to trying to get through the rape. In retrospect, these victims may blame themselves for not being able to see the danger and escape, or for not being able to fight off the attack. By examining how their own misconceptions about rape contribute to their self-blame, they can lessen their shame and guilt, and begin to appreciate what they did to survive. Victims' sharing the details of their rapes with a nonblaming counselor, while difficult, helps them to feel less isolated, alone, and less guilty.

## Stage Three: Crisis and Disorganization

Stage Three, Crisis and Disorganization, encompasses the crisis period immediately following the rape. Victims are often in a state of shock and feel helpless, out of control, ashamed, confused, and guilty. Their feeling reactions may vary from numbness to hysterical crying. This stage may vary in length from a few hours to a year, depending on the choices the survivor makes (e.g., whether to prosecute) and the coping strategies she uses. During this stage, she is especially vulnerable to negative, blaming reactions by others. Negative reactions revictimize the survivor. These "second wounds" (P. Brickman et al., 1982; Sanchez-Hucles & Hudgins, 2001) become part of the rape trauma that needs to be healed.

Women may contact rape crisis centers during this stage. A therapist counseling a recent survivor may benefit from consultation with a rape crisis center, if one is available. The victim's needs during this stage include regaining a sense of control over self, making decisions about reporting, medical care and disclosure to others, being accepted and understood, and not being revictimized. Decisions about reporting and disclosure are especially conflict-laden, because victims often accurately fear that others will blame them for being raped. Useful counseling strategies at this stage include information-giving about legal and medical procedures and about community support services available, teaching decision-making skills, open-ended questions, primary empathy, and supporting the victim as she implements her decisions. Therapists must be careful to allow and/or encourage survivors to make their own decisions about disclosures and pursuing medical and legal services. Attempts to steer clients in a particular direction take away their control yet another time and, thus, revictimize them.

## Stage Four: Outward Satisfactory Adjustment and Denial

Anger. Rage.

A fire buried deep.

Buried under politeness.

"Don't make a scene."

Buried under fear,

Frozen in a sea of foggy threats:

"We can do this the easy way or . . ."

Buried in a heap of self-blame:

"Why did I . . . ?"

"Why didn't I . . . ?"

A fire smoldering under years of female socialization.

A fire buried, threatening to rise up and name itself.*

Survivors attempt to get their lives back to normal in Stage Four. To accomplish this, they attempt to avoid thinking about the rape through various uses of denial, suppression, and minimization. These avoidance strategies can include forgetting they were raped, not defining what happened to them as rape, denying there were any negative consequences to them from the rape, believing they have "made up" their memories of being raped, minimizing the impact of their rape by seeing themselves as "less hurt" than other survivors, and repressing some details of the rape. While this stage is often a useful resting place and a time in which survivors regain some sense of control over their lives, there are often negative impacts of the rape (e.g., nightmares or unexplained depression) that they may or may not connect to their rapes. Some survivors move on to Stage Five in a matter of months. Others, like Anna, may stay in the denial stage for many years. Many women never move beyond Stage Four. A survivor's needs in Stage Four are to have a sense of control over her life and to be allowed to cope with the rape memories as she is able. Therapists need to respect the client's coping strategies as well as help the client begin to see connections between her symptoms and her rape. This is a tightrope walk for the therapist. Because violence against women is a common occurrence, assessment for traumatic experiences is an important part of EFT.

## Stage Five: Reliving and Working Through

Sadness and anger.

About my losses,

About the losses of other victims.

Shattered trust in self and others.

Stolen sexual spontaneity.

Mountains to be climbed that sap energy.

A sense of invulnerability and safety gone forever.

Victims living in constant fear of being raped.

Illusions replaced with reality.*

The victim's denial gradually or suddenly lifts in Stage Five. She often begins to have intrusive nightmares and flashbacks about the rape, reliving vividly the rape events. In many ways, her reactions are similar to those of the crisis stage and, in fact, many survivors report feeling as if they had been raped "yesterday" instead of years earlier. Victims who have a delayed reaction often report that they do not understand having such strong, delayed emotional reactions and wonder whether they are going crazy. Therapists need to assure the survivor that her reactions are normal and are typical delayed responses to traumatization. In Stage Five, the rape event must be described and processed. In addition, successful resolution of Stage Five involves the survivor challenging her self-blame and shame. Self-blame has been found by researchers to have differential effects on the long-term recovery process. For example, Janoff-Bulman (1979, 1985) found that characterological self-blame (e.g., "I was raped because I am a slut") was associated with more positive coping outcomes. In contrast, C. Meyer and Taylor (1986) identified three kinds of blame attributions: (a) judgment or behavioral self-blame; (b) victim type or characterological self-blame; and (c) societal factors or nonself-blame. In general, rape survivors in their study who used behavioral or characterological self-blame displayed more negative adjustment than did survivors who attributed blame to societal factors. Their findings suggest that therapists should work at helping clients change both kinds of internal self-blame attributions to external ones. Moving the focus of blame to external cause (e.g., to society or to the rapist) is compatible with EFT principle II, *The Personal Is Political.*

## Stage Six: Resolution and Integration

Powerlessness and violation finally balanced with strength and self-empowerment.

Never the same; yet, now, more.

That is my truth.

Joining hands with other survivors.

Joining hands to cleanse our shame and fight our demons of self-blame.

Joining hands to change laws and attitudes.

Working together on the battlefield of healing,

At one moment, healers; in the next moment, the one being healed.

Fighting a never-ending battle,

Survivors, victims, and healers melded into one.*

The negative effects of the rape must be processed and changed for the survivor to move to Stage Six. The survivor positively integrates the rape into her life in Stage Six, making it an undenied part of her identity. She has worked through most of the negative consequences of the rape and comes to accept the rape as a part of her life. This process involves making existential sense of the meaning of having been raped. (See Table 8.2 for examples of changes in existential beliefs.) She enhances her existing coping skills. In addition, she comes to a fuller appreciation of the strengths that helped her survive the rape and heal from it. She moves from being a *victim* to being a *survivor.* She does not "recover" from the rape, but rather "integrates" it. Additionally, survivors often get involved in bringing about societal changes regarding rape or in helping other rape victims. Many of these societal changes worked for by survivors during Stage Six cycle back to become preventive strategies for Stage One. In writing about her own rape, J. Katz (1984) captured the essence of this coming back full circle: "It is only through shared experience, understanding and action that we can create change. That is the purpose of this testimony. For I am a survivor and the role of the survivor is to testify" (p. 102). Stages Five and Six are described in more detail as Anna's therapy is summarized.

**Table 8.2   Pre-rape, post-rape, and reconstructed existential beliefs for Anna**

| Pre-Rape Existential Beliefs (Pre-Rape Assumptions That Are Shattered) | Post-Rape Existential Beliefs | Reconstructed Existential Beliefs |
| --- | --- | --- |
| The world is positive and ordered. | The world is negative and chaotic. | The world is somewhat ordered and somewhat chaotic. It is made up of positive and negative elements. |
| The world is just: Good things happen to good people, bad things to bad people. | A bad thing happened to me, so I am a bad person. | The world is not just: Bad things can happen to good people. I am still a good person. |

## FEMINIST EMPOWERMENT RAPE THERAPY: AN OVERVIEW

The EFT approach to counseling Anna is firmly built on the four EFT principles. First, in accordance with Principle I, *Personal and Social Identities Are Interdependent,* the client's social locations and respective identity development levels must be assessed and explored. As we have emphasized in the cultural analysis section, clients' cultural contexts strongly impact the existence of rape, victims' responses to rape, and the healing process. Second, in accordance with Principle II, *The Personal Is Political,* the societal context of rape is explored with the client. The rapist is held fully responsible for his actions and the victim is never blamed. The victim is helped to see that the rape was not her fault and to challenge others' negative reactions to her. In relation to Principles III and IV, *Relationships Are Egalitarian* and *Women's Female Perspectives Are Valued,* the client is treated as an expert on her own experience by being believed and not blamed, and by being encouraged to trust her perceptions of what happened during the rape, even though they do not fit society's views of rape. She is helped to develop a definition of rape that encompasses her own experience. The client's coping strategies are redefined as positive and as survival-oriented. The client is a full, collaborative partner in setting therapy goals. She is encouraged to take back control of her life. The therapist teaches the client about the trauma recovery process and helps her to see how her reactions are normal given the trauma she has survived. She is not pathologized. The therapist self-discloses appropriately, sharing her own related experiences to living in a rape-prone culture. If she is a survivor herself, she shares relevant aspects of her rape and of her reactions. Clients are encouraged to join a rape therapy or support group to help reduce their isolation and stigmatization.

## MULTICULTURAL CONSIDERATIONS

Membership in multiple disadvantaged societal groups (e.g., being a woman and a Person of Color, being a lesbian, living in poverty, having a disability, having been traumatized previously) puts people at increased risk for victimization (Ginorio, 1998; D. M. Greene & Navarrim, 1998; Sanchez-Hucles & Hudgins, 2001). According to Angela Ginorio, some social locations increase exposure to risk because these locations "reflect the values and structures of inequality existing in the culture" (p. 81). Research findings on prevalence rates for rape for women from diverse groups are sparse. Hispanic women appear to have lower risks for rape than non-Hispanic women, but they are also less likely to report (Tjaden & Thoennes, 2000). The prevalence rates for Caucasian women and African American women appear to be similar although the research findings are somewhat inconsistent (Holzman, 1996; McNair & Neville, 1996). Women living in poverty are at increased risk for rape probably because their living circumstances (e.g., using public transportation or walking) are less safe (Ginorio, 1998). Rape also occurs in lesbian relationships although its gendered contexts vary from heterosexual rapes. Research yields inconsistent results about whether ethnicity affects recovery from rape. In her review of the literature, Koss (1993) pointed out that some researchers found that rape victims who belong to cultures that intensely shame women who have been raped have more difficulty recovering while other researchers have found no recovery differences. Sanchez-Hucles and Hudgins (2001) summarize resiliency factors found by Fairbank, Schlegner, Saigh, and Davidson that facilitate individuals' trauma recoveries. These factors are strongly related to cultural context and include "stable families, safe environments, community support, little or no substance use, and belonging to a cultural group that is open to discussion of trauma and that values survivors but does not stigmatize victims of PTSD" (p. 1162).

Counseling survivors of rape must be based on an understanding of the survivor's unique cultural context and the impact of her interacting social locations. Definitions of rape, gender-role prescriptions, views of the legal system, values, perceptions of rape survivors, and norms about seeking and accepting help vary across cultures (Holzman, 1996). Janis Sanchez-Hucles and Patrick Hudgins (2001) recommend that culturally appropriate treatment for traumatic experiences include:

1. Interventions that embrace the family and community, especially for survivors from collectivist cultures.
2. "Approaches that address immediate survival issues and the ongoing trauma of sexism, racism, and economic, educational, and political disenfranchisement" (p. 1168).
3. Healing rituals based on cultural practice.
4. Support groups.

In Diane's counseling of Anna, we summarize how Diane used her understanding of Latina/Latino culture to facilitate Anna's healing. While it is beyond the scope of this chapter to review the therapeutic cultural considerations for all groups of women, we chose to highlight as examples two additional cultural groups—Native Americans and African Americans.

## African American and Native American Rape Survivors

Several writers (Holzman, 1996; McNair & Neville, 1996) point out the importance of focusing on the intersection of gender, race, and class and on understanding the historical context of rape when counseling African American and Native American rape survivors. Historically, African American women were sexually exploited during slavery, are not viewed as credible complainants, and are stereotyped (e.g., as promiscuous) in ways that blame them for their rapes. Rape of Native American women was also a significant part of White domination of Native Americans in the United States (Holzman, 1996). For both African Americans and Native Americans, sexism and racism interact to complicate recovery from rape. Lily McNair and Helen Neville (1996) and Clare Holzman (1996) identified factors that complicate the therapeutic process. For example, rage felt by Men of Color as a result of racism may be targeted at women in their own ethnic group (Sanchez-Hucles & Hudgins, 2001). In addition, many African American women do not trust therapists. If their perpetrator was an African American man, they also may experience conflicts around self-disclosure and legal reporting because of wanting to protect male members of their community. For Native American survivors, Holzman (1996) asserted that counseling interventions emphasizing the therapist's quiet presence are more appropriate for Native Americans than feeling expressive ones. She also advocated group treatment for survivors from collectivist cultures.

## ANNA'S THERAPEUTIC JOURNEY

Anna was in Stage Five, Reliving and Working Through, when she initiated therapy. We chose to focus on Anna's case because she was a survivor of acquaintance rape (the most prevalent form of rape), because it is during Stage Five that many women seek counseling, and because very little is written about therapeutic interventions for Stages Five and Six. Space does not allow us to present a comprehensive therapeutic plan for working with Anna. Rather, we highlight the aspects of her therapy that emphasize EFT Principles. Anna's therapist, Diane, is an EF therapist and a psychodramatist. Although we earlier describe Remer's six stages of coping with rape, we now apply them more specifically (especially Stages Five and Six) as we explore Anna's therapy.

Diane is a 50-year-old, White, heterosexual, Methodist woman. In her private practice, Diane specializes in counseling women who have experienced rape or childhood sexual abuse. She has read extensively and attended training workshops on treatment of trauma, on violence against women, and on sexual assault. Diane is also aware that rape occurs in a cultural context. Thus, she has read about the experience and impact of rape for diverse women. She has worked diligently to integrate EFT perspectives into her counseling of sexual assault survivors. As a rape survivor herself, Diane has attended carefully to her own healing by completing therapy and through ongoing self-reflection. When Diane accepted Anna as a client, she educated herself further about Hispanic views of, and responses to, rape.

### Stage Five: Reliving and Working Through

Behavioral, cognitive, and affective counseling techniques facilitate a survivor's resolution of rape trauma. Since the trauma usually taxes the victim's coping skills, survivors often need to learn additional coping skills, especially strategies for managing flashbacks. Recapitulating and processing of the rape experience need to be a primary focus of therapeutic interventions. Previous beliefs about self, the world, and rape often need to be restructured to incorporate and resolve the trauma. Feelings related to the rape and its aftermath need to be expressed, accepted, and validated. Thus, Anna's counseling included behavioral, cognitive, and affective-focused interventions.

## Assessing for Traumatic Experiences and Their Impacts

Anna's nightmares, flashbacks, feelings of fear, and negative reactions during sex are consistent with a delayed PTSD reaction to her rape experience. Although the details of Anna's nightmares allowed her to connect them with her earlier rape, many survivors experience symptoms that are not as clearly related to their rapes. Thus, EF therapists must be knowledgeable about typical reactions connected with sexual trauma. These reactions include depression, sleep disturbance, nightmares, flashbacks, anxiety or fear reactions, avoidance of rape-related stimuli, inability to concentrate, sexual dysfunction, interpersonal conflicts, guilt and shame, anger and rage, lowered self-esteem, loss of trust in self and others, disturbance in typical eating patterns, and a range of physical/health related problems (Koss, 1993; Koss, Heise, et al., 1994; Resick, 1993). Therapists who encounter clients displaying several of these symptoms should ask them about previous unwanted or unpleasant sexual experiences. Further, women who suffer abuse in childhood, especially childhood sexual abuse, are about twice as likely as women without such a history to be raped as adults (D. M. Greene & Navarrim, 1998; Koss, 1993; Russell, 1986b). Thus, any client who has been raped as an adult should be assessed for possible childhood sexual abuse.

Since depression is a common long-term reaction to rape, instruments like the Beck Depression Inventory (BDI-II; Beck et al., 1996) are often useful diagnostic tools with rape survivors. They can also help assess for suicide risk. Anna was given the BDI-II at several points in her therapy. In addition, she was given the Trauma Symptom Inventory (TSI; Briere, 1995) to assess a range of reactions common for trauma survivors. Anna also completed a life history questionnaire that inquired about her developmental history, her current functioning in a variety of areas, and her use of various drugs, including alcohol. At the beginning of therapy, Anna had clinically elevated scores on the Intrusive Experiences, Anxious Arousal, Defensive Avoidance, and Sexual Concerns scales of the TSI, indicating that the memories of her rape were intruding psychologically, and that, in part, she was trying to cope by avoiding them. Her BDI score indicated that she was not clinically depressed initially, although she did become mildly depressed at several points in therapy. Her life history questionnaire seemed to indicate a relatively happy childhood, although she did grow up feeling less physically attractive than her older sister. Nothing else was remarkable on the questionnaire. Based in part on these assessments, Anna and her therapist decided to focus therapeutically on the rape experience with Raul and its traumatic aftereffects.

## Normalizing Responses to Trauma

Diane's first focus was to build a collaborative and trusting relationship with Anna. Rape survivors need a safe place to heal, and having a therapist who believes and does not blame them is an important part of that safety. Since Diane was a rape survivor herself, when therapeutically appropriate, she disclosed to Anna relevant aspects of her own experience and healing process. In addition, because Diane was Caucasian and Anna was Latina, Diane raised the issue of their cultural differences and its possible impact on their counseling relationship, a topic they revisited several times during their sessions. To be a culturally competent therapist for Anna, Diane had to became more knowledgeable about the Latino cultural context of rape; she read relevant material and consulted with a Latina colleague. After building a trust relationship with Anna, Diane began to give Anna information about the trauma recovery process so that Anna could see the normality of her reactions. Diane shared the six stages of the Remer model with Anna, encouraging her to comment on how the model fit or did not fit with her experience. Diane's therapeutic approach was in part based on the trauma stress models proposed by Figley (1985) and Scurfield (1985). These models emphasize common "normal" reactions to trauma experiences, as opposed to describing survivors' reactions as pathological, an approach that is compatible with EFT's value of treating the client as an expert on herself. Diane showed her Scurfield's six educational statements about trauma reactions. These include the ideas that trauma can produce symptoms in anyone, flashbacks and other reactions are expected and normal, and healing from rape is possible. Further, Diane shared with Anna information from research on Latina rape survivors that indicates they often have a more difficult healing process because of Hispanic cultural beliefs about rape (e.g., being raped brings shame to the family; Lira, Koss, & Russo, 1999). Anna was relieved to learn that her reactions were normal and to have both a map and hope for her recovery.

## Exploring Social Locations

Diane also assessed for Anna's rape-relevant social locations. Anna perceived her primary social location to be a Latina. Anna appeared to be in Level 3, Immersion, of ethnic identity development as she was very aware of ethnic discrimination and oppression of Hispanic people and identified closely with her Latina/Latino community. Anna listed her Catholic religious identity as her second most important identity. She also identified with being a woman, but had limited, but growing awareness, of societal sexism. Thus, Diane assessed that Anna was probably in early Level 2, Encounter, of gender-role identity development. Diane understood that from Anna's perspective, racism and was more important than sexism. However, Diane also understood that rape is strongly affected by dominant societal and ethnic sexism and that raising Ann's awareness about sexism was crucial to her healing. Diane also expected that because social locations are interdependent (EFT Principle I), consciousness raising about sexism would impact both Ann's gender identity development and her racial identity development.

Anna's experience of being raped was influenced by her social identities in that she had learned and internalized the sociocultural values about rape associated with all her identities (Ginorio, 1998). The aftermath of rape is also influenced by her social identities and their sociocultural contexts. That is, will she be believed, blamed, shamed, and/or supported? Anna had minimized the possibilities of others' reacting negatively to her rape by initially not telling anyone. By analyzing her cultural contexts (e.g., her Latina/Latino views of rape victims), Anna began to understand better her choices before, during, and after the rape. Exploration of Anna's social locations eventually led to a challenging of both the norms and practices of our dominant U.S. culture and of Anna's Latina/Latino culture. Understanding Anna's Latina/Latino and Catholic cultural values did not prohibit Diane from challenging their patriarchal structures and negative impacts on Anna.

## Making the Personal Political

Anna and Diane did a cultural analysis of rape, which followed the format we presented previously. Information-giving by Diane and self-analysis by Anna were the foundation of this analysis. Anna's cultural analysis included what she had learned about rape from the dominant culture and from her Latina culture (Lira et al., 1999). Anna discovered that she had learned and internalized that rapists were always strangers who jumped their victims in dark alleys, that women should be able to fight off rape attacks, that it is the woman's fault if she allows herself to get in a dangerous situation, and that forced types of sexual activity that were not vaginal-penile intercourse were not rape. Her Latina socialization especially had emphasized the importance of being a virgin until marriage. Her Catholic religious teachings included stories of Maria Goretti, a woman who died defending herself during a rape and who was later elevated to sainthood (Lira et al., 1999). Anna had internalized that good women do not let themselves be raped, and she feared that disclosure of her rape would bring shame to her family. Originally, Anna had not classified her experience with Raul as "rape" because it did not match any of her learned messages about rape. As a female who was raised to be polite, to trust male acquaintances as her protectors, and not to be physically aggressive, Anna had a difficult time perceiving that she was in danger and needed to physically defend herself. She also believed that she should have been able to identify that Raul was dangerous. Diane shared facts about rape with Anna (e.g., that about 60% of rapes are acquaintance rapes, that rapists generally are not crazy men who are readily identifiable). Further, she explained that acquaintance rapists often deliberately behave in a trustworthy manner so as to gain the intended victim's trust. Thus, Anna was able to see that she did not have clear signals to let her know she was in danger. Diane also gave Anna information about victims often fearing for their lives (Zollicoffer, 1989). Diane reframed the fact that Anna had stopped struggling during the rape as a life survival strategy rather than as a sign she had consented.

Processing all of this analysis and information helped Anna change her self-blame attributions and reduce her guilt. (See Table 8.3 for examples of cognition changes Anna made as a part of her healing process.) Further, her actions during and after the rape began to make more sense to her. She began to appreciate that by stopping her struggling,

**Table 8.3  Anna's restructured cognitions**

| Self-Blame Cognitions | Restructured Cognitions |
| --- | --- |
| I should have been able to see that he was dangerous. | He deliberately portrayed himself as trustworthy and hid his dangerousness from me. Society misled me to believe that only strangers commit rape. |
| I should have prosecuted. | Given the laws at the time and the circumstances of my rape, he probably would not have been convicted, and I probably would have been traumatized further. I made a good decision. |
| I should have fought harder and longer. | He was larger and stronger than I. If I had fought more, I might have been more physically hurt and I probably still wouldn't have been able to avoid being raped. |
| The rape was my fault. | I did nothing for which I deserved to be raped. Raul is fully responsible for having raped me. |

she protected herself from further physical and psychological damage and possible death. She began to understand that her decision not to report the rape or tell anyone about it were typical responses for an acquaintance rape victim and were also based on her Latina/Latino gender-role and sexual messages. Her silence may have shielded her from probable blame and stigmatization. She also realized her initial choice to remain silent about being raped was based on her realistic fear that her Latino father and brothers might have sought revenge defending "her honor." Thus, she also began to perceive that many of her responses during and after the rape, rather than being inadequate, were actually effective coping strategies.

## Clarifying Flashbacks

Understanding Anna's nightmares and flashbacks was another important aspect of her therapy. Diane began by explaining Horowitz' avoidance-intrusion cycle to Anna. Horowitz (1979) theorized that survivors respond to the trauma by cycling between avoidance (i.e., denial of and emotional numbing to the rape) and intrusion (i.e., unwanted recall of the rape). The intrusion of the rape into conscious thought usually occurs through nightmares, flashbacks, and unwanted thoughts. The avoidance responses, which include numbing of emotional responses to the rape, denial or suppression of memories of the rape, and minimization of the trauma of the rape, allow the survivor to ward off psychologically the reality of the rape. On the one hand, avoidance responses can offer respite for the survivor from being overwhelmed by the rape trauma and allow her time to build the resources needed to deal with its reality. On the other hand, avoidance responses interrupt full processing of and cognitively integrating the rape. The intrusion cycle continues until the survivor has integrated the trauma emotionally and cognitively.

Anna's understanding that her avoidance-intrusion cycle was a normal reaction to trauma and that it is part of a healthy organismic tendency to heal helped Anna feel less out of control and crazy. With this new knowledge, Anna decided to learn strategies for coping with the intrusions, made a commitment to decrease her use of avoidance responses, and agreed to work in therapy on cognitively integrating her rape.

## Coping with Flashbacks

Although Anna's nightmares and flashbacks eventually diminished, she initially needed to learn ways to gain some control of them. First, Diane told Anna that flashbacks and nightmares, while painful to experience, are often indicators of where to focus in counseling. From this perspective and in accordance with EFT Principle III (Relationships Are Egalitarian), Diane suggested that Anna trust these intrusions (and herself) as road signs to guide them. Second, Anna learned that her flashbacks were often triggered by present stimuli in her life that were similar to stimuli present during her rape. For example, during her rape, the rapist held her down by her wrists. One evening her husband playfully tugged on her right wrist. Anna felt trapped and angry and snapped at her husband. Understanding how her strong reaction got triggered helped Anna feel less out of control and able to trust herself more. Because of this interpersonal triggering, Diane and Anna discussed the pros and cons of telling Anna's husband, Tomas, about her rape. In a joint session with Tomas, Diane helped Anna disclose to him and to share her reactions to the rape. Diane gave Tomas information about the rape recovery process, about how he could support Anna's recovery, and about potential vicarious traumatization reactions he might experience (R. Remer & Ferguson, 1996). Anna was able to talk with Tomas about how he had triggered her, and he avoided touching her in that way again.

In Chapter 6, we introduced the mood ratings sheets. Diane used these sheets with Anna to help her identify the rape-related triggers for her strong emotional reactions and for her flashbacks. Once Anna identified her triggers, she was able to anticipate, modify, and/or avoid them, thus reducing her flashbacks. For example, by asking her husband not to grab her wrists, Anna created a way for her to avoid that trigger. Anna was able to anticipate that driving down a gravel road to a friend's farmhouse might be triggering. She modified this potential trigger by using relaxation techniques while approaching the road and by focusing on the wildflowers in the field instead of on the sound of the tires on the gravel.

## Enhancing Social Support

Diane knew that healing from rape can be facilitated by supportive environments, while blaming environments may retard recovery and revictimize the survivor. Significant others are especially important. Thus, as we described in an earlier section, Diane suggested that Anna's husband, Tomas, be included in several sessions throughout the course of therapy. In addition to giving him information about the rape healing process, Diane also taught him about potentially destructive responses. Two examples of possibly destructive responses he should avoid using with Anna were: "You shouldn't have gone out with him" and "You should be over this by now."

## Identifying and Sharing the Traumatic Events

As a part of Stage Five, Anna was encouraged to share (recapitulate) the details of rape at her own pace. Diane facilitated this process by asking Anna to be as specific as possible and by psychodramatically doubling Anna's feelings. Psychodramatic enactment of parts of the rape helped Anna reclaim some pieces of the rape event that she had forgotten, as well as to begin to express the feelings she had not been able to express during and after the rape. Feelings that Anna, like many rape survivors, needed to express include fear and powerlessness, rage, anger, sadness, shame, guilt, and isolation. Expression of these feelings associated with her rape and its aftermath in the presence of Diane, a nonblaming, believing, and supportive other, facilitated Anna's healing. Reexperiencing feelings associated with her rape also helped her to confront cognitions that had served to minimize the severity of her rape and its aftermath. For example, Anna initially stated, "My rape wasn't too bad. I got off lucky because he didn't force me to have intercourse." After sharing her rape event details with Diane and expressing her anguish and rage, Anna said, "I was very traumatized by my rape. I felt paralyzed with fear and was so invaded by him. He robbed me of my relaxed enjoyment of sex even before I got to know much about it. I feel so angry with him." Recapitulation of the details of the trauma and the accompanying feelings also facilitated Anna's desensitization to the trauma. Diane's knowledge of the details of Anna's rape was also crucial to helping her refute her self-blame and to helping her identify the triggers for her flashbacks.

Through both the cultural analysis and event detailing, Anna developed her own definition of rape that encompassed what had happened to her. Her definition, "sexual intimacy forced on one person by another," included being attacked by a date and having forced oral sexual activity instead of intercourse. She began to use the word *rape* in reference to herself. Diane was careful to respect Anna's own labeling and so did not use the word *rape* to refer to Raul's behavior until Anna did.

*Coping with Fear*

Rape victims usually score higher on fear measures, especially on rape-specific fear measures, than do non-raped women (Resick, 1993). One of Anna's strongest responses to being raped was feeling anxious. At the beginning of therapy, she was having difficulty going out alone, especially at night. She also had strong fear responses when she had flashbacks. From a feminist perspective, working with a rape survivor's fear responses is tricky business. On the one hand, Diane knew it was important to reduce Anna's fear responses (e.g., experiences of intense anxiety) so that she could function in her daily life and not feel continually overwhelmed. On the other hand, Diane knew that women who have not been raped tend to live in denial about the prevalence of rape and of their risk to being raped. Because of these conflicting issues related to rape fears, Diane used a two-prong approach with Anna. First, she taught Anna relaxation and desensitization techniques for reducing her intense fear responses. Second, she and Anna discussed societal denial of rape; and Diane acknowledged that as a survivor, Anna had a more realistic appraisal of the need to be fearful of rape. Diane's acknowledgment that Anna's appraisal was accurate was important, because it facilitated Anna's rebuilding trust in her own reactions. This appraisal can also be motivation for getting politically involved to bring about societal changes related to rape. For example, Anna began to work with other women from the local rape crisis center to develop rape prevention programs specifically designed for Latino men and Latina women in the community.

Survivors move out of Stage Five when they have alleviated most of the negative consequences of the rape. They may move back and forth between Stages Five and Six as new issues emerge.

## Stage Six: Resolution and Integration

*Confronting Existential Beliefs*

Anna's pre-rape beliefs included: (a) viewing the world as benign, orderly, and just; (b) believing herself to be invulnerable to harm; and (c) having a positive view of herself. Initially, Anna's experience with Raul did not fit with these core beliefs; therefore, to cope, she minimized his violation of her by not labeling the experience as *rape,* thus maintaining her pre-rape schemas. As a result of Anna's therapy work in Stage Five, she no longer denied the reality of her rape experience. This new perspective led to Anna's need to restructure her schemas in such a way that her rape could be integrated into them (McCann et al., 1988).

Anna had always felt in control of what happened to her. She believed that she was a good person and that the world was basically a good place. She believed that rape was something that happened to other women who were careless or promiscuous. Her rape disrupted her existential view of herself and her world. As she learned more about the prevalence of rape and talked with other rape survivors, she began to change her existing cognitive schemas. She still saw herself as a good person, but came to see that bad things can happen to good people. She grieved over the loss of the part of herself that believed that she could prevent bad things from happening.

This schematic integration of the trauma is a highly individualized process for each survivor. (See Table 8.3 for examples of Anna's changes in beliefs.) Treating the individual as an expert on herself is especially important to this process. This integration occurs over a long period of time, encompassing both Stages Five and Six. For a more detailed explanation of cognitively integrating the trauma, see McCann et al. (1988).

## Positively Integrating the Trauma

Positive integration of the rape experience into their lives is the major goal of Stage Six. This positive integration can take many forms: identifying strengths and coping strategies used to survive and to resolve the rape; becoming involved in bringing about social or legal changes related to rape; helping another survivor; self-disclosing to others about the rape; confronting others who perpetuate rape myths; developing a self-enhancing, nonself-blaming perspective on the rape; and finding positive meaning for the rape. Figley (1985) referred to this process as one of moving from being a victim to becoming a survivor. Part of moving from being a victim to a survivor is finding positive meaning in the rape. In discovering positive meanings for the rape, survivors make sense of the trauma, gain mastery, and increase self-esteem. Scurfield (1985) proposed that positive outcomes of a trauma may include a healthy reassessment about the direction of the survivor's life, appreciation of the ability to cope with adverse circumstances, and sensitization to human trauma and dehumanization. Once Anna acknowledged that she had indeed survived a terrifying and traumatic experience, she was able to identify many strengths she had used to cope with it. For example, she was able to own what fortitude she had displayed to continue with school and excel scholastically. As a result of her counseling work on her rape, Anna came to several new insights. For example, Anna realized that she rarely allowed others to support her during trying times. Because she felt so overwhelmed by feelings in Stage Five, she learned to reach out, ask for, and take in support from others. Because of this experience, she was able to balance her autonomy and self-sufficiency with interpersonal connectedness. Anna's involvement as a volunteer at a local rape crisis center and her involvement in developing rape prevention programs for her community were two ways she used to find positive meaning from her rape. Being able to use her own experience to connect with other victims and to change society through prevention programs brought special meaning to Anna's life. Anna felt empowered by these positive transformations in her life and replaced her earlier feelings of shame about having been raped with feelings of pride about her survivorship.

## Evaluating Therapeutic Outcomes

Anna was in therapy weekly for about nine months. Although some sessions focused on areas of her life not directly related to her rape, the majority of her sessions did focus on rape-related issues. In addition, Anna attended an eight-week, time limited group for rape survivors. At the end of therapy, Anna believed she had accomplished the following goals. She had:

1. Defined herself as having been raped and had acknowledged the traumatization she experienced.
2. Understood the societal factors that contribute to the existence of rape and that complicate recovery from rape.
3. Challenged and replaced detrimental gender-role messages.
4. Replaced self-blame statements with external blame ones.
5. Replaced beliefs in learned rape myths with ones based on rape facts.
6. Felt less stigmatized and isolated.

7. Perceived her post-rape reactions as normal and as a validation of her victimization.
8. Decreased her flashbacks and nightmares.
9. Grieved the loss of her pre-rape self.
10. Identified and learned to appreciate the strengths that she used to survive the rape and to work through the resolution process.
11. Increased her self-esteem.
12. Revised her existential beliefs to incorporate her rape.
13. Engaged in social action to change rape-related aspects of society.
14. Identified positive meanings from her rape.
15. Increased her behavioral repertoire of coping skills.
16. Improved her marital intimacy.
17. Progressed to higher levels of identity development on rape-relevant social locations.

Anna continued to deal with several rape-related issues, including struggling with how to respond to people who tell jokes about rape and deciding whom to tell about her rape. She summed up her progress by saying, "As a result of having survived my rape and having worked to resolve it, I feel stronger than I did before I was raped. I am a survivor!"

## FEMINIST PERSPECTIVES ON HEALING

We believe that resolving a rape experience is an ongoing, lifelong process. From a feminist perspective, the meaning of recovery and resolution is best individually determined by each survivor. In a study by Alice Zollicoffer and Pam Remer (1989), rape survivors were asked what recovery, resolution, and healing meant to them. Their qualitative answers give insight into possible definitions for these terms and into the process of working through a rape.

First, 20% of the respondents indicated that they did not believe that a woman ever fully recovers from rape. Second, while there were commonalities among survivors' responses, there were also many individual differences. Resolution and healing seem to be multidimensional processes. The following categories represent some of the commonalities among survivors, responses to what constituted recovery, healing, and resolution for them:

1. Working through feelings so that the survivor is no longer overwhelmed by rape-related emotions.
2. Integrating the rape into her life so that the rape is no longer controlling her life.
3. Accepting the reality of the rape, including acknowledging that she was raped and that it was a traumatic experience.
4. Helping others by counseling and supporting others who have been raped.
5. Perceiving support from others as the survivor shared her feelings and thoughts about the rape. If she could share, not be blamed or judged, and be listened to empathically, then the survivor felt validated and less isolated and stigmatized.

6. Loving, appreciating, and forgiving herself; learning to trust herself to perceive accurately and to make good decisions and judgments.

One other finding from this study sheds further light on the meanings of recovery and resolution. Some participants who rated themselves as high on resolution also had moderate or high avoidance and intrusion scores. Thus, even among survivors who perceived themselves to be resolved, some continued to experience rape-related effects.

We believe that a woman does not go back to being the same person she was before the rape. She is changed by it. Resolution involves finding ways to alleviate the negative consequences of the rape, integrating the reality of the rape, and finding positive meaning from the rape in her life.

## SUMMARY

The EFT approach to counseling rape survivors begins with a feminist analysis of the cultural context in which rape exists. Rape myths, gender-role socialization, and power differentials between women and men all contribute to the prevalence of rape. EF therapists empower rape survivors by validating their experience, educating them about trauma, confronting client's internalization of societal rape myths, and identifying and appreciating client strengths in coping with the rape.

Counseling sexual assault survivors is both a challenge and a privilege. In our work with survivors, we have felt challenged to confront our own biases, myths, and the need to believe that we are invulnerable to any future victimization. We have felt challenged to apply the EFT principles and rewarded when we succeeded. In our work with sexual assault survivors, we have been able to see most clearly the effects of societal oppression of women, of institutionalized sexism and racism, and of gender-role-stereotyping. More importantly, we feel privileged to counsel survivors. We appreciate the trust they place in us by being vulnerable as they share their stories and feelings with us. Finally, we are awed by the courage and inner strength of these survivors—testimonies to the strength and courage of all women.

## ACTIVITIES

With a friend or in small classroom groups, complete one or more of the following exercises:

Remember and share joking comments about rape that you have heard, admonitions about protecting yourself from rape that you have been given, and the portrayal of rape in movies you have seen. Discuss how the jokes, movies, and admonitions reflect various rape myths and facts. Discuss how you have internalized these messages.

Identify what things you do or do not do currently that are precautions against being raped (e.g., not going out at night alone). Be aware of how much the threat of being raped influences your actions. If you are a male, identify how your life has been influenced by women living in fear of rape.

The threat of the possibility of rape is a part of women's lives. Remember and share any of the following:

1. A time you were alone and began to worry about being raped.
2. Having someone you were dating become overly sexually aggressive and not listening to or discounting your choice not to be sexually involved.
3. Sexual and verbal abuses you have encountered on the street, at parties, at work, and so on, that make you feel sexually violated.
4. Physical sexual abuses (even minor ones) that made you feel sexually violated.
5. Any situation you have been in where you became afraid you might be raped.

The prevalence of gender-based violence against women is so high that most people have first-hand knowledge of such an experience (i.e., a trauma that happened to you directly, one you witnessed, or one you had disclosed to you). Write an account of this experience. Notice how you feel as you write the account and how you feel after you finish writing it. In a group setting or a class, these accounts can be typed and handed in anonymously. They can be distributed, read aloud, and discussed. This exercise, which is adapted from one developed by Angela Ginorio (1998), brings the *Personal Is Political* principle to life.

*Excerpts from a poem by Pam Remer, 1993.

## FURTHER READINGS

Holzman, C. G. (1996). Counseling adult women rape survivors: Issues of race, ethnicity, and class. *Women and Therapy, 19,* 47–63.

Koss, M. P., Goodman, L. A., Browne, A., Fitzgerald, L. F., Keita, G. P., & Russo, N. F. (1994). *No safe haven: Male violence against women at home, at work, and in the community.* Washington, DC: American Psychological Association.

Koss, M. P., Heise, L., & Russo, N. F. (1994). The global health burden of rape. *Psychology of Women Quarterly, 18,* 509–538.

McCann, I. L., Sakheim, D. K., & Abrahamson, D. S. (1988). Trauma and victimization: A model of psychological adaptation. *Counseling Psychologist, 16,* 531–594.

# Chapter 9

# *CONFRONTING ABUSE*

*You are more likely to be physically assaulted, beaten, and killed in your own home at the hands of a loved one than any place else, or by anyone else in our society.*

Richard Gelles and Murray Strauss, 1988

*Battering and the values supporting it cannot be understood apart from other aspects of the culture that sanction male superiority. Once male privilege is granted, the right to enforce it directly follows.*

Neil Jacobson and John Gottman, 1998

## SELF-ASSESSMENT: BELIEFS ABOUT ABUSE IN CLOSE RELATIONSHIPS

Common beliefs about the causes and consequences of interpersonal abuse are frequently invoked by the victim, the abuser, friends, and family, as well as the law enforcement and legal systems, to excuse and maintain the abuse. For each of the following statements, determine whether you believe it is mostly true (T) or mostly false (F) by circling the appropriate letter on the right.

| | | | |
|---|---|:---:|:---:|
| 1. | The abuser is seldom pathological or mentally ill. | T | F |
| 2. | Physical abuse occurs in families from all socioeconomic levels. | T | F |
| 3. | The victim could leave safely if she really wanted to. | T | F |
| 4. | Women who are in abusive relationships are masochistic and secretly enjoy being dominated. | T | F |
| 5. | Some women provoke their abuse by nagging and being overly critical. | T | F |
| 6. | Since the abuser is after only the woman, the children are safe. | T | F |
| 7. | The police and legal system will protect her from further abuse if she will only report it. | T | F |

| | | |
|---|---|---|
| 8. Once a battered woman leaves her abuser, she is safe. | T | F |
| 9. Neighbors and friends would help her if they knew about the abuse. | T | F |
| 10. A woman can avoid getting her partner angry and violent by her own reactions. | T | F |
| 11. The abuser is not responsible for his violent behavior if he has been drinking. | T | F |
| 12. Abusers are usually unemployed or under extreme personal stress. | T | F |
| 13. Abused women usually grew up in abusive homes and are therefore predisposed to accept further abuse. | T | F |
| 14. The abused woman stays only for the sake of the children. | T | F |
| 15. The abuser will change for the better when he is under less stress. | T | F |
| 16. A woman who earns more than her spouse threatens his self-esteem and thus provokes the abuse. | T | F |
| 17. Some men slap their partners occasionally but they seldom cause serious injury. | T | F |
| 18. Woman battering occurs in 20% to 50% of North American families. | T | F |
| 19. Victims who seek shelter in a safe house frequently return home to the abuser. | T | F |
| 20. Children who observe or experience family violence are at risk for cognitive, emotional, and behavioral problems. | T | F |

## Scoring

Of the previous statements, only the following are true: 1, 2, 18, 19, and 20. The remaining statements are false, but reflect commonly held myths about partner abuse. Refer to the chapter text and to Tables 9.1 and 9.2 and Figures 9.1 and 9.2 for further information on items you may have missed.

## OVERVIEW

Estimates of woman abuse suggest that over half of the clients who seek counseling have experienced interpersonal violence in a close relationship (Walker, 1994). Many clients, however, shield the facts of physical, emotional, or sexual abuse behind other presenting issues. All initial assessments with women clients should include screening for possible violence and abuse. When clients in your initial screening and assessment do not reveal apparent abuse, as in the case of Rachel that follows, clinicians should remain vigilant for further cues that suggest its presence. In this chapter, we discuss the dimensions of violence in close relationships, including definitions of abuse, incidence rates, and psychological effects on the victim. We present a model of abuse in close relationships that includes societal, situational, and maintaining factors in the initiation and persistence of abusive behaviors toward women.

Once the existence of current abuse is revealed, intervention is focused on: (a) ensuring and planning for the safety of the woman, (b) exploring the dimensions of her current situation and her responses to her victimization; (c) reempowering her by reframing her "symptoms" as strengths and resilient coping, (d) assisting in the decision-making process by exploring resources and helping her to consider alternatives and their possible outcomes, and (e) restructuring her situation and planning for action. When there appears to be a risk of imminent danger to the client, considerations of personal and social identity status may be deferred and then integrated into the sessions as they become relevant.

We consider the story of Rachel, who came to us initially because she understood that we had a Jewish woman therapist on staff, and she preferred to see someone with a religious background similar to her own. Fortunately, it was possible to honor Rachel's request, and she was scheduled to see Karen, who described herself as Jewish from both an ethnic and a liberal religious perspective. At 30 years of age, Karen was single and living alone but involved in a long-term heterosexual relationship. As a committed Empowerment Feminist Therapy (EFT) practitioner with five years of postdoctoral experience, Karen preferred to work with issues relevant to women and tended to see a broad range of clients. This was her first experience with a service request related to her ethnic identity, and she wondered how this factor would impact either the therapeutic relationship or her own ability to be helpful to this client.

Rachel's presenting issues were twofold: She wanted help in deciding whether to modify or change her job (career counseling), and she also wanted to deal with her weight problem. Karen raised the issue of Rachel's request for a particular religious orientation early in the sessions in the process of exploring Rachel's personal and social identities. What was the importance of having a Jewish therapist? How did she wish her ethnicity to be understood and appreciated? Rachel proceeded to elaborate on her Jewish identity and about how she felt very uncomfortable in self-disclosing to those she considered to be "outsiders." Rachel indicated that she was a second-generation American, with immigrant grandparents who escaped from the horrors of the Holocaust in Germany to establish a new and better life for their children. Her concern was that personal problems should not be aired outside the family, that others might be nonaccepting and critical and thus judge her entire community more harshly. Karen then disclosed briefly the nature of her own Judaic background and asked for feedback if at any point Rachel felt misunderstood or at risk in the relationship. At that point, Rachel seemed satisfied that she could trust Karen with her story.

Here, we focus the intervention with Rachel on the phases following the session in which she revealed a history of severe physical abuse by her husband. Intervention strategies for Rachel included responding to crisis, ensuring safety, power and gender-role analysis, cultural and spiritual analysis, bibliotherapy, cognitive restructuring, assertiveness coaching, reattribution training, problem solving, career exploration, contact with police and community agencies, legal consultation, and entrance into a spouse abuse support group.

After reading this chapter, you will be able to:

1. Identify the characteristics of the Battered Woman Syndrome (BWS).
2. List and describe external factors that support abusive relationships.
3. Explain the theory and effects of entrapment.

4. Outline a plan for enabling women to terminate abuse in their close relationships.
5. Discuss the issues to consider when the abuse is supported by an appeal to the client's religious or cultural identity.

## RACHEL'S STORY: THE STRUGGLE TOWARD FREEDOM FROM ABUSE

### Denying Abuse

Rachel's request for counseling was typical for many women who are living in abusive relationships. Experiencing terror, abuse, and alternating attacks of anxiety and depression, she wanted to change something about herself. "I think I need some help in deciding what to do about my job. I'm also much too fat and I'd like some help in losing weight." At that point, she was unable (or unwilling) to locate the source of her dissatisfaction in the home situation. In searching for the causes of her distress, she decided that: (a) she was "too fat," which was associated with periodic depressive episodes; and (b) that her job required too much evening and overtime work (she was an assistant credit manager in a large discount store), and she was finding it increasingly difficult to concentrate on her work.

In the course of assessment and some exploratory sessions, Rachel's two presenting issues were accepted as initial counseling goals. We had some reservations about her weight reduction goal. However, for many women, the excessive concern about weight can become the focus of therapeutic intervention in itself. Rachel's reasons for wanting to lose weight, her current and past strategies for approaching the problem, and the underlying self-concept reflected in her weight-related concerns were all topics of relevance to her situation. Early sessions revealed that Rachel had little awareness of sociocultural gender issues for women (gender identity level I, Preawareness) but was very invested in being a "good Jewish wife and mother" (ethnic identity level 3, Immersion). Throughout the sessions, Karen was careful to interject the relevance of these two social locations to the ways in which Rachel conceptualized and coped with her concerns (Principle I). Preliminary steps in the assessment and counseling of career decision making comprised the second set of counseling strategies. (See Chapter 8 for more details on career counseling.)

During the first two months of counseling, Rachel began to drop hints about her relationship with her husband, Stan, that led her therapist to "listen with a third ear." Rachel gradually revealed that her feelings of dissatisfaction with her appearance and her job were related to Stan's reactions. It became clear that Stan was saying she was too fat. Stan was also annoyed with her night work. He wanted her home when he came home and objected to having to "baby-sit" or leave their six-year-old daughter with a sitter at night. Rachel periodically dieted to try to lose weight, and she finally agreed with Stan that her investment in her job, which required her to stay until 10:00 P.M. on alternate weekends, was the source of many of their problems.

The multiple cues about Rachel's investment in pleasing Stan led Karen to probe further for evidences of psychological intimidation and the possibilities of more serious abuse. Rachel's response was to defend Stan, providing "good reasons" for his concern about her and the welfare of their daughter, Sherry. Rachel believed that Stan's love for her and Sherry led him to be concerned with how she looked and with having her safely home at night whether or not he was there. Stan also spent many late evenings at medical school, where he was a fourth-year student. She also viewed his jealousy of one of her coworkers as further indication of his love. Stan started asking her about this man frequently and monitored her telephone calls carefully ("Who was that you were just talking to on the phone?"). Rachel assured Stan that the man was "just a friend," but Stan accused her of having an affair. The new piece of information concerning Stan's jealousy further alerted Karen, who then kept an open ear for evidences of abuse.

Eight weeks into counseling, Rachel arrived one day wearing dark glasses. Behind the camouflage, Karen could detect obvious lacerations on the side of Rachel's forehead and what appeared to be evidence of a black eye. It required very little probing to break through Rachel's mask of a happy marriage and to encourage Rachel to share the burden of her misery.

## Uncovering Abuse

Rachel and Stan were married shortly before he applied to medical school. After Sherry was born, Rachel continued to work as assistant credit manager and was the major source of their limited income during Stan's medical training. She recalls that over time, Stan became withdrawn and irritable and began to shout obscenities at her for small mistakes. Since she knew that medical school was difficult and demanding, she attributed these abusive reactions to his stressful situation. He grew increasingly critical of her, targeting her appearance, habits, housekeeping, mothering, cooking, family, and the conditions of her job. He became demanding of sex, frequently waking her up late at night to insist that she engage in various sexual practices with him, some of which she found painful or unpleasant. He became angry if she declined, telling her she was a "cold fish," and he would coerce her into satisfying his demands. The next morning he would act as though nothing unusual had occurred, convincing her that she must be "crazy." With each new source of dissatisfaction, she attempted to appease and please him. "Things seemed to go smoothly as long as I could figure out ways to keep him from getting angry," she said.

But over time, Rachel's efforts to placate Stan failed to control his outbursts of anger. A heated argument one evening over her late work hours ended in his pushing her violently across the room, hitting and seriously cutting her head on the corner of a table. Rachel recalls that "Stan was really scared, because I was bleeding really bad, and Sherry woke up and saw me like that and she was crying. He picked me up and hugged me and told me to go in and clean it with water. The whole next week he was really good to me and things went along just fine."

The next physical battering incident occurred almost three months later, when they were arguing about her telephone calls to friends in the evening. "Stan just hated me to talk to my friends when he was home, and he kept trying to pull the phone away from me but I wouldn't let him, so when I didn't get off the phone right away, he just ripped it off the wall and threw the whole thing at me. I was so mad, him tearing up the phone like that, I started screaming at him and he hit me in the mouth and told me to shut up, and some other foul things too, and then threw me down on the floor and kicked me over and over in the stomach and on my breasts. I was crying so hard by then, and screaming too, I knew I had lost a tooth or something, but he just picked up and left the house, yelling at me through the door."

As she told this story, Rachel began to sob, raising her voice as she described the violence of the scene. Having been able to disclose these early acts of violence toward her,

Rachel could not seem to stop, and began repeating the details of each subsequent abusive incident, enacting her fears, escalating terror, and feelings of isolation and hopelessness. She was beginning to realize that she could not find ways to escape the increasingly angry outbursts; threats of violence; destruction of household objects (throwing dishes); and periodic slapping, hitting, and sexual coercion. Her reasons for entering counseling were thus to improve the situation by making herself more attractive to Stan, so that "he would want to be loving with me again."

## Confronting Abuse

Now, the focus of counseling shifted. Karen communicated her concern for Rachel's safety, as well as for Sherry's and suggested that they renegotiate their counseling goals. Rachel's reaction was to deny that the abuse was the major problem. She retreated into a defense of Stan, his difficult childhood, their economic insufficiencies, and his stress in medical school. She denied that he ever hit Sherry except to discipline her. She was certain that something could be done to help him, as well as to continue her efforts to modify her own behaviors. "I just want to make it easier for both of us. I know he'll come around when he's finished with school and he's under less stress," she insisted. "Please help me to make it better now." In many ways, Rachel's situation and her reactions were similar to those described by Lenore Walker (1979) as the *cycle of violence*. Figure 9.1 displays how the victim's denial and attempts to deal with the violence are followed by escalation and eventual repetition of the violent episodes. We caution that this model is useful in conceptualizing some, but not all, abusive relationships.

The uncovering of serious and possibly lethal abuse to both Rachel and Sherry triggered a major change in the direction of counseling. Karen initiated a discussion of how Rachel might take precautions to reduce the risk of physical endangerment. Rachel listened politely, but remained unconvinced that she or Sherry was in danger of serious harm. Stan came from a "good Orthodox family," she insisted, and she would not want to disgrace him or his parents by allowing any of her family problems to be revealed. Further, she did not want to compromise his progress in medical school or his important position as president of the youth brotherhood in his synagogue. At this point, Karen checked the abuse literature and consulted with someone more experienced in wife battering, and together they identified a self-report index on intimate violence that might help Rachel to place her personal experiences into a broader context (EFT Principle II). Rachel was willing to complete the abuse index to prove she was not at risk.

## Assessment

Rachel had been administered a routine assessment when she first entered counseling, which had not uncovered direct evidence of abuse. In the light of new information, we introduced additional assessment for battering with a modification of the Center for Social Research (CSR) Abuse Index (Stacey & Shupe, 1983), which provided Rachel with objective feedback on Stan's behavior in the context of abusive relationships (see Table 9.1).

There are several other standardized and reliable instruments to assess the extent of woman battering, such as the Index of Spouse Abuse (Hudson & McIntosh, 1981). However, we like to use the CSR index in situations such as Rachel's, where her denial had led to the abuse being hidden. The initial CSR items reflect partner suspicion and control rather than direct physical abuse, which enables many clients to see a reflection

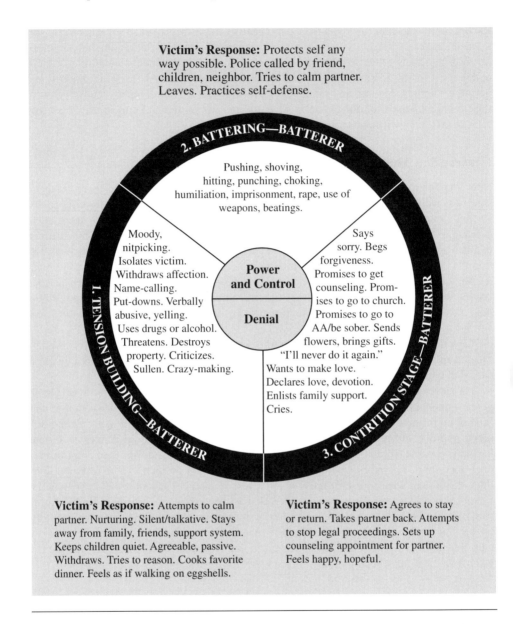

**Victim's Response:** Protects self any way possible. Police called by friend, children, neighbor. Tries to calm partner. Leaves. Practices self-defense.

**2. BATTERING—BATTERER**

Pushing, shoving, hitting, punching, choking, humiliation, imprisonment, rape, use of weapons, beatings.

**1. TENSION BUILDING—BATTERER**

Moody, nitpicking. Isolates victim. Withdraws affection. Name-calling. Put-downs. Verbally abusive, yelling. Uses drugs or alcohol. Threatens. Destroys property. Criticizes. Sullen. Crazy-making.

**Power and Control**

**Denial**

**3. CONTRITION STAGE—BATTERER**

Says sorry. Begs forgiveness. Promises to get counseling. Promises to go to church. Promises to go to AA/be sober. Sends flowers, brings gifts. "I'll never do it again." Wants to make love. Declares love, devotion. Enlists family support. Cries.

**Victim's Response:** Attempts to calm partner. Nurturing. Silent/talkative. Stays away from family, friends, support system. Keeps children quiet. Agreeable, passive. Withdraws. Tries to reason. Cooks favorite dinner. Feels as if walking on eggshells.

**Victim's Response:** Agrees to stay or return. Takes partner back. Attempts to stop legal proceedings. Sets up counseling appointment for partner. Feels happy, hopeful.

**Figure 9.1    Cycle of violence.** *Source: Violence and Control in Intimate Relationships,* **by D. G. Dutton, 1995, New York: Guilford Press. Reproduced with permission.**

of themselves. The items become increasingly coercive and violent, which some clients might reject if they were presented initially. Rachel was visibly shaken by her score on the CSR (81), which indicated a seriously abusive situation, and she agreed to the need for further assessment and a change in the direction of the counseling sessions.

Karen used a structured interview procedure in evaluating for the presence of the Battered Woman Syndrome (BWS) (Douglas, 1987; Walker, 1994) and for the symptoms

**Table 9.1    Revised CSR Abuse Index**

*Questions 1–14*

3 = Frequently        2 = Sometimes        1 = Rarely        0 = Never

_____ 1. Does he continually monitor your time and make you account for every minute (when you run errands, visit friends, commute to work, etc.)?

_____ 2. Does he ever accuse you of having affairs with other men or act suspiciously of you?

_____ 3. Is he ever rude to your friends?

_____ 4. Does he ever discourage you from starting friendships with other women?

_____ 5. Is he ever critical of things such as your cooking, clothes, or appearance?

_____ 6. Does he demand a strict account of how you spend money?

_____ 7. Do his moods change radically, from very calm to very angry, or vice versa?

_____ 8. Is he disturbed by your working?

_____ 9. Does he become angry more easily when he drinks?

_____ 10. Does he pressure you for sex much more often than you like?

_____ 11. Does he become angry if you do not want to go along with his requests for sex?

_____ 12. Do you and your partner quarrel much over financial matters?

_____ 13. Do you quarrel much about having children or raising them?

_____ 14. Does he ever strike you with his hands or feet (slap, punch, etc.)?

*Questions 15–26*

6 = Frequently        5 = Sometimes        4 = Rarely        0 = Never

_____ 15. Does he ever strike you with an object?

_____ 16. Does he ever threaten you with an object or weapon?

_____ 17. Has he ever threatened to kill either you or himself?

_____ 18. Does he ever give you visible injuries (such as welts, bruises, cuts, etc.)?

_____ 19. Have you ever had to treat any injuries from his violence with first aid?

_____ 20. Have you ever had to seek professional aid for any injury at a medical clinic, doctor's office, or hospital emergency room?

_____ 21. Has he ever hurt you sexually or made you have intercourse against your will?

_____ 22. Is he ever violent toward the children?

_____ 23. Is he ever violent toward other people outside your home and family?

_____ 24. Does he ever throw objects or break things when he is angry?

_____ 25. Has he ever been in trouble with the police?

_____ 26. Have you ever called the police, or tried to call them, because you felt you or members of your family were in danger?

_____ Total

Scoring:  To score responses, add up the points for each question. This sum of the points is your Abuse Index Score. To get some idea of how abusive your relationship is, compare your Index score with the following:

120–92    Dangerously abusive
91–35      Seriously abusive
34–13      Moderately abusive
12–0        Not abusive

*Source: The Family Secret,* by A. Stacey & A. Shupe. Copyright 1983 by W. A. Stacey & A. Shupe. Reprinted by permission of Beacon Press.

of physical, psychological, and sexual abuse. Some sample interview questions that clinicians might use to encourage clients to explore the abuse and its effects on her life activities and psychological well-being are displayed in Table 9.2. Douglas defined BWS in terms of the effects of physical abuse that reduce the woman's ability to respond proactively to the violence against her. The BWS includes three categories of response:

1. The effects of repeated trauma (cognitive and affective, such as distorted memory and high arousal, depression, or anxiety).
2. "Learned helplessness" deficits in which the woman simply gives up the possibility of change.
3. Coping responses to violence that appear to be self-destructive, such as avoidance, withdrawal, and self-blame.

Some of these responses are similar to those in clients diagnosed for Posttraumatic Stress Disorder (PTSD), but the BWS extends beyond to a wider range of reactions. We explore these characteristics in the following sections in the context of Rachel's experiences.

Karen then took the opportunity to introduce the *Power and Control Wheel* (presented in Chapter 5) to explore with Rachel how Stan's abusive behaviors were designed to control and coerce her. This diagram, which compliments the factors depicted in Figure 9.1, provides a useful technique for depicting the many faces of coercive control. Finally, Karen readministered the Personal Progress Scale (PPS-R) as a measure of empowerment,

**Table 9.2   Assessing abuse**

**Obtain Patterns and Details of Abuse**
- Invite the woman to tell her own story without pressure.
- Encourage details to her narrative gradually.
- First time the abuse occurred.
- The worst or most frightening incident.
- Frequency of abuse within time spans (week, month, year, etc.).
- Circumstances surrounding abuse (substance abuse, pregnancy, etc.).
- Abuse of children, animals, destruction of property.
- Violence or abusive behavior toward others.

**Obtain Effects of Abuse**
- Physical injury.
- PTSD symptoms, anxiety, depression, panic, dissociation.
- Avoidance of places or people, hypervigilance, fears for safety.
- Changes in relationships with partner and/or children.
- Strategies used to avoid or escape abuse.
- Self-injurious reactions (suicide attempts, substance abuse).
- Other coping strategies (denial, placating, leaving home).
- Perceived changes in self, hopelessness, fears of going crazy.
- Contact with others about abuse (police, family, friends).

both to assess Rachel's further progress and to provide feedback to her on her journey toward health and liberty.

## Precautions in Assessment

Precautions are important in the assessment and record keeping procedures when a client's issues might involve future court proceedings. In Rachel's case, the issue of custody for Sherry could be influenced by our diagnosis of Rachel and the implications of pathology for her future fitness as a parent. The apparent similarities of the Minnesota Multiphasic Personality Inventory (MMPI) profiles of abused women with schizophrenic and borderline patients has been documented (Rosewater, 1988). However, Lynne Rosewater cautioned that clinicians remain sensitive to subtle differences and to the possibilities that abuse histories are not accurately reflected in these profiles. For clients such as Rachel, the interpretation of these data has been that the observed pathology (increased anger, confusion, depression, and paranoia) is the outcome of a history of abuse rather than representing preexisting psychological conditions (Walker, 1994). Some cautions are also in order regarding the use of the BWS for all clients. Edward Gondolph (1998) pointed out that the learned helplessness paradigm does not match the experiences of many women, such as African Americans, who have responded to woman battering with active attempts to cope, such as fighting back, calling the police, or leaving the abuser. In Rachel's case, her placement of family and community loyalty over her individual needs prevented her from using such self-protective strategies.

In view of the high incidence of child abuse in violent relationships, Karen recommended a separate evaluation for Sherry. Although Rachel protested that Stan had never abused Sherry, Karen pointed out how a child's knowledge and observation of family violence may result in traumatic reactions for her (Grych, Jouriles, Swank, McDonald, & Norwood, 2000). Karen assured Rachel that this evaluation was fairly routine in their clinic and that it might help Sherry in coping with her parents' conflict. Karen also showed Rachel a format for children's possible responses to family violence (presented in Figure 9.2) and emphasized again that no action would be taken unless Rachel and Sherry agreed that further help was needed.

## Goals of Assessment

The nine goals of the abuse assessment were to:

1. Evaluate the importance of Rachel's social locations, especially her religious ideology and commitment, to the alternatives that would be acceptable to her.
2. Obtain the history, frequency, and extent of abuse to both Rachel and Sherry.
3. Evaluate the medical status of the client with respect to past physical injury and especially trauma to the head.
4. Uncover Rachel's cognitive reactions to the situation (attributions, self-blame, locus of control, minimization).
5. Evaluate her psychological status (depression, anxiety, anger, and hopelessness).
6. Assess the range and outcomes of her previous coping strategies and efforts to end the abuse (leaving home, contacting others, calling police).

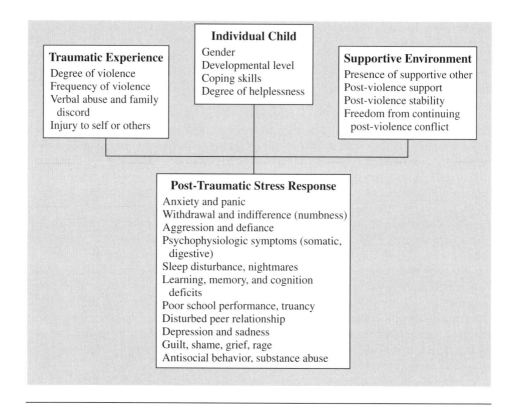

**Figure 9.2    A model of children's response to family violence.**

7. Assess the risk of serious self-injury or suicide, and of homicidal ideation or intention with respect to Stan.
8. Assess the range of her personal strengths (self-esteem, self-efficacy, coping strategies).
9. Evaluate her social support network and economic resources.

## Assessment Outcomes

Because Rachel's personal and social identity was closely tied to her religious commitment, the first goal addressed this concern. Each of the other assessment goals was designed to provide information to Rachel, as well as to Karen, about the potential for serious outcomes for herself and Sherry, to identify and support her strengths, and to assist in further intervention plans. Karen believed that normative feedback on her situation might motivate Rachel to adopt safety precautions and to arrive at difficult decisions. Rachel was certain that Sherry was not being harmed physically but agreed to have her evaluated by another therapist with child-assessment experience.

Rachel was referred for a medical evaluation for evidence of persisting injury. In previous routine medical checkups, Rachel had not disclosed her circumstances of abuse.

The current medical review uncovered numerous body bruises, especially to the abdomen and breasts where they were not apparent to the casual observer. However, the scars on her face were accompanied by bruises and festering cuts under her hairline that required additional medical attention. The structured interview questions revealed evidence of moderate depression, anxiety, low trust of others, and intermittent anger and hopelessness. Further questions uncovered her minimization of the abuse ("He's really a good man under stress"), denial ("I don't think he'd really hurt me seriously; sometimes he can be so sweet and loving"), and evidence of global self-blame ("I guess I'll never be all the things he wanted in a wife"). On the other hand, she did not take responsibility for the abuse ("I know he shouldn't act like that; he's got to realize he's wrong about me"), and she asserted her determination to change the relationship ("I don't want to live like this"). Here we see that assessment can become an effective part of the intervention. The outcome of the assessment procedures moved Rachel to a new stage of counseling, in which she was able to self-identify as a battered woman, to begin to come to terms with that realization, and to agree to work on the abuse as her primary issue.

## Impression

Rachel's story is one that is repeated, in different forms, in many intimate relationships. The early part of her marriage was generally a satisfying experience for Rachel. Her parents were pleased with Stan's similar religious background, his father's prominent position in the Jewish community, and Stan's ambitious academic and career aspirations. During their last year of college, Stan had courted her with intensity and persistence, convincing her to marry before he entered medical school so that they would "belong to each other forever." Rachel felt attractive and loved, reflected in the eyes of the man who had chosen her. When they were with her family, he was charming, courteous, and eager to please. All their relatives and friends believed that this was a good match. When the first abusive incident occurred, she found it difficult to believe that this was the "real Stan" and discounted his behavior as due to external circumstances (academic stress), the facts of his childhood (an only son with a strict and demanding father), and her own failure to meet his needs (self-blame). Rather than being afraid for her safety, her initial reaction was to intensify her commitment to Stan in an effort to "help him be a happier person." Over time, her perception that Stan frequently followed his violent outbursts with remorse and renewed demonstrations of affection (usually sexual) maintained her belief in the viability of the marriage and strengthened her determination to improve their relationship and keep the family together.

To the external observer, this increased commitment by Rachel may appear to be a masochistic reaction, suggesting that she really enjoyed the abuse and needed to experience pain in relationships. However, viewed from her personal experience, all alternatives seemed insurmountable to Rachel: the fear of humiliation, shame, and disgrace to her family if she revealed the abuse; the risks for Stan of losing his medical school standing; and the unacceptability in her family and religious community of separation and divorce. Further, Stan's periodic affection was sufficient to maintain her belief that he would change, and she reasoned that Sherry needed a father. Thus, the forces that kept her in the marriage were supported by her traditional religious and relationship beliefs and not by the enjoyment of pain. The use of masochism to explain women's apparent attachment to an abusive relationship is another example of a victim-blaming attribution and serves to excuse and condone the behavior of the abuser, rather than to confront him with his responsibility for the violence. (See Chapter 5 on diagnosis for further discussion of woman-blaming categories.)

As the abuse escalated, Rachel continued to believe that she was somehow at fault (reinforced by Stan's criticism), and she reciprocally escalated her efforts to please him and to avoid conflict. These efforts took the form of increased silence and withdrawal at home, eliminating calls to family and friends in the evenings (further isolating her from sources of potential support), agreeing to have him take her to work and pick her up at night so that she lost access to her own car, and her obsessive dieting to lose weight.

Rachel's investment in keeping the relationship viable, being a good partner for Stan, and providing a stable home for Sherry, and her embarrassment, guilt, and shame about the abusive events all kept her from sharing her unhappy situation with family, physician, and friends. Her firm Jewish identity encouraged a commitment to her religious and ethnic community that prevented her from exposing them to external criticism and increased stereotyping. As a religious minority group in a dominant Christian community, Rachel was well aware of their vulnerability to further discrimination and public exclusion. She once revealed a violent incident to her rabbi, when she thought she was pregnant again and Stan threw her down and kicked her in the stomach ("Whose baby is that?"). The rabbi assured her that Stan was a "fine young man from a good family." He admonished her to try to be a better wife, to smooth it over, and preserve *shalom bayis,* or peace in the family. He advised her not to talk about this to anyone, because airing such matters publicly would represent a *"chilul Hashem,* a disgrace to the sanctity of Judaism" (Twerski, 1996, p. 3). She was advised to tolerate his "irritability" until he graduated: "He'll feel better when he's the wage earner and you can stay home with Sherry" (see Alsdurf, 1985, for research on pastoral advice in wife battering; also Twerski, 1996 and Sternoff, 2000, for the incidence and dynamics of hidden wife abuse in Jewish families). Supported by her own desires for a happy marriage, Rachel wanted to believe her rabbi and never again revealed her abuse or sought help from others until she entered counseling.

The outcomes for Rachel were both physical and psychological entrapment (see Figure 9.3). The more she invested in maintaining the relationship, the greater was her loss of freedom of movement and sense of competence and independence. As she responded to verbal intimidation and physical violence with increased compliance, isolation, and withdrawal, her self-confidence was eroded. She increasingly doubted her perceptions of reality and her ability to make clear decisions. The tactics that she adopted for personal survival became the very ones that consolidated her entrapment.

## FACTS ABOUT THE ABUSE OF WOMEN

### Incidence

> On September 7, 2001, a man in Amherst, New Hampshire, crashed a small plane into the home of his wife and daughter after she had filed for a protective order and divorce. Luckily, they were not home. (Faragher, 2001)

Although most of us are taught to fear danger and assault from strangers in the streets, documented violence to a woman is most likely to be inflicted by someone she knows and frequently loves (Walker, 1994). As evidenced by the air crash incident, when battered women attempt to separate or leave home, they are more than twice as likely to be

# CONFRONTING ABUSE

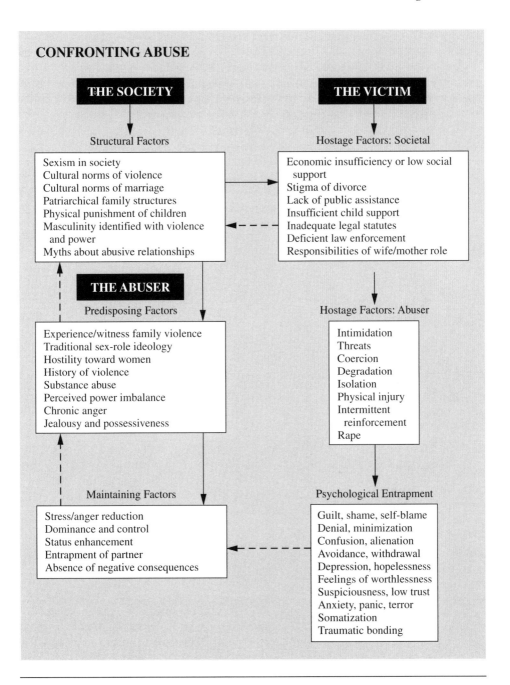

Figure 9.3    A model of violence toward women.

killed than if they remain with the abuser (Walker, 2001; M. Wilson & Daly, 1993). In the United States, more women are injured or killed from partner abuse than from vehicle crashes, mugging, and rapes combined (Ferris, 1994; Harway & Hansen, 1994). Similar violence against women has been reported worldwide. In post-Soviet Russia, for example, 14,000 women are reported killed each year by male partners, which substantially exceeds the murder rate in all other countries (Horne, 1999).

Estimates of abuse and violence in close heterosexual relationships depend on the populations surveyed and the kinds of questions that are asked. A telephone survey of nearly 2,000 women in Kentucky was conducted by the Harris Poll for the Kentucky Commission on Women (Shulman, 1979). Of the respondents, 23% had been physically abused by a husband or partner, and more than two-thirds of those who had been separated or divorced the previous year experienced physical violence in that relationship.

## Marital Abuse

In a large national survey, an estimated 1.8 million wives in the United States were beaten by their husbands each year (Strauss, Gelles, & Steinmetz, 1980). Using the Conflict Tactics Scale (CTS), the survey researchers conducted face-to-face interviews with more than 2,000 randomly selected families. Their data indicated that one in six wives had been struck by her husband during the course of their marriage, and the "average battered wife is attacked three times each year" (Gelles & Strauss, 1988, p. 104). A subsequent telephone survey by these researchers with more than 6,000 respondents found similar rates of violence toward wives.

In evaluating these reported incidence rates, we note at least five problems with the use of the CTS:

1. The CTS documents only single instances of physical violence and, therefore, may underestimate the frequency of violence to wives and overestimate the frequency of violence by wives toward their partners (Dobash & Dobash, 1992). Their finding of relatively "equal" violence by wives ignores the evidence that biting is the most frequent attack used by women and is in the service of their own defense (Yllo, 1988).

2. Because the CTS does not include degree of injury to the victim, it omits documentation of severe injury such as broken bones, teeth knocked out, and need for extensive surgery and restoration. Women are more likely than men to be severely injured by physical conflict.

3. The CTS is limited by its omission of the multiple forms of violence reported by battered women: hair-pulling, smothering, burning, attempts to drown, throwing the woman across the room or down the stairs, stomping or jumping on her, twisting her arms and legs, forcing her to crawl on the floor, throwing her out of a moving car, and sexual assault or genital mutilation (Walker, 1994).

4. The CTS fails to assess many aspects of coercion and intimidation, such as bondage, locking the woman in the car or closet, surveillance of her activities when away from home, destruction of her property, and threats of violence or death to her, the children, pets, or other loved ones.

5. Limiting these rates of violence to currently married women underestimates the total extent of woman abuse. Based on an accumulation of data over the years,

Mary Koss and her associates (1994a) estimated that one in every three women in the United States is physically assaulted by an intimate partner during her lifetime. Further, the incidence of sexual abuse in marriage has been seriously underreported. In samples of battered women, the incidence of sexual abuse is high, ranging from 28% (Gondolph, 1998) to 58% (Walker, 1994). In a survey of 800 community women, Russell (1982) found that 12% of the women reported marital rape. Married women are twice as likely to be raped by a spouse than by a stranger or acquaintance. Similar to reports of physical violence, the variation in reported sexual abuse across samples is probably due in part to differences in how the women defined sexual abuse and how the researchers presented the questions to respondents.

## Nonmarital Abuse

Premarital or dating abuse has been reported mainly for college populations, probably because they are easily available to researchers. Across a range of studies, interpersonal violence occurs in 20% to 60% of dating couples, depending on whether only physical abuse is considered, or verbal and sexual abuse are included (Cate, Henton, Koval, Christopher, & Lloyd, 1982; Witt & Worell, 1986, 1988). Thus, woman abuse in nonmarital relationships appears to be even higher than in marital arrangements (Koss et al., 1994a).

We have limited information about the extent of abuse and violence toward women from diverse groups. Extensive reviews of woman battering across various social and cultural groups (e.g., Gondolph, 1998; Koss et al., 1994b) suggest that there are many factors that enter into the equation when comparing across population samples. Such factors may include how the abuse is defined by victims and/or researchers, and the degree of poverty, educational levels, employment status, living arrangements, immigration or acculturation status, cultural norms of family allegiance that preclude exposure such as in Rachel's story, reluctance to seek help or report the abuse, access to services, and fear of police intervention. Further, differing patterns of abuse may occur in each cultural or ethnic group. The limited evidence about battering in lesbian relationships suggests that it may be as frequent as heterosexual abuse, involving similar patterns of interpersonal dominance and control (Harway & Hansen, 1994). When working with clients who are culturally dissimilar to themselves, clinicians are cautioned to avoid stereotypes about violence within and across diverse groups by remaining close to the data provided by the victim herself.

## The Last Resort

Survey research does not tell us about the most violent form of woman abuse—murder. More than 1,500 women in the United States are murdered every year by a current or former partner (American Association of University Women, 2001). In a historic study, Jones (1980) reported that four out of five women who are killed by men are murdered at home, and three-fourths of all murdered women are killed by husbands or lovers. Although most violent conflicts occur in the home, many women are stalked and killed once they leave the abusive situation (Walker, 1994). Danger exists also to the men in these relationships as the woman turns to a last desperate move for freedom from terror: About 10% of all homicides in the United States are perpetrated by women, many of whose victims were former husbands or lovers (Thyfault, Browne, & Walker, 1987). The therapist who sees a battered woman must consider that her client's life is always in danger, whether she is at home with the abuser or has followed through with her decision to leave. The documented danger to a battered woman's life is essential to remember when helping the woman to consider the stay-or-leave decision.

The relatively high incidence of abuse and violence in close interpersonal relationships reinforces our suggestion that therapists routinely screen for such abuse with all female clients. Although we have no indication that Rachel would have admitted to the violence at an earlier stage of counseling before sufficient trust had been established, the screening questions can frequently set the stage for client self-disclosure. Once the disclosure of violence occurs, further screening for life-threatening danger is essential.

## DEFINING ABUSE AND VIOLENCE

We are using the concept of *abuse* in a broad sense to include any threats or acts of coercion (controlling another's behavior), aggression (intent to cause harm to another), or violence (perpetration of damage or injury to another or to their belongings and property) that are unwanted by the victim. We thus include three factors, *coercive control, intention to harm,* and *injury outcome,* as well as physical, emotional, and sexual categories of abuse.

Definitions of abuse exist in all state legislative regulations in the United States. Only in the 1980s did the federal government enact legislation denoting violence against women as a crime rather than as a "domestic disturbance." However, there is still inconsistency in defining threats, stalking, and abuse to wives and partners as either misdemeanors (mild infractions of the law) or felonies (more serious criminal behavior). There is also considerable controversy over how to define abuse for either children or adults, especially with respect to (a) intentionality to harm and (b) demonstrated injury. We believe that both intent and injury are important to consider, since neither one may cover all instances of interpersonal abuse. In addition, we include the concept of *control,* since many abusive behaviors include holding the other person against her will, locking her in or out of spaces, stalking and following her wherever she goes, removing her car keys so that she cannot drive, tearing out the telephone, and otherwise restricting her freedom of movement and access to communication with others. These control behaviors inflict harm on the victim by relegating her to the status of a prisoner or hostage in her own life space.

Gelles and Strauss (1988) contend that the concept of *abuse* is political rather than scientific, reflecting the values and norms of a particular society at a particular time. We concur with this view, noting that even at the time of revising this book, laws regarding violence toward women are uneven across legislatures and communities. Thus, behavior regarded as criminally violent in some communities, such as wife rape, is both legal and sanctioned in other regions. Likewise, the prosecution of violence toward women is frequently colored by the legal relationship between the woman and her abuser (Erez, 1986). Violence perpetrated by a stranger is likely to be taken more seriously by police, for example, than domestic violence, which is frequently believed to be in the private domain of the home. Incidents of violence toward women or wives is not routinely reported in most communities, so that the true epidemiology of violence toward women is currently unknown and probably underestimated (American Psychological Association, 1996). Of particular concern in all cases of apparent abuse are local or cultural norms that condone practices with and toward women that isolate, demean, or injure them. Service providers need to be especially sensitive to such norms and how to intervene ethically and effectively.

## ISSUES IN THE ABUSE OF WOMEN

Few issues in counseling women generate as much concern, consternation, and coordination of resources as woman battering. First, intervention with partners of violent men always involves risk. There is an overriding issue of danger—not only to the woman, but often to her partner, and potentially to the therapist or other help-givers as well. Second, because a large proportion of abused women remain with or return to their battering partners (Harway & Hansen, 1994), help-givers often feel frustrated and ineffective. A common reaction here is to blame the woman for undermining her own counseling by "allowing" herself to continue the abusive relationship. Third, the decision to leave an abusive relationship frequently requires a concerted organization of economic, social, and physical resources that many clinicians believe are beyond their scope and experience. These three factors combine to create a unique challenge to the professional who works with abused and battered women.

### A Model of Abuse toward Women

We have conceptualized the abusive process as a three-part model, involving the society at large, the violence-prone abuser, and the female victim of abuse. Figure 9.3 displays the hypothesized relationship among the three variables, in which the straight lines represent a direct influence of one factor on another. The dotted lines signify a feedback loop in which the consequences of the societal and abuser factors provide reinforcement and repetition of the violence and oppression. The hypothesized outcomes of the model, if not attenuated at some juncture, provide for a continuation of violence to women. In the following sections, we offer a brief description of each factor.

### Societal Support of Male Violence

The societal factors include cultural norms of violence, norms of inequality between women and men, and general institutionalized sexism that promote the dominance and entitlement of men and devalue and subordinate women (American Psychological Association, 1996; Jacobson & Gottman, 1998; Koss et al., 1994a). Rather than asking why Stan batters Rachel, we ask first why men in general use violence against women (Principle II). How does this violence serve in most cultures to maintain traditional family and societal structures by keeping women in relatively powerless and subordinate position (Principles I and II)? As stated by Mary Koss and her associates, "To understand violence against women, one must understand why men believe they are entitled to control women and why they feel they may use intimidation, coercion, threats, and force to do so" (p. 4). Jacobson and Gottman (1998) further describe battering as "physical aggression with a purpose: that purpose is to control, intimidate, and subjugate one's intimate partner" (p. 35).

We examine the cultural norms of heterosexual partnerships and marriage, which generally provide for male-advantaged arrangements and the sanctity of the home. We take the position that abuse is a matter of public concern, not private privilege. The control of women and children through physical punishment is widely accepted in most cultures, and the identification of masculinity with the use of force further supports this view of the right to control. In a study with 300 college students, Finn (1986) reported a correlation of +.65 between traditional gender-role beliefs and endorsement of violence toward wives. In a study of 1,000 battered women, Bowker, Arbitell, and McFerron (1988) found that in 70% of the families with children present, men who beat their wives also physically abused their children.

These sociocultural variables work together to: (a) increase the potential for violent, dominant, and controlling behavior by males who grow up in a violence-prone and patriarchical culture; and (b) keep women intimidated, powerless, economically insufficient, and lacking in community and legal recourse and police protection in the face of violence.

## A View of the Abuser

The abuser in Figure 9.3 is conceptualized by: (a) the range of characteristics that have been reported in the literature on woman-battering, not all of which apply to a particular individual (e.g., see Ganley, 1987; Gondolph, 1988; Jacobson & Gottman, 1998; O'Neil & Harway, 1999; Sonkin, Martin, & Walker, 1885); and (b) the variables that appear to maintain his abusive behavior. Men with a history of family and personal violence, traditional ideology about the position of women and the rights of men to dominate through the use of physical force, and a sensitization to minimal cues of male-female power imbalance may be prone to resort to violence in the effort to control their women.

Gondolph (1988), reporting on a cluster analysis of the characteristics of 500 male batterers, divided these men into four groups based on their history of arrests and patterns of violence in and outside the relationship. These types include the sociopath, the antisocial batterer, the chronic batterer, and the sporadic batterer. Table 9.3 displays these four types and their frequencies of battering behaviors. The sociopathic group represents only 5% of the sample. The sporadic batterer, however, is the only type that is likely to be remorseful and to benefit from counseling. Gondolph maintained that "the pursuit of a unitary batterer profile is in vain" (p. 74).

More recently, Jacobson and Gottman (1998) presented a detailed study of married couples, divided into groups of severe male batterers, mildly abusive males, dissatisfied marriages, and the happily married. On the basis of interviews, videotapes, and assessment of physiological responses, they categorized the severe batterers into two groups that they named the *Cobras* and the *Pit Bulls*. They described the Cobras as more severely violent both in and outside the home. These men appeared similar to Gondolph's sociopath and antisocial groups. Rather than being emotionally distraught when angry, they were internally calm and focused. In contrast, the men in the Pit Bull group were more likely to be insecure and emotionally dependent on the spouse. They feared betrayal and abandonment and were more likely to be emotionally aroused when angered. Since Stan was not directly our client, we have insufficient information with which to understand his particular pattern of violence. However, he fits many aspects of the Pit Bull profile, using intimidation, force, and coercion to maintain his control and power over Rachel.

What maintains the violence once it is initiated? Walker (1979) proposed a *cycle of violence theory,* in which each successive round of violence is followed by (a) remorse and apologies by the batterer, and (b) a "honeymoon" period in which the wife believes

**Table 9.3   Frequency of battering by type of male woman abusers**

| Cluster of Sample | Cluster | | | | |
|---|---|---|---|---|---|
| | I 5% | II 32% | III 30% | IV 33% | Total 100% |
| Length of relationship (more than 5 years)** | 36 | 38 | 45 | 28 | 37 |
| Weekly abuse* | 68 | 50 | 49 | 35 | 46 |
| Kicked* | 46 | 96 | 56 | 32 | 61 |
| Weapon used* | 36 | 80 | 26 | 17 | 43 |
| Sexual abuse* | 59 | 36 | 34 | 20 | 31 |
| Child abuse* | 46 | 26 | 24 | 17 | 23 |
| Threaten or blame (in response to abuse)* | 91 | 62 | 76 | 9 | 50 |
| Broken bones* | 46 | 23 | 7 | 5 | 13 |
| Drug abuse* | 60 | 37 | 28 | 22 | 30 |
| Nonfamily violence* | 68 | 54 | 43 | 25 | 42 |
| Arrest for nonfamily violence* | 64 | 23 | 15 | 13 | 19 |

$n = 550$, *$p < .001$; **$p < .01$
Batterer Types: I = Sociopathic, II = Antisocial, III = Chronic, IV = Sporadic.
*Source: Battered Women as Survivors: An Alternative to Treating Learned Helplessness*, by E. W. Gondolph and E. R. Fisher. Copyright 1988 by Lexington Books. Reprinted with permission.

that he loves her and that things will improve (see Figure 9.1). This intermittent reinforcement functions to maintain her hopes and to keep her attached in the relationship. Her compliance with his demands also reinforces the batterer in believing that he can be successful in deploying violence in the future as a means of control. Gondolph (1988) questioned the cycle theory, suggesting that only a small proportion of male batterers, the sporadic group, express remorse for their actions, and that those who do may be over-represented in research because they are more receptive to counseling.

*Social exchange theory* uses a cost-benefit analysis, predicting that a balance of reward over punishment encourages the behavior to continue. The "normal" or typical survival strategies of battered women include increased compliance and submission to abuser demands, and hypervigilance to avoid displeasing him. Once the abuser uses violence successfully to establish dominance and control with no negative contingencies, the reinforcement of his power and the absence of negative consequences ensure that further violence follows.

In support of a social exchange view, Edna Erez (1986) reviewed all domestic incident reports filed with a county prosecutor's office for one year, a total of 3,021 reports. Across all female-male intimate relationships, the frequency of arrest of the assaultive party did not exceed 13%. Police intervention with domestic violence in all communities has been notoriously deficient, and police responses to women who are personally violated frequently increases the woman's distress (Wyatt, Notgrass, & Newcomb, 1990). In contrast, a pilot project in Minnesota (L. Sherman & Berk, 1984) found that immediate arrest of the batterer, with a minimum of 24 hours' incarceration, reduced subsequent violence in these men by 50%. However, mandatory arrest in the United States is neither universal nor is it uniformly enforced where it exists. As long as the rewards of power and control outweigh the costs of perpetrating abuse, violence against women will not abate.

## The Victim's Dilemma

The victim in Figure 9.3 is viewed in the context of the "hostage syndrome" or traumatic bonding, which leads to a psychological state we call *entrapment*. The hostage syndrome, originally developed to explain the paradoxical attachment of hostages to their captors, has been applied to the situation experienced by battered women (Dutton & Painter, 1981; Graham, Rawlings, & Rimini, 1988; Resick, 1983). The "hostage syndrome" is created by both society and the individual abuser.

First, as a hostage of society, the battered woman is unable to leave her abuser when external circumstances deny her access to resources that would enable her to escape the violence and to live independently. These external variables include norms of marriage and motherhood, low social support from community and family, lack of economic equity that enables her to subsist independently, the unavailability of abuse shelters in many communities, and inadequate legal and police protection against the batterer.

In Rachel's case, she received little support from the one person to whom she revealed the abuse, her rabbi. The rabbi's advice for her to stay with Stan was traditional in its alliance with the sanctity of marriage and the wife/mother role (Twerski, 1996). Rachel felt guilty for wanting to deny her daughter's need for a father and for not being patient with Stan under his medical school pressures. She rationalized his violence as a "natural" reaction to stress, thus buying into cultural norms of justification for male violence. Further, she had internalized the gender-role belief that women are primarily responsible for the success of marital relationships: "I will be a failure as a woman if this relationship does not succeed" (Worell, 1988a).

Second, as a hostage to the abuser, the battered woman is alternately intimidated, terrorized, isolated, violated, and injured. Intermittently, her abuser may encourage her to stay by providing some affection, attention, and promises to reform. According to the hostage syndrome theory, the victim responds to this life-threatening relationship by reactions that (a) ensure her safety and survival, and (b) increase her commitment to her abuser (traumatic bonding). As hostage to the abuser, she feels unable to leave him when she fears for her life and that of her children, and she believes as well that she loves him (Graham et al., 1988). She may be grateful to her abuser for not harming her more than he did ("At least I'm still alive"). In denying the real danger to herself and her children, she can still believe that she has some control over his violence in a situation in which she really has no control at all.

Rachel was clearly intimidated and terrorized by Stan's unpredictable outbursts of anger, humiliating remarks, and periodic violence. He was able to control her movements, her conversations, and access to her car and friends. She was also clearly attached to Stan and wanted to continue the marriage. She believed that under all the abuse, he loved her and would return to his former self when medical school was behind them.

The outcome for the victim of this dual hostage situation is the psychological state we call *entrapment*. (For a fuller discussion of entrapment theory, see Brockner & Rubin, 1985; Strube, 1989.) In psychological entrapment, the individual feels committed to a course of action and escalates attempts to improve the situation as goal attainment fails. In abusive marriages, traditional gender-role messages encourage the woman to believe that it is her responsibility to make the relationship run smoothly; if the relationship is failing, she may then conclude that she is not trying hard enough. The more time and effort the woman invests, the harder it is to give up without success and the less likely that a battered woman will leave the relationship. Perceived personal responsibility and the belief that alternatives are risky or unavailable serve to strengthen her commitment and increase her inability to leave. In Rachel's case, her religious commitment provided a further barrier to any serious consideration of leaving Stan and further bound her to the relationship.

The entrapped victim of repeated abuse experiences a variety of internal negative states, including shame, guilt, self-blame, and worthlessness. She may use withdrawal and avoidance strategies to reduce the abusive incidents, but she experiences periodic attacks of anxiety and panic when violence threatens to erupt. We use the term *entrapment* to point out that the psychological outcomes of repeated abuse and the lack of resources for escape convince her that she is unable to leave. In addition, the strategies she uses in her desperate attempt at survival and safety are the same ones that reinforce the batterer and further reduce her personal power. No matter what she does to survive in the relationship, the violence eventually returns. The model of hostage and entrapment are clearly appropriate to our understanding of Rachel's dilemma.

## INTERVENTION STRATEGIES

As we suggested earlier, treatment with violently abused women can be problematic for many help-givers. Those who work with abused women require specific training that is designed to develop skills in competent, effective, and ethical practice with battered clients.

### Counseling Competencies

The competent counselor of women in battering relationships requires: (a) knowledge about abuse in close relationships; (b) attitudes toward woman abuse that contribute to, rather than deter from, the process of therapy; (c) skills in assisting the process of decision making and in coordinating personal and community resources; and (d) personal resources that include therapist awareness of her own abuse history and sufficient access to personal safety, consultation, and support (Walker, 1979, 1994).

#### Knowledge

In many locales in the United States, licensure of psychologists and other mental health professionals requires mandatory training in "domestic abuse." In the Commonwealth of Kentucky, this training is accompanied by extensive materials for increasing clinician knowledge about family violence as well as providing a set of useful resources for referral and client education. As a psychologist-in-training, you may be able to attend such sessions or to avail yourself of other training opportunities in your area.

We developed the model in Figure 9.3 to summarize information that is minimally important in understanding the issues in the abuse of women. Each topic in the model encompasses a background of theory, research, and clinical data with which the therapist should become familiar. In particular, you should know the facts that challenge the validity of the myths listed in the self-assessment section and be able to present these facts to your clients. In accordance with Principle II, you should be able to untangle the political from the personal in the individual lives of each client, thus helping clients see their situation as a relatively normal extension of societal structure and attitudes, as well as involving their responsibility for change. In accordance with Principle I, you should also be aware of your client's important identities, particularly those that engage strong ethnic, cultural, or religious beliefs. It is important to explore with clients any conflicts they may have between their important identities and actions they may need to take for their safety and well-being.

*Attitudes*

Dealing with violence and anger is emotionally draining and frequently frightening. As a competent counselor, you should be able to:

1. Listen empathically to extended stories of horror, bloodshed, and violence, and allow the client to recount full details without premature foreclosure. Detailed recapitulation of traumatic events is crucial to client recovery.
2. Confront and deal with your own fears of violence and be willing to share and self-disclose where appropriate, especially for the counselor who was herself violently abused (Principle III).
3. Allow the client to work through her issues without pushing her to arrive at decisions you feel she should make (Principles I and III).
4. View the woman's "pathology" as the probable outcome of her abuse and not the cause of it (Principles II and IV).
5. Accept and encourage the client's expression of anger and rage (Principles II and IV).
6. View the client's reactions as normal survival strategies that anyone might use to cope with terrorizing and life-threatening events (Principles II and IV).
7. Advocate actively for the client and avoid blaming her for "provoking" the abuse. Share with her your conviction that violence is always inflicted, not provoked (Principles II and IV).
8. Avoid reacting with annoyance and frustration if the client decides to remain or return to the abusive relationship (Principles I, III, and IV).
9. Respect and affirm the client's power to arrive at decisions that are appropriate for her life at this time (Principles I, III, and IV).
10. Support and validate her capacity for change (Principles III and IV).

*Skills and Personal Resources*

In addition to the broad range of skills required for all feminist counseling, working with battered women also challenges you to:

1. Be knowledgeable about federal, state, and community laws regarding woman abuse and the procedures for obtaining police protection.
2. Maintain contact with legal service resources and be willing to assist your client in following through with legal procedures to protect her safety.
3. Maintain contacts with other community professionals who deal with battered women, especially women's shelter personnel.

4. Be competent in collaborating with a variety of other professionals and laypersons in planning for your clients' future well-being.

5. Develop a network of community resources for child care, financial and living assistance, and whatever else is required to assist your client to live apart from her abuser should she choose to do so.

6. Maintain resources for recommending abuser treatment groups, abuse survivor groups, or couples counseling if the client wishes to explore these options. Be aware that treatment of the abuser requires specialization and is most effectively accomplished in groups. Further, couples therapy is not indicated until the abuser has taken full responsibility for his violence and has worked sufficiently on his issues.

7. Develop and maintain a personal support group with whom you can discuss and validate your intervention strategies and concerns with abused clients.

8. Protect yourself from secondary trauma by diversifying your client load so that abused women are interspersed with clients presenting other issues.

9. Establish careful assessment data and record keeping that anticipate the possibility of legal actions and child custody litigation.

10. Maintain personal well-being with nourishing leisure activities and relationships.

These four areas of knowledge, attitudes, skills, and personal resources related to working with abused women form the basis of your intervention plans. In the remainder of our discussion, we briefly summarize how Karen helped Rachel through the process of confronting her abuse and coming to some decisions about the future directions of her life.

## A Model of Intervention for Violent Abuse

Once the violence in the marriage became the focal point in Rachel's counseling, new goals were considered. In the negotiation and implementation of new goals, Karen followed a five-phase plan for intervention:

1. Crisis intervention that included assessment of potential danger and lethality to all family members, and planning for Rachel and Sherry's safety.

2. Further exploration of Rachel's experience of the marital abuse history and how she had dealt with each event within the context of her religious and gender-role beliefs.

3. Reempowering her through reframing her responses as strengths and effective coping strategies.

4. Consideration of alternatives and constructive decision making.

5. Planning for action.

In practice, these phases may overlap or merge, as the client moves at a pace that is comfortable and nonthreatening to her. The four principles of EFT were used liberally throughout the sessions. You are now sufficiently skilled to detect the use of each principle and to be able to support the context in which it appears. For purposes of simplicity, we have condensed the interventions into three phases: crises intervention, exploration and decision making, and resolution and restructuring.

*Crisis Intervention*

When violence to the client is present, crisis intervention procedures become paramount. In crisis intervention with Rachel, Karen had three major goals: (a) increasing her safety, (b) documenting the violence, and (c) providing information and support.

**Increasing Safety**    Karen's first concern for Rachel was to ensure her safety as well as that of her daughter, Sherry. Although Rachel had previously denied injury to Sherry, the data on the high frequency of child abuse by battering men was presented to her as a cautionary measure. In assessing the risks, Karen pointed out to Rachel that Stan had seriously injured her in the past, had access to guns and knives, and sometimes appeared to be "out of control" of his anger. We do not subscribe to the myth that battering men are "unable to control" their violence, since they exhibit violent behavior only under certain circumstances and toward their wives and children rather than toward more powerful others. Further, the violence at home usually escalates over time. Stan, for example, was a model medical student and maintained a warm and comfortable relationship with his family. However, it was important to affirm for Rachel that nothing she could do would necessarily be effective in controlling Stan's future violence toward her.

Karen also asked Rachel for a written suicide/homicide contract, in which she agreed not to inflict lethal harm on either herself or Stan during the course of our sessions with her. Although our assessment for suicide risk was minimal, Rachel expressed intense rage at this point and indicated her wish to see Stan "burn in H____." Karen interpreted this statement as a wish rather than a threat, but Karen knew that predictions of dangerousness are unreliable. In response to Rachel's insistence that she could control Stan's

---

**Table 9.4    Planning for safety**

- Identify Situations
  Notice cues, occasions, locations where abuse has occurred.
  Notice drug or alcohol signals, behavioral cues (voice, posture).

- Identify Possible Escape Routes
  Plan for quick exits, know best ways out of the house, rehearse.
  Keep money, car keys, and house keys available for emergency exit.
  Prepare to remove children quickly and quietly.

- Seek Protection
  Inform children of how to make emergency calls (911).
  Inform neighbors of possible emergency calls.
  Develop plan of where to stay (family, friends, shelter).
  Plan what to tell police.

- Seek Support
  Know women's shelter hotline number in advance.
  Know how to obtain an emergency protection order.
  Know location of closest hospital and how to get there.
  Identify persons who can accompany you if necessary.

outbursts, Karen kept repeating, "I'm afraid for your safety. If Sherry were my daughter, I would be afraid for her, too." Karen also validated Rachel's anger toward Stan, saying, "I feel very angry that he did that to you."

Rachel was helped to develop a plan of escape should the violence reoccur (see Table 9.4). She found a place to hide a set of car keys, memorized the number of the local women's shelter hotline, and agreed to explore the possibilities of calling her mother or younger sister. Rachel was encouraged to consider how to deal with the next violent episode, including calling the police ("Assault is a crime," said Karen), visiting the hospital to document injury, and swearing out a warrant for Stan's arrest. Rachel was unwilling at this point either to inform her mother, leave the home, or ask Stan to leave.

**Documenting the Violence**   The process of uncovering the abuse and detailing the violence had begun prior to crisis intervention. Now, Karen encouraged Rachel to tell her entire story in detail, having her describe each incident of violence and everything she could recall about it. Her ability to recall and recount the incidents of abuse, sexual coercion, and violence increased with each session, and she had difficulty stopping at the end of the hour. Karen took copious notes of the violence and, with Rachel's permission, included them in her clinic records. The documentation of violence provided information to the therapist but also served as a therapeutic step in helping Rachel to break through her denial and to confront the realities of her situation.

The process of documenting the violence is a painful one for both client and counselor. Karen was mindful of asking clarifying questions, but also of focusing on Rachel's feelings of anger, shame, guilt, terror, and reactions of denial and minimization. She noted when Rachel made excuses for Stan and carefully labeled him as the batterer and Rachel as a battered women. Table 9.2 details the questions and areas that may be covered in this phase of the counseling. Throughout this process, Karen and Rachel considered how the position of women within families and the broader cultural milieu provide or deny women their freedom and safety. The process of documentation, then, leads naturally into an educative and supportive phase.

**Information and Support**   Here, Karen used all four EFT principles. She gave Rachel a fact sheet that provided facts to challenge the myths of wife battering and offered two short books for Rachel when she felt ready to read them. (See the Further Readings section.) Rachel was encouraged to keep these materials at work until the battering issues were brought out openly with Stan. Rachel was amazed to discover how the incidence and details of wife abuse matched her own situation. This information led into some discussions of Rachel's anxiety, panic attacks, and depressive episodes; and together they developed some strategies to help her relax. (See Chapter 6 for strategies with anxiety and depression.) In particular, Karen modeled some cognitive stress inoculation techniques that Rachel could use to affirm her determination to take care of herself and Sherry and to reduce her self-blame ("This wasn't my fault," "I can take care of myself," "I'm not to blame for his anger," etc.).

Karen invoked Principles III and IV by affirming Rachel's caring and supportive approach to Sherry and Stan, pointing to her attempts to maintain the family as a woman-valued approach. She also supported Rachel's ambivalence about leaving the relationship, but reminded Rachel that she was strong and competent (Hadn't she coped effectively until now?) and that she had many career and interpersonal skills that would enable her to live independently should she choose to do so.

Karen then self-disclosed that she was a formerly abused wife. Rachel was surprised and wanted to hear more details. Karen gave a brief account of her experiences, how difficult it was for her to either remain or leave a long-term marriage, and how she had filed twice for divorce before she found the strength and determination to go through with it. She also modeled the successful outcome of her independent living but cautioned Rachel that each person must arrive at her own individual solution that fits her situation and her values. This discussion led naturally into the next phase—exploration and decision making.

## Exploration and Decision Making

The self-disclosure of personal history of violence in Karen's marriage served as a catalyst for Rachel. However, for therapists without such a personal history, self-involving responses of personal feelings about the violence can be quite effective ("I am feeling very afraid for your safety," etc.). For the first time, Rachel seriously considered the option of separation. Karen pointed out that separation, even if temporary, is a desirable interim step if further violence is anticipated (and it was in this case). Temporary separation while the woman (and possibly the man) explores the situation and options can send a clear message to the batterer that his violent behavior will not be tolerated. Separation may either increase or jeopardize the woman's safety, however. Although it provides her with psychological space in which to arrive at rational decisions, the batterer may follow and continue to harass and threaten her. Other options for safety include changing jobs or going to a women's shelter where she cannot be located by the abuser. A separation was explored but rejected by Rachel, who feared that it was too final and that she would lose Stan. She was still interested in helping him and wanted him to seek counseling.

Feminist therapists are generally opposed to couples counseling with battering men, unless the woman has had sufficient time and assistance to arrive at firm decisions for herself. Certain conditions for the abuser's behavior should be in place before he is included in couples counseling. We are particularly concerned about the use of traditional family systems approaches that place equal responsibility on both partners for the abuse, or that locate the causes of the abuse solely in the transactions between the partners. Couples therapy that is aimed at reestablishing homeostasis and that ignores the dynamics of unequal power in the relationship, is detrimental to the woman (Bograd, 1986; Jacobson & Gottman, 1998). Advocates of feminist family therapy have revised these traditional formats, enabling them to employ a systems approach that remains sensitive to gender imbalances (Goldner, 1985; Goodrich, Rampage, Elman, & Halstead, 1988).

Karen judged that couples therapy would not be advisable for Rachel and Stan at this time for the following reasons:

1. The power imbalance between them could make it difficult for Rachel to assert her ideas and true feelings.
2. Rachel's disclosure in couples sessions of violence could trigger more violence and retaliation by Stan.
3. Terrorizing at home by Stan could then reduce Rachel's disclosure in session.
4. Couples counseling sends a message to both that the goal for Rachel is to remain in and repair the marriage before she has had the opportunity to complete a careful decision-making process.

5. Stan's anticipated criticisms of her behavior may encourage her further attempts to placate him.
6. Couples counseling would require a new therapist, possibly cotherapists, and would remove an important source of personal support for Rachel unless she also continued with individual counseling.
7. Stan first needs to acknowledge and take responsibility for his violence and possibly participate actively in an abuser's group.

Karen advised Rachel of her approach, suggesting that once Rachel had come to a fuller understanding of her situation and felt strong enough (and safe enough) to confront Stan openly, couples counseling might be an option. However, Karen emphasized that she did not recommend couples counseling unless Stan first signed and adhered to a no-violence contract.

In the interim, Karen suggested that Rachel join a spouse abuser survivor group, in which six to eight women survivors shared experiences and provided mutual support. There, she would meet other women like herself, some of whom had remained with their abusers and some who had left. In this context, she would have exposure to different kinds of solutions and strategies. In the group, she could receive validation and support for her own situation, as well as being in a position to view the choices made by other women. Karen also proposed an abuser group for Stan. Rachel was eager for a group experience for herself, but when Rachel suggested this for Stan, he scoffed at her and said it was all her problem, not his. Rachel did attend several group sessions but reported to Karen that she listened to the stories of other women rather than disclose her own situation to strangers.

In the remainder of the decision-making phase, Rachel and Karen explored possible options and her accumulated feelings of helplessness, ambivalence, depression, and intermittent rage. Rachel needed time and opportunity to mourn the ideal marriage she never had, and she began to look more realistically at what positive qualities remained of her relationship with Stan. Together, they examined Rachel's cognitions about blame, abuse, guilt, and denial. They reviewed cognitions related to Rachel's self-efficacy and self-esteem and the probability that Rachel could either (a) forgive Stan and live with him amicably if the abuse terminated, or (b) live independently as a single parent. Neither choice was attractive to Rachel.

Karen showed Rachel how to complete a cost-benefit analysis according to a social exchange paradigm (Rusbult, 1983), looking at each option and its possible outcomes. Rachel determined that her job was indeed a good one and that she did not need any more career counseling. She also decided that her income, with child support, would suffice for both herself and Sherry should she decide to make a break. They covered some aspects of assertiveness, so that Rachel could feel more competent in expressing her position and eventual decision to Stan. They explored community resources for child care, costs of apartments, and so on. Rachel continued to monitor Stan's behavior to document physical, sexual, and psychological abuse; and one day she came into session with new bruises on her head and arms.

Rachel repeated her earlier statement, "I've had enough, I'm not going to take any more of this," but was still reluctant to seek a temporary separation. Karen then suggested that Rachel consider other support systems, such as women in her synagogue. Rachel had been active in a women's group there, *Hadassah,* but had not attended recently because of Stan's demands that she stay home. Karen encouraged her to rejoin the group and attend their meetings. Two sessions later, Rachel came in jubilantly. "At the Hadassah meeting last week, a woman I know, Naomi, approached me asking about my bruises, saying that they were similar to those she had sustained when she was married. I was taken aback but immediately I felt the urge to spill it all to her." Rachel then described how she had taken the risk to disclose her situation to Naomi, again crying uncontrollably, and how good it felt to share her misery. Through the next few sessions, with Karen's encouragement, Rachel and Naomi decided to talk to several other women in the group, with the result that a small committee was formed to consult with the rabbi. To Rachel's surprise, the visit was a success; once her rabbi was convinced that a number of women in the congregation were experiencing terrors similar to those that Rachel reported to him earlier, he agreed to help disseminate educational materials on wife abuse that the Hadassah women volunteered to provide. Karen pointed out to Rachel how "the personal is political" (Principle II) was taking place. What appeared to Rachel as "her problem" now became a women's problem, thus deflecting the blame from her to a larger system of inequality and patriarchy.

*Resolution and Restructuring*

Now the sessions moved to a new level. In the final phase of Rachel's counseling, she became very task-orientated and proactive. She refused to file assault charges against Stan, but asked him to leave the house. She obtained a restraining order that required Stan to remain away from the home for a predetermined period of time. He was furious and threatened to sue for custody of Sherry. For many women, this step in restraining the man from access to his home triggers increased violence and anger. Rachel was made aware of this, but Stan suddenly reacted with compliance and even agreed to attend an abuser's group to try to reinstate their relationship. This move by Stan was an encouraging sign for Rachel, and she began to feel more optimistic.

The remainder of this phase was concerned with developing Rachel's self-confidence and self-sufficiency. She had many skills in dealing with others and in independent living that required only that she believe in herself and agree to attempt new behaviors. Counseling at this point was concentrated on helping Rachel to identify herself as a caring and competent woman who could make rational and wise choices, either to remain with Stan or to leave and live on her own. Because she had submerged her needs and desires so heavily with his in the past few years, time was devoted to helping Rachel nurture herself by attending a sports clinic and going to dinner and theater with friends. As she continued her Hadassah group attendance, she found new friends and a new view of herself that belied the incompetent and unattractive woman that Stan tried to fashion for her.

At the end of six months, Rachel announced that she was ready to take Stan back. She wanted one more chance to mend the relationship and to make her marriage work (She confronted Karen: "You did that too, didn't you?"). Rachel decided to terminate her counseling and to recontact Karen if she needed further support.

## CONCLUSIONS

Rachel's story is one that is told over and over in many counseling experiences. During the six months she worked with Karen, Rachel gained considerable insight into the dynamics of her battering relationship with Stan and was no longer in a state of denial. She labeled him as a batterer and warned him at the reunion that she would not tolerate another episode or it would be truly the end of the marriage. Her view of herself had changed dramatically, from a frightened and self-effacing "fat person who needed a new job," to a relatively self-confident professional woman who could rehearse her strong points and who liked the way she looked and the career she had originally chosen. However, she decided to return to the marriage with the hopes that Stan would change. For Rachel and Sherry's sake, Karen hoped so also. However, research with battering men, even following group therapy, suggests that the battering will continue in a majority of cases (Gondolph, 1988, 1998; D. K. Snyder & Fruchtman, 1981). This was information that Rachel had to determine for herself. We believed that, armed with her new view of herself and with a background of information and support from the counseling sessions and her women's support group, she would make a wise choice if the battering did repeat itself.

## SUMMARY

The abuse of women in close relationships is sufficiently frequent to be viewed as normative in Western society. In this chapter, we reviewed the incidence and theories about violence toward women. A three-part model of violence and entrapment includes the larger society, the male batterer, and the abused victim. In this model, the violence and sexism of society and the abuser combine to create a hostage situation for the woman. As hostage to terror and violence, she escalates her attempts to placate and please; and in doing so, she increases her powerlessness and becomes psychologically and physically entrapped in a relationship from which she feels unable to extricate herself.

We presented the case of Rachel, who was physically, psychologically, and sexually abused by her husband, and applied the theory of hostage and entrapment to her situation. The counseling followed a model of crisis intervention, exploration and decision making, and resolution and restructuring. Karen combined these phases with EFT principles and cognitive-behavioral strategies to support and validate Rachel as a strong and worthwhile individual, and to assist her in the process of decision making about the course of her life. At the end of six months, Rachel decided to give her marriage another try, and Karen lost contact with her. We judged that, at the end of this period, her depression and anxiety were decreased and her self-efficacy and self-esteem were much higher. She had learned to provide herself with nonblaming self-statements, had found a helpful group of supportive friends in her religious community, and was determined not to live with abuse again. Karen wished her well and hoped for a positive outcome. She did not return for further counseling.

## ACTIVITIES

**A.** Review the phases of counseling with Rachel. For each phase, identify one procedure or topic that represents an EFT principle. List the principle and explain how it was used here in the counseling process.

**B.** With a partner, role-play a session in which you are Rachel and have decided to stay in the relationship with Stan at the termination of counseling. Although he has been violent once more, you have decided that the rewards are higher than the anticipated costs of leaving. You want your therapist to help you now in managing this relationship. Then reverse roles and play the therapist.

With a partner, role-play Rachel. You have returned to counseling because Stan has continued to be violent and you want help in the decision about whether to leave him. Then reverse roles.

For each part you played, what were your affective reactions (feelings)? What were your thoughts? What do you believe you would have done in each situation?

**C.** Challenging myths: For each myth (false statement) in the self-assessment at the beginning of the chapter, prepare a written response you would give to a client (female or male) who believed the myth to be true. Role-play your challenges with a partner and be prepared to deal with counter-challenges.

## FURTHER READINGS

There are many good books on battering relationships. Read at least one of the following to expand your understanding:

Dutton, M. A. (1992). *Empowering and healing the battered woman: A model for assessment and intervention.* New York: Guilford Press.

Gelles, R. J., & Strauss, M. A. (1988). *Intimate violence: The causes and consequences of abuse in American families.* New York: Simon & Schuster.

Gondolf, E. W. (1998). *Assessing woman battering in mental health services.* Thousand Oaks, CA: Sage.

Walker, L. E. A. (1994). *The abused woman and survivor therapy: A practical guide for the psychotherapist.* Washington, DC: American Psychological Association.

Yllo, K., & Bograd, M. (Eds.). (1988). *Feminist perspectives on wife abuse.* Newbury Park, CA: Sage.

### Resources for Abused Clients

Jones, A., & Schechter, S. (1992). *When love goes wrong: Strategies for women with controlling partners.* New York: HarperCollins.

NiCarthy, G. (1986). *Getting free: A handbook for women in abusive relationships.* Seattle, WA: Seal.

# PART 3

# BECOMING AN EMPOWERMENT FEMINIST THERAPIST

Becoming an EF therapist is a lifelong, challenging process. One of our goals in writing this book is to give you a structure for learning about and applying a feminist therapy perspective to women's counseling issues. Once you have learned the basic theory, principles, and techniques of EF therapy covered in Part 1, you are ready to apply these perspectives to various issues women bring to therapy. In Part 2, we provided samples of this application process. In Part 3, we cover issues related to research, practice, and training. Chapter 10 discusses traditional approaches to and feminist transformations of research. We then describe current research on evaluating the process and outcomes of feminist therapy. In Chapter 11, we explore additional challenges in applying an EFT perspective. We focus on feminist perspectives of ethics. Then, we explore the impact of power on client-counselor relationships. Finally, we discuss professional labels and conflicting client and counselor goals. In Chapter 12, we discuss feminist identity development. We propose a model for training feminist-diversity therapists that enhances the process of developing attitudes, knowledge, and skills needed to become an EF therapist.

As we end our part of your journey to becoming a feminist therapist, we are keenly aware of the topics we have been unable to include in this book. For example, we did not have space to address the application of an EFT perspective to marriage and family therapy, eating disorders, body image, women's groups, older women, substance abuse, and agoraphobia, as well as to a variety of women's health issues such as menarche, menopause, mastectomy, infertility, and unwanted pregnancy. You will want to become more informed about each of these areas. In addition, you will benefit from expanded reading on the gender and ethnocultural bias often present in traditional approaches to research and alternative models for research congruent with a feminist perspective.

Our book is only a part of your journey to becoming a feminist therapist. We hope we have given you a different set of lenses with which to view yourself, the world, and the issues your clients bring to counseling. We encourage you to continue your journey through further reading, discussions with colleagues, and workshops and classes. If our professional paths should cross, we shall be interested in hearing about your journey. Bon voyage!

# Chapter 10 ———————————————————

# *RECONSIDERING RESEARCH*

*Advocacy and scholarship are not incompatible activities, despite what we have been social-
ized to believe . . . indeed, we want to do research that will change the world.*

Mary Crawford and Ellen Kimmel, 1999

## SELF-ASSESSMENT: EVALUATING RESEARCH FOR BIAS

1. What is your concept of gender bias in research? List at least four examples of
   gender bias in research and share your ideas with a partner.
2. Select one research study with which you are familiar from your graduate education or from continuing education experiences, and analyze its topic, content,
   methods, and conclusions for evidence of gender bias. Report your findings to the
   class or to a colleague.
3. Select any source of bias from the SEARCH list (sexism, ethnocentrism, ableism
   and ageism, racism, classism, and heterosexism) and identify how it appears in
   one research study according to the criteria for analysis in (2).
4. Reconstruct each of the studies used in (2) and (3) to correct the examples of bias
   that you have identified.

## OVERVIEW

Knowledge about human behavior can be gained from many sources. As an empirical
and databased science, psychology has emphasized the importance of objective observation and measurement, and a value-free science. In this chapter, we review the requirements of traditional scientific procedures, and we raise some issues related to
their utility and validity for studying the psychology of women and gender. In reconsid-
ering psychological research, we present a set of criteria that reframes our perspectives
and reintroduces a diverse universe of women and their issues into the knowledge base
of psychology. A final section considers how we can proceed to evaluate the outcomes

of feminist interventions with clients in the absence of a clear match between the goals of feminist-diversity counseling and those of many traditional psychotherapy approaches.

## RECONSIDERING RESEARCH

The foundation of every graduate program in psychology rests on the integration and application of scientific research. Using an empirical and databased science, psychologists seek to understand human behavior and the variables that influence its form and change. Research activities form the cornerstone without which this science and its theories cannot flourish. Our psychological theories provide us with frameworks for considering what to observe in the universe around us, what questions to ask, and how to interpret and apply the information that we obtain.

Why should you be concerned about research if you are studying to be a feminist practitioner? Janice Yoder (1999) writes:

> Systematic research defines our scholarship and underlies the therapies we practice, the courses we teach, and the consulting work we do as expert witnesses in business, in education, and in government as well. (p. 18)

Throughout this book, we typically support our discussions and practical applications with reference to relevant research studies. It has become an adage in psychology that science and practice go hand-in-hand, each being reciprocally informed by the other. That is, many of the techniques and strategies that you apply in the counseling session are based on a background of research that supports its utility. In turn, the issues and concerns that arise in the therapy session provide a rich source of data for further testing and theoretical development. Thus, the relationship can and should be a reciprocal one (Hadley & Mitchell, 1995). We provide examples of this process later in the chapter.

### Questioning Traditional Assumptions

As the feminist movement expanded, questions arose concerning the appropriate definition of science, the adequacy of our theorizing, the values of traditional empiricism, and the established methods of psychological inquiry. The body of knowledge that we call *psychology* was also brought into question as it reflects the limitations of our theories and methods. Feminist scholars have pointed to the ways in which our science has been biased, androcentric, classist, ethnocentric, and heterosexist in its content and methods, and have called for revisions in the manner in which research is conceptualized, conducted, and taught (M. C. Crawford & Kimmel, 1999; M. C. Crawford & Marecek, 1989; Riger, 1992; D. L. Tolman & Brydon-Miller, 1997).

In this chapter, we look at feminist revisions in the traditional scientific research paradigm and the ways in which these alternative approaches have helped to construct new knowledge by looking through another lens. We consider first traditional views of scientific psychology, which represent the medium in which most of us learned our science. We then review the ways in which biases such as those attributable to the SEARCH variables have influenced the content and methods of psychology. In contrast, we present some emergent feminist revisions of research methods, content, and process. Finally, we address the issue of evaluating the process and outcomes of feminist-diversity counseling in the context of a revised understanding of the research paradigms.

## Science as Objective and Value-Free

Contemporary scientific inquiry is based on logical positivism, which assumes that knowledge about the universe should be both objective and value-free. From this perspective, scientific knowledge is valid only when it is gained through "objective" observation. It is assumed that the values and beliefs of the observer do not impinge on the scientific process of observation, so that the researcher remains independent of the object of inquiry. The outcomes of the scientific method are intended as universal truths or laws of behavior that can apply to a wide range of individuals and across situations and historical time.

In the service of these scientific goals, research methods in psychology have emphasized careful quantitative measurement that is assumed to be free of subjective or personal bias. It has also been expected that findings will be generalizable to other persons and situations, and can be replicated and thus verified and validated by other researchers. Considerable importance is placed on the deductive method that expects linear relationships (e.g., if A, then B) and testing the Null Hypothesis.

## Evaluating the Ethic of Objectivity

The assumption of a value-free and objective science is to accumulate a body of knowledge that represents the discipline and informs us correctly about the nature of human behavior. The experimental laboratory, in which conditions that might influence the response under investigation are controlled or minimized, is still regarded by many researchers as the ideal locus of research activity. Stripped of the daily contexts of their normal lives, it is assumed that individuals will respond to experimental conditions in a relatively uniform manner that will reveal universal laws or principles of behavior.

### Advantages

There are several advantages of these traditional approaches to the scientific enterprise. Researchers from diverse locales can communicate and replicate the findings of others. Methods reported do not have to be explained and defended, since the scientific community agrees on the rules of research conduct (population sampling, reliability and validity of measures, etc.). And for the individual researcher, publication and dissemination of experimental findings are facilitated by editorial adherence to widely accepted methods and topics of research (Worell, 1994).

### Drawbacks

The disadvantages of traditional scientific psychology have been voiced by many scholars (see M. C. Crawford & Kimmel, 2001; Grossman et al., 1997). In particular, researchers have raised questions about the assumptions of its epistemology, or ways of knowing what we think we know. In Chapter 1, we discussed the social construction approach to knowledge (all knowledge is relative), which contrasts boldly with the logical positive view of knowing (all knowledge is absolute). Here, we consider some of the many questions raised by the community of feminist scholars, whose objections to

Table 10.1   Feminist critique of traditional approaches
to research

| | |
|---|---|
| Androcentric: | Constructs a womanless psychology. |
| Ethnocentric: | Fails to consider diverse populations. |
| Restrictive: | Accepts a limited range of methods. |
| Hierarchal: | Treats participants as objects, uses deception. |
| Context-free: | Observes people outside the realities of their lives. |

traditional modes of psychological inquiry are based on at least five major factors (see Table 10.1) (M. C. Crawford & Marecek, 1989; Ohye & Daniel, 1999; Reid et al., 1995):

1. Androcentric and biased methods that reflect the values of the dominant culture.
2. An ethnocentric science that fails to be inclusive of the lives of diverse populations.
3. A narrow science that neglects subjective methods and alternative routes to gaining knowledge about human behavior.
4. An exploitive approach to participants, treating them as objects to be acted on, and using deceptive methods of inquiry.
5. Context-stripping by examining people's behavior without respect to the realities of their lives.

## SOURCES OF BIAS IN RESEARCH

The call for revisions in traditional psychological inquiry comes from many sources. In the following discussion, we draw on the insights of many feminist scholars, both within psychology and from other related social science disciplines. We start by considering the ethic of objectivity and the implicit bias in its assumptions. We then review four major activities that are common to all research efforts:

1. Theory-building and generation of hypotheses.
2. Selection of samples to be studied.
3. Research methods, including relevant social locations of the researcher (such as sex and ethnicity), conditions of the investigation, and instrumentation.
4. Analysis and interpretation of the data, and dissemination of results.

### Objectivity Reconsidered

The assumption that science can be objective is a myth. All thinking and theorizing flow from a position of valuing, and they are fashioned by the history and culture from which the observer is positioned. In the social sciences, the researcher determines what topics are important to study, what questions to ask, how to proceed in finding answers to those questions, and what populations to study. Each of these elements of the research design reflects the value orientation of the researcher.

## What Topics Should We Study?

A great deal of research activity in the period from 1950 to 1975 was centered on aggression and achievement—both Western and male-valued topics that received a disproportionate amount of attention. They were studied with biased methods that ignored female achievement and the motivation and display of aggression by women. Further, the theories from which the research was generated were constructed from a dominant culture and male-oriented framework, the instrumentation was both culturally and gender biased, and the samples used were primarily or exclusively male students from an Ivy league college. When women did not fit the paradigms or respond as did men, they were dropped from the samples. Was this an example of objective science? Had the researchers themselves been poor, Latino, or female, what different topics, methods, and conclusions might have eventuated? Where was the research on sexual assault, wife-battering, unplanned pregnancy, or child care?

## What Are the Questions?

A major area of biased research is in the formulation of questions to be examined. We cite here the research on single parenting and its outcomes for the well-being of children. Early research in this area was titled "Father-absent boys" that looked at the consequences to young boys in terms of impairment of aggression, masculinity, and school achievement. The hypotheses were drawn mainly from Freudian theory, which presented the father as the prototype of masculinity and the identification of boys with their fathers and their values as prerequisite to appropriate male development. The finding that boys raised primarily by single mothers were less aggressive and less masculine than boys raised in two-parent families was accepted as evidence of the inadequacy of mother-headed families. Male identity was presumed to be at risk in mother-headed families. What do you suppose was the research agenda here?

Ethnocultural, gender, heterosexual, and social class bias entered into this research when multiple variables that affect mother-headed families were ignored or unacknowledged. For example, in 1999, nearly half of mother-headed families with young children were living below the poverty line (U.S. Census, 2000). Of the mothers who were divorced, fewer than half received full child support. The results of the "father-absent" type of research were disseminated as though they represented "reality" rather than only one perspective. Gender and ethnocultural bias was also evident in the assumption that a reduction in male aggression is undesirable or change worthy, and in the lack of concern for the well-being of the mothers and daughters in these families.

Revised versions of this approach explored the strengths, rather than the liabilities, of the female-headed family. Such research examined child well-being in terms of variations in ethnic identity, family structure and transitional living arrangements, maternal education and employment, economic stress, social support, availability and quality of child care, paternal involvement, and contact and conflict between the separated parents (E. M. Hetherington, Cox, & Cox, 1982; Steil, 2001; Worell, 1988b). To what extent, for example, are any negative outcomes of single parenting related to poverty and limited resources? Later research looked at positive characteristics of the children, including increased cooperativeness, empathy, interpersonal skills, and helpfulness of both girls and boys in single mother-headed families. Alternative ways of viewing the mother-headed family throw a different light on the effects of single parenting on the psychological development of children.

## Implications for Intervention

Consider the implications of the differences in research perspective and results for family counseling had we focused on fatherless boys instead of on single-parent families. In the one case, we might encourage these boys to engage in more masculine and aggressive activities, such as football. We might also encourage conflicted, abusive, and dysfunctional families to remain intact on the assumption that the male children needed a father present in the home. We are aware of examples of court-mandated joint custody following divorce in battering relationships, with the expressed interest of keeping the male children in contact with their fathers.

Alternative formulations might propose that some of the difficulties in adjustment of children from separated families are related to maternal stress, loneliness, isolation, inadequate housing and economic insufficiency, and continuing interparental conflict. Interventions in these situations would focus on assisting the mother in obtaining adequate child support and affordable housing, and assisting with employment opportunities, child management, social support networks, and self-nurturance. Each alternative framework provides a different set of conclusions and different recommendations for intervention. Moreover, concern for the children's well-being would extend to girls as well as boys and would focus on opportunities for family strengthening and empowerment.

## What Populations Are Sampled?

Gender bias is reflected in sampling procedures in which (a) only males are included and the results are generalized to all persons; (b) both females and males are studied but the similarities and differences in their responses are ignored and results are summed to apply to all participants; and (c) females are compared to males in situations in which their responses are judged as deviant or deficient because they do not match "normative" male responses. Examples of the first problem appear in early influential research on moral development (Kohlberg, 1966). Lawrence Kohlberg used only male participants in his early studies and then assumed that the results applied to everyone. Subsequent studies using mixed-sex samples produced some very different outcomes (e.g., Carol Gilligan's 1982 work on the moral development of women).

The second bias appears in research on marital satisfaction, in which summed satisfaction scores of couples have frequently masked the individual scores of the wives, assuming that wife satisfaction is equated with couple satisfaction (Steil, 1997; Worell, 1988a). Examples of the third problem are found in some studies on interpersonal skills, in which women were evaluated as unassertive because they talked less than the men. Here, women were evaluated as "deficient" when their responses were compared to the "male as norm." Later research with women and men in mixed sex groups found that there are many situational variables aside from gender that determine "talk time" (Carli, 2001). Alternative approaches might consider each participant's role in listening, providing verbal and nonverbal positive feedback, or seeking conflict-reducing strategies. In all three examples, alternative research frameworks have revealed new information on women's experiences and behavior that were ignored or missing from the original research.

Ethnocultural bias in sampling is evidenced by:

1. The relative absence of women and men of color as participants in most published studies.
2. Omission of information in most published studies on the ethnocultural composition of their samples.
3. The dearth of studies that use community or noncollege samples.
4. Selection of topics to study that emphasize the deficiencies, rather than the strengths, of minority populations.

In a search of the psychological literature on adolescent identity, Bonnie Ohye and Jessica Daniel (1999) reported that "two thirds of these published studies did not mention ethnic minority groups or discuss the limitations of their findings due to the racial-ethnic characteristics of their samples" (p. 123). Identifying broad categories of ethnocultural groups, however, may prove to be an ineffective approach. Richard Dana (2000) points out that these general descriptions ignore critical variable such as socioeconomic, immigrant, or acculturation status. We would add that within any socially identified group, ethnocultural identity level also influences response characteristics. For example, Shanette Harris (1995) found that African American women who had a secure Black identity status and few anti-White feelings (Immersion level) held more favorable attitudes toward their own physical appearance and engaged in more health-promoting behaviors than women who were less secure in their Black identity (Preencounter). These authors point out the importance of alternative approaches to psychological inquiry and the explicit inclusion of those who do not represent the dominant majority population.

## HOW DOES TRADITIONAL RESEARCH REFLECT GENDER AND ETHNOCULTURAL BIAS?

A broad range of methods and procedures have provided opportunities for gender and ethnocultural bias. We cite only a few examples here.

### Characteristics of the Researchers

Several researcher variables may influence respondent performance. The sex of the experimenter has been shown to be a variable in the responses of women. In particular, female and male researchers may "pull" for different research outcomes. Until well into the 1980s, researchers were primarily male (Kessler & McKenna, 1985). Likewise, little attention has been given to the effects of the match between the researcher and participants on the responses of minority samples. Sensitivity to this issue is reflected in a study on well-being and resilience in single African American mothers (Todd & Worell, 2000). Because the interviewer (Janet Todd) is White, she trained an African American researcher to interview half of her participants and compared the two interviewers on the responses of the mothers. In this case, the response differences of participants were attributable to researcher training rather than to ethnicity of the interviewers. This type of researcher control is rare, but reflects a desirable way to acknowledge the possible bias effects of researcher characteristics.

Feminist researchers have also pointed to the hierarchal relationship in most traditional research between the researcher and the subjects. Reference to research volunteers as *subjects* to be acted on appears to place them in a subordinate position and treats them as objects in the experimental situation. Recognition of this perception led to the revision of the *Publication Manual* (1983) of the American Psychological Association to require that *subjects* be replaced by *participants* in all research publications. This revision acknowledges the fact that these are live human beings who also have intent and purpose in the situation, rather than objects to be acted on. Further, many psychological studies employ deception as an integral part of the design. Thus, providing false information about the purpose or intent of the research shows disrespect for the intelligence, autonomy, and dignity of the participants.

## Characteristics of the Task

Sources of bias in research can stem from the nature of the tasks presented. The gender typing of the experimental tasks can influence responses by females if the task is perceived as male-oriented. Conclusions drawn from male-typed tasks, such as drawing machine parts, can lead researchers to the wrong conclusions regarding achievement motivation in women asked to draw these parts quickly and accurately. Sharon Nash (1979) found that high school girls fared less well than boys on spatial skills tasks, but that girls who perceived that "math is for girls as well as for boys" did as well as the boys on these tasks. In Chapter 5, we discussed the concept of *stereotype threat* (Steele, 1997), whereby individuals who believe that they are expected as a group to do poorly on the task at hand (math, academics, etc.) may demonstrate reduced performance. For some individuals, stereotype task threat functions as a self-fulfilling prophecy and may interfere with effective performance.

Multiple characteristics of experimental tasks may reflect bias. In particular, the "meaning" of verbal stimuli on any self-report scale may differ not only across individual responses, but across various social location groups. For example, the Bem Sex-Role Inventory (BSRI; 1974) was constructed to reveal differences in response tendencies due to gender. However, a comparison of the meaning of terms between White women and diverse groups of Women of Color (WOC) revealed significant differences in their interpretations. Terms such as *passive* and *assertive* were viewed differently by the two groups. White Women tended to describe their experience of *passive* as "easygoing," while the WOC members were more likely to describe this as "not saying what one thinks" (Landrine, Klonoff, & Brown-Collins, 1995). Although these authors did not analyze differences in meanings among the differing WOC groups, we might anticipate the ethnocultural individualities would surface among them as well.

On the basis of their research, Landrine et al. emphasized that qualitative and person-centered approaches are "prerequisites for a culturally diverse and culture-sensitive feminist psychology" (p. 60). They pointed out that from a Western viewpoint, observation of other cultures is interpreted from the perspective of the dominant "cultural dictionary" for understanding behavior. The result is "stereotypes masquerading as scientific evidence" (p. 61). Feminist psychologists, seeking to understand the experienced lives of women, have been mindful of the importance of alternative approaches to standardized and "objective" measurement (such as Crawford & Kimmel's [2000] two issues of the *Psychology of Women Quarterly* devoted to innovative methods). In a similar spirit, Judith Worell and Redonna Chandler (1996) revised their measure of women's empowerment, the Personal Progress Scale (PPS) to incorporate each woman's social locations by asking respondents to answer all questions from the perspective of their own relevant personal identities (PPS-R; Worell & Chandler, 1999). In this manner, we can look at both individuals and groups by selectively partitioning their responses according to the social identity locations they have selected.

## Instrumentation

Researchers may draw inaccurate conclusions when both females and males are assessed with biased instrumentation. A gendered example is the well-known scale on negative life events (Holmes & Rahe, 1967), which was developed with an all-male sample to predict heart disease. The scale has also been used frequently with women, and gender comparisons have inaccurately predicted women's stress responses. The insistence on "objective" measurement can lead researchers to ignore important variables in the lives of individuals that have not been explored prior to instrument development. Thus, such variables as unemployment, retirement, and difficulties with children may have differing stress contributions for women and men that are not elicited by this scale (Murrell, Norris, & Hutchins, 1984). Further, areas of stress commonly experienced by diverse groups of women—such as poverty, single parenting, sexual assault, battering, homelessness, and sexual or ethnocultural harassment—are not represented by items in this scale. Inclusion of such relevant items might produce a very different scale for predicting women's heart disease. Chapter 5 explored assessment bias more fully. As an emerging or seasoned researcher, you should be aware and knowledgeable about the sources of bias in your measuring instruments and take steps to correct or modify your approach to observation and data collection.

## Data Analysis and Interpretation

Analysis of the data may be influenced by unacknowledged assumptions. There are a number of problems in analyzing data for gender or ethnocultural differences, some of which are displayed in Table 10.2. First, if no hypotheses about gender or group membership were originally generated, obtained groups differences may be random or incidental and the results misleading or uninterpretable. Second, if group differences, rather than similarities, are highlighted, readers are further misled into polarizing and stereotyping women and men or members of diverse groups. Most researchers are aware that studies reporting no significant differences between experimental groups are less likely to be accepted for publication in most scientific journals. When I (JW) was editor of the

**Table 10.2    Problems in analyzing for gender or ethnocultural differences**

- Theories or hypotheses are missing.
- Similarities between groups are ignored.
- Difference leads to polarity and stereotypes.
- Difference may be interpreted as deficiency.
- Difference may be interpreted as biological or genetic.
- Difference may lead to essentialism.
- Difference may mask mediating variables.

*Psychology of Women Quarterly,* a journal of feminist research, I became aware very early that it was common for researchers to report group differences but to ignore many similarities in responses between their groups. Even the titles of articles typically included the term *difference.* In a somewhat controversial decision, all authors were asked to use the term *comparisons* among groups to reflect that both similarities and differences were usually found between groups. As we have emphasized throughout this book, terminology and the "power to name" is a critical factor in framing people's thoughts and beliefs.

As displayed in Table 10.2, additional problems exist with "difference" research. We have discussed previously that *difference* has often been interpreted as "deficient," as in the previous example of the sons of single mothers. Rather than view their less aggressive responses as reflecting positive qualities, these boys were viewed as deficient in masculinity. Difference research also leads frequently to *essentialism,* or assumptions about the biological or genetic characteristics of the groups. Thus, when women's higher nurturance is attributed to being a genetic female, the cultural, social, or situational variables that might mediate her caretaking responses are overlooked. Likewise, the lower scores on ability tests of certain ethnic groups in the United States have been attributed by some to genetic inferiority, neglecting the facts of other variables such as widespread poverty and oppression. (See the discussion in Chapter 5 of stereotype threat.) Finally, reports of group differences may fail to identify the specific aspects of these group variables that mediate the proposed relationship (Betancourt & Lopez, 1993).

Analysis of gender or group-related differences leads back to our discussion in Chapter 1 of Alpha and Beta bias. Thus, rather than *difference,* we prefer to use the concept of gender or culturally related *comparisons* to emphasize that (a) most studies that report differences also find similarities on some responses, (b) most obtained differences between socially defined groups are group-*related* rather than group-*determined,* and (c) most studies that report group differences find a relatively small effect due to gender or ethnicity. For example, the majority of metanalyses in psychological research on sex differences have found little more than 5% of the variance to be attributable to gender. However, Diane Halpern (1995) pointed out that relatively few of the studies included in metanalyses are inclusive of diverse populations. Thus, the conclusions based on such broad analyses may reveal little about women from all the social locations we have discussed.

The thoughtful consideration of widespread bias in research has lead to revisions in conceptualization and implementation of research activities. As feminist scholars from many disciplines consider alternative solutions to the limitations of traditional research paradigms, we consider these proposals to represent a work in progress. Although there is some controversy in the feminist community concerning whether we revise or entirely reconstruct our science (cf. Peplau & Conrad, 1989), our recommendations are based on general consensus across a variety of views.

## FEMINIST AND DIVERSITY REVISIONS

### Questioning a Value-Free Science

In contrast to traditional views of science, feminists of all persuasions insist that science cannot be value-free. Rather, the values that enter our science should be stated explicitly and consciously entered into the research process (M. C. Crawford & Kimmel, 2001; Lott, 1985b; Peplau & Conrad, 1989). We take the position that all research serves a political purpose, whether explicit or implicit, and has social implications related to the culture in which it is embedded as well as in the individual mind frames and worldviews of the researchers (Betancourt & Lopez, 1993; M. C. Crawford & Marecek, 1989). These purposes and values should be brought forward and acknowledged.

## Feminist-Diversity Values Introduced

Feminist-diversity research is open in its values and proclaims an explicit purpose. A primary purpose is to introduce women from all social locations and with diverse gender-related issues into a traditionally culture-free and womanless psychology. Established truths about women's lives are revisited, entertaining the validity of constructed realities. Feminist theories contribute to the discovery of problems that begged for solutions, to questions with no ready answers, and to hypotheses that framed new questions.

Feminist research aims to view women in a variety of contexts that frees our understanding of women from comparisons with norms for behavior that are derived from restricted and sanitized populations. Such research looks at women's issues previously ignored: sexual assault, sexual harassment, dual-career partners, women's health, and women of low social status (ethnically and culturally diverse, poor, old, disabled, lesbian, bisexual, etc.). Feminist research also looks at women in the context of their personal experience, such as in their interactions with others: women, men, lovers, children, supervisors, students, employees, and so on. Feminist values of gender equity, for example, opened the doors of academic inquiry into questions that were never asked or examined. These values fueled new areas of research, such as on marital equality and the division of household labor (Steil, 1997); on girls' diminished academic aspirations and self confidence (Eccles et al., 1999); on inequities in employment opportunities and salary allocation (Gutek, 2001a); and on the implications of sexual desire in the experiences of young women (M. Fine, 1988; D. L. Tolman, 1999).

Finally, feminist research takes into consideration the hierarchy of sociocultural power arrangements that have dominated the scientific literature and seeks to provide an alternative lens through which to view women's realities. In this context, women from all social locations are viewed in terms of their strengths, their contributions, and their positive qualities. Women's vulnerabilities may be reframed in the light of the social and institutional constraints on their behavior and opportunities. Thus, rape is examined less from the consideration of "what she was wearing and how she behaved" than on the situational, cultural, and structural variables that mediate the rape event and the woman's experience of it. From the sum of these revisionist viewpoints and activities, feminist researchers aim to reconstruct and transform the knowledge base of their disciplines.

## FEMINIST-DIVERSITY TRANSFORMATIONS

Feminist principles, beliefs, and values form the basis of transformations in theory and research related to women. An overarching goal is to respect and represent the perspectives of women from all social locations. To this end, Claire Etaugh and I (JW) (1994) proposed a set of six themes that underlie feminist research and over 40 variations of these themes that represent a broad consensus of the feminist research community. These themes and their variations are displayed in Table 10.3.

### Table 10.3   Feminist research themes and variations

1. *Challenging the Tenets of Traditional Scientific Inquiry*
   a. Recognizing that values enter into all scientific enterprises and that these values should be explicit.
   b. Rejecting the assumption of a truly objective science free from the culture, history, and experience of the observer.
   c. Restructuring the polarity of objective-subjective; pointing out how "subjects" should not become objects to be manipulated by the researcher but collaborators in the process.
   d. Identifying and correcting multiple elements of sexism and bias in scientific research procedures.
   e. Affirming that the raw data never speak for themselves and that all data require categorization and interpretation.
   f. Emphasizing the researcher as an individual who interacts with participants in meaningful ways that enrich both observer and observed.
   g. Producing a more inclusive science that reflects alternative realities; including multiple perspectives by both researcher and participants; expanding the diversity of all persons involved; recognizing that reality is created, in part, by the scientific process.
   h. Extending the populations studied beyond White middle class, college student samples; studying populations that are relevant to the questions being asked.
   i. Admitting a range of research methods as legitimate; asserting that qualitative, quantitative, ethnographic, and other methods of gathering data may be useful for different purposes and may reveal unique information.

2. *Focus on the Experience and Lives of Women*
   a. Discovering the contributions of women to research and the history of psychology.
   b. Valuing women as a legitimate target of study.
   c. Studying women apart from the standard of male as norm.
   d. Questioning the category of woman as representative of all women, thus recognizing and exploring the sources of variation among us; looking at women who differ from the majority group, such as in ethnic and racial identities, socioeconomic status, sexual orientation, disability, age, parenthood, and employment status.
   e. Encouraging research questions that are grounded in personal experiences of women researchers; asking questions that were never imagined about women's lives.
   f. Exploring research questions that are relevant to women's lives, such as rape, incest, sexual harassment, reproductive processes, sexual decision making, employment segregation, discrimination, and so on.
   g. Rejecting sex difference research as basic to our understanding of women or of men; recognizing that differences among women, and among men, are greater than those between them.
   h. Constructing methods of research that target issues of importance to women's lives, such as measures of rape myth, hostility to women, traditional gender.
   i. Studying women in the context of their lives and natural milieu; avoiding "context-stripping" through laboratory approaches that reduce complexity and individuality.
   j. Attending to women's strengths and capabilities as well as their problems; researching variables related to women's competency and resilience.
   k. Viewing observed gender differences in the context of power dynamics and women's expected socialized role behaviors rather than as differences embedded in biology.

3. *Viewing Power Relations as the Basis of Patriarchal Political Social Arrangements*
   a. Recognizing that women's subordinate status in society is based on unequal distribution of power rather than on women's deficiencies; exploring the dimensions of power as influences on the quality of women's lives.
   b. Considering differences among women as mediated by power differentials related to opportunities available based on color, economic sufficiency, age, sexual orientation, and so on.

**Table 10.3**  *(Continued)*

    c. Attending to privilege and privation as sources of research questions.

    d. Examining women's health concerns in the context of power arrangements. Examples include challenging the assignment of women with normative behavior to the "sick" role and the neglect of many of their legitimate health concerns.

    e. Focusing research in interpersonal relationships in the context of patriarchal power arrangements, such as marital inequality, definitions of consent in rape, and so on.

    f. Exploring the basis of stereotyped female characteristics, such as sociability, nurturance, or passivity in the context of unequal power relations; pointing out that what appears naturally may be framed by the politics of power.

    g. Shifting attributions of responsibility and blame from victim to perpetrator.

    h. Seeking strategies that lead to women's empowerment.

4. *Recognizing Gender as an Essential Category of Analysis*

    a. Pointing out the multiple conceptions of gender; challenging the use of gender only as an independent variable that explains observed behavior.

    b. Exploring the functions of gender as a stimulus variable that frames expectations, evaluations, and response patterns.

    c. Recognizing gender as a social construction based on power arrangements; viewing observations attributed to gender in the context of power asymmetries.

    d. Emphasizing the situational context of gender and gendering as an active process that structures social interactions.

5. *Attention to the Use of Language and the Power to "Name"*

    a. Creating public awareness of hidden phenomena by identifying and naming them, as in sexual harassment, woman battering, date rape; initiating research on hidden phenomena based on the process of naming.

    b. Restructuring language to be inclusive of women; rejecting the generic masculine and promoting a gender-free language system.

    c. Renaming and restructuring research topics, such as translating rape as an act of aggression rather than an expression of natural sexuality.

    d. Reducing the polarity between private and public in women's lives, such as renaming women's work, concepts of family, and the appropriate placement of these in private and public domains.

    e. Recognizing that language frames thought and vice versa; attention to syntax as power-driven, such as reversing the obligatory ordering of male/female, boy/girl, men/women.

6. *Promoting Social Activism toward the Goal of Societal Change*

    a. Reconceptualizing theories, methods, and goals to encompass possibilities for social change, toward reductions in power asymmetries and promotion of gender justice.

    b. Creating a science that will benefit rather than oppress women and that will correct as well as document prevalence of inequity, illness, violence, and so on.

    c. Remaining cognizant of how research results may be used, and promoting responsible applications of research findings.

    d. Directing personal involvement and action to initiate or support changes in policies, practices, and institutional structures that will benefit women and correct injustices.

*Source:* "Transforming Theory and Research with Women: Themes and Variations," by J. Worell and C. Etaugh, 1994, *Psychology of Women Quarterly, 18,* pp. 443–450. Reprinted with permission.

We do not reject established scientific criteria for valid research procedures, but we advance a step beyond. We agree with Anne Peplau and Eva Conrad (1989) that "all methods can be feminist," and that no research method is inherently feminist or nonfeminist. That is, bias due to the SEARCH (see Chapter 2) or other variables can be injected into research through any method, depending on how that method is applied.

Laboratory studies may be revealing if contextual and situational variables are considered. Controlled experimental methods are particularly useful when exploring evidence of bias in participants because of their attitudes or beliefs about another socially identified group. For example, in a carefully controlled experiment, Heather Bullock and Julian Fernald (1998) found that women and men tend to perceive sexual intent differently. Compared to women participants, men "rated women targets as more promiscuous and seductive regardless of clothing style, alcohol use, or social class status" (p. 12). This type of controlled study is useful in trying to understand differences in women's and men's interpretations of cross-gender interactions such as in heterosexual harassment and date rape.

Both quantitative and qualitative approaches may be appropriate for particular questions. Quantitative methods tend to use standardized or numerical measurement and statistical analysis based on probability theory, such as using the Null Hypothesis and alpha levels to determine the significance of group difference. Qualitative methods, anchored in women's voices, employ a wide range of alternative routes to exploring individual and group experience and may summarize their findings in terms of categories or themes rather than in numbers. The themes or categories of qualitative research may also be summarized into quantitative terms that can be submitted to standard statistical analyses. Both quantitative and qualitative approaches are frequently employed in the same study to provide alternative and expanded views of the topic under investigation. For example, Faye Crosby and I (JW) employed both intensive interviews and responses to written questionnaires to explore questions about whether feminist psychology professors "walk the talk" in their teaching practices and social activism (Crosby, Todd, & Worell, 1996; Kmeic, Crosby, & Worell, 1996). And yes, they do! Their responses to open-ended questions about activism, for example, resulted in a list of more than 40 different activities in which they participated, relating to interpersonal and community change from a feminist perspective.

Other researchers may approach a well-researched topic, such as female eating disorders, with a fresh point of view that integrates unexamined contextual variables of importance in the lives of women and measures them with both quantitative and intensive qualitative methods. For example, Niva Piran and her associates (1999) have been using multiple methods to explore factors that can help prevent the onset of eating disorders in adolescent girls. Starting with a pilot study to assess personal experiences, they analyzed process notes from more than 200 focus groups in which diverse samples of girls expressed feelings about their bodies. Three themes emerged: (a) violations of the body territory (such as sexual harassment); (b) prejudicial treatment (sexism, weightism, racism), and (c) the social construction of women, which leaves them feeling silenced and out of control of their lives. Building on these themes, the second step in the research program involved selecting a wide range of measures relevant to these issues and administering them to a large sample of 900 community women. Included in the assessment were scales for unwanted sexual attention, sexual coercion, childhood sexual abuse, marital or partner abuse, racism, sexism, heterosexism, self-silencing, self-esteem, body appearance, eating disorders, and health-related behaviors such as smoking, alcohol, self injury, and safer sex. Combined with analysis of these measures was an intensive interview procedure on life history events that might be associated with any of the variables measured quantitatively. Among all these measures, the "objectified experience of the body" was the strongest predictor of disordered eating (Piran, 2001, p. 375). These creative efforts demonstrate how a feminist approach to an issue of concern to many girls and women can be approached from a multiplicity of methods.

From the broad range of possible approaches to the study of women's lives, we developed the research themes and variations displayed in Table 10.3 (Worell & Etaugh, 1994). They are emergent, in that we are still in the process of shaping and refining them. They serve as goals or guideposts rather than as fixed principles. We remain open to further revision as new scholars and new data provide alternative visions of how better to define and clarify the feminist science agenda. The themes affirm the study of women in all their diversities as a legitimate activity, validate alternative approaches to inquiry, focus on the social construction of gender and ethnocultural identity, insist on attention to societal and power issues, open the selection of research topics and participants to broad and diverse populations, engage participants in a collaborative adventure, resist blaming women for their vulnerabilities, recognize the power of language to name women's experience, and openly declare the role of social change in designing and implementing psychological research. We view these themes and their variations as increasing the visibility of women and the realities of their lives into the knowledge base of the behavioral sciences. In considering women of all groups that were previously ignored and in opening up topics for research never before questioned, feminist-diversity research expands the domains of the feminist journey. It allows us to construct new realities in which women and men from all social locations may view themselves in a different light.

## Research Utilization

In graduate educational programs, feminist research reviews and renews the study of human behavior and the process of behavior change. In a feminist framework, new views of research are built on the foundations of traditional psychological knowledge to expand our understanding and interventions. Students are introduced to feminist, cross-cultural, and gender-related journals and are encouraged to build their own models of research using revised criteria for seeking topics and methods appropriate to their interests. Students are encouraged to explore their personal experience in the search for appropriate research questions, thus uncovering the hidden and personal and moving it into the realm of open and common experience. The research produced by graduate trainees thus reflects a reconstructed conception of women's and men's lives and feeds back in a recursive process into the furthering of new knowledge about human existence. Some of the most creative research on women and gender has been produced by students with whom we have been privileged to collaborate.

Research outcomes are also extrapolated to effect the public policies that govern the lives of women. These policies can include such concerns as education and employment equity, violence against women, reproductive freedom, child care and child custody arrangements, affordable housing, mental and physical health and hospitalization, criminal justice systems, law enforcement, sexuality, and the public media, as well as many other areas. Several examples follow.

As a public policy fellow at the American Psychological Association (APA), Jeanine Cogan (1997) collated the extant research on women's eating disorders and arranged for three feminist psychologists to testify in a briefing before a committee of the U.S. Congress in support of upcoming legislation on disordered eating. Another outstanding example of the dissemination of feminist research into public policy domains is the extensive report by members of the Society for the Psychology of Women, a division of the APA. Based on hundreds of published research studies, the published document, *Making Welfare to Work Really Work* (Rice & Wyche, 1998) included policy recommendations related to job training, child care, and intimate violence and was distributed to psychologists and policymakers at both state and federal levels. One of the outstanding goals of feminist research is to influence changes in the social and institutional structures that affect women's health and well-being.

## EVALUATING COUNSELING AND PSYCHOTHERAPY PROCESS AND OUTCOME

> Without theory, the facets of therapy that can be used to improve treatment will be difficult to identify. (Allen E. Kazdin, 2001)

Across the range of psychological interventions, there appear to be a number of factors that are common among them. Lambert and Bergin (1994) defined *common factors* as those dimensions that are not specific to any one mode of treatment. These factors include such variables as the therapeutic alliance, therapist warmth, attentiveness, credibility, and skill, as well as client expectancy effects, talk-time, and degree of engagement. To demonstrate the effectiveness of any particular approach, it is necessary to document that specific procedures beyond these common factors are responsible for client change (Stevens, Hynan, & Allen, 2000). Therein lies the challenge for feminist therapies.

As is true of most applied procedures, the development of feminist interventions at the scholarly and practice levels exceeds their empirical support. Some outcome studies have appeared for programs designed to treat specific conditions, such as childhood sexual abuse (Westbury & Tutty, 1999) or irritable bowel syndrome (Toner, Segal, Emmott, & Myron, 2000). The average feminist practitioner, however, typically treats a wide range of women's problems. We found relatively little research providing empirical support for most of the feminist approaches to intervention. What is the evidence that any of these feminist approaches to therapy are as effective as more traditional and established interventions?

If Empowerment Feminist Therapy (EFT) or any of the various forms of feminist therapy are to take their places among the major intervention approaches, it is essential to establish their accountability. By *accountability,* we mean providing assurance to those who receive, support, or are informed of these services, that specific interventions "work" and are effective in helping particular clients and/or communities to reach personal and social goals. Effectiveness studies relate to accountability by validating that some or all of the therapeutic goals have been accomplished. These goals vary, of course, with the type or level of intervention.

## Levels of Feminist Intervention

Although we have been discussing counseling and therapy throughout this book, we know that feminist interventions can occur in differing venues and in at least five different but overlapping levels: prevention, education, remediation, empowerment, and community change (Worell, 2001). Evaluation procedures for these levels of intervention may differ depending on the level and purpose of the intervention.

Prevention appears to be the most logical location at which to initiate change (R. M. Kaplan, 2000). The violence against women legislation during the 1980s was shown to increase the number of community-based remedial programs for woman-battering men (Gondolph, 1998). In turn, these programs were found to increase efforts across many communities to reduce violence against women (R. Tolman & Bennet, 1990). There are primary prevention programs that meet a feminist agenda, such as workshops for reducing sexual coercion and harassment in schools, colleges, and in the workplace. These programs are typically assessed with outcome data on attitude change or reduced incidence of noxious behaviors. Educational programs have been shown to modify gender and ethnocultural attitudes and behaviors. Chapter 12 discusses research designed to evaluate a feminist doctoral training program. Feminist remediation, empowerment, and community change all combine in the programs developed by rape crisis centers and battered spouse shelters. Outcome assessment on the effectiveness of these programs for women might be reflected in reduced hospital emergency room visits or increased community awareness campaigns. We note, however, that the construction and evaluation of prevention programs target general populations and are seldom informed by considerations of diversity.

We believe that for each client that we have discussed in this book, all five levels of intervention are incorporated by our EFT model. We educate clients with information about gender and ethnocultural relationships within societal institutional structures. We remediate distress with therapeutic techniques that teach clients how to manage stress, self-nurture, and problem-solve effectively. We empower clients by practicing all four of the EFT principles throughout the therapeutic encounter. We model and encourage community change strategies at both micro- and macrolevels; and we anticipate that the integration of all these strategies will assist clients in becoming more resilient, leading to improved skills in daily living and prevention of further distress. Thus, the five levels are interrelated and all are engaged in the process of EFT. Evaluation of outcomes and the effectiveness of feminist therapy, therefore, can occur singly or combined, within and across any of these levels.

Research on the effectiveness of psychotherapy suggests that a wide range of interventions may be helpful to clients with a variety of problems (Nathan & Gorman, 1998). Not all clients benefit equally, of course, and some may not be helped at all or may become worse following certain interventions. Sol Garfield (1992) pointed out that the complexity of evaluating the outcomes of therapeutic interventions is complicated by the existence of more than 200 kinds of psychotherapy. Further, many variables enter into the therapeutic process and may be targets of evaluation. These variables include characteristics of the clients (e.g., family and cultural background, severity and complexity of problems), the therapist (e.g., experience, persona style), the therapeutic alliance, presenting symptoms and concerns, the treatment setting, the purpose and length of intervention or treatment, and family and community support (Kazdin, 2001). Chapter 11 discusses some of the client characteristics that may influence client counselor interaction, such as gender and ethnicity, but many other variables influence this relationship as well. For feminist approaches, the complexity in evaluating outcomes is compounded by several additional factors.

## Challenges in Evaluating Feminist Therapy Outcomes

First, feminist outcome research presents a challenge in that feminist approaches to intervention are typically integrated within a number of dissimilar theoretical approaches (see Chapter 4). In designing an effectiveness study, identification of specific integrative approaches presents an obstacle unless all the counselors or therapists in the study apply the same theory to be combined with a feminist format. Second, many feminist practitioners are reluctant to apply the *Diagnostic and Statistical Manual of Mental Disorders, 4th Edition (DSM-IV)* psychiatric diagnoses that pathologize their clients, as expected in controlled clinical trials (Caplan, 1995; Lerman, 1996). A major issue in this context is the demonstrated gender or ethnocultural bias inherent in several *DSM* diagnostic categories (e.g., see Becker & Lamb, 1994, Chapter 4; Potts, Burnam, & Wells, 1991). Third, even in the feminist practice community, approaches to therapeutic intervention differ in some major ways. For example, in an open-ended interview study with a group of self-identified feminist therapists, Jeanne Marecek and Diane Kravetz (1996) found that many of the principles that characterize feminist-diversity interventions were not articulated, especially a commitment to social and structural change. Thus, aside from self-identification as a feminist therapist, effectiveness studies need to assess the specific beliefs and behaviors of their respondents by means of quantified measurement and/or direct observation. We discuss some of these approaches next.

## OPENING DOORS TO EVALUATION RESEARCH

The prospects for well-controlled effectiveness research in feminist practice are encouraging. At a minimum, three avenues of research are essential:

1. Identify the unique parameters of feminist practice by establishing reliable and valid measures of therapist beliefs and behaviors.
2. Identify measures or procedures to validate client experience of these behaviors.
3. Develop outcome assessments that extend beyond symptom reduction.

These assessments might cover positive and strength-reflecting variables such as optimism, resilience, quality of life, personal well-being, or empowerment. Once these assessment tools are available, they can be applied in the service of designing effective outcome research. In the following sections, we review a sample of research studies that were designed to measure the unique parameters of feminist therapy from the perspectives of both therapists and clients, and to assess the effectiveness of feminist practice using short- and long-term outcome data.

The first issue addresses a commonly stated view that feminist therapy or counseling is no different than any other "good therapy." In response to this concern, we review several studies that have developed instrumentation to compare the attitudes and behaviors of feminists with nonfeminists who practice counseling and psychotherapy.

### Therapist and Client Reports of Therapy Behaviors

As a preliminary step in the evaluation process, there is a clear need for assessment instruments to measure the behaviors and strategies employed by clinicians who practice feminist modes of therapy. Given such instrumentation, we can then proceed to examine the process of the therapeutic experience and to select or develop further measures to evaluate its outcomes. We summarize several structured rating scales that have been developed to elicit information directly from practitioners about their beliefs and behaviors. In many of these studies, researchers also developed measures to validate client experience of these behaviors (EFT Principle IV), thus integrating both objective and subjective methods.

First, in response to the aspects of family therapy that "reinforce a traditional, patriarchal value system," Laura Black and Fred Piercy (1991, p. 112) constructed the *Feminist Family Therapy Scale* (FFTS). This 17-item unidimensional scale contains general belief statements such as "Therapists reinforce traditional sex roles by not addressing them." The authors validated the scale by showing that FFTS scores were higher for respondents with more gender-related training and lower for respondents with high scores on a sexism inventory. Client validation of feminist behaviors would have been inappropriate with this scale, since the items reflect broad feminist views of the family rather than identifying specific therapist strategies.

At about the same time, Damon Robinson and I (JW) constructed the Therapy with Women Scale (TWS; D. Robinson & Worell, 1991) following an intensive review of the principles, beliefs, and strategies reported in the literature on feminist therapy. The TWS contains 40 declarative statements such as "I consider my clients' problems through a gender-role perspective." From the responses of a large randomized sample of both female and male practitioners, two factors were extracted; we named them *Empowerment of the Client* and *Advocacy for Women*. Both factors of the TWS discriminated between practitioners who identified as either feminist or woman-centered (FWC), and those who did not (NOT; D. Robinson, 1994). FWC therapists were also more likely than NOT to diagnose a sample case as Posttraumatic Stress Disorder rather than histrionic or borderline, suggesting that these therapists considered situational or environmental variables rather than internal pathology in their diagnostic decision-making (EFT Principle II).

In a follow-up study with 15 university counseling center therapists and a diverse group of their clients, we asked to what extent clients of feminist therapists experience in sessions the behaviors and strategies identified by their therapists. To validate client perceptions of their therapists' behavior in session, we constructed the Client Therapy with Women Scale (CTWS) to mirror the TWS statements of their therapists. The CTWS matches clients' reported experiences of the same behaviors their therapists' indicated on the TWS (e.g., "My therapist helps me explore my self-identity"). Regardless of variation across clients in referral problems and diagnoses, client and therapist responses did not differ significantly on 85% of the item ratings, suggesting that clients did experience in session most of the behaviors as reported by their therapists (Worell, Chandler. Robinson, & Blount, 1996). Thus, we were able to validate one critical aspect of feminist therapy as both an identifiable set of therapeutic strategies and a lived experience for clients. When employed as independent variables, either scale may be considered a measure of feminist therapist process. However, from a feminist standpoint, client report of session process may be a more clinically relevant measure than that of the therapist. On the TWS, therapists report their typical strategies across clients, whereas on the CTWS, clients report their personal experience with a particular provider.

From a more recent survey of practicing psychologists with a selected set of TWS items, six factors were extracted that characterized therapist behaviors. Five of the factors differentiated self-identified FWC from NOT groups: Affirming the Client, Taking a Gender-Role Perspective, Woman-Centered Activism, Therapist Self-Disclosure, and Egalitarian Stance. Similarly, FWC practitioners were more likely than NOT to endorse the following four goals for their clients that reflect feminist therapy goals: improved self-esteem and self-regard, improved well-being or quality of life, flexible use of gendered behaviors, and personal activism toward social change (Feminist Therapy Process and Outcomes, 1999).

Client experience in feminist therapy can also be assessed with the Feminist Frame Scale, which asks 43 specific questions about the therapy experience in the form of "Did your therapist ask you about . . ." (Piran, 1999). This scale revealed three major factors: Respectful Validation, Empowerment, and Unsilencing Trauma. Piran found that adherence to these three principles was significantly higher by feminist therapists than by either a humanistic or traditional therapist comparison group. Once again, clients validated their therapists' feminist stance. Finally, in a creative study on feminist therapy by Anne Cummings (1999), novice counselors were instructed and coached on the use of four feminist strategies:

1. Empowering the client.
2. Decreasing power differentials.
3. Exploring gender-role conflict.
4. Placing client concerns in a sociocultural context.

At the end of training, counselor scores on the TWS (D. Robinson & Worell, 1991) and their written diaries following each session confirmed that they were using feminist strategies. Further, client responses on the CTWS further confirmed that clients experienced these strategies in their sessions. These three studies corroborate that feminist therapy principles can be reliably measured, can be taught to novice counselors, are experienced as feminist by clients, and are more likely to be implemented by feminist, as compared to nonfeminist, practitioners.

We concluded that despite the variations among feminist therapists in theoretical stance, professional training, or years of experience, certain beliefs and behaviors are common across them and can be reliably assessed. Further, irrespective of differences in client presenting issues and clinical diagnoses, the feminist beliefs and behaviors of their therapists are experienced as such by their clients. These studies confirm our position that (a) feminist practitioners differ substantially in their beliefs and self-reported behaviors from nonfeminists, (b) they communicate these beliefs and behaviors to their clients, and (c) these therapist differences can be measured reliably.

## Measures for Assessing Outcomes of Feminist Interventions

The crux of assessment for accountability rests with the availability of instruments appropriate to the goals of the intervention. For traditional interventions such as those based on a medical model, assessment tools are selected based on client diagnosis, such as assessing for depression. However, since desirable outcomes in feminist therapy are based only partially on symptom reduction, feminist goals require creative new strategies for evaluating outcomes. Although feminist therapists aim to reduce personal distress, they tend to focus on client strengths rather than deficits. As we discussed in Chapters 1 and 3, they regard symptoms as adaptive strategies in the context of an oppressive environment (Wyche & Rice, 1997). An overall goal is to affirm client empowerment. The experience of empowerment prepares individuals to confront and deal with both internal and external threats to their current and future well-being. Standard measures of therapy outcome that assess only symptom reduction are therefore unsuitable for most feminist therapy goals.

Several collaborative research programs are in the process of developing assessment tools that measure women's empowerment (e.g., PPS-R; Worell & Chandler, 1999) and women's socialized roles (the Gender Socialization Scale; Toner, 1999). Using such measures, a number of studies have reported data on feminist psychotherapy outcomes that show clear support for creative new assessments of women's experience and women's empowerment (Cummings, 1999; D. M. Johnson, 2001; Worell et al., in press).

For example, Worell et al. (in press) used the 32-item objective measure of empowerment (PPS) based on the ten goals of the empowerment model presented in Chapter 1 to assess outcomes for adult women in counseling with feminist and woman-centered therapists. Following either brief therapy (four sessions or fewer) or extended therapy (more than seven sessions), clients reported moderate to high scores on the PPS, suggesting that even brief intervention from a feminist perspective can impact a sense of personal empowerment. In a long-term follow-up of feminist therapy outcomes (Chandler, Worell, Johnson, Blount, & Lusk, 1999), scores on the PPS correlated well with client self-ratings of improvement over time. Scores on the PPS also increased over time significantly more than scores on a standard measure of personal well-being. In both studies, women's written reactions indicated that they experienced progress on most components of the empowerment goals. We were encouraged to find support for the empowerment model as a template for women's well-being and as a useful tool in the evaluation of feminist therapy outcomes.

A serious limitation of this research was a study sample that was primarily White and middle class. To address the need for more culturally sensitive measures, we revised the scale to address each respondent's personal identities. Dawn Johnson (2001) tested a revised multicultural version of the PPS (PPS-R) with a diverse college, clinical, and community sample. Through factor analysis, she was able to validate factors for 8 of the 10 empowerment goals. The results of these studies would not be evident had we used more traditional measures that assess only symptom reduction.

Finally, from a more qualitative approach, Angela Browne developed a Strengths Assessment Inventory for evaluation and intervention with battered women. The measure addresses the self-perceived strengths of the battered woman, recognizes the woman as an expert on herself, and identifies coping skills and personal resources that these women may have to deal with trauma and abuse (cited in Gondolph, 1998).

## CONCLUSIONS

Researchers have just begun to explore the process and outcomes of feminist therapy. We are left with more questions than answers. An overall task for researchers in this arena is to validate the applied practices of feminist therapists with research that establishes the effectiveness of their procedures for women's well-being. We envision many challenges to this research.

First, we emphasize the continuing search for more valid and reliable instruments to assess the process, content, and outcomes of feminist therapy. The measures we report here are exploratory in that their application is untested for diverse groups and cultures, for whom empowerment and well-being may have very different meanings. These instruments need to be assessed directly with carefully selected groups who differ in their language expression and cultural expectations.

We need to move away from symptom-focused research toward more inclusive variables that predict personal strength and empowerment, positive thriving, resilience in the face of stress, and maintenance of psychological well-being over time. Symptom-focused practice has been shown to result in immediate relief, but high relapse rates. In contrast, we need to articulate useful and testable models of the healthy woman in a healthy environment and work toward achieving this goal.

Next, we need to envision more sophisticated measures of the therapy outcomes that extend beyond simple symptom reduction. Our approach to well-being is promising, but reflects a particular model of women's psychological well-being. As well, we need more research on feminist intervention with specific diagnoses and presenting problems.

We also need to initiate dismantling studies that can reveal which components of feminist therapy are most and least effective. Since feminist therapy providers function from a variety of other theoretical perspectives, it is important that we evaluate their effectiveness when compared with one another.

Finally, we need to initiate more training programs in which feminist therapy is at least one modality of education in how to provide skilled, ethical, and caring service to individuals in pain and distress. At the present time, only a few graduate programs in the United States provide training in feminist approaches to research and intervention. We challenge both researchers and practitioners to contribute their expertise and their energy to filling this void. Chapter 12 discusses our conception of a viable training program for feminist psychological practitioners and presents research that supports the effectiveness of programs that educate for gender and diversity.

## SUMMARY

We have reviewed the basis for traditional and feminist approaches to research. Some of the traditional scientific values and procedures in research include objectivity, reliability, validity, generalizability, replicability, and independence of the researcher from the "object" of study. Bias due to SEARCH variables in past and current research includes topics and content, formulation of hypotheses, sample selection and inclusiveness, methodology, sex and ethnicity of researchers, and statistical analysis and dissemination of the research.

We discussed some of the feminist revisions in approaches to research, which are based on the position that values enter into all science and should be made explicit rather than remain unacknowledged. We offered a model of feminist themes and variations in research that aims to transform the traditional agenda. The final section considered issues in the evaluation of process and outcomes for feminist counseling and psychotherapy. We reviewed some recent approaches to measurement of the process of feminist therapy, of client experience of this process, and of the outcomes of feminist therapy that extend beyond symptom reduction. An agenda for further research on feminist process and outcome is needed.

## ACTIVITIES

1. Go to the library or your own bookshelf and review an entire recent issue of the following two journals: *Psychology of Women Quarterly* and *Sex Roles*. Who is

the editor of each journal? Who publishes in these journals? To what extent do they contain topics related to the SEARCH variables?

2. Select one article from each journal and answer the following questions:
   a. What was the general topic?
   b. Where was the study conducted?
   c. What population was used?
   d. What were the general methods used?
   e. How were the results interpreted?
   f. How did these and other studies in these journals differ from any you have read in more traditional journals?

## FURTHER READINGS

Crawford, M. C., & Kimmel, E. B. (1999). Promoting methodological diversity in feminist research. *Psychology of Women Quarterly, 23,* 1–6.

Crawford, M. C., & Kimmel, E. B. (2001). Methods for studying gender. In J. Worell (Ed.), *Encyclopedia of women and gender: Sex similarities and differences and the impact of society on gender* (pp. 749–758). San Diego, CA: Academic Press.

Peplau, L. A., & Conrad, E. (1989). Beyond nonsexist research: The peril of feminist methods in psychology. *Psychology of Women Quarterly, 13,* 379–400.

Worell, J. (1996). Opening doors to feminist research. *Psychology of Women Quarterly, 20,* 469–486.

Worell, J., & Etaugh, C. (1994). Transforming theory and research with women: Themes and variations. *Psychology of Women Quarterly, 18,* 443–450.

# Chapter 11 ————————————————————————

# *EXPLORING ETHICS AND PRACTICE ISSUES*

> *All ethical acts must be understood within sociopolitical contexts. . . . When an ethical person discerns a wrong against an individual or a group, he or she is obligated to act.*
>
> Mary Brabeck and Kathleen Ting, 2000, pp. 28–29

> *. . . almost every cultural tradition is oppressive to women; insofar as any tradition is destructive to women, it is not to be respected but changed so that it will offer full human rights to women.*
>
> Susan Contratto and Jane Hassinger, 1995, p. 129

## SELF-ASSESSMENT: ETHICAL ISSUES

For the following client case: (a) Identify possible or potential ethical violations using the standard of the ethical guidelines of your profession; (b) review the four principles of Empowerment Feminist Therapy (EFT); and (c) identify possible or potential violations of the four EFT principles. What would be the advantages and disadvantages for the client if the client's second therapist is a female? A male? A person of color? If the client is a lesbian woman and the therapist is a heterosexual woman? If possible, discuss your answers with a colleague or in small groups in class.

> You have had eight counseling sessions with an adult survivor of childhood sexual abuse. In her last session, she disclosed having had a sexual experience with her previous White, male therapist while in therapy with him. She felt uncomfortable with the experience and terminated counseling. She feels guilty and responsible about the encounter, saying she didn't physically resist and must have sent him "come on" signals. She has disclosed to you because she didn't want to be secretive, but she doesn't want to pursue the matter with an ethics or licensing board.

## OVERVIEW

In this chapter, we explore some of the issues associated with practicing feminist-diversity therapy. We begin by focusing on ethical issues. The unique perspectives that a feminist orientation brings to the field of ethics are delineated. A feminist decision-making model is presented. Then, several feminist therapy guidelines/ethical principles relevant to the practice of EFT are described, and we summarize the commonalities in these guidelines. Next, we discuss ethical and practice issues that have special relevance for feminist therapists. In these latter sections, our approach is to raise tough questions and review a variety of perspectives on these issues. Our goal is to stimulate your thinking about these issues and to facilitate you in reaching your own conclusions. After reading Chapter 11, you will be able to:

1. Describe feminist perspectives of ethics and a feminist model of ethical decision making.
2. List several practice guidelines relevant to counseling diverse women.
3. Incorporate a feminist therapy perspective into your own professional code of ethics.
4. Understand the debilitating effects on clients of therapists' sexual misconduct.
5. Analyze the potential problems that may accompany overlapping relationships with clients.
6. Recognize the influences of social locations' power on the counseling relationship.
7. Reach your own decisions about difficult practice issues, such as overlapping relationships, self-identifying professional labels, and conflicts between client and counselor therapy goals.

The structure, perspective, and resources we bring to this chapter are tied to our training and practice as psychologists. For example, several of the guidelines we present come from psychological organizations. Our basic understanding of professional ethics is rooted in the Ethical Principles of the American Psychological Association (1992). Because many of you come from different mental health professions, we have decided to stay in the limits of our expertise by offering these psychologist-oriented materials and perspectives as samples of ways to approach the questions explored in this chapter. We encourage you to review your own codes of professional ethics, to evaluate the strengths and weaknesses of those documents from a feminist-diversity therapy viewpoint, and to integrate the principles of EFT into your applications of your profession's ethical code.

## ETHICAL ISSUES

### Feminist Perspectives on Ethics

Many writers (e.g., Brabeck & Ting, 2000; Mahalik, Van Ormer, & Simi, 2000; Meara & Day, 2000) have asserted that ethics should attend to more than what not to do and should not focus primarily on ethical dilemmas. They described a higher level of ethics that focuses on desirable ethical behaviors toward which therapists should aim, that is, "aspirational ethics" (Mahalik et al., 2000, p. 198) or "feminist moral vision" (Meara &

Day, 2000, p. 256). Feminist aspirational ethics include: (a) maintaining a therapeutic relationship that is conducted for the welfare of the client, (b) attending to counselor self-care, (c) being inclusive of diverse value orientations, (d) collaborating and sharing power with clients, (e) self-reflecting on the impacts of social locations and values positions, (f) attending to oppressive power structures and dynamics, (g) valuing the uniqueness of all people, (h) reducing the effects of oppression and privilege in ourselves and others, (i) honoring the importance of human relationships, (j) using phenomenological and empathic approaches to understanding the life of each woman in its cultural context, (k) honoring experiential, intuitive knowledge, (l) working to achieve social justice, and (m) moving beyond remediating dysfunctions to embracing empowerment (Brabeck & Ting, 2000; Mahalik et al., 2000; Meara & Day, 2000). Table 11.1 lists five feminist ethic themes identified by Brabeck and Ting (2000). These feminist inspirational ethics reflect EFT's four principles. Among these feminist inspirational ethics, social justice is considered a hallmark of feminist-diversity ethical approaches. Valuing social justice involves a moral responsibility to critique all societal discrimination and to reduce various forms of oppression. Empowerment Feminist Therapists have an obligation to take action once they become aware of inequities.

## Ethical Challenges in Integrating Feminist and Multicultural Perspectives

### Theoretical Dilemmas

As described in several chapters, EFT and multicultural/diversity approaches share several assumptions and perspectives. For example, both view women's lives through a contextual lens that recognizes the complex and intersecting impacts of various forms of oppressions (sexism, ethnocentrism, ableism and ageism, racism, classism, and heterosexism [SEARCH] variables), respects cultural diversity, analyzes power dynamics in human relationships and institutions, emphasizes the importance of therapist self-awareness, and stresses the importance of social action (Sparks & Park, 2000). Thus, many of the feminist ethical aspirations discussed previously are also ideals for diversity therapists.

However, differences also exist between the values of multicultural and feminist approaches. For example, feminist values are viewed by some as individualistic while

**Table 11.1    Five feminist ethical themes**

1. The assumption that women and their experiences have moral significance.
2. The assertion that attentiveness, subjective knowledge, can illuminate moral issues.
3. The claim that a feminist critique of male distortion must be accompanied by a critique of all discriminatory distortions.
4. The admonition that feminist ethics engage in analysis of the context and attend to the power dynamics of that context.
5. The injunction that feminist ethics require action directed at achieving social justice.

*Source:* "Feminist Ethics: Lenses for Examining Ethical Psychological Practice" (pp. 17–35), by M. M. Brabeck and K. Ting, 2000, in *Practicing Feminist Ethics in Psychology,* M. M. Brabeck (Ed.), Washington, DC: American Psychological Association. Copyright © 2000.

multicultural orientations are more likely to embrace collectivism. Thus, ethical conflicts can arise between multicultural and feminist values for therapists who embrace both orientations. Further, ethical conflicts can occur in a feminist approach and in a multicultural approach. For instance, feminist therapists value challenging oppressive societal practices, and they also value being respectful of clients' values. Similarly, multicultural therapists value being aware of the impact of culture on individual experience, and they also value being sensitive to individuals' cultural values. For both groups of therapists, these sets of values can come into conflict, especially when the cultural context condones the oppression of women. Elizabeth Sparks and Aileen Park (2000) referred to these ethical dilemmas or conflicts as "borderland" issues (p. 204). "Feminist practitioners enter the metaphorical borderland when they must decide how to act in situations where a womans or man's adherence to cultural norms and values is jeopardizing her or his psychological or physical well-being" (p. 212).

This conflict between culture and feminist values is often found in the setting of goals for therapy. Throughout this book, we address the importance of client self-determination and collaborative goal setting by the client and counselor. Collaborative goal setting is a relatively easy process when the client and counselor agree on the direction of therapy. However, major difficulties may arise when our clients want to achieve therapy goals that violate our feminist values. For example, encountering a client whose therapy goal is to lose weight may be challenging for an EFT therapist. Understanding the impact of cultural messages that extol thinness and objectify women's bodies, the EFT therapist's goals would be for this client to accept and love her body as it is and to treat her body in a more physically healthy way. While these goal discrepancies can be navigated, resolving them can be challenging.

## Resolving Borderland Dilemmas

While the borderlands are difficult territory for both feminist and multicultural therapists to navigate, Sparks and Park (2000) offered several landmarks or strategies for dealing with these dilemmas. Their landmarks are displayed in Table 11.2 and can be viewed as a part of aspirational ethics. Additionally, in the next section, we introduce a model for feminist ethical decision making to resolve these borderland dilemmas.

While borderland issues require sensitivity and creativity to resolve, many feminist practitioners believe there are cultural values that must be challenged. For example, Olivia Espin (1994) asserted that violence against women is always unacceptable no

---

**Table 11.2   Landmarks to navigate through ethical borderlands**

Landmark 1: Understanding the cultural context of the client.

Landmark 2: Awareness of oppressive forces in U.S. cultural context and their impact on clients.

Landmark 3: Enhancing counselor self-awareness of values.

Landmark 4: Flexibility in determining solutions.

*Source:* "The Integration of Feminism and Multiculturalism: Ethical Dilemmas at the Border" (pp. 203–224), by E. E. Sparks and A. H. Park, 2000, in *Practicing Feminist Ethics in Psychology,* M. M. Brabeck (Ed.), Washington, DC: American Psychological Association.

matter what specific cultural values may apply. Similarly, Contratto and Hassinger (1995) declared that all feminists decry tolerance for violence against women, and cultural sensitivity does not mean giving "universal respect" (p. 147). This perspective is compatible with those that we articulated in Chapter 3 when we discussed our decision rules for integrating EFT with a diversity perspective. There we asserted that all cultures have both positive and toxic elements.

## GUIDELINES RELEVANT TO COUNSELING WOMEN

Several professional groups have adopted guidelines for competent and ethical practice for diverse groups. We begin by presenting some of these guidelines and then summarizing their commonalities.

### American Psychological Association's Principles Concerning the Counseling and Psychotherapy of Women

The Division of Counseling Psychology of the American Psychological Association adopted the 13 Principles Concerning the Counseling/Psychotherapy of Women in 1978 (see Table 11.3; Fitzgerald & Nutt, 1986). In brackets following each of the 13 principles, we have added the numbers of the EFT principles that pertain. These 13 principles stress the importance of therapists being knowledgeable about the effects of sexism on female clients and on the therapeutic relationship, and being aware of their own values and personal functioning. As this book goes to press, these guidelines are being revised by a joint task force of two divisions of the American Psychological Association: the Society for the Psychology of Women and the Division of Counseling Psychology.

### Feminist Therapy Network Code of Ethics

The introductory section of the Feminist Therapy Network's Code of Ethics (1988) is shown in Table 11.4. The table also includes a summary of four subsequent specific issues that are addressed by the code.

### Feminist Therapy Institute Code of Ethics

The Feminist Therapy Code of Ethics, developed by the Feminist Therapy Institute (1987), consists of a preamble and five ethical guidelines for feminist therapy practice. The preamble stresses the importance of applying feminist analyses of the effects of sexism on client issues and understanding both the internal and external aspects of client issues. The five ethical guidelines, shown in Table 11.5, address cultural diversities and oppressions, power differentials, overlapping relationships, therapist accountability, and social change.

### Guidelines for Psychotherapy with Lesbian, Gay, and Bisexual Clients

In 2000, the American Psychological Association Council of Representatives adopted the Guidelines for Psychotherapy with Lesbian, Gay, and Bisexual Clients, which are depicted in Table 11.6. These guidelines were developed by the Division 44 Committee on Lesbian,

**Table 11.3    Principles concerning the counseling/psychotherapy of women**

*Principle I.* Counselors/therapists should be knowledgeable about women, particularly with regard to biological, psychological, and social issues which have impact on women in general or on particular groups of women in our society. (EFT Principles, I, II, IV)

*Principle II.* Counselors/therapists are aware that the assumptions and precepts of theories relevant to their practice may apply differently to men and women. Counselors/therapists are aware of those theories and models that prescribe or limit the potential of women clients, as well as those that may have particular usefulness for women clients. (EFT Principles I, II, III, IV)

*Principle III.* After formal training, counselors/therapists continue to explore and learn of issues related to women, including the special problems of female subgroups, throughout their professional careers. (EFT Principles I, II, III, IV)

*Principle IV.* Counselors/therapists recognize and are aware of all forms of oppression and how these interact with sexism. (EFT Principles I, II)

*Principle V.* Counselors/therapists are knowledgeable and aware of verbal and nonverbal process variables (particularly with regard to power in the relationship) as these affect women in counseling/therapy so that the counselor/therapist interactions are not adversely affected. The need for shared responsibility between clients and counselors/therapists is acknowledged and implemented. (EFT Principles I, II, III)

*Principle VI.* Counselors/therapists have the capability of utilizing skills that are particularly facilitative to women in general and to particular subgroups of women. (EFT Principles I, II, III, IV)

*Principle VII.* Counselors/therapists ascribe no preconceived limitations on the direction or nature of potential changes or goals in counseling/therapy for women. (EFT Principles I, II, III, IV)

*Principle VIII.* Counselors/therapists are sensitive to circumstances where it is more desirable for a woman client to be seen by a female or male counselor/therapist. (EFT Principles I, II, III, IV)

*Principle IX.* Counselors/therapists use nonsexist language in counseling/therapy, supervision, teaching, and journal publication. (EFT Principles I, II, IV)

*Principle X.* Counselors/therapists do not engage in sexual activity with their women clients under any circumstances. (EFT Principles I, II, III)

*Principle XI.* Counselors/therapists are aware of and continually review their own values and biases and the effects of these on their women clients. Counselors/therapists understand the effects of sex-role socialization upon their own development and functioning and the consequent values and attitudes they hold for themselves and others. They recognize that behaviors and roles need not be sex-based. (EFT Principles I, II, III)

*Principle XII.* Counselors/therapists are aware of how their personal functioning may influence their effectiveness in counseling/therapy with women clients. They monitor their functioning through consultation, supervision, or therapy so that it does not adversely affect their work with women clients. (EFT Principles I, II, III)

*Principle XIII.* Counselors/therapists support the elimination of sex bias within institutions and individuals. (EFT Principles I, II)

*Source:* Adapted from "The Division 17 Principles Concerning the Counseling/Psychotherapy of Women: Rational and Implementation," by L. F. Fitzgerald and R. Nutt, 1986, *Counseling Psychologist, 14,* pp. 180–216.

**Table 11.4    Feminist therapy network code of ethics**

I. *Introductory Section*
   1. The name of the organization is the Feminist Therapy Network.
   2. A Feminist Therapy Network member is expected to adhere to the Code of Ethics of whichever professional societies she is a member.

      As feminist therapists we assume the following principles in therapy practice with clients:
      (a) Feminist therapy is directed toward growth, self-actualization, and self-empowerment.
      (b) Feminist therapy affirms the importance of the process of dealing with the following issues: ageism, sexism, heterosexism, racism, and classism.
   3. Feminist therapy emphasizes the importance of sharing of common experiences among women and among men, to contribute to the changing dialogue between women, between men, and between sexes.
   4. Feminist therapy supports the formation of nonexploitive relationships which are more equal and respectful, including those with children, parents, partners, and friends.
   5. Feminist therapy values and requires a relationship between client and therapist which is nonauthoritarian and in which the therapist serves as facilitator, advocate, and educator.

II. *Summary of Specific Issues*
   1. Friendship and boundaries

      The differences between friend and therapy relationships are noted. Therapists are prohibited from doing therapy with a friend and are warned of the complexities of posttherapy friendships.
   2. Sexuality in and out of therapy

      Therapists are prohibited from engaging in sexual contact in therapy and are cautioned about the problems associated with posttherapy sexual relationships. It is recommended that *at least* six months elapse between the end of therapy and the beginning of a sexual relationship.
   3. Touching

      The healing power of and potential problems with touch are discussed. The importance of respect for the client is stressed. They suggest using discussions of appropriate touching, exploration of boundary issues for both client and therapist, getting permission for physical contact, and stopping any kind of self-abusive behavior.
   4. Business ethics: Barter guidelines
      The use of barter in psychotherapy is opposed.

*Source:* Adapted from *Feminist Therapy Network Code of Ethics,* 1988, Milwaukee, WI: Author.

**Table 11.5    Feminist therapy code of ethics: Ethical guidelines for feminist therapists**

I. Cultural Diversities and Oppressions (Feminist Therapy Principles I, II)

   A. A feminist therapist increases her accessibility to and for a wide range of clients from her own and other identified groups through flexible delivery of services. When appropriate, the feminist therapists assists clients in accessing other services.

   B. A feminist therapist is aware of the meaning and impact of her own ethnic and cultural background, gender, class, and sexual orientation, and actively attempts to become knowledgeable about alternatives from sources other than her clients. The therapist's goal is to uncover and respect cultural and experiential differences.

   C. A feminist therapist evaluates her ongoing interactions with her clientele for any evidence of the therapist's biases or discriminatory attitudes and practice. The feminist therapist accepts responsibility for taking action to confront and change any interfering or oppressing biases she has.

II. Power Differentials

   A. A feminist therapist acknowledges the inherent power differentials between client and therapist, and models effective use of personal power. In using the power differential to the benefit of the client, she does not take control or power which rightfully belongs to her client.

   B. A feminist therapist discloses information to the client which facilitates the therapeutic process. The therapist is responsible for using self-disclosure with purpose and discretion in the interests of the client.

   C. A feminist therapist negotiates and renegotiates formal and/or informal contacts with clients in an ongoing mutual process.

   D. A feminist therapist educates her clients regarding their rights as consumers of therapy, including procedures for resolving differences and filing grievances.

III. Overlapping Relationships

   A. A feminist therapist recognizes the complexity and conflicting priorities inherent in multiple or overlapping relationships. The therapist accepts responsibility for monitoring such relationships to prevent potential abuse of or harm to the client.

   B. A feminist therapist is actively involved in her community. As a result, she is especially sensitive about confidentiality. Recognizing that her client's concerns and general well-being are primary, she self-monitors both public and private statements and comments.

   C. A feminist therapist does not engage in sexual intimacies nor any overtly or covertly sexualized behaviors with a client or former client.

IV. Therapist Accountability

   A. A feminist therapist works only with those issues and clients within the realm of her competencies.

   B. A feminist therapist recognizes her personal and professional needs, and utilizes ongoing self-evaluation, peer support, consultation, supervision, continuing education, and/or personal therapy to evaluate, maintain, and improve her work with clients, her competencies, and her emotional well-being.

*(continued)*

**Table 11.5**    *(Continued)*

   C. A feminist therapist continually reevaluates her training, theoretical background, and research to include developments in feminist knowledge. She integrates feminism into psychological theory, receives ongoing therapy training, and acknowledges the limits of her competencies.

   D. A feminist therapist engages in self-care activities in an ongoing manner. She acknowledges her own vulnerabilities and seeks to care for herself outside of the therapy setting. She models for the ability and willingness to self-nurture in appropriate and self-empowering ways.

V. Social Change

   A. A feminist therapist actively questions other therapeutic practices in her community that appear abusive to clients or therapists, and when possible, intervenes as early as appropriate or feasible, or assists clients in intervening when it is facilitative to their growth.

   B. A feminist therapist seeks multiple avenues for impacting change, including public education and advocacy within professional organizations, lobbying for legislative actions, and other appropriate activities.

*Source:* The Feminist Therapy Institute, Inc., 1987. Used with permission.

Gay, and Bisexual Concerns Joint Task Force on Guidelines for Psychotherapy with Lesbian, Gay, and Bisexual Clients (JTF; see the task force's description of these guidelines, 2000). The JTF described these guidelines as "aspirational in intent" (p. 1440).

## Guidelines for Culturally Competent Practice, Education and Training, and Research

The Guidelines for Culturally Competent Practice, Education and Training, and Research were developed by a task force of the Division of Counseling Psychology of the American Psychological Association and will be submitted to APA Council of Representatives for approval in the near future. Because a main focus of this book is the integration of multicultural and feminist perspectives, we include these guidelines although they had not been officially approved at the time of publication of this book. (See Table 11.7 for a summary of the major tenets for culturally competent psychological practice.) These guidelines use a narrow definition of *multicultural,* which is limited to racially and ethnically diverse clients. Gender, sexual orientation, disability, age, and class are not included.

## Commonalities among the Guidelines

The five sets of guidelines we presented have several similarities. First, all incorporate aspects of the four EFT principles. Indeed, the first three seem to be ways to integrate EFT principles into an ethical code. The guidelines give specific definitions to the more general professional ethical principles of competence, confidentiality, client welfare, and counselor responsibility. Second, all the guidelines focus on the importance of acquiring special knowledge and skills related to counseling diverse populations. Third,

**Table 11.6   Guidelines for psychotherapy with lesbian, gay, and bisexual clients**

*Guidelines*

1. Psychologist understand that homosexuality and bisexuality are not indicative of mental illness.

2. Psychologists are encouraged to recognize how their attitudes and knowledge about lesbian, gay, and bisexual issues may be relevant to assessment and treatment and seek consultation or make appropriate referrals when indicated.

3. Psychologists strive to understand the ways in which social stigmatization (i.e., prejudice, discrimination, and violence) poses risks to the mental health and well-being of lesbian, gay, and bisexual clients.

4. Psychologists strive to understand how inaccurate or prejudicial views of homosexuality or bisexuality may affect the client's presentation in treatment and the therapeutic process.

5. Psychologists strive to be knowledgeable about and respect the importance of lesbian, gay, and bisexual relationships.

6. Psychologists strive to understand the particular circumstances and challenges faced by lesbian, gay, and bisexual parents.

7. Psychologists recognize that the families of lesbian, gay, and bisexual people may include people who are not legally or biologically related.

8. Psychologists strive to understand how a person's homosexual or bisexual orientation may have an impact on his or her family of origin and the relationship to that family of origin.

9. Psychologists are encouraged to recognize the particular life issues or challenges that are related to multiple and often conflicting cultural norms, values, and beliefs that lesbian, gay, and bisexual members of racial and ethnic minorities face.

10. Psychologists are encouraged to recognize the particular challenges that bisexual individuals experience.

11. Psychologists strive to understand the special problems and risks that exist for lesbian, gay, and bisexual youth.

12. Psychologists consider generational differences with lesbian, gay, and bisexual populations and the particular challenges that lesbian, gay, and bisexual older adults may experience.

13. Psychologists are encouraged to recognize the particular challenges that lesbian, gay, and bisexual individuals experience with physical, sensory, and cognitive-emotional disabilities.

14. Psychologists support the provision of professional education and training on lesbian, gay, and bisexual issues.

15. Psychologists are encouraged to increase their knowledge and understanding of homosexuality and bisexuality through continuing education, training, supervision, and consultation.

16. Psychologists make reasonable efforts to familiarize themselves with relevant mental health, educational, and community resources for lesbian, gay, and bisexual people.

*Source:* "Guidelines for Psychotherapy with Lesbian, Gay, and Bisexual Clients," Division 44/Committee on Lesbian, Gay, and Bisexual Concerns Joint Task Force on Guidelines for Psychotherapy with Lesbian, Gay, and Bisexual Clients (JTF), 2000, *American Psychologist, 55,* pp. 1440–1451. Reprinted with permission.

**Table 11.7    Guidelines for culturally-competent psychological practice**

The practicing psychologist shall:

1. Make a lifelong commitment to maintaining cultural expertise.
2. Continually develop awareness of issues of discrimination and oppression (e.g., racism, sexism, homophobia) that clients might experience and develop an understanding of how these issues relate to presenting psychological concerns. In addition, psychologists are urged to find ways to address and dismantle oppression as part of their responsibility as competent professionals.
3. Pay special attention to the unique worldview and cultural backgrounds of clients.
4. Recognize the client-in-context.
5. Recognize that contextual therapy may often require nontraditional interventions.
6. Examine traditional practice interventions for their cultural appropriateness (e.g., person-centered, cognitive-behavioral, psychodynamic) and contextual awareness.
7. Receive ongoing feedback and assessment on personal cultural competence. Such review shall include the following mechanisms: peer review; review of one's practice by members of the community with special attention to multicultural issues; client evaluation; working on a team of culturally diverse professionals so that feedback becomes part of the work setting.
8. Affirm the importance of empirical research to culturally competent practice.

*Source: Guidelines for Culturally Competent Practice,* Task Force of Division 17, Washington, DC: American Psychological Association, 2001.

most of the guidelines address the importance of therapists knowing themselves, resolving their own personal issues that may harm clients, and being aware of, and open about, their value systems.

The guidelines presented here also have several differences. These approaches vary in the level of specificity of the issues addressed and in whether they are gender-inclusive. Three are labeled *guidelines for psychotherapy* while the other two are labeled *ethical codes.*

We are concerned that diverse client counseling needs are being addressed in three separate sets of guidelines (women, LGB, and multicultural) because individual clinicians must integrate them before they can be used with clients who have diverse multiple subordinate social locations. Further, many diverse social locations (e.g., clients with disabilities, clients living in poverty) are not addressed by these guidelines. While we believe these three sets of guidelines are important improvements toward ethical practice, we believe there is much more work to be done.

## A FEMINIST MODEL FOR ETHICAL DECISION MAKING

Feminist ethics can provide perspectives for dealing with conflicts between ethical principles or with conflicts between ethical codes, legal codes, counselor values, or client values. Resolution of ethical dilemmas requires having a way to apply ethical principles (Hill, Glaser, & Harden, 1995). We believe the Feminist Model for Ethical Decision Making presented in Table 11.8 is an excellent tool for choosing how to handle ethical

**Table 11.8   Feminist ethical decision-making model**

| Rational-Evaluative Process | Feeling-Intuitive Process |
| --- | --- |
| *Recognizing a Problem* | |
| Information from therapist's knowledge; advice from supervisor or colleague. | Uncertainty about how to proceed in situation. |
| | Identify what stands in the way of working through the problem; feelings about the nature of the issue; feelings about the consultant or about asking for help. |
| *(Decision to consult may occur here)* | |
| *Defining the Problem* | |
| What is the conflict? Who are the players? What are the relevant standards? (rules, codes, principles) | What else is my discomfort about? What do my feelings tell me about the situation? What am I worried about? |
| What personal characteristics and cultural values do I bring to this decision? How do these factors influence my definition of the problem? | |
| How does the client define the problem? | What are the client's feelings about the dilemma? |
| *(Decision to consult may occur here)* | |
| What personal characteristics, values does the consultant bring to this process? | How do the consultant's characteristics affect me? |
| *Developing Solutions* | |
| Brainstorm possibilities. Cost-benefit analysis. Prioritize values. | What do my reactions to each choice tell me? |
| *Choosing a Solution* | |
| What is the best fit emotionally and rationally? Does this solution meet everyone's needs, including mine? Can I implement and live with the effects? | |
| *Reviewing Process* | |
| Would I want to be treated this way? | Does the decision feel right? |
| Is the decision universalizable? Would this decision withstand the scrutiny of others? | Have I given myself time to let reservations emerge? |
| How are my values, personal characteristics influencing my choice? How am I using my power? | Does the manner in which I carry out this decision fit my style? |
| Have I taken the client's perspective into account? | |

*(continued)*

**Table 11.8**   *(Continued)*

| Rational-Evaluative Process | Feeling-Intuitive Process |
|---|---|
| *Implementing and Evaluating the Decision* | |
| Carry out the decision. | Is this solution the best I can do? |
| Observe consequences. | |
| Reassess the decision. | Does the outcome continue to feel right? |
| How has this decision affected the therapeutic process? | |
| *Continuing Reflection* | |
| What did I learn? | Have I changed as a result of this process? How? |
| What would I do differently? | How might this experience affect me in the future? |

*Source:* "A Feminist Model for Ethical Decision Making" by M. Hill, K. Glaser, and J. Harden, 1995. In E. J. Rave and C. C. Larsen (Eds.), *Ethical Decision Making in Therapy: Feminist Perspectives*. New York: Guilford Press. Reprinted with permission.

conflicts in a way that is compatible with EFT principles. Marcia Hill, Kristin Glaser, and Judy Harden have based this model on the following assumptions: (a) There is no one right strategy for resolving an ethical conflict; (b) both rational and intuitive processes are needed to reach the best decisions; (c) "values, beliefs, and factors such as gender, race, class, and sexual/affectional preferences of the people involved are assumed to affect the various aspects of the ethical dilemma" (p. 19); and (d) the client is involved in the decision-making process. They believed that every aspect of ethics is influenced by context, personal cultural values, power status, and so on. Given that most ethical decision-making models do not consider the influence of cultural factors, their model is an important tool for feminist and diversity therapists.

## CHALLENGING SPECIAL ISSUES FOR FEMINIST THERAPISTS

We devote the remainder of the chapter to exploring difficult issues related to the practice of feminist-diversity therapy. We begin with some issues raised by the ethical codes reviewed and conclude with several issues that are less related to ethics, but are, nevertheless, very challenging concerns for EF therapists.

## DUAL AND OVERLAPPING RELATIONSHIPS

Conflicting roles and relationships with clients are an important area of concern for all therapists. Berman (1985) used the term *overlapping relationships* to describe counselors having more than one role or relationship with a client (i.e., an overlapping of personal, professional, and social roles). We view overlapping relationships as existing on a continuum. One end of this continuum is anchored by overlapping relationships in which the therapist does not have power over the client in more than one of the relationships (e.g., a therapy relationship and a peer relationship, as volunteers at a rape crisis agency). The other end (the "dual" end) of the continuum is characterized by the psychologist having power over the client in both (or in multiple) of the overlapping relationships (e.g., a therapy relationship and a business relationship where the therapist is the boss of the client). Thus, there are many kinds of overlapping relationships, with ones at the dual end of the continuum being more problematic and likely to violate the client. The use of the terms *overlapping, dual,* and *multiple* relationships are not uniformly applied in the literature. The Ethical Principles of Psychologists (American Psychological Association, 1992) uses the term *multiple relationships* to refer to relationships that had previously been called *dual relationships.* Kenneth Pope (as cited in Biaggio & Greene, 1995) defined *dual relationship* as one that "occurs when the therapist engages in another, significantly different relationship with the patient" (p. 89). Given the confusion, we use *overlapping relationships* as the general category and *dual relationships* to refer to ones that involve conflicting power roles.

## Sexual Misconduct with Clients

Almost all mental health professional ethical codes have prohibitions against sexual contact between counselors and clients. Prohibitions against sexual contact are relatively new to most of these codes and have usually been added at the urging and lobbying of women's committees within these organizations. In addition, many North American states have passed laws making sexual contact with a client by a therapist illegal.

Clients are in a very vulnerable role, and therapists who engage in sexual relationships with clients obscure their therapeutic objectivity and take advantage of their clients' vulnerability. For example, sexual abuse survivors have a greater likelihood of revictimization by authority figures (Russell, 1986; Whetsell, 1990). Whetsell found that 20% of the adult survivors of sexual abuse in her study had been sexually abused by at least one therapist. Further, these women identified sexual involvement with their therapists as traumatic. In a national survey of 1,320 psychologists, Pope and Vetter (1991) found that half of the respondents reported assessing or treating at least one client who had had sexual involvement with a previous therapist. Ninety percent of these cases involved harm to the client as a result of the sexual misconduct by former therapists.

While most mental health professional codes prohibit sexual contact with a current client, there is debate about what time limits should be placed on the therapeutic relationship. For example, if the therapeutic relationship is terminated on one day, can the therapist ethically be sexual with the "former" client the next day? Or, given that clients may want to return to therapy at another time in the future, does the therapeutic relationship last for life? Can the power imbalance in the therapeutic relationship ever be overcome, even in posttherapy relationships? Might the counselor terminate therapy to establish a sexual relationship, thereby doubly disadvantaging the client? The Feminist Therapy Network Code of Ethics recommends an elapse of at least six months between the termination of therapy and the initiation of sexual activity between a counselor and a former client. On the other hand, many psychologists believe "once a client, always a client." The American Psychological Association's Ethical Principles of Psychologists and Code of Conduct (1992) state that psychologists may not have a sexual relationship until at least two years after the termination of therapy; and except in the most unusual circumstances, therapists should not ever have a sexual relationship with a former client. Sexual relationships with clients is a dual relationship that is harmful to clients.

## Nonsexual Overlapping Relationships

Examples of nonsexual overlapping relationships with clients include friendships, social network contacts, business relationships, social action involvement, and having two or more separate clients involved in relationships outside of therapy with each other. While these situations are not at the "dual end" of the continuum, clients may feel uncomfortable or violated by the overlapping relationship, the counselor may feel caught between the roles and even feel triangulated between two clients, or the client may suffer negative consequences as a result of the overlap. On the other hand, avoidance of an overlapping relationship may have negative consequences for clients. For example, if a current client wants to accept employment in a feminist organization where her therapist is a board member, to avoid the overlapping relationship, the client might have to terminate therapy prematurely or decline the job offer. Or a third alternative might be for her therapist to resign from the board, resulting in a loss to the therapist and the board.

Most of these examples of overlapping relationships apply primarily to ongoing therapeutic relationships; however, some of them may pertain to posttherapy relationships as well. For example, if the counselor is or becomes the employer of a current client, the dual relationships put the client at risk professionally and therapeutically. If the counselor becomes the employer of a former client, the client may still be at risk, yet the complications of the overlapping relationships are not as clear. Many of these concerns about overlapping relationships apply to professional situations other than client-counselor (e.g., student-teacher, supervisee-supervisor).

These overlapping roles are diverse and complex. Some overlapping relationships and boundary issues cannot be avoided completely. Therapists who work in small communities have an especially difficult time avoiding these overlaps. For example, lesbian therapists who counsel lesbian clients often find their personal and professional roles overlapping. Because of the small size of most lesbian communities and because of the importance of the shared values and support in the lesbian community, lesbian therapists often find themselves making tough decisions about the overlaps. Further, feminist therapy principles and techniques may increase the likelihood of occurrence of several of these situations. For example, as feminist therapists join social action groups, they find themselves working side by side with current and former clients whom they have encouraged to work for institutional change. Moreover, because feminist therapists may publicly declare or own their value systems, individuals who have existing relationships with therapists (friends, colleagues, business associates) may actively seek them as therapists because of their values (Berman, 1985).

## Resolving Boundary Dilemmas

Simple "do and don't" rules for therapists are inadequate to address the complexities of overlapping relationships and boundary violations. Thus, feminist therapists must weigh and resolve these issues for themselves. They must assess the consequences of the issues individually in the context of each unique situation. Laura Brown (1991) outlined a three-step process for approaching these role and boundary issues. First, therapists need to acknowledge the existence of, and potential problems with, the overlapping relationship. Second, in a planned manner, therapists must assess the risks and benefits of the overlapping relationships for the client, for the counselor, and for the client-counselor relationship. Third, therapists must have effective ways to take care of themselves to maintain their own mental health and not depend on relationships with clients to meet their needs.

We propose that feminist therapists consider the following five areas in reaching effective decisions about overlapping relationships. These areas cover the specific characteristics of the overlapping relationships, of the people involved, and of the context in which the relationships exist. Under each of the five areas, we have posed a series of relevant questions. Therapists may use these questions to reach effective decisions about overlapping relationships.

1. *The nature of the therapeutic relationship.* What is the status of the client's mental health? What is the focus of therapy? How long did the therapy relationship last, or how long is it anticipated to last? Is the client in individual or group therapy? How egalitarian is the therapy relationship? In general, the more vulnerable the client is, the more important it is to avoid overlapping relationships.

2. *The nature of the overlapping relationships.* Do the overlapping relationships involve a power differential? What negative consequences might accrue to the client and/or counselor as a result of the overlapping relationships? In general, if the overlapping relationships involve a substantial power differential (e.g., employer-employee, teacher-student), a therapy relationship should not be initiated. On the other hand, while a friend-to-friend relationship does not involve a power differential, there are many potential problems when counselors are friends with clients.

3. *Health of therapist.* What is the mental health status of the therapist? How effectively does the therapist take care of self? Therapists who are psychologically impaired or who are not getting their personal needs met outside the therapeutic relationship are more likely to engage in practices that are damaging to their clients.

4. *Context variables.* What is the nature of the community shared by the counselor and client? What is the size of the community? What are the norms of the community and how might they contribute to problems with the overlapping relationships?

5. *Therapist theoretical orientation.* What assumptions or important constructs (e.g., transference) of the therapist's theoretical orientation are violated or complicated by the overlapping relationship?

The Feminist Therapy Code of Ethics (Feminist Therapy Institute, 1987) highlighted the "unavoidable nature" of overlapping relationships. Taking this unavoidability into account, therapists need strategies for handling them. These strategies include: (a) planning with the client for how to handle outside encounters, (b) being careful about the use of power in other relationships with the client, (c) putting the welfare of the client in the forefront of all decisions, (d) being self-aware and meeting needs apart from therapy relationships, and (e) consulting with colleagues (Biaggio & Greene, 1995).

In this assessment and decision process, priority must be given to the impact of all decisions on the client. The more vulnerable status of the client must be kept in mind. Therapists must acknowledge and own their special power and status and must ensure that they do not abuse that power and their client's trust. Even in egalitarian or collaborative relationships, the therapist has expert power and this power differential must be used in service of the client. Further, the questions posed previously may best be answered in the context of Hill and colleagues' (1995) feminist decision-making model. In many cases, collaboration with the client may be appropriate.

## Client-Counselor Power Issues

The general societal power imbalances between diverse groups affect the more specific dynamics of the therapy relationship as well. The therapist's and client's social locations have potentially different impacts on the outcome of therapy. The impact of gender, ethnicity, sexual orientation, age, ability, and class sources of power on the process and outcome of therapy are especially important in feminist-diversity therapy because of its emphasis on egalitarian counseling relationships. In this section, we highlight the role of power in counseling.

In Chapter 3, we posited several reasons for the importance feminist therapists give to building egalitarian relationships with clients. First, egalitarian relationships reduce the social control aspects of therapy, whereby therapists misuse their power to get clients to comply and adapt to an oppressive society. In egalitarian relationships, therapists have less of a power base from which to impose their values on clients. Second and most important, feminist therapists believe that the therapy relationship should not recreate the power imbalance women and members of subordinate groups experience in society. Client-counselor relationships should be models for egalitarian relationships in general. Because of the central role that power plays in therapeutic relationships, it is important to understand the power differentials between clients and therapists.

### Gender Power Imbalances in Therapeutic Relationships

Mary Ann Douglas (1985) defined different kinds of power present in the therapist role and pointed out the ramifications of these power sources in four different therapy dyads. Douglas noted that although feminist therapists strive to build egalitarian relationships with clients, they still retain greater power than clients because clients are dependent on receiving something from therapists. Acknowledgment and owning of this power differential by therapists is important in order for therapists to minimize the misuse and abuse of their power. Reward, coercive, informational, expert, legitimate, and referent powers are either inherent to the therapist role or are available sources of power for therapists. To these six sources of power, Douglas added gender power, reflecting the general greater power status of men vis-à-vis women in most societies. The power dynamics of any heterosexual relationship exist ". . . within a context of permanent inequality between the sexes" (p. 244). The interactive effects of therapist role power and gender power is summarized in Douglas' model, presented in Table 11.9.

Although a feminist therapy approach seeks to build egalitarian relationships, the degree to which therapist role power and gender power can actually be reduced in the therapy relationship needs to be investigated empirically. At present, a feminist therapist analysis of advantages and disadvantages of same- and cross-sex therapy dyads must take into account these power differentials. In the following analysis of the advantages and disadvantages of the different client-counselor gender pairings, we assume that both the female and male therapists are feminist therapists. We believe that men can be effective feminist psychological health practitioners.

The potential advantages to a female client-feminist female counselor pairing are: (a) the therapist has increased empathy for the client due to similarities in life experiences,

**Table 11.9   Relative power of therapist vis-à-vis the client, based on therapist and gender roles**

| | Female Therapist | | Male Therapist | |
|---|---|---|---|---|
| Sources of Power | Female Client | Male Client | Female Client | Male Client |
| Therapist role | GT | GT | GT | GT |
| Gender role | EQ | GC | GT | EQ |
| Total relative power of therapist vis-à-vis client | GT | — | GT | GT |

Key: GT = greater therapist power; GC = greater client power; EQ = equal client/therapist power.
*Source:* "The Role of Power in Feminist Therapy: A Reformulation," by M. A. Douglas, 1985, in *Handbook of Feminist Therapy,* 1985, L. B. Rosewater and L. E. A. Walker (Eds.), New York: Springer. Reprinted with permission.

(b) the therapist can serve as an effective nonstereotyped role model with whom the client can identify, (c) an egalitarian therapeutic relationship is easier to develop since the gender power is equal, and (d) some female clients may feel more comfortable disclosing about sensitive topics to a female therapist. Potential disadvantages are: (a) the possible lack of clear distinctions between therapist and client issues and (b) failure to clarify the meaning of a client's statement because the therapist assumes their experiences are the same. In the feminist male counselor and male client dyad, there are advantages similar to the female matched pair: (a) the male therapist can be an effective nontraditional male role model, (b) there may be increased empathy due to a common life experience base, and (c) an egalitarian therapy relationship may be easier to establish. Reluctance of the male client and counselor to express sadness and fear in the presence of another man is an important potential disadvantage. Further, similar to the matched female dyad, the male counselor in the matched male dyad may erroneously assume similarity between him and his client, obscuring actual differences.

The cross-sex pairings generally have more potential problems than same-sex pairings. When the client is female and the feminist counselor is male, one potential advantage is that the therapist can be an effective nonstereotyped male role model, thus providing the client with a positive experience relating to a man. However, an egalitarian relationship is more difficult to achieve because of the gender power imbalance. Power inequality is heightened by the male therapist-female client dyad (Fitzgerald & Nutt, 1986). Female clients may feel intimidated by and unsafe with a male counselor and may fall into a female stereotypic behavior pattern of acquiescence. Further, there are specific issues or life experiences that the female client may have that make it difficult or impossible for her to trust a male therapist, no matter how sensitive and empathic the therapist is. Women who have been raped, sexually abused, or a victim of spouse abuse frequently request a female therapist. As the female client's consciousness is raised as a result of counseling, she may become angry with the men in her life, including her male therapist. If the therapist fails to validate that anger because of his own defensiveness, the client's progress may be hindered. Male counselors must be aware of their nonverbal messages, especially ones that convey dominant-subordinate power status (Fitzgerald & Nutt, 1986).

When the client is male and the feminist counselor is female, there are several potential advantages: (a) the client learns to appreciate and relate to a nonstereotyped woman, and (b) male clients may find it easier to express feelings in the presence of a female therapist than with a male therapist. As shown in Douglas' (1985) chart in Table 11.9, the overall power balance of this dyad is unknown or may vary depending on the specific individuals involved. Potential disadvantages to this pairing are: (a) the male client may discount or devalue the female counselor and/or her interventions, and (b) the female counselor may feel intimidated by the male client and fail to confront or challenge him.

Issues emerging from same- and cross-sex counseling pairings become even more complex in couples and family counseling. For example, in studies of female and male family therapist trainees, Warburton, Newberry, and Alexander (1989) found that both female and male trainees "can expect pulls for affiliation with the same-sex parent and defensiveness from the opposite-sex (sic) parent" (p. 153). However, the female trainee is likely to experience more defensiveness from the father than the male trainee is from the mother. Gender power imbalances may be present not only between the counselor and each family member, but also among family members. Further, EFT therapists who colead groups need to model an egalitarian relationship with their cotherapists. When the therapists' social locations are representative of a privileged and oppressed status (e.g., male-female, White, Person of Color), they must take care not to reflect these societal power imbalances in their interactions and work together.

### Other Seats of Oppression and Privilege

In accordance with EFT Principles I and II, clients' and therapists' social locations need to be identified and their impact on the therapeutic relationship explored. While Douglas (1985) focused on gender power issues only, her model about sources of power in the therapeutic relationship can be extended to other sources of privilege and oppression. Thus, every relevant social location dimension would be a potential source of power that would affect therapeutic interactions. Indeed, the multiple social locations of both therapist and client have interactional effects. For example, even Douglas's power analysis for gender effects may vary across cultural groups because of differing cultural views of female and male roles. The costs and benefits outlined for the various gender combinations would also roughly apply to combinations of therapists' and clients' multiple social locations. Obviously, a chart depicting all relevant social locations and the relative power of the client vis-à-vis the therapist becomes very complex to construct once we move beyond one social location dimension. Nevertheless, exploring this complex territory with the client is at the heart of EFT and of Principle I. The social location exploration interventions discussed in Chapters 2 and 3 are important starting points for this dialogue. Addressing the negative effects of racism, sexism, heterosexism, classism, ableism, and so on, is also crucial to helping clients talk about their relationship with the therapist and to facilitating their movement through the identities' levels (Espin, 1994).

## Summary of Power Issues

An awareness of how positions of privilege and oppression may impact therapy relationships and outcomes has several implications for therapists. First, this awareness adds additional layers of complexity to the delivery of psychological services. Second, the importance of exploring the seats of oppression and privilege associated with the social locations of both clients and therapists is crucial to achieving effective therapeutic outcomes. Note that this exploration involves discussing both oppressed and privileged social locations of the client (and of the therapist). For instance, asking a White female client who has a Woman of Color therapist to address how her privileged White status and internalized racism may be affecting their therapeutic work may be uncomfortable, but very necessary. (See Olivia Espin's 1994 description of her work with a White female client for a detailed example.) Parallel issues may be present with male clients who have female therapists or with heterosexual clients who have lesbian, gay, or bisexual therapists. Third, complete similarity of social locations (and thus, of equal social location power distributions) between clients and therapists is rare and even more rare for Women of Color, lesbian women, lower socioeconomic status women, and for women with disabilities. When social location client-counselor matches are available and requested by the client, we believe priority and respect must be given to client's preferences for a counselor. In reality, almost all therapy is cross-cultural in nature. Fourth, therapists must be aware of all of their social locations and own both their seats of oppression and privilege. These are not easy tasks, especially the unpacking of privilege (McIntosh, 1986). But they are crucial to the delivery of competent services.

While we have focused on therapy issues in our discussions in this chapter, power issues also impact other psychological practices (e.g., teaching, supervision, assessment, research). For all these areas of practice, supervision by an EF therapist can be helpful to identifying and dealing with the diversity of social locations and their impact on psychological practice.

## PREASSESSMENT EXERCISE UPDATE

Now that we have discussed dual relationships and client-counselor power issues, we return to the client case presented at the beginning of this chapter. At this point, you are probably very aware that the first therapist's sexual involvement with the client was unethical and was a revictimization of the client, in that many of the dynamics of the client's childhood sexual abuse experiences were recreated by the therapist's sexual exploitation of her. EFT Principles I, II, III, and IV have been violated by the therapist's misuse of both his professional and gender power. In addition to the harm done to this particular client, this therapist may be likely to violate other clients as well. Since the client does not want to pursue the issue further, several other ethical issues are raised. Because of the client privilege of confidentiality, the second therapist cannot confront the first therapist without the client's permission. One possible goal for therapy with this client is to help her restructure her self-blaming cognitions about the encounter to cognitions that hold the therapist responsible for his behavior. Gender-role analysis, power analysis, and confrontation of sexual abuse myths may help empower this client to confront her former therapist and/or take her case to an ethics review board. Her current therapist must be careful to support her in her decision making, as undue pressure to take action revictimizes the client.

## "COMING OUT" AS A FEMINIST THERAPIST

If you decide to embrace the four EFT principles, you need to decide how to label yourself in relation to these values. There is a continuum of choices: (a) Labeling yourself as a feminist (EFT) therapist; (b) labeling yourself as a diversity-feminist therapist; (c) listing yourself as a therapist specializing in women's issues; (d) calling yourself a nonsexist therapist; (e) not labeling yourself, but stating your feminist therapy values to clients. You need to decide how to label yourself not only to clients, but also to colleagues, to your community, and to yourself.

The decision about how to label oneself is a choice encountered by all feminist psychological health practitioners. Pam Remer and Sharon Rostosky (2000, 2001) have collected psychologists' experiences with, and their reasons for, using or not using a feminist label. On the negative side, some practitioners worry about the label being a "red flag" or about negative associations that people have to the *feminist* label. They fear it may unnecessarily restrict potential clients from choosing them for therapy. One female psychologist talked about the fear of creating barriers with clients based on clients' misunderstanding of what feminist means; thus, she does not publicly label herself as feminist. Another psychologist says she usually does disclose to clients that she is feminist unless she has a reason not to (e.g., an older woman client with traditional values). Another female psychologist discussed her work in a small, rural, southern U.S. community. Because most of the people in this town belong to one conservative denominational church, she refrains from being public about being a feminist because she fears the whole religious community might be dissuaded from coming to her. Another psychologist worried that potential clients might believe that feminist therapy is only for women. Several male psychologists who do label themselves as *feminist* described being censored by both female and male colleagues. Their male colleagues denigrated them for being interested in frivolous areas of inquiry while their feminist female colleagues questioned their motives and abilities to be a "real feminist."

On the positive side of identifying as a feminist therapist, one psychologist said she makes a point to label herself a feminist with professional colleagues. "If colleagues have trouble with the word, then I'm pleased to set up a little dissonance whereby they have to open their minds a little or dismiss me . . . I say *feminist* in training settings to model, advocate, teach . . ." (Remer & Rostosky, 2000, p. 7). Other psychologists who do label themselves as feminists point out the importance of using a label that is consistent with their values. One psychologist labels herself a *feminist/multicultural therapist,* indicating her integration of these two perspectives. Using the label may attract clients who want a therapist with this values' orientation, and using the label most accurately reflects the therapist's values system, allowing clients to make a more informed decision in choosing a therapist.

Other possible labels have advantages and disadvantages. A *specialist in women's issues* designation may exclude male clients unnecessarily. The label *nonsexist therapist* also has interpretation problems by potential consumers.

A study by Carolyn Enns and Gail Hackett (1990) provides data to support positive outcomes associated with feminist therapist value orientation and therapists explicit disclosures about their values. Using an analogue study format, in which college women viewed videotaped counseling vignettes of a female client and female counselor, Enns and Hackett investigated the differential effects of nonsexist, liberal, feminist, and radical feminist counseling approaches. The vignettes were varied by counseling orientation and by the explicitness of the counselors' value statements. Participants were grouped into a feminist or nonfeminist stance, based on their responses to the Attitudes Toward Feminism Scale developed by the authors. All participants (feminist and nonfeminist) preferred to see the two feminist counselors for career and sexual assault concerns; no differences were found for personal-interpersonal concerns. Counselors who made explicit value statements were seen as more helpful than any counselor in the implicit value condition. Both types of feminist counselors were seen as significantly more helpful, expert, and trustworthy than was the nonsexist therapist. However, note that these participants were college students and thus may differ from community women. Having acknowledged this limitation of the study, these findings suggest that both feminist and nonfeminist clients may perceive feminist therapists more favorably and that the "red flag" worries about the feminist therapist label may be exaggerated.

Thus, the choice to come out as a feminist therapist is a complex one. While we acknowledge the risks that may be encountered by using a *feminist* label, we do not believe these anticipated risks are always actualized. Moreover, we believe that when we label ourselves as feminist practitioners, we create opportunities to challenge others' stereotypes and myths about feminist therapists and we own our unique perspectives. Further, in the psychological literature, we have encountered treatment interventions that were based on feminist principles, but were not labeled feminist (or the label was buried deep in the article). If we do not find the courage to label our feminist-based interventions as feminist (to our clients, to our colleagues, to our communities, and in our publications), then we will not have a sufficient and identifiable base on which to demonstrate the effectiveness of feminist interventions, and myths about feminists and feminist therapy will go unchallenged. In many respects, the future of feminist psychological practice will be influenced by the decision feminist practitioners make about "coming out" in their professional endeavors.

Your labeling decision may fit currently, but may change over time and with your experience. The following questions may help you decide what to call yourself. How closely do your beliefs and values match the four principles of EFT? What does being a feminist therapist or being a diversity therapist mean to you? Will each of the labels that you are considering attract or repel the clients with whom you want to work? Which label will contribute most to your effectiveness in your professional work? Which label will contribute most to your professional identity? Which label will most accurately reflect the values you hold and the interventions you use? Which label will contribute most to the development of your specialty or theoretical orientation?

## SUMMARY

Having a feminist-diversity therapy perspective of ethical practices permits us to behave more congruently with our chosen value system. We have ". . . added to the definition of *ethics* the concept that sexist, racist, homophobic, or other discriminatory attitudes on the part of the therapist could be evidence of unethical behavior" (L. S. Brown, 1991). Feminist therapy ethical guidelines give additional protection to clients, especially female clients, from the possible misuse of power by therapists.

Being a feminist therapist has many unique challenges. How do we define our relationships to our clients both inside and outside the therapy relationship? How do we own and positively use our professional power to facilitate our clients' growth? How do we cope with the impact of our social locations on our roles as therapists? How do we resolve the inevitable borderland issues we encounter and creatively integrate feminist and diversity perspectives? How shall we respond when our goals and values do not match those of our clients? What shall we call ourselves? We each must answer these questions for ourselves within our own understanding and application of the four EFT principles. In our answers to these questions, we each define more specifically not only our relationships to our present and potential clients, but also our relationships to ourselves and to our communities.

## ACTIVITIES

### Case Application

Read the following case, which describes a therapy dilemma of conflicting goals, and answer the questions.

A White, Catholic, 35-year-old woman comes to you for therapy, saying she wants to stop criticizing her husband and stop arguing with him. In the initial assessment phase of therapy, you discover that: (a) She and her husband have a traditional he-dominant, she-submissive relationship; (b) he has been physically abusive to her; (c) she feels responsible for provoking his attacks on her; and (d) she appears to be in the first level (preawareness) of gender identity development. Your desired goals for her are to take steps to ensure her physical safety, increase her self-esteem, decrease her economic dependency, and increase her self-assertion. You also want to facilitate her movement in the levels of gender identity development.

Given this situation, how would you answer the following question? What impact is the social locations having on your respective discrepant goals? At what point, if any, in the therapy process would you disclose your goals for her? How would you go about resolving the goal discrepancies? If the conflict cannot be resolved, would you counsel her in working toward her goals? Your goals? Would you begin by working toward her goals with the hope of convincing her of the importance of your goals? Would you refer her to another counselor, and if so, at what point? How would your answers to these questions change if the ethnicity, religion, immigration status, or age of the client were changed? You may want to review the case of Rachel in Chapter 9 as an example of how a similar dilemma was resolved.

Think about and/or discuss with others the following questions:

1. How do you relate differently in your female and male relationships? In your relationships with people of differing social class, ethnicity, age, ability, sexual orientation?

2. Given the person that you are and the professional attitudes and skills that you possess, what do you see as the strengths and weaknesses you bring to your work with female clients? With male clients? With clients from other social locations?

3. How do the various ethical code models presented in this chapter fit with your own profession's ethical code? What problems would you anticipate in trying to have a feminist therapy set of ethical principles added to your profession's existing ethical code?

## FURTHER READINGS

Biaggio, M., & Greene, B. (1995). Overlapping/dual relationships. In E. J. Rave & C. C. Larsen (Eds.), *Ethical decision making in therapy: Feminist perspectives* (pp. 88–123). New York: Guilford Press.

Brabeck, M. M. (2000). *Practicing feminist ethics in psychology.* Washington, DC: American Psychological Association.

Fitzgerald, L. F., & Nutt, R. (1986). The Division 17 principles concerning the counseling/psychotherapy of women: Rationale and implementation. *Counseling Psychologist, 14,* 180–216.

Sparks, E. E., & Park, A. H. (2000). The integration of feminism and multiculturalism: Ethical dilemmas at the border. In M. M. Brabeck (Ed.), *Practicing feminist ethics in psychology.* Washington, DC: American Psychological Association.

# Chapter 12 ———————————————————————

# *IMPLEMENTING A FEMINIST-DIVERSITY MODEL OF TRAINING*

> *Feminism is a way of being in the world . . . it involves breaking silences and taking a stance that automatic power should be challenged and that knowledge or expertise should be used in the service of learning and teaching on the part of both teacher and learner.*
>
> Ellen Kimmel and Judith Worell, 1997

## SELF-ASSESSMENT: EVALUATING CURRENT EDUCATIONAL PROGRAMS

Consider both your undergraduate and graduate education in responding to the following questions:

1. How was feminist theory and the psychology of women, gender, and multiculturalism included or integrated into your regular college curriculum?
2. Identify the ways in which your undergraduate and graduate education reflected oppressive or insensitive practices. These would include those reflecting any of the SEARCH (sexism, ethnocentrism, ableism and ageism, racism, classism, and heterosexism) variables with regard to students, faculty, resources, curriculum, clinical practice and supervision, research, and interpersonal relationships. Share your perceptions with a partner and ask for feedback. As you read this chapter, determine whether your answers to these two questions should be expanded, reconsidered, or revised.

## OVERVIEW

We consider the process of becoming a feminist psychological practitioner in terms of personal values, beliefs and attitudes, knowledge base, interpersonal behavior, community action, and applied practice. We suggest that an educational agenda with respect to feminist and culturally sensitive counseling/psychotherapy requires attention to all these variables. First, we explore the development of a feminist perspective, and we introduce a model of feminist identity development and its application to educational practice. Next, we propose a four-factor model of feminist professional training that promotes coordination of student, faculty, departmental, university, and community resources. The model emphasizes a broad band of interventions across the student's educational experiences that integrates attitudes, knowledge, and skills toward the implementation of a feminist and culturally sensitive graduate counseling program.

## DEVELOPING A FEMINIST PERSPECTIVE

The process of becoming an EF therapist requires that you first develop an understanding, acceptance, and integration of a general feminist perspective. The application of this viewpoint to the client-counselor process then follows a clear rationale. How does the process of feminist identity occur, and how can we encourage a broad feminist-diversity view of psychology in graduate educational programs?

### Prefeminist Awareness

We know that learning can occur in many ways and under diverse learning conditions (Kimmel & Worell, 1997; Worell & Stilwell, 1981). Many of the professionals who currently identify themselves as feminist psychological practitioners were educated and trained in traditional psychology programs. For some of us, there were no women faculty or mentors, no texts or research literature on women and their issues, and we were trained and supervised with traditional practices in research, assessment, and psychological intervention.

If we were aware of gender or ethnocultural discrimination, sexual harassment, or the contributions of societal structures and practices to women's psychological health problems, we were unable to articulate this awareness into a cohesive theory or to translate it into action. How did we revise our thinking to become active as feminist psychologists, as competent in developing a new field of the Psychology of Women? Do we need new programs to prepare psychologists to meet new goals for the health and psychological well-being of diverse women and men in the twenty-first century?

Early recognition of an emerging feminist consciousness among psychologists paralleled general interest in the 1970s Women's Movement. This awareness raised questions in many quarters about what kinds of women were these who dared to confront traditional values, to challenge the scientific establishment, and to ask for an equal place in the social order? To explore this intriguing question, Judith Worell and Leonard Worell (1977) conducted a study with 979 female and male university students. We found that certain personality traits did differentiate those who supported or opposed the Women's Movement. Supporting women (emergent feminists?) differed from college women's norms on only one trait: They described themselves as more independent and autonomous. In contrast, opposing women scored as more autocratic and dogmatic, more concerned with external sources of approval, more conventional, less rational, and more cautious in risky choice situations. These characteristics tend to suggest that opposers were individuals who were generally resistant to new ideas and to social change. Early results were encouraging to those of us who thought of ourselves as supporters of equal status for women and who were still in the process of creating a personal feminist identity. A subsequent review of relevant research by Lucia Gilbert (1980) found feminists, in contrast to nonfeminists, to be more politically liberal and active, achieving, self-confident, autonomous, self-actualizing, and higher in self-esteem. From diverse sequences of research, theory building, and organizational structures, gradual images of a feminist perspective emerged.

## Feminist Identity Development

A feminist identity is forged, in part, from an understanding and commitment to the values and ideals of feminism. In Chapter 1, we defined and discussed feminism and feminist psychology. We proposed eight tenets or values that characterize feminist psychology and that provide the foundation for empowerment feminist therapy (EFT). We recognize that not all women (and men) who consider themselves to be feminist subscribe to all eight of these tenets and that many persons who support one or more of these values do not identify themselves as feminists. How can we then understand the differing positions of individuals with respect to feminist values and goals? Given our values about feminist identity as an important personal and social location for the practice of EFT, what are the conditions that foster its development? We turn first to models of feminist identity development to help us consider this question.

## A Model of Feminist Identity Development

A format for conceptualizing feminist identity development for women, patterned after that constructed for Nigrescence, or Black identity, was proposed by Nancy Downing and Kristin Roush (1985). Table 12.1 displays the five stages of the model, which coincide with the stages of Black identity development defined by Cross (1980). A summary of the Downing and Roush stages follows:

*Stage I: Passive Acceptance* "describes the woman who is either unaware of or denies the individual, institutional, and cultural prejudice and discrimination against her" (p. 669). She is likely to accept her subordinate position with respect to men and appears to enjoy traditional gender-role arrangements.

*Stage II: Revelation* is precipitated by consciousness-raising experiences that invalidate her previous perceptions. These experiences may include personal discrimination, loss of a relationship, or contact with feminist ideas. At this stage, she becomes angry at the realization of her oppression and guilty for her own role in having collaborated with patriarchal power structures. She is likely to polarize gender by valuing women and devaluing men.

*Stage III: Embeddedness-Emanation* describes the woman who immerses herself in women's culture and increases her social and emotional connections with other women. The authors point out that the immersion process is difficult for most women, since social structures prevent them from avoiding male contact entirely. If she is married or has male children, she may see herself as imprisoned with her oppressor. As women emanate from this stage, they relinquish their polarized position and begin to reintegrate themselves into a new personhood.

**Table 12.1  Parallels between the identity development stages for women and Blacks**

*Stages for Women*

| Passive Acceptance | Revelation | Embeddedness-Emanation | Synthesis | Active Commitment |
|---|---|---|---|---|
| Passive acceptance of traditional sex roles and discrimination; belief that traditional roles are advantageous; men are considered superior. | Catalyzed by a series of crises, resulting in open questioning of self and roles and feelings of anger and guilt; dualistic thinking; men are perceived as negative. | Characterized by connectedness with other select women, affirmation and strengthening of new identity. Eventually more relativistic thinking and cautious interaction with men. | Development of an authentic and positive feminist identity; sex-role transcendence; "flexible truce" with the world; evaluate men on an individual basis. | Consolidation of feminist identity; commitment to meaningful action, to a nonsexist world. Actions are personalized and rational. Men are considered equal but not the same as women. |

*Stages for Blacks*

| Preencounter | Encounter | Immersion-Emersion | Internalization | Internalization-Commitment |
|---|---|---|---|---|
| The unaware person; acceptance of oppression as justified; values assimilation into majority culture; negative self-concept. | Catalyzed by profound event(s) resulting in increased awareness, rejection of oppression, and feelings of guilt and anger. | Initially characterized by withdrawal from the dominant culture, immersion in one's heritage and hostility toward Whites. Eventually greater cognitive flexibility and pride emerge. | Development of an integrated, more positive self-image; adoption of a pluralistic, nonracist perspective. | Commitment of the new self to meaningful action for the benefit of the minority community. |

*Source:* "From Passive Acceptance to Active Commitment: A Model of Feminist Identity Development," by N. E. Downing and K. L. Roush, 1985, *Counseling Psychologist, 13*, pp. 695–709. Reprinted with permission.

In *Stage IV: Synthesis,* the woman has arrived at a flexible and positive feminist identity and increasingly values her female self. She is still aware of societal oppression, but is "able to transcend traditional sex roles, make choices . . . based on well-defined personal values, and evaluates men on an individual, rather than a stereotypic, basis" (p. 702).

Finally, *Stage V* describes a position of *active commitment* to social change. The woman becomes involved in working for women's rights and "in creating a future in which sex-role transcendence is a valued and encouraged goal" (p. 702).

The authors point out that most women alternately advance and then retreat to earlier stages, as they progressively encounter new situations and develop new skills. Thus, feminist identity becomes a process through which we evolve gradually and in which we continually seek new perspectives. In a study of feminist identity development in psychology graduate students (Worell, Stilwell, Oakley, & Robinson, 1999), the stage model was not as well-supported as was a dimensional model, in which individual scores varied across dimensions of feminist commitment but did not follow a step-up progression. The issue of whether these are stages or dimensions has been raised by others, pointing out that stage theories imply (a) higher stages are "better" than lower ones, and (b) having reached a higher stage, one cannot revert to a lower one (Hyde, 2002). Since we have evidence that neither of these conditions have been met, we prefer to regard these as levels or dimensions that can each be measured separately. This conclusion suggests that individuals can be positioned at differing levels of these "stages" at various times and in different situations. As we have discussed with respect to other social locations, the salience of the situation to feminist identity development varies across situations. As well, the importance or core value of a person's feminist position varies across life experiences, so that a new encounter with sexism for a woman who is high in *Active Commitment* may infuse her with renewed anger, throwing her back to the *Revelation* position.

As a cautionary note, we recognize that the model does not take into account individual differences in feminist orientations due to ethnocultural values, religion, nationality, sexual orientation, age, socioeconomic class, or the fact of being male. From the perspective of a professional Woman of Color, Beverly Vandiver (2002) questioned the utility of the Downing and Roush model for diverse populations. She also questioned whether the model is applicable to young women of the twenty-first century, who are presumably more aware of sexism and thus less likely to have a "revelation." Finally, she pointed out that the model implies that feminism is a *personal* identity, rather than a *reference group* orientation. Many Women of Color, for example, subscribe to a Womanist identity, which connects the woman to a larger reference community. Referring to EFT Principle I, we maintain that personal and social identities are not independent, but are interconnected and interdependent. Thus, feminist identity is a social location that incorporates both aspects. It provides an index for "who am I" that engages awareness and appreciation of connection to a reference group outside of the self.

A model of feminist identity development for men also remains to be explored. We believe that men as well as women can be feminist therapists. Arnold Kahn (1984), a self-identified feminist, has pointed out that for many men, the possession of power—in society and over women—is central to their self-definition, self-esteem, and concept of masculinity. To acknowledge and advocate women's equality, such men must relinquish the goal of power and find sources of identity and self-esteem in ways that are independent of their gender. Men also have to confront and accept their privileged position in most societies, and White men in particular need to deal with privileges that result from their being White. Thus, men's feminist identity development may require a stage that includes consideration of power and its potential loss. To the extent that a range of variables enters into the feminist identity process, modifications in the format and measurement of the model should be considered. You may wish to compare the Downing and Roush (1985) model with our more articulated model of Personal/Social Identity/Development (PSID) presented in Chapter 2. The PSID model is designed on a similar progression of attitudes and behaviors, but we assume that these are dimensions or levels of a person's various social locations rather than stages specifically related to feminism. Feminist identity may be one of the core social locations for some individuals, as it is for the authors of this book. Further, the PSID incorporates the variables of oppression and privilege for each identity as a means of connecting the level of each social location to personal outcomes of pride and self-esteem or shame and self-negation.

## Applying the Model

Adena Bargad and Janet Hyde (1991) took an initial approach to evaluating the feminist identity model. They constructed the 39-item Feminist Identity Development Scale (FIDS) to test the application of the model to the effects of college courses centering on women's studies. They administered the FIDS to women in three different classes pre- and postcompletion of these courses, comparing their responses with those of a control group who did not enroll in a women's studies course. The overall goals of the courses were to raise student consciousness of feminist perspectives and to empower students through increased self-awareness.

The pre- and post scores of the groups on each of the five stages of feminist identity are displayed in Figure 12.1. At pretest, the control group did not differ from the three women's studies groups, and at posttest, the controls did not differ from their own pretest scores. In contrast, the experimental groups changed on all five stage measures, supporting the effectiveness of a university course curriculum in promoting a feminist perspective. This study supports previous research that reported significant changes in student attitudes, values, and activism following courses related to gender and women (Henderson-King & Stewart, 1999; S. E. Kahn & Theurer, 1985; Stake & Gerner, 1987; Stake, Roades, Rose, Ellis, & West, 1994; Vedovato & Vaughter, 1980; Worell, Stilwell, Oakley, & Robinson, 1999).

We referred earlier to a study conducted by Worell and her associates (1999) to support and validate the effectiveness of training and exposure to feminist concepts. We hypothesized that this feminist training program would impact several areas of student development, including cognitive, personal, and professional outcomes. In support of these hypotheses, we found that field and program exposure to gender-related content and issues was positively related to (a) students' personal epistemology or belief in a social construction approach to knowledge; (b) performance self-esteem or self-efficacy beliefs about one's academic abilities; (c) endorsement of feminist therapy goals as measured by the Therapy with Women Scale (TWS); and (d) higher scores on feminist identity on a four-level version of the Bargad and Hyde FIDS. We also revised the FIDS items to be applicable to male as well as female participants. The self-assessment scale at the beginning of this book is our revision of the FIDS.

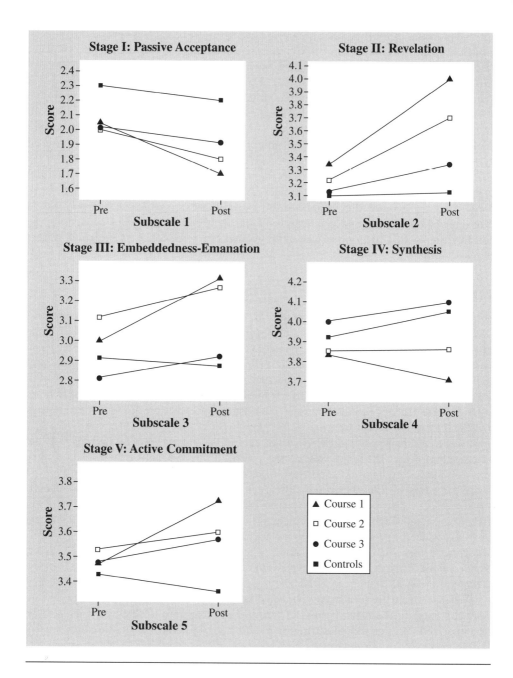

Figure 12.1  Mean subscale scores by course at pre- and posttests. *Source:* From
"Women's Studies: A Study of Feminist Identity Development," by
A. Bargad and J. S. Hyde, 1991, *Psychology of Women Quarterly, 15,*
pp. 181–201. Used with permission of Cambridge University Press.

We reviewed these studies in some detail to highlight the effectiveness of university courses with a feminist perspective on changes in student self-awareness, endorsement of feminist principles, and, in some cases, student activism. These research findings also suggest that a curriculum that incorporates gender and feminist-diversity perspectives across a range of attitudes, knowledge, and skill areas should be effective in promoting the goals of a feminist counseling training program.

## A FEMINIST-DIVERSITY TRAINING MODEL

The foregoing studies suggest strongly that exposure to theory and research on gender, ethnocultural, and feminist perspectives can influence student awareness and attitudes. Michelle Harway (1979), Worell (1980), and Worell and Remer (1992) have proposed models of feminist training in counseling psychology that contain similar components. The models are designed to enable students to gain the knowledge, attitudes, and skills that facilitate their effective functioning in feminist-oriented research and practice. In addition, the training models focus on issues of personal identity, autonomy, and creative growth for all students and faculty involved.

The four major components of a graduate program, displayed in Figure 12.2, are:

1. Attitudes and values.
2. Structures.
3. Resources.
4. Outreach.

### Attitudes and Values

All educational and training programs are built on a foundation of attitudes and values, whether implicit or explicit. In feminist education, values about equity, diversity, attention to process, and social justice are clearly delineated and are prerequisites for initiating a feminist-diversity training program. Relevant attitudes may be held by only one or two faculty members, who disseminate information to others (students, faculty, administration) in a consciousness-raising effort to encourage interest and motivation for change. Soliciting interested women faculty to teach a course on gender or multicultural topics is a viable way to increase awareness in interested but uncommitted faculty. Mary Walsh (1985) reported that faculty who teach modules or courses on gender become more knowledgeable and demonstrate significant attitude changes as a result of their preparations for the course. Other departmental faculty and some administrators, while not initially interested, need to be informed and integrated toward a common effort so that new courses can be added to existing programs.

Strategies for accomplishing the task of modifying attitudes vary with institutional structures and may be more difficult in some situations than in others. In a recent study of feminist professors across three types of academic settings (universities, colleges, and women's colleges), the explicit support by female administrators for faculty in women's colleges was the only predictor of differences in academic satisfaction among them (Gross, Kmeic, Worell, & Crosby, 2001). Circulation of brief readings, invited speakers, volunteering to present guest lectures in their classes, personal confrontation,

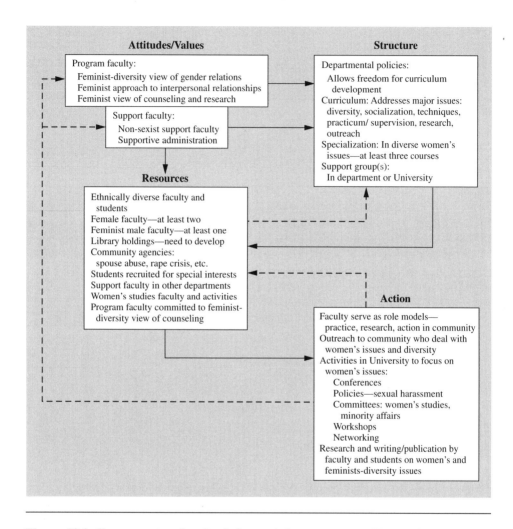

**Figure 12.2  Components of a feminist training program. Heavy lines indicate direct influence. Dotted lines propose recursive feedback loops and subsequent influences.**

and persistence may be necessary to convince an otherwise negative or disinterested faculty of the legitimacy of the program. Many years ago, when one of the authors proposed a new course on gender development in her academic department, a statistics faculty member commented: "Can't you just integrate that material as a lecture or module into your Social Development course?" In response, he was asked: "You teach Multivariate Analysis as a semester course; can't you just integrate that content into a seminar in your ANOVA class?" The point was clear; the new course was approved and implemented.

*Infusing Feminist Pedagogy*

Is feminist teaching "just good teaching"? Integral to the issue of value and attitudes are the principles and strategies of pedagogy. The feminist-diversity teacher is committed to a feminist process in the classroom. This commitment engenders both progress and problems, as the pedagogy working group at the First National Conference on Feminist Practice discovered (see Chapter 1). However, from the conscious application of a feminist process of decision making that required open minds and consensus on all issues, a template of feminist principles and practices emerged (Kimmel & Worell, 1997). Fourteen principles and 28 strategies to articulate these principles into feminist-informed teaching practices emerged from a four-day meeting. Table 12.2 presents a summary of the 14 principles. The working group on feminist pedagogy also developed a matrix of how the 14 principles and 28 strategies can be implemented by indexing them to a list of 168 references. We recommend this matrix to those of you who are involved in the teaching-learning process.

## Dealing with Academic Challenges

We would be remiss, however, in pretending that the road to a successful teaching career as a feminist scholar is a smooth one. Considerable research supports our earlier discussions about the problems facing all women as they enter domains previously reserved for White men (Kite, 2001). Despite our fantasies about the intellectual protections provided by the proverbial "ivory tower," academia is no different from other traditionally patriarchal organizations. The American Psychological Association (APA) Task Force on

**Table 12.2    Principles of feminist pedagogy**

1. Differentials of power and privilege are made explicit through articulation of values and classroom policies.
2. Feminists acknowledge the power inherent in their teaching role and seek ways to empower students in the learning process.
3. All voices are encouraged, valued, and heard. A climate of respect for differences in fostered.
4. Multiple styles of learning are recognized and accommodated. Differences in the contexts of students' lives are respected.
5. Learning should integrate cognitions, feelings, and experience.
6. Connections between personal experience and social reality are made explicit.
7. Both teachers and students are engaged in a mutual learning process.
8. Feminist teachers strive to increase their knowledge of and sensitivity to diverse cultural realities.
9. Feminist teachers model an acceptance of their own authority and expertise.
10. Feminist teachers are committed to including multiple sources of knowledge.
11. Learning is in the service of social change.
12. Feminist teachers help to reclaim women's histories and cultures.
13. Learning is in the service of increasing self awareness and personal growth.
14. Feminist pedagogy is aimed at transforming the discipline.

*Source:* "Preaching What We Practice: Principles and Strategies of Feminist Pedagogy," by E. Kimmel and J. Worell, 1997, *Shaping the Future of Feminist Psychology: Education, Research and Practice,* pp. 121–153, in J. Worell and N. G. Johnson (Eds.), Washington, DC: American Psychological Association. Reprinted with permission.

Women in Academe (2001) began their report with this statement: "Historically, academe has been an inhospitable place for women . . . [and] inequities still exist" (p. 1080). The report documented these inequities in detail. There are rewards as well as risks, of course, for feminist teaching as for all women in academia. Table 12.3 summarizes some of the major risks, challenges, rewards, and needed support for feminist teachers (Kimmel & Worell, 1997). Other sources for support are offered by the book *Career Strategies for Women in Academe: Arming Athena* (Collins, Chrisler, & Quina, 1998).

## Structure

When there are at least two committed faculty (and some interested and supportive students), policies and curriculum can be set in place. Evidence on the experiences of lone or isolated female faculty, especially those with feminist values, suggests strongly that there should be support and strength in numbers (Makowsky & Paludi, 1990). Many decisions require planning with others: about what courses to develop, appropriate breadth and depth for an adequate curriculum, and strategies for implementing the revised curriculum. Factors that require attention include: (a) departmental and university policies; (b) curriculum development; (c) research activities; (d) practice, supervision, and internships; (e) mentoring and social support; and (f) community outreach.

### Policies

Departmental and university policies may need revision toward current practices. First, a commitment to increasing female and ethnically diverse faculty is essential. Although women comprise nearly half of the membership of the American Psychological Association, for example, fewer than 25% of the faculty of accredited university training programs in the United States are women, and fewer still are ethnic minorities. Further, current student body distribution suggests that women are entering the field at a higher rate than are men, so that women students and especially Women of Color are underrepresented by the insufficient proportion of diverse female faculty (Ostertag & McNemara, 1991). Especially important here are the functions they offer of support, mentoring, and the creation of innovative research relevant to the lives of a diverse range of women.

Second, departmental and university policies need to address issues of persisting ethnocentric bias and sexism in language, textbook, allocation of resources, and incidence of sexual harassment of students by faculty. A departmental policy on use of nonsexist language in all student writings and faculty documents and memos, for example, is essential. Despite the official guidelines detailed in the *Publication Manual* of the American Psychological Association (1994, 2001) on how to avoid bias in written language with respect to gender, sexual orientation, ethnic identity, disabilities, and age, the use of the generic *he* is still in evidence in some of our graduate student papers as well as in more scholarly scientific writings. For example, in a review of research that is frequently assigned for graduate student reading on the effectiveness of psychotherapy, the therapist was routinely referred to as *he* (Lambert, Shapiro, & Bergin, 1985).

More recently, Rebecca Campbell and Pamela Schram (1995) conducted a content analysis of 40 textbooks on research methods to determine if these texts used nonsexist language and if they contained discussion on how to avoid gender bias in research. They reported that 18% of these texts still contained sexist language such as "The statistician . . . if he is wise" (p. 93). None of the texts discussed how to avoid gender bias in research. A Task Force of the American Psychological Association (Textbook Task Force,

**Table 12.3   Dimensions of the personal experience of being a feminist teacher**

*Risks*

   Backlash from negative reactions to feminism.

   Unrealistic student expectations for unconditional support.

   Institutional sanctions in tenure and promotion decisions.

   Sexual harassment as a visible and vulnerable target.

   Stigmatization and devaluing of feminist scholarship.

   Professional liabilities in feminist publishing.

   Marginalization of career and scholarship efforts.

   Overextension from too many demands on time and energy.

*Challenges*

   Struggling with appropriate use of power with peers and students.

   Negotiating the special dynamics of faculty—student interactions and relationships: Ethics and boundaries.

   Becoming a realistic and useful role model for students.

   Attending to the impact of feminist teaching on students' academic and personal lives.

   Assessing the effects of feminist pedagogy on the individual, the institution and the larger social system.

   Developing resources and methods to meet the goals of feminist pedagogy.

*Rewards*

   Affirmation of self in the pursuit of important goals.

   Congruence between personal values and professional life.

   Visibility and voice within the institution and community.

   A sense of meaning and purpose associated with membership in a revolutionary social movement.

   Connection to the feminist community.

   Being a midwife to the emergence of feminist consciousness in student.

   Participating in students' personal growth and empowerment.

   Learning from students.

   Collaborating with students and colleagues.

*Needed supports*

   Institutional resources for research, library, assistance.

   More feminist faculty.

   Strong women's studies program.

   More feminists in leadership roles.

   Modifications in evaluation forms to reflect feminist pedagogy.

   Strategies for thriving in hostile environments.

*Source:* "Preaching What We Practice: Principles and Strategies of Feminist Pedagogy," by E. Kimmel and J. Worell, 1997, *Shaping the Future of Feminist Psychology: Education, Research and Practice,* pp. 121–153, in J. Worell and N. G. Johnson (Eds.), Washington, DC: American Psychological Association. Reprinted with permission.

2002) studied college texts for five types of bias related to gender, ethnicity, ageism, sexual orientation, and disability. The degree of omission and/or stereotyping across content areas and across texts reported by the Task Force suggests that departments establish a textbook selection policy with respect to the appropriate inclusion of these variables.

Funding resources need to be monitored continuously to ensure that women faculty and students receive their fair share of financial assistance and research support. Finally, despite federal laws and institutional policies to the contrary, sexual harassment of women faculty and students has not disappeared from college campuses (Lott & Roccio, 1998; Malovich & Stake, 1990; Paludi, 1990). Evidence of sexual harassment needs to be continuously monitored, exposed, and censured. At the university where the authors teach, no sexual harassment policy was in place until one of us pioneered a university policy that, despite considerable administrative protests that it was unnecessary, finally made its way into the student, staff, and faculty codes. It is worthwhile to note that mentoring and modeling played an active role in student development through the planned collaboration of several graduate students in this example of feminist faculty activism.

## Curriculum

There are two major approaches to curriculum development in feminist psychology that reflect *infusion* and *expansion.* We believe that both approaches are essential. The infusion approach implies that the inclusion of concepts, issues, and research related to gender and diversity is relevant to all educational experiences, from course work to field work. Faculty in areas such as human development, history and systems, psychopathology, or assessment can be persuaded to remedy gender or ethnically biased and/or womanless and diversityless readings and texts, and to introduce modules into existing courses that emphasize gender and ethnic-sensitive content. The advantages of infusion are multiple. Primarily, it establishes multiple realities as the norm rather than as a marginal or nonexistent concern. It removes the dominant lens and replaces it with a broader focus that allows all perspectives to be included in the intellectual domain. Infusion is only the first step, however; it does not ensure that critical theory and content necessary for a grounded feminist-diversity understanding and skill development are offered. The expansion approach proposes specific courses on the psychology of women, gender, and diversity are essential.

Celia Foxley (1979) suggested a minimum of four courses for developing an adequate curriculum in "nonsexist" counseling. How much more do we need today as the information explosion produces new theory and research, and the interests of a diverse range of women are introduced? Ideally, a feminist training program requires specific courses that cover life span gender development; gender and multicultural analysis of contemporary society, issues, and techniques in counseling and psychotherapy with women; applied feminist research using current student and faculty projects; and at least one practicum that includes feminist supervision of clients. Specific topics in these courses may vary, but fundamental principles of feminist process, theory, therapy, and research would permeate all elements of the curriculum. Excellent sources are now available for developing and infusing materials and course work in gender and ethnicity into psychology programs (see for example, Margaret Madden and Janet Hyde's special issue of the *Psychology of Women Quarterly,* 1998).

Although there is still controversy about whether the new scholarship on women and ethnically diverse groups should be segregated into separate courses or into mainstream academia (Makowsky & Paludi, 1990; Walsh, 1985), we take side with both positions.

Specialized course work can explore important ethnocultural and gender-related issues with both breadth and depth; infusion into mainstream curriculum can expand these findings to related topics and makes them available to the broader student population. Students in all areas benefit from a balanced view of human behavior that takes into consideration the full range of human experience.

We are particularly concerned with the absence of feminist and diversity content and practice in applied internships and postdoctoral programs. Norine Johnson and Pam Remer and their colleagues (1997) provided a detailed discussion of current practices in postdoctoral training for practice; they offered a model that embodies the values, principles, and procedures that we cover in this book. For both beginning and advanced trainees, programs to match prior experience, interests, and expertise in feminist practice need to be integrated at both internship and postdoctoral levels. Aside from our commitment to feminist-diversity practice, one goal of this training would be to prepare advanced practitioners and scholars to qualify for accreditation by the Board of Professional Psychology. Although no such accreditation exists at the present time for feminist psychological practice, active steps are being taken to meet the requirements for such accreditation (Remer, Enns, Fisher, Nutt, & Worell, 2001).

## Research Activities

Feminist scholars have pointed to the ways in which our science has been gender-biased, androcentric, and ethnocentric in its content and methods and have called for revisions in the manner in which research is conceptualized, conducted, and taught. Chapter 10 discusses these issues in detail and provides a format for transforming traditional research toward more feminist content and form. It is particularly helpful to include an applied feminist research course or research teams in which students and interested faculty work together to plan research, react to one another's ideas, and provide constructive feedback to developing research projects. In our experience, many talented students become anxious, unfocused, and frequently immobilized by the challenges in developing and completing a dissertation thesis. A feminist research group can be useful in sharing and allaying some of this impediment to student progress. Such a group is especially important in providing support to students whose feminist-diversity research may be challenged by nonfeminist faculty.

## Practice Issues

Practice in feminist theory and process is encouraged through four broad procedures:

1. Assignment of a wide range of diverse clients to provide opportunities for practicing feminist and multicultural skills.
2. Supervision that employs a feminist process and focuses on issues related to diversity and feminist perspectives.
3. Placement in agencies that specialize in women's issues and that serve a diverse range of clients (women's shelters, rape crisis centers, women's health centers, eating disorders, and reproductive planning clinics, etc.).
4. Monitoring of predoctoral internship sites to facilitate a feminist, cross-cultural, or gender-sensitive placement.

Qualifying examinations can contribute to this unfolding process by including written or oral questions on how the student's theoretical orientation is compatible with feminist and multicultural counseling theory and practice. As an example of feminist process in practice training, we center on supervision.

## Supervision

Contrasting models of clinical supervision tend to differ in terms of their emphasis on process, procedures, relationships, or didactics (Hess, 1980). Feminist supervision may include aspects of all these models, but it also includes unique characteristics. In particular, feminist-diversity supervision is sensitive to power differential between trainee and supervisor, to issues presented by cross-cultural dyads, as well as to broadly valued philosophical goals. Natalie Porter (1995) offered a four-stage model of feminist supervision that was designed to promote awareness and competence in integrating issues of gender, race, class, and ethnicity into practice. Her approach included information and didactics, understanding of the "other," exploring one's own biases and how they might affect one's clinical work, and encouraging an active approach to confront and overcome these internalized biases.

Feminist supervision can consist of direct observation or cotherapy, audiotape and/or videotape review, case conference, and case analysis. We believe that group supervision is particularly appropriate because it is relatively efficient in faculty resource allocation, it exposes a larger number of students to the process of feminist analysis, and it provides for peer, as well as faculty, feedback. In any feminist model, each of the following components should be included:

1. Attention to process (between counselor and client, between trainee and faculty, and among trainees) to facilitate egalitarian, open, and flexible interactions.
2. Application of gender and cultural analyses with respect to trainee-client interactions with both females and males, ethnic or culturally different clients, and those who have a different sexual orientation to that of the trainee.
3. Exploration of how the trainee's current theoretical orientation matches with feminist and diversity goals.
4. Examination of contracted therapy goals with respect to client-counselor collaboration; analysis of problematic goals proposed by client (such as client's goal to avoid making her husband angry).
5. Redefining health and pathology; attention to assessment and diagnosis to monitor potentially damaging labels and procedures (such as the tendency to describe women in problematic relationships as nagging or codependent, mothers as controlling and enmeshed, and ambivalent clients as passive-aggressive).
6. Focus on external as well as internal sources of client problems; looking at how current issues trace back to institutionalized SEARCH factors and internalized cultural and gender-role messages.
7. Evaluation of progress that provides continuous and constructive feedback to client and that emphasizes her strengths; focusing on the process of change toward personal empowerment, autonomy, and community connectedness.
8. Assistance in designing and developing specialized women's groups, workshops, and educational formats for reaching a wider range of public consumers. Emphasis on prevention as well as on remediation.
9. Respect and validation for the strengths of the trainee; assisting trainee to trust own experience.

A set of principles to guide these activities in feminist supervision was adopted at the First National Conference on Feminist Practice (see Worell & Johnson, 1997). These principles provide a useful format when implementing the feminist supervision activities listed previously. Table 12.4 displays these principles.

## Social Support

Support groups for students with feminist counseling focus are important for (a) dealing with personal issues related to being a woman, lesbian or bisexual, ethnic or cultural minority, and/or a developing feminist; (b) continued consciousness-raising for applications of their program to personal and professional issues; and (c) personal support for surviving in a nonfeminist environment. A woman's group that includes both students and interested faculty becomes a useful and sometimes critical mechanism for meeting these needs and can be a vehicle for introducing newer students to the possibilities of the program. In particular, we emphasize that interactions within such a group can turn the personal into the political, as students discover that many of their "personal" issues are experienced by others as well.

**Table 12.4   Principles guiding feminist supervision**

| Principle | Description |
| --- | --- |
| Principle 1 | Feminist supervisors are proactive in analyzing power dynamics and differentials between the supervisors and the supervisee, model the use of power in the service of the supervisee, and vigilantly avoid abuses of power. |
| Principle 2 | Feminist supervision is based on a collaborative relationship, defined as mutually respectful, where the supervisee's autonomy and diverse perspectives are encouraged. |
| Principle 3 | Feminist supervisors facilitate reflexive interactions and supervisee self-examination by modeling openness, authenticity, reflexivity, and the value of lifelong learning and self-examination. |
| Principle 4 | Supervision occurs in a social context that attends to and emphasizes the diversity of women's lives and context. |
| Principle 5 | Feminist supervisors attend to the social construction of gender and the role of language in maintaining a gendered society. |
| Principle 6 | Feminist supervisors advance and model the feminist principle of advocacy and activism. |
| Principle 7 | Feminist supervisors maintain standards that ensure their supervisees' competent and ethical practice. |
| Principle 8 | Feminist supervisors attend to the developmental shifts occurring in the supervisory process and provide input as a function of the skill level, developmental level, and maturational level of the supervisee. |
| Principle 9 | Feminist supervisors advocate for their supervisees and clients in the educational and training settings with which they practice. |

*Source:* From "Covision: Feminist Supervision, Process, and Collaboration," by N. Porter and M. Vasquez, 1997, in *Shaping the Future of Feminist Psychology: Education, Research, and Practice* (pp. 155–172), by J. Worell and N. G. Johnson (Eds.), Washington, DC: American Psychological Association. Reprinted with permission.

Modifications in social support groups may be required for programs in which men have decided to become feminist in their orientation and wish to join the support group. Women's groups frequently reject the inclusion of men because of their experiences of mixed-sex groups and consequent difficulties in interaction. We know of no evidence, however, of mixed-sex support groups for feminist counselors, a model that is potentially useful and might increase awareness for both women and men. Scholars in teaching the Psychology of Women, however, recommend that even in mixed-sex groups, women and men should be provided with the opportunity to meet separately for periods of time to facilitate open and uninhibited self-disclosure (Paludi, 1990).

## Resources

Resources can be minimal or lavish, but basic prerequisites need to be in place before a fully functioning feminist program can operate. These resources include: at least two feminist faculty members, one or more ethnic minority faculty, one or more supportive male faculty, departmental support with respect to allocation of course work and service responsibilities, support faculty in other university departments for committee participation, students recruited for special interest in the program, adequate library holdings including gender and culturally focused periodicals, cooperating community agencies, and professional contacts with other feminist psychologists. The process of developing, acquiring, and conserving current resources is typically gradual and continuous.

Finally, the program is enriched if other curriculum and faculty resources are available in the university. Gender and culturally related course work can include offerings from perspectives other than psychology: sociology, anthropology, education, women's studies, social work, and political science. Students are encouraged to attend cross-departmental and external seminars, colloquia, and workshops. Early in their program, students are encouraged to expand their professional commitment through membership and participation in relevant organizations that provide professional contacts related to women's issues, such as the Association for Women in Psychology, or the Society for the Psychology of Women (a Division of the American Psychological Association).

## Outreach

A fully functioning graduate psychology program for preparing feminist therapists requires concerted activism and outreach on the part of both faculty and students. First, faculty serve as role models, not only for their research and practice approaches, but for their visibility in local, regional, and national activities. Feminist faculty join and take active steps in organizations that articulate and facilitate their goals, and they make students aware of these activities (Crosby et al., 1996). Faculty serve on boards and committees in the community that further feminist goals, such as rape crisis or spouse abuse centers or a teenage mothers' project. Feminist faculty may organize or become part of other local professional groups that are working for women's equity and professional advancement. All of these activities are communicated to students, who are mentored and encouraged to participate as well.

Feminist faculty also become involved in university affairs dealing with women. They participate on committees that investigate women faculty salaries, tenure procedures, policies affecting women (such as sexual harassment or maternity leave), and employment of diverse female faculty. They initiate or collaborate in developing workshops, seminars, and conferences relevant to the diversity of women. They volunteer time to speak to other classes, thereby helping to infuse women's content into mainstream academia. And feminist faculty focus on networking with other university, community, national, and international women who can serve as resources and support systems for the program and its participants.

## Addendum

If this training program seems ambitious and demanding of time, effort, and dedication, the implications for expansion are clear. In the absence of considerable personal

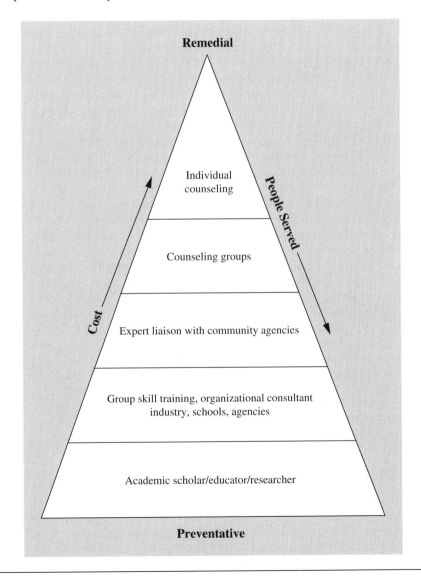

**Figure 12.3   A cascade model of intervention for social change.**

commitment, networking with other feminist professionals, and support from the home university, such programs are difficult to implement and maintain. The few women faculty can become overburdened with more responsibilities than are possible to fulfill, especially those related to outreach and social activism. The program outlined here represents more of an ideal than a reality until women and diverse feminist faculty are no longer a minority in academia.

## Evaluating Outcomes

We envision multiple outcomes of a training program in feminist counseling. We propose a cascade model that depicts a triad of training outcomes in terms of (a) types of service provided (educational, preventative or remedial); (b) populations served (many to few); and (c) ratio of intervention cost to size of population served. Within these dimensions, the attitudes, knowledge, and skills produced by the training program are integrated within each service-provider function: researcher/scholar, educator, consultant, administrator, change agent, or direct counseling practice. Graduates are prepared to function effectively in any of these areas, but in practice will probably select a few areas for personal commitment. The cascade model is displayed in Figure 12.3.

At the broadest level of intervention, the researcher/scholar function produces new knowledge about women, men, and their social and ethnocultural environments that is disseminated through research reports and written documentation. This information becomes available nationally as well as internationally and survives over time to influence the development of the discipline. At the narrowest level, personal counseling is provided for individual clients in a clinical practice or agency. Across the functions within the model, the training program aims to produce a cadre of specialists in the psychology and life-career development of diverse women who will interface with organizations, community agencies, and individuals to create a collaborative network for implementing social change.

Evaluations of the model and training program outcomes are accomplished by means of within-program assessment of attitudes, knowledge, and skills, and periodic follow-up of graduates to determine the implementation and distribution of their skills and activities. Earlier, we reviewed briefly a program evaluation study (Worell et al., 1999) supporting our contention that education about gender and the diversity of women can significantly influence multiple aspects of student development. It remains for further research to document how training in EFT will impact these students as they pursue their careers in practice, research, social policy, or in academic arenas.

## SUMMARY AND CONCLUSIONS

In this chapter, we reviewed some of the variables that influence individuals toward developing a feminist awareness. We presented a model of feminist identity development and some support for its applications to personal change. Measures of feminist identity development are available and can be combined with other assessments to evaluate selected outcomes of a gender and culturally sensitive curriculum. We outlined a model program of graduate training in feminist counseling containing four factors: attitudes and values, structures, resources, and outreach. Suggestions for a preliminary evaluation of a feminist training program, in the form of a Cascade Model of intervention, were offered.

## ACTIVITIES

**A.** With a partner, review the model training program and compare its contents and process with your current or past programs. How do they differ and how are they similar?

**B.** Prepare and present three suggestions for revising your current or former graduate program to match the goals of a feminist-diversity agenda.

**C.** Retake the Self and World Views self-assessment (Feminist Identity Development Scale) at the beginning of this book and compare your scores on each factor with your previous scores before you read the book. Please recall that the scale presented here is a shortened version of the Bargad and Hyde (1991) scale. We dropped stage four and revised the gender content of some items so that men, as well as women, can respond. Share your observations with a partner and compare how each of you has changed.

## FURTHER READINGS

Downing, N. E., & Roush, K. L. (1985). From passive acceptance to active commitment: A model of feminist identity development for women. *Counseling Psychologist, 13,* 665–670.

Johnson, N. G., & Remer, P. (1997). Postdoctoral training in feminist psychological practice. In J. Worell & N. G. Johnson (Eds.), *Shaping the future of feminist psychology: Research, education, and practice* (pp. 203–226). Washington, DC: American Psychological Association.

Kimmel, E., & Worell, J. (1997). Practicing what we preach: Principles and strategies of feminist pedagogy. In J. Worell & N. G. Johnson (Eds.), *Shaping the future of feminist psychology: Research, education, and practice* (pp. 121–154). Washington, DC: American Psychological Association.

Porter, N. (1995). Supervision of psychotherapists: Integrating anti-racist, feminist, and multicultural perspectives. In H. Landrine (Ed.), *Bringing cultural diversity to feminist psychology: Theory, research, and practice* (pp. 163–176). Washington, DC: American Psychological Association.

# References

Abbey, A., McAuslan, P., & Ross, L. T. (1998). Sexual assault perpetration by college men: The role of alcohol, misperception of sexual intent, and sexual beliefs and experience. *Journal of Social and Clinical Psychology, 2,* 167–195.

Abramson, L. Y., Seligman, M. E. P., & Teasdale, J. D. (1978). Learned helplessness in humans: Critique and reformulation. *Journal of Abnormal Psychology, 87,* 49–74.

Allen, F. (1995). Feminist theory and cognitive behaviorism. In W. O'Donohue & L. Krasner (Eds.), *Theories of behavior therapy* (pp. 495–528). Washington, DC: American Psychological Association.

Alloy, L. B., & Abramson, L. Y. (1988). Depressive realism: Four theoretical perspectives. In L. B. Alloy (Ed.), *Cognitive processes in depression* (pp. 223–265). New York: Guilford Press.

Alsdurf, J. M. (1985, Winter). Wife abuse and the church: The response of pastors. *Response,* 9–11.

American Association of University Women. (1992). *The AAUW report: How school shortchanges girls.* Washington, DC: American Association of University Women Educational Foundation.

American Association of University Women. (1993). *Hostile hallways: AAUW survey on sexual harassment in American schools.* Washington, DC: American Association of University Women Educational Foundation.

American Association of University Women. (1995). *Growing smart: What's working for girls in school.* Washington, DC: American Association of University Women Educational Foundation.

American Association of University Women. (2001). Wife-beaters.com. *Outlook, 95,* 12.

American Psychiatric Association. (1980). *Diagnostic and statistical manual of mental disorders* (2nd ed.). Washington, DC: Author.

American Psychiatric Association. (1994). *Diagnostic and statistical manual of mental disorders* (4th ed.). Washington, DC: Author.

American Psychological Association. (1975). Report of the Task Force on Sex Bias and Sex-Role Stereotyping in Psychotherapeutic Practice. *American Psychologist, 30,* 1169–1175.

American Psychological Association. (1983). *Publication manual of the American Psychological Association* (3rd ed.). Washington, DC: Author.

American Psychological Association. (1992). Ethical principles of psychologists and code of conduct. *American Psychologist, 47,* 1597–1611.

American Psychological Association. (1996). *Violence and the family: Report of the presidential task force.* Washington, DC: Author.

American Psychological Association. (2001). *Publication manual of the American Psychological Association* (5th ed.). Washington, DC: Author.

American Psychological Association. (2002). *Proceedings: Summit on women and depression.* Washington, DC: Author.

Astin, H. S. (1984). The meaning of work in women's lives: A sociopsychological model of career choice and work behaviors. *Counseling Psychology, 12,* 117–126.

Astin, H. S., & Lindholm, J. A. (2001). Academic aspirations and degree attainment of women. In J. Worell (Ed.), *Encyclopedia of women and gender: Sex similarities and differences and the impact of society on gender* (Vol. 1, pp. 15–27). San Diego, CA: Academic Press.

Atkinson, D. R., Morton, G., & Sue, D. W. (1998). *Counseling American minorities* (5th ed.). Boston: McGraw-Hill.

Auster, E. R. (2001). Professional women's midcareer satisfaction: Toward an explanatory framework. *Sex Roles, 44,* 719–750.

Baltes, P. B., Staudinger, U. M., & Lindenberger, U. (1999). Lifespan psychology: Theory and application to intellectual functioning. In J. T. Spence, J. M. Darley, & D. L. Foss (Eds.), *Annual review of psychology* (Vol. 50, pp. 471–507). Palo Alto, CA: Annual Reviews.

Bandura, A. (1977a). Self-efficacy: Toward a unifying theory of behavior change. *Psychological Review, 84,* 191–215.

Bandura, A. (1977b). *Social learning theory.* Englewood Cliffs, NJ: Prentice-Hall.

Bandura, A. (1978). The self system in reciprocal determinism. *American Psychologist, 33,* 344–358.

Bandura, A. (1986). *Social foundations of thought and action.* Englewood Cliffs, NJ: Prentice-Hall.

Bandura, A. (1997). *Self-efficacy: The exercise of control.* New York: Freeman.

Bandura, A. (2001). Social cognitive theory: An agentic perspective. In S. T. Fiske, D. L. Schacter, & C. Zahn-Waxler (Eds.), *Annual review of psychology* (Vol. 52, pp. 1–26). Palo Alto, CA: Annual Reviews.

Bargad, A., & Hyde, J. S. (1991). Women's studies: A study of feminist identity development. *Psychology of Women Quarterly, 15,* 181–201.

Barnard, C. P. (1994). Resiliency: A shift in our perception? *American Journal of Family Therapy, 22,* 135–144.

Barnett, R. C., & Hyde, J. S. (2001). Women, men, work, and family: An expansionist theory. *American Psychologist, 56,* 781–796.

Barnett, R. C., & Rivers, C. (1998). *She works/he works: How two-income families are happy, healthy, and thriving.* Cambridge, MA: Harvard University Press.

Barry, R. J. (1980). Stereotyping of sex role in preschoolers in relation to age, family structure, and parental sexism. *Sex Roles, 6,* 975–976.

Baruth, L. G., & Manning, M. L. (1999). *Multicultural counseling and psychotherapy: A lifespan perspective* (2nd ed.). Columbus, OH: Merrill.

Basow, S. A. (1992). *Gender stereotypes and roles* (3rd ed.). Pacific Grove, CA: Brooks/Cole.

Basow, S. A., & Rubin, L. R. (1999). Gender influences on adolescent development. In N. G. Johnson, M. C. Roberts, & J. Worell (Eds.), *Beyond appearance: A new look at adolescent girls* (pp. 25–52). Washington, DC: American Psychological Association.

Baucom, D. H., Epstein, N., Daiuto, A. D., Carels, R. A., Rankink, L. A., & Burnett, C. K. (1996). Cognitions in marriage: The relationship between standards and attributions. *Journal of Family Psychology, 10,* 209–222.

Beck, A. T. (1976). *Cognitive therapy and the emotional disorders.* New York: International Universities Press.

Beck, A. T., Steer, R. A., & Brown, G. K. (1996). *Beck Depression Inventory* (2nd ed.). San Antonio, TX: Psychological Corporation.

Becker, D. (2001). Diagnosis of psychological disorders: *DSM* and gender. In J. Worell (Ed.), *Encyclopedia of women and gender: Sex similarities and differences and the impact of society on gender* (Vol. 1, pp. 333–343). San Diego, CA: Academic Press.

Becker, D., & Lamb, S. (1994). Sex bias in the diagnosis of borderline personality disorder and post traumatic stress disorder. *Professional Psychology: Research and Practice, 25,* 56–61.

Belenky, M. F., Clinchey, B. M., Goldberger, N. R., & Tarule, J. M. (1986). *Women's ways of knowing: Development of self, voice, and mind.* New York: Basic Books.

Bem, S. L. (1974). The measurement of psychological androgyny. *Journal of Consulting and Clinical Psychology, 47,* 155–162.

Bem, S. L. (1983). Gender schema theory and its implications for child development: Raising gender-aschematic children in a gender schematic society. *Signs, 8,* 598–616.

Bem, S. L. (1993). *The lenses of gender: Transforming the debate on sexual inequality.* New Haven, CT: Yale University Press.

Benedetto, B., & Tittle, C. K. (1990). Gender and adult roles: Role commitment of women and men in a job-family trade-off context. *Journal of Counseling Psychology, 37,* 41–48.

Benokraitis, N. V., & Feagin, J. R. (1986). *Modern sexism: Blatant, covert, and subtle discrimination.* Englewood Cliffs, NJ: Prentice-Hall.

Berkowitz, A. (1992). College men as perpetrators of acquaintance rape and sexual assault: A review of recent research. *College Health, 40,* 175–181.

Berman, J. R. S. (1985). Ethical feminist perspectives on dual relationships with clients. In L. B. Rosewater & L. E. A. Walker (Eds.), *Handbook of feminist therapy* (pp. 287–296). New York: Springer.

Betancourt, H., & Lopez, S. R. (1993). The study of culture, ethnicity, and race in American psychology. *American Psychologist, 48,* 629–637.

Betz, N. E. (1992). Counseling uses of career self-efficacy theory. *Career Development Quarterly, 41,* 22–26.

Betz, N. E. (1993). Issues in the use of ability and interest measures with women. *Journal of Career Assessment, 1,* 217–232.

Betz, N. E. (1994). Self-concept theory in career development and counseling. *Career Development Quarterly, 43,* 32–42.

Betz, N. E., & Hackett, G. (1981). The relationship of career-related self-efficacy expectations to perceived career options in college women and men. *Journal of Counseling Psychology, 28,* 399–410.

Betz, N. E., & Hackett, G. (1987). Concept of agency in educational and career development. *Journal of Counseling Psychology, 34,* 299–304.

Biaggio, M., & Greene, B. (1995). Overlapping/dual relationships. In E. J. Rave & C. C. Larsen (Eds.), *Ethical decision making in therapy: Feminist perspectives* (pp. 88–123). New York: Guilford Press.

Black, L., & Piercy, F. P. (1991). A feminists family therapy scale. *Journal of Marriage and Family Therapy, 17,* 111–120.

Blatner, A. (1996). *Acting-in: Practical applications of psychodramatic methods* (2nd ed.). New York: Springer.

Blatner, A. (2000). *Foundations of psychodrama: History, theory, and practice.* New York: Springer.

Blatner, A., & Blatner, A. (1988). *Foundations of psychodrama: History, theory, & practice.* New York: Springer.

Blatner, H. A. (1973). *Acting-in: Practical applications of psychodramatic methods.* New York: Springer.

Bleier, R. (1984). *Science and gender: A critique of biology and its theories on women.* Elmsford, NY: Pergamon Press.

Bleier, R. (1988). Sex differences research: Science or belief. In R. Bleier (Ed.), *Feminist approaches to science* (pp. 147–164). New York: Pergamon Press.

Block, J. H. (1979). Another look at sex differentiation in the socialization behavior of mothers and fathers. In J. Sherman & F. F. Denmark (Eds.), *Psychology of women: Future directions for research.* New York: Psychological Dimensions.

Block, J. H. (1983). Differential premises arising from differential socializations of the sexes: Some conjectures. *Child Development, 54,* 1335–1354.

Block, J. H., Block, J., & Harrington, D. (1975). Sex-role typing and instrumental behavior: A developmental study. *Child Development, 54,* 1335–1354.

Blumstein, P., & Schwartz, P. (1983). *American couples: Money, work, and sex.* New York: Morrow.

Bograd, M. (1986). A feminist examination of family therapy: What is women's place? In D. Howard (Ed.), *Dynamics of feminist therapy* (pp. 95–106). New York: Haworth.

Bograd, M. (1988). Feminist perspectives on wife abuse: An introduction. In K. Yllo & M. Bograd (Eds.), *Feminist perspectives on wife abuse* (pp. 11–26). Newbury Park, CA: Sage.

Bornstein, M. H., Cote, L. R., & Venuti, P. (2001). Parenting beliefs and behaviors in northern and southern groups of Italian mothers of young infants. *Journal of Family Psychology, 15,* 663–675.

Bowker, L. H., Arbitell, M., & McFerron, J. R. (1988). On the relationship between wife beating and child abuse. In K. Yllo & M. Bograd (Eds.), *Feminist perspectives on wife abuse* (pp. 158–174). Newbury Park, CA: Sage.

Brabeck, M. M., & Ting, K. (2000). Feminist ethics: Lenses for examining ethical psychological practice. In M. M. Brabeck (Ed.), *Practicing feminist ethics in psychology* (pp. 17–35). Washington, DC: American Psychological Association.

Brickman, J. (1984). Feminist, non-sexist, and traditional model of therapy: Implications for working with incest. *Women and Therapy, 3,* 49–67.

Brickman, P., Rabinowitz, V. C., Karuza, J., Coates, D., Cohn, E., & Kikker, L. (1982). Models of helping and coping. *American Psychologist, 37,* 368–384.

Briere, J. (1995). *Trauma Symptom Inventory.* Odessa, FL: Psychological Assessment Resources.

Briere, J., & Malamuth, N. (1983). Self-reported likelihood of sexually aggressive behavior: Attitudinal vs. sexual explanations. *Journal of Research in Personality, 17,* 315–323.

Brockner, J., & Rubin, J. Z. (1985). *Entrapment in escalating conflicts: A social psychological analysis.* New York: Springer.

Brodsky, A. M. (1973). The consciousness-raising group as a model for therapy with women. *Psychotherapy: Therapy, Research, and Practice, 10,* 24–29.

Brodsky, A. M., & Hare-Mustin, R. T. (1980). *Psychotherapy with women: An assessment of research and practice.* New York: Guilford Press.

Bronstein, P. (2001). Parenting. In J. Worell (Ed.), *Encyclopedia of women and gender: Sex similarities and differences and the impact of society on gender* (Vol. 1, pp. 798–808). San Diego, CA: Academic Press.

Brooks-Gunn, J. (1986). The relationship of maternal beliefs about sex-typing to maternal and young children's behavior. *Sex Roles, 14,* 21–35.

Broverman, I. K., Broverman, D. M., Clarkson, F. E., Rosenkrantz, P. S., & Vogel, S. R. (1970). Sex-role stereotypes and clinical judgments of mental health. *Journal of Consulting and Clinical Psychology, 34,* 1–7.

Brown, G. W., & Harris, T. (1978). *The social origins of depression: A study of psychiatric disorder in women.* London: Tavistock.

Brown, L. (1996, January). *The feminist academy.* Proposal presented at the midwinter meeting of the Society for the Psychology of Women, Seattle, WA.

Brown, L. S. (1987, August). *Towards a new conceptual paradigm for the Axis II diagnoses.* Paper presented at the annual meeting of the American Psychological Association, New York.

Brown, L. S. (1991). Ethical issues in feminist therapy: Selected topics. *Psychology of Women Quarterly, 15,* 323–336.

Brown, L. S. (1994). *Subversive dialogues: Theory in feminist therapy.* New York: Basic Books.

Brown, L., & Root, M. (Eds.). (1990). *Diversity and complexity in feminist therapy.* New York: Haworth.

Browne, A. (1993). Violence against women by male partners. *American Psychologist, 48,* 1077–1087.

Brownmiller, S. (1975). *Against our will: Men, women, and rape.* New York: Simon & Schuster.

Burkhart, B. R., & Fromuth, M. E. (1991). Individual and social psychological understandings of sexual coercion. In E. Gruerholz & M. A. Koralewski (Eds.), *Sexual coercion: A sourcebook on its nature, causes, and prevention* (pp. 75–89). Lexington, MA: Lexington Books.

Burn, S. M. (1996). *The social psychology of gender.* New York: McGraw-Hill.

Burnam, M. A., Stein, J. A., Golding, J. M., Siegel, J. M., Sorenson, S. B., Forsythe, A. B., et al. (1988). Sexual assault and mental disorders in a community population. *Journal of Consulting and Clinical Psychology, 56,* 843–850.

Buss, D. (1996). The evolutionary psychology of human social strategies. In E. T. Higgins & A. W. Kruglanski (Eds.), *Social psychology: Handbook of basic principles* (p. 38). New York: Guilford Press.

Bussey, K., & Bandura, A. (1999). Social cognitive theory of gender development and differentiation. *Psychological Bulletin, 106,* 676–713.

Byars, A. M., & Hackett, G. (1998). Applications of social cognitive theory to the career development of women of color. *Applied and Preventive Psychology, 7,* 255–267.

Calhoun, L. G., & Tedeschi, R. G. (1998). Beyond recovery from trauma: Implications for clinical practice and research. *Journal of Social Issues, 54,* 357–371.

Campbell, B., Shellenberg, E. G., & Senn, C. Y. (1997). Evaluating measures of contemporary sexism. *Psychology of Women Quarterly, 21,* 89–102.

Campbell, R., & Schram, P. J. (1995). Feminist research methods: A content analysis of psychology and social science textbooks. *Psychology of Women Quarterly, 19,* 85–106.

Cancian, F. M. (1987). *Love in America: Gender and self-development.* Cambridge, MA: Cambridge University Press.

Caplan, P. J. (1985). *The myth of women's masochism.* New York: Signet.

Caplan, P. J. (1995). *They say you're crazy: How the world's most powerful psychiatrists decide who's normal.* Reading, MA: Addison-Wesley.

Caplan, P. J., & Hall-McCorquodale, I. (1985). Mother-blaming in major clinical journals. *American Journal of Orthopsychiatry, 55,* 345–353.

Carli, L. (2001). Assertiveness. In J. Worell (Ed.), *Encyclopedia of women and gender: Sex similarities and differences and the impact of society on gender* (Vol. 1, pp. 157–168). San Diego, CA: Academic Press.

Carr, J. G., Gilroy, F. D., & Sherman, M. F. (1996). Silencing the self and depression among women: The moderating role of race. *Psychology of Women Quartely, 20,* 375–392.

Cass, V. (1979). Homosexual identity formation: A theoretical model. *Journal of Homosexuality, 4,* 219–235.

Cate, R. M., Henton, J. M., Koval, J., Christopher, F. S., & Lloyd, S. (1982). Premarital abuse: A social psychological perspective. *Journal of Family Issues, 3,* 79–90.

Cauce, A. M., Hiraga, Y., Graves, D., Gonzales, N., Ryan-Finn, K., & Grove, K. (1996). Mothers and their adolescent daughters: Closeness, conflict, and control. In B. J. R. Leadbeater & N. Way (Eds.), *Urban girls: Resisting stereotypes, creating identities* (pp. 100–116). New York: New York University Press.

Chambless, D. L., & Hollon, S. D. (1998). Defining empirically supported therapies. *Journal of Consulting and Clinical Psychology, 66,* 7–18.

Chambless, D. L., & Ollendick, T. H. (2001). Empirically supported psychological interventions: Controversies and evidence. In S. T. Fiske, D. L. Schacter, & C. Zahn-Waxler (Eds.), *Annual review of psychology* (Vol. 52, pp. 685–716). Palo Alto, CA: Annual Reviews.

Chandler, R., Worell, J., Johnson, D., Blount, A., & Lusk, M. (1999, August). Measuring long-term outcomes of feminist counseling and psychotherapy. In J. Worell (Chair), *Measuring process and outcomes of feminist counseling and therapy.* Presented at the annual meeting of the American Psychological Association as part of a symposium, Boston.

Chard, K., Weaver, T. L., & Resick, P. A. (1997). Adapting cognitive processing therapy and child sexual abuse survivors. *Cognitive and Behavioral Practice, 4,* 31–52.

Chodorow, N. (1978). *The reproduction of mothering: Psychoanalysis and the sociology of gender.* Berkeley: University of California Press.

Clance, P. R., & Imes, S. A. (1978). The impostor phenomenon in high achieving women: Dynamics and therapeutic interventions. *Psychotherapy: Theory, Research, and Practice, 15,* 241–247.

Clance, P. R., & O'Toole, M. A. (1987). The imposter phenomenon: An internal barrier to empowerment and achievement. *Women and Therapy, 6,* 51–64.

Clark, M. C., Caffarella, R. S., & Ingram, P. B. (1999). Women in leadership: Living with the constraint of the glass ceiling. *Initiatives, 59,* 65–76.

Cogan, J. (1997). *A conceptual framework for eating disorders.* Washington, DC: American Psychological Association.

Cole, N. S., & Hanson, G. R. (1978). Impact of interest inventories on career choice. In L. S. Hansen & R. S. Rapoza (Eds.), *Career development and counseling of women* (pp. 487–509). Springfield, IL: Charles C Thomas.

Collins, L. H., Chrisler, J. C., & Quina, K. (1998). *Career strategies for women in academe: Arming Athena.* Thousand Oaks, CA: Sage.

Comas-Diaz, L. (1991). Feminism and diversity in psychology: The case of women of color. *Psychology of Women Quarterly, 15,* 594–610.

Comas-Diaz, L., & Greene, B. (1994). *Women of color: Integrating ethnic and gender identities in psychotherapy.* New York: Guilford Press.

Constantinople, A. (1973). Masculinity–femininity: An exception to a famous dictum? *Psychological Bulletin, 80,* 309–407.

Contratto, S., & Hassinger, J. (1995). Violence against women. In E. J. Rave & C. C. Larsen (Eds.), *Ethical decision making in therapy: Feminist perspectives* (pp. 124–152). New York: Guilford Press.

Cortina, L. H., Swan, S., Fitzgerald, L. F., & Waldo, C. (1998). Sexual harassment and assault: Chilling the climate for women in academia. *Psychology of Women Quarterly, 22,* 419–441.

Cowan, G., Lee, C., Levy, D., & Snyder, D. (1988). Dominance and inequality in X-rated videocassettes. *Psychology of Women Quarterly, 12,* 299–311.

Craighead, L. W., Craighead, W. E., Kazdin, A. E., & Mahoney, M. J. (1994). *Cognitive and behavioral interventions: An empirical approach to mental health problems.* Boston: Allyn & Bacon.

Crawford, I., McLeod, A., Zamboni, B. D., & Jordan, M. B. (1999). Psychologists' attitudes toward gay and lesbian parenting. *Professional Psychology: Research and Practice, 30,* 394–401.

Crawford, M. C. (2001). Gender and language. In R. K. Unger (Ed.), *Handbook of the psychology of women and gender* (pp. 228–241). New York: Wiley.

Crawford, M. C., & Kimmel, E. B. (Eds.). (1999). Innovations in feminist research [Special issue]. *Psychology of Women Quarterly, 23*(1/2, Whole).

Crawford, M. C., & Kimmel, E. B. (2001). Methods for studying gender. In J. Worell (Ed.), *Encyclopedia of women and gender: Sex similarities and differences and the impact of society on gender* (Vol. 2, pp. 749–758). San Diego, CA: Academic Press.

Crawford, M. C., & Marecek, J. (1989). Psychology reconstructs the female: 1968–1988. *Psychology of Women Quarterly, 13,* 147–167.

Crosby, F. J. (1982). *Relative deprivation and working women.* New York: Oxford University Press.

Crosby, F. J. (1991). *Juggling: The unexpected advantage of balancing career and home for women and their families.* New York: Free Press.

Crosby, F. J., Todd, J., & Worell, J. (1996). Have feminists abandoned social activism? Voices from the academy. In L. Montada & L. J. Lerner (Eds.), *Current societal concerns about justice* (pp. 85–102). New York: Plenum Press.

Cross, W. E. (1980). Models of psychological nigrescence. In R. L. Jones (Ed.), *Black psychology* (pp. 81–98). New York: Harper & Row.

Cummings, A. L. (1999, August). Assessing the process and outcome of short-term feminist therapy. In J. Worell (Chair), *Measuring process and outcomes in feminist counseling and therapy.* Symposium presented at the annual meeting of the American Psychological Association, Boston.

Dana, R. H. (2000). Culture and methodology in personality assessment. In I. Cuellar & F. A. Paniagua (Eds.), *Handbook of multicultural mental health: Assessment and treatment of diverse populations* (pp. 97–120). San Diego, CA: Academic Press.

Dattilio, F. M. (2000). Cognitive-behavioral strategies. In J. Carlson & L. Sperry (Eds.), *Brief therapy with individuals and couples* (pp. 33–70). Phoenix, AZ: Zeig, Tucker & Theisen.

de las Fuentes, C., & Vasquez, M. J. T. (1999). Immigrant adolescent girls of color: Facing American challenges. In N. G. Johnson, M. C. Roberts, & J. Worell (Eds.), *Beyond appearance: A new look at adolescent girls* (pp. 131–150). Washington, DC: American Psychological Association.

Deaux, K. (1984). From individual differences to social categories: Analysis of a decade's research on gender. *American Psychologist, 39,* 105–116.

Deaux, K. (1985). Sex and gender. In M. R. Rosensweig & L. W. Porter (Eds.), *Annual review of psychology* (Vol. 36, pp. 49–82). Palo Alto, CA: Annual Reviews.

Deaux, K. (1993). Reconstructing social identity. *Personality and Social Psychology Bulletin, 19,* 4–12.

Deaux, K. (1996). Social identification. In E. T. Higgins & A. W. Kruglanski (Eds.), *Social psychology: Handbook of basic principles* (pp. 777–795). New York: Guilford Press.

Deaux, K., & Major, B. (1987). Putting gender into context: An interactional model of gender-related behavior. *Psychological Bulletin, 94,* 369–389.

Deaux, K., & Stewart, A. J. (2001). Framing gendered identities. In R. K. Unger (Ed.), *Handbook of the psychology of women and gender* (pp. 84–100). New York: Wiley.

Delaney, W., & Lee, C. (1995). Self esteem and sex roles among male and female high school students: Their relationships to physical activity. *Australian Psychologist, 30,* 84–87.

DeRubeis, R. J. (1999). Cognitive-behavioral therapy is comparable to antidepressants. *American Journal of Psychiatry, 156,* 1007–1013.

Deutsch, F. M., & Saxon, S. E. (1998). The double standard of praise and criticism for mothers and fathers. *Psychology of Women Quarterly, 22,* 665–683.

Dewey, C. R. (1974). Exploring interests: A non-sexist method. *Personnel and Guidance Journal, 52,* 311–315.

DeZolt, D. M., & Henning-Stout, M. (1999). Adolescent girls experiences in school and community settings. In N. G. Johnson, M. C. Roberts, & J. Worell (Eds.), *Beyond appearance: A new look at adolescent girls* (pp. 253–275). Washington, DC: American Psychological Association.

Dion, K. K., & Dion, K. L. (2001). Gender and relationships. In R. K. Unger (Ed.), *Handbook of the psychology of women and gender* (pp. 256–271). New York: Wiley.

Division 17 Task Force. (2001). *Guidelines for culturally competent practice.* Unpublished document. Washington, DC: American Psychological Association.

Division 44/Committee on Lesbian, Gay, and Bisexual Concerns Joint Task Force. (2000). Guidelines for psychotherapy with lesbian, gay, and bisexual clients. *American Psychologist, 55,* 1440–1451.

Dobash, R. E., & Dobash, R. P. (1992). *Women, violence, and social change.* New York: Routledge.

Doherty, M. A. (1978). Sexual bias in personality theory. In L. W. Harmon, J. M. Birk, L. E. Fitzgerald, & M. F. Tanney (Eds.), *Counseling women* (pp. 94–105). Monterey, CA: Brooks/Cole.

Domestic Abuse Intervention Program. (n.d.). *Power and control wheel.* Duluth, MN: Author.

Donnerstein, E. (2001). Media violence. In J. Worell (Ed.), *Encyclopedia of women and gender: Sex similarities and differences and the impact of society on gender* (Vol. 2, pp. 709–715). San Diego, CA: Academic Press.

Douglas, M. A. (1985). The role of power in feminist therapy: A reformulation. In L. B. Rosewater & L. E. A. Walker (Eds.), *Handbook of feminist therapy* (pp. 241–249). New York: Springer.

Douglas, M. A. (1987). The battered woman syndrome. In D. J. Sonkin (Ed.), *Domestic violence on trial: Psychological and legal dimensions of family violence* (pp. 39–54). New York: Springer.

Douglas, M. A., & Strom, J. (1988). Cognitive therapy with battered women. *Journal of Rational–Emotive and Cognitive–Behavioral Therapy, 6,* 33–49.

Downing, N. E., & Roush, K. L. (1985). From passive acceptance to active commitment: A model of feminist identity development. *Counseling Psychologist, 13,* 695–709.

Dutton, D. G. (1995). *Violence and control in intimate relationships.* New York: Guilford Press.

Dutton, D., & Painter, S. L. (1981). Traumatic bonding: The development of emotional attachments in battered women and other relationships of intermittent abuse. *Victimology, 6,* 139–155.

Dweck, C. S. (1986). Motivational processes affecting learning. *American Psychologist, 10,* 1040–1048.

Eagly, A. H. (1987). *Sex differences in social behavior: A social role interpretation.* Hillsdale, NJ: Erlbaum.

Eccles, J., Barber, B., Jozefowicz, D., Malenchuck, O., & Vida, M. (1999). Self-evaluation of competence, task values, and self-esteem. In N. G. Johnson, M. C. Roberts, & J. Worell (Eds.), *Beyond appearance: A new look at adolescent girls* (pp. 53–84). Washington, DC: American Psychological Association.

Eccles, J. S. (1994). Understanding educational and occupational choices: Applying the Eccles et al. Model of achievement-related choices. *Psychology of Women Quarterly, 18,* 585–609.

Eccles, J. S. (2001). Achievement. In J. Worell (Ed.), *Encyclopedia of women and gender: Sex similarities and differences and the impact of society on gender* (Vol. 1, pp. 43–53). San Diego, CA: Academic Press.

Eccles, J. S., & Hoffman, L. W. (1984). Sex roles, socialization, and occupational behavior. In H. W. Stevenson & A. E. Siegel (Eds.), *Child development research and social policy* (Vol. 1). Chicago: University of Chicago Press.

Economic and Social Council. (1992). *Report to the working group on violence against women.* Vienna: United Nations. (E/CN.6/WG.21/1992/L.3)

Ellis, A. (1962). *Reason and emotion in psychotherapy.* New York: Lyle Stuart.

Elshtain, J. B. (1991). Ethics in the women's movement. *Annuals of the American Academy, 515,* 126–139.

Enns, C. Z. (1997). *Feminist theories and feminist psychotherapies: Origins, themes, and variations.* New York: Harrington Park.

Enns, C. Z. (2000). Gender issues in counseling. In S. D. Brown & R. W. Lent (Eds.), *Handbook of counseling psychology* (3rd ed., pp. 601–637). New York: Wiley.

Enns, C. Z., & Hackett, G. (1990). Comparison of feminist and non-feminist women's reactions to variants of non-sexist and feminist counseling. *Journal of Counseling Psychology, 37,* 33–40.

Enns, C. Z., Nutt, R., & Rice, T. (2002). *Guidelines for counseling women.* Dallas, TX.

Epstein, C. F. (1997). The multiple realities of sameness and difference: Ideology and practice. *Journal of Social Issues, 53,* 259–278.

Epstein, N., Schlesinger, S. E., & Dryden, W. (1988). *Cognitive-behavioral therapy with families.* New York: Brunner/Mazel.

Erez, E. (1986). Police reports of domestic violence. In D. J. Sonkin (Ed.), *Domestic violence on trial.* New York: Springer.

Erikson, E. (1963). *Childhood and society* (2nd ed.). New York: Norton.

Erikson, E. (1968). *Identity: Youth and crisis.* New York: Norton.

Espin, O. M. (1984). Cultural and historical influences of sexuality in Hispanic/Latina women: Implications for psychotherapy. In C. Vance (Ed.), *Pleasure and danger: Exploring female sexuality* (pp. 149–163). London: Routledge & Kegan Paul.

Espin, O. M. (1994). Feminist approaches. In L. Comas-Diaz & B. Greene (Eds.), *Integrating ethnic and gender identities in psychotherapy* (pp. 265–286). New York: Gilbert Press.

Ewing, K. M., Richardson, T. Q., James-Meyers, L., & Russell, R. K. (1996). The relationship between racial identity attitudes, worldview, and African American graduate students' experience of the imposter phenomenon. *Journal of Black Psychology, 22,* 53–66.

Fagot, B. (1978). The influence of sex of child on parental reactions to toddler behaviors. *Child Development, 49,* 459–465.

Fagot, B. I., & Hagen, R. (1991). Observations of parent reactions to sex-stereotyped behaviors: Age and sex effects. *Child Development, 62,* 663–672.

Faragher, T. (2001, September 15). Too many know terror at home. *Lexington, KY Herald Leader.*

Farmer, H. S. (1997). *Diversity and women's career development: From adolescence to adulthood.* Thousand Oaks, CA: Sage.

Fassinger, R. E. (2001). Women in non-traditional occupational fields. In J. Worell (Ed.), *Encyclopedia of women and gender: Sex similarities and differences and the impact of society on gender* (Vol. 2, pp. 1269–1280). San Diego, CA: Academic Press.

Fassinger, R. E., & Miller, B. A. (1996). Validation of an inclusive model of sexual minority identity formation on a sample of gay men. *Journal of Homosexuality, 32,* 53–78.

Feingold, A. (1994). Gender differences in variability in intellectual abilities: A cross-cultural perspective. *Sex Roles, 40,* 81–92.

Feminist Therapy Institute. (1987). *Feminist therapy code of ethics.* Denver, CO: Author.

Feminist Therapy Network. (1988). *Feminist therapy network code of ethics.* Milwaukee, WI: Author.

Feminist Therapy Process and Outcome. (1999, January). Report to the executive committee of the Society for the Psychology of Women, Boulder, CO.

Ferris, L. E. (1994). Canadian family physicians' and general practitioners' perceptions of their effectiveness in identifying and treating wife abuse. *Medical Care, 32,* 1163–1172.

Figler, H. E. (1979). *Path: A career workbook for liberal arts students.* Cranston, RI: Carroll.

Figley, C. R. (1985). From victim to survivor: Social responsibility in the wake of catastrophe. In C. R. Figley (Ed.), *Trauma and its wake: The study and treatment of post-traumatic stress disorder* (pp. 398–415). New York: Brunner/Mazel.

Fine, L. J. (1979). Psychodrama. In R. Corsini (Ed.), *Current psychotherapies* (pp. 428–459). Ithaca, IL: Peacock.

Fine, M. (1988). Sexuality, schooling, and adolescent females: The missing discourse of desire. *Harvard Educational Review, 58,* 29–53.

Finn, J. (1986). The relationship between sex role attitudes and attitudes supporting marital violence. *Sex Roles, 24,* 235–244.

Fiske, S. T., & Stevens, L. E. (1998). What's so special about sex? Gender stereotyping and discrimination. In D. L. Anselmi & A. L. Law (Eds.), *Questions of gender: Perspectives and paradoxes* (pp. 232–246). New York: McGraw-Hill.

Fitzgerald, L. (1993). Sexual harassment: Violence against women in the workplace. *American Psychologist, 48,* 1070–1076.

Fitzgerald, L. F., & Betz, N. E. (1994). Career development in cultural context: The role of gender, race, class, and sexual orientation. In M. Savickas & R. Lent (Eds.), *Convergence in career development theories: Implications for science and practice* (pp. 103–115). Palo Alto, CA: Consulting Psychologists Press.

Fitzgerald, L. F., Collinsworth, L. L., & Harned, M. S. (2001). Sexual harassment. In J. Worell (Ed.), *Encyclopedia of women and gender: Sex similarities and differences and the impact of society on gender* (Vol. 2, pp. 991–1004). San Diego, CA: Academic Press.

Fitzgerald, L. F., & Crites, J. O. (1980). Toward a career psychology of women: What do we know? What do we need to know? *Journal of Counseling Psychology 27,* 44–62.

Fitzgerald, L. F., & Nutt, R. (1986). The Division 17 principles concerning the counseling/psychotherapy of women: Rational and implementation: *Counseling Psychologist, 14,* 180–216.

Ford, M., & Widiger, T. (1989). Sex bias in the diagnosis of histrionic and antisocial personality disorders. *Journal of Consulting and Clinical Psychology, 57,* 301–305.

Foxley, C. H. (1979). *Non-sexist counseling: Helping women and men redefine their roles.* Dubuque, IA: Kendall/Hunt.

Franks, V. (1986). Sex-stereotyping and diagnosis of psychopathology. *Women and Therapy, 5,* 219–232.

Freud, S. (1948). Some psychological consequences of the anatomical distinction between the sexes. In *Collected papers* (Vol. 5). London: Hogarth.

Freud, S. (1965). *New introductory lectures on psychoanalysis.* New York: Norton.

Friedland, S. I. (1991). Date rape and the culture of acceptance. *Florida Law Review, 43,* 487–527.

Frieze, I. H., Bailey, S., Mamula, P., & Noss, M. (1989). Perceptions of daily life scripts and their effects on college women's desires for children. In R. K. Unger (Ed.), *Representations: Social constructions of gender* (pp. 222–235). Amityville, NY: Baywood.

Ganley, A. L. (1987). Perpetrators of domestic violence: An overview of counseling the court-mandated client. In D. J. Sonkin (Ed.), *Domestic violence on trial: Psychological and legal dimensions of family violence* (pp. 156–173). New York: Springer.

Garfield, S. L. (1992). Major issues in psychotherapy research. In D. K. Freedman (Ed.), *History of psychotherapy: A century of change* (pp. 335–359). Washington, DC: American Psychological Association.

Gelles, R. J., & Strauss, M. A. (1988). *Intimate violence: The definitive study of the causes and consequences of abuse in the American family.* New York: Simon & Schuster.

Georgeson, J. C., & Harris, M. J. (2000). The balance of power: Interpersonal consequences of differential power and expectancies. *Personality and Social Psychology Bulletin, 26,* 1239–1257.

Gergen, K. J. (1985). The social constructionist movement in modern psychology. *American Psychologist, 40,* 266–275.

Gergen, M. (2001). Social construction theory. In J. Worell (Ed.), *Encyclopedia of women and gender: Sex similarities and differences and the impact of society on gender* (Vol. 2, pp. 1043–1058). San Diego, CA: Academic Press.

Gilbert, L. A. (1980). Feminist therapy. In A.M Brodsky & R. T. Hare-Mustin (Eds.), *Women and psychotherapy: An assessment of research and practice* (pp. 245–265). New York: Guilford Press.

Gilligan, C. (1982). *In a different voice: Psychological theory and women's development.* Cambridge, MA: Harvard University Press.

Ginorio, A. B. (1998). Contextualizing violence in a participatory classroom: A socially defined identities approach. *Psychology of Women Quarterly, 22,* 77–96.

Ginorio, A. B., Gutierrez, L., Cauce, A. M., & Acosta, M. (1995). Psychological issues for Latinas. In H. Landrine (Ed.), *Bringing cultural diversity to feminist psychology: Theory, research, and practice* (pp. 241–264). Washington, DC: American Psychological Association.

Glick, P., & Fiske, S. T. (1996). The Ambivalent Sexism Inventory: Differentiating hostile and benevolent sexism. *Journal of Personality and Social Psychology, 70,* 491–512.

Glick, P., & Fiske, S. T. (1997). Hostile and benevolent sexism: Measuring ambivalent sexist attitudes toward women. *Psychology of Women Quarterly, 21,* 119–138.

Goldman, E. E., & Morrison, D. S. (1984). *Psychodrama: Experience and process.* Dubuque, IA: Kendall/Hunt.

Goldner, V. (1985). Warning: Family therapy may be dangerous to your health. *Family Therapy Networker, 9,* 19–23.

Gollwitzer, P. M., & Moskowitz, G. B. (1996). Goal effects on action and cognition. In E. T. Higgins & A. W. Kruglanski (Eds.), *Social psychology: Handbook of basic principles.* New York: Guilford Press.

Gondolf, E. W. (1998). *Assessing woman battering in mental health services.* Thousand Oaks, CA: Sage.

Gondolph, E. W. (1988). *Battered women as survivors: An alternative to treating learned helplessness.* Lexington, MA: Lexington Books.

Good, G. E., & Sherrod, N. B. (2001). Men and masculinity. In R. K. Unger (Ed.), *Handbook of the psychology of women and gender* (pp. 201–214). New York: Wiley.

Goodrich, T. J., Rampage, C., Elman, B., & Halstead, K. (1988). *Feminist family therapy.* New York: Norton.

Graber, J. A., Lewinsohn, P. M., Seeley, J. R., & Brooks-Gunn, J. (1997). Is psychopathology associated with the timing of puberty? *Journal of the American Academy of Child and Adolescent Psychiatry, 36,* 1768–1776.

Grady, K. E. (1981). Sex bias in research design. *Psychology of Women Quarterly, 5,* 628–636.

Graham, D. L. R., Rawlings, E., & Rimini, N. (1988). Survivors of terror: Battered women, hostages, and the Stockholm syndrome. In K. Yllo & M. Bograd (Eds.), *Feminist perspectives on wife abuse* (pp. 217–233). Newbury Park, CA: Sage.

Greene, B. (1994a). African-American women. In L. Comas-Diaz & B. Greene (Eds.), *Integrating ethnic and gender identities in psychotherapy* (pp. 10–29). New York: Gilbert Press.

Greene, B. (1994b). Lesbian women of color: Triple jeopardy. In L. Comas-Diaz & B. Greene (Eds.), *Women of color: Integrating ethnic and gender issues in psychotherapy* (pp. 389–427). New York: Guilford Press.

Greene, B., & Croom, G. L. (2000). *Education, research, and practice in lesbian, gay, bisexual, and trangendered psychology: A resource manual.* Thousand Oaks, CA: Sage.

Greene, B., & Sanchez-Hucles, J. (1997). Diversity: Advancing an inclusive feminist psychology. In J. Worell & N. G. Johnson (Eds.), *Shaping the future of feminist psychology: Education, research, and practice* (pp. 173–202). Washington, DC: American Psychological Association.

Greene, B. A. (1986). When the therapist is White and the patient is Black: Considerations for psychotherapy in the feminist heterosexual and lesbian communities. In D. Howard (Ed.), *The dynamics of feminist therapy* (pp. 41–66). New York: Haworth.

Greene, D. M., & Navarrim, R. L. (1998). Situation-specific assertiveness in the epidemiology of sexual victimization among university women. *Psychology of Women Quarterly, 22,* 589–604.

Greenspan, M. (1983). *A new approach to women and therapy.* New York: McGraw-Hill.

Greenspan, M. (1986). Should therapists be personal? Self-disclosure and therapeutic distance in feminist therapy. *Women and Therapy, 5,* 5–18.

Gross, R., Kmeic, J., Worell, J., & Crosby, F. J. (2001). Institutional affiliation and satisfaction among feminist professors: Is there an advantage to women's colleges? *Psychology of Women Quarterly, 25,* 20–26.

Grossman, F. K., Gilbert, L. A., Genero, N. P., Hawes, S. E., Hyde, J. S., & Marecek, J. (1997). Feminist research: Practice and problems. In J. Worell & N. Johnson (Eds.), *Shaping the future of feminist psychology: Education, research, and practice* (pp. 73–92). Washington, DC: American Psychological Association.

Groth, A. N., Burgess, A. W., & Holmstrom, L. L. (1977). Rape: Power, anger, and sexuality. *American Journal of Psychiatry, 134*(11), 1239–1243.

Grunebaum, H., & Chasin, R. (1978). Relabeling and reframing reconsidered: The beneficial effects of a pathological label. *Family Process, 17,* 449–456.

Grych, J. H., Jouriles, E. N., Swank, P. R., McDonald, R., & Norwood, W. D. (2000). Patterns of adjustment among children of battered women. *Journal of Consulting and Clinical Psychology, 68,* 84–94.

Gutek, B. A. (2001a). Women and paid work. *Psychology of Women Quarterly, 25,* 379–393.

Gutek, B. A. (2001b). Working environments. In J. Worell (Ed.), *Encyclopedia of women and gender: Sex similarities and differences and the impact of society on gender* (Vol. 2, pp. 1191–1204). San Diego, CA: Academic Press.

Gutek, B. A., & Done, R. S. (2001). Sexual harassment. In R. K. Unger (Ed.), *Handbook of the psychology of women and gender* (pp. 367–387). New York: Wiley.

Hadley, R. G., & Mitchell, L. K. (1995). *Counseling research and program evaluation.* Pacific Grove, CA: Brooks/Cole.

Halpern, D. F. (1995). Cognitive gender differences: Why diversity is a critical issue. In H. Landrine (Ed.), *Bringing cultural diversity to feminist psychology: Theory, research, and practice* (pp. 77–92). Washington, DC: American Psychological Association.

Hamilton, S., Rothbart, M., & Dawes, R. M. (1986). Sex bias, diagnosis, and *DSM-III. Sex Roles, 15,* 269–274.

Hammen, C. (1988). Depression and personal cognitions about personal stressful events. In L. B. Alloy (Ed.), *Cognitive processes in depression* (pp. 77–108). New York: Guilford Press.

Hansen, J. C., Stevic, R. R., & Warner, R. W. (1986). *Counseling theory and process.* Boston: Allyn & Bacon.

Hare-Mustin, R. T. (1978). A feminist approach to family therapy. *Family Process, 17,* 181–194.

Hare-Mustin, R. T. (1983). An appraisal of the relationship between women and psychotherapy; 80 years after the case of Dora. *American Psychologist, 38,* 594–601.

Hare-Mustin, R. T., & Marecek, J. (1988). The meaning of difference: Gender theory, postmodernism, and psychology. *American Psychologist, 43,* 455–464.

Hare-Mustin, R. T., & Marecek, J. (1990). *Making a difference: Psychology and the construction of gender.* New Haven, CT: Yale University Press.

Hare-Mustin, R. T., Marecek, J., Kaplan, A. G., & Liso-Levinson, N. (1979). Rights of clients, responsibilities of therapists. *American Psychologist, 34,* 3–16.

Harrigan, B. L. (1977). *Games your mother never taught you: Corporate games-manship for women.* New York: Warren Books.

Harris, S. M. (1995). Family, self, and sociocultural contributors to body-image attitudes of African-American women. *Psychology of Women Quarterly, 19,* 139–145.

Hartmann, H., Allen, K., & Owens, C. (1999). *Equal pay for working families: National and state data on the pay gap and its costs*. Washington, DC: Institute for Women's Policy Research and American Federation of Labor and Congress of Industrial Organizations. (ERIC Document Reproduction Service No. ED429231)

Hartung, C. M., & Widiger, T. A. (1998). Gender differences in the diagnosis of mental disorders: Conclusions and controversies of the *DSM-IV. Psychological Bulletin, 123,* 260–278.

Harway, M. (1979). Training counselors. *Counseling Psychologist, 8,* 8–10.

Harway, M., & Hansen, M. (1994). *Spouse abuse: Assessing and treating battered women, batterers, and their children.* Sarasota, FL: Professional Resources Press.

Hayes, K. M., & Davis, S. F. (1993). Interpersonal flexibility, Type A individuals, and the impostor phenomenon. *Bulletin of the Psychonomic Society, 31,* 323–325.

Hayes, S. C. (1987). A contextual approach to therapeutic change. In N. S. Jacobson (Ed.), *Psychotherapists in therapeutic practice: Cognitive and behavioral perspctives* (pp. 327–387). New York: Guilford Press.

Healy, J. F. (1997). *Race, ethnicity, and gender in the United States: Inequality, group conflict, and power.* Thousand Oaks, CA: Pine Forge Press.

Heilmann, M. E. (2001). Description and prescription: How gender stereotypes prevent women's ascent up the organizational ladder. *Journal of Social Issues, 57,* 657–674.

Helms, J. E. (1990). *Black and White racial identity: Theory, research, and practice.* New York: Greenwood Press.

Helwig, A. A. (1998). Gender-role stereotyping: Testing theory with a longitudinal sample. *Sex Roles, 38,* 403–424.

Henderson-King, D., & Stewart, A. J. (1999). Educational experiences and shifts in group consciousness: Studying women. *Personality and Social Psychology Bulletin, 25,* 390–399.

Henley, N. M. (1977). *Body politics: Power, sex, and non-verbal communication.* Englewood Cliffs, NJ: Prentice-Hall.

Herman, J. (1981). Father-daughter incest. *Professional Psychology, 12,* 76–80.

Hess, A. K. (1980). *Psychotherapy supervision: Theory, research, and practice.* New York: Wiley.

Hetherington, E. M., Cox, M., & Cox, R. (1986). Longterm effects of divorce and remarriage on the adjustment of children. *Journal of the American Academy of Child Psychiatry, 24,* 518–530.

Hill, M., Glaser, K., & Harden, J. (1995). A feminist model for ethical decision making. In E. J. Rave & C. C. Larsen (Eds.), *Ethical decision making in therapy: Feminist perspectives* (pp. 18–37). New York: Guilford Press.

Hoffman, L. W. (1979). Maternal employment: 1979. *American Psychologist, 34,* 644–657.

Holland, D., & Davidson, D. (1984). Prestige and intimacy: The fold models behind Americans' talk about gender types. In N. Quinn & D. Holland (Eds.), *Cultural models in language and thought.* New York: Cambridge University Press.

Holland, J. L. (1994). *Self-directed search (SDS), Form R.* Odessa, FL: Psychological Assessment Resources.

Holmes, T. H., & Rahe, R. H. (1967). The Social Readjustment Scale. *Journal of Psychosomatic Research, 11,* 218–218.

Holroyd, J. (1978). Psychotherapy and women's liberation. In L. W. Harmon, J. M. Birk, L. E. Fitzgerald, & M. F. Tanney (Eds.), *Counseling women* (pp. 193–207). Monterey, CA: Brooks/Cole.

Holzman, C. G. (1996). Counseling adult women rape survivors: Issues of race, ethnicity, and class. *Women and Therapy, 19,* 47–62.

Horne, C. M. (1999, June). Post-soviet Russian violence toward women. *Boston Globe.* Boston, MA.

Horner, M. S. (1972). Toward an understanding of achievement-related conflicts in women. *Journal of Social Issues, 28,* 157–175.

Horowitz, M. J. (1979). Psychological responses to serious life events. In V. Hamilton & D. Warburton (Eds.), *Human stress and cognition: An information processing approach* (pp. 235–263). New York: Wiley.

Hossain, Z., & Roopnarine, J. L. (1993). Division of household labor and child care in dual-earner African American families with infants. *Sex Roles, 29,* 571–584.

Hudson, W., & McIntosh, S. (1981). The assessment of spouse abuse: Two quantifiable dimensions. *Journal of Marriage and the Family, 43,* 873–884.

Hughes, B. M. (1999). The prediction of suicidal behaviors in adults who were sexually abused as children. *Dissertation Abstracts International, 50,* 11B-5775.

Hughes, D. L., & Galinsky, E. (1994). Gender, job and family conditions, and psychological symptoms. *Psychology of Women Quarterly, 18,* 251–270.

Hurtado, A. (1997). Understanding multiple group identities: Inserting women into cultural transformations. *Journal of Social Issues, 53,* 299–328.

Huston, A. C. (1983). Sex-typing. In P. H. Mussen & E. M. Hetherington (Eds.), *Handbook of child psychology: Socialization, personality, and social development* (4th ed., Vol. 4, pp. 387–468). New York: Wiley.

Huston, A. C. (1988). Gender, socialization, and the transmission of culture. In S. Brehm (Ed.), *Seeing female: Social roles and personal lives* (pp. 7–19). New York: Greenwood Press.

Hyde, J. S. (1994). Should psychologists study gender differences? Yes, with some guidelines. *Feminism and Psychology, 4,* 507–512.

Hyde, J. S. (2002). Feminist identity development: The current state of theory, research, and practice. *Counseling Psychologist, 30,* 105–110.

Hyde, J. S., & Kling, K. (2001). Women, motivation, and achievement. *Psychology of Women Quarterly, 25,* 364–378.

Hyde, J. S., & Linn, M. (1986). *The psychology of gender: Advances through meta-analysis.* Baltimore: Johns Hopkins University Press.

Ingram, K. M., Corning, A. F., & Schmidt, L. D. (1996). The relationship of victimization experiences to psychological well-being among homeless women and low-income housed women. *Journal of Counseling Psychology, 43,* 218–227.

Jack, D. C. (1991). *Silencing the self: Women and depression.* Cambridge, MA: Harvard University Press.

Jackson, L. A. (1992). *Physical appearance and gender: Sociobiological and sociocultural perspectives.* Albany: State University of New York Press.

Jackson, L. A., Ialongo, N., & Stollak, G. E. (1986). Parental correlates of gender roles: The relation between parents' masculinity, femininity, and childrearing behaviors and their children's gender roles. *Journal of Social and Clinical Psychology, 4,* 204–224.

Jacobson, N. (Ed.). (1987). *Psychotherapists in clinical practice: Cognitive and behavioral perspectives.* New York: Guilford Press.

Jacobson, N. S., & Christensen, D. K. (1995). Studying the effectiveness of psychotherapy: How well can clinical trials do the job? *American Psychologist, 51,* 1031–1040.

Jacobson, N. S., & Gottman, J. M. (1998). *When men batter women: New insights into ending abusive relationships.* New York: Simon & Schuster.

Jacobson, N. S., & Hollon, S. D. (1996). Cognitive-behavioral therapy vs. pharmacotherapy: Now that the jury's returned its verdict, it's time to present the rest of the evidence. *Journal of Consulting and Clinical Psychology, 64,* 74–80.

Jacobson, N. S., Holzworth-Munroe, A., & Schmaling, K. B. (1989). Marital therapy and spouse involvement in the treatment of depression, agoraphobia, and alcoholism. *Journal of Consulting and Clinical Psychology, 57,* 5–10.

Jacobson, N. S., & Margolin, G. (1979). *Marital therapy: Strategies based on social learning and behavioral exchange principles.* New York: Brunner/Mazel.

Jacobson, N. S., Martell, C. R., & Dimidjian, S. (2001). Behavioral activation treatment for depression: Returning to contextual roots. *Clinical Psychology: Science and Practice, 8,* 255–270.

Jakubowski, P. A. (1977). Self-assertion training procedures for women. In E. I. Rawlings & D. K. Carter (Eds.), *Psychotherapy for women* (pp. 168–190). Springfield, IL: Charles C Thomas.

Janoff-Bulman, R. (1979). Characterological versus behavioral self-blame: Inquiries into depression and rape. *Journal of Personality and Social Psychology, 37,* 1798–1809.

Janoff-Bulman, R. (1985). The aftermath of victimization: Rebuilding shattered assumptions. In C. R. Figley (Ed.), *Trauma and its wake: The study and treatment of posttraumatic stress disorder* (pp. 15–35). New York: Brunner/Mazel.

John, D., Sheldon, B. A., & Luschen, K. (1995). Race, ethnicity, gender, and perceptions of fairness. *Journal of Family Issues, 16,* 357–379.

Johnson, D. M. (2001). *Exploring women's empowerment and resilience: Beyond symptom reduction.* Unpublished doctoral dissertation, University of Kentucky, Lexington.

Johnson, N. G., & Remer, P. (1997). Post-doctoral training in feminist psychological practice. In J. Worell & N. G. Johnson (Eds.), *Shaping the future of feminist psychology: Education, research, and practice* (pp. 203–225). Washington, DC: American Psychological Association.

Johnson, N. G., Roberts, M. C., & Worell, J. (1999). *Beyond appearance: A new look at adolescent girls.* Washington, DC: American Psychological Association.

Johnson, P. B. (1976). Women and power: Toward a theory of effectiveness. *Journal of Social Issues, 32,* 99–100.

Jones, A. (1980). *Women who kill.* New York: Fawcett Columbine Books.

Jordan, J., Kaplan, A. G., Miller, J. B., Stiver, I. P., & Surrey, J. L. (1991). *Women's growth in connection: Writings from the Stone Center.* New York: Guilford Press.

Kahn, A. (1984). The power of war: Male response to power loss under equality. *Psychology of Women Quarterly, 8,* 234–247.

Kahn, S. E., & Theurer, G. M. (1985). Evaluation research in a course on counseling women: A case study. In L. B. Rosewater & L. E. A. Walker (Eds.), *Handbook of feminist therapy: Women's issues in psychotherapy* (pp. 321–331). New York: Springer.

Kanagawa, C., Cross, S., & Marcus, H. R. (2001). "Who am I?" The cultural psychology of the conceptual self. *Personality and Social Psychology Bulletin, 27,* 90–103.

Kanfer, F. H., & Schefft, B. K. (1988). *Guiding the process of therapeutic change.* Champaign, IL: Research Press.

Kanter, R. M. (1977). *Men and women of the corporation.* New York: Basic Books.

Kaplan, M. (1983). A woman's view of *DSM-III. American Psychologist, 38,* 786–792.

Kaplan, R. M. (2000). Two pathways to prevention. *American Psychologist, 55,* 382–396.

Karraker, H., Vogel, D. A., & Lake, M. A. (1995). Parents' gender-stereotyped perceptions of newborns: The eye of the beholder revisited. *Sex Roles, 33,* 687–701.

Kaslow, N. (1989, August). *Treatment of depressed women.* Symposium paper presented at the annual convention of the American Psychological Association, New Orleans, LA.

Katz, J. (1984). *No fairy godmothers, no magic wands: The healing process after rape.* Saratoga, NY: R & E.

Katz, P. A. (1979). The development of female identity. *Sex Roles, 5,* 155–178.

Katz, P. A., & Boswell, S. L. (1986). Flexibility and fractionality in children's gender roles. *Genetic, Social, and General Psychology Monographs, 112,* 105–147.

Katz, P. A., & Ksansnak, K. (1994). Developmental aspects of gender role flexibility and traditionality in middle childhood and adolescence. *Developmental Psychology, 30,* 272–282.

Kazdin, A. E. (2001). Progression of therapy research and clinical application of treatment require better understanding of the change process. *Clinical Psychology: Research and Practice, 8,* 143–151.

Kelly, J. A., & Worell, L. (1976). Parent behaviors related to masculine, feminine, and androgynous sex-role orientations. *Journal of Consulting and Clinical Psychology, 44,* 843–851.

Kendall, P. C. (1998). Empirically supported psychological therapies. *Journal of Consulting and Clinical Psychology, 66,* 3–6.

Kendrick, D. T., & Trost, M. R. (1993). The evolutionary perspective. In A. E. Beall & R. J. Sternberg (Eds.), *The psychology of gender* (pp. 149–172). New York: Guilford Press.

Kessler, S., & McKenna, W. (1985). *Gender: An ethnomethodological approach.* Chicago: University of Chicago Press.

Kimmel, E., & Worell, J. (1997). Preaching what we practice: Principles and strategies of feminist pedagogy. In J. Worell & N. G. Johnson (Eds.), *Shaping the future of feminist psychology: Education, research, and practice* (pp. 121–153). Washington, DC: American Psychological Association.

King, J. E., & Cooley, E. L. (1995). Achievement orientation and the impostor phenomenon among college students. *Contemporary Educational Psychology, 20,* 304–312.

King, K. R. (1998, August). *Effects of prejudice attributions on self-esteem and stress among African American females.* Poster presented at the annual meeting of the American Psychological Association, San Francisco.

Kite, M. (2001). Changing times, changing gender roles: What do we want women and men to be? In R. K. Unger (Ed.), *Handbook of the psychology of women and gender* (pp. 215–227). New York: Wiley.

Kitzinger, C., & Wilkinson, S. (1993). Theorizing heterosexuality. In S. Wilkinson & C. Kitzinger (Eds.), *Heterosexuality* (pp. 1–32). London: Sage.

Kmeic, J., Crosby, F. J., & Worell, J. (1996). Walking the talk: On stage and behind the scenes. In K. F. Wyche & F. J. Crosby (Eds.), *Women's ethnicities: Journeys through psychology* (pp. 49–62). Boulder, CO: Westview Press.

Kohlberg, L. A. (1966). A cognitive-developmental analysis of children's sex-role concepts and attitudes. In E. E. Maccoby (Ed.), *The development of sex differences* (pp. 83–173). Palo Alto, CA: Stanford University Press.

Koss, M. P. (1985). The hidden rape victim: Personality, attitudinal, and situational characteristics. *Psychology of Women Quarterly, 9,* 193–212.

Koss, M. P. (1993). Rape: Scope, impact, interventions, and public policy responses. *American Psychologist, 48,* 1062–1069.

Koss, M. P., & Burkhart, B. R. (1989). A conceptual analysis of rape victimization: Long-term effects and implications for treatment. *Psychology of Women Quarterly, 13,* 27–40.

Koss, M. P., Goodman, L. A., Browne, A., Fitzgerald, L. F., Keita, G. P., & Russo, N. F. (1994). *No safe haven: Male violence against women at home, at work, and in the community.* Washington, DC: American Psychological Association.

Koss, M. P., Heise, L., & Russo, N. F. (1994). The global health burden of rape. *Psychology of Women Quarterly, 18,* 509–537.

Krantz, S. E. (1985). When depressive cognitions reflect negative realities. *Cognitive Theory and Research, 9,* 595–610.

Kravetz, D. (1980). Consciousness-raising and self-help. In A. M. Brodsky & R. T. Hare-Mustin (Eds.), *Women and psychotherapy: An assessment of research and practice* (pp. 268–284). New York: Guilford Press.

Kravetz, D., Marecek, J., & Finn, S. E. (1983). Factors influencing women's participation in consciousness-raising groups. *Psychology of Women Quarterly, 7,* 257–271.

Kurdek, L. A., & Schmitt, J. P. (1986). Relationship quality of partners in heterosexual married, heterosexual cohabiting, gay, and lesbian relationships. *Journal of Personality and Social Psychology, 51,* 711–720.

Lambert, M. J., & Bergin, A. E. (1994). The effectiveness of psychotherapy. In A. E. Begin & S. L. Garfield (Eds.), *Handbook of psychotherapy and behavior change* (4th ed., pp. 143–189). New York: Wiley.

Lambert, M. J., Shapiro, D. A., & Bergin, A. E. (1985). The effectiveness of psychotherapy. In S. L. Garfield & A. E. Bergin (Eds.), *Handbook of psychotherapy and behavior change* (pp. 157–212). New York: Wiley.

Landrine, H. (1989). The politics of personality disorder. *Psychology of Women Quarterly, 13,* 325–329.

Landrine, H. (1995). *Bringing cultural diversity to feminist psychology: Theory, research, and practice.* Washington, DC: American Psychological Association.

Landrine, H. (1999). Race x class stereotypes of women. In L. A. Peplau, S. C. DeBro, R. C. Veniegas, & P. L. Taylor (Eds.), *Gender, culture, and ethnicity: Current research about women and men* (pp. 38–47). Mountain View, CA: Mayfield.

Landrine, H., Klonoff, E. A., & Brown-Collins, A. (1995). Cultural diversity and methodology in feminist psychology: Critique, proposal, empirical example. In H. Landrine (Ed.), *Bringing cultural diversity to feminist psychology: Theory, research, and practice* (pp. 55–76). Washington, DC: American Psychological Association.

Landrine, H., Klonoff, E. A., Gibbs, J., Manning, V., & Lund, M. (1995). Physical and psychiatric correlates of gender discrimination: An application of the Schedule of Sexist Events. *Psychology of Women Quarterly, 19,* 473–492.

Lange, S. J., & Worell, J. (1990, August). *Satisfaction and commitment in lesbian and heterosexual relationships.* Paper presented at the annual meeting of the American Psychological Association, Boston.

Langlois, J. H., & Downs, A. C. (1980). Mothers, fathers, and peers as socialization agents of sex-typed play behavior in young children. *Child Development, 51,* 1237–1247.

Laumann, E. O., Gagnon, J. H., Michael, R. T., & Michaels, S. (1994). *The social organization of sexuality: Sexual practices in the United States.* Chicago: University of Chicago Press.

Lavine, H., Sweeney, D., & Wagner, S. H. (1999). Depicting women as sex objects in television advertising: Effects on body dissatisfaction. *Personality and Social Psychology Bulletin, 25,* 1049–1058.

Lazarus, R. S., & Folkman, S. (1984). *Stress, appraisal, and coping.* New York: Springer.

Lerman, H. (1996). *Pigeonholing women's misery: A history and critical analysis of the psychodiagnosis of women in the twentieth century.* New York: Basic Books.

Levant, R. F. (1984). *Family therapy: A comprehensive overview.* Englewood Cliffs, CA: Prentice-Hall.

Levant, R. F. (2001). Men and masculinity. In J. Worell (Ed.), *Encyclopedia of women and gender: Sex similarities and differences and the impact of society on gender* (Vol. 2, pp. 717–728). San Diego, CA: Academic Press.

Levy, L. (1970). *Conceptions of personality: Theories and research.* New York: Random House.

Lewinsohn, P. M. (1974). A behavioral approach to depression. In R. J. Friedman & M. M. Katz (Eds.), *The psychology of depression: Contemporary theory and reseach* (pp. 157–178). New York: Wiley.

Lewinsohn, P. M., Antonuccio, D. O., Steinmetz, J. L., & Teri, L. (1984). *Coping with depression: A psychoeducational intervention for unipolar depression.* Eugene, OR: Castalia.

Lewinsohn, P. M., Munoz, R. F., Youngren, M. A., & Zeiss, A. M. (1978). *Control your depression.* Englewood Cliff, NJ: Prentice-Hall.

Liberman, R. P., & Roberts, J. (1976). Contingency management of neurotic depression and marital disharmony. In H. J. Eysenck (Ed.), *Case studies in behavior therapy.* London: Routledge & Kegan Paul.

Linz, D., Donnerstein, E., Bross, M., & Chapin, M. (1986). Mitigating the influence of violence on television and sexual violence in the media. In R. J. Blanchard & D. C. Blanchard (Eds.), *Advances in the study of aggression* (Vol. 2, pp. 165–194). New York: Academic Press.

Lipman-Blumen, J., & Leavitt, H. J. (1978). Vicarious and direct achievement patterns in adulthood. In L. S. Hansen & R. S. Rapoza (Eds.), *Career development and counseling of women* (pp. 132–148). Springfield, IL: Charles C Thomas.

Lips, H. M. (1999). *A new psychology of women: Gender, culture, and ethnicity.* Mountain View, CA: Mayfield.

Lira, L. R., Koss, M. P., & Russo, N. F. (1999). Mexican American women's definition of rape and sexual abuse. *Hispanic Journal of Behavioral Sciences, 21,* 236–265.

Lonsway, K. A., & Fitzgerald, L. F. (1994). Rape myths: In review. *Psychology of Women Quarterly, 18,* 133–164.

Lopez, P. (1992). He said. She said: An overview of date rape from commission through prosecution through verdict. *Criminal Justice Journal, 13,* 275–302.

Lopez, S. R., & Guarnaccia, P. J. J. (2000). Cultural psychopathology: Uncovering the social world of mental illness. *Annual Review of Psychology, 51,* 571–598.

Lorber, J. (1994). *Paradoxes of gender.* New Haven, CT: Yale University Press.

Lott, B. (1985a). The devaluation of women's competence. *Journal of Social Issues, 41,* 43–60.

Lott, B. (1985b). The potential enrichment of social/personality psychology through feminist research and vice versa. *American Psychologist, 40,* 155–164.

Lott, B. (1997). The personal and social correlates of a gender difference ideology. *Journal of Social Issues, 53,* 279–299.

Lott, B., & Roccio, L. M. (1998). Standing up, taking charge, and talking back: Strategies and outcomes in collective action against sexual harassment. In L. H. Collins, J. C. Chrisler, & K. Quina (Eds.), *Arming Athena: Career strategies for women in academe* (pp. 249–270). Thousand Oaks, CA: Sage.

Lykes, M. B., & Qin, D. (2001). Individualism and collectivism. In J. Worell (Ed.), *Encyclopedia of women and gender: Sex similarities, differences, and the impact of culture on gender* (Vol. 1, pp. 625–632). San Diego, CA: Academic Press.

Lytton, H., & Romney, D. M. (1991). Parents' differential socialization of boys and girls: A meta-analysis. *Psychological Bulletin, 109,* 267–296.

Maccoby, E. E., & Jacklin, C. N. (1974). *The psychology of sex differences* Stanford, CA: Stanford University Press.

MacDonald, M. L. (1984). Behavioral assessment with women clients. In E. A. Blechman (Ed.), *Behavior modification with women* (pp. 60–93). New York: Guilford Press.

MacKay, D. G. (1980). Language, thought, and social attitudes. In H. Giles, P. Robinson, & P. M. Smith (Eds.), *Language: Social psychological perspectives.* Oxford, England: Pergamon Press.

Madden, M., & Hyde, J. S. (1998). Integrating gender and ethnicity into psychology courses. *Psychology of Women Quarterly, 22*(1).

Mahalik, J. R., Van Ormer, E. A., & Simi, N. L. (2000). Ethical issues in using self-disclosure in feminsit therapy. In M. M. Brabeck (Ed.), *Practicing feminist ethics in psychology* (pp. 189–201). Washington, DC: American Psychological Association.

Major, B. (1987). Gender, justice, and the psychology of entitlement. In P. Shaver & C. Hendrick (Eds.), *Sex and gender. Review of personality and social psychology* (Vol. 7, pp. 124–148). Newbury Park, CA: Sage.

Makowsky, V. P., & Paludi, M. A. (1990). Feminism and women's studies in the academy. In M. Paludi & G. A. Stuernagel (Eds.), *Foundations for a feminist restructuring of the academic disciplines* (pp. 1–38). New York: Harrington Park Press.

Malamuth, N. M. (1981). Rape proclivity among males. *Journal of Social Issues, 37,* 138–157.

Malamuth, N. M. (1998). The confluence model as an organizing framework for research on sexually aggressive men: Risk moderators, imagined aggression, and pornography consumption. In R. H. Geen & E. Donnerstein (Eds.), *Human aggression: Theories, research, and implications for social policy* (pp. 229–245). San Diego, CA: Academic Press.

Malovich, N. J., & Stake, J. E. (1990). Sexual harassment on campus: Individual differences in attitudes and beliefs. *Psychology of Women Quarterly, 14,* 63–81.

Marcus, B. F. (1987). Object relations theory. In R. Formanek & A. Gurian (Eds.), *Women and depression: A lifespan perspective* (pp. 27–40). New York: Springer.

Marecek, J., & Kravetz, D. (1996, August). *A room of one's own: Power and agency in feminist therapy.* Paper presented at the annual meeting of the American Psychological Association, Toronto, Ontario, Canada.

Margolin, G. (1982). Ethical and legal considerations in marital and family therapy. *American Psychologist, 37,* 788–801.

Margolin, G., Fernandez, V., Talovec, S., & Onorato, R. (1983). Sex-role considerations and behavioral marital therapy: Equal does not mean identical. *Journal of Marital and Family Therapy, 9,* 131–145.

Markus, H. R., Kitayama, S., & Heiman, R. (1996). Culture and basic psychological principles. In E. T. Higgins & A. W. Kruglanski (Eds.), *Social psychology: Handbook of basic principles* (pp. 857–914). New York: Guilford Press.

Mazure, C. M. (1998). Life stress and risk factors for depression. *Clinical Psychology: Research and Practice, 5,* 291–313.

McBride, A. B. (1987). Position paper. In A. Eichler & D. L. Perron (Eds.), *Women's mental health: Agenda for research* (pp. 28–41). Rockville, MD: National Institute of Mental Health.

McBride, A. B. (1990). Mental health effects of women's multiple roles. *American Psychologist, 45,* 381–384.

McCann, I. L., Sakheim, D. K., & Abrahamson, D. S. (1988). Trauma and victimization: A model of psychological adaptation. *Counseling Psychologist, 16,* 531–594.

McGhee, P. E., & Freuh, T. (1980). Television viewing and the learning of sex role stereotypes. *Sex Roles, 6,* 179–188.

McGrath, E., Keita, G. P., Strickland, B. R., & Russo, N. F. (1990). *Women and depression: Risk factors and treatment issues.* Washington, DC: American Psychological Association.

McHugh, M. C., Frieze, I. H., & Browne, A. (1993). Research on battered women and their assailants. In F. L. Denmark & M. A. Paludi (Eds.), *Psychology of women: A handbook of issues and theories* (pp. 513–552). Westport, CT: Greenwood Press.

McHugh, M. C., Koeske, R. D., & Frieze, I. H. (1986). Issues to consider in conducting non-sexist psychological research. *American Psychologist, 41,* 879–890.

McIntosh, P. (1986). *Unpacking the invisible knapsack.* Wellesley, MA: Stone Center Working Papers.

McLennan, N. A. (1999). Applying the cognitive information processing approach to career problem solving and decision making to women's career development. *Journal of Employment Counseling, 36,* 82–96.

McNair, L. D., & Neville, H. A. (1996). African American women survivors of sexual assault: The intersection of race and class. *Women and Therapy, 19,* 107–118.

McNeill, B. W., Prieto, L. R., Niemann, Y. F., Pizarro, M., Vera, E. M., & Gomez, S. P. (2001). Current directions in Chicana/o psychology. *Counseling Psychologist, 29,* 5–17.

Meara, N. M., & Day, J. D. (2000). Epilogue: Feminist visions and virtues of ethical psychological practice. In M. M. Brabeck (Ed.), *Practicing feminist ethics in psychology* (pp. 249–268). Washington, DC: American Psychological Association.

Meichenbaum, D. (1977). *Cognitive-behavioral modification: An integrative approach.* New York: Plenum Press.

Meichenbaum, D. (1986). Cognitive-behavioral modification. In F. H. Kanfer & A. P. Goldstein (Eds.), *Helping people change: A textbook of methods* (pp. 346–380). New York: Pergamon Press.

Metalsky, G. I., Laird, R. S., Heck, P. M., & Joiner, T. E. (1995). Attribution therapy: Clinical applications. In W. O'Donohue & L. Krasner (Eds.), *Theories of behavior: Exploring behavior change* (pp. 385–414). Washington, DC: American Psychological Association.

Meyer, C. B., & Taylor, S. E. (1986). Adjustment to rape. *Journal of Personality and Social Psychology, 50,* 1226–1234.

Meyer, G. J., Finn, S. E., Eyde, L. D., Kay, G. G., Moreland, K. L., Dies, R. R., et al. (2001). Psychological testing and psychological assessment: A review of evidence and issues. *American Psychologist, 56,* 128–165.

Miles, A. (1988). *The neurotic woman: The role of gender in psychiatric illness.* Worchester, England: New York University Press.

Miller, J. B. (1976). *Toward a new psychology of women.* Boston: Beacon Press.

Mills, C. S., & Granoff, B. J. (1992). Date and acquaintance rape among a sample of college students. *Social Work, 37,* 504–509.

Mineka, S., Watson, D., & Clark, L. A. (1998). Comorbidity of anxiety and unipolar depression. In J. T. Spence, J. M. Darley, & D. L. Foss (Eds.), *Annual Review of Psychology,* (Vol. 49, pp. 377–412). Palo Alto, CA: Annual Reviews.

Moreno, J. L. (1975). *Psychodrama: Foundations of psychodrama* (Vol. 2). Beacon, NY: Beacon House. (Original work published 1959)

Moreno, J. L. (1985). *Psychodrama.* Beacon, NY: Beacon House. (Original work published 1946)

Morgan, K. S., & Brown, L. (1991). Lesbian career development, work behavior, and vocational counseling. *Counseling Psychologist, 19,* 273–291.

Morgan, M. (1982). Television and adolescents' sex-role stereotypes: A longitudinal study. *Journal of Personality and Social Psychology, 43,* 947–955.

Morowski, J. G. (1987). The troubled quest for masculinity, feminity, and androgyny. In P. Shaver & C. Hendricks (Eds.), *Sex and gender: Review of personality and social psychology* (Vol. 7, pp. 44–69). Beverly Hills, CA: Sage.

Morowski, J. G., & Bayer, B. M. (1995). Stirring trouble and making theory. In H. Landrine (Ed.), *Bringing cultural diversity to feminist psychology: Theory, research, and practice* (pp. 113–138). Washington, DC: American Psychological Association.

Murrell, A. J. (2001). Career achievement: Opportunities and barriers. In J. Worell (Ed.), *Encyclopedia of women and gender: Sex similarities and differences and the impact of society on gender* (Vol. 1, pp. 211–218). San Diego, CA: Academic Press.

Murrell, S. A. (1984). Distribution and desirability of life events in older adults: Population and policy implications. *Journal of Community Psychology, 12,* 301–311.

Mynatt, C. R., & Algeier, E. R. (1990). Risk factors, self-attributions, and adjustment problems among victims of sexual coercion. *Journal of Applied Psychology, 20,* 130–153.

Nash, S. (1979). Sex roles as a mediator of intellectual functioning. In M. A. Wittig & A. C. Peterson (Eds.), *Sex-related differences in cognitive functioning: Developmental issues.* New York: Academic Press.

Nathan, P. E., & Gorman, J. M. (Eds.). (1998). *A guide to treatments that work.* New York: Oxford University Press.

New York Chapter of National Organization of Women. (1978). *A consumer's guide to non-sexist therapy.* New York: Service Fund of the National Organization of Women.

Nolen-Hoeksema, S., & Girgus, J. S. (1994). The emergence of gender differences in depression during adolescence. *Psychological Bulletin, 115,* 424–443.

Nolen-Hoeksema, S., & Jackson, B. (2001). Mediators of the gender differences in rumination. *Psychology of Women Quarterly, 25,* 37–47.

O'Hara, M. W. (1989, August). *Postpartum depression.* Paper presented at the annual meeting of the American Psychological Association, New Orleans, LA.

Ohye, B. Y., & Daniel, J. H. (1999). The "other" adolescent girls: Who are they? In N. G. Johnson, M. C. Roberts, & J. Worell (Eds.), *Beyond appearance: A new look at adolescent girls* (pp. 115–130). Washington, DC: American Psychological Association.

O'Neil, J. M., & Harway, M. (1997). A multivariate model explaining men's violence toward women. *Violence Against Women, 3,* 182–203.

Ostertag, P. A., & McNemara, J. R. (1991). "Feminization" of psychology: The changing sex ratio and its implications for the profession. *Psychology of Women Quarterly, 15,* 349–369.

Pacheco, S., & Hurtado, A. (2001). Media stereotypes. In J. Worell (Ed.), *Encyclopedia of women and gender: Sex similarities and differences and the impact of society on gender* (Vol. 2, pp. 703–709). San Diego, CA: Academic Press.

Paludi, M. A. (1990). *Ivory power: Sexual harassment on campus.* Albany: State University of New York Press.

Payne, D. L., Lonsway, K. A., & Fitzgerald, L. F. (1999). Rape myth acceptance: Exploration of its structure and its measurement using the Illinois Rape Myth Acceptance Scale. *Journal of Research in Personality, 33,* 27–68.

Payne, R. K. (1998). *A framework for understanding poverty.* Highlands, TX: RFT Publishing.

Pearson, J. C. (1985). *Gender and communication.* Dubuque, IA: William C. Brown.

Pederson, P. B. (1997). Recent trends in cultural theories. *Applied and Preventative Psychology, 6,* 221–231.

Peplau, L. A., & Beals, K. P. (2001). Lesbians, gay men, and bisexuals in relationships. In J. Worell (Ed.), *Encyclopedia of women and gender: Sex similarities and differences and the impact of society on gender* (Vol. 2, pp. 657–666). San Diego, CA: Academic Press.

Peplau, L. A., & Conrad, E. (1989). Beyond non-sexist research: The perils of feminist methods in psychology. *Psychology of Women Quarterly, 13,* 379–400.

Peplau, L. A., & Garnetts, L. D. (2000). New paradigm for understanding women's sexuality and sexual orientation. *Journal of Social Issues, 56,* 329–350.

Peplau, L. A., Veniegas, R. C., Taylor, P. L., & DeBro, S. C. (1999). Sociocultural perspectives on the lives of women and men. In L. A. Peplau, S. C. DeBro, R. C. Veniegas, & P. L. Taylor

(Eds.), *Gender, culture, and ethnicity: Current research about women and men* (pp. 23–37). Mountain View, CA: Mayfield.

Phinney, J. S. (1996). When we think about American ethnic groups, what do we mean? *American Psychologist, 51,* 918–927.

Piasecki, J., & Hollon, S. D. (1987). Cognitive therapy for depression: Unexplicated schemata and scripts. In N. S. Jacobson (Ed.), *Psychotherapists in clinical practice: Cognitive and behavioral perspectives* (pp. 121–152). New York: Guilford Press.

Piran, N. (1999, August). The Feminist Frame Scale. In J. Worell (Chair), *Measuring process and outcomes in feminist counseling and therapy.* Paper presented at the annual meeting of the American Psychological Association as part of a symposium, Boston.

Piran, N. (2001). Eating disorders and disordered eating. In J. Worell (Ed.), *Encyclopedia of women and gender: Sex similarities and differences and the impact of society on gender* (Vol. 1, pp. 369–378). San Diego, CA: Academic Press.

Piran, N., Levine, M. P., & Steiner-Adair, C. (1999). *Preventing eating disorders: A handbook of interventions and special challenges.* Philadelphia: Brunner/Mazel.

Pleck, J. H. (1985). *The myth of masculinity.* Cambridge, MA: MIT Press.

Pope, K., & Vetter, V. A. (1991). Prior therapist-patient sexual involvement among patients seen by psychologists. *Psychotherapy: Theory, Research, and Practice, 28,* 429–438.

Pope, K. F. M., & Vasquez, M. J. T. (1998). *Ethics in psychotherapy and counseling: A practical guide* (2nd ed.). San Francisco: Jossey-Bass.

Porter, N., & Vasquez, M. (1997). Covision: Feminist supervision, process, and collaboration. In J. Worell & N. G. Johnson (Eds.), *Shaping the future of feminist psychology: Education, research and practice* (pp. 155–172). Washington, DC: American Psychological Association.

Potts, M. K., Burnam, M. A., & Wells, K. B. (1991). Gender differences in depression detection: A comparison of clinician diagnosis and standardized assessment. *Psychological Assessment, 3,* 609–615.

Powlishta, K. K., Sen, M. G., Serbin, L. A., Poulin-Dubois, D., & Eichstedt, J. A. (2001). The role of social and cognitive factors in becoming gendered. In R. K. Unger (Ed.), *Handbook of the psychology of women and gender* (pp. 116–132). New York: Wiley.

Price-Bonham, S., & Skeen, P. (1982). Black and White fathers' attitudes toward children's sex roles. *Psychological Reports, 50,* 1187–1190.

Raag, T., & Rackliff, C. (1998). Preschoolers' awareness of social expectations of gender: Relationships to toy choices. *Sex Roles, 41,* 809–831.

Ragins, B. R., & Sundstrom, E. (1989). Gender and power in organization: A longitudinal perspective. *Psychological Bulletin, 105,* 51–88.

Rapaport, K. R., & Posey, C. D. (1991). Sexually coercive college males. In A. Parrot & L. Bechhofer (Eds.), *Acquaintance rape: The hidden crime* (pp. 217–228). New York: Wiley.

Rave, E. J., & Larson, C. C. (1995). *Ethical decision-making in therapy: Feminist perspectives.* New York: Guilford Press.

Rawlings, E. I., & Carter, D. K. (1977). Feminist and non-sexist psychotherapy. In E. I. Rawlings & D. K. Carter (Eds.), *Psychotherapy for women* (pp. 19–76). Springfield, IL: Charles C Thomas.

Reame, N. K. (2001). Menstruation. In J. Worell (Ed.), *Encyclopedia of women and gender: Sex similarities and differences and the impact of society on gender* (Vol. 2, pp. 739–742). San Diego, CA: Academic Press.

Reed, M. K., McLeod, S., Randall, Y., & Walker, B. (1996). Depressive symptoms in African American women. *Journal of Multicultural Counseling and Development, 24,* 6–14.

Rehm, L. P. (1988). Self-management and cognitive processes in depression. In L. B. Alloy (Ed.), *Cognitive processes in depression* (pp. 143–176). New York: Guilford Press.

Reid, P. T., Haritos, C., Kelly, E., & Holland, N. E. (1995). Socialization of girls: Issues of ethnicity in gender development. In H. Landrine (Ed.), *Bringing cultural diversity to feminist psychology: Theory, research, and practice* (pp. 93–111). Washington, DC: American Psychological Association.

Reid, P. T., & Zalk, S. R. (2001). Academic environments: Gender and ethnicity in U.S. higher education. In J. Worell (Ed.), *Encyclopedia of women and gender: Sex similarities and differences and the impact of society on gender* (Vol. 1, pp. 29–42). San Diego, CA: Academic Press.

Reinharz, S. (1992). *Feminist methods in social research.* New York: Oxford University Press.

Remer, P. (1986). *Stages in coping with rape.* Unpublished manuscript, University of Kentucky, Lexington.

Remer, P. (1993). *Victim, survivor, healer.* Unpublished manuscript, University of Kentucky, Lexington.

Remer, P., Enns, R., Fisher, A., Nutt, R., & Worell, J. (2001). *Specialty in feminist psychological practice.* Washington, DC: American Psychological Association.

Remer, P., & O'Neill, C. D. (1978). *A counseling companion for self-guided career decision-making.* Lexington, KY: Author.

Remer, P., & O'Neill, C. D. (1980). Clients as change agents: What color could your parachute be? *Personnel and Guidance Journal, 58,* 425–429.

Remer, P., O'Neill, C. D., & Gohs, D. E. (1984). Multiple outcome evaluation of a life-career development course. *Journal of Counseling Psychology, 31,* 532–540.

Remer, P., & Remer, R. (2000). The alien invasion exercise: Creating an experience of diversity. *International Journal of Action Methods: Psychodrama, Skill Training, and Role Playing, 52,* 147–154.

Remer, P., & Rostosky, S. (2000, Fall). Practice talk. *Psychology of Women Newsletter, 27*(4), 7.

Remer, P., & Rostosky, S. (2001, Fall). Practice talk: The fears of labeling ourselves feminist practitioners. *Feminist Psychologist, 28*(4), 30.

Remer, R., & Ferguson, R. (1996). Becoming a secondary survivor of sexual assault. *Journal of Counseling and Development, 7,* 407–414.

Remer, R., & Witten, B. J. (1988). Conceptions of rape. *Violence and Victims, 3,* 217–232.

Resick, P. A. (1983). Sex-role stereotypes and violence against women. In V. Franks & E. D. Rothblum (Eds.), *The stereotyping of women: Its effects on mental health* (pp. 230–256). New York: Springer.

Resick, P. A. (1993). The psychological impact of rape. *Journal of Interpersonal Violence, 8,* 223–255.

Resick, P. A., & Schnicke, M. K. (1993). *Cognitive processing therapy for rape victims: A treatment manual.* Newbury Park, CA: Sage.

Rice, J. K. (1997). Including education in welfare reform. In APA Division 35 Task Force on Women, Poverty, and Public Assistance (Eds.), *Implementing welfare policy to insure long-term independence and well-being* (pp. 7–21). Washington, DC: American Psychological Association.

Rice, J. K., & Wyche, K. (1998). *Making welfare to work really work.* Washington, DC: American Psychological Association.

Richie, B. S., Fassinger, R. E., Lin, S. G., Johnson, J., Prosser, J., & Robinson, S. (1997). Persistence, connection, and passion: A qualitative study of the career development of highly achieving African-American Black and White women. *Journal of Counseling Psychology, 44,* 133–148.

Ridley, C. R., Li, L. C., & Hill, C. L. (1998). Multicultural assessment: Reexamination, reconceptualization, and practical application. *Counseling Psychologist, 26,* 827–910.

Riger, S. (1992). Epistemological debates, feminist voices: Science, social values, and the study of women. *American Psychologist, 47,* 730–740.

Riggs, N. (2000). Analysis of 1076 cases of sexual assault. *Journal of American Medical Association, 283,* 30–48.

Robinson, D. (1994). *Therapy with women: Empirical validation of a clinical expertise.* Unpublished doctoral dissertation, University of Kentucky, Lexington.

Robinson, D., & Worell, J. (1991). *The Therapy with Women Scale (TWS).* Unpublished manuscript, University of Kentucky, Lexington.

Robinson, D., & Worell, J. (2002). Clinical assessment with women: Practical approaches. In J. N. Butcher (Ed.), *Clinical personality assessment* (2nd ed., pp. 190–207). New York: Oxford University Press.

Robinson, T. L. (1999). The intersection of dominant discourses across race, gender, and other identities. *Journal of Counseling and Development, 77,* 73–79.

Robinson, T. L., & Howard-Hamilton, M. F. (2000). *The convergence of race, ethnicity, and gender: Multiples identities in counseling.* Upper Saddle River, NJ: Merrill.

Robinson, T. L., & Ward, J. V. (1995). African American adolescents and skin color. *Journal of Black Psychology, 21,* 256–274.

Rosenthal, R. (1994). Interpersonal expectancy effects: A 30-year perspective. *Current Directions in Psychological Science, 3,* 176–179.

Rosewater, L. B. (1985a). Feminist interpretation of traditional testing. In L. B. Rosewater & L. E. A. Walker (Eds.), *Handbook of feminist therapy: Women's issues in psychotherapy* (pp. 266–273). New York: Springer.

Rosewater, L. B. (1985b). Schizophrenic, borderline, or battered. In L. B. Rosewater & L. E. A. Walker (Eds.), *Handbook of feminist therapy: Women's issues in psychotherapy* (pp. 215–225). New York: Springer.

Rosewater, L. B. (1988). Battered or schizophrenic? Psychological tests can't tell you. In K. Yllo & M. Bograd (Eds.), *Feminist perspectives on wife abuse* (pp. 200–216). Newbury Park, CA: Sage.

Rosewater, L. B., & Walker, L. E. A. (1985). *Handbook of feminist therapy: Women's issues in psychotherapy.* New York: Springer.

Rosser, S. V. (1990). *Female-friendly science: Applying women's studies methods and theories to attract students.* New York: Pergamon Press.

Rostosky, S. S., & Riggle, E. D. B. (in press). Out at work: The relation of actor and partner workplace policy and homophobia to disclosure status. *Journal of Counseling Psychology.*

Rotter, J. B. (1954). *Social learning and clinical psychology.* Englewood Cliffs, NJ: Prentice-Hall.

Rozee, P. D. (1993). Forbidden or forgiven? Rape in cross-cultural perspective. *Psychology of Women Quarterly, 17,* 499–514.

Ruble, D., & Martin, C. L. (1998). Gender development. In W. Damon & N. Eisenberg (Eds.), *Handbook of child psychology: Social, emotional and personality development* (5th ed., Vol. 3, pp. 933–1016). New York: Wiley.

Ruble, T. (1983). Sex stereotypes: Issues of change in the 1970s. *Sex Roles, 9,* 397–402.

Rusbult, C. E. (1983). A longitudinal test of the investment model: The development and deterioration of satisfaction and commitment in heterosexual involvements. *Journal of Personality and Social Psychology, 45,* 101–117.

Russell, D. (1982). *Rape in marriage.* New York: Macmillan.

Russell, D. (1984). *Sexual exploitation: Rape, child sexual abuse and workplace harassment.* Beverly Hills, CA: Sage.

Russell, D. (1986). *The secret trauma: Incest in the lives of girls and women.* New York: Basic Books.

Russell, D. E. H., & Howell, N. (1983). The prevalence of rape in the United States revisited. *Signs: Journal of Women in Culture and Society, 8,* 688–695.

Rust, P. C. R. (2000). Bisexuality: A contemporary paradox for women. *Journal of Social Issues, 56,* 205–222.

Sadker, D., & Sadker, M. (1994). *Failing at fairness: How America's schools cheat girls.* New York: Scribner.

Sampson, E. E. (2000). Reinterpreting individualism and collectivism: Their religious roots and monologic vs. dialogic person-other relationships. *American Psychologist, 55,* 1425–1432.

Sanchez-Hucles, J., & Hudgins, P. (2001). Trauma across diverse settings. In J. Worell (Ed.), *Encyclopedia of women and gender: Sex similarities and differences and the impact of society on gender* (Vol. 2, pp. 1151–1168). San Diego, CA: Academic Press.

Sanday, P. R. (1981). *Female power and male dominance: On the origins of sexual inequality.* New York: Cambridge University Press.

Sandler, B. (1982). *Project on the education and status of women.* Washington, DC: U.S. Government Printing Office.

Santos de Barona, M., & Dutton, M. A. (1997). Feminist perspectives on assessment. In J. Worell & N. G. Johnson (Eds.), *Shaping the future of feminist psychology: Education, research, and practice* (pp. 37–56). Washington, DC: American Psychological Association.

Schein, V. E. (2001). A global look at psychological barriers to women's progress in management. *Journal of Social Issues, 57,* 675–688.

Schissel, B. (1993). Coping with adversity: Testing the origins of resiliency in mental health. *International Journal of Social Psychiatry, 39,* 34–46.

Schlossberg, N. K., & Pietrofesa, J. J. (1978). Perspectives on counseling bias: Implications for counselor education. In L. W. Harmon, J. M. Birk, L. E. Fitzgerald, & M. F. Tanney (Eds.), *Counseling women* (pp. 59–74). Monterey, CA: Brooks/Cole.

Scott, B. A. (2000). Women and pornography: What we don't know can hurt us. In J. C. Chrisler, C. Golden, & P. D. Rozee (Eds.), *Lectures on the psychology of women* (pp. 271–287). Boston: McGraw-Hill.

Scurfield, R. (1985). Post-trauma stress assessment and treatment: Overview and formulations. In C. R. Figley (Ed.), *Trauma and its wake: The study and treatment of posttraumatic stress disorder* (pp. 219–256). New York: Brunner/Mazel.

Seager, J., & Olson, A. (1986). *Atlas: Women in the world.* New York: Simon & Schuster.

Segall, M. H., Lonner, W. J., & Berry, J. W. (1998). Cross-cultural psychology as a scholarly discipline: On the flowering of culture in behavioral research. *American Psychologist, 53,* 1101–1110.

Seligman, M. E. P. (1975). *Helplessness: On depression, development, and death.* San Francisco: Freeman.

Seligman, M. E. P. (1981). A learned helplessness point of view. In L. P. Rehm (Ed.), *Behavior therapy for depression.* New York: Academic Press.

Seligman, M. E. P. (1998). *Learned optimism.* New York: Pocket Books.

Serbin, L. A., Powlishta, K. K., & Gulko, J. (1993). The development of sex-typing in middle childhood. *Monographs of the Society for Research in Child Development, 58* (2, Serial No. 232).

Sherif, C. (1982). Needed concepts in the study of gender identity. *Psychology of Women Quarterly, 6,* 375–395.

Sherman, J. A. (1980). Therapist attitudes and sex-role stereotyping. In A. M. Brodsky & R. T. Hare-Mustin (Eds.), *Women and psychotherapy: An assessment of research and practice* (pp. 35–66). New York: Guilford Press.

Sherman, J. A. (1987). Achievement-related fears: Gender roles and individual dynamics. *Women and Therapy, 6,* 97–105.

Sherman, L., & Berk, R. (1984). The deterrent effects of arrest for domestic assault. *American Sociological Review, 49,* 261–272.

Shulman, M. A. (1979). *A survey of spousal violence against women in Kentucky.* Louis Harris and Associates.

Sidhu, G. (2000). Challenging power: A new WEDO campaign pushes for equal representation in governments. *Women's Environment and Development Organization, 13,* 1–11.

Silverstein, L. B. (1996). Fathering is a feminist issue. *Psychology of Women Quarterly, 20,* 3–38.

Smith, A. J., & Siegel, R. F. (1985). Feminist therapy: Redefining power for the powerless. In L. B. Rosewater & L. E. A. Walker (Eds.), *Handbook of feminist therapy: Women's issues in psychotherapy* (pp. 13–21). New York: Springer.

Smolak, L., & Striegel-Moore, R. H. (2001). Body image concerns. In J. Worell (Ed.), *Encyclopedia of women and gender: Sex similarities and differences and the impact of society on gender* (Vol. 1, pp. 201–210). San Diego, CA: Academic Press.

Snyder, D. K., & Fruchtman, L. A. (1981). Differential patterns of wife abuse: A data-based topology. *Journal of consulting and Clinical Psychology, 49,* 878–885.

Snyder, M., & Dyamot, C. M., Jr. (2001). Self-fulfilling prophecies. In J. Worell (Ed.), *Encyclopedia of women and gender: Sex similarities and differences and the impact of society on gender* (Vol. 2, pp. 945–953). San Diego, CA: Academic Press.

Sobel, S. B., & Russo, N. F. (1981). Sex roles, equality, and mental health: An introduction. *Professional Psychology, 12,* 1–5.

Sommer, B. (2001). Menopause. In J. Worell (Ed.), *Encyclopedia of women and gender: Sex similarities and differences and the impact of society on gender* (Vol. 2, pp. 729–738). San Diego, CA: Academic Press.

Sonkin, D., Martin, D., & Walker, L. E. A. (1985). *The male battered.* New York: Springer.

Sparks, E. E., & Park, A. H. (2000). The integration of feminism and multiculturalism: Ethical dilemmas at the border. In M. M. Brabeck (Ed.), *Practicing feminist ethics in psychology* (pp. 203–224). Washington, DC: American Psychological Association.

Spence, J. T., & Hahn, E. D. (1997). The Attitudes Toward Women Scale and attitude changes in college students. *Psychology of Women Quarterly, 21,* 17–34.

Spence, J. T., & Helmreich, R. L. (1978). *Masculinity and femininity: Their psychological dimensions, correlates, and antecedents.* Austin: University of Texas Press.

Spielberger, C., Gorsuch, R., & Luchins, R. (1970). *Test manual for the State-Trail Anxiety Inventory.* Palo Alto, CA: Consulting Psychologist Press.

Srebnik, D. S., & Salzberg, E. A. (1994). Feminist cognitive-behavioral therapy for negative body image. *Women and Therapy, 15,* 117–134.

Stacey, W. A., & Shupe, A. (1983). *The family secret: Domestic violence in America.* Boston: Beacon Press.

Stake, J. E., & Gerner, M. A. (1987). The women's studies experience: Personal and professional gains for women and men. *Psychology of Women Quarterly, 11,* 277–284.

Stake, J. E., Roades, L., Rose, S., Ellis, L., & West, C. (1994). The women's studies experience: Impetus for feminist action. *Psychology of Women Quarterly, 19,* 17–24.

Starrels, M. E. (1994). Gender differences in parent-child relations. *Journal of Family Issues, 15,* 148–165.

Steele, C. M. (1997). A threat in the air: How stereotypes shape intellectual identity and performance. *American Psychologist, 52,* 613–629.

Steil, J. M. (1997). *Marital equality.* Thousand Oaks, CA: Sage.

Steil, J. M. (2001). Family forms and member well-being: A research agenda for the decade of behavior. *Psychology of Women Quarterly, 25,* 344–363.

Sternoff, N. S. (2000, November). Abuse in the Jewish community: *Shalom.* Lexington: Central Kentucky Jewish Federation.

Stevens, S. E., Hynan, M. T., & Allen, M. (2000). A meta-analysis of common factor and specific treatment effects across the outcome domains of the phase model of psychotherapy. *Clinical Psychology: Science and Practice, 7,* 273–290.

Stitt-Gohdes, W. L. (1997). *Career development: Issues of gender, race, and class.* Columbus, OH: ERIC Clearinghouse on Adult, Career, and Vocational Education. (ERIC Document Reproduction Service No. ED413533)

Stockard, J., Schmuck, P. A., Kempner, K., Williams, P., Edson, S. A., & Smith, M. A. (1980). *Sex equity in education.* New York: Academic Press.

Stokes, J., Riger, S., & Sullivan, M. (1995). Measuring perceptions of the working environment for women in corporate settings. *Psychology of Women Quarterly, 19,* 533–550.

Strauss, M. A., Gelles, R. J., & Steinmetz, S. K. (1980). *Behind closed doors: Violence in the American family.* New York: Doubleday.

Strickland, B. R. (2000). Misassumptions, misadventures, and the misuse of psychology. *American Psychologist, 55,* 331–338.

Striegel-Moore, R. H., & Cachelin, F. M. (1999). Body image and disordered eating in adolescent girls: Risk and protective factors. In N. G. Johnson, M. C. Roberts, & J. Worell (Eds.), *Beyond appearance: A new look at adolescent girls* (pp. 85–108). Washington, DC: American Psychological Association.

Strube, M. J. (1989). The decision to leave an abusive relationship: Empirical evidence and theoretical issues. *Psychological Bulletin, 104,* 236–250.

Sturdivant, S. (1980). *Therapy with women: A feminist philosophy of treatment.* New York: Springer.

Sue, D. W., & Sue, D. (1999). *Counseling the culturally different: Theory and practice.* New York: Wiley.

Sugihara, Y., & Katsurada, E. (2000). Gender-role personality traits in Japanese culture. *Psychology of Women Quarterly, 24,* 309–318.

Super, D. E. (1957). *The psychology of careers.* New York: Harper & Row.

Super, D. E. (1976). *Career education and the meaning of work.* Monographs on career education. Washington, DC: U.S. Office of Education, Office of Career Education.

Surrey, J. L. (1991). The self-in-relation: A theory of women's development. In J. V. Jordan, A. G. Kaplan, J. B. Miller, I. P. Stiver, & J. L. Surrey (Eds.), *Women's growth in connection: Writings from the Stone Center* (pp. 51–66). New York: Guilford Press.

Sweeney, P. D., Anderson, K., & Bailey, S. (1986). Attributional style in depression: A meta-analytic review. *Journal of Personality and Social Psychology, 50,* 974–991.

Swim, J. K., & Cohen, L. L. (1997). Overt, covert, and subtle sexism: A comparison between the Attitudes Toward Women Scale and Modern Sexism Scales. *Psychology of Women Quarterly, 21,* 103–118.

Tanaka-Matsumi, J., Seiden, D. Y., & Lam, K. N. (1996). The culturally-informed functional assessment (CIFA) interview: A strategy for cross-cultural behavioral practice. *Cognitive and Behavioral Practice, 3,* 215–233.

Tedeschi, R. G., & Calhoun, L. G. (1995). *Trauma and transformation: Growth in the aftermath of suffering.* Thousand Oaks, CA: Sage.

Terlau, M. T. (1991). Effects of career self-efficacy and sex-role beliefs on nontraditionality of women's occupational choices. *Dissertation Abstracts International, 52,* 10A-1216. (UMI No. DA 9126904)

Textbook Task Force on integrating diversity into introductory psychology texts. (2002). Report to the American Psychological Association, Washington, DC: Author.

Thompson, T., Davis, H., & Davidson, J. (1997). Attributional and affective responses of impostors to academic success and failure outcomes. *Personality and Individual Differences, 25,* 381–396.

Thoreson, C. E., & Mahoney, M. J. (1974). *Behavioral self-control.* New York: Holt, Rinehart and Winston.

Thyfault, R. K., Browne, A., & Walker, L. E. A. (1987). When battered women kill: Evaluation and expert witness testimony techniques. In D. J. Sonkin (Ed.), *Domestic violence on trial: Psychological and legal dimensions of family violence* (pp. 71–85). New York: Springer.

Tjaden, P., & Thoennes, N. (2000). Prevalence and consequences of male-to-female and female-to-male intimate partner violence as measured by the National Violence Against Women Survey. *Violence Against Women, 6,* 142–161.

Todd, J. L., & Worell, J. (2000). Resilience in low-income, employed, African American mothers. *Psychology of Women Quarterly, 24,* 119–128.

Tolman, D. L. (1999). Female adolescent sexuality in relational context: Beyond sexual decision-making. In N. G. Johnson, M. C. Roberts, & J. Worell (Eds.), *Beyond appearance: A new look at adolescent girls* (pp. 227–246.) Washington, DC: American Psychological Association.

Tolman, D. L., & Brown, L. M. (2001). Adolescent girls' voices: Resonating resistance in body and soul. In R. K. Unger (Ed.), *Handbook of the psychology of women and gender* (pp. 133–155). New York: Wiley.

Tolman, D. L., & Brydon-Miller, M. (Eds.). (1997). Transforming psychology: Interpretive and participatory research methods. *Journal of Social Issues, 53*(Whole No. 4).

Tolman, R., & Bennet, L. W. (1990). A review of quantitative research on men who batter. *Journal of Interpersonal Violence, 5,* 87–118.

Toner, B. B. (1999, August). The Gender Socialization Scale. In J. Worell (Chair), *Measuring process and outcomes in feminist counseling and therapy.* Paper presented at the annual meeting of the American Psychological Association as part of a symposium, Boston.

Toner, B. B., Segal, Z. V., Emmott, S. D., & Myron, D. (2000). *Cognitive-behavioral treatment of irritable bowel syndrome: The brain-gut connection.* New York: Guilford Press.

Tougas, F., Brown, R., Beaton, A. M., & Joly, S. (1995). Neosexism: Plus ca change, plus c'est pareil. *Personality and Social Psychology Bulletin, 21,* 842–849.

Towsen, S. M. J., Zanna, M. P., & MacDonald, G. (1989). Self-fulfilling prophecies: Sex-role stereotypes as expectations for behavior. In R. K. Unger (Ed.), *Representations: Social constructions of gender* (pp. 97–107). Amityville, NY: Baywood.

Travis, C. B. (1988). *Women and health: Mental health issues.* Hillsdale, NJ: Erlbaum.

Travis, C. B. (2001). Beauty politics and patriarchy: The impact on women's lives. In J. Worell (Ed.), *Encyclopedia of women and gender: Sex similarities and differences and the impact of society on gender* (Vol. 1, pp. 189–200). San Diego, CA: Academic Press.

Triandis, H. C. (1995). *Individualism and collectivism.* Boulder, CO: Westview Press.

Twenge, J. M. (1997). Attitudes toward women, 1970–1995: A meta-analysis. *Psychology of Women Quarterly, 21,* 35–52.

Twenge, J. M. (1999). Mapping gender: The multifactorial approach and the organization of gender-related attributes. *Psychology of Women Quarterly, 23,* 485–502.

Twerski, A. J. (1996). *The shame borne in silence: Spouse abuse in the Jewish community.* Pittsburgh, PA: Mirkov.

U.S. Bureau of the Census. (2000). *Statistical abstract of the U.S.: 2000.* Washington, DC: Congressional Information Service.

U.S. Department of Labor. (1999). *Highlights of women's earnings in 1998.* Washington, DC: Bureau of Labor Statistics.

Unger, R. K. (1979). *Female and male: Psychological perspectives.* New York: Harper & Row.

Unger, R. K. (1983). Through the looking glass: No wonderland yet! *Psychology of Women Quarterly, 8,* 9–32.

Unger, R. K. (1989). Sex in psychological paradigms: From behavior to cognition. In R. K. Unger (Ed.), *Representations: Social constructions of gender* (pp. 15–20). Amityville, NY: Baywood.

Unger, R. K. (1995). Cultural diversity and the future of feminist psychology. In H. Landrine (Ed.), *Bringing cultural diversity to feminist psychology* (pp. 413–431). Washington, DC: American Psychological Association.

Unger, R. K., & Crawford, M. (1993). Sex and gender: The troubled relationship between sex and gender. *Psychological Science, 4,* 122–124.

United Nations. (1995). *The world's women 1995: Trends and statistics.* New York: Author.

Vandello, J. A., & Cohen, D. (1999). Patterns of individualism and collectivism across the United States. *Journal of Personality and Social Psychology, 77,* 279–292.

Vandiver, B. (2002). What do we know and where do we go? *Counseling Psychologist, 30,* 96–104.

van Wormer, K. (1990). Co-dependency: Implications for women and therapy. *Women and Therapy, 8,* 51–63.

Vasquez, M. J. T. (2001). 1999 Division 35 presidential address: Leveling of the playing field— Toward the emancipation of women. *Psychology of Women Quarterly, 25,* 89–97.

Vasquez, M. J. T., & de las Fuentes, C. (1999). American-born Asian, African, Latina, and American Indian adolescent girls: Challenges and strengths. In N. G. Johnson, M. C. Roberts, & J. Worell (Eds.), *Beyond appearance: A new look at adolescent girls* (pp. 151–174). Washington, DC: American Psychological Association.

Vedovato, S. L., & Vaughter, R. M. (1980). Psychology of women courses changing sexist and sex-typed attitudes. *Psychology of Women Quarterly, 4,* 587–590.

Wade, M. E. (2001). Women and salary negotiation: The costs of self-advocacy. *Psychology of Women Quarterly, 25,* 65–76.

Walker, L. E. A. (1979). *The battered woman.* New York: Harper & Row.

Walker, L. E. A. (1989a). Psychology and violence against women. *American Psychologist, 44,* 695–702.

Walker, L. E. A. (1989b). *Terrifying love: Why battered women kill and how society responds.* New York: Harper.

Walker, L. E. A. (1994). *The abused woman and survivor therapy: A practical guide for the psychotherapist.* Washington, DC: American Psychological Association.

Walker, L. E. A. (2001). Battering in adult relationships. In J. Worell (Ed.), *Encyclopedia of women and gender: Sex similarities and differences and the impact of society on gender* (Vol. 1, pp. 169–188). San Diego, CA: Academic Press.

Wallston, B. S. (1986). *What's in a name revisited: The psychology of women vs. feminist psychology.* Invited address, annual meeting of the Association for Women in Psychology, Oakland, CA.

Walsh, M. R. (1985). The psychology of women course: A continuing catalyst for change. *Teaching of Psychology, 12,* 198–202.

Walz, J., & Jacobson, N. S. (1994). Behavioral couples therapy. In L. W. Craighead, W. E. Craighead, A. E. Kazdin, & M. J. Mahoney (Eds.), *Cognitive and behavioral interventions: An empirical approach to mental health problems* (pp. 1169–182). Boston: Allyn & Bacon.

Warburton, J., Newberry, A., & Alexander, J. (1989). Women as therapists, trainees, and supervisors. In M. McGoldrick, C. Anderson, & F. Walsh (Eds.), *Women in families: A framework for family therapy* (pp. 152–165). Scranton, PA: Norton.

Ward, L. M., & Caruthers, A. (2001). Media influences. In J. Worell (Ed.), *Encyclopedia of women and gender: Sex similarities and differences and the impact of society on gender* (Vol. 2, pp. 687–702). San Diego, CA: Academic Press.

Ward, V. (1996). Raising resisters: The role of truth telling in the development of African American girls. In J. R. Leadbeater & N. Way (Eds.), *Urban girls: Resisting stereotypes, creating identities* (pp. 85–99). New York: New York University Press.

Warshaw, R. (1988). *I never called it rape.* New York: Harper & Row.

Waters, M. (1996). The intersection of gender, race, and ethnicity in identity development in Carribean American teens. In J. R. Leadbeater & N. Way (Eds.), *Urban girls: Resisting stereotypes, creating identities* (pp. 65–84). New York: New York University Press.

*Webster's new world dictionary of the english language.* (1978). New York: Collins, World.

Weinraub, M., & Brown, L. M. (1983). The development of sex-role stereotypes in children: Crushing realities. In V. Franks & E. D. Rothblum (Eds.), *The stereotyping of women: Its effects on mental health* (pp. 30–58). New York: Springer.

Weis, K., & Borges, S. S. (1977). Victimology and rape: The case of the legitimate victims. In D. R. Nass (Ed.), *The rape victim* (pp. 35–75). Dubuque, IA: Kendall-Hunt.

Weisner, T. S., Garnier, H., & Loucky, J. (1994). Domestic tasks, gender egalitarian values, and children's gender typing in conventional and nonconventional families. *Sex Roles, 30,* 23–54.

Weissman, M. M. (1980). Depression. In A. M. Brodsky & R. T. Hare-Mustin (Eds.), *Women and psychotherapy: An assessment of research and practice* (pp. 97–112). New York: Guilford Press.

Westbury, E., & Tutty, L. M. (1999). The efficacy of group treatment for survivors of childhood abuse. *Childhood Abuse and Neglect, 23,* 31–44.

Whaley, R. B. (1998). Sexual assault on the college campus: The role of male peer support. *Gender and Society, 12,* 601–602.

Whetsell, M. S. (1990). The relationship of abuse factors and revictimization to the long-term effects of childhood sexual abuse in women. *Dissertation Abstracts International, 51,* 10B–5047. (UMI No. AAC 9034199.)

Whiffen, V. E. (2001). Depression. In J. Worell (Ed.), *Encyclopedia of women and gender: Sex similarities and differences and the impact of society on gender* (Vol. 1, pp. 303–315). San Diego, CA: Academic Press.

Widiger, T. A., & Spitzer, R. L. (1991). Sex bias in the diagnosis of personality disorders: Conceptual and methodological issues. *Clinical Psychology Review, 11,* 1–22.

Wilkinson, S., & Kitzinger, C. (1993). *Heterosexuality: A feminism and psychology reader.* London: Sage.

Williams, J. E., & Best, D. L. (1990). *Measuring sex stereotypes: A multinational study.* Beverly Hills, CA: Sage.

Wilson, E., & Ng, S. H. (1988). Sex bias in visual images evoked by generics: A New Zealand study. *Sex Roles, 18,* 159–168.

Wilson, M., & Daly, M. (1993). Spousal homicide risk and estrangement. *Violence and Victims, 8,* 3–16.

Witt, V., & Worell, J. (1986, March). *Premarital and marital abuse: Factors in common.* Paper presented at the annual meeting of the Southeastern Psychological Association, New Orleans, LA.

Witt, V., & Worell, J. (1988, March). *Antecedents and correlates of premarital abuse.* Paper presented at the annual meeting of the Southeastern Psychological Association, New Orleans, LA.

Wolleatt, A., & Marshall, H. (2001). Motherhood and mothering. In R. K. Unger (Ed.), *Handbook of the psychology of women and gender* (pp. 170–182). New York: Wiley.

Worell, J. (1980). New directions in counseling women. *Personnel and Guidance Journal, 58,* 477–484.

Worell, J. (1981). Lifespan sex roles: Development, continuity, and change. In R. M. Lerner & N. A. Busch-Rossnagel (Eds.), *Individuals as producers of their development* (pp. 313–346). New York: Academic Press.

Worell, J. (1982). Psychological sex roles: Significance and change. In J. Worell (Ed.), *Psychological development in the elementary years* (pp. 3–52). New York: Academic Press.

Worell, J. (1986, November). *The DSM III-R: Controversies in gender bias.* Invited paper presented at the annual meeting of the Association for the Advancement of Behavior Therapy, Chicago.

Worell, J. (1988a). Satisfaction in women's close relationships. *Clinical Psychology Review, 8,* 477–498.

Worell, J. (1988b). Single mothers: From problems to policies. *Women and Therapy, 7,* 3–14.

Worell, J. (1989a). Images of women in psychology. In M. A. Paludi & G. A. Stuernagel (Eds.), *Foundations for a feminist restructuring of the academic disciplines* (pp. 185–224). New York: Harrington Park.

Worell, J. (1989b). Sex roles in transition. In J. Worell & F. Danner (Eds.), *The adolescent as decision-maker: Applications for development and education* (pp. 246–280). New York: Academic Press.

Worell, J. (1990). Feminist frameworks. *Psychology of Women Quarterly, 14,* 1–6.

Worell, J. (1993a, June). *Children's response to family violence.* Conference paper presented to the Reproductive Choice Coalition, Louisville, KY.

Worell, J. (1993b, November). *What do we really know about feminist therapists? Approaches to research on process and outcome.* Invited presentation, Texas Psychological Association, Austin.

Worell, J. (1994). Feminist journals: Academic empowerment or professional liability. In S. M. Deats & L. T. Lenker (Eds.), *Gender and academe: Feminist pedagogy and politics* (pp. 197–216). Lanham, MD: Rowan and Littlefield.

Worell, J. (1996a). Feminist identity in a gendered world. In J. C. Chrisler, C. Golden, & P. D. Rozee (Eds.), *Lectures on the psychology of women* (pp. 358–370). New York: McGraw-Hill.

Worell, J. (1996b). Opening doors to feminist research. *Psychology of Women Quarterly, 20,* 469–486.

Worell, J. (2000). Feminism in psychology: Evolution or revolution? *The Annals of the American Academy of Social and Political Science.* In C. L. Williams (Ed.), *Feminist views of the social sciences* [Special issue]. Thousand Oaks, CA: Sage.

Worell, J. (2001). Feminist interventions: Accountability beyond symptom reduction. *Psychology of Women Quarterly, 25,* 335–343.

Worell, J., & Chandler, R. (1999). *The Personal Progress Scale, Revised (PPS-R).* Unpublished manuscript, University of Kentucky, Lexington.

Worell, J., Chandler, R., Johnson, D. M., & Blount, A. (in press). Measuring process and outcomes in feminist therapy. *Psychology of Women Quarterly.*

Worell, J., Chandler, R., Robinson, D., & Blount, A. (1996, August). Measuring beliefs and behaviors of feminist therapists. In J. Worell (Chair), *Evaluating process and outcomes in feminist therapy and counseling.* Symposium presented at the annual meeting of the American Psychological Association, Toronto, Ontario, Canada.

Worell, J., & Etaugh, C. (1994). Transforming theory and research with women: Themes and variations. *Psychology of Women Quarterly, 18,* 443–450.

Worell, J., & Johnson, D. M. (2001). Therapy with women: Feminist frameworks. In R. K. Unger (Ed.), *Handbook of the psychology of women and gender* (pp. 317–329). New York: Wiley.

Worell, J., & Johnson, N. G. (1997). *Shaping the future of feminist psychology: Education, research, and practice.* Washington, DC: American Psychological Association.

Worell, J., & Remer, P. (1992). *Feminist perspectives in therapy: An empowerment model for women.* Chichester, England: Wiley.

Worell, J., Stilwell, D., Oakley, D., & Robinson, D. (1999). Educating about women and gender: Cognitive, personal, and professional outcomes. *Psychology of Women Quarterly, 23,* 797–812.

Worell, J., & Stilwell, W. S. (1981). *Psychology for teachers and students.* New York: McGraw-Hill.

Worell, J., & Worell, L. (1977). Support and opposition to the women's liberation movement: Some personality and parental characteristics. *Journal of Research in Personality, 11,* 10–20.

Wyatt, G. E., Guthrie, D., & Notgrass, C. M. (1992). Differential effects of women's childhood sexual abuse and subsequent sexual revictimization. *Journal of Consulting and Clinical Psychology, 60,* 167–173.

Wyatt, G. E., Notgrass, C. M., & Newcomb, M. (1990). Internal and external mediators of women's rape experiences. *Psychology of Women Quarterly, 14,* 153–176.

Wyche, K. F. (2001). Sociocultural issues in counseling for women of color. In R. K. Unger (Ed.), *Handbook of the psychology of women and gender* (pp. 330–340). New York: Wiley.

Wyche, K. F., & Rice, J. K. (1997). Feminist therapy: From dialogue to tenets. In J. Worell & N. G. Johnson (Eds.), *Shaping the future of feminist psychology: Education, research, and practice* (pp. 57–72). Washington, DC: American Psychological Association.

Yee, D., & Eccles, J. (1983, August). *A comparison of parents' and children's attributions for successful and unsuccessful math performances.* Paper presented at the annual meeting of the American Psychological Association, Anaheim, CA.

Yllo, K. (1988). Political and methodological debates in wife abuse research. In K. Yllo & M. Bograd (Eds.), *Feminist perspectives on wife abuse* (pp. 28–50). Newbury Park, CA: Sage.

Yoder, J. D. (1999). *Women and gender: Transforming psychology.* Upper Saddle River, NJ: Prentice-Hall.

Young, J. E. (1982). Loneliness, depression, and cognitive therapy. In L. A. Peplau & D. A. Perlman (Eds.), *Loneliness: A sourcebook of current theory, research and therapy* (pp. 379–404). New York: Wiley.

Yuen, L. M., & Depper, D. S. (1987). Fear of failure. *Women and Therapy, 6,* 21–39.

Zollicoffer, A. M. (1989). Factors affecting long-term avoidant and intrusive responses and the process of resolution for women who have been raped. *Dissertation Abstracts International, 50,* 12A–4126. (UMI No. AAC-9008-780.)

Zollicoffer, A. M., & Remer, P. (1989). Unpublished manuscript, University of Kentucky, Lexington.

Zunker, V. G. (1998). *Career counseling: Applied concepts of life planning.* Pacific Grove, CA: Brooks/Cole.

# Author Index

# Subject Index ——————————————————

Scholastic Assessment Test, 119–120
Schools:
  differential expectations, 178–181
  gender messages, 53
  sexism, implications for counseling,
    178–181
  sexual and gender harassment in, 54
  teacher stereotypes, 54–55, 178–181
  textbook stereotypes, 53
Science:
  empirical, 268
  feminist approaches to, 274–280
  as objective, 266
SEARCH variables, 33, 182, 187, 266, 278,
    290, 312, 326
Self-assessments:
  analyzing your career development,
    173–174
  assessment of client descriptions, 87–88
  beliefs about abuse in close relationships,
    232–233
  beliefs about rape, 203–204
  beliefs and facts about depression, 145–146
  clarifying your theoretical position,
    116–117
  ethical issues, 288
  evaluating current educational programs,
    312
  evaluating research for bias, 265
  exploring personal identity, 29–30
  relationships between women and men, 3–4
  self and world views, xiii–xv
  therapy with women, 60–61
Self-confidence, 147–148, 149–151, 190–191
Self-Directed Search, 121
Self-disclosure, therapist, 71–72, 76, 167, 258
Self-efficacy, 259
  career, 190
  in Cognitive Behavioral theory, 101, 103,
    105
  in Empowerment model, 26
Self-esteem, 12, 149, 156, 190–191, 259
Self-fulfilling prophecy, 11, 272
Self-in-Relation theory, 90
Self-involving responses, 72, 76
Self-management, 101, 105
Self-monitoring, 81, 150,
Self-reinforcement, 104
Sex:
  biological bases, 14
  definition, 9–10
  differences, 8–9, 273–274
  evolutionary theory of, 14
  and gender, 8–10
Sexism:
  ambivalent, 43
  benevolent, 43

definition, 13
hostile, 44
institutionalized, 177–178, 181–187, 200
modern, 43
Sexual abuse, 222. *See also* Incest; Rape;
    Sexual assault
  by therapists, 301–302, 310
Sexual assault. *See* Incest; Rape
Sexual harassment, 138, 186–187
  adverse reactions, 54, 158
  definition, 158
  in schools, 54
Sexual orientation, 7. *See also* Bisexual;
    Lesbian
Sexuality, 92
Sexual needs, 75
Sexual orientation, 7, 188–189. *See also*
    Lesbian; Bisexual
Sexual victimization, categories of, 211–212
Sharing, 113
Silencing the Self Scale, 148
Single women, 19, 47, 49, 152, 269–270
Single-parent families, 19, 47–49, 279–270
Social change, 27, 69–70, 74, 130, 133,
    227–228, 290
Social construction:
  of gender, 5, 10, 11
  of race, 13
Social dominance hypothesis, vs. opportunity
    dominance, 120–122
Social exchange theory, 251
Social identity analysis, 76
Social institutions, gender rules, 45
Social learning theory, 102–105
Social locations 11–13, 66–67, 75, 116
  Cognitive Behavioral interventions,
    101–102
  diagrams, 31, 83, 168
  feminist format, 104
  Psychodrama, 111–12
  Salience, 32, 33, 53, 66
Social support:
  for African American women, 169
  for battered women, 259–260
  for graduate students, 328
  in Empowerment Feminist therapy, 74
Socialization for womanhood, 44–50. *See also*
    Gender roles
  cognitive outcomes, 48–49
  encouragement, 48
  in families, 45–50
  modeling, 47–48
  relationship training, 48–49
Society for the Psychology of Women, 64, 69
Society, 109
Sociodrama, 111, 112
Sociometry, 109, 112